Clinical Negligence

A Practical Guide

To my mother,

ac i Nicola,
f'anwylyd am byth

Clinical Negligence

A Practical Guide

Sixth Edition

Charles J Lewis, MA

of the Middle Temple, Barrister
former open classical scholar of Oriel College, Oxford

Tottel
publishing

Tottel Publishing, Maxwelton House, 41–43 Boltro Road, Haywards Heath, West Sussex, RH16 1BJ

© Tottel Publishing Ltd 2006

A CIP Catalogue record for this book is available from the British Library.

ISBN 1 84592 237 9

Typeset by Phoenix Photosetting, Chatham, Kent
Printed and bound in Great Britain by Antony Rowe, Chippenham, Wiltshire

Foreword

This book is a comprehensive and up to date guide through the complexities of the legal and procedural difficulties facing practitioners in this field. As previous Forewords have said, its outstanding characteristic is its readability. Charles Lewis has the great gift of engaging the reader's interest and informing the reader interestingly. As before, this edition comes after a period of great change in the clinical negligence landscape. The main features are described and discussed in Chapter 2, interlaced with the author's invigorating comments. The last four years have seen important legal developments not only in decisions directly concerned with medical matters but also in analogous areas such as dyslexia and other educational matters. Perhaps of more day to day importance have been the procedural developments and the growing impact of conditional fee arrangements which have the capacity to distort litigation as we have traditionally practised it. And not, I fear, for the better.

Change will continue. There is no doubt that the cost of litigation is an obstacle to rational resolution of disputes. The State, as the main paymaster, is bound to seek alternative methods of providing sensible solutions. We are addicted to a Rolls Royce model. I understand the author's concerns about what he sees as unrealistic demands made by the courts in terms of time and other case management decisions. But they are necessary if litigation is to be conducted effectively. And mediation is one of the dispute resolution tools which can help, despite the author's reservations. Not all cases are conducted responsibly by experienced practitioners with the objective of a just outcome. And even when they are, perspectives can become distorted. I believe from personal experience that it can be the least bad way of resolving difficult cases.

As always this book ends with an elegant epilogue which is well worth reading whether one agrees with the author's views or not. I therefore have no hesitation in commending it and congratulating Charles Lewis on his achievement. As a practical guide it is impeccable; and as a stimulating tour of this fascinating area of the law it is extremely enjoyable which is not something which one can say of many text books.

David Latham
Royal Courts of Justice
London WC2A 2LL

January 2006

Preface

I had not intended to write a 6th edition of this my modest opus. But over recent months the clamour grew so strong that I finally yielded. Surely as I now, like Wotan, prepare to enter my Valhalla, the paradise to which all good and faithful legal hacks are conveyed by amazonian beauties, I can exclaim, like the god: *Vollendet das ewige Werk*. And, thus escorted, I depart the legal scene, bequeathing my work, like a hair from Caesar's head, as a rich legacy unto my heirs at Old Square Chambers and across the globe.

What a changing scene we have here beheld. *Tempora mutantur, nos et mutamur in illis*. For Lord Woolf and others we can translate that as *Times change and we with them*.

The hottest topic as we go to press is, of course, *Redress*. The Bill is being debated. The Conservatives are making an attempt to remove all compensation from the scheme. Even if, as is likely, the Bill is not heavily amended, it does no more than provide the power to create a scheme. The likely scheme, and its consequences for the injured patient, are discussed at some length in the body of the text of this edition. At the moment it looks as if it will be limited to small claims at the outset and in that context may be helpful to patients. Of one thing we can be sure: it will be deployed more widely sooner or later by the legal aid authority as an additional, probably their principal, tool for the further hampering of patient litigation.

We may briefly note here significant recent developments. We have a raft of decisions from the House of Lords: *Chester v Afshar* on consent to treatment, *Rees v Darlington Memorial Hospital NHS Trust* on the unplanned child, the *Fairchild* case on causation and increasing the risk of injury, and *Gregg v Scott* on loss of a chance, We have *Thompson v Bradford* from the Court of Appeal on relevant breach of duty, and developments in the vexed areas of nervous shock. In the area of practice, we have the important Protocol from the Civil Justice Council on the instruction of experts. And, of course, human rights continue to invest, some might say infest, every corner of litigation. And so it will go on, until the ending of time, or at least of civilisation as we know it. Change, and, to an extent, decay, but also, let it be said, some hope for the future, in all around I see. One can only wait each time for next month's package.

Stop-press cases

This month's package, too late for the main body of the text, offers three significant decisions of the Court of Appeal.

Relevant breach and foreseeability (Chapter 18)

A breach of duty has to be relevant to the injury claimed. Just because an injury would not have occurred if the defendant had not been negligent it does not necessarily follow that he is liable for it. For example, if a route planner is so badly designed that it sends a motorist on a roundabout route from A to B, the company may be liable for wasted petrol but not for a motoring accident that just happens to occur on the way. Obviously it would not have occurred if the route offered had been a reasonable one, but the injury has to have a relevant connection with the breach. This was recently considered in the Court of Appeal in the interesting, but very sad, case of *Thompson v Bradford* [2005] EWCA Civ 1439. The trial judge had found that a GP had not been negligent when he did not consider that a buttock abscess was a good reason for advising against a polio vaccination on an 8-week old baby but he had been negligent in not advising the parents that such an abscess was unusual and might need surgery, ie after the vaccination. In the event the child contracted poliomyelitis from the vaccine, the judge finding that, although no doctor could have foreseen that the lancing of the abscess might provide a portal of entrance for the germ, that was in fact what had happened. The judge found that, if the parents had been given the information that the abscess might require surgery, they would not have gone ahead at that time with the vaccination and the baby would therefore not have contracted the illness. Therefore the GP was liable for this having happened. The fallacy in this reasoning is not hard to spot. The Court of Appeal said that it was important that the reason for giving the information about the abscess was not that it could be a risk factor for contracting polio but simply that it might be uncomfortable for the baby to have surgery a short time after his vaccination. The judge did not deal with the relevance of foreseeability to the advice that the GP was accused of failing to give. The only relevant branch of duty was one that would render him liable for the contraction of polio. There was no relevant breach of duty, ie relevant to the injury sustained. The relevant breach of duty depended on what the GP could reasonably have foreseen as the consequences of his failure to give the relevant information.

It is interesting to note that the real thrust of the pleading and the opening address of claimant's counsel was that the defendant should have advised against the immunisation. It would seem that it was only when this proved a weak contention that the other line, based merely on failure to give information, was actively pursued, a line that would seem to me to have always suffered from an obvious defect – as the Court of Appeal judgment showed.

The inquest (Chapter 7)

In *R (on the application of Takoushis) v HM Coroner for Inner North London and Guys and St Thomas' Hospital NHS Trust* [2005] EWCA Civ

1440, the Court of Appeal said that, where a person died as a result of what was arguably medical negligence in a NHS hospital, the state had to have a system that provided for the practical and effective investigation of the facts and for the determination of civil liability. Unlike in the cases of deaths in custody the system did not have to provide for an investigation initiated by the state but might include such investigation. The question in each case was whether the system as a whole, including both any investigation initiated by the state and the possibility of civil and criminal proceedings , satisfied the requirements of article 2 as identified by the European Court. The system in operation in England, including both the possibility of civil process and the inquest, met those requirements. There was an important difference between those who were being detained by the state and those who were not.

Then, by judgment of 7 December 2005, we have the majority decision in *Lillywhite v University College London Hospitals NHS Trust* MLC 1300, reversing the judgment of Jacks J (MLC 1117) in favour of the defendants. The claim was brought by parents of a baby girl born severely disabled in 1992, on the basis that the prenatal ultrasound scan report by a consultant sonologist at a tertiary referral centre had been prepared negligently in that it reported that the necessary fetal structures had been seen (it was agreed that they had not in fact been present). It was contended that due care would have yielded a contrary conclusion and a termination would then have been sought and obtained. The trial judge had found that the defendants' explanation of how such an admitted error could reasonably have been made was enough to displace the prima facie allegation of negligence . However the majority of the Court of Appeal disagreed, saying that the expert evidence could not support such a conclusion. The full judgments should be carefully read by all medical negligence practitioners, most particularly as the judges were totally in conflict about what the trial judge could and what he could not reasonably conclude from the evidence. In terms of procedure, we may note that the 'explanation' referred to above given by the defendants was only advanced during the trial. Not surprisingly the appeal court strongly disapproved, saying that in these days of Woolf where careful pre-trial preparation and exchange of evidence was the order of the day, litigation in that form was completely unacceptable. The court also said that it was not open to the judge to prefer one expert over two other experts without making clear the basis on which he reached that conclusion.

I will also take the opportunity to note *Codent v Lyson*, 8 December 2005, CA, on the topic of Calderbank offers and payments in, from which, following *Trustees of Stokes Pension Fund v Western Power Distribution (South West) plc* [2005] 1 WLR 3595, it appears that a defendant can get some advantage as to costs from a mere offer made less than 21 days before the trial.

Coda

I would like at this point to record my gratitude to Lord Justice Latham (coincidentally himself among the majority in the above *Lillywhite* case) for agreeing to write the foreword to this edition. He will not mind my saying that I find it particularly appropriate that it is he who does this, as he was there at my time of coming in — we were law students together – and so he is here now at the time of my going out.

It has been a labour of love, this involvement of mine in medical negligence, over the past twenty years. They say that *amor vincit omnia,* and certain it is that the gently persistent efforts of patient-oriented groups and individuals over the years has produced a huge, we may say a seismic, shift in the scenario of medical litigation. I have seen the patient's claim, at first so beset around with difficulties that it was well nigh unwinnable, grow in stature, and in number, to a point where it demanded a re-thinking of the doctor/patient relationship and a re-assessment by the medical profession of the strategies for risk assessment and accident avoidance. Much of the response of the NHS in this connection merits praise, as does the work of the lawyers and groups that support patients, most notable among which has been Action against Medical Accidents, formerly Action for Victims of Medical Accidents. Lately we have been fighting a recession, not because the law is being used to deprive patients of their rights, but through the machinations of the legal aid authority, seeking, at government insistence, ever more ploys to avoid supporting these claims, and in so doing, of course, to assist the NHS to avoid paying out on claims. They do not pay out on claims that are not brought!

The future is uncertain. But then it always has been uncertain in this branch of the law. Heraclitus, my dear old Carian guest, would recognise the situation. 'As I keep telling you', he would exclaim, 'everything is in a state of flux'.

Well, it will have to flux without me, now. Perhaps I have been able to bring a little 'rough magic' to my task. But

Now my charms are all o'erthrown,
And what strength I have's mine own,
Which is most faint.

Charles Lewis
Gray's Inn
London

January 2006

Acronyms

BMLR   Butterworths' *Medico-Legal Reports*, published from June 1992.

JPIL   *Journal of Personal Injury Litigation.*

Med LR   The *Medical Law Reports*. From the beginning of 1998 the series has been published by Lloyds of London Press (the citation has been changed to [2001] Lloyd's Rep Med).

ML   *Medical Litigation*: this is the journal that since the beginning of 1998 kept practitioners up to date with all the latest developments in the medical negligence field – judgments with commentaries, writs, settlements, appeals set down, news and views, articles, etc. It ceased hard copy publication at the end of 2004. Its management continues to run two websites: www.medneg.com for practitioners, and www.medicalclaims.co.uk for the public.

MLC   *Medical Litigation Cases*: this is the invaluable database of full transcripts on the Internet at *www.medneg.com*, originally conceived by *Medical Litigation* and now run by *Medical Litigation Online*. Access is by subscription and every UK judgment relevant to medical claims since the end of 1997, as well as many overseas judgments, is posted in full transcript. Also, significant older medical cases are currently being posted all the while. In addition, every other UK medical negligence decision from every available hard copy source appears in summary form in the medical negligence index section. In line with the switch to electronic publishing and citation, MLC will be dropping the citation of the year and will only read, eg, *A* v *B* MLC 00999, rather than *A* v *B* [2001] MLC 00999. For that reason some MLC cases in the text are given a year reference and others are not. Where I have given only a MLC reference for a case I have in any event added the year as I think that information is helpful. The website also contains many articles, news items, and indexed lists of lawyers and experts. The site has an excellent search engine. Anyone practising in the field of medical claims needs to subscribe to this website.

Contents

PROCEDURE

Table of statutes

References at the right-hand side of the column are to page numbers.

Table of statutory instruments

References at the right-hand side of the column are to page numbers.

Table of cases

References at the right-hand side of the column are to page numbers.

B

C

D

G

H

K

L

M

N

Q

R

T

X

Y

Z

Quotations

On law

In law, what plea so tainted and corrupt,
But, being seasoned with a gracious voice,
Obscures the show of evil?

The Merchant of Venice (Bassanio)

I must say that, as a litigant, I should dread a lawsuit beyond almost anything
else, short of sickness and death.

Judge Learned Hand

The definition of the duty of care is a matter for the law and the courts. They
cannot stand idly by if the profession, by an excess of paternalism, denies their
patients a real choice. In a word, the law will not permit the medical profession
to play God.

Sir John Donaldson MR

The problem with Bolam *is that it inhibited the courts exercising a restraining*
influence. The courts must recognise that theirs is essentially a regulatory role
and they should not interfere unless interference is justified. But when
interference is justified they must not be deterred from doing so by any principle
such as the fact that what has been done is in accord with a practice approved
of by a respectable body of medical opinion.

Lord Woolf (January 2001)

On medicine

Physicians of all men are most happy. What good success soever they have, the
world proclaimeth, and what faults they commit, the earth covereth.

Francis Quarles (1592–1644)

In the practice of surgery particularly, the public are exposed to great risks from
the number of ignorant persons professing a knowledge of the art, without the
least pretensions to the necessary qualifications, and they often inflict very
serious injury on those who are so unfortunate as to fall into their hands.

Baron Garrow (1822)

The doctor is often more to be feared than the disease.

Old French proverb

Doctors are men who prescribe medicine of which they know little to human beings of whom they know nothing.

Voltaire

The primary function of the doctor is to entertain the patient while he gets better on his own.

Voltaire

Proper treatment will cure a cold in not more than seven days, but left to itself it will hang on for a week.

HG Felsen

It is unwise to place any profession or other body providing services to the public on a pedestal where their actions cannot be subject to close scrutiny. The greater the power the body has, the more important is this need.

Lord Woolf (January 2001)

Chapter 1

Introduction

A FASCINATING SUBJECT

There is probably no area of law that provokes such interest, and so immediately, from the non-lawyer as medical negligence. The lawyer has only to mention in conversation with non-lawyers, whether professional people or from any other walk of life, that he does that sort of work for him to be met with interested and informed opinions, the most striking aspect of which is the enthusiasm with which they are offered. His companions will tell him of the experiences they, their relatives and friends have had with the medical profession, usually those that have left the patient unsatisfied (the other sort is less memorable and not so much of a talking point); everyone will have a view on whether doctors are by and large a good or a bad thing; the spectre of American medical malpractice law will be raised – everyone seems to 'know' that vast sums are awarded at the drop of a hat to claimants in US courts, insurance premiums for the doctors are astronomical and not a few are driven or choose to go out of business. 'We don't want to get like America', one hears.

Within the profession, the work has a cachet that ordinary personal injury does not. Lawyers, particularly counsel, are quick to say that they specialise in the field even if their involvement is modest. Many of the solicitors who are qualified to do the work form a tight-knit group, striving to outdo their rivals with some striking victory, and ever on the look-out for new ways of extending the boundaries of the medical negligence claim.

Why does this branch of the law attract such interest and evoke so keen, often so emotional, a response from the lay person? It is partly because it is almost everyone's experience to have at one time or another been in the hands of the doctors, but, more importantly, it stems above all from the nature of the doctor's role. The healer is an archetype, just as the judge is. He is part priest, part parent; he is the object of an unstated love-hate relationship.

The patient looks to the physician on the one hand as the comforter and healer who will make him well and happy; he has the learning and the magic that will bring relief from fear and pain. The patient, whether consciously acknowledging it or not, longs to be relieved or comforted. All this gives the physician a hierophantic status. On the other hand, the patient resents his dependence and is not averse to debunking the myth; a myth, be it noted, that he has himself created. This relationship is not entirely dissimilar to the emotional duality that a child feels towards his parents. In an age where the child has learnt that obedience to parents is not necessarily the norm, parental control is less and less effective, and for today's children anything is permissible, it is not surprising that the divine aspect of the medical profession has taken a beating (aided enormously by their own well-publicised malpractices). There is perhaps something of a temptation when specialising in cases against the medical profession to regard it as a sort of crusade, as do many of those who specialise in actions against the police, as if not only policemen but also doctors represent some sort of authority figures with which one has not within oneself completely come to terms; and when that happens one forgets too easily the marvellous skills and devoted care that generally characterise the practice of medicine. But this is not a textbook on psychology; the issues raised here are merely by way of explanation for the fascination that lawsuits against the medical profession have for the ordinary member of the public and for the almost emotional response that they can arouse in lawyer and non-lawyer alike.

A similar attitude, based on archetypes, is found in respect of judges, where the archetype invests ordinary people with a patina of awful superiority. Because the unconscious mind is affected by the archetype of judge as stern dispenser of both wisdom and punishment the reality of the average judge is not perceived. While proper respect is due to every person, of whatever station in life, the holder of judicial office is not by reason of his appointment alone imbued with any special qualities. All that one might conclude is that the judge, as indeed the lawyer, is likely to be more in his head than the average person, who has not spent most of their life arguing, as Swift said of lawyers, 'in words multiplied for the purpose and in a language no other mortal understands, that black is white and white is black, according as he is paid'.

The above, largely philosophical, passage was written in 1987 for the first edition of this work. It remains valid comment today, nearly twenty years later, even though the practical picture of medical negligence, at ground level as it were, and the workings of the courts and the lawyers involved, as well as the attitude of the public to suing for compensation, has radically altered.

THE GROWTH OF LITIGATION

There is no doubt that medical negligence litigation has grown enormously over the last twenty five years. In earlier times such a claim was unusual and stood little chance of success. That was partly because it was not within the current ethos to accuse the god-like doctors of incompetent treatment: patients shrank from such a course and judges did not approve of it. Lord Denning used to say that to prove a doctor guilty of negligence required a higher standard of proof than if the accusation was levelled against a non-professional.[1] In 1953 Finnemore J said:

> It is the duty of a doctor to exercise reasonable skill and care, but a simple mistake in diagnosis or treatment is not of itself negligence. The court is not bound to shut its eyes to the fact that there are quite a few cases at the present time in which doctors are sued for negligence. That may arise from the changing relationship between doctor and patient, but it matters not. There is a considerable onus on the court to see that persons do not easily obtain damages simply because there is some medical or surgical mistake made. But the court will not shrink from facing the issue if it finds that the doctor has failed to give to a case the proper skill and care which patients have a right to expect.[2]

That represented the traditional view: insistence that medical mistakes did not necessarily involve negligence, regardless of the consequences, and a friendly nod in the direction of the patient.

Practicalities, both social and legal, were also against the patient. Few doctors were prepared to give evidence for the patient. It took years to create lists of fair-minded specialists who would give an impartial opinion on the standard of care. Even now, if the patient goes to the wrong expert, he or she will get a whitewash (whitewashes are still the forte of a fair number of oft-appearing defence experts, regardless of their parroting their impartial duty owed to the court). In earlier years statements of witnesses and the evidence of experts were not disclosed until they came to the witness box. It was trial by ambush. Gradually the scene changed, thanks to the persistent efforts of those, like Action for Victims of Medical Accidents (now known as Action against Medical Accidents – AvMA) and the lawyers who supported it, who fought unrelentingly for the rights of the patient. Now, due particularly to the recent Woolf reforms, a cards-on-the-table approach is a living and mandatory reality. But there are still one or two judges, usually appointed from a successful defence practice at the Bar, who are unreasonably slow to find for the patient and who will always, if at all possible, 'prefer' the evidence of the defence expert to that of the claimant's expert.

What is more difficult to pinpoint is the growth of medical negligence litigation, if any, over the last few years. Governments will produce statistics purporting to prove whatever they want to prove, for example exponential growth in NHS liability for medical claims; but usually their statistics are biased, often demonstrably so, because they are politicians and their statistics are therefore unreliable. It is unlikely, with substantial reductions in the eligibility of legal aid for medical claims and the reluctance of the Legal Services Commission to give the green light to any claim, that there has been any growth in this litigation over the last few years or that there will be any in the future. What has pushed up substantially the amount of total NHS outlay on claims (so that awards of

---

1   In *Hucks* v *Cole* [1993] 4 Med LR 393, CA, Lord Denning said that a charge of negligence against a professional man was serious. It stood on a different footing to a charge of negligence against the driver of a motor car. The consequences were far more serious. It affected his professional status and reputation. The burden of proof was correspondingly greater. As the charge was so grave, so should the proof be clear.

2   *Edler* v *Greenwich and Deptford Hospital Management Committee* (1953) Times, 7 March.

well over £4m no longer occasion surprise) is the general increase in the calculation of future loss (due to judicial acceptance of what is known as the 2.5% multiplier), and increased life expectancy for injured persons thanks to progress in medical care. Beside the effect of this change the parsimonious increase in general damages authorised not long ago by the Court of Appeal pales into insignificance.

Such evidence as there is strongly suggests that the actual number of claims has been falling over the last two or more years. This is hardly surprising given the aforesaid reluctance of the legal aid authority to fund these claims and the grudging way they authorise any increase in the scope of a legal aid certificate. More positively, the availability of mediation for small claims where money is not the main objective, the expert handling of most claims by certificated solicitors and the early clarification of claims and defences under the clinical negligence protocol have all helped to reduce the number of claims commenced, and, even more so, the number of claims actually brought to trial.[3]

A note on aggravated and exemplary damages

In some legal claims, substantial further amounts can be awarded on top of general damages for aggravated or exemplary damages, though well short of the huge jury awards for punitive damages that are made from time to time in USA jurisdictions.[4] The suggestion is not infrequently made in medical claims that aggravated or exemplary damages should be claimed, usually on the basis that, as perceived by the patient, the negligence has been gross or the behaviour of the medical personnel highly offensive. As explained below, such claims will rarely be successful.

The distinction between the two sorts of damages is that aggravated damages are given to compensate the claimant when the harm done to him by a wrongful act has been aggravated by the manner in which the act was done. Exemplary damages, on the other hand, are intended (within defined limits – see below) to punish the defendant for opprobrious conduct, ie a form of punitive damages.

It has been said more than once that neither aggravated nor exemplary damages have any place in medical negligence actions in this country (see *Barbara* v *Home Office* (1984) 134 NLJ 888; *G* v *North Tees Health Authority* [1989] FCR 53; *Kralj* v *McGrath* [1986] 1 All ER 54). In *H* v *Ministry of Defence* [1991] 2 QB 103 the Court of Appeal did suggest that exemplary damages might be awarded if the defendants had abused their authority. The ambit of exemplary damages as laid down by the House of Lords in the two leading cases of *Rookes* v *Barnard* [1964] AC 1129 and *Cassell Co Ltd* v *Broome* [1972] AC 1027 is narrow (only available where there had been oppressive conduct by the executive or similar body, or the defendant had sought to make a

---

3   There is an interesting editorial on this topic by Peter Walsh in Clinical Risk Vol 9 Issue 3 page 108.

4   Punitive damages in the USA are of a different order. In October 1997 a South Carolina jury awarded $262.5m against the Chrysler Corporation in favour of the parents of a six year old boy who was thrown to his death out of a Dodge Caravan when the lock failed. £250m of this award was punitive damages.

profit from his wrongdoing).[5] In *Kuddus* v *Chief Constable of Leicestershire Constabulary* [2001] 2 WLR 1789 the House of Lords extended the catchment area for exemplary damages somewhat by holding that their relevance was not limited to torts where the claim had already been recognised before 1964 as one to which exemplary damages could be applicable. However, the judges were clearly unhappy about the general confusion over exemplary damages, and certainly there is nothing in their speeches to benefit the claimant in a medical negligence action. Nevertheless we may usefully note that Dyson J awarded aggravated damages (15% of his award of general damages) against a dentist who, callously and simply for his own profit, recommended and carried out all manner of unnecessary treatments on a variety of patients (*Appleton* v *Garrett* [1997] 8 Med LR 75).

In *Hunter Area Health Service* v *Marchewski* [2001] MLC 0296 the New South Wales Court of Appeal considered the question whether aggravated damages were ever appropriate to a negligence claim. The judge had awarded a further 20% on top of general damages on the ground that the hospital's decision not to resuscitate a doomed child without telling the parents (who would not have consented to such a course) callously increased their suffering (it was otherwise a reasonable medical decision). In the event, the appeal court did not decide the broad issue (though it signified its agreement with the English authorities), but set aside the award on the narrower ground that to admit aggravated damages where the claim was being brought for pure psychiatric injury would be inconsistent with the current parameters prescribed for claims for psychiatric injury.[6]

The common law in New Zealand is different. There they are not, as we are, 'still toiling in the chains of *Rookes* v *Barnard*', to borrow the expression used in the judgment in September 2002 of the Privy Council in the medical case of *A* v *Bottrill* MLC 0854, [2000] UKPC 44. Free from such constraints, the court decided in that case that even intentional misconduct or conscious recklessness was not in principle an essential prerequisite of the court's discretionary jurisdiction to award exemplary damages, for it extended to all cases of tortious wrongdoing where the defendant's conduct satisfied a criterion of outrageousness. In this case the doctor, whose false reporting rate on pap smears in relation to cervical cancer was 50% or higher, had clearly been outrageously negligent, but the New Zealand Court of Appeal had wrongly held that the claim must fail as he had not been shown to have been consciously reckless. So the issue fell to be re-determined by that Court. It is clear, however, that without intentional misconduct or conscious recklessness the conduct would have to be, by objective standards, quite appalling to justify an award and so such cases will be very rare. If ever English law escapes the trammels of *Rookes* v *Barnard*, this Privy Council judgment is likely to be much in point.

---

5   The court said in *Kralj* v *McGrath* (supra) that there was no precedent for awarding damages for anger and indignation aroused by a defendant's high-handed way of dealing with the relevant incident (in this case the obstetric negligence at the delivery of a child had been horrific and the defendant's response thereafter highly unsatisfactory).

6   The Law Commission produced a report on exemplary and aggravated damages in 1997 (Cmnd No. 247).

THE EXPENSE OF LITIGATION

Whoever wins a medical negligence action the taxpayer, and/or other patients, are the losers. The lawyers always get something out of it, but who would begrudge them that? If the patient achieves compensation the NHS has to pay the costs of both sides as well as the compensation. If the patient does not achieve compensation the NHS still has to pay its own costs and the Legal Services Commission (LSC) has to pay the patient's costs (albeit at a reduced rate). Medical and administrative staff are likely to have to take time off their specialised duties to give their input where relevant to the defence process. No wonder various schemes are being proposed, or have already been implemented, to cut the cost of medical negligence litigation. There was a voluntary pilot scheme in the North of England not long ago called *Resolve* which was intended to provide a speedy process for settling medical claims. However that seems to have foundered, largely because its sponsors, the NHS Litigation Authority, were perceived as selecting experts to decide the issues who were not impartial. The outlines put forward by the Chief Medical Officer in June 2003 for a not dissimilar scheme (at any rate as far as liability is concerned), this time called *Redress,* though no doubt to be pounced upon in due course by the LSC as an excuse for them not to fund medical negligence litigation, is likely to suffer from the same fundamental objection. Some authorities still argue every so often that a no-fault system of compensation would be a great improvement, grappling as best they can with the clear arguments that have shown on every previous occasion this has been proposed that this is unlikely to be the case (see Chapter 28). One of the objections to the proposals of the *Redress* document was that it seemed to be offering a largely no fault basis for birth injury – how on earth the overstretched NHS would have afforded the necessary payments even on a somewhat parsimonious tariff system was unclear. Anyway that (large) aspect of the scheme was hastily abandoned.

Medical negligence claims, like all legal aid litigation, were originally attacked by the activities of Lord Mackay, but then hostilities were redoubled in earnest by Lord Irvine. The government's first 'success' was to abolish all legal aid for personal injury claims, forcing claimants into conditional fee agreements. But most personal injury claims succeed in one way or another, so that the legal aid funds were in any event being reimbursed their costs. That hasn't saved them much. Since then the government has been trying to find ways of avoiding paying for medical mistakes without losing political support in the process. They would dearly like to abolish the common law right to sue for medical mistakes (but they dare not – human rights and all that); they would like to put all medical claims on a miserly tariff for compensation as they did for criminal injuries, and they would like to give the NHS, through the NHS Litigation Authority, the sole right to decide if compensation should be paid. They would like to deny all funded support to all medical claims, reserving the limited legal aid funds for more important issues than disabled children, such as asylum seekers, immigration and human rights claims (all of which continue to multiply like flies).

Redress proposes a system whereby whether to pay compensation and, if so, how much, would be decided by a panel for the benefit of an injured patient who would have no expertise to assess the proposals, let alone any rights to challenge it. How much of this will come to pass remains to be seen and, in particular, how independent or dependent the panel will be, overtly or covertly, is an interesting question. What, however, is clear is that the LSC is already preparing to use *Redress*, when it comes into being in some shape or another, to deny funds for litigation to an injured patient for as long as possible, if not for ever. That explains why they disingenuously announce that they no longer propose to require a patient to proceed after the investigative stage by way of a conditional fee agreement. They have their sticky fingers in quite another pie now.

All the recent changes to funding and to the NHS generally, as well as to legal procedures, are dealt with in more detail in the next few chapters. But however medical litigation is funded and whatever the rules of procedure, it will always be expensive because every medical claim with apparent potential requires from the outset that the medical records be obtained, sorted and carefully investigated, that at least one and probably more than one expert report be obtained from carefully selected independent experts, and that then, unless liability is admitted, the claim be subjected to protracted and complex argument over the content, acceptability and consequences of the medical care afforded to the patient. None of this comes cheap. It is all worlds away from the comparatively straightforward scenario of a road traffic accident. As I wrote in the last edition of this book: 'The only way in which the cost of medical litigation could be substantially cut would be to take medical claims out of the litigation arena entirely, whether by outlawing any such claims (an unwise move politically, as well as an unjust one running counter to the fundamental principles of the English legal system [and probably human rights as well, we may now add], or by handing them over to simple scrutiny by some sort of medical assessment board and subjecting them to a set tariff of compensation (similar to the procedures of the Criminal Injuries Compensation Board).'

ON THE OTHER HAND

The cry is often heard from certain quarters to the effect that greedy patients, over-indulgent judges and, worst of all, unprincipled lawyers, are bringing the NHS to its knees, to the general detriment of the public, and that something has to be done about the growth of medical claims and the huge rise in the number and the quantum of compensation awards. Yet some of the foremost authorities on the subject offer a different view. In January 2001 at University College, London, Lord Woolf said that in the past courts had been excessively deferential to the medical profession but that this automatic assumption of beneficence had been dented. He said it was unwise to place any profession or other body providing services to the public on a pedestal where their actions could not be subject to close scrutiny. The courts should take a more robust view of negligence by the medical profession and not be deterred by the accepted test for negligence that asked whether what had been done was in accord with a respectable body of medical opinion. He said he could not help believing that the behaviour of the medical personnel involved in recent scandals betrayed a lack of appreciation of the limits of their responsibility.

Though not motivated by personal gain, they had lost sight of their power and authority, and had acted as though they were able to take any action they thought desirable, irrespective of the views of others. That over-deferential approach was captured by the phrase 'doctor knows best'. The contemporary approach was a more critical one. It could be said that doctor knows best if he acted reasonably and logically and got his facts right. Lord Woolf also pointed out the increase of more than 30% over the previous year in the number of complaints to the General Medical Council and said this had called the very future of that body into question. He said other factors had made judges less deferential: the difficulties people had in bringing successful claims; increasing awareness of patients' rights; the closer scrutiny of doctors by courts in places such as Canada and Australia, and the scale of medical negligence litigation, which was a 'disaster area'. Lord Woolf said all this indicated that the health service was not giving sufficient priority to avoiding medical mishap and treating patients justly when mishaps occurred (for the full text, see (2001) 9 *Medical Law Review*).

At about the same time, Sir Donald Irving, chairman of the GMC, accused doctors of 'deep-seated flaws', including excessive paternalism, secrecy and lack of respect for patients. Dr Michael Wilkes, chairman of the BMA's medical committee, responded, saying that no one in the medical profession expected the public – or the courts – to put doctors on a pedestal, and that the medical profession was working very hard to improve the quality of practice and to ensure that cases of incompetence were dealt with swiftly and fairly.

Over the last few years the element of hostility between lawyers and doctors has reduced to an appreciable extent owing to better liaison, communication and association. In other words, the two professions talk to each other more, rather than just waving their assegais. There is now a greater understanding that the litigation war arises principally from medical mistakes rather than greedy lawyers or ungrateful patients and that therefore eradicating mistakes by a combination of risk assessment, clinical governance and proper training (and not overworking the staff) is the way to turn a war into an alliance, which would benefit not only the public coffers but also the patients.

So the truth lies somewhere between the opposing views. The medical profession is largely good, often marvellous, but sometimes less than satisfactory. The lawyers, on both sides, are largely fair-minded and responsible, but sometimes too quick and too keen to sue or to defend. The judges are on the whole astute and impartial, but sometimes neither one nor the other. However, the practice of the courts in assigning medical trials to whomever is available, rather than to a judge with at least some experience of medical claims, is not conducive to an informed judgment, but only to a guaranteed lottery. But at least the inexperienced judges usually demonstrate a degree of humility in the face of the wide experience of the lawyers appearing before them. Some experienced judges, on the other hand, are overweening in their arrogance, acting the great panjandrum. This gentle criticism does not apply, I hasten to add, to any of the High Court judges, but rather to one or two big fish in little ponds out in the provinces.

Chapter 2

The changes

INTRODUCTION

Medical negligence has undergone huge changes over the last few years. These changes have involved the substantive law, in cases such as *Gregg* v *Scott* [2005] 2 WLR 268, MLC 1202 and *Chester* v *Afshar* [2005] 1 AC 134, MLC 1170, and the wrongful birth cases after *McFarlane* v *Tayside Health Board* [2000] 2 AC 59, MLC 0127, HL, and, in fields only slightly removed and certainly relevant to medical negligence, dyslexia and stress at work have provided a fund of new material and possibilities for the imaginative medical lawyer (not an oxymoron, I hope). The changes have involved further developments in the attack on public funding of medical claims, with the threat of something even nastier in store when the system of *Redress* takes shape in some form or another; and, although the procedural rules after the Woolf report have now largely bedded down, we have also seen the rise and rise of the new vogue of mediation. Human rights, as originally forecast from Lord Denning onwards, occupy a large part of the judicial time; no claim is considered complete unless within it at some point can be discerned a complaint that some form of human right to which the claimant is entitled has been traversed. Needless to say, the NHS, in the hands of the current government (not to say any other would be better, though), undergoes ceaseless change, restless like Homer's ocean. Health bodies are forever merging and separating in a hypnotic eddy of tides, with names and nomenclature forever changing, services reviewed and altered, targets disastrously introduced leading to serious distortion of clinical priorities, meaningless (indeed harmful) comparisons of hospitals and of practitioners created by eager bureaucrats, ten-year plans proudly proclaimed, and vote-catching initiatives started with flags flying and political tails wagging only to be quietly forgotten in due course. Quangos proliferate, administrators outnumber practitioners, and rules and regulations for the governance of society spew forth endlessly from the legislative maw in this as in every other aspect of community life. In April 2005 a Fellow of the Royal College of Surgeons wrote to a daily newspaper, saying that the government had set NHS targets for short-term political gain, and that priorities were now set by politicians and administrators, if not by doctors. Restriction of working hours, interference with medical training and farming out routine work to the private sector made training the next generation of doctors near impossible. Diversion of funds from hospitals, and the next wave of NHS changes (including funding according to a national tariff) would leave trusts unable to provide a basic emergency service. The Prime Minister knew all that, but ignored it. History would record that the demise of the NHS was caused by a Labour party obsessed with power, not policy.

THE GENERAL CHANGES

Reform of the rules of court

The Woolf reforms were originally forced upon us before their full implications had been worked out, even before the civil procedure rules (CPR) had been fully scripted. There was for a period a chaotic deluge of amendments,[1] but, to be fair, as stated above they are to a large, though not a comprehensive, extent bedded in by now. They are intended to reduce the twin evils of litigation identified by Woolf; namely expense and delay. They are intended to be user-friendly, consistent with the general dumbing down of the legal process (Latin is now frowned upon if not actually outlawed, despite the unrivalled clarity it offers in identifying legal rules and concepts and despite the fact that highly placed judges remain happy to use the lingo in their judgments and speeches). We were initially given inconsistent messages from the appeal courts about the relevance of the large body of law built up from earlier decisions of the courts under the previous Rules of the Supreme Court, being told one moment that they had all become irrelevant, the next that some of them could still be useful (reminiscent of babies and bath water).[2] Now it is appreciated that the rules have a lot in common with the Chancellor's foot, their interpretation owing more to judicial discretion than to legislative certainty, being based on the humorous concept that comprehensive and arbitrary (ie uncontrolled) judicial case management will cure all ills, and that therefore judges should intervene at every pre-trial stage rather than leaving the progress of the case up to the lawyers as they have been the ones responsible for the problems in the first place. What has all this resulted in? Couching the new rules in general terms and referring every issue to the so-called 'overriding objective' (piously but hopelessly vaguely expressed as the objective of enabling the courts to deal with cases 'justly'

---

1   For example, we have been told that to get to grips with the procedural law on civil appeals the practitioner must consult the Access to Justice Act 1999; Part 52 of the CPR, together with rr 27.12 and 27.13 and section VIII of Pt 47; Practice Direction 42 and the Access to Justice Act 1999 (Destination of Appeals) Order 2000 (*per* Brooke LJ in his long and helpful judgment unravelling the infinite complexity of the current law in *Tanfern Ltd* v *Cameron-MacDonald* [2000] 1 WLR 1311, CA). See also *Copeland* v *Smith* [2000] 1 WLR 1371, CA, for the burden placed on counsel to keep up with the deluge, so that, *inter alia*, an end will be put to 'the endless appeals in interlocutory matters which characterised the pre-26 April 1999 regime' (*per* Brooke LJ, again).

2   Throughout the book I have tried to retain such old procedural law as probably remains relevant and omit what is not. But often enough it is anyone's guess which is which. A New Age position was recently adopted by Curtis J in *Marsh* v *Frenchay Healthcare NHS Trust* (2001) Times, 13 March, when he declined to consider the old law in respect of an application to withdraw a payment.

– as to what is just, we may say '*quot homines* (or rather *iudices*), *tot sententiae*'), denying the validity of previous judge-made law, requiring the judges at the interlocutory levels to dictate the pre-trial progress and preparation of a case and giving them almost unfettered discretion on every issue (with the Court of Appeal constantly telling us it is reluctant to interfere – see footnote 1 above and the Access to Justice Act 1999, s 55(1)(a) and (b)), has had the following results:

- there is complete unpredictability as to how a court will decide an interlocutory issue. At one time claims were being struck out for minor infringements of the rules, the theory being that if lawyers were hit hard enough and often enough, they would come into line; but, when it was perceived that this was a good way to present the lawyers with extra fees from appeals (ie a whole new satellite industry, born of draconian decisions and the general uncertainty how the new rules should be interpreted), wiser counsels prevailed. Even so, unpredictability remains, and the natural response to uncertainty is to litigate in an attempt to gain some certainty.[3] That is what precedent is all about. It is all very well starting over in this bright new age of litigation with *tabulae rasae*, but the nature of English jurisprudence means that one will litigate twice as hard to fill them. Otherwise the situation is totally chaotic with each decision depending on nothing more stable than the length of the judge's foot, or which side of the bed he or she got out of that morning. That, however, may be what the rules intend, seeing how reluctant the Court of Appeal is to entertain appeals on points of procedure, particularly if a district judge and a county court judge have already ruled on the issue.

- judges dealing with medical negligence cases (and perhaps other types of case) often impose impossible deadlines in order to meet unrealistic 'target' dates, deliberately ignoring or just plain ignorant of what time is needed to arrange this or that stage, eg obtaining an expert report. Counsel's availability is now usually ignored, which means that the patient, who has relied on her counsel for probably two years and more, has to change horse mid-stream. Sometimes experts' availability is ignored (leaving the litigant to go and find another expert), all for the overriding objective of avoiding delay. Targets must be met, *ruat justitia*. The irony in practice is that, when the lawyers have managed to meet unreasonable deadlines, they often find when the day for the trial dawns that the court administration (outside the High Court in London) is so shambolic that no court or judge can be found for the trial and so it is postponed for (in my experience) up to a year.

- judges often refuse to allow reports to be obtained from necessary experts or, if already obtained, to be used, thus prejudicing the patient's claim. The knee jerk reaction of many judges is to reduce the number of experts requested by the claimant's lawyers, however few they ask for. Many judges have insufficient understanding or

---

3   A recent example of this 'uncertainty' syndrome can be found in the judicial history of mediation, which is dealt with in detail below.

experience of medical cases; yet, paradoxically, it is they who have been given control of the preparation of a claim rather than the experienced lawyers (the accreditation system means that now only highly experienced lawyers are permitted to handle legal aid medical negligence claims for the patient). Some of the orders made are little short of ridiculous. One district judge ordered a joint report on causation in a perinatal brain damage case (the order was reversed by a High Court judge on appeal); one county court judge refused to allow experts on liability in a medical claim to be called to give oral evidence; another recently insisted, despite objections from both sides, on a joint report on vascular causation where the injury alleged was amputation of a leg (he was reversed in short order by the Court of Appeal).

If all this sounds very depressing, it is. The only glimmer of light lies in the hope that these are teething problems, that the judiciary will gradually understand what can reasonably and what cannot be done, and within what time limits, and what needs to be done, if medical cases are to be processed properly. However, to redress the balance a little, let us acknowledge that the situation since I wrote the above rodomontade for the last edition some five years ago has improved (I thought it too fine a Philippic to delete it though). The Court of Appeal has shown a good understanding of the just requirements of the medical suitor and his claim and there are judges at the lower levels, most particularly the specialist Masters of the High Court, whose interventions are sensible and helpful and in that manner validate Lord Woolf's intentions. Let us hope their wisdom is garnered in due course by those who exercise similar functions in the further reaches of the jurisdiction.

Reform of the legal aid system

The Woolf reforms, though created under the rubric of 'access to justice', had at least as much to do with saving money as benefiting the consumer. The examples given in CPR 1.1(2) of what dealing with a case 'justly' involves relate largely to the financial implications of litigation and the principle of proportionality (the expense of bringing a claim should not be disproportionate to its value). Yet the general thrust of the rules, if interpreted and implemented sensibly, is now seen to be beneficial. The general objectives of reducing expense and delay are valid.[4] Specific benefits for the medical negligence action can be found in particular rules, often relating to the need for transparency and a cards-on-the-table approach rather than tight-lipped combat.[5]

The legal aid reforms, however, though presented by the Government as intended to benefit the consumer, appear wholly concerned with

---

4   One does wonder at some of the new concepts, however. For example, the recommendation to assess at each stage the costs of interlocutory hearings has been said by no less an authority than HH Judge Cook to involve in many cases the expenditure of more time and money than the case itself.

5   Lord Woolf considered that medical negligence was sui generis, a special category of its own, not to be lumped under the rubric of personal injury. He devoted a whole chapter in *Access to Justice* to medical claims (see Appendix VI).

saving money. Despite claims of the Government's interest in 'access to justice', it remains hard for impoverished litigants to afford the court fees. Further, that interest does not accord with the speedy abolition of legal aid for personal injury claims. Similarly, the 'benefits' of conditional fees warrant more research if conclusions may be drawn from the fact that amendments to the rules are forever being produced at short notice under pressure from this or that lobby – eg the complex rules about recovery of the success fee. The Government's original idea was to include medical negligence within the personal injury exclusion, but fortunately wiser counsels prevailed. It was grudgingly acknowledged that conditional fees were not yet – if ever they would be – a viable basis for suing for medical injury except in a small minority of cases. Now it appears that the legal aid authority has turned its lethal gaze away from conditional fee arrangements (CFAs) to rely in due course on defeating the litigant with measures based on the *Redress* system when it is in place.

The current situation regarding funding and availability of legal aid for what they are now pleased to call 'clinical negligence'[6] claims is explained in the next chapter.

THE SPECIFIC CHANGES

The specialist panels

The most significant practical change over the last few years has been the requirement, operative from July 1999, that only a firm with a clinical negligence franchise can take new clinical negligence cases on legal aid. In order to obtain a franchise it is a necessary, but not a sufficient, condition that at least one of the members of the firm should have been admitted to one of the two expert panels, that run by the Law Society or that run by Action against Medical Accidents (AvMA). It was obviously necessary to have some form of accreditation for solicitors in this field, as too many, through inexperience or inefficiency, were making a compete mess of potential claims, not processing them properly and wasting a lot of public money. Horror stories used to abound. However, a lot of capable practitioners have now been excluded because the criteria for acceptance on the panels are so strict (both panels have written criteria and some sort of appeal procedure). Large swathes of the country are without a franchised firm, with the result that patients in those areas have to travel a long way to get to see a qualified solicitor. Solicitors who on application to the panel have not satisfied the experience criteria are not able then to take on more work which would enable them to satisfy the criteria. The result is that they gravitate towards the established players, or, probably more frequently, give up the work. A non-panel practitioner who wants to do this work will have to join a firm with a franchise or whatever

---

6   The definition of clinical negligence for the franchise category adds nothing to what everyone had understood by the term medical negligence: a claim for damages in respect of an alleged breach of duty of care or trespass to the person committed in the course of the provision of clinical or medical services (including dental or nursing services); or a claim for damages for alleged professional negligence in the conduct of such a claim.

form of contract is the current LSC norm. Thus the work becomes concentrated in the hands of a small group of practitioners. At the time of writing there are only about 250 firms with the relevant authority for legal aid work. There cannot be any reasonable expectation that that number will increase, for the reasons just stated.

Procedural changes

Procedural changes are dealt with in the main text at the relevant points. The most significant is the clinical negligence protocol, which provides for the manner in which a claim may be commenced. Also important is the new guidance protocol for experts, drafted by the Civil Justice Council (see Appendix II). Many other rules are highly relevant to medical negligence claims, though not specific to them, such as the new rules on pleading (particularly those that outlaw blanket defences by requiring specific responses to the allegations of negligence).

Progress (?) in NHS services

Before going further, it may be helpful to cast an eye over what progress in NHS services we have seen over the last few years. The Labour government has certainly increased spending on the NHS. It stood, in England, at £34 billion before the 1997 election. It is now at about £69 billion and is planned to rise to £90 billion in two years. There are more doctors and more nurses (though many are only part time). But a lot of that money has little bearing on patient care. It goes to increase wages or fund the legions of administrators. Of the 12% budget increase for the NHS in 2004/05 only 2.4% was left for new hospital services. Of course, there have been some improvements. Waiting times are shorter in casualty and in GP practice, if not for in-patient treatment. But doctors hate the way the system has become so politicised and centralised, with ministers setting targets leading to the distortion of clinical priorities, at the same time employing a great host of managers whose overriding objective is to ensure that the targets are met and the appropriate handful of stars achieved, come what may (there are now 37,000 of these bureaucrats, double what there were in 1997). The pressure to meet these wretched targets is so intense that eight out of ten doctors claim it has resulted in threats to patient safety. Hospitals risk losing funds and managers their jobs if they aren't met. So, among other dodges, non-urgent cases are now often treated first to avoid missing a target; and a report by the National Audit Office found that one in ten decisions to close wards in an effort to check MRSA outbreaks was overruled by hospital managers, often because to close a ward would risk transgressing targets for how long patients wait for an operation. One hospital cancelled operations that had been booked well in advance as it would not look good for its figures if it had to cancel them late, and then the inspectors might not award them the coveted three stars. Those of us who watched *Bodies*, the recent black comedy on television, may wonder why it was not billed as a documentary. Labour has failed to live up to its promise to scrap the internal market introduced by the Tories in an attempt to control expenditure, but the fact of the matter is that every government finds that, however much money one pours into the NHS, it is never enough. Aneurin Bevan's dream is not realisable in the real world (though it has to be said that it is a lot better than having no public healthcare at all).

Meanwhile the incessant tinkering, often amounting to radical re-organising of the service – particularly under this regulation-mad government – will continue. One of the latest bright ideas is 'foundation' status for hospitals and trusts. We are told that foundation hospitals are new types of hospitals that will have more independence from the government. They are different from other NHS hospitals in that local people, hospital staff, patients and, in some cases, carers, can become members of the hospital. The members can choose a board of governors to run the hospital. Foundation hospitals are not managed by the Department of Health. This means hospital managers are able to choose how they spend money, and make decisions based on the needs of the local community. Foundation hospitals, says the Government, give patients, staff and members of the public more choice over how the hospital is run. They want all NHS trusts to have foundation status within the next five years.

Alan Milburn, then health secretary, said:

> Freeing NHS Foundation Trusts from day-to-day Whitehall control will encourage greater local innovation in how services are delivered. They will help put doctors, nurses and other frontline staff in the driving seat and give a far greater say to local communities over how hospitals are run. NHS Foundation Trusts are part of our wider reform programme to open up the NHS so that it provides more responsive services to patients.

What baffles me is how it is supposed to be a step forward to give local people and patients power over how a hospital is run. What expertise do they possibly have to offer? On this principle maybe local people and litigants should be offered the running of legal services.

It is still very early days but it does not seem to be going very well for the few trusts that have already applied and been granted the status.

Generally, financial problems abound. The dual quango report of June 2005 from the National Audit Office and the Audit Commission told us that more than a hundred NHS bodies were in deficit, 16 by more than £5m. Government reforms such as foundation trusts, new staff contracts and changes to the funding system were putting 'unprecedented pressure' on NHS finances.

As this edition reached its final stages (December 2005), we heard that the latest 'cost-cutting' reforms are going to cost the NHS £320m in redundancies. This situation arises out of a pre-election promise to save £250m a year in management costs and involves merging primary care trusts with strategic health authorities. The plan, *Commissioning a Patient-led NHS*, proposes that PCTs should abandon the task of delivering services, handing it over to private or voluntary groups or to hospital trusts (300 PCTs would reduce to 100, and strategic health authorities from 28 to 11). In theory, therefore, the savings should be substantial by the third year. If you believe that ...

BODIES (NON-CORPOREAL)

A number of organisations, some new and some not so new, have been created in an attempt to produce swifter and fairer resolution of medical claims. Some have arisen in the medical arena, some in the legal, and some halfway between. The medico-legal bodies concentrate on creating a smooth interface between the professions. They include the Clinical Disputes Forum (CDF) and the Expert Witness Institute (EWI).

The legal bodies include the NHS Litigation Authority.

The medical bodies concentrate on risk management and clinical governance (there is a note below on this current buzzword), so that, one hopes, fewer mistakes will be made. They involve a multitude of quangos.

Clinical Disputes Forum (CDF)

The Clinical Disputes Forum labels itself a unique organisation, being a group of the key people in the field of clinical negligence litigation working together to try to improve its procedures and reduce the number of patients who have to go to law to resolve their disputes with their doctors and other healthcare providers.

It originated with the Woolf Inquiry into Access to Justice in 1994-96 and was founded in January 1996. It consists of representatives of the various groups involved in clinical negligence: patients' and consumers' representatives, managers and doctors and dentists; the lawyers on both sides, the experts, the NHS Litigation Authority and the legal aid authority. Also the Lord Chancellor's Department, the General Medical Council, the Law Society and the UKCC (the Central Council for Nursing, Midwifery and Health Visiting, which regulates the nursing professions).

The Forum works to find solutions that will be acceptable to all the groups in the field. It establishes an agenda of work and sets up working parties. Its projects have included the pre-action protocol, the interface between complaints and litigation, experts' meetings, lump sum damages and mediation. It produced draft guidelines on experts' discussions in the context of clinical disputes but does not appear to have done much lately.

The Expert Witness Institute (EWI)

The Expert Witness Institute was launched in November 1996 to service and support experts. It acts as a voice for the expert witness community, supporting experts from all professional disciplines and lawyers who use the services of experts. Its functions are to encourage, train and educate experts and to improve and maintain their standards and status. The EWI works with a wide range of professional bodies to achieve this. It is independent of outside commercial interests and is democratic, transparent and fully accountable to its members. It is a non-profit making company limited by guarantee. Its objective is the support of the proper administration of justice and the early resolution of disputes through fair and unbiased expert evidence. To achieve this it:

- acts as a voice for expert witnesses, especially in communicating with the media;
- provides support to experts of all professional disciplines and other occupations requiring skills and judgment;
- encourages lawyers to make use of experts wherever specialised knowledge is required;

- engages in the training of experts to maintain and enhance standards and their status;
- works actively with other allied professional bodies and associations;
- makes representations to Government and to professional bodies and associations wherever appropriate.

The Institute produced a general *Code of Guidance for Experts* under the CPR, and it publishes an informative newsletter on the internet.

The NHS Litigation Authority (NHSLA)

This is the special health authority set up to oversee the workings of the Clinical Negligence Scheme for Trusts, a sort of 'pay-as-you-go' scheme for helping trusts to discharge the financial burdens of medical negligence claims. It also has a role to play in risk management and may get involved, through the independent Professional Advisory Panel it is setting up, in law reform (its chief executive is a member of the Clinical Disputes Forum).

However, it is in the context of active litigation that the NHSLA plays its most controversial role. It has complete authority over the defence of medical claims against the NHS.[7] It has its own 'gatekeeper' firms who instruct a firm of solicitors on their small panel of accredited firms to conduct the defence.[8] But, unlike earlier days, that firm has no authority to do anything much without referring back to the NHSLA's solicitors, so an additional level of bureaucracy is created.

This aspect of the work of the NHSLA was intended to speed up the process of early identification and settlement of valid claims. This intention has only partly been realised. There are still many cases which are defended (for a while, or up to and sometimes through trial) on the evidence of a hired gun, ie an expert who writes to order and sees his task as that of finding some sort of defence for his client and maintaining it, often in the face of all reason, until instructed to desist. Such witnesses feature regularly in medical cases (the truly impartial expert owing a duty only to the court, as hopefully envisaged by the new rules of court, is the exception rather than the rule). There are still too many cases where admission of breach of duty should have been made years before; when it eventually is made there is no reasonable explanation why it took so long.

Further, settlements are more difficult to achieve. The NHSLA appears to make up its mind at an early stage, on whatever information it has at that point, whether or not the case should be defended. If it decides not to settle it is thereafter immovable, unless and until, in some few cases, the immediate prospect of a trial and the incurring of counsel's fees by delivery of the brief (which is usually held back until the last minute) concentrates the collective mind. Quite often the NHSLA will make an early offer (which, the appeal court recently declared, was in their case to be

---

7   From April 1999 the responsibilities of the NHSLA were augmented to include non-clinical claims.

8   This panel was revamped not long ago to the surprise of leading medical negligence claimants' solicitors who had come over the years to establish good relations with and to trust many defence firms who were no longer to be accepted on the panel, there emerging in their place insurance-based firms who have yet to earn any approbation from the claimants' side.

equated with a payment into court – *Crouch* v *King's Healthcare NHS Trust* [2004] EWCA Civ 1332, [2005] Lloyds Rep Med 50) well before any schedules of loss have been prepared, based on an apparent gut feeling as to what the case is worth. This is not in itself to be criticised. It is their right; it is an insurers' tactic, and they come from the insurance industry. But patients' lawyers are not accustomed to settle, nor should they, on gut reactions as to what the case is worth. They need to prepare the necessary quantum reports and proper schedules of loss. The result is that the offer, often accompanied by disingenuous protestations from the defence in front of the district judge that they are really eager to negotiate a settlement and so there should be a (highly premature) meeting between the lawyers (a round table meeting, as it is called) has served no purpose in terms of facilitating settlement. With the NHSLA thereafter being immovable, the normal process of gradually settling a case as it goes on through the pre-trial process, whereby the defence solicitor reassesses the merits at every stage and is available for productive discussions with the other side, is not available. The process, however, will still be available when the defendant falls outside the purview of the NHSLA, eg if a doctor is sued in his own name. As for settling a case at the door of the court or during a trial – which often used to happen to the advantage of both parties – now the trust's solicitors, who, being closer to the management of the case, have a clearer view of where the case is going, often cannot get instructions at that stage from the NHSLA, and, if they do, the instructions are unlikely to be informed by any frontline grasp of the realities of the situation. Why the NHSLA are not willing to rely on the experience and expertise of the trusts' lawyers, who after all have been accredited by them for the conduct of such litigation, is a mystery.

A number of standard defences have emerged since the NHSLA came into being (I appreciate that *post hoc* is not always *propter hoc*[9]). For example, failed sterilisation cases are often defended, by the same expert, with arguments to the effect that instant fistulae can arise, providing a passage for egg to meet sperm or that the operator cannot be blamed if the clip does not occlude the tube because it can be hard to see (both wrong). A claim for negligently causing brachial plexus injury at birth following shoulder dystocia has been defended on the basis that recent studies show that such an injury can arise in the womb (very rarely), and, most recently, and most spectacularly, the rise and rise of the theory of the maternal propulsive forces (as causing the injury rather than operator traction) has made it much harder to win these cases. No doubt the so-called international consensus on causation in cerebral palsy (to the effect that it cannot be shown it was due to perinatal asphyxia unless one can prove a metabolic acidosis of a certain degree) would now be used to defend cases had it not promptly been demolished in the pages of *Clinical Risk*.

It is fair to add that I have also had experience of more than a few claims where liability has been promptly admitted and settlement swiftly agreed and of claims which have been reasonably, and sometimes even successfully, defended.[10]

---

9 I'd like to hear Lord Woolf put that into equally concise and meaningful English!
10 For the NHSLA's own, and less jaundiced, assessment of their achievements the reader is referred to Chapter 8 of Powers and Harris *Clinical Negligence* (3rd edn, 2000).

A note on clinical governance

Clinical governance has been defined as:

A framework through which NHS organisations are accountable for continuously improving the quality of their services and safeguarding high standards of care by creating an environment in which excellence in clinical care will flourish. (NHS White Paper: A First Class Service. Dept of Health, 1998).

The programme of clinical governance introduced in all NHS organisations from April 1999 is designed to ensure that all clinical staff, including doctors, participate in the review of the quality of their services and in planning ways to improve it.

The Clinical Governance Research and Development Unit, reconstituted in April 1999 at Leicester University, builds on the former Eli Lilly National Clinical Audit Centre. The new body's principal function is research and development within the emerging field of clinical governance.

NHS QUANGOS

This term was originally invented as a joke but fell into common usage in the United Kingdom to describe the agencies produced by the growing trend of government devolving power to appointed or self-appointed bodies. The definition of a quango by the government is 'a body which has a role in the processes of a national government, but is not a government department or part of one, and which accordingly operates to a greater or lesser extent at arm's length from ministers'. Since most of such bodies are in fact part of the government in terms of funding, appointment and function, the acronym does not work as a description – they are generally not non-governmental organisations and they will often have less autonomy than those that are. It has been suggested that 'quasi-autonomous non-ministerial governmental organisation' would be a better description. As is to be expected, the NHS is awash with quangos. The government, following one of its electoral pledges, has been making half-hearted attempts to reduce their number. One result of this is that one can never know whether this or that quango is still functioning or has been abolished or merged with some other. I append notes on one or two of the most important quangos. I also offer a summary of the quango position, which no doubt will be out of date by the time this book is in print.

The National Institute for Clinical Excellence (NICE)

This important body was set up as a Special Health Authority for England and Wales on 1 April 1999. It is part of the NHS; its role is to identify clear national standards and to provide patients, health professionals and the public with authoritative, robust and reliable guidance on current 'best practice'. The guidance covers both individual health technologies (including medicines, medical devices, diagnostic techniques, and procedures) and the clinical management of specific conditions. NICE joined with the Health Development Agency in April 2005 to become the new National Institute for Health And Clinical Excellence (helpfully also to be known as NICE).

NICE aims to promote clinical and cost effectiveness through guidance and audit, to support frontline staff. It advises on best practice in the use of existing treatment options, appraises new health interventions, and advises the NHS on how they can be implemented and how best these might fit alongside existing treatments. It has a key role in co-ordinating the range of current activity in both the active dissemination of information and in responding to specific inquiries, and provides a single reference point for information on standards and audit methodologies. It purports to create a new partnership between the government, the NHS and clinical professionals. By establishing NICE, the government said it intended to take responsibility for helping to clarify, both for patients and professionals, which treatments worked best for which patients and those which did not. For the first time in the history of the NHS, so it said, the government, working with clinical bodies, would systematically appraise clinical interventions before these were introduced into the NHS. Clear, authoritative guidance on clinical and cost effectiveness would be offered to frontline clinicians.

We are told that NICE aims to set clear national standards of what patients can expect to receive from the NHS, the aim being to improve clinical governance alongside the Commission for Health Improvement (meaning now, presumably, the Healthcare Commission), the National Performance Framework, and the National Patient and User Survey.

The Healthcare Commission

The Healthcare Commission is an independent body, set up to promote and drive improvement in the quality of healthcare and public health. It aims to do this by becoming an authoritative and trusted source of information and by ensuring that this information is used to drive improvement.

It inspects the quality and value for money of healthcare and public health and aims to equip patients and the public with the best possible information about the provision of healthcare. It promotes improvements in healthcare and public health.

Its main duties in England are to:

- assess the management, provision and quality of NHS healthcare and public health services;
- review the performance of each NHS trust and award an annual performance rating;
- regulate the independent healthcare sector through registration, annual inspection, monitoring complaints and enforcement;
- publish information about the state of healthcare;
- consider complaints about NHS organisations that the organisations themselves have not resolved;
- promote the co-ordination of reviews and assessments carried out by ourselves and others; and
- carry out investigations of serious failures in the provision of healthcare.

In carrying out its duties, it is required to pay particular attention to:

- the availability of, access to, quality and effectiveness of healthcare;
- the economy and efficiency of the provision of healthcare;
- the availability and quality of information provided to the public about healthcare; and

- the need to safeguard and promote the rights and welfare of children and the effectiveness of measures taken to do so.

As a public body, the Healthcare Commission also has important positive obligations under the Race Relations (Amendment) Act 2000 and the Human Rights Act 1998 to take active steps to promote respect for human rights and equality of opportunity and good relations between all racial groups.

The Healthcare Commission works in close partnership with the Mental Health Act Commission (MHAC), whose role is to ensure that there is adequate and effective protection of patients detained under the Mental Health Act 1983. Under the government's review of legislation on mental health, it is expected that most of the functions of MHAC will transfer to the Healthcare Commission and that MHAC will be abolished, though not before April 2007. In the meantime, each organisation will maintain its separate statutory responsibilities but work together on a coherent overall programme for the assessment of the provision of care in the field of mental health.

The Healthcare Commission's legal name is the 'Commission for Healthcare Audit and Inspection', which not long ago was the new name for the Commission for Health Improvement. It was formed by the Health and Social Care (Community Health and Standards) Act 2003, and launched on 1 April 2004.

National Patient Safety Agency (NPSA)

The NPSA is a Special Health Authority created in July 2001 to co-ordinate the efforts of the entire country to report, and more importantly to learn from, mistakes and problems that affect patient safety.

As well as making sure errors are reported in the first place, the NPSA is trying to promote an open and fair culture in the NHS, encouraging all healthcare staff to report incidents without undue fear of personal reprimand. It will then collect reports from throughout the country and initiate preventative measures, so that the whole country can learn from each case, and patient safety throughout the NHS can be improved.

From 1 April 2005 the NPSA has expanded, giving it greater scope to improve patient safety in the NHS.

The NPSA's work now encompasses:

- safety aspects of hospital design, cleanliness and food (transferred from NHS Estates);
- ensuring research is carried out safely, through its responsibility for the Central Office for Research Ethics Committees; and
- supporting local organisations in addressing their concerns about the performance of individual doctors and dentists, through its responsibility for the National Clinical Assessment Service.

It also manages the contracts with the three confidential enquiries. This responsibility has been transferred from NICE.

Commission for Social Care Inspection (CSCI)

Launched in April 2004, CSCI is the single, independent inspectorate for all social care services in England. The commission was created by the

Health and Social Care (Community Health and Standards) Act 2003. CSCI incorporates the work formerly carried out by:

- The Social Services Inspectorate (SSI);
- SSI/Audit Commission Joint Review Team;
- The National Care Standards Commission.

The Commission has a much wider remit than its predecessor organisations and its creation is a significant milestone for social care. Bringing together the inspection, regulation and review of all social care services into one organisation allows for a more rational and integrated system.

For the first time, one single organisation has a total overview of the whole social care industry. The Commission provides a complete picture of social care in England: locally and nationally, in adult services and children's services, for people who use social services, for local councils, voluntary and private providers, and for government.

CSCI's primary function is to promote improvements in social care, which it aims to do by putting the people who use social care services firmly at the centre of their work.

The National Clinical Assessment Service (NCAS)

The National Clinical Assessment Authority was established on 1 April 2001 following recommendations made in the Chief Medical Officer's reports 'Supporting Doctors, Protecting Patients' (November 1999) and 'Assuring the Quality of Medical Practice: Implementing Supporting Doctors, Protecting Patients' (January 2001). The National Clinical Assessment Service is its new name; it is a division of the National Patient Safety Agency. NCAS was set up as one of the central elements of the NHS' modernisation plan to ensure the high quality of healthcare.

Health Protection Agency

The Agency was created in April 2003 to provide better protection against infectious diseases and other dangers to health, including chemical hazards, poisons and radiation. Its core functions are to:

- identify and respond to health hazards and emergencies;
- anticipate and prepare for emerging and future threats;
- alert and advise the public and government on health protection;
- provide specialist health protection services; and
- support others in their health protection roles.

Its aim is to protect health, prevent harm and prepare for threats. Its staff include specialists in:

- communicable disease control, who tackle outbreaks of infectious diseases and prevent the spread of disease through vaccination and other measures;
- public health specialists;
- infection control nurses;
- emergency planning advisers;
- epidemiologists, who monitor the spread of disease;
- toxicologists;
- laboratory scientists and technicians;

- information specialists; and
- information technologists.

The Commission for Patient and Public Involvement in Health (CPPIH)

The Commission for Patient and Public Involvement in Health was set up in January 2003. It is an independent, non-departmental public body, sponsored by the Department of Health.

The Commission's role is to make sure the public is involved in decision making about health and health services in England. There are 572 Patient and Public Involvement (PPI) Forums, one for each NHS Trust in England, and they are putting into practice improved health which will only come through continuous engagement of people and communities.

PPI Forums are made up of groups of volunteers in local communities who are enthusiastic about helping patients and members of the public to influence the way that local healthcare is organised and delivered. Forum members come from a broad variety of backgrounds and have a range of experiences and skills.

The Commission is responsible for submitting reports to and advising the government on how the PPI system is functioning. It liaises with national bodies such as the Healthcare Commission on patient and public involvement issues, and makes recommendations to these bodies and the Department of Health as appropriate. The Commission gathers information and opinion from PPI Forums, channelled through its shared information system in order to ensure that the bodies it reports to are acting upon patients' and the public's views.

This body is on death row (see below).

Arm's length bodies

It is not surprising that the government dislikes the term quango; so they have coined the expression 'arm's length bodies' (known, mysteriously, as ALBs).

Note, by way of summary, first that NICE joined with the Health Development Agency in April 2005 to become the new National Institute for Health and Clinical Excellence (helpfully also to be known as NICE). The Commission for Patient and Public Involvement in Health, with its budget of £23 million and up to 150 staff, is under sentence of death, announced after a mere six months had expired since its widely publicised creation. Execution has recently been postponed to August 2007. We are told that the future of its almost 600 patient forums will be preserved; it is merely that they will be directly controlled by the Department of Health. They say they intend a 50% reduction of these ALBs by 2008. Now, let us get ourselves really confused. The Commission for Health Improvement was abolished in March 2004, as was the National Standards of Care Commission. But then we got the Commission for Social Care Inspection and the Healthcare Commission, which is the new short and, of course, confusing name for the Commission for Health Audit and Inspection. The Health and Social Care Information Centre has been created to reduce administrative burdens on frontline NHS staff and improve the quality of information. It will aim to keep form-filling to a minimum and improve accessibility by acting as a central point for everyone who needs information, including patients, clinicians and regulators. The Health Protection Agency swallows the National Radiological Protection Board. The National Patient Safety Agency takes on the functions of the National Clinical Assessment Authority and various other NHS bodies. Got that?

Community Health Services (CHCs)

We cannot leave this short survey without sorrowfully acknowledging the passing of the Community Health Councils. It was the NHS ten-year plan to establish a new system of PPI that saw them off as part of the 'modernisation programme'. The CPPIH was to replace the CHCs and manage patient forums, which I suppose are the same thing as Patient and Public Involvement Forums (yes, PPIFs), but, as already stated, the CPPIH's future was curtailed after only six months. No-one knows yet how the patient fora will be managed. We are told they are working in every NHS Trust and Primary Care Trust (PCT) area to get the views of local people about local health services and that over 5000 people are currently members of fora. And here we must bring in PALS – what a lovely (fortuitous, do you think?) acronym for Patient Advice and Liaison Services.

PALS are a central part of the new system of PPI in England. They are available in all trusts.

PALS provide:

- confidential advice and support to patients, families and their carers;
- information on the NHS and health-related matters; confidential assistance in resolving problems and concerns quickly;
- information on and explanations of NHS complaints procedures and how to get in touch with someone who can help;
- a focal point for feedback from patients to inform service developments; and
- an early warning system for NHS Trusts, PCTs and PPIFs by monitoring trends and gaps in services and reporting these to the trust management for action.

PALS act on behalf of their service users when handling patient and family concerns. They liaise with staff, managers and, where appropriate, other relevant organisations, to negotiate speedy solutions and to help bring about changes to the way that services are delivered. PALS will also refer patients and families to local or national-based support agencies, as appropriate.

Mediation

That mediation, amicable and speedy, might resolve most of our medical claims is a consummation devoutly to be wished. Its virtues are loudly trumpeted by those who stand to gain from its widespread acceptance. Practitioners do not agree. Compare what Tony Allen has written about the invaluable services of the Centre for Dispute Resolution in *Medical Litigation* Issue 11/99 with the riposte of Roger Wicks in Issue 3/00 of the same journal. The former tells that 'the time has come for an exponential increase in the use of mediation as a primary means of resolving clinical disputes'. The latter replies that it is more expensive than litigation (as the mediator has to be paid); and there will be inequality of arms unless the patient's lawyers have obtained all the necessary reports, at which time one might just as well follow the normal course of negotiation.

The fact of the matter is that mediation is not a useful way of resolving claims between patient and the NHS where substantial compensation is sought (although it may be helpful where substantial compensation is not relevant). It has achieved so far neither success nor acceptance. The pilot scheme attracted virtually no takers. Except in small cases, it is doubtful if mediation in medical claims will achieve anything that sensible communication between the parties' solicitors, followed perhaps in the bigger cases by a round-table discussion, cannot achieve.

It is interesting to see what the view of the Clinical Disputes Forum special group is:

> The special project mediation group within the Clinical Disputes Forum was first formed in the early days of the Woolf Inquiry, to monitor such initiatives as were already exploring the possibilities for mediation in this area, notably the NHS Mediation Pilot Scheme. The group tells us that mediation is seen as offering the means to speedier resolution; through a flexible process over which the parties themselves can retain ultimate control, to yield a flexible range of possible outcomes far beyond that which would be available at law. It notes regretfully that, although support – at least in principle – remains widespread, this has (so far) failed to translate into any significant volume of actual referrals. Such reticence, manifest perhaps particularly in the legal profession, may be rooted in – or at least fuelled by – some of the persistent concerns regarding integrity of the process, in which inequality of information and experience may be open to exploitation; in an area where parties may be felt to be especially vulnerable.[11]

The LSC now intends to require explanation from solicitors if in any particular case resort is not had to mediation. Let us hope that they are, or learn to become, aware of the limited scope for mediation in medical negligence cases. Judges at first instance have given widely different decisions where a party has earlier refused to mediate, some seeing the refusal as demanding that a successful party be denied his costs, others taking a less draconian view.

Halsey v Milton Keynes

Fortunately we now have the first judgment of the Court of Appeal on this issue, *Halsey* v *Milton Keynes General NHS Trust* [2004] 1 WLR 302.

A widow was suing for the death in hospital of her 83 year-old husband. It was clearly a very small claim. Her solicitors wrote a number of letters, including one to the Secretary of State for Health, asking for mediation. At all times the defendants, in reality the NHSLA, refused to accept liability, refused to offer any money at all and refused to mediate. In due course the trial took place and the judge found for the defendants. Given how the virtues of mediation in medical cases (as well as in all other cases, about which I am not qualified to speak) have been trumpeted around, one might have thought the Court of Appeal would have been

---

11 A short but useful treatment of the current position and attitudes can be found in [2000] *Clinical Risk* 257.

critical of the obduracy of these defendants. But not a bit of it. The court accepted that active case management included 'encouraging the parties to use an alternative dispute resolution procedure if the court considers that appropriate and facilitating the use of such a procedure' (Rule 1.4(2)(e)) and said it was in no doubt that it should proceed on the basis that there were many disputes which were suitable for mediation. The court also said it was well aware of the ADR pledge, announced by the Lord Chancellor in March 2001, which led to the NHSLA proclaiming that it would encourage greater use of mediation. Apparently, since May 2000, the NHSLA has been requiring solicitors representing NHS bodies in medical claims to offer mediation in appropriate cases and to provide clear reasons to the authority if a case is considered inappropriate. It may therefore be thought somewhat surprising that the defence solicitors in this case took the attitude that they did. Nevertheless the court fully supported their attitude and made no criticism of them at all. Rather, it criticised the claimant's solicitors for what it saw as a tactical use of their many requests in the case for mediation.

The court said, first, that there was no power to force parties into mediation: 'It seems to us that to oblige truly unwilling parties to refer their disputes to mediation would be to impose an unacceptable obstruction on the right of access to the court', ie it would contravene Article 6 of the European Convention on Human Rights. The Court of Appeal also said that, even if there were such power, it found it difficult to conceive of circumstances in which it would be appropriate to exercise it, though the court could encourage parties to mediate in as strong terms as the court might think appropriate.

Next, on the costs issue, the court said that one must bear in mind that depriving a successful party of his costs would be an exception to the general rule and it should only be done where that party had acted unreasonably in refusing to agree to mediation. There could, incidentally, be no criticism of any position that a party chose to adopt in the actual mediation. The court also said – which has always been my main contention – that most cases were settled by negotiation in the ordinary way. Mediation provided litigants with a wider range of solutions than those that were available in litigation, for example, an apology, and an explanation. The court said that mediation and other alternative dispute resolution processes did not offer a panacea and could have disadvantages as well as advantages; they were not appropriate for every case. Those who stand to gain by mediation, that is to say the mediators' organisation, whose costs are by no means low, presumptuously tried but failed to get the court to accept that there should be a presumption in favour of mediation. The court said that factors to consider in deciding whether the refusal to mediate had been reasonable would include the nature of the dispute, the merits of the case, the extent to which other settlement methods had been attempted, whether the costs of the mediation would be disproportionately high, whether any delay in setting up and attending the mediation would have been prejudicial, and whether it had had a reasonable prospect of success.

Turning to the facts of the case, the court said that the defendants had been justified in refusing to mediate, despite the ADR pledge mentioned above. The pledge was no more than an undertaking that ADR would be considered and used in all suitable cases. The reasons justifying the defendants' refusal to mediate in this case were that they were entitled to defend the claim and to have no intention of settling it, so that this was not a case where mediation would be likely to be successful, and they were entitled to take the view that, compared to the value of the claim and the likely costs of a short trial, the costs of mediation would be disproportionately high. The claimant had the burden of proving there was a reasonable prospect that the mediation would have been successful and that the defendant had behaved unreasonably and she got nowhere near doing that. So her appeal was dismissed.

In some ways this is a remarkable judgment from the Court of Appeal. When mediation was being trumpeted, largely by mediators but also by a number of judges, as the panacea for the expense and delay of litigation, I pointed out in no uncertain terms in the journal *Medical Litigation*, on more than one occasion, that the NHSLA knew perfectly well whether they wanted to make an offer in a case or not and what that offer should be, and nothing would be served by having a third party trotting between the parties to try and persuade them to offer something that they would not otherwise have been willing to do.[12] The short fact of the matter is that in the larger medical negligence claims compensation is almost 100% of the claimant's purpose, the parties almost always will be able to confer amicably and reasonably with each other, and a round table meeting between the experienced lawyers in the case is going to be at least as productive as, and probably more productive than, a mediation. It seems to me that this decision by the Court of Appeal has vindicated the stance I adopted.[13]

It is interesting to note that in the personal injury case of *Steel* v *Joy*, which the court heard at the same time, the party who had refused to mediate was exonerated on the grounds that he had acted reasonably in taking his stand on a point of law which he successfully maintained in the court below, that the cost of mediation would have been disproportionately high in respect of a case where the trial took only some two hours, and that the offer to mediate had come late in the proceedings when substantial costs had already been incurred.

Redress

In June 2003 the Chief Medical Officer unveiled his proposals for an alternative system of providing redress for patients injured by medical negligence. The framework lacked detail, but it was clear enough what it envisaged – a scheme whereby patients would put themselves in the hands of a NHS panel (whose independence is a matter of conjecture, and concern) who would decide if redress (ie rehabilitation services and/or compensation) should be offered, and, if so, what and how much. It seems to be envisaged that the patient would be financed to the extent of taking

---

12 In two mediations forced upon solicitors who had instructed me in the cases the strong impression the solicitors obtained was that the aim of the mediator was to get the claimant to compromise, not the NHSLA.

13 It is fair to note that ADR procedures enabled a settlement of the group of 18 cases brought for negligent diagnosis and treatment by a consultant pediatrician in respect of epilepsy at the defendant's hospital between 1990 and 2001: see *A* v *University Hospitals of Leicester NHS Trust* [2005] MLC 1258. Awards ranged from £4,000 to £48,000.

legal advice on any offer made, but how any offer could be evaluated, short of comparing it with the sort of sum litigation might result in (which is not the basis for a *Redress* offer) is unclear in the extreme. Rehabilitative treatment and services would be offered within the NHS, not privately (as is so often sought and achieved in a legal action), and we all know what limited rehabilitative services are for the most part currently on offer to a disabled person. However, it is worth bearing in mind that the statutory provision which enforces disregard of the availability of NHS services for an injured person if he intends to avail himself of private services may be repealed in due course (the lobby for such a repeal is currently growing in strength).

One of the two principal proposals of the scheme has already been dropped. There will not be any scheme to compensate for perinatal injuries, ie children handicapped at birth by way of avoidable brain injury. The powers that be eventually realised the obvious fact that such a scheme would be impossible given the restricted availability of rehabilitative services within the NHS and the huge cost of bringing them up to any useful level. One has only to think of the minimum assistance currently offered to the family of a non-negligently brain-injured child, compared with the millions of pounds worth of assistance that the common law permits where there has been negligence.

What is left is a proposal to offer redress of a limited sort to claims that can be valued at less than £30,000 (it is envisaged that that limit will be raised, perhaps to £50,000). Where will it stop, though? The patient will not be forced into the scheme. He can still sue, but one wonders on what funding. A CFA will still be possible. Or he may have legal expenses insurance. Or his own funds (unlikely). But not, it is envisaged, legal aid. We can expect that for the less than huge cases he will not be offered legal aid (this is indeed more or less what one of the recommendations proposes). Short of other alternatives he will have to accept the redress scheme, and have to accept what the panel is prepared to offer. Some redress!

The first recommendation is that a scheme should be introduced 'to provide investigations when things go wrong; remedial treatment, rehabilitation and care where needed, explanations and apologies; and financial compensation in certain circumstances'. The NHSLA would have to be satisfied that the harm could (presumably should) have been avoided and that the adverse outcome was not the natural progression of the illness. It is fair to say that one of the recommendations is that a national body should oversee the scheme and manage the financial compensation element at national level, but one may seriously doubt to what extent such a body would be independent and uninfluenced by political and financial considerations akin to those affecting the NHSLA. Are we supposed to forget the words of the Lord Chief Justice in a lecture in January 2001 that 'the medical profession could not be relied on to resolve justified complaints justly'?

This scheme has echoes of the voluntary *Resolve* scheme, which foundered as patients' advisers felt that the investigators were biased towards the defendants, ie the NHSLA. What a surprise!

Other recommendations include abandoning the rule applying currently in respect of the internal complaints procedure, that such investigation must stop if legal action is begun. If a patient accepts an offered package of redress, he loses the right to litigate. There is a recommendation that doctors should be immune from disciplinary action when reporting an error, presumably because they cannot be trusted to do the honourable thing if they might get into trouble for it. Maybe such a reluctance to report incidents is why we do not yet have the comprehensive centralised NHS claim reporting system which the Clinical Negligence Scheme for trusts was supposed to be setting up.

There is an unattractive provision seeking to trespass on the law on disclosure by proposing that documents and information collected for identifying adverse events should be protected from disclosure in court. More secrecy and non-accountability? The proviso does little to sweeten this proposal: it is to apply only where full information on the event is also included in the medical records.

And the CMO cannot resist putting his oar into the murky waters of mediation, recommending that it should be 'seriously considered for the majority of claims which do not fall within the *Redress* system'. He obviously hasn't read what I and claimants' solicitors have written about mediation for the larger cases. Not content with this intrusion, he also tells us that the common law should no longer countenance private care in awarding compensation. What chutzpah! But then he is the voice of the medical profession at governmental level, so what could one expect? Particularly as this report was so severely delayed one could only expect that his masters were dictating to the CMO what they wanted him to write.

Not satisfied with all his proposals, he ends with the suggestion that ways of yet further reducing costs in medical negligence cases should be considered by the Department for Constitutional Affairs, the LSC and the Civil Justice Council – no mention of any patients' representative body here!

We cannot do better finally than to read the words of the supremely well informed editor of *Medical Litigation*, when he writes:

> The real concern one must have about the proposals is that the new body which will administer the redress scheme replacing the NHSLA is not going to be independent. ...The overall impressions of the proposals is that the government has sailed as close as possible to the human rights wind in order to reduce the costs of clinical negligence by taking away the right of injured patients to have remedial treatment provided by the private sector and use the already over-stretched NHS, and to sweep more medical blunders under the carpet.

As we were going to press we were privileged to be offered the government's view on *Redress* and their NHS Redress Bill. According to the Labour Party website, www.labour.org.uk, under the NHS Redress Bill, published on 13 October 2005, patients will no longer have to go to court to get compensation, care, apologies and investigations if something goes wrong with their NHS hospital treatment or care. The Bill gives the Secretary of State the power to establish an NHS Redress Scheme and to place a duty on providers and commissioners of hospital services to ensure patients receive a more consistent, speedy and appropriate response to clinical negligence. The scheme will cover low monetary value claims, with the initial upper limit expected to be set at £20,000. It is designed to offer patients a real alternative to litigation, avoiding the long delays and legal costs typical of the current system. Other key elements of the NHS Redress Bill and Scheme include:

- Provision for patients to receive redress in the form of care.
- A duty on all scheme members to appoint an appropriate person responsible for learning from mistakes.
- A more proactive approach to clinical negligence, with the onus no longer on the patient to initiate a claim. All scheme members will be required to review adverse incidents and trigger the scheme themselves, where appropriate.

The aim of the scheme is not to cut costs, but to ensure NHS money goes directly on benefitting the patient with less spent on legal costs.

Health Minister, Jane Kennedy said:

> The NHS Redress Bill means fairness for patients, not fees for lawyers. It is an important step in preventing a US-style litigation culture.

> The vast majority of NHS patients receive safe and effective care, but we have to recognise that in our modern, increasingly complex health service, mistakes do happen.

> We want to improve patients' experience of the NHS by giving patients what they tell us they want when something goes wrong with their care – an apology, an explanation of what's happened and action to put things right. We need to move away from the current way of responding to clinical negligence, which is characterised by variations in outcomes, long and complicated processes and legal costs that often exceed amounts paid out to patients.

> The NHS Redress Bill enables us to provide a better and more consistent response to patients when something goes wrong with their NHS care. By understanding the implications of clinical negligence and giving practical support to patients and their families when things go wrong, the NHS will be in a better position to learn from mistakes and drive up the standard and quality of care provided in the future.

> The NHS Litigation Authority (NHSLA) will be responsible for overseeing the Scheme and managing the financial compensation. Scheme members will be required to report all cases which may fall within the Scheme to the NHSLA. The NHSLA will then establish liability and, if appropriate, the level of compensation. If financial compensation is not appropriate, the patient will still have the right to receive an investigation, explanation, apology and, if appropriate, remedial care.

Steve Walker, Chief Executive of the NHS Litigation Authority said:

> The NHS Redress Scheme should enable us to deliver access to justice even faster and more economically in future.

The NHS Redress Bill builds on a commitment made in 2001 to reform the current clinical negligence system and the proposals set out in the Chief Medical Officer's report, 'Making Amends'. The NHS Redress Scheme is expected to come into force in 2007/08.

Jane Kennedy has clearly been trained in the same school of spin as her boss. Note the devious vote-catching reference to lawyers. They, of course, are the people who take money away from the patients and the NHS. It will be interesting in due course to compare the compensation a lawyer might get for an injured patient in various cases with what the NHS will generously offer. The only purpose of *Redress* is to save the government money. It may well do so, but at the expense of the patient. And then wait to see how the availability of legal aid, already curtailed by all manner of ploys devised by the LSC,[14] becomes virtually unattainable.

The Bill is not the scheme, of course. It merely permits the creation of a scheme and will no doubt undergo changes during the parliamentary process. Then the scheme will be set up. At worst the scheme will limit compensation to the paltry sum of £20,000, and all aspects of the process will be managed by the defendants, ie the NHSLA. They will provide advice to a scheme applicant, they will appoint the 'independent' panel, and they will decide what they are willing to offer. At best there will be some degree of free and independent advice provided to the applicant and the panel will in time come to be seen to be giving impartial and reliable judgments. I do not actually think this last will happen. The difficulty we have had over the years in finding impartial and reliable experts to review a patient's management speaks volumes in his connection! It is fair to add that while *Redress* is limited to small claims that would be unlikely to satisfy the costs benefit ratio for legal aid in any event, it provides at least some avenue for the patient to follow. But who believes it will remain so limited?

---

14 The latest of these immoral acts that I have come across is when a member of the staff of the LSC who is not legally trained but has nevertheless been given the task of assessing cases announces to the lawyers acting for a patient that he does not think there is a valid case, despite a positive and fully argued advice from counsel.

Chapter 3

Funding

A LITTLE HISTORY

The Lord Chancellor before Lord Irvine, Lord Mackay, made some inroads into the legal aid system, making the financial eligibility criteria stricter and introducing the conditional fee system, whereby lawyers were permitted to conduct cases on the basis that they would take an uplift to their fees out of any damages recovered for the client, but if the case was not successful they would get nothing. This was a revolutionary idea and completely contrary to the traditional ethos of the legal profession which did not permit lawyers to be financially interested in the outcome of a case (at least, not openly). Although this system is not the same as the American contingency fee system, because there they take a percentage of the damages recovered whereas here the lawyer is merely entitled to charge additional fees, this is only an insignificant distinction in the way in which success enables higher profits and failure may result in bankruptcy for the lawyer. The ethical considerations are the same. The lawyer is under pressure to get a settlement. Pronouncements from the Government to the effect that lawyers can be trusted not to sell the client short simply in order to recover their fees are part of the hypocrisy which has all along accompanied the destruction of the legal aid system that has been undertaken solely for economic reasons, and they are hardly consistent with the vicious attacks on lawyers that the Government has mounted when trying to win the hearts and minds of the people in support of their 'reforms'. They tell the people that the 'greedy lawyers' are being made to put their money where their mouth is, so that they will no longer push invalid claims forward simply to earn fees without risks, and that, in any event, they are earning far too much from the system. One can only hope that an informed and intelligent public will continue to draw their own conclusions.

However, few people foresaw the vigour, not to say savagery, with which the legal profession and the legal aid system would be attacked by Lord Mackay's successor, Lord Irvine, successful commercial silk and friend and ex-pupil-master of the then Prime Minister, Mr Blair. As a result, legal aid for personal injury claims is now virtually unobtainable. That would also have been the fate of clinical negligence claims, had he not been forced to acknowledge that such claims are far too complex and unpredictable for a solicitor to be able to conduct on a conditional fee basis in more than a few clearly indefensible cases. The feasibility of any conditional fee scheme remains questionable, particularly with regard to the insurance arrangements necessary to protect the client – and the solicitor – from the threat of bankruptcy.[1] Further reforms are likely to threaten the preservation of legal aid for medical negligence, most particularly when the system proposed by the Chief Medical Officer called *Redress* comes eventually into effect.

It is something of a coincidence that a lot of this has been going on at the same time as the Woolf reforms have been implemented. These are intended to ameliorate the expense and delays of litigation. However, the way in which this is primarily being done is founded on a misconception, particularly inappropriate in the context of medical negligence. The reformers create a panel of expert lawyers who alone are permitted to handle legal aid medical negligence cases. At the same time they introduce the concept of judicial case management on the basis that the real problem with litigation was the dilatory and inefficient lawyers running up unnecessary expense. The result is that experienced lawyers can be prevented from preparing cases properly, thwarted by judges inexperienced in processing medical negligence cases who impose impossible deadlines, in order, it would appear, to be seen to be committed to the Woolfian objective of bringing cases on quickly, and who deny the patient the necessary experts for the proper preparation and presentation of the claim, because money is thereby saved.

At one point it seemed that any minor infraction of the new rules or an order of the court would result in the case being struck out (*pour encourager les autres*) but, largely because it was seen that that sort of draconian attitude ('smacking the heads of the lawyers to bring them into line') was going to spawn a satellite industry of appeals, recent judgments from the Court of Appeal have promulgated wiser counsel. The most recent example of this is their interesting judgment on the issue of costs penalties for a party who refuses to mediate (*Halsey* v *Milton Keynes General NHS Trust* MLC 1115).

Pluses

It has to be said that some form of accreditation was necessary for solicitors (and remains necessary for barristers). History is full of horror stories of cases abandoned, lost or simply left to wither because of the lack of experience, enthusiasm and effort of the lawyers involved. So the need for specialist lawyers alone to handle medical negligence cases was clear. However, what is not clear is to what extent such change is going to save money. There is little evidence that inexperienced lawyers were processing invalid cases. Rather the opposite. They were failing to process valid cases. Experienced lawyers are more likely to unearth a cause of action. So, one can actually expect as much if not more litigation. Any downturn is likely to be due to other factors, such as effective procedures for early disclosure and settlement, or the refusal of legal aid. The ingenuity of the

---

1 One or two legal aid offices have tried to refuse legal aid on the basis that a CFA should be entered into, but the chief executive of the LSC has said that is not an appropriate decision for clinical negligence cases.

experienced lawyer in unearthing new causes of the ordinary action, such as the dyslexia cases and the stress at work cases, as well as that ubiquitous maid of all work, the human rights plea, and new causes of the very expensive group action, such as the MMR action, hardly suggest that money is being saved.

However, it is also clear that the weaknesses of the adversarial procedure and ineffective monitoring of the progress of litigation had in certain cases led to the ills highlighted by Woolf – principally delay and expense. If sensibly deployed, the new rules, coupled with the accreditation system, could ensure that cases are managed fairly and reasonably speedily, and that the costs remain proportionate to the value of the claim (the principle of proportionality that lies at the heart of the Woolf reforms).

One may also allow that the introduction of the conditional fee system can enable a small class of injured parties to bring an action where they would not in any event have qualified for legal aid for financial reasons and could not have afforded to sue from their own resources. However, they must have the sort of strong case that would tempt lawyer and insurer to take the risk, and their number is bound to be small. Despite sporadic trumpeting from the insurers, there is still no published evidence, even barely convincing evidence, that conditional fees are a success in the medical negligence arena. Even in the area of personal injury it has been said that only the easy cases get accepted for conditional fee agreements (CFAs).

THE LEGAL AID SYSTEM

Before the implementation of the Access to Justice Act 1999 in April 2000, the Legal Aid Board acted pursuant to the provisions of the Legal Aid Act 1988, granting certificates to any solicitor whose client was financially eligible for legal aid and whose proposed claim satisfied the test of reasonableness.

At the same time, the right to conduct medical negligence claims on legal aid was being restricted to firms that numbered among their personnel a solicitor who had succeeded in gaining entry to one of the two specialist medical negligence panels and who could therefore hope to obtain a 'clinical negligence franchise'. The panel run by AvMA[2] had been going a long time. The Law Society Clinical Negligence Panel has a published set of criteria, which were originally drafted with the help of AvMA. Not surprisingly, the two sets of criteria are similar. They are not easy to satisfy. This means that the assessors of the Law Society panel, themselves all solicitors with large medical negligence practices, retain a discretion to admit or refuse many of the applicants for admission

---

2   AVMA is a charitable organisation which from minimal beginnings has campaigned with considerable success since its inception in 1982 to improve the lot of the patient in litigation and generally. It has acquired considerable influence in various important quarters, such as with the legal aid authority and conditional fee insurers (CFIs). It recently changed its name, in line with the mood of the times and the spirit of the age, to Action against Medical Accidents (AvMA).

because they do not strictly satisfy the criteria. Many able solicitors have been refused admission on the ground of failure to satisfy the criteria. In short, the total number of solicitors on the panels (there is much duplication) is low, about 250. These solicitors tend to gravitate towards the big firms as it is not easy to run a medical negligence practice as a sole practitioner or as the only fee earner doing that sort of work in the firm (assuming the firm has already been able to satisfy the criteria relating to backup). The result is that fewer and fewer firms are doing the work. Patients in some areas have to travel a long way to get to the nearest accredited firm. New applicants for panel admission are not likely to be successful unless they have been trained by and so have acquired the relevant experience in one of the big firms.

Since July 1999, no firm may be granted a legal aid certificate for a medical negligence claim unless they have a fee earner on their staff and can persuade the Legal Services Commission to give them a clinical negligence franchise.[3] It is not clear why the term 'medical negligence' had to be changed. The definition of clinical negligence used by the legal aid authority could just as well define medical negligence. It has been said that a new term was needed to embrace dentists. But the old term could easily enough have done that. The truth of the matter is that the reformers wanted a term of art; jargon goes down very well with such people, particularly as a new nomenclature persuades them that they are creating something radically new and helps them to think it is an animal which they can control (rather like the insistence on Latin by the clergy of old, or the belief of primitive peoples that if they give something a name they acquire power over it). It does not go down so well with the consumer though, who readily understands the term medical negligence, but for whom clinical negligence suggests very little.

Under the Access to Justice Act 1999, the previous legal aid scheme is replaced by the Community Legal Service, and the Legal Services Commission takes the place of the Legal Aid Board. The Commission's role is more pro-active (not my word) than the Board's was. The Commission plans how the available money is to be spent by setting priorities, which is given effect through a combination of contracts and the Funding Code.

Criteria for funding

The Funding Code offers seven levels of service to be funded by the Community Legal Service, two of which are relevant to clinical negligence cases: Legal Help – roughly equivalent to the present advice and assistance; and Legal Representation. Legal Representation is Licensed Work and may only be undertaken by firms with a clinical negligence contract. Legal Representation can be granted in one of two forms, each with its own criteria. One form is Investigative Help – available where a case needs substantial investigation before its prospects of success can be deter-

---

3   Now, a new piece of jargon has taken the place of 'franchisees'. They are now known as Specialist Quality Mark holders. The Quality Mark for Specialist Help Services (eg lawyer) is equivalent to the old Legal Aid Franchise Quality Assurance Standard plus additional requirements covering referral and client satisfaction.

mined. The other is Full Representation – available only for strong cases. The General Funding Code sets out the criteria, which apply to all cases, subject to any variation by special criteria for particular subject areas. Clinical Negligence has its own special criteria in the Funding Code. The Guidance to the Funding Code explains the position in section 18.

Criteria for Investigative Help

Investigative Help may only be granted where the prospects of success of the claim are uncertain, and substantial investigative work is required before those prospects can be determined. In clinical negligence claims, of course, the investigative stage is of vital importance, and special criteria apply to this level of service.

Although under the general criteria the Commission would appear to be entitled to refuse funding for Investigative Help in certain cases on the grounds that a conditional fee agreement should be obtained rather than public funding, the availability of a conditional fee agreement is, happily, not now a ground for refusing aid for clinical negligence cases. This is partly because it is recognised that, whilst a number of insurance products exist for clinical negligence claims, many of these are relatively new and many solicitors' firms may not yet be financially structured in a way that would enable them to bear these investigative costs, and partly because the LSC has plans to make it more difficult (I should say even more difficult) to get legal aid once the system of *Redress* is in place.

If the claim is primarily for damages and has no significant wider public interest, Investigative Help will be refused unless the damages are likely to exceed £5,000. Note that under the General Funding Code, the £5,000 damages cut-off does not apply to claims, which have a significant wider public interest, or are of overwhelming importance to the client. Clinical negligence claims involving infant death come within this category.

The Commission may take the view on an application for Investigative Help that the (new) NHS complaints procedure is more appropriate for the client than litigation. This is particularly likely to be the case with small claims, ie under £5,000. However, the legal aid authority now recognises that the internal complaints procedure is irrelevant to the obtaining of compensation, and so they no longer take the view that all cases worth less than £10,000 must go first by way of the internal procedures.

Criteria for Full Representation

As we have seen, the availability of conditional fees is not now a ground for refusal in clinical negligence cases. However, the approach to the prospect of success will be the same as in the General Funding Code in that Full Representation will be refused if:

- prospects of success are unclear (Investigative Help may be appropriate);
- prospects of success are borderline and the case does not appear to have a significant wider public interest or to be of overwhelming importance to the client; or
- prospects of success are poor.

Cost-benefit ratio

A key issue has been whether the cost benefit criteria for quantifiable claims should be different for clinical negligence.

When clinical negligence work was restricted to specialist firms in February 1999, the guidance published under the Legal Aid Act 1988 recommended minimum cost-benefit ratios. These ratios of damages to costs are:

1:1   for cases with 80% plus prospects (very good);

1.5:1   for the 60–80% bracket (good) (this is the bracket into which almost all medical negligence cases thought viable by the expert solicitor will fall);

2:1   for the 50–60% range (moderate).

The ratio is 4:1 for Very High Cost Cases (see below).

The proposed cost-benefit thresholds in the General Funding Code are more stringent:

damages must exceed costs   for cases with 80% plus prospects;
2:1   for the 60–80% bracket;
4:1   for the 50–60% range.

There has been concern that the use of these cost-benefit thresholds could have a marked impact on clinical negligence claims, because of the higher costs of these claims when compared with average costs for claims in other categories. So, for the time being, the cost-benefit criteria in the code for clinical negligence will be the ratios from the Board's *existing* guidance. The LSC has recently said that the ratios for clinical negligence cases will be raised to the same level as that applicable to other types of case (just one more of their devious little ploys designed to reduce their obligation to fund medical negligence claims). This means that the 1.5:1 ratio that currently applies to the 60–80% bracket will become 2:1.

Criteria for settlement

Although the Board's existing guidance suggests different cost-benefit ratios for claims that will be settled compared with those that will proceed to trial, this position is not followed under the Code. The ratios suggested in the special criteria apply throughout the life of a clinical negligence claim. One of the reasons for this is that it has been suggested that different criteria might encourage opponents to delay settlement in the hope that funding may be withdrawn because of a failure to meet the more stringent ratios for cases proceeding to trial.

Very High Cost Civil Cases

Very expensive cases (known as Very High Cost Civil Cases) may receive special treatment by being referred to the Special Cases Unit, where likely or actual costs to disposal exceed £25,000. Thus many medical negligence cases will fall into this bracket. Cases referred to the Unit will need to include a detailed costed case plan,[4] reviewable at every stage,

---

4   There are helpful specimen plans downloadable at www.legalservices.gov.uk.

and will be subject to the affordability criterion. This criterion is expressed as whether it is reasonable for the case to be funded in the light of the resources available. Clinical negligence claims in the 50–60% merits bracket may only be funded out of the central budget where the cost-benefit ratio is the same as that in the General Funding Code, namely 4:1.[5] Conducting such a case involves a bureaucratic nightmare of form-filling, a strait-jacket of costs, and the necessary prescience to be able to predict every step that will require to be taken in the conduct of the case.

Mediation

There is a detailed section in the Code and the Guidance on alternative dispute resolution, where likely to be thought suitable and where not. This is clearly a course currently much in favour with the LSC. However, they do also seem to understand that it may well be unsuitable for a med-ical negligence action, even if they do not appreciate that fact to the same degree to which I appreciate it.

The public interest advisory panel

Even if a case would otherwise fall outside the scope of legal aid (eg a per-sonal injury case, or one where the costs-benefit ratio cannot be satisfied, or even one where the merits might raise a question mark), it may be pos-sible to qualify for legal aid on the ground that the case has 'significant wider public interest' as assessed for the LSC by this special panel it has set up. The opinion given by the panel (which includes representatives of the Consumers Association, the Bar Council, the Law Society, Liberty and JUSTICE) is only advisory, but regional offices will naturally take it into account in reaching any decision. The conclusions of the panel, which are published in *Focus*, make interesting reading. One case that fulfilled the criterion was a claim for surrogacy costs (presumably the *Briody*[6] case). Another piece of litigation that qualified was the multi-party per-sonal injury proceedings in respect of the oral contraceptive pill. It will be interesting to watch developments as the panel's function must play a significant part, in one direction or another, in the Government's cam-paign to reduce legal aid costs dramatically.

Guidance for solicitors

The legal aid authority produced rules, which they called guidance, which narrowly and in great detail circumscribed the manner in which legal aid medical negligence cases might be processed, what might be done, and what might be spent. This document ('Guidance: Exercise of Devolved

---

5   The lawyers should be particularly careful not to lose these high value cases as the solicitors' legal aid remuneration beyond their first £25,000 costs will be at a low 'at risks' rate (which is not new), while counsel's rate of reimbursement after the first £5,000 of his costs will be at subsistence level, about one-third of his proper fees (the first £5,000 of his costs is remunerated at the standard rate) – which is a new ploy by the legal aid authority.

6   *Briody* v *St Helens and Knowsley Health Authority* (2000) 53 BMLR 108.

Powers'), which featured in the last edition of this book, is now archived for historical reference only. Reference may now be made to the General Civil Contract, section 15.

Three stages of processing a medical negligence claim

Three stages of processing a medical negligence claim are envisaged. They are initial screening, preliminary investigation and full investigation.

The first stage

Initial screening (which can be carried out under what used to be called the 'green form' scheme, then legal advice and assistance, now legal help) will take place even before disclosure of medical records. It will determine whether the fee-paying client of moderate means would be advised to incur the costs of further investigation. The specialist solicitor is expected to be able to make this judgment, therefore, on nothing more than the patient's statement. Presumably only obvious non-starters would be rejected. Initial screening is expected to be carried out within two hours (taking instructions, considering any medical records if the patient has them, advising initially on law, procedure, costs and statutory charge, and applying for legal aid).

The solicitor must be satisfied that the primary purpose of the patient is to claim damages for medical negligence. The solicitor is expected to direct the client to other forms of redress if appropriate.

What is rather odd is that the solicitor is told to reject cases 'if there is no *prima facie* evidence of negligence', and yet often in practice, upon investigation it is established that a complaint is valid where at first there was no supporting evidence. The solicitor must also, at this early stage as at all stages, have in mind the cost-benefit ratio (equated at this stage, though not at later stages, with the test of the fee-paying client of moderate means). Therefore, at this stage the solicitor, before applying for civil legal aid, must be satisfied there is *prima facie* evidence of negligence, and that it is reasonable from a cost-benefit view to proceed further.

We are told that to satisfy the test for *prima facie* evidence of negligence there must be some information to indicate to the specialist practitioner the possibility that negligent acts or omissions were responsible for the injury or an unacceptable outcome. It is expressly stated that the mere fact of an unsatisfactory or unexpected outcome is not sufficient reason for granting legal aid in the absence of *prima facie* evidence of negligence. But, as we know, the majority of successful medical negligence cases are investigated and processed for the precise reason that the outcome has been unsatisfactory. What other *prima facie* evidence of negligence does the legal aid authority expect the solicitor, in the vast majority of cases, to discern in the exiguous information he will have at the initial stage?

The rules then distinguish between 'uncertainty over the merits' at the initial screening stage and 'there being no *prima facie* evidence'. In the former case, the solicitor may take the application forward, particularly in a serious case.

Solicitors may be expected to interpret these rules fairly liberally at this early stage in the proceedings. If not, they will not have much business.

AvMA, ever quick to assist in and, if desired, to oversee every aspect of medical negligence litigation, offer a screening service whereby a suitable expert from their database will give an initial view of the proposed case based on sufficient but not extensive evidence at a cost of £250.

As to small cases, disputed claims worth less than £5,000 are unlikely to be granted legal aid. For claims up to £10,000 legal aid is unlikely to be granted 'if there is little *prima facie* evidence of negligence'.

The second stage

The solicitor may now apply for legal aid to proceed to the second stage, namely preliminary investigation, costing not more than £2,000. He may obtain the medical records and a preliminary view from an expert, but he should not investigate subsidiary issues in detail until a positive view has been obtained. This second, but fuller, screening is said to be particularly relevant for cases worth less than £25,000, or where there are already specific concerns about the merits of the case.

The third stage

Stage three is the full pre-issue investigation, for which the solicitor will be paid £5,000 (including disbursements – the ceiling can be extended for good reason upon application). He must provide the legal aid area office with a record of his views of the case as they developed during the time he was processing it.

Note that full investigation is unlikely to be granted where costs exceed likely damages. Once full investigation is granted, the solicitor is expected to work in accordance with the Clinical Disputes Pre-Action Protocol (see Appendix I, and Health Service Circular 1998/183).

Amendment to permit issue

At the end of the full pre-issue investigation we come to the first precise statistical analysis. The legal aid authority will not permit issue if the case stands less than a 50% chance of success. If the chance of success is between 50 and 60% the estimated damages must be at least one and a half times the likely costs. If the estimate of success is more than 60% (I have not recommended cases for issue unless the chance of success has been at least 65%) the estimated damages must be at least equal to costs. The assessment of costs may take into account the prospects of a settlement. It is appreciated by the Board that a far more realistic assessment can be given later when all the evidence has been exchanged.

Note that the solicitor is not required, though he is entitled, to get an opinion from counsel.

Amendment for trial

The only other amendment to the legal aid certificate is that required to cover trial, the amendment permitting issue having authorised all steps up to exchange of all evidence. In order to go to trial the solicitor must be satisfied where the chance of success is between 50 and 60% that damages will be at least twice the figure for costs; between 60 and 80%, damages must be at least one-and-a-half times likely costs; and, in the unlikely event that the solicitor can really believe that in a disputed case he is going to trial with more than an 80% chance of success, damages must be at least equal to costs. Reason suggests that in most cases that go to trial, likely damages must be at least one-and-a-half times the likely costs to be incurred by the claimant by the end of the trial. As a claimant's costs for an average medical negligence case (say, three or four days) are likely to be not less than £25,000 and as much as £40,000, it would seem that no case worth less than £37,500 can go to trial.

The AvMA interface

Where there is an appeal from the refusal of a certificate or an amendment, AvMA, who have for years worked to create a close association with the legal aid authority, are now employed to vet for reward applications or appeals for legal aid where the authority are doubtful which way to decide the issue. They provide a 'merits screening report' (ie a screening report on the merits of the case). AvMA's role is then to provide a report for the area office, and, if legal aid is still not granted, for the area committee on appeal. It appears that AvMA will not be involved where legal aid has been refused 'solely upon grounds of reasonableness', as opposed to 'legal merits'. Doubts have been raised about a conflict of interest, given that AvMA's raison d'être has always been to devote itself entirely to the interests of the patient and to push the cause of the patient forward with all means at its disposal; yet now it has accepted a position where it owes what appears to be a conflicting duty to the legal aid authority. (AvMA has also accepted an even more surprising position, namely that it advises a leading medical negligence insurer on the merits of applications for insurance in proposals for conditional fee claims.)

The peripatetic client

Finally, we may note that the authority will no longer (without very good reason) support the peregrination of the patient from one solicitor to another – seeing that the whole purpose of the franchise scheme (now the Specialist Quality Mark scheme) is that the patient should from the outset be in the hands of a specialist.

CONDITIONAL FEE AGREEMENTS (CFAs)

The history

At common law any sort of contingency or conditional fee agreement (CFA) between solicitor and client was anathema. It was said by the courts time and again that it was totally unacceptable for the lawyer to have a financial interest in the outcome of a case. This applied equally to the simple situation where it was agreed or understood that the solicitor would only get paid or would only get his full fee if he won the case as to the obviously more contentious situation where he would get more than his full fee if he won and less or nothing if he lost. The terminology is unclear. Semantically all these agreements could be called either contingency or conditional fee agreements. However, contingency fee is usually reserved these days for the American system, unknown here (as yet), whereby the lawyer gets a share of the damages if he wins and nothing if he loses. Nevertheless, the Law Society's rules use the word contingency when outlawing any arrangement whereby a solicitor enters into any arrangement to receive a contingency fee, defined as 'any sum (whether fixed, or calculated either as a percentage of the proceeds or otherwise howsoever) payable only in the event of success in the prosecution of any action' (Solicitors' Practice Rules 1999, as amended, rr 8(1), 18(2)).

Two points need to be made: first, this prohibition, which has the force of law (*Swain* v *Law Society* [1983] 1 AC 598, HL) applies only to contentious business. Solicitors have long been entitled to arrange a conditional fee in non-contentious business. Second, there has never been anything wrong, indeed it has been applauded, where a solicitor agrees to act for an impecunious client, it being well understood that he will not get paid if the case is lost. The sin lies in the subtle distinction that he was not entitled to agree that that should be the basis on which he would act.

Maintenance and champerty

Maintenance consisted in supporting a case financially when having no proper interest to do so ('improperly stirring up litigation and strife by giving aid to one party to bring or defend a claim without just cause or excuse').[7] It was permissible if the person concerned had a legitimate interest in supporting the action, whether financial or social or whatever. Champerty was a form of maintenance whereby the person maintaining the action took as a reward a share in the property recovered (ie it adds to maintenance 'the notion of a division of the spoils').[8]

Both used to be both tortious and criminal until the Criminal Law Act 1967. However, that Act preserved the common law rule that they were contrary to public policy.[9]

Lord Denning more than once expressed his horror of champerty, particularly in respect of the lawyer who charged a fee that would only be payable if his client was successful, whether as a portion of the damages recovered or merely his normal fee payable only if he won, or by way of uplift to his normal fee. It is really extraordinary that the contingency fee, traditionally outlawed to protect the client from the lawyer being tempted to cut corners to achieve success and 'in order to preserve the honour and honesty of the profession'[10] should now, for economic reasons only, be sanctified as the panacea for the problems of litigation with the lawyers being held up as men and women of such virtue that they could never be tempted to act other than in the client's best interests – the

---

7   *Per* Lord Denning in *Re Trepca Mines Ltd (No 2)* [1963] Ch 199 at 219, CA.
8   *Per* Lord Mustill in *Giles* v *Thompson* [1994] 1 AC 142 at 161, HL.
9   For the current position see *Giles* v *Thompson* [1994] 1 AC 142 at 161, HL.
10   *Per* Lord Esher in *Pittman* v *Prudential Deposit Bank* (1896) 13 TLR 110 at 111, CA.

Government sings a very different tune when it wants to inflame the public against lawyers and their fees, as it does from time to time.[11]

In *R v Secretary of State for Transport, ex p Factortame* [2002] EWCA Civ 22, Lord Phillips MR explored the history of champerty, the court concluding that an arrangement under which accountants provided forensic accountancy services to litigants on a contingent fee basis was not one to which s 58 of the Courts and Legal Services Act 1990 had any application and was not void for champerty.

Recent cases decided under the old law

Conditional fees were first introduced by the Courts and Legal Services Act 1990, which by s 58 (which came into force in July 1993) provided that a lawyer could agree in writing for fees and expenses to be payable only in specified circumstances (any increase above normal fees, ie any uplift, had to be specified as a percentage). The situations in which a conditional fee agreement was permissible were first specified by regulations in 1995, which were amended to cover all proceedings in 1998.

So there was as yet no statutory authorisation for the agreements found to have been made in the *Thai Trading* case or in *Geraghty* v *Awwad* (see below). Those agreements therefore fell to be considered at common law.

In *Thai Trading Co* v *Taylor* [1998] QB 781 the arrangement was that the solicitor would recover his profit costs only if the claim succeeded (this may be called a normal costs conditional agreement). The Court of Appeal reversed the trial judge and held that in the context of the current perception of public policy with regard to conditional fees the agreement was not unenforceable (in this case, unlike the *Geraghty* case – see below). It was not a question of the solicitor seeking his fees against his client, who was his wife, but of claiming costs against the other side – if his client was not legally bound to pay his costs, the losing party would not be bound to pay them either. However, as the Court of Appeal later pointed out in *Awwad* v *Geraghty & Co* [2000] 3 WLR 1041, an essential plank in the reasoning of the court had been that the prohibition in the Solicitors Practice Rules against any sort of contingency fee did not have the force of law.[12] Unfortunately, the court had not been referred to the House of Lords decision in *Swain* v *Law Society* [1983] 1 AC 598 at 608, which established exactly the opposite.[13]

In *Geraghty*, Schiemann LJ listed powerful arguments for holding that in 1993 when the relevant normal fee conditional agreement was made between Geraghty and Co and their client, Mr Awwad, ie before such an agreement was authorised by the relevant statutory

---

11 'A legal adviser who acquires a personal financial interest in the outcome of litigation may obviously find himself in a situation in which that interest conflicts with that obligation' (*per* Buckley LJ in *Wallersteiner* v *Moir (no 2)* [1975] QB 373, CA).

12 The Rules have naturally since been amended to permit a contingency agreement where authorised by statute.

13 As a footnote to *Swain,* reference may be made to *Mohamed* v *Alaga & Co* [2000] 1 WLR 1815, where the Court of Appeal refused to validate a contract in breach of the Solicitors' Practice Rules 1990 for payment to the claimant for introducing clients to the defendant firm (but they allowed a *quantum meruit* claim for services rendered).

instrument, the agreement, although outlawed by the Solicitors Rules, was not unenforceable. Particularly noticeable is the judge's acknowledgement that:

> It seems odd that an open contractual statement of what is unobjectionably in a solicitor's mind should render unenforceable an agreement which would have been enforceable had the solicitor not shared his thoughts with his client and promised not to change his mind.

The arguments he listed in support of his conclusion that the agreement was unenforceable seem far less cogent. In particular, it seems most surprising that he listed the traditional reason, namely that the lawyer might be tempted to cut corners to achieve success if his fee depended on succeeding, seeing that that is precisely the temptation that we are all now exposed to by the introduction of conditional fees.[14] However, he concluded that in 1993, despite the changing public perception and the clear indications given by the 1990 Act, any sort of conditional fee arrangement, even a normal fee agreement (I get my normal costs if I win but nothing if I lose) was against public policy and so unenforceable at common law.[15]

In *Geraghty* May LJ spoke of 'the difficulties and delays surrounding the introduction of conditional fee agreements', and it is to that aspect of the subject that we now turn.

What are the problems of conditional fee agreements?

Not looking before they leap

Conditional fees were introduced by Lord Mackay, but his reforms to the legal aid system had not gone very far before his Government lost power. The present Government has pushed them forward precipitately without full consideration of or sufficient foresight about the many difficult issues they raise, particularly in the unpredictable context of medical claims (they are less of a problem in the context of simple personal injury claims where the issues, of liability and causation at least, are usually much clearer and far less often capable of sensible dispute). Seemingly unaware how complex the situation was that they were creating, the present Government would have abolished legal aid by now for medical negligence claims had they not been forced by persistent lobbying to acknowledge that, although removing legal aid support for medical negligence claims would certainly have the desired effect of reducing the legal aid bill, it was going to leave injured patients without a remedy, simply because the nuts and bolts necessary to create a usable conditional fee system had not even been found, let alone put in place. Those nuts and

---

14   The reader will not need any reminding that the Government has had no interest at all in 'access to justice' when legislating for conditional fees, merely in reducing the legal aid bill. If some few litigants are enabled to sue who would not have been able to do so under the old legal aid rules, that is an irrelevant by-product of the legislation.

15   The court plainly found it to be not without significance that the solicitor had endeavoured to conceal the fact of the agreement (that she would charge her lower normal rate if she lost (£90 per hour) but her higher normal rate if she won (£150)).

bolts are for the most part reasonably affordable and effective insurance policies. Even now, some years down the line, the manner in which the few solicitors who do apparently conduct medical negligence cases on CFAs operate (no doubt cherry-picking the best cases and declining the others) remains mysteriously obscure, with cryptic talk of such matters as special deals with banks and special terms from insurers (this despite my having asked some of them more than once to write an article on their practices).

Stages towards a conditional fee case

The patient who goes to a solicitor with a complaint needs first to satisfy him that there is something to investigate. Heretofore it could be said that lawyers were too ready to apply for legal aid certificates where they might have been able, using their experience, to conclude that the proposed claim was not worth investigating, because liability or causation appeared very likely to be non-starters. In such cases, the internal complaints procedure (which has just been revamped – see Chapter 6) may be the only reasonable course for the patient to follow. But, assuming the case appears to warrant investigation after what we, like the legal aid authority, may call the initial screening (ie the first interview with the client), the question is who is to pay for the investigation. At first it was blithely assumed that the solicitor would have to put his money where his mouth was. But it then became clear that virtually no solicitor could afford to fund medical cases in that manner. Some patients could afford the few thousand pounds it costs to investigate a claim, but many could not. So legal aid had to be kept for the time being, for the investigative stage at least. Not only that; there was then the question of insurance if legal aid was not available for further work on the case.

There is no legal requirement that insurance must be taken out to support a conditional fee agreement (CFA).[16] But virtually all claimants in medical cases will need to be protected against having to pay the defence costs upon losing the case. So a simple form of policy would involve a premium paid by the claimant which would be irrecoverable in the event of success, but would require the insurers to discharge the claimant's liability to the defendant in the event of failure. The claimant would still, however, be liable for his own disbursements (eg to pay his own experts), if his solicitor had not agreed to cover them himself; so these, too, would need to be covered by the policy. A standard policy with a CFA will therefore cover defence costs and own disbursements (including counsel's fees if he is not on a CFA himself).

But the premium for a CFA medical claim remains expensive, currently about 8% of the cover required (more than five times the cost of an

---

16 Just as a case could always be processed tacitly on a conditional fee basis (as explained above), so also can a case be covered by after-the-event insurance without there being a CFA. Such policies have been on offer for years. But they are expensive, with the premium starting at 15% of the cover required. In that event the claimant's legal fees (as well as the defendant's costs) will be paid by the insurers if the case is lost.

ordinary personal injury action).[17] Cover for any more than a modest medical claim should be at least £60,000 and probably substantially more. Cover can be paid for in stages. Nevertheless, the financing is far more than the average patient can afford. It is unlikely that any solicitor could afford to advance the money. So, a product has been devised which lends the premium to the claimant. If the case is lost, the claimant pays nothing, often not even the interest on the loan of the premium. If the case is won, the premium and interest can be taken from the damages (or charged to the defendant where the law permits such recovery). Naturally, a policy of that sort (sometimes termed a 'bullet' policy) involves a higher premium.

If the solicitor is willing to take the case on a CFA, he will enter into a contract with the client. The contract will permit the solicitor to take his success fee (which may well be a 100% uplift to his normal rates, as the outcome of medical cases is always highly unpredictable) from the compensation awarded, up to a limit of 25% of the damages recovered. There will be an arrangement between solicitor and counsel permitting counsel's fees to gain a similar uplift (unless counsel is not acting under a CFA). Therefore, the claimant is likely to lose a substantial chunk of his damages in this way, when premium and interest and success fees are deducted. That might be thought not unreasonable, as the price of getting the claim processed in the first place. However, the Government appeared to see it as a vote loser and preferred to hold the unsuccessful defendant liable for a substantial part of the success fee and the premium (though not the interest on the premium, if any). By the same token this represents a sizeable increase in the amount of damages payable by a losing defendant.

The insurers' decision

Insurers will only cover disbursements once a policy has been granted (but most policies will be backdated once granted, ie to cover disbursements already incurred). But a policy will not be granted until the insurers are satisfied, following investigation, that a claim should be supported. They are free to make up their own minds about that. They seek help from a variety of sources, including the reports, if any, obtained already by the solicitor, their own qualified staff, and external assistance, including vetting on their behalf by AvMA (who one would have thought would perceive something of a divided duty between their lifelong commitment to the cause of the patient and their newly acquired duty under their contract with the insurers to advise them about the merits of a proposed claim). If the insurers decline to support

---

17 There is little information available currently on the creation, progress and outcome of CFAs generally and virtually none on CFAs in medical actions. Occasionally, one reads the odd anecdote, such as the sad story of the action by the Newcastle United fans to preserve their debenture seating. They sued the club on a CFA. They bought £118,000 of after-the-event cover, for which they paid £26,000 (excluding insurance premium tax), ie 22% of the costs covered, and, to cover their unsuccessful appeal, a further £14,000 for £40,000 of cover, ie 35%. Unfortunately, the defendants raised a bill for £200,000, and their own solicitor a bill for £75,000 (which was generously waived).

a claim, the costs of the investigation remain the liability of whoever commissioned them, depending on the agreement between patient and solicitor. Experts, be it noted, are not permitted to write reports on a conditional fee basis.

Solicitor's duty to advise client about available products

Assuming the insurers are interested to support the case, the question then arises as to what products are on the market, what each involves (for they are many and varied), and what suits the particular client best. There are currently different views as to the duty of the solicitor to understand the market and so give informed advice to the client. Some say that is not his function – he is not an insurance broker. Others say he must learn to be one.

The contracts between client and solicitor, and between solicitor and counsel, of both these types have gone through manifold draft stages and are likely to continue to do so as further problems come to light. The contract between client and solicitor will have to state who picks up the bill for the investigation (the initial screening is unlikely to cost the client anything – it should be completed within two hours), assuming the insurers decline. It will have to state – and this must be made absolutely clear to the client – that there will be a percentage uplift to the solicitor's fees in the event of success. Success needs to be defined. Is any settlement a success? The client will have to be told that, if the insurers take the case, the client will have to pay a premium (or it will be funded in some other way), which is usually in the order of a few thousand pounds. There may also be a fee for the insurer's assessment of the application. If the law enables success fee and premium to be recovered in the event of success this will also be explained. If the solicitor hopes to get a product which will not require the premium, but only interest on the premium, to be paid in the event of the claim failing, and assuming it is the client who will be responsible for the interest, this, too, needs to be explained.

The contract between solicitor and counsel is only necessary if counsel is being asked to do any work on a conditional fee basis. He may well be prepared to spend an hour or two assessing the case for nothing in the investigative stage. Thereafter, if the case is going ahead, the insurance product may specify that counsel's fees are to be treated as a disbursement, in which case he will be paid in any event. The solicitor may, however, want counsel to be in the same boat as he is, even though counsel has so little control over a case compared with the solicitor. Or a product that treats counsel's fees as disbursements may not be available. A conditional fee contract between counsel and solicitor has to be carefully worded to cover all eventualities, including, for example, disputes between them as to the value or the direction, or the merits at any stage, of the case, or as to what the rules are if the brief has to be returned (unlikely, though, in the context of a medical negligence trial). Counsel needs to have a sophisticated system in place in chambers for assessing the risk and therefore the uplift to his fees in the event of success. He also needs to assess likely quantum as the lawyers are not expected in any event to take by way of uplift more than 25% of the damages awarded, of which counsel will probably be limited to 10%.

Assuming the lawyers are on conditional fee contracts,[18] the matter proceeds.

The insurance policy

Products are continually being developed by the various companies offering insurance for clinical negligence claims. Policies can sometimes be taken out without there being a CFA. Own costs can be covered, in full or up to a percentage. Naturally, the premium is higher than for a CFA policy where the insurer has no risk of paying the claimant's costs. Simple loans are available to the solicitor for the cost of the initial investigation so that, although they will need to be paid back with interest if no insurance policy is taken out at a later stage, the firm's cash-flow situation will be alleviated. In this type of non-CFA policy funding may also be available for the premium.

CFA policies

Policy terms are Protean, ie many and varied and constantly changing. Different terms are offered under different schemes, often depending on whether the solicitor is on one of the two specialist panels (AvMA or the Law Society) or has got himself directly accredited by the insurer (ie is on the insurer's own panel) or is on no panel at all. The premium is likely to vary between 8% and 15%. A panel solicitor may well find better terms than a non-panel solicitor. As we have seen, the policy may provide the money up front for the premium, and the claimant pays nothing unless the case is won, in which event premium and interest are taken from the damages or, insofar as the law permits, added to the compensation. An assessment fee may be payable to the insurer, which will be deducted from the premium if a policy is granted.

Are conditional fees attractive to medical negligence lawyers?

Despite sporadic anecdotal boasting from insurers and occasionally from solicitors there is no proper evidence at all – none being made available by solicitors who are thought to be doing work on conditional fees (despite their having been asked more than once to provide it)[19] that the conditional fee facility is regarded as a reasonably profitable line of work by lawyers. The basic problem with a conditional fee claim is not so much that expensive investigation has to be funded by someone before a reasonably useful preliminary assessment of the proposed claim can be made (that problem can usually be overcome in one way or another), but,

---

18 It may be that the case has been processed a fair way on legal expenses insurance, which then runs out. It is possible to create a conditional fee scheme at that point if the insurers agree, or even without involving insurers; the desire on the part of the lawyers not to have to drop the case at an advanced stage may motivate them to unwonted acts of selflessness. Insofar as there is funding under an insurance contract which happens to include legal expenses, the litigant will be in a happier position than the claimant who has to go straight to a CFA or drop his claim.

19 By me and by the editor of *Medical Litigation*.

more significantly, that the outcome of a medical negligence claim always remains unpredictable. It is a common occurrence that, in their original reports, patients' experts condemn the management and confirm that proper management would probably have avoided the injury, but then, 18 months down the line, the defence come up with an expert report that says the opposite. It is unlikely that that will cause patients' lawyers to drop the claim, provided their experts maintain their position. If production of a contrary defence report was enough to invalidate the claim, very few claims would succeed. Many claims go on to successful settlement in the face of an apparently strong defence report. It is often not possible to know if the defence report is genuine or written to order, by way of an attempt to gain time or facilitate a reduced settlement. Assuming it cannot be discounted as a concoction, it is normally quite impossible to predict what will happen at the trial, ie how the evidence will come out, or how the judge will react to it, given that almost all medical claims are complex and, as the trial approaches and during the trial, all manner of small but important points and fresh arguments will emerge, anyone of which could scupper the claim. As the trial progresses it usually becomes clear by the second day or so what has until then been no more than a more or less informed guess, namely what the chances of success actually are. If the case is then lost the solicitor gets nothing for all the work he has done over the years on the case. Most cases succeed early, by way of admission and settlement, and so the profit costs to the solicitor are low. Cases that fail fail late, ie at trial, and so the solicitor loses a lot by way of unpaid costs.[20] One calculation has told us that the solicitor needs to win 30 cases to compensate for losing one. The true figure is probably about ten to one.

So it can be seen that litigating medical claims on conditional fees does not appear to be an attractive commercial proposition.[21]

THE FUTURE FOR LEGAL AID

The LSC told us recently of its proposals for the future. It no longer proposes to leave a litigant to hunt for a CFA after the investigative stage has been funded by legal aid. That sounds like a generous concession. However, it says it will be taking advantage of *Redress* as and when appropriate. What this entails remains to be seen. If *Redress*, now that that part of the scheme which proposed redress for all perinatal injury has been abandoned (they eventually got the point as to the astronomical cost of this vote-catching idea), is to be confined to cases worth less than

---

20 There are schemes by way of which the solicitor can insure himself against complete loss of his costs. But to what extent that is a profitable course for him has not been publicly made known yet.

21 The situation is very different in ordinary personal injury cases, where claims have long been profitably taken on a conditional basis. The reason is that the outcome of such cases, by and large, is not difficult to predict as their simpler facts do not present the same opportunity for complex and subtle argument as do medical claims. In addition there is not so much emotion involved in deciding whether a motorist or employer or local authority should be defended against a claim as for a doctor.

a certain amount, perhaps £50,000, legal aid may not be available for claims which do not exceed that amount. The patient will then have to rely entirely on the *Redress* panel and its carefully chosen members for appropriate compensation in respect of the injuries the NHS has caused him – and how independent will they turn out to be?

Human rights

The obvious question to ask in this context is whether human rights, that Protean horse of many colours (to mix a metaphor), can be invoked to challenge the refusal of legal aid. The answer in any medical case is likely to be no. The Court of Appeal has held, in what it described as an exceptional case[22] that the family of the deceased were entitled to be funded by the state at the inquest by virtue of the state's obligations under Article 2 of the European Convention on Human Rights even though death had occurred before the Human Rights Act came into force (*R (on the application of Mohammed Farooq Khan)* v *Secretary of State for Health* [2003] EWCA Civ 1129; [2004] Lloyds Rep Med 159).[23] *Contra* in another case where the death occurred before the Act came into force Richards J held that there was no obligation to provide funding (*R (on the application of Challender* v *Legal Services Commission* [2004] EWHC 925 (Admin)).[24] An unsuccessful challenge to the refusal of legal aid, relying among other grounds on Article 6 of the Convention, was launched over a claim in respect of a disputed property transfer in *Oakes* v *Legal Services Commission* [2003] EWHC 1948 (Admin). In *Perotti* v *Collyer-Bristow* [2003] EWCA Civ 1521 the Court of Appeal said the court had no power in civil proceedings to grant a right to representation. The decision whether or not to fund legal services in civil proceedings was a matter for the LSC, and it was not for the court to direct the Commission to exercise its discretion to provide funding. The state's obligation to provide legal aid arose if the fact of presenting his own case could be said to prevent the litigant from having effective access to the court. The test under Article 6(1) of the Convention was whether the court was put in a position where it really could not do justice in the case because it had no confidence in its ability to grasp the facts and principles of the matter on which it had to rule.

---

22   The case involved the death of a child of three from apparent gross medical negligence
      in the over-administration of potassium as part of the treatment for B cell lymphoma.
23   Overruled, though, by the House of Lords in a later case. See Chapter 7.
24   See further Chapter 7 on inquests.

Chapter 4

The structure of the National Health Service

PROMISES, PROMISES

Every government feels the need to tinker with the NHS, if only to ensure an impression of concern and to give employment to quangos and the like. The current Government is no exception. It makes many vote-catching promises, to pour money into the service (often deliberately counting the same money several times), to improve management, to cut waiting lists, and so forth, promises which are manifestly impossible to keep on any reasonable economic or social basis. Meanwhile it tinkers – and more – with the dramatic market reforms of the last Conservative Government, particularly in the GP field, producing a host of free pamphlets trumpeting the virtues of their new 'ten-year plan'.

ORIGINS

The NHS is a statutory creation. It came into force on 5 July 1948, by virtue of the National Health Service Act 1946. It brought into being a social benefit unique in Europe. Its purpose was to provide free medical services wherever needed, nationalising the voluntary and the local authority hospitals, and achieving a more efficient distribution over the country of GPs, specialists, doctors and opticians.

Its division of management between local authorities and health authorities was amended by the National Health Service Reorganisation Act of 1973 into the three levels of Region, Area and District. Family Practitioner committees (now Family Health Services Authorities) and Community Health Councils were set up. The district level was the operational level of the 1973 reorganisation. The Area Health Authority had a supervisory role; the District management team were the workers on the ground. The National Health Service Act 1977 consolidated this position. Acting under the Health Services Act 1980, the Secretary of State abolished the Area Health Authority and put in its place the District Health Authority.

Fundamental changes were made by the Conservative administration. The National Health Service and Community Care Act 1990 gave hospitals the right to opt out of health authority control and become self-governing trusts. That was more a matter of hopefully improved efficiency and economy within the NHS, for these units nevertheless remain firmly within the framework of the NHS (see below). The funding arrangements, which created the dichotomy between purchasers of healthcare (principally health authorities and GPs) and providers of health care (the hospitals), and which were designed to create a market economy in the field of care provision, do not directly affect the medical negligence scene. Under the current Government, GP collectives and community nurses (the GP fundholder as such is phased out) are given the power (ie the funds) to buy all treatments except very specialised ones (eg heart, lung and kidney transplants and specialist pediatric services).

Bureaucracy was simplified by the Health Authorities Act 1995, which took effect in April 1996, in that there is now only one level of health authority. Regional health authorities were abolished, and district health authorities were merged with family health services authorities to form a single purchasing authority, responsible for securing health services for their local populations

Hospitals are now self-governing trusts, as are most other health bodies (eg ambulance services and community-based services). The division between purchasers and providers of healthcare is complete.

CURRENTLY

By way of summary, we may see the Department of Health as leading direction and reform of the NHS, setting standards, securing resources and working with the Healthcare Commission (described as an independent inspection body for the NHS in England and Wales) to help ensure quality of services. The Department is responsible for 'special health authorities', involving national services such as the National Blood Authority, and for the 'strategic health authorities' (28 of them), which are themselves responsible for ensuring that local trusts are performing well. These local trusts comprise NHS trusts, ambulance trusts, mental health trusts and care trusts. Primary care trusts (PCTs) (302 in number) provide GP, dental and optical care, along with pharmacists, walk in centres and NHS Direct. They have the main responsibility for funding secondary care from the trusts. 75% of the NHS budget goes to PCTs.

We spoke of the 'reforms' to the NHS in Chapter 2. We may note here the expansion in many directions of private funding and services. Of 132 new hospitals, 121 are being funded through private initiative. PCTs can fund surgery privately, from an independent sector treatment centre, or from 'flying surgeons' brought in from overseas, and even by sending the patient abroad. Complaint has been made that the private sector cherry-picks the patients and is paid more than the former providers, the hospitals, while often offering questionable levels of service. As with the radical new development of foundation hospitals, only time will tell if what look like ominous beginnings improve so as to live up to the Government's proud boasts. Further material on the NHS and its various components can be found in Chapter 2.

AT GOVERNMENTAL LEVEL

The widest issues, including national health policies and the general organisation of the NHS, are decided by Parliament. The Secretary of State for Health is the cabinet-level minister who is in charge of health matters, assisted by a Minister of State for Health. The Secretary of State is in charge of the work of the Department of Health, which is responsible for central planning of the health services and for monitoring their performance.[1] Two select committees in Parliament deal with health matters – the Select Committee on Health and the Select Committee on the Parliamentary Commissioner for Administration, which examines the reports of the Ombudsman.

The provision of health care is legally the function of the Secretary of State for Health. The principal Acts, the National Health Service Act 1977 (still the principal Act) and the National Health Service and Community Care Act 1990, afford the Minister extremely broad and extensive discretionary powers. These powers need to be delegated to appropriate bodies. The paramount power of the Secretary of State is the control of NHS expenditure through the use of cash limits.

Section 1 of the 1977 Act imposes the duty to continue to promote a free, comprehensive health service designed to improve our physical and mental health and to improve the prevention, diagnosis and treatment of illness, and the Secretary of State has the duty to provide for that purpose services in accordance with the Act. Section 2 gives him power to provide such services as he considers appropriate for the purposes of discharging any of his statutory duties, and to do anything calculated to facilitate, or conducive or incidental to, the discharge of any of his duties.

Section 3 imposes the particular duty to provide, to such extent as he considers necessary to meet all reasonable requirements:

- hospital accommodation;
- other accommodation for the purposes of any service provided under the Act;
- medical, dental, nursing and ambulance services;
- facilities for the care of expectant and nursing mothers and young children, such as he considers appropriate as part of the health service;
- facilities for the prevention of illness and the care and after-care of patients, such as he considers appropriate;
- such other services as are required for the diagnosis and treatment of illness.

Section 4 requires the Secretary of State to maintain special security hospitals for dangerous, violent or criminal patients. Section 5 requires him to arrange for medical and dental inspection and treatment of schoolchildren, and, in an unhappy juxtaposition, to provide advisory

---

1   He is also Chairman of the NHS Policy Board (the other important organ is the NHS Executive chaired by the NHS Chief Executive). The Policy Board and the NHS Executive are intended to provide clear leadership of the NHS at the centre.

and medical services and appliances to those interested in contraception.[2]

Overall supervision of the NHS is the function of the NHS Executive,[3] whose basic functions relate to strategic planning and market regulation. It is a branch of the Department of Health whose remit is to work within the framework set by the Department of Health and the NHS Policy Board. The Board is chaired by the Health Secretary. Its workings are shrouded in secrecy. It establishes policy, priorities, and standards for the NHS. Responsibility for assessing local health needs and securing services for local populations is delegated to health authorities. Since April 1996 the responsibility for monitoring the operation of the NHS market, both purchasing and providing, has been that of the NHS Executive. It issues strategic and operational guidelines to health authorities, develops and advises the Policy Board of resource policies and needs, proposes the distribution of funds to the regions, deals with pay and personnel issues, and sets health authority targets and monitors their achievement through regional planning and review processes. The role of the NHS Executive now includes responsibility for primary care as well as acute and community health services.

TRUSTS

Trusts are statutory corporations, run by their own board of directors, who have responsibility for determining overall policy, monitoring implementation and maintaining the financial viability of the trust. They are not trusts in the legal sense. The term was chosen, and substituted for 'self-governing hospital', because it was perceived (by government) as having a ring about it of public service rather than personal profit (rather like the National Lottery). They are the main providers of NHS services, together with some organisations independent of the NHS. Their principal duties are to assume responsibility for providing and managing services.

They are free to determine their own management structures, to employ their own staff and set their own terms and conditions of service, to acquire, own and sell their own assets, to retain surpluses, and to borrow money subject to annual limits. Each trust is run by its own board of directors, independent of district and regional management.

Though separate from a health authority, a trust remains accountable to the Health Secretary via the NHS Executive, although the principal accountability measures are concerned with fiscal rather than organisational or administrative matters. In its annual report a trust needs to

---

2   In *Danns* v *Department of Health* [1996] PIQR P69; affd [1998] PIQR P226, CA the claimant in an ingenious argument (as to which see Chapter 5) based the claim on the Ministry of Health Act 1919, s 2, whereby a duty is laid on the Minister ' to take all such steps as may be desirable to secure ... the collection, preparation, publication and dissemination of information and statistics relating thereto' (ie to public health generally).

3   If you have been wondering what became of the NHS Management Executive, the answer is that they decided that that title was not user-friendly and so, at great public expense, the logo, letterheads and anything else displaying the offending word were changed.

demonstrate that it is striking a fair balance between quality of services and expenditure.

It is possible for a trust to go bankrupt, but its liabilities will be accepted by the NHS pursuant to the National Health Service (Residual Liabilities) Act 1996 (this is an important reassurance for a patient accepting from a trust a self-funded structured settlement).

Guidance is given to health bodies from time to time by the Department of Health in health circulars and executive letters from the NHS Executive, fundamental matters of policy having been decided at governmental level. Hospitals were the original beneficiaries of the trust status. Now trusts for every aspect of healthcare proliferate.

HEALTH AUTHORITIES

The duty of health authorities is to ensure that the services provided meet the needs of those resident or present in their area. This includes the provision of ambulance and emergency services. These powers are delegated by the Secretary of State to implement his obligations to provide services under the 1977 Act. Health authorities are expected to work with GPs and with local people and organisations. They retain managerial factions in relation to matters such as transfer of patients between lists and are responsible for ensuring that doctors and dentists keep to the terms of their contracts. They also operate the independent review stage of the complaints procedures.

GPS

The more radical role for GPs and the push towards a primary care-led health service has left many practitioners uncertain of their role and dissatisfied with both the administrative and clinical overload. The GP fund-holder, as was, now collective, is both purchaser and provider of services, which is inconsistent with one of the primary principles of the reforms. Some observers feel that the fundamental values of general practice are being eroded. Others question the rising cost of management and administration. Perhaps the new facility for opting out of night duty may be taking some pressure off GPs now.

THE NHS AND THE CROWN

The NHS is a Crown body. The NHS authorities exercise their functions on behalf of the Crown. By virtue of the Crown Proceedings Act 1947 the Crown may be sued in the ordinary way in tort and contract. But legislation does not bind the Crown unless expressly so stated, or necessarily implied. Coercive orders, such as execution of a judgment or an order for specific performance or an injunction, cannot issue against the Crown. Before February 1987 the Crown could not be prosecuted for breach of safety or health regulations. There was a procedure, in use since 1978, whereby inspectors could issue improvement or prohibition notices to Crown undertakings, including NHS hospitals, and these would not be ignored. Under the National Health Service (Amendment) Act 1986 Crown immunity was removed, to the extent that health authorities might thereafter be prosecuted for breaches of the food, health and safety legislation.

The House of Lords decision in *Pfizer Corpn* v *Ministry of Health* [1965] AC 512 established that the NHS was a Crown service. It was held that the use of drugs in the NHS was a use 'for the service of the Crown', and therefore a patented drug could be made use of under the Patents Act 1949 subject to appropriate payment to the owner of the patent. In *Wood* v *Leeds Area Health Authority* [1974] ICR 535 the National Industrial Relations Court held that a NHS employee was a servant of the Crown and that therefore he could not take advantage of the Contracts of Employment Act 1972. In *Dory* v *Sheffield Health Authority* (1988) 11 BMLR 93 the health authority's use of patented medical equipment was held to be use by the Crown for the purposes of s 55 of the Patents Act 1977. Compare *British Medical Association* v *Greater Glasgow Health Board* [1989] AC 1211 where the House of Lords held that proceedings for an interdict against a health board (the Scottish version of a health authority) did not constitute 'proceedings against the Crown' within the meaning of s 21(1) of the Crown Proceedings Act 1947.

Section 60 of the National Health Service and Community Care Act 1990 provides that from the appointed day no health service body shall be regarded as the servant or agent of the Crown or as enjoying any status, immunity or privilege of the Crown. It therefore follows that, whether or not the matter was arguable before, by virtue of this section a health authority can be made subject, for example, to an injunction, to summary judgment, and to contempt proceedings.[4]

THE ARMED FORCES

The position in respect of matters arising before 1987

Members of the armed forces, pursuant to s 10 of the Crown Proceedings Act 1947, may not be sued, nor may the Crown, for causing death or personal injury when on duty to another member of the armed forces, provided the injured party was on duty at the time or was on premises for the time being used for the purposes of the armed forces. So a soldier may not sue for mistreatment he received in an army hospital. In *Bell* v *Secretary of State for Defence* [1986] QB 322 an injured serviceman, stationed in West Germany, was transferred from an army medical reception centre to a civilian hospital where he died, allegedly as a result of totally inadequate notes provided to the hospital by the army doctor. On a preliminary issue the Secretary of State for Defence was held not to be entitled to immunity from the suit brought by the dead soldier's father because, said a majority of the Court of Appeal, the failure to provide

---

4   It may be noted that in *R* v *Licensing Authority established under the Medicines Act 1968, ex p Smith Kline & French Laboratories Ltd (No 2)* [1990] 1 QB 574, the Court of Appeal said that the prohibition in the Crown Proceedings Act 1947 against granting declaratory and injunctive relief against the Crown did not apply to judicial review proceedings.

proper notes had occurred at the civilian hospital and not on Crown premises (a decision which is a little difficult to understand on the facts). In *Pearce* – see below – the court said that *Bell* was wrongly decided.

This immunity only applies if the minister certifies that the injury will be attributed to service as a member of the armed forces for the purposes of disablement or death benefit (it is intended that a serviceman who has the benefit of the service pension scheme should not also have a right to sue at common law). Immunity is not to be accorded if the court is satisfied that the alleged negligence was not 'connected with' the execution of army, etc duties.

In *Pearce* v *Secretary of State for Defence* [1988] AC 755, Caulfield J ruled on a preliminary point in a claim backed by the Nuclear Test Victims Association. The claimant, then an NCO in the Royal Engineers, had been exposed to radiation from the atomic tests carried out on Christmas Island in the late 1950s. The tests had been carried out by the now defunct Atomic Energy Commission, which had not been a Crown body, though its functions were transferred to the Ministry of Defence in 1973. The judge said that s 10 of the Act of 1947 did not afford immunity to the Crown upon the claim, because sub-s(1) was restricted to acts by members of the armed forces, and sub-s(2), which included a prohibition on legal action by members of the armed forces for death or personal injury arising out of the nature or condition of military equipment being used in connection with the armed forces, was not in point because the 'thing suffered' by the claimant within the meaning of the provision was the continuing omission of the authority to warn of the hazard (the actual injury was not the 'thing suffered' but the consequence of it), and so the 'thing suffered' was not by or in consequence of the nature or condition of land, premises, ship, aircraft, vehicle, equipment or supplies (the result may be attractive, but the argument is strained). The Court of Appeal by a majority dismissed the defendant's appeal on the basis that the claimant's accrued right to sue the Atomic Energy Commission survived as against the Ministry of Defence ([1988] AC 755) and the House of Lords upheld their decision on the same ground, while holding also that the construction given by the trial judge to the words 'thing suffered' was wrong. That construction had followed the reasoning of the Court of Appeal in the *Bell* case, which therefore had been wrongly decided ([1988] AC 755). In *Quinn* v *Ministry of Defence* [1998] PIQR P387 the Court of Appeal followed *Pearce* in its interpretation of the words 'thing suffered'.

It was said in *Trawnik* v *Lennox* [1985] 1 WLR 532, CA, that there was no right of action against the Crown in tort apart from that arising by virtue of the Act of 1947.

In *Derry* v *Ministry of Defence* [1999] PIQR P204, CA, the old s 10 was still in force at the time of the alleged negligence in 1985. The defendants successfully pleaded the active duty defence.

Human rights had, of course, to pop its head up in this context (as in all others). In *Matthews* v *Ministry of Defence* MLC 0905, [2003] PIQRP 392 the House of Lords held, in respect of a serviceman's claim for injury acquired before 1987, that a s 10 certificate was a substantive and not a procedural bar to legal action and that therefore it was not incompatible with Article 6(1) of the European Convention on Human Rights.

In the complex and important case of *Multiple Claimants* v *Ministry of Defence* [2003] EWHC 1134 (QB) Owen J held that the Crown was protected by the immunity under s 10 of the 1947 Act in respect of claims by former members of the armed forces for damages for psychiatric illness caused by the stress of combat where the act or omission relied on occurred before 15 May 1987.

The position after May 1987

This immunity was repealed by the Crown Proceedings (Armed Forces) Act 1987, which received royal assent on 15 May 1987, but the statute does not have retrospective effect (the Crown accepts *ex gratia* claims arising after 8 December 1986).

FOREIGN FORCES

In *Littrell* v *United States of America (No 2)* [1994] PIQR P141, CA, the court declined to exercise jurisdiction over the complaint by an American staff sergeant that he had been injured by negligent medical treatment carried out in 1987 at the military hospital at the United States air base at Lakenheath. It is surprising that the claimant's advisers thought they had any chance of defeating a plea of *acta iure imperii* (ie that, in respect of the acts complained of, the defendant state was acting in the exercise of its sovereign power and was therefore not subject to the jurisdiction of our courts – see Lewis *State and Diplomatic Immunity* (Lloyd's of London Press, 3rd edn, 1990)).

In *A (a child)* v *Ministry of Defence* MLC 1007, Bell J held that, where the dependant child of a British serviceman posted to Germany was injured at birth by the negligence of a German health carer in a Designated German Provider Hospital (DGP) procured by Guy's and St Thomas' Hospital NHS Trust to whom the Ministry of Defence had subcontracted procuring of secondary hospital healthcare in DGPs, proceedings by that dependant in respect of that negligence must be brought in Germany. The Court of Appeal upheld the judge's decision: MLC 1259 ([2004] Lloyds Rep Med 351).[5]

---

5   This decision is more fully considered in Chapter 21.

Chapter 5

Suing over policy decisions

This chapter looks at claims that are not rooted in alleged clinical negligence but relate more to policy decisions or alleged system or administration failures, whether by government or the NHS or a particular health body. In this context fall claims over the allocation of resources, over closures of units, over inadequacies of infrastructure, over refusals to authorise a particular treatment, and so forth. The grounds for any such claim may now be more extensive thanks to the human rights aspect, though lawyers need to handle this aspect of any proposed claim with caution (see Chapter 27 on human rights).

In *R* v *Secretary of State for Social Services, ex p Hincks* (1979) 123 Sol Jo 436; affd (1980) 1 BMLR 93, CA, four orthopedic patients at a Birmingham hospital, who were being obliged to wait longer than was medically advisable for treatment because of a shortage of facilities due in part to a policy decision not to build a new hospital block for economic reasons, applied for declarations against the Minister, and Regional and Area Health Authorities, that the statutory duties imposed by ss 1 and 3 of the National Health Service Act 1977 (see above and Appendix I) had not been discharged. The patients needed to establish in the first place that they had a *locus standi* to bring the action; if they had, they asked for a declaration that the authorities were in breach of their statutory duties, and they sought both an order requiring them to perform their duties, and also damages for the pain and suffering caused to them by the delay in treatment. They failed. Wien J said that the Minister's duty was to provide such services as he considered necessary and that such a wording gave him a discretion as to how financial resources were to be used. If there was not enough money then all needs could not be met. In those circumstances it was impossible to say that the Minister, or any other body, was in breach of statutory duty. The court would only interfere where the Minister had acted as no reasonable Minister could possibly act, or had acted so as to frustrate the policy of the Act. Nor did he take the view that the Act gave any right of action to the individual patient to sue in respect of an alleged breach of the Minister's general duties.

The Court of Appeal agreed with the trial judge; Bridge LJ pointed out that the Minister must be entitled to make policy decisions about the allocation of financial resources in the light of overall long-term planning or he would be called upon to disburse funds that were not in fact available. This surely is the complete answer to the human rights enthusiasts who predict that patients will now be entitled to demand any treatment, regardless of the cost.

In *Department of Health and Social Security* v *Kinnear* (1984) 134 NLJ 886, sufferers from the whooping cough vaccine brought an action against the Department in relation to the manner of promoting the vaccine. Stuart-Smith LJ struck out their claim in so far as it involved an attack on the exercise by the Department under s 26 of the National Health Service Act 1946 of their discretion as to whether arrangements should be made for immunisation against such a disease. The judge said that it was in the bona fide exercise of that discretion that the department had adopted a policy of promoting immunisation against whooping cough. That policy, being within the limits of the discretion and the result of its bona fide exercise, could not give rise to a cause of action (though one may note that that part of the claim that regarded actions of an operational rather than a policy nature, allegations *inter alia* that negligent or misleading advice had been given by the Department as to the manner and circumstances in which immunisations were to be performed, was not struck out).

The Kinnear decision was followed in part in the Scottish Court of Session in *Ross* v *Secretary of State for Scotland* [1990] 1 Med LR 235, where a pursuer's direct case against the Scottish Home and Health Department alleging that she suffered brain damage as a result of being vaccinated against smallpox was dismissed because it was based on considerations of ministerial policy and matters of discretion and was, therefore, irrelevant in the absence of averments of bad faith. The Kinnear decision was distinguished in part in that the judge, Lord Milligan, said that that part of the Kinnear claim that was permitted to proceed appeared to be of an 'operational' nature and so not of assistance in his case. A similar decision on the main issue had been reached by Lord Grive in the Scottish case of *Bonthrone* v *Secretary of State for Scotland* 1987 SLT 34, where the pursuer's claim for injury allegedly sustained as a result of vaccination against whooping cough, diphtheria and tetanus without there having been given adequate warning of the risk of encephalopathy or other side effects had been struck out as attacking the ambit of exercise of a discretion rather than action taken to implement a discretionary decision.

In *Re HIV Haemophiliac Litigation* (1990) 41 BMLR 171, [1990] NLJR 1349, CA, Ralph Gibson LJ said that in appropriate circumstances a duty of care might be imposed in regard to the discharge of functions under the Act of 1977.

In *Danns* v *Department of Health* [1996] PIQR P69, a claim that owed more to the creative imagination of the claimant's advisers than to any realistic assessment of the prospect of success was brought, following a late recanalisation after a vasectomy and the consequent birth of a child to the claimant's wife, against the Department on the ground that it should have publicised the risk of failure of such a procedure by the time of the vasectomy in 1983. The claim was based in part on s 2 of the Ministry of Health Act 1919 which provides:

> It shall be the duty of the Minister ... to take all such steps as may be desirable to secure the preparation, effective carrying out and co-ordination of measures conducive to the health of the people, including measures for the prevention and cure of diseases ... the treatment of physical and mental defects ... the

initiation and direction of research, the collection, preparation, publication and dissemination of information and statistics relating thereto, and the training of persons for health services.

The usual action where it is alleged that the patient should have been told of the risk of late recanalisation is an action against the doctor or hospital responsible for the procedure (see Chapter 24). Presumably in this case the claimant's advisers had concluded that the facts did not permit such a claim, and therefore they chanced their arm on an action against the Department of Health, *faute de mieux* one might say.

Not surprisingly, Wright J held that a breach of this section would not give rise to a private law right of action, that it clearly conferred upon the Minister a discretion to decide what steps he should or should not take in discharge of his ministerial function, and that in the present context any decisions by the Minister as to what materials were to be disseminated under the provisions of the section were entirely a question of policy in respect of which he was entitled to exercise his discretion. In any event, he was fully entitled to leave it to the medical profession to decide what advice or counselling it should give to those coming forward for a vasectomy. The Court of Appeal, agreeing with the judge and stating that the Department did not owe the claimant a duty of care as there was no sufficient relationship of proximity, dismissed the appeal, saying that the prospects of success on appeal had been slight ([1998] PIQR P226).

In *R v Central Birmingham Health Authority, ex p Walker* (1987) 3 BMLR 32, CA, an unsuccessful application was made for judicial review of the health authority's decision that, although it was agreed that baby Walker needed a certain operation, it could not carry it out at that time for resource reasons. The Master of the Rolls said:

> It is not for this court, or indeed any court, to substitute its own judgment for the judgment of those who are responsible for the allocation of resources. This court could only intervene where it was satisfied that there was a *prima facie* case, not only of failing to allocate resources in the way in which others think that resources should be allocated, but of a failure to allocate resources to an extent which was '*Wednesbury* unreasonable', to use the lawyers' jargon, or, in simpler words, which involves a breach of a public law duty. Even then, of course, the court has to exercise a judicial discretion. It has to take account of all the circumstances of the particular case with which it is concerned.[1]

In another case against the same health authority less than two months later, the father of four-year-old Matthew Collier failed to persuade the Court of Appeal to intervene where desperately needed open-heart surgery was delayed for months, even though Matthew had been placed at the top of the waiting list, due to shortage of intensive care beds and nurses. The court said that there was no evidence that the health

---

1   Under the well-established *Wednesbury* principle the court will only intervene if it is shown that the decision taken was one which no reasonable body could have arrived at if it had been taking into account all relevant matters – in other words, the decision must be shown to be irrational (see *Associated Provincial Picture Houses v Wednesbury Corpn* [1948] 1 KB 223, CA).

authority had acted unreasonably or in breach of any public duty (*R* v *Central Birmingham Health Authority, ex p Collier* [1988] CA transcript 6 January).[2]

In *R* v *North West Thames Regional Health Authority, ex p Daniels* [1993] 4 Med LR 364 the Divisional Court, despite sympathising with the predicament of the boy, Rhys Daniels, and actually finding that the District Health Authority had failed, contrary to Regulation 19(1) of the Community Health Councils Regulations, SI 1985/304, to consult the community health council before closing the bone marrow unit at Westminster Children's Hospital, was, predictably, unwilling to order the reopening of the unit because making an order would not benefit the boy. The court said it was sure that the unit at Bristol would do all it could. Although one understands that the proceedings had the useful effect of getting the NHS to ensure that appropriate treatment was speedily made available, the parents, most sadly, had to decide in September 1997 that no further treatment should be attempted and Rhys died just before Christmas 1998, aged nearly eight.

In *R* v *Sheffield Health Authority, ex p Seale* (1994) 25 BMLR 1, Auld J held that it was not unreasonable for the health authority to limit IVF treatment to women between the ages of 25 and 35 in view of their limited budget. He said that although they had undertaken to provide such treatment for patients within their area, that did not mean they were bound to provide the service on demand and regardless of financial and other concerns.[3]

In *R* v *Cambridge District Health Authority, ex p B* [1995] 1 WLR 898, CA, the father of a 10-year-old girl, who had already been treated with two courses of chemotherapy, applied for an order compelling the health authority to fund a third course and a second bone marrow transplant when she suffered a relapse of her acute myeloid leukemia. The health authority had declined to treat, principally on the basis that the proposed treatment, being of an experimental nature, was not in the child's best interests, and also on the ground that the huge expense involved would not be an appropriate use of their limited resources. The trial judge, Laws J, while not being prepared to order the health authority to treat, required them to reconsider their decision on the ground that their

---

2 Reference may also be made to *Wyatt* v *Hillingdon London Borough Council* (1978) 76 LGR 727, CA, where it was held that provisions in the Chronically Sick and Disabled Persons Act 1970 gave default powers over the health authority to the Minister that precluded the remedy sought from the courts. In *R* v *Inner London Education Authority, ex p F* (1988) Times, 28 November, the Divisional Court declined to review a consultant psychiatrist's decision to transfer a patient. In *R* v *Ealing District Health Authority, ex p F* (1992) 11 BMLR 59 the court made it clear that it would not compel psychiatric supervision of a patient. In *X* v *A, B and C* (1991) 9 BMLR 91 the court declined to order treatment requested by a pedophile, stating that wrongful acts within the context of public law afforded no remedy to the individual.

3 On the fringe of this 'resource' question we can note *R* v *Secretary of State for Health, ex p Keen* [1990] 1 Med LR 455, where Professor Keen, Director of the Unit for Metabolic Medicine and Director of Clinical Services/Medicine at Guy's Hospital, failed in an application for judicial review of the expenditure of resources on the preparation, before the National Health Care and Community Service Bill became law, for a change of the hospital's status to that of self-governing NHS Trust.

reasoning had been flawed because the treatment was not experimental and because they had not properly explained their funding priorities. The Court of Appeal reversed his decision. The Master of the Rolls provided what at that time might have been thought to be the last word on the attitude of the courts to decisions on funding by health authorities:

I have no doubt that in a perfect world any treatment which a patient, or a patient's family, sought would be provided if doctors were willing to give it, no matter how much it cost, particularly when a life was potentially at stake. It would however, in my view, be shutting one's eyes to the real world if the court were to proceed on the basis that we do live in such a world. It is common knowledge that health authorities of all kinds are constantly pressed to make ends meet. They cannot pay their nurses as much as they would like; they cannot provide all the treatments they would like; they cannot purchase all the extremely expensive medical equipment they would like; they cannot carry out all the research they would like; they cannot build all the hospitals and specialist units they would like. Difficult and agonising judgments have to be made as to how a limited budget is best allocated to the maximum advantage of the maximum number of patients. That is not a judgment which the court can make. In my judgment, it is not something that a health authority such as this authority can be fairly criticised for not advancing before the court.

And Sir Stephen Brown said:

After the most critical, anxious consideration, I feel bound to say that I am unable to say that the authority in this case acted in a way that exceeded its powers or which was unreasonable in the legal sense. The powers of this court are not such as to enable it to substitute its own decision in a matter of this kind for that of the authority which is legally charged with making the decision.

It is understood that in the event money was provided by a benefactor for the necessary treatment, but that, most sadly, the child did not survive.

However, perhaps presaging the current greater willingness of the courts to intervene, Dyson J held in *R v North Derbyshire Health Authority, ex p Fisher* [1997] 8 Med LR 327 that the policy of the health authority relating to the administration to patients suffering from multiple sclerosis of the drug beta interferon was unlawful because it failed to give serious consideration to the advice offered in the relevant NHS Circular. That Circular requested purchasing authorities and providers within the NHS to develop and manage the entry of such drugs into the NHS and in particular to initiate and continue prescribing beta interferon to hospitals. Insofar as the health authority had any policy at all, the judge was satisfied that it amounted in effect to a blanket ban on the prescription of the drug. It is clear that the judge found the evidence produced by the health authority to be wholly unsatisfactory. He was understandably unimpressed by a weasel-speak minute from the health authority which, having accepted that in the light of a speech by the Secretary of State for Health a blanket ban was not acceptable, noted: 'However it might be possible to have creative constraints'. The judge granted a declaration that the policy of the health authority was unlawful, quashed its decision to decline to prescribe the drug to Mr Fisher, and ordered it to form and implement a policy which took into account the policy of the circular. He did not, of course, order the health authority to treat the patient.[4]

In *R* v *Brent and Harrow Health Authority, ex p London Borough of Harrow* [1997] 3 FCR 765, 34 BMLR 9, the local education authority, who were being sued by a pupil in an attempt to compel them to provide speech, occupational and physiotherapy, as required by s 16 of the Education Act 1993, brought a similar action against the health authority requiring them to allocate resources for that purpose. Turner J said that allocation of resources must be done according to a number of competing priorities, of which the provision of services under the Education Act was only one. The health authority could not reasonably be expected to recalculate and reallocate resources according to a particular demand which arose at any particular moment. They were entitled to ration their scarce resources as they had done in the present case.

However if funds are used for a clearly unauthorised purpose the court will take appropriate action. In *R* v *Secretary of State for Health, ex p Manchester Local Medical Committee* (1995) 25 BMLR 77, Collins J acceded to an application for judicial review of the refusal of the Secretary of State to take action when he was informed that the surplus funds allocated to a Family Health Services Authority for the provision of general medical services and the reimbursement of claims by GPs for practice staff costs, rent and premises improvement grants had in fact been used by the authority for the (unlawful) appointment of facilitators to arrange or assist in the provision of general medical services in the region.

More recently

Latterly the courts have shown themselves even readier to oversee and, where considered appropriate, invalidate administrative decisions, including decisions as to the allocation of resources, and on various grounds to set them aside. But whether they would ever be willing to make a direct order for allocation to a particular purpose, whether on human rights grounds or any other, remains very doubtful.

In *R* v *North and East Devon Health Authority, ex p Coughlan* [2000] 2 WLR 622, [1999] MLC 0105 the Court of Appeal set aside a decision by the health authority to close a home for disabled residents, on the ground that, having told the residents at an earlier date that it would be a permanent home for them, there was no sufficient 'over-reaching public interest' which would justify the health authority breaking that 'home for life promise'. A further ground, involving highly complex argument, was that the health authority had misinterpreted its responsibilities under the National Health Service Act 1977. The judge below, Hidden J, had also been satisfied that the necessary elements for consultation had not

---

4   In *R (on application of Longstaff)* v *Newcastle PCT* [2003] EWHC 3252 (Admin); [2004] Lloyds Rep Med 400 Charles J held in December 2003 that the defendant NHS trust, who had refused to provide funding for the applicant haemophiliac to be treated with the recombinant Factor VIII, had not been under a duty to seek further information as to the reasons for his decision to refuse to accept treatment with plasma derived Factor VIII products.

been satisfied. He had said that he accepted entirely that the respondent authority was master of its own resources, but the decisions it made as to its own resources had to be made reasonably. A reasonable resolution of the problem would have to include a conclusion on all relevant arguments and the exclusion of all irrelevant ones. He had said the approach of the authority was flawed from the outset as it treated a promise of a permanent home merely as a promise to provide care. The assessments the authority carried out were not proper multi-disciplinary assessments, as required by the relevant Guidance, and no regard was paid to the Social Services assessment that the home 'ideally suited' the applicant. In relation to the process of decision-making the judge had said that the procedures were 'far from the stuff of which true consultation is made'.

In *R* v *North West Lancashire Health Authority, ex p Miss A, D and G* [2000] 1 WLR 977, [1999] MLC 0111 the Court of Appeal again upheld a decision of Hidden J, on this occasion invalidating a decision by the health authority in relation to the treatment it was or was not prepared to provide to transsexuals, ie a decision on the allocation of its limited resources. The health authority had refused the applicants gender reassignment surgery, from male to female. Suffering as they did from an inability to accept the gender they were born with, they were in principle entitled to be considered for treatment under the NHS. However this health authority had decided upon a policy that such surgery would be refused unless there were exceptional circumstances over and above the clinical need.

The court said that the allocation and weighting of priorities in funding different treatments from finite resources was a matter of judgment for the health authority; that it was proper for an authority to adopt a general policy; that a policy to allocate a low priority to gender reassignment surgery was not in principle irrational; but that in this case the policy was undermined and invalidated by evidence which showed that the health authority did not in fact regard gender dysphoria as a genuine illness requiring more than psychiatric reassurance, an approach that did not reflect its own medical judgment. The court therefore quashed the relevant resource allocation policies and all decisions based on them and required the health authority to give proper weight to its acknowledgement that gender dysphoria was an illness, to address the clinical evidence as to the need for and effectiveness of gender reassignment procedures, to indicate reasons in broad terms for the priority to be given to providing such treatment, and to make effective provision for exceptions in individual cases from any general policy restricting funding for such treatment.[5]

Once again, Hidden J's approach at first instance is worth studying. He accepted that it was for the health authority and not the court to allocate limited budgets to the maximum advantage for the number of patients. Nevertheless, he said, in formulating or applying policy to any particular case before it the authority had to consider whether there was a demonstrable medical need for the treatment in question. Although the court

---

5   For the human rights aspect of these cases, see Chapter 27.

would not seek to allocate scarce resources in a tight budget, it would ensure that the health authority had asked the right questions and had addressed the right issues before arriving at its policy. In this case the authority was unable to define or exemplify what it meant by the proviso of 'overriding clinical need'. The judge said that it was not entitled to limit its treatment to counselling and so to exclude hormone treatment and surgery. Therefore its decision was unlawful and irrational, arrived at with without consideration of relevant matters such as the question of what was the proper treatment or what was actually recognised as the illness of gender identity dysphoria. Relevant considerations were not taken into account and irrelevant ones were. The policy unlawfully fettered the discretion of the health authority in its duty towards each particular patient of providing treatment and facilities for the prevention of illness and the cure of persons suffering from gender identity dysphoria.

Jackson J followed the lead of the Court of Appeal when he declared unlawful a decision by a health authority to close a long-stay hospital for patients with profound learning disabilities. He said that the health authority had failed to have regard to promises previously made that the patients would have a home for life at the hospital or to the specific needs of those patients in relation to their relocation (*R* v *Merton, Sutton and Wandsworth Health Authority, ex p Perry* [2001] Lloyd's Rep Med 73).

In *R* v *Secretary of State for Health, ex p Pfizer Ltd* [1999] MLC 0103, 51 BMLR 189, Collins held that a Department of Health Circular 1998/158 advising that doctors should not prescribe Viagra was unlawful both as seeking to override a doctor's professional judgment as to what treatment would best benefit his patient, and also as being in breach of the European Directive 89/105/EEC (which required that publicity be given to the criteria applied in measures to restrict or exclude from the public domain medicinal products for human use).

In *Cowl* v *Plymouth City Council* [2001] EWCA Civ 1935, the Court of Appeal, perhaps tiring of the many appeals against closure of homes and the like, now as a matter of course padding out the claim with a human rights plea, refusing an application for judicial review of a council's decision to close one of their residential homes for the elderly, said that, where the lawfulness of a decision to close such a home was in question, the lawyers on both sides were under a heavy obligation to resort to litigation only if it was really unavoidable. They should strive to resolve the issues, or a significant part of them, outside the litigation process. A decision to similar negative effect was *R (on application of Haggerty)* v *St Helen's Council* [2003] EWHC 803 (Admin), Silber J.

R v *Brent, Kensington & Chelsea & Westminster Mental NHS Trust, ex p C* [2002] EWHC 18, Newman J, was an unsuccessful application for judicial review of the mental health trust's decision to close a residential lodge. *R (on the application of Dudley)* v *East Sussex County Council* [2003] EWHC 1093 (Admin), was an unsuccessful application for judicial review of the council's decision to close a long-term residential care home for the elderly. Maurice Kay J said there was no breach of any human rights in the process.

On this vexed question of allocation of resources we may also note *Wilsher* v *Essex Area Health Authority* [1987] QB 730, CA, which is authority for the proposition that the employment through lack of funds of relatively inexperienced young doctors in responsible positions does not reduce the level of the standard of care which the patient has a right to expect. And even though the Secretary of State would not himself be responsible, it appears from the judgments of Glidewell LJ and Sir Nicolas Browne-Wilkinson VC that in an appropriate case a hospital management committee might be itself directly liable in negligence for failing to provide sufficient qualified and competent medical staff, it being said that there was no reason in principle why a health authority should not be liable if its organisation were at fault in that way. Consider also *Bull and Wakeham* v *Devon Health Authority* [1993] 4 Med LR 117, MLC 0022 where the Court of Appeal, upholding the judge's decision in favour of the claimant, said that the system of obstetric cover provided by the hospital had given rise to a real inherent risk that an obstetrician might not attend reasonably promptly. But what if the hospital had alleged that its budget could not cover any better system?

The question of defective systems also arose in *Robertson* v *Nottingham Health Authority* [1997] 8 Med LR 1, CA, where significant breakdowns in the defendants' systems of communication in respect of obstetric care were proved and shown to constitute breaches of proper practice. Brooke LJ said that a health authority had a non-delegable duty to establish a proper system of care just as much as it had a duty to engage competent staff and a duty to provide proper and safe equipment, safe premises and a reasonable regime of care, ie a regime of a standard that could reasonably be expected of a hospital of the size and type in question – in the present case a large teaching centre of excellence. It mattered not whether those at fault could be individually identified. If they could, the hospital would be vicariously liable for their negligence, but, if not, the hospital would be in breach of its own duty of care for failing to provide a proper system.[6] But what the judge did not say is that those obligations were regardless of whether sufficient funds had been made available.[7]

See also the section 'Lack of funds' in Chapter 16.

---

6 One would like to think that successful claims could be brought against hospitals based on unacceptable standards of hygiene (and that the defence would not have the chutzpah to plead lack of funds); but such claims are hard to prove in terms of causation, not so much in the sense of showing that the patient contracted a specific infection while in hospital but in the sense of showing that it was contracted from a hospital source that would not have been infective given proper management. Hence the lack of success so far for MRSA claims.

7 In *Mercer* v *Royal Surrey County and St Luke's Hospitals NHS Trust* [2000] MLC 0289 the system for contacting an obstetric anesthetist when needed was held to be defective. In *Ocloo* v *Royal Brompton and Harefield Hospital NHS Trust* [2001] MLC 0539, there was admitted system negligence in failing to arrange a follow-up appointment for a heart patient (however the claim failed on causation).

Procedure

Chapter 6

The initial complaint

A patient needs to decide as soon as possible whether he wishes to seek financial compensation or just moral satisfaction. If the former, he should go to a solicitor accredited for medical negligence work. If the latter, or if he is not sure, he can get help initially from Citizens' Advice Bureaux, the Patients' Association or AvMA. But only legal action offers financial compensation. The private patient must think in terms of the General Medical Council (GMC) or a solicitor. One can always write, initially at least, to the hospital or doctor to ventilate a complaint or uncertainty.

THE PATIENT FEELS UNHAPPY

Where a patient has received treatment at the hands of the medical profession (and in 'treatment' I include non-treatment such as refusal to visit, give an appointment, treat, prescribe, etc) with which he is not satisfied, he has a number of choices of action.

He needs first to decide, if he can, whether he is looking for financial compensation or for satisfaction of another sort, eg by way of explanation, reassurance or apology.[1] If he knows that he has not suffered more than minimal damage, or if for any reason he is not interested in launching a claim for financial reparation, then there are a number of courses he can follow, depending on the type of complaint he wishes to make, ie against whom and in relation to what. These courses will not get him compensation; they are investigations into the conduct of the medical service, with a view to correcting any mistake, maladministration or misconduct for the future. This correction may also involve offering him further treatment as well as explanations and, where appropriate, apologies.

If on the other hand he wishes to claim compensation, or at any rate to take advice to see if he has a claim for compensation, he should go to an accredited solicitor straight away – see the section 'Accredited solicitors' below. He may, if he wishes, write an informal letter to the hospital or practitioner first, to see if that gets him anywhere. The newly prescribed course to follow as per the new regulations are explained below.

---

1   It cannot be emphasised enough how important it is to a patient to get an explanation of what went wrong. This is often his or her chief, and sometimes only, objective.

POSSIBLE COURSES OF ACTION

There are various organisations who will help the patient in the first place decide how he wants to make his complaint.

Citizens' Advice Bureaux (CABs) will point him in the right direction, perhaps to the local Independent Complaints Advisory Service (ICAS), another of this Government's recent innovations, or AvMA (see below). The CAB address can be found under 'Citizens' Advice Bureaux' in the telephone book, or the relevant Town Hall or local library will have the necessary information.

The Patients' Association

This body also represents the interests of the consumer, and will assist as far as it can a patient who feels aggrieved. Its motto is 'puts patients first'. It is an advice service and collective voice for the patients, independent of government, the health professions and the drug industry, and is financed by members' subscriptions, donations and a government grant. Its aims are to represent and further the interests of patients; to give information and advice to individuals; to acquire and spread information about patients' interests; to promote understanding and goodwill between patients and everyone in medical practice, and related activities. Founded in 1963, its campaigns have led or contributed to action in such areas as the appointment of an NHS Ombudsman; a code of practice for the medical profession in using hospital patients for teaching; improved hospital visiting hours; improvements in drug safety; and reductions in hospital waiting lists. It does not, be it noted, give medical advice. The subscription is modest, and the Association's address is PO Box 935, Harrow, Middx HA1 3YJ, helpline 0845 608 4455.

The Ombudsman

The Office of Health Service Ombudsman (or Health Service Commissioner as it is officially known) was established by the Act of 1973, and the relevant statutory provisions are now found in the Health Service Commissioners Act 1993 (as amended in 1996). His function is to investigate and report and make recommendations on complaints about the activities of health authorities and those for whom they are responsible. There are separate offices for England, Wales and Scotland, ie the posts are legally separate, but the same person may, and does currently, fill all three positions. He is the Parliamentary Commissioner, too, so he has a lot on his plate. He will consider and investigate a complaint if you feel that the patient has suffered injustice or hardship as a result of a failure in a service provided by certain authorities, or a failure by one of those authorities to provide a service which it has a duty to provide, or maladministration which has affected any other action taken by or on behalf of such an authority. The authorities whose actions he may investigate are extensive and include health authorities, NHS trusts and family health service providers. But he is not permitted to investigate grievances for which there is or has been a remedy in the courts or some other legal tribunal, unless he thinks it unreasonable for the matter to go to court. And, again unless he thinks it unreasonable, the complaint must be made first through the NHS complaints procedure.

In respect of matters arising before April 1996, the Ombudsman cannot investigate clinical complaints, ie complaints about treatment afforded or withheld, nor can he investigate complaints against family health service providers. The wide extensions to his catchment area afforded by the amending Act of 1996 apply only to complaints arising after March 1996.

Other matters he cannot investigate are: personnel matters, such as staff appointments or removals, pay, discipline and superannuation; contractual or other commercial transactions; properly taken discretionary decisions which an authority has a right to take (but the Ombudsman can look at whether the authority has followed proper procedures and considered all relevant aspects in reaching its decision); action which has been or is the subject of an inquiry set up by the Secretary of State in any circumstances where he thinks it advisable to do so, such as a serious incident or major breakdown in service.

The patient should write to 'The Health Service Commissioner for England' at Church House, Great Smith Street, London SW1, tel: 020 7212 7676; for Wales the address is Pearl Assurance, Greyfriars Road, Cardiff, tel: 01222 394621.

There is a time limit: the complaint should be made within one year of the date on which the matter first came to the notice of the complainant (though the Ombudsman may if he thinks fit waive this requirement). The patient will discuss his complaint with the Ombudsman's representative, and at the end of the investigation he and the 'other side' will receive his written report.

The General Medical Council (GMC)

Complaints about serious professional misconduct by a GP or hospital doctor may be addressed to the GMC (44 Hallam Street, London W1, tel: 020 7580 7642). In its publication *Professional Conduct and Discipline*, 1981, the GMC gives examples of serious professional misconduct, including serious neglect or disregard of responsibilities to patients for their care and treatment, abuse of professional privileges in prescribing drugs or issuing medical certificates, abuse of professional confidence, abuse of the financial opportunities of medical practice, abuse of the doctor/patient relationship, and personal behaviour that could bring the profession into disrepute. The Medical (Professional Performance) Act 1995 has empowered the GMC to impose penalties where they find a doctor's standard of professional performance to have been seriously deficient.[2] On a complaint the GMC can refer the matter to the professional conduct committee for a formal inquiry, send the doctor a warning letter, refer the matter to the Health Committee of the GMC (where it appears that a doctor's fitness to practise is impaired by a physical or mental condition), or take no action. The hearing is governed by the formal rules of evidence. Sanctions where the complaint is adjudged proved range from issuing a

---

2   It was held by the Privy Council in *McCandless* v *General Medical Council* [1996] 1 WLR 167 that falling hopelessly below the standard of care that patients had a right to expect could amount to 'serious professional misconduct'.

warning to striking off. The doctor has a right of appeal to the Privy Council.

Recent highly publicised instances of highly deficient management by hospitals and individual doctors over long periods, and continued despite many warning signals, have given a much needed impetus to the GMC's attempts to ensure effective monitoring of performance standards to accord with the public's reasonable expectations. New procedures are being implemented for that purpose, and also to conform to human rights, among which is the plan for ongoing revalidation of all doctors, whereby they must be prepared to provide continuing evidence of fitness to practice. Even if one feels compelled to add the words 'at last', one must acknowledge that the GMC is making substantial progress towards putting its house in order and to end its image as a closed shop protecting its own (it has to be said that in the light of the recent extraordinary spate of revelations about mismanagement by various individual doctors and hospitals it has had little choice if it wanted to survive). Consideration is being given to the appropriate standard of proof in complaints against individual doctors, which at the moment requires proof beyond reasonable doubt.

For an example of the care with which the court will examine the workings of the GMC in respect of patient's complaints and the importance it attaches to the procedure, see *R* v *General Medical Council, ex p Toth* [2000] Lloyd's Rep Med 368 (Lightman J). The case involved consideration, in relation to a complaint brought, of the proper functions of the preliminary screener, the Preliminary Proceedings Committee and the Professional Conduct Committee. For similar scrutiny by the Privy Council of the discharge of its functions by the Professional Performance Committee see *Krippendorf* v *General Medical Council* [2001] Lloyd's Rep Med 9.

The GMC tends to be seen as biased in favour of the profession, doing too little and too late. This is not necessarily a fair preconception.

The statutory inquiry

An individual complaint may, though rarely, bring to the attention of the Secretary of State matters into which he decides to hold an inquiry. He has power to do this in relation to any matter arising from the National Health Service Act 1977 (by s 84). If the Minister thinks that any health body has failed to carry out any of its functions under the relevant legislation he can declare it to be in default and replace its members. A recent example is the Shipman inquiry.

Member of Parliament

This can be a useful avenue of complaint, particularly where the patient is getting no response to inquiries or letters. It can be used at any time to stir things up.

Internal complaints procedure

The patient may choose to make a formal complaint through the NHS complaints procedure. This has very recently been completely revamped (see the section below for further details). If he is unhappy with the treatment or service received from the NHS he is entitled to make his complaint, have it considered, and receive a response from the NHS organisation or primary care practitioner concerned. A Patient Advice and Liaison Service (PALS) has been established in every NHS Trust and primary care trust. PALS are not part of the complaints procedure itself but they might be able to resolve concerns informally and they can tell the patient more about the complaints procedure and independent complaints advocacy services.

The NHS complaints procedure covers complaints made by a person about any matter connected with the provision of NHS services by NHS organisations or primary care practitioners (GPs, dentists, opticians and pharmacists). The procedure also covers services provided overseas or by the private sector where the NHS has paid for them. The patient should normally complain within six months of the event(s) concerned or within six months of becoming aware that there is something to complain about. Primary care practitioners and complaints managers in NHS organisations have discretion to waive this time limit if there are good reasons for not complaining earlier.

The first stage of the NHS complaints procedure is 'local resolution'. The complaint should be made in the first instance to the organisation or primary care practitioner providing the service. Local resolution aims to resolve complaints quickly and as close to the source of the complaint as possible using the most appropriate means; for example, use of conciliation.

The patient can raise his concerns immediately by speaking to a member of staff (eg doctor, nurse, dentist, GP or practice manager) or someone else, eg PALS. They may be able to resolve his concerns without the need to make a more formal complaint. However, if the patient does want to continue with his complaint he can do this orally or by writing (including email) to the primary care practitioner or the NHS organisation concerned. If he makes his complaint orally a written record should be made by the complaints manager. He should receive a response from a primary care practitioner within 10 working days or from the chief executive of the NHS organisation concerned within 20 working days. He should be kept informed of progress if this is not going to happen.

NHS Foundation Trusts, however, will have their own systems for the internal handling of complaints, which may differ from the 'local resolution' process described above. For a complaint about an NHS Foundation Trust, the patient should contact it for advice on how to make the complaint. But the 'independent review' stage carried out by the Healthcare Commission does apply to NHS Foundation Trusts, which are also covered by the Health Service Ombudsman.

It used to be the case that a hospital would discontinue a review if the patient appeared to be about to sue. For example, in *R* v *Canterbury and Thanet District Health Authority* [1994] 5 Med LR 132, the Divisional Court upheld the discontinuance by the defendants of an independent review when it became clear that the complainants were contemplating legal proceedings (the complaints were against a psychiatrist for negligent diagnoses of sexual abuse). The court said that the procedure depended upon the co-operation of the consultant whose actions were the subject of the inquiry and that his co-operation would clearly not now be forthcoming. The primary purpose of the procedure was either to get a second opinion and thereby a change of diagnosis or treatment, or to enable the health authority to change its procedures in the light of what transpired at the inquiry. Further, if the matter was likely to go to court that would provide a far more searching inquiry than the independent review procedure.

Independent review: If the patient is unhappy with the response to his complaint, including a complaint about an NHS Foundation Trust, he can ask the Healthcare Commission for an 'independent review' of the case. The Healthcare Commission is an independent body established to promote improvements in healthcare. One can contact the Commission at: Healthcare Commission, FREEPOST NAT 18958, Complaints Investigation Team, Manchester M1 9XZ. Tel: 0845 601 3012. Email: complaints@healthcarecommission.org.uk. Website: www.healthcarecommission.org.uk.

Experience under the old scheme suggested that there were fundamental flaws in the procedure that resulted in less than wholly impartial analysis of the complaint at the 'independent review' stage. The convenor who decided whether or not to convene a panel was not independent of the trust, and the review panel itself was regarded as 'a committee of the trust', which hardly suggested or promoted independence. To what extent reviews undertaken by the Healthcare Commission will inspire confidence in the patient remains to be seen.

The Health Service Ombudsman

If the patient remains unhappy after local resolution and independent review[3] he can complain to the Health Service Ombudsman. The Ombudsman is completely independent of the NHS and government. He can be contacted at: Millbank Tower, Millbank, London, SW1P 4QP. Tel: 0845 015 4033. Email: OHSC.Enquiries@ombudsman.gsi.gov.uk. Website: www.ombudsman.org.uk.

Further advice and help: The PALS or complaints manager at the NHS organisation the subject of the complaint can provide advice, including advice about local independent complaints advocacy services. The local primary care trust can also advise in respect of a complaint about a primary care practitioner. ICAS provides advice and support to people who want to complain about the NHS. Details are at www.dh.gov.uk or you can call NHS Direct on 0845 4647, or contact the local Citizens Advice Bureau.

Current legislation

The National Health Service (Complaints) Regulations 2004 came into force on 30 July 2004. The Complaints Regulations derive from powers

---

3   In *R (on the application of Kellett)* v *Southampton and South West Hampshire Health Authority* (2001) MLC 0543 the applicant, representing herself, took the unusual step of applying for judicial review of the decision of the defendants not to hold a further independent review panel of her complaint about the treatment they had given her. She was not successful.

given to the Secretary of State for Health in the National Health Service (Community Health and Standards) Act 2003 to make provision for the handling and consideration of complaints by NHS bodies in England (or a cross-border Special Health Authority). Chapter 9, Regulations 113 to 119 deal with complaints about health and social care. The Complaints Regulations do not apply to the handling of complaints by primary care practitioners at local resolution (GPs, dentists, opticians and pharmacists) and apply only in part to NHS Foundation Trusts (see below). Although the intention had been to implement the Complaints Regulations in full from June 2004, Ministers decided on a phased implementation following an approach from the Shipman Inquiry. Therefore, the Local Resolution stage of the complaints procedure remains broadly unchanged across all services. The Complaints Regulations consolidate and rationalise the statutory requirements set out in the various Directions referred to in Regulation 24 for Local Resolution by NHS bodies and introduce the reformed independent review stage carried out by the Healthcare Commission. Separate regulations setting out the requirements for Local Resolution of complaints by primary care practitioners and in relation to personal medical services continue to apply. Amended Complaints Regulations will be issued in due course once the Department has been able to give proper consideration to any recommendations made by the Shipman Inquiry, which published its fifth report on 9 December 2004.

Bear in mind that substantial amendments are expected once the implications of the Shipman, Neale and other inquiries into health scandals have been digested.

Currently the Regulations deal in Part II with the handling and consideration of complaints by NHS bodies, and in Part III with the handling and consideration of complaints by the Healthcare Commission. Part II is as above explained. The Healthcare Commission cannot deal with a complaint where the complainant has stated in writing that he intends to take legal proceedings. The CMO in his consultative paper *Redress* has proposed that that restriction should be repealed. Nor may the Commission deal with a complaint where the subject of it is being disciplined. The basic time limit for applying to the Commission is two months from the final response of the trust. Among the courses of action the Commission is empowered to take is no action at all, and, at the other end of the spectrum, to conduct an investigation itself whether by setting up a panel or otherwise. It must keep an up-to-date list of persons considered suitable for membership of an independent lay panel. A panel would consist of three people with no connection with the health service. It is not immediately clear to me how adjudicators with no experience of the health service have the necessary expertise to fairly adjudicate on a complaint about the provision of health services. They may indeed be independent, though.

Primary care practitioners and personal medical services

The regulations listed below set out the statutory framework for the handling of complaints at a *local* level by *primary care practitioners* and about personal medical services. They will *continue to be in force* until the amended Complaints Regulations are issued:

- SI 1996/698 – National Health Service (Pharmaceutical Services) Amendment Regulations 1996;
- SI 1996/704 – National Health Service (General Dental Services) Amendment Regulations 1996;
- SI 1996/705 – National Health Service (General Ophthalmic Services) Amendment Regulations 1996;
- SI 2004/291 – National Health Service (General Medical Services Contracts) Regulations 2004;
- SI 2004/627 – National Health Service (Personal Medical Services Agreements) Regulations 2004;
- SI 2004/865 – General Medical Services and Personal Medical Services Transitional and Consequential Provisions Order 2004.

NHS Foundation Trusts

NHS Foundation Trusts have their own systems for the internal handling of complaints, which may differ from the 'Local Resolution' procedure outlined in the Regulations. Anyone wishing to make a complaint about an NHS Foundation Trust should contact the Trust for advice on how to make their complaint. The 'Independent Review' stage operated by the Healthcare Commission does apply to NHS Foundation Trusts, which are also covered by the Health Service Ombudsman.

Private patients

Remember that these procedures (the new ones just as the previous ones) are applicable in respect of NHS treatment; they do not apply to private patients. Further, it can readily be seen that these procedures, while they may result in satisfaction for the not inconsiderable number of complainants who are more interested in an explanation, apology, or assurance that the same thing will not happen to other patients, are of no use in the more serious case, where the aggrieved patient wants substantial financial compensation. At one time the legal aid authority, by way of ploy intended, like so many, to reduce the legal aid bill for medical negligence cases, was requiring, though perhaps only through a small number of area committees, that the patient first use the internal complaints procedure before being granted legal aid. It is not known whose brainchild that was, but it was apparent to patients' lawyers from the outset, and soon enough became apparent even to the legal aid authority, that such a requirement was unfair, unproductive and illogical. Nevertheless the authority still retains to itself the right and power to require recourse to the internal procedure first. And, given the radical changes made to the complaints procedures, the LSC may again find it attractive to hamper the patient by such a device.

Action against Medical Accidents (AvMA)

AvMA is a charitable organisation that exists to help those who have been injured as a result of medical treatment. In an appropriate case, AvMA may give advice that does not involve legal proceedings. But in the main the cases that are referred to it call for the intervention of a lawyer, and to that end AvMA is able to refer the patient, or his representative, to a suitably qualified solicitor. AvMA's address is 44 High St, Croydon, CR0 1YB, tel 020 8686 8333.

Accredited solicitors

If the claim is likely to be funded on legal aid, it has to be conducted by a solicitor who is accredited for that purpose by the LSC. A list of such solicitors, and of other solicitors who have had relevant experience of handling medical negligence claims, can be found, together with a regional map, on the website of Medical Litigation at www.medicalclaims.co.uk. The Law Society would also give appropriate advice.

Chapter 7

The inquest

AN OPPORTUNITY NOT TO BE MISSED

If there is going to be an inquest, efforts should be made to make the most of the opportunity to find out what the hospital says about the circumstances surrounding the death. It is, of course, not a trial, and one is very much at the 'mercy' of the coroner as to what may be asked of the doctors, by him and by the family. If possible, copies of the medical records should be obtained before the inquest, whether by asking the coroner to call for them (this is a bit chancey) or by demanding them, if there is time for this before the inquest (or any adjournment), by way of pre-action disclosure. In *Stobart* v *Nottingham Health Authority* [1993] PIQR P259, Rougier J held that it was a proper use of the old pre-action disclosure provisions to seek the medical records prior to the inquest.

The impact of the Human Rights Act

The Act, which came into force on 2 October 2000, has had an enormous impact on UK inquest law. It has given scope to the kin of the deceased to challenge all aspects of an inquest, from the decision to hold or not hold one through the manner in which an inquest is conducted, to the way in which a verdict is given, even including the issue of legal representation. The cases have concerned the shoot-to-kill deaths in Northern Ireland, the deaths of prisoners in custody, and, more directly to our purpose, deaths in hospital. So vulnerable to criticism on human rights grounds does our inquest system appear to be that a number of judges have doubted its ability to adapt so as to conform to human rights law. The human rights issues are explored below after a short summary of inquest law according to the common law, ie minus the human rights factor.

THE LAW

Natural causes

The Coroners Act 1988 requires an inquest to be held where information has been received upon which there is reasonable cause to suspect that the deceased died (*inter alia*) an unnatural death, or a sudden death of which the cause is unknown. That information may come from any person, eg a doctor or relative of the deceased. It is often difficult to define the relevant cause of death, particularly in a 'medical' context (it is not necessarily the proximate or terminal cause): there is no statutory definition of natural or unnatural. 'Unnatural' has been defined in recent times as 'wholly or partly caused, or accelerated, by any act, intervention or omission other than a properly executed measure intended to prolong life' (Pilling, *Medical Science and the Law*, April 1967). In *R v Poplar Coroner, ex p Thomas* [1993] QB 610, the Court of Appeal said that the late arrival of the ambulance following a terminal asthmatic attack did not make the death 'unnatural' within the meaning of s 8(1)(a) of the Act of 1988, even though the evidence indicated that if it had arrived earlier the deceased, a 17-year-old girl, could probably have been saved. Simon Brown LJ added that if the late arrival had constituted a more extreme failure of the service than in fact it had, common sense would dictate that the death be deemed unnatural. In *R v Coroner for Birmingham and Solihull, ex p Benton* [1997] 8 Med LR 362, Kay J distinguished between the situation where a person was suffering from a potentially fatal condition and medical intervention did no more than fail to prevent death (in which case the appropriate verdict would be natural causes) and the situation where a person was suffering from a non-life-threatening condition but underwent treatment which caused death, in which case the appropriate verdict would be death by accident/misadventure (assuming there was no question of unlawful killing). The judge found the verdict of the coroner to be flawed because he had not explained to the jury the distinction between the two situations. He had been wrong to conclude that the child's death came so clearly within the first category that there could be no other verdict than death by natural causes.

In *R v HM Avon Coroner, ex p Smith* (1998) 162 JP 403 Ognall J, invalidating the decision of the coroner not to hold an inquest where a child died in hospital from a cerebellar hematoma, said he was not satisfied that the coroner had adequately addressed the vital question whether the death was from the natural cause of the disease or, unnaturally, from a failure of care such as a delay in performing the CT scan. In *Terry v East Sussex Coroner* [2001] EWCA Civ 1094 the Court of Appeal upheld the coroner's refusal to hold an inquest where he had concluded that the deceased, a former asbestos moulder, had died from natural causes in 1994 and that it was not an asbestos-related death. Where a deceased suffered a fatal fall in hospital in 1997 and an Independent Review Panel and all the expert evidence concluded that he had received all appropriate care, the Divisional Court upheld the coroner's decision not to hold an inquest (*R (Harris) v HM Coroner for Swansea* MLC 0545).

Coroner's function

It is the coroner's function to examine the witnesses on oath – the right to cross-examine or otherwise intervene on the part of others is within the coroner's discretion; but he must exercise that discretion judicially. The inquest is intended to ascertain not culpability for the death, but, principally, who the deceased was, and how, when and where he came by his death.

A coroner has power to order the production of the hospital records, by a *subpoena duces tecum* (the Latin denotes an order 'that you bring with you ...', ie the specified documents to the court), and he can be criticised if he ignores the relatives' request for them (see *R* v *Southwark Coroner, ex p Hicks* [1987] 1 WLR 1624, DC).

Verdicts

Among the verdicts that can be returned are (relevant for our purposes) 'want of attention at birth', and 'accident or misadventure' (it appears to be the better view that these last two verdicts are not distinguishable and that 'accident' is the preferable term). The 'lack of care' verdict can cause problems: it is unclear whether it is a verdict in its own right or a rider which may be added to some or all of the other verdicts (Coroners Rules 1984, SI 1984/552, r 42). In any event no verdict should be framed in such a way as to determine any question of civil liability (Coroners Rules 1984, SI 1984/552, r 42) though, as the court said in the *Linnane* case (see below), the issue of lack of care can properly be raised so long as no one is identified in the verdict as being responsible for it.

Cases on 'lack of care'

Decisions given before the Human Rights Act came into force in October 2000 need to be regarded with circumspection. One at least, the heretofore important case of *Jamieson* (see below), has been expressly disapproved in an important respect by the House of Lords.

Croom Johnson J said in the *Hicks* case (above) that the prime meaning of 'lack of care' was that of a failure of physical attention, such as a failure to prevent death from starvation or exposure, bad nursing or medical care, there being no difference between a failure to give enough nourishment and a failure to give enough medicine.[1]

In *R* v *HM Coroner for Inner London North, ex p Linnane (No 2)* (1990) 155 JP 343, the Divisional Court said that a coroner had erred in refusing to call a particular doctor as a witness: although it was up to the coroner to decide whom he wished to hear, his reasons for refusing to hear this witness were invalid, they being that the doctor had been selected by the deceased's family and that he, the coroner, being a doctor himself with experience of infectious diseases, did not need the assistance of any other doctor. Further, the issue of death from acute myocarditis aggravated by lack of care should have been left to the jury. However, in view of the fact that the death had been some 21 months earlier and that the doctor's report in fact gave little support to the contention that lack of care on the part of the police had been responsible for the death of the deceased in police custody, the court refused to exercise its discretion to order a new inquest.

In *R* v *North Humberside and Scunthorpe Coroner, ex p Jamieson*

---

1   In two fairly recent cases where prisoners died in custody the Court of Appeal criticised the lack of a structure or guidance for coroners when dealing with complex medical issues – *R* v *Inner London South Coroner, ex p Douglas-Williams* [1999] 1 All ER 344; *R* v *HM Coroner for Lincolnshire, ex p Hay* [2000] MLC 0190.

[1995] QB 1, the Court of Appeal, in a full review and restatement of the relevant law, emphasised the limited ambit of the inquest (solely directed to establishing the identity of the deceased, and where, when and how he came by his death) and said that 'lack of care' or 'neglect', as it should more appropriately be expressed, is the obverse of self-neglect and connotes gross failure to provide sustenance, shelter or necessary medical attention for a person who was dependent by reason of age, illness or incarceration. Neglect could rarely, if ever, be a free-standing verdict and only is appropriate as ancillary to any verdict where there was a direct causal connection between the relevant conduct and the cause of death. Where, as here, a person had killed himself (while in prison), neglect could not form part of a verdict of suicide merely because he had been given an opportunity to kill himself.

On the other hand, in *R v HM Coroner for East Berkshire, ex p Buckley* (1992) 157 JP 425, (1992) Times, 1 December, the Divisional Court said that counsel should have been allowed to ask the jury for a verdict of lack of care, the deceased having died at Broadmoor mental hospital after injections of Phenothiazine.

In *R v HM Coroner for Surrey, ex p Wright* [1997] QB 786, where the inquest concerned the death of a patient under anesthetic as a result of failure to maintain his airway, Tucker J held that it was permissible for a coroner to call for the assistance of an assessor (here a consultant anaesthetist) if he considered it necessary having regard to the technical nature of the evidence which might have to be considered, and that the assessor could ask any witness any relevant questions but should not give evidence himself. The judge also held that it was no longer open to a coroner to record a verdict of lack of care; and that, although it was open to a coroner to record a verdict of death as a result of neglect, 'neglect' meant continuous or at least non-transient neglect, which was not an appropriate description of the negligent lack of care which was alleged to have led to the deceased's death. Although it might seem difficult to understand why a coroner in the case of obvious anesthetic negligence should be limited to a verdict of accidental death, some explanation may be found, as Tucker J seems to have found it, in the judgment of the Court of Appeal in the *Jamieson* case where the Master of the Rolls said:

> Much of the difficulty to which verdicts of lack of care have given rise appears to be due to an almost inevitable confusion between this expression and the lack of care which is the foundation for a successful claim in common law negligence. Since many of those seeking that verdict do so as a stepping-stone towards such a claim the boundary is bound to become blurred. But lack of care in the context of an inquest has been correctly described as the obverse of self-neglect. It is to be hoped that in future the expression 'lack of care' may for practical purposes be deleted from the lexicon of inquests and replaced by 'neglect'.

In *R v HM Coroner for Inner West London, ex p Scott* (2001) EWHC (Admin) 105; (2001) BMLR 22, a fresh inquest was ordered where the coroner had not left a neglect verdict to the jury despite clear evidence of that possibility. The known suicidal tendencies of a person in custody had been overlooked in that his shoelaces, which had been removed while he was at the magistrates court, had been returned to him when he got back to prison. He then used them to hang himself.

In *R* v *HM Coroner for Coventry, ex p Chief Constable of Staffordshire Constabulary* [2000] MLC 0233, Tomlinson J said that lack of care in the context of an inquest does not connote lack of care sufficient to found an action for negligence: it was simply the obverse of self-neglect.

Human rights

By Article 1 of the Convention, member states bound themselves to secure to everyone within their respective jurisdictions the rights and freedoms defined in Section 1 of the Convention. The first of those rights, expressed in Article 2(1), is the right to life:

> Everyone's right to life shall be protected by law. No one shall be deprived of his life intentionally save in the execution of a sentence of a court following his conviction of a crime for which this penalty is provided by law.

But, notwithstanding the apparently limited ambit of these (deceptively simple) words, the scope of the Article goes, in typical European fashion, well beyond the primary purposes thus defined. It is clear from decisions of the European Court (see the full exegesis from the House of Lords in *R (on the application of Amin)* v *Home Secretary* [2004] 1 AC 653) that the obligation imposed on the state that everyone's right to life shall be 'protected by law' includes a procedural aspect. It includes the minimum requirement of a mechanism whereby the circumstances of a deprivation of life by the agents of a state may receive public and independent scrutiny. The nature and degree of scrutiny which satisfies this minimum threshold will depend on the circumstances of the particular case. There may be cases where the facts surrounding a deprivation of life are clear and undisputed and the subsequent inquisitorial examination may legitimately be reduced to a minimum formality. But equally, there may be other cases where a victim dies in circumstances which are unclear, in which event the lack of any effective procedure to investigate the cause of the deprivation of life could by itself raise an issue under Article 2 of the Convention. It will be noted that the state's duty is not restricted to cases of intentional killing. That is why it can be relevant where the death occurs in the context of medical treatment. However, note well that the European Commission has said that, where the state has made adequate provision for securing high professional standards among health professionals and for the protection of the lives of patients, the state's duty cannot be engaged merely by such matters as errors of judgement on the part of a health professional or negligent co-ordination among heath professionals in the treatment of a particular patient (*Powell* v *UK* (App No 45305/99)).

As the House of Lords said in *R (on the application of Middleton)* v *HM Coroner for the Western District of Somerset* (2004) UKHL 10 :

> The European Court of Human Rights has repeatedly interpreted Article 2 of the European Convention as imposing on member states substantive obligations not to take life without justification and also to establish a framework of laws, precautions, procedures and means of enforcement which will, to the greatest extent reasonably practicable, protect life. See, for example, *LCB* v *United Kingdom* (1998) 27 EHRR 212, para 36; *Osman* v *United Kingdom* (1998) 29 EHRR 245; *Powell* v *United Kingdom* (App No 45305/99, unreported, 4 May 2000), 16-17; *Keenan* v *United Kingdom* (2001) 33 EHRR 913, paras

88–90; *Edwards* v *United Kingdom* (2002) 35 EHRR 487, para 54; *Calvelli and Ciglio* v *Italy* (App No 32967/96, unreported, 17 January 2002); *Öneryildiz* v *Turkey* (App No 48939/99, unreported, 18 June 2002).

The European Court has also interpreted Article 2 as imposing on member states a procedural obligation to initiate an effective public investigation by an independent official body into any death occurring in circumstances in which it appears that one or other of the foregoing substantive obligations has been, or may have been, violated and it appears that agents of the state are, or may be, in some way implicated. See, for example, *Taylor* v *United Kingdom* (1994) 79-A DR 127, 137; *McCann* v *United Kingdom* (1995) 21 EHRR 97, para 161; *Powell* v *United Kingdom*, supra p 17; *Salman* v *Turkey* (2000) 34 EHRR 425, para 104; *Sieminska* v *Poland* (App No 37602/97, unreported, 29 March 2001); *Jordan* v *United Kingdom* (2001) 37 EHRR 52, para 105; *Edwards* v *United Kingdom*, supra, para 69; *Öneryildiz* v *Turkey*, supra, paras 90-91; *Mastromatteo* v *Italy* (App No 37703/97, unreported, 24 October 2002).

The European Court has repeatedly recognised that there are many different ways in which a state may discharge its procedural obligation to investigate under Article 2. In England and Wales an inquest is the means by which the state ordinarily discharges that obligation, save where a criminal prosecution intervenes or a public enquiry is ordered into a major accident, usually involving multiple fatalities. To meet the procedural requirement of Article 2 an inquest ought ordinarily to culminate in an expression, however brief, of the jury's conclusion on the disputed factual issues at the heart of the case.

It can be seen, therefore, that human rights law offers considerable scope for challenges to various aspects of the inquest. No doubt case law will increase exponentially as scores of the bereaved apply for legal aid to challenge the decision not to hold an inquest, or how to conduct the inquest or how to invite, receive or record a verdict, and also extending, be it noted, to any decision not to grant legal aid or other public funding for representation by the next of kin at an inquest.

Case law

The first thing to note is that the human rights provision cannot be invoked in our courts (as opposed to by excursion to Strasbourg) for deaths occurring before the Act came into force (In *Re McKerr* [2004] UKHL 12, overruling, on this point, the Court of Appeal in *R (on the application of Khan)* v *Secretary of State for Health* [2003] EWCA Civ 1129. See also *R (on the application of Challender* v *Legal Service Commission* [2004] EWHC 925 (Admin), Richards J.

In *R (on the application of Amin)* v *Home Secretary* [2003] UKHL 51, where an inquest into the death of a prisoner at the hands of his cellmate had been adjourned and not resumed, the House of Lords found that there had been no effective official investigation as would comply with the state's obligation under Article 2(1) (neither the police investigation nor the murder verdict at trial nor the general investigation into racial discrimination in the prison service by the Commission for Racial Equality sufficed). In another case of death in custody (*R (on the application of Middleton)* v *HM Coroner for the Western District of Somerset* [2004] UKHL 10), the House of Lords said that an inquest had ordinarily to culminate in an expression of the jury's conclusions on the disputed factual issues at the heart of the case in order to be compliant with the Convention. This could be achieved not by substantive changes to the common law but, abiding by the statutory rules for conducting inquests, by re-interpreting the word 'how' in the Coroners Act 1988, s 11(5)(b)(ii) in a broader sense so as to mean 'by what means and in what circumstances' rather than simply 'by what means' the deceased came to his death. The same reasoning was applied to a case of suicide in custody in *R (on the application of Sacker)* v *HM Coroner for County of West Yorkshire* [2004] UKHL 11. In a later case arising out of a death occurring in a home for elderly mentally disabled people, *R (on the application of Longfield Care Homes* v *HM Coroner for Blackburn* [2004] EWHC 2467 (Admin), Mitting J said that where the death resulted from more than one cause of different types a narrative verdict would often be required.

In *Goodson* v *HM Coroner for Bedfordshire and Luton* [2004] EWHC 2931 (Admin), where a patient had died in hospital after an elective treatment to treat gallstones, Richards J said that in the case of a death in hospital there was no separate procedural obligation to investigate under Article 2 where the death raised no more than a potential liability in negligence. In the instant case the investigative obligation under Article 2 was not engaged. There was at most a possibility of simple negligence. Although the coroner had been wrong to hold that the hospital was not a state body or agent of the state for the purposes of Article 2, his refusal to conduct the inquest as an Article 2 investigation was justified. Further, even if the inquest had been required to be an Article 2 investigation, it fulfilled that role, the objection of the claimant that the coroner should have engaged an independent medical expert to give evidence on the treatment received by the deceased being unsustainable. This case highlights two important considerations: the first is that there has to be more than a possibility of medical negligence for a death in hospital to engage Article 2; second, as has been said more than once by the House of Lords, in most cases a properly conducted inquest in accordance with the ordinary rules will itself also fulfil any Article 2 requirements.

There is an interesting decision by Jackson J in *R* v *Home Office, ex parte Wright* [2001] EWHC Admin 520 (you will observe from the form of the title of the case that it was begun before the general dumbing down of the legal profession). There had been an inquest in 1997 resulting in a verdict of natural causes on the death in 1996 of a prisoner due to negligent medical attention to his asthmatic condition. The judge held that the inquest had signally failed to comply with Article 2 obligations. The cellmate had not been called as a witness; there had been no independent expert medical evidence; no proper investigation of the relevant prison medical officer; and the deceased's aunt had not been represented or even given a proper explanation of the issues. The judge ordered an independent investigation into the circumstances of the death. What happened thereafter I do not know; at that time, of course, it was not appreciated that the Human Rights Act did not apply to deaths before it came into force (in October 2000 – see above). It was certainly imaginative of the aunt's advisers on any view to challenge the findings of an inquest more than three years after the verdict.

The cost of representation

To be legally represented at an inquest naturally involves costs. But will public funding, whether by legal aid or express provision of the Secretary of State, be made available for representation at an inquest? Apart from human rights law, funding for advocacy services at an inquest (ie going beyond the legal help service which is available for preparation for an inquest) will not normally be granted, though there is power to do so if the case appears to be an exceptional one, for example involving an issue of wider public interest. But the position is not the same under human rights law. The European Court has said more than once that for the official investigation to be effective the next-of-kin must be involved in any procedure to the extent necessary to safeguard their legitimate interests. This does not mean, however, that they must always be represented. It is clear that the general expectation is that the coroner will be able in most cases to conduct an effective investigation without such representation.

In the *Khan* case, overruled as explained above on a different point, the Court of Appeal saw an exceptional case where the highly distraught parents of a girl of three who died (apparently) due to medical negligence in the excessive administration of potassium as part of the treatment for B cell lymphoma, were entitled to be funded by the state at the inquest by virtue of the state's obligations under Article 2 of the European Convention. The court said that the forthcoming inquest, which clearly was the means by which the state intended to fulfil its Article 2 obligations, would not be an effective one unless the family could play an effective part in it. The issues were so complex that the coroner had rightly enlisted an independent medical expert to help him. The trust would have the benefit of legal representation, there was a possibility there had been a cover-up, and the family themselves were in no state to cope effectively with the inquest.

In the *Challender* case (above), where death had occurred in a flat belonging to a friend of the deceased as a result of an injection of drugs (self-administered, or possibly enforced by an alien hand), Richards J said *obiter* that the Article 2 obligation applied even in cases where there had been no state involvement or the use of force (it remains to be seen if this very wide interpretation will be accepted by the appeal courts). But, quite apart from his conclusion that the claim must fail as death had occurred before the Human Rights Act came into effect, the judge was for dismissing the claim for funding at the inquest on the basis that the case was not an exceptional one, ie not a *Khan*-type case, there was little factual or legal complexity, no suggestion of a cover-up, and no evidence that the next of kin were unlikely to be able to cope with the inquest. In the overwhelming majority of cases, as was said in *Khan*, the coroner could conduct an effective judicial investigation himself.

Costs of inquest on assessment

Note finally that in *Stewart* v *Medway NHS Trust,* Supreme Court Costs Office 6 April 2004, Master O'Hare held that the costs of attending an inquest could be recoverable under a costs order following later clinical negligence proceedings; and in *King* v *Milton Keynes NHS Trust* (MLC 1132, Supreme Court Costs Office 13 May 2004) Master Gordon-Saker, to similar effect, held that the court, when assessing the costs of civil proceedings, had jurisdiction to award the costs of attendance at an inquest if a material purpose of that attendance was to obtain information or evidence for use in the civil proceedings.

Chapter 8

The medical records

THE RECORDS OF TREATMENT

The patient's medical records are the backbone of almost all medical negligence claims. They must be obtained, intelligently sorted and read.
After that, they will be submitted to an expert, who will make his report
based on them and any other relevant information such as witness statements from patient and family. The pre-action protocol sets out profor-
mas for requesting records and for responding to such a request. It is not
mandatory to use the proforma, but it would be unwise not to (see
Appendix I). The box that asks the patient to give grounds for his claim
need not be taken too seriously. It is not a legal requirement, and is in any
event unlikely to be able to be clearly answered at such a preliminary
stage.

All relevant records should be obtained. Records of treatment at other
hospitals earlier or later than the impugned treatment may well illuminate aspects of the claim. On the other hand, they may relate to conditions not pertinent to the claim, in which case one would expect the
expert solicitor not to spend money getting them. GP records are almost
always relevant.

Copy records should be checked against the originals. Originals will
often yield a better insight into the medical events by revealing more
clearly the appearance of the entries (eg colours, writing pressures).
Often the photocopying will not extend to the dates in the left margin of
the nursing notes, or will show only the last of the two digits for the day
of the month – which creates confusion. In one case the parties were misled in that way when the hole-puncher had obliterated the first digit
(*Johnson* v *John and Waltham Forest Health Authority* (1998) MLC 0244,
CA).

Often certain records will be missing. If relevant, they should be chased
up with vigour. It is amazing what turns up eventually. The law on getting such documents is explained below. But what if records have been
lost for good or destroyed?

Records lost or destroyed

HC(80)7 advises a minimum retention period of 25 years for obstetrics
records; until the twenty-fifth birthday or eight years after the last entry

for children and young people; for mentally disordered persons 20 years from the date of cure; and in any other case eight years.

In *Malhotra* v *Dhawan* [1997] 8 Med LR 319, the Court of Appeal, considering the maxim *omnia praesumuntur contra spoliatorem*, indicated that inferences could be drawn against a party who had destroyed relevant evidence (although the court said the maxim only applied where that had been done to stop the other party showing how much of his property had been taken).[1] In *Le Page* v *Kingston and Richmond Health Authority* MLC 0610, [1997] 8 Med LR 229, John Samuels QC, sitting as a Deputy Judge of the Queen's Bench Division, said that the defendants could not properly complain if he drew inferences from surviving documentation which might have been contradicted by other records which they had improperly destroyed.

In *Skelton* v *Lewisham and North Southwark Health Authority* [1999] MLC 0662, [1998] Lloyd's Rep Med 324, the inadequacy of the anesthetic notes (brief, unsigned, without a record of key events and pressures), although not causative of the damage, was said by the judge to be indicative of an unexplained carelessness. In *Rhodes* v *Spokes and Farbridge* MLC 0640, [1996] 7 Med LR 135, Smith J said:

> A doctor's contemporaneous record of a consultation should form a reliable evidential base in a case such as this. I regret to say that Dr Farbridge's notes of the plaintiff's attendances do not provide any such firm foundation. They are scanty in the extreme. He rarely recorded her complaints or symptoms; he rarely recorded any observations; usually he noted only the drug he prescribed ... The failure to take a proper note is not evidence of a doctor's negligence or of the inadequacy of treatment. But a doctor who fails to keep an adequate note of a consultation lays himself open to a finding that his recollection is faulty and someone else's is correct. After all, a patient has only to remember his or her own case, whereas the doctor has to remember one case out of hundreds which occupied his mind at the material time.

Do the records prove themselves?

The answer is no, strictly. But normally in a trial it is tacitly accepted that they are not going to be challenged, unless one party has put the other side on notice that the timing or content or authoring of a particular note is not accepted. In *Arrowsmith* v *Beeston* (18 June 1998, unreported), CA, it was said that GP records are not evidence of the correctness of the diagnosis made unless the maker of the record is called to give evidence. In *Steele* v *Millbrook Proving Ground Ltd* (6 May 1999, unreported), CA, the relevant issue was whether the rotator cuff syndrome from which the claimant in an employment accident case was suffering was due to the accident or not. In concluding that it was, the judge had relied to an extent on GP records which tended to confirm the claimant's account. Upon objection by the defendants, the Court of Appeal said that there was no doubt that medical records were evidence of the facts recorded in them, and the weight to be attached to the records

---

1   In *Dobson* v *North Tyneside Health Authority* [1997] 1 WLR 596 the Court of Appeal said that for the maxim to apply it had to be shown that the spoliator was a 'wrongdoer'.

in this case, given that neither party called the GP to give evidence, was a matter for the judge.

Occasionally a party to a medical negligence action will serve a notice to admit medical records (the Treasury Solicitor has been known to do this). As I have indicated, that is probably the correct procedure, strictly speaking.

The Data Protection Act 1998 and the Freedom of Information Act 2000

The Act of 1998, intended to implement Directive 95/46/EC,[2] repealed the Data Protection Act 1984 and the Access to Health Records Act 1990 with effect from 1 March 2000, except to the extent that it applied to deceased patients. So the new Act is the route for access to medical records. It has its own jargon. A patient is a 'data subject', the holder of the records is a 'data controller', and the records are 'information constituting data'. Clinical records include 'all paper and computer records whenever created'.[3] A health record means any record which consists of information relating to the physical or mental health or condition of an individual and which has been made by or on behalf of a health professional in connection with the care of that individual (s 68). A health professional includes, by s 69, all forms of medical practitioners (eg doctors, dentists, opticians, nurses, midwives, osteopaths, chiropractors, speech therapists, physiotherapists) and anyone registered as a member of a profession supplementary to medicine (within the catchment of the Professions Supplementary to Medicine Act 1960). Under s 7, an individual or his representative has a right to access and get a copy of his clinical records on making a request in writing with the prescribed fee. Copies are to be supplied within 40 days unless such supply would involve disproportionate effort. An explanation must be supplied where the records contain terms otherwise unintelligible. There are provisions for an application to the court by either party.

The Act is drafted in general terms. The Data Protection (Subject Access Modification) (Health) Order 2000, SI 2000/413 sets out specific rules concerning health records. Disclosure may be refused where serious harm might be caused to the physical or mental health of the patient. Medical records that have been created in the expectation that they would not be disclosed to the person making the request are exempt from the Act. In *Hubble* v *Peterborough Hospital NHS Trust* (2001) MLC 0347, a Recorder held that X-rays fell within the Act and so no extra charge for copying them could be levied. Although not expressly decided, the same reasoning would seem to apply to the CTG traces, in respect of which an additional charge had already been paid. A charge beyond the £50 maximum (currently under review) is possible pursuant to s 8(2) if 'disproportionate effect' is required to supply the record.

---

2   Note that the human rights aspect of accessing medical records is considered in Chapter 27.

3   The Data Protection Act 1984 did not apply to paper records; one had to turn to the Access to Health Records Act 1990 for them. (See the Court of Appeal's judgment in *R* v *Mid-Glamorgan Family Health Services Authority, ex p Martin* [1994] 5 Med LR 383.) The 1984 Act was also limited to records created after October 1991.

The Freedom of Information Act 2000, now in force, applies, by and large, to non-personal data. Although most documents which might be helpful to a medical claim can be obtained under normal disclosure rules, it is not difficult to see that some might fall outside the ambit of those rules in the more complex or wide-ranging claim, and the Act of 2000 could be particularly useful in accessing information previously undivulged relating (for example) to trust or health authority systems and data or Department of Health and government management, thus assisting in the investigation and formulation of a claim. This might well be particularly helpful to group claims, where the budget for such an investigation is so much greater than for the single claim. Though on the surface exceptionally wide-ranging, the Act is complex and hedged about with exceptions. This is not the place to offer more than a brief summary.

Individuals already have the right to access information about themselves (personal data) which is held on computer and in some paper files under the Data Protection Act 1998. The Act of 2000 extends this right of access (as far as public authorities are concerned) to allow access to all the types of information held, whether personal or non-personal. This may include information about third parties, although the public authority will have to take account of the Data Protection Act 1998 before releasing any personal information. The Act gives two related rights:

- the right to be told whether the information exists; and
- the right to receive that information.

The right to access the information held by public authorities can be exercised by anyone, worldwide. The Act is also retrospective. This right to access information came into effect on 1 January 2005.

The Act is 'challenged with the task of reversing the working premise that everything is secret, unless otherwise stated, to a position where everything is public unless it falls into specified excepted cases' (Lord Chancellor's first Annual Report on the implementation of the Act, November 2001). It was passed on 30 November 2000. As indicated, it gives a general right of access to all types of recorded information held by public authorities, sets out exemptions from that right and places a number of obligations on public authorities (health bodies are, of course, included in the term 'public authority'). The Act also makes appropriate amendments to the Data Protection Act 1998 and the Public Records Act 1958. Subject to the exemptions, any person who makes a request to a public authority for information must be informed whether the public authority holds that information. If it does, that information must be supplied, subject to certain conditions.

Every public authority is required to adopt and maintain a publication scheme setting out how it intends to publish the different classes of information it holds, and whether there is a charge for the information. Some trusts have already put their publication schemes online. Two codes of practice issued under the Act provide guidance to public authorities about responding to requests for information and records management. The Act is enforced by the Information Commissioner and was brought into force in two parts, with full implementation on 1 January 2005. The requirement to publish and maintain a publication scheme was phased in during 2003 and 2004. Individual rights of access to information came into force across all public authorities in January 2005.

Before 2005, there were Codes that gave the public access to some information held by government departments. These were little used and were considered to be exclusive rather than inclusive. The Freedom of Information Act covers over 100,000 public bodies. It is proclaimed that the Act will ensure that much more information will be routinely and freely available about the way in which we are governed and the way decisions that affect all our lives are reached, at both national and local levels. With the introduction of publication schemes in 2003/04, a vast amount of information not previously accessible became available as a matter of routine. Publication schemes mean that public bodies have to ensure that information which they say is available through their publication scheme is truly and easily available, and they will have to indicate in their schemes how they will achieve this. The legislation allows for public bodies to charge for access subject to certain restrictions but this too should be notified in the publication scheme.

The main features of the individual right of access are:

1. Every written request for information, including emails, will be considered to be an access request under the Freedom of Information Act. There is no set format, nor is there any requirement to justify the request. There are no citizenship or residency restrictions and the only requirement is that applicants provide a name and address.
2. Access requests must be dealt with within 20 working days.
3. If the information is not available or the information is not supplied the applicant must be told why.
4. In cases where either the precise information covered by the request is unclear or where the scope is so wide as to make it likely that the request would be refused on the grounds of cost, public bodies are encouraged to discuss with the applicant the nature of their request to see whether it can be redefined to lead to a positive outcome.
5. The Act requires public bodies to set up an appeals procedure to review refusals at the request of the applicants and, if the applicant remains unhappy at the refusal, there is an avenue of recourse to the Information Commissioner.

The modest hope has been offered to the effect that the Act will encourage transparency in decision-making, leading to a re-establishment of the trust between national and local public bodies and the people they serve.

THE RIGHT TO PRE-ACTION DISCLOSURE

The Access to Health Records Act 1990 did not apply to records created before November 1991, as to which the old law remained in force. Given that the 1998 Act applies to all clinical records whenever created, the old law has assumed considerably less significance in medical negligence claims. However, there may from time to time be documents the patient wants to see which do not comprise data caught by the Act. For example, in *Hewlett-Parker* v *St George's Healthcare NHS Trust* [1998] MLC 0072, Owen J ordered disclosure of an NHS complaints file (pursuant to the then current RSC Ord 24, r 8). It is therefore useful to summarise the old law.

Pre-action disclosure is provided for by the Supreme Court Act 19 s 33, the County Courts Act 1984, s 52, and CPR 31.16. Note that this facility is only available against a likely party to future proceedings. Disclosure against a non-party can only be obtained after action is commenced[4] – apart of course from any rights under the 1998 Act. Disclosure against a non-party is governed by the Supreme Court Act 1981, s 34, the County Courts Act 1984, s 53, and CPR 31.17.

Pre-action disclosure is no longer limited to personal injury cases. In *Burrells Wharf Freeholds Ltd* v *Galliards Homes Ltd* [1999] 33 EG 82, the court rejected the submission that Art 5 of the Civil Procedure (Modification of Enactments) Order 1998, which removed the former restriction to personal injury cases, was *ultra vires.*

Any application must be supported by evidence. The applicant must show that he and the respondent are likely to be parties to proceedings, that the documents he seeks fall within the ambit of disclosable documents under the general provisions of r 31.6, and that early disclosure is desirable in order to dispose fairly of the anticipated proceedings or to assist the dispute to be resolved without proceedings or to save costs.

On an application for disclosure against a non-party, it must be shown that the documents sought are likely to support the case of the applicant or adversely affect *another* [my emphasis] party's case, and that disclosure is necessary in order to dispose fairly of the claim or to save costs.[5]

The Court of Appeal considered the ambit of the Act of 1981 and the new rules in the case of *American Home Products Corpn and Professor Sir Roy Calne* v *Novartis Pharma AG* (2001) IPD 24021. This was an action for alleged infringement of a patent for the use of rapamycin in the preparation of a drug for inhibiting organ or tissue transplant rejection. The court found a similar limitation to the Act's 'any documents which are relevant to an issue' in the words of rule 31.17 enabling the court to make an order 'only where the documents ... are likely to support the case for the applicant or adversely affect the case of one of the other parties to the proceedings'.

Confidentiality of medical records

It goes without saying that a person's medical records are confidential and normally not to be disclosed to anyone but his doctors. The main exception to this is that in a personal injury action or a clinical negligence action he is taken to have waived his right to confidentiality so that the defendants are entitled to see all relevant records (and in most cases that will embrace all his records). Any unacceptable disclosure is likely also to be a contravention of the right to privacy under Article 8 of the Convention.

In *R* v *Plymouth City Council ex parte Stevens* [2002] EWCA Civ 388, where a mother sought to see the medical records of her adult son who was in the guardianship of the respondent council, the court said that although there was a legitimate interest in protecting the

le to join a party simply to get disclosure (*Douihech* v *Findlay* [1990]

ds considered the relevant principles in *O'Sullivan* v *Herdmans Ltd* :7.

confidentiality of personal information about a person in the guardian-ship of his local authority, his nearest relative was entitled to have direct access to that information when she needed it in order to deter-mine whether she should oppose the renewal of the guardianship. This reasoning was followed by Sumner J in *Re R (a Child)* [2004] EWHC 2085 (Fam), where the judge made an order for pre-action disclosure under CPR rule 31.16, subject to conditions, in respect of a potential claim by a child against the respondent trust for failing to diagnose his condition. The judge said that the balance came down in favour of full disclosure even though the trust's notes contained sensitive material about the applicant's mother.[6]

In *A Health Authority* v *X & Ors* [2001] EWCA Civ 2014 the Court of Appeal said that a judge who had ordered the disclosure to a health authority of case material used in care proceedings and GP patient records had correctly balanced the public interest in effective disciplinary procedures for the investigation and eradication of medical malpractice against the confidentiality of the documents, and had correctly used his power to attach conditions to the disclosure. In the absence of exceptional circumstances an application for the release of papers in care proceedings should be determined by the trial judge.

In *A* v *X & B (non-party)* [2004] EWHC 447 (QB) a defendant who had admitted causing injury by his negligent driving sought to reduce the victim's damages by proving, by way of disclosure of the medical records of the victim's brother, that the victim's brain disability was familial (genetic) and would have arisen in any event. Morland J, refus-ing the application, said that only in a very exceptional factual situa-tion would a court be justified in civil proceedings in ordering disclosure of a non-party's confidential medical data and that this was not such a case. In *Bennett* v *Compass Group UK* [2002] EWCA Civ 642 defendants to a claim in respect of an accident at work had sought, rea-sonably enough one would have thought, to obtain disclosure of the employee's medical records. The records had been referred to in an expert medical orthopaedic report served on behalf of the claimant. The Court of Appeal said that the judge had had jurisdiction to make his order that the claimant provide the defendant with a signed form of authority for release of her GP and hospital records direct to the defen-dant, although care was to be taken in the exercise of that jurisdiction. The defendant had a right to inspect the records under CPR 31.3, and also as records relied on by the claimant's expert in his report, under CPR 31.14(e).[7]

In *Ashworth Security Hospital* v *MGN Ltd* (2002) MLC 0800 the House of Lords agreed with the Court of Appeal in upholding the judge's order

---

6   It is also worth noting the costs point: the judge said that ordinarily a party required to provide pre-action disclosure would be awarded his costs but in the circumstances each side should pay its own costs. It is not the practice in my experience that a party who successfully challenges the refusal of a likely party to proceedings bears the costs of the application.

7   Note that in care proceedings it will generally be the case that the court should be pro-vided with medical records of parents (see *Re B (disclosure to other parties)* (2001) 2 FLR 1017 and *Re B, R and C (Children)* 12 November 2002, CA).

that a journalist's employer at the *Daily Mirror* should disclose the identity of an intermediary as a means of identifying the source of information on a patient detained under the Mental Health Act 1983. The court said that the disclosure of confidential medical records to the press was misconduct which was not merely of concern to the individual establishment in which it occurred; it was an attack on an area of confidentiality which should be safeguarded in any democratic society and the protection of patient information was of vital concern to the National Health Service. However, when the hospital sought to compel the intermediary journalist who had originally obtained the information from hospital sources, ie information derived from the patient's records, to disclose the identity of those sources the Court of Appeal, managing to distinguish the House of Lords decision, declined to make the order sought, saying that protection of journalistic sources was one of the basic conditions of press freedom and there was no overriding requirement in the case to allow what would otherwise be a breach of Article 10 of the European Convention on Human Rights (*Ackroyd* v *Mersey Care NHS Trust* [2003] Lloyds Rep Med 379).[8]

Misleading disclosure

Where a health authority had grossly misled the claimant's medical and legal advisers in their disclosure of X-rays, the Court of Appeal ordered a new trial (*Cunningham* v *North Manchester Health Authority* [1997] 8 Med LR 135).

OTHER PRE-ACTION FACILITIES

By s 33(1) of the Act of 1981, the court may make orders for:

- the inspection, photographing, preservation, custody and detention of property which by section 35(5) includes any land chattel or other corporeal property of any description [possibilities of inspection of hospital premises and machines here] that appears to the court to be property which may become the subject matter of subsequent proceedings or as to which any question may arise in any such proceedings; and
- taking samples of any such property and carrying out any experiment on or with it.

In *Ash* v *Buxted Poultry Ltd* (1989) Times, 29 November, Brooke J held that the court had power to order one party to a personal injury action to permit the other to make a video recording of a relevant industrial process so as to facilitate the judge's understanding of the case. This power could be of use in the odd medical case, eg to film the process of a machine in hospital.

---

8   There is some fear for confidentiality as the Government proposes at huge expense to put all health records on a central database. But such fear is unwarranted. If the Government's track record on IT is taken into account, in the civil service and defence, for example, as well as in health, it won't work.

In *Dobson* v *North Tyneside Health Authority* [1997] 1 WLR 596, the Court of Appeal held that there was no right of property in the brain of a deceased and that there was no duty to preserve the brain after *post mortem* and after the rest of the body had been buried. The claim was therefore struck out.[9] In *AB* v *Leeds Teaching Hospital NHS Trust and Cardiff and Vale NHS Trust* (2004) MLC 1101, an imaginative group action by parents of deceased children whose organs had been removed at post-mortem, the claim was for psychiatric injury caused on discovery of the removal of the organs. Gage J held that the parents had no possessory rights in the organs (although a duty of care could exist in such circumstances – see Chapter 15).[10]

The reverse side of the coin

Subject to any conflict with human rights (see Chapter 27), we may note *Dunn* v *British Coal Corpn* [1993] PIQR P275, in which the Court of Appeal held that where a claim for damages for an industrial accident included a substantial claim for loss of earnings, the claimant was obliged to disclose all his medical records and not just those relating to the accident (the Court of Appeal has confirmed that the duty to disclose medical records in this type of situation was a duty to disclose not only to the medical advisers for the other party but also to the legal advisers – *Hipwood* v *Gloucester Health Authority* MLC 0708, [1995] 6 Med LR 187).

In the Irish case of *Irvin* v *Donaghy* [1996] PIQR P207, where the application by the defendants for the claimant's medical records was made direct to the GP and hospital, it was said that a sensible practice had grown up of providing that the documents were in the first instance to be inspected by the claimant who could object to the production on grounds of privilege. The court had to seek to ensure that only the relevant parts of confidential documents were made available to the applicant. There was no objection in principle to the claimant having a right to object to the production of irrelevant material and he should have the opportunity to cover up entries in the medical records which were irrelevant, just as the claimant could in the traditional context of discovery between parties.

Section 35(1) provides that the court is not to make an order for disclosure if it considers that compliance with the order would be likely to be injurious to the public interest. As the court has a general discretion whether to exercise its power to order disclosure or not, this provision seems otiose.

Disclosure should not be refused on the ground that the claim is time-barred unless that is clear beyond reasonable argument,

---

9 In *R* v *Kelly* (1998) 51 BMLR 142, it was held that parts of a dead body can be property within s 4 of the Theft Act 1968 if they have acquired different attributes as a result of the application of skill, such as dissection or preservation techniques, for exhibition or teaching purposes.

10 A breach of the human right to family life under Article 8 was included in the plea, of course.

particularly as discovery might reveal material which would affect the position *(Harris* v *Newcastle upon Tyne Health Authority* [1989] 1 WLR 96, CA).

PRIVILEGE

Privileged documents must be disclosed but can be withheld from inspection. Rule 31(3) acknowledges this, but, if challenged, the existence of privilege has to be proved. The two classes of privilege that are likely to be relevant to disclosure of medical records are legal professional privilege and public interest.

Legal professional privilege

Correspondence and other communications between a solicitor and his client are privileged from production even though no litigation was contemplated or pending at the time, provided that they are of a confidential nature and the solicitor was acting in his professional capacity for the purpose of giving legal advice or getting it on behalf of the client, as from counsel. If a document to which legal professional privilege attaches does find its way into the hands of the defendant, he may use it as desired, regardless of the privilege, but if he has not yet made use of it, he can be restrained from so doing *(Goddard* v *Nationwide Building Society* [1987] QB 670, CA; *English and American Insurance Co* v *Herbert Smith & Co* [1988] FSR 232; and see also *Guinness Peat Properties* v *Fitzroy Robinson Partnership* [1987] 1 WLR 1027, CA – and see below the section on documents obtained by mistake).

But it is in the class of documents that are only privileged if made when litigation was contemplated or pending that any problems on disclosure of medical records are likely to arise. The general principle is that communications between a solicitor and third party, whether directly or through an agent, which come into existence after litigation is contemplated or commenced and are made with a view to such litigation, either for the purpose of giving or obtaining advice in regard to that litigation, or of obtaining or collecting evidence to be used in it, or obtaining information which may lead to the obtaining of such evidence, are privileged. This privilege includes documents which are obtained by a solicitor with a view to enabling him to prosecute or defend an action, or to give advice with reference to existing or contemplated litigation, but does not include copies he obtains of documents that are not themselves privileged. It is with reference to reports of accidents and similar documents which are made before litigation is commenced and generally have the purpose of putting the senior personnel or the solicitors of the potential defendants fully in the picture that problems have arisen. Such reports have a dual purpose at least, that of producing as clear an account of the incident as possible and as soon as possible so that the facts may be ascertained and any necessary action taken, and that of providing a basis on which solicitors may be instructed if necessary and proceedings defended (or settled) if they are instituted. It is not easy to discern in the shifting sands of the law what the legal rules are for defining the test of 'made with a view to litigation'. Similarly, it is not clear at what point litigation may be said to have begun to be 'contemplated'.[11]

Dominant purpose

In *Waugh* v *British Railways Board* [1980] AC 521, the defendants sought privilege for an internal report that was made in accordance with their usual practice after an accident. It contained contemporary accounts from witnesses. The defendants deposed that one of the principal purposes in preparing it had been so that it could be passed to their chief solicitor to enable him to advise the Board on their legal liability and defend any proceedings if so advised. After considerable dissension below, the House of Lords, agreeing with Lord Denning MR's judgment in the Court of Appeal, said that the due administration of justice strongly required that a contemporary report such as this, which would almost certainly be the best evidence as to the cause of the accident, should be disclosed, and that for that important public interest to be overridden by a claim of privilege the purpose of submission to the party's legal advisers in anticipation of litigation must be at least the dominant purpose for which it had been prepared; that in that particular case that purpose had been of no more than equal weight with the purpose of facilitating proper railway operation and safety. Therefore, the claim to privilege failed. The court added that the fact that the report stated on its face that it had finally to be sent to the solicitor for advice could not be conclusive as to what in fact the dominant purpose of its creation was.[12]

This principle was applied to a health authority report in *Lask* v *Gloucester Health Authority* [1991] 2 Med LR 379. The Court of Appeal held that a confidential accident report, which NHS circulars required to be completed by health authorities both for the use of solicitors in case litigation arose in respect of the accident and also to enable action to be taken to avoid a repetition of the accident, was not privileged since the dominant purpose of its preparation had not been for submission to solicitors in anticipation of litigation, and this was so decided even though both health authority and solicitor had deposed that that had in fact been its dominant purpose and the report itself referred only to that purpose (the court saw in the wording of the relevant Health Circular material which enabled it to reject the sworn statements in the affidavits). This may be contrasted with *McAvan* v *London Transport Executive* (1983) 133 NLJ 1101, CA, in which reports that had been prepared by a bus crew and an inspector after an accident had occurred were held by the court to

---

11 Privilege does not attach to pre-existing documents obtained, but not created, for the purposes of litigation (*Ventouris* v *Mountain* [1991] 1 WLR 607, CA). Note also that the Court of Appeal stated that just because a document had to be disclosed, it did not automatically follow that production or inspection would be ordered. Privilege, as opposed to admissibility, becomes irrelevant once a document has in fact been disclosed (*Black & Decker Inc* v *Flymo Ltd* [1991] 1 WLR 753).

12 In *Secretary of State for Trade and Industry* v *Baker* [1998] Ch 356, the Vice-Chancellor said that it would not be enough to establish 'dominant purpose' if production of the document did not involve a risk of impinging upon the inviolability of lawyer/client communications.

be privileged as the dominant purpose in their preparation was to ascertain blame in the event of a claim being made.

In *Green* v *Post Office* (15 June 1987, unreported), the Court of Appeal ordered disclosure of an accident report brought into existence by an employer for the dual purpose of providing information not only on which legal advice could be obtained if a claim for personal injuries was made by the employee but also on which the employer could consider whether any remedial action was required to avoid a repetition of the accident at work.

Medical reports

Although Lord Woolf wanted all communications between patients' solicitors and medical experts to be disclosed, that has fortunately not become the law.[13] Medical reports, whether on liability or prognosis, and indeed any expert report that a party has commissioned, are privileged and he cannot be required to produce them (*Worrall* v *Reich* [1955] 1 QB 296, CA; *Causton* v *Mann Egerton (Johnsons) Ltd* [1974] 1 WLR 162, CA). If you want a sight of the defendants' doctor's report when you show them yours or agree to send the client to a medical examination, you must get their agreement first. It is not safe to rely on an implied agreement, even though Lord Denning MR said in the *Causton* case in a strong dissenting judgment:

> I hope that in future the solicitors for every plaintiff will refuse to allow any defendants to have any medical examination of the plaintiff except on the terms that the defendants will disclose the medical reports following the examination. This has become so usual in practice that I think it may be said to have become the 'usual terms'. This is most desirable. We know that the medical men of this country give their reports honestly and impartially by whichever side they are instructed, and it is only fair that if one side shows his the other should reciprocate.

The usual order for disclosure of medical reports on the claimant's condition and prognosis means only that if a party does in fact intend to produce such evidence in court, he must disclose it first.

If the reports are not prepared in anticipation of litigation, eg where they have been made by an employer in order to establish whether an employee is able to return to work, the court may order disclosure if that is necessary for the fair disposal of the case (*Ford Motor Co* v *X Nawaz* [1987] ICR 434, EAT).

In *Jackson* v *Marley Davenport Ltd* [2004] 1 WLR 2926 the Court of Appeal said that CPR r 35.13 did not provide the courts with the power to order disclosure of earlier reports made by experts in preparation of a final report. Where an expert made a report for legal advisers of for the purposes of a conference, such a report was subject to litigation privilege at the time it was made. It was not intended that the CPR should abrogate privilege, and references to the disclosure of experts' reports in CPR r 35.10(2) had to be references to the expert's actual evidence and not to

---

13　Note, however, that in certain circumstances the court can order disclosure of an expert's instructions under r 35(10)4 (see Chapter 9).

earlier draft reports (*Carlson* v *Townsend* [2001] PIQR P346 applied). A bold attempt had already been made in *Linstead* v *East Sussex, Brighton and Hove Health Authority* [2001] PIQR P356 to consign legal professional privilege to the waste bin using the ubiquitous human rights plea, here under Article 6, the right to a fair trial. The claimant sought to force disclosure of an earlier statement made by a midwife to the defendants at a time when clearly proceedings were pending. Forbes J refused the application, saying that the privilege was paramount and absolute when not waived or abrogated. The right to a fair trial did not entitle interference with the right to legal confidentiality. The Human Rights Act did not alter the nature and effect of legal privilege, which was not subject to any balancing exercise of weighing competing public interests.

The House of Lords has three times recently had occasion to consider legal professional privilege. In *B* v *Auckland District Law Society* [2003] 2 AC 736, a case on appeal from New Zealand, they held that privilege had not been waived where documents had voluntarily been made available expressly for limited purposes. In *Medcalf* v *Weatherill* [2002] 3 WLR 172, they held that it was unfair to make wasted costs orders against counsel for pursuing allegations of fraud where legal professional privilege prevented counsel from adducing evidence as to whether they had any reasonably credible material before them to prove those allegations. Reference may also be made to *Dempsey* v *Johnstone* [2003] EWCA Civ 1134 where the Court of Appeal held that the question whether counsel had been negligent in pursuing a claim could only be resolved by a sight of counsel's written advice and that was not permitted as the document was privileged.

The third House of Lords decision is *Three Rivers Council* v *Bank of Credit and Commerce International* [2004] 3 WLR 1274. The court said that legal advice privilege attached to advice given by solicitors about the preparation and presentation of evidence to be submitted to an inquiry since legal advice for the purposes of privilege included advice as to what should prudently and sensibly be done in the relevant legal context. Legal professional privilege was not an extension of litigation privilege, but a single integral privilege whose sub-heads were legal advice privilege and litigation privilege; it was litigation privilege that was restricted to proceedings or anticipated proceedings in a court of law.

Proceedings contemplated

The other question – at what point can one say that proceedings are contemplated? – can also give rise to difficulties. It can be said that as soon as any accident has occurred there is a prospect of litigation. Some cases have endorsed that approach, principally *Seabrook* v *British Transport Commission* [1959] 1 WLR 509 ('I think that, whenever a man is fatally injured in the course of his work on the railway line, there is at least a possibility that litigation will ensue', *per* Havers J); but it is doubtful if that case is authority for anything any more in view of *Waugh* v *British Railways Board* (above); *Alfred Crompton Amusement Machines Ltd* v *Customs and Excise Comrs (No 2)* [1974] AC 405, HL, which would appear to be authority for the proposition that, where a decision needs to be taken by a potential defendant before solicitors are instructed, documents coming into existence before that decision is taken cannot be said to have been made when litigation was in contemplation and are therefore not privileged. There would appear to be scope for arguing on that basis for the disclosure of a great many accident reports (the documents in the *Alfred Crompton* case comprised material collected for the purpose of preparing a valuation of the claimant's goods for an assessment to purchase tax, but the principle is equally applicable to accident or medical reports).

Whose privilege?

The general rule is that the privilege is that of the client and of no-one else; only the client can waive the privilege (though the privilege is not lost by reason of the death of the client). The somewhat complex facts of *Lee* v *South West Thames Regional Health Authority* [1985] 1 WLR 845, CA, illustrate what appears to be an exception to the principle that privilege may be claimed only by the party for whose benefit the document was prepared, or at any rate a limit upon that principle.

> Pre-action disclosure was sought on behalf of a small boy who suffered brain damage, probably through lack of oxygen when he was on a respirator either in hospital or in the ambulance. The health authority for the hospital had, after litigation was contemplated against them, required from the defendants, who were responsible for the ambulance service, a report on what had or might have happened. That report was agreed by the parties to be privileged as far as the hospital health authority was concerned; but its disclosure was sought against the defendants, it being argued that the privilege was not theirs to assert. The Court of Appeal refused to order disclosure, saying that, although the defendants appeared to be advancing the other authority's claim to privilege, the cause of action being asserted against the defendants was not a wholly independent cause of action, but arose out of the same incident as that which rendered the hospital authority a likely defendant. However, that conclusion was 'reached with undisguised reluctance because we think that there is something seriously wrong with the law if Marlon's mother cannot find out exactly what caused this brain damage'.

Public interest privilege

It is all too easy for a public body that wishes to avoid embarrassing disclosures, or to create or preserve a sense of mystique, to claim that disclosure of certain important documents would be damaging to the public interest. Where the claim is based on the ground of national security, it may well succeed as that is an argument which our courts take very seriously. So, too, where the interests of children are involved. But in all cases, such a claim must be carefully scrutinised so that public bodies that are seeking to take the easy way out should not be encouraged to expect to succeed.

Strictly, this is not a claim for privilege that a party may advance, but rather an immunity from production that the court should invoke of its own accord if the party does not, on the basis that such production would be injurious to the public interest, ie that withholding the documents is necessary to the proper functioning of the public service. It features most frequently in the area of governmental decisions or policy, and police or similar investigations, but it could be found occasionally in the medical negligence action. Every potential claim to immunity will be considered on its own facts, but a decision as to a particular type of document is likely to be of persuasive authority when a similar situation occurs later. There are many reported cases on public interest privilege. One example, in the medical field, must suffice here.

> In September 1990 haemophiliacs seeking compensation for having been infected with the HIV virus from contaminated clotting agents secured in the Court of Appeal the release of many important documents that the government were unjustly trying to withhold from them on the factitious ground, so dear to government, that the public interest demanded that they remain secret (see *Re HIV Haemophiliac Litigation* (1990) 41 BMLR 171, [1990] NLJR 1349).

Documents obtained by mistake

It is not unusual to find privileged documents among the medical records, such as memos or letters from the 'accused' doctor to the hospital administrator, health authority solicitor or MDU, which have clearly been included through oversight – someone has simply copied everything in the file without properly scrutinising the documents. In such a case, the general rule is that you cannot take advantage of their oversight and must send back the documents and any copies, though that rule seems to admit of the strange exception that if you did not realise when you saw the document that it had been supplied by mistake, you need not give it back (see *Guinness Peat Properties Ltd* v *Fitzroy Robinson Partnership* [1987] 1 WLR 1027, CA, and *Derby & Co* v *Weldon (No 8)* [1991] 1 WLR 73). In *Kenning* v *Eve Construction Ltd* [1989] 1 WLR 1189, Michael Wright J refused to order the return of a clearly privileged covering letter from an expert which had been inadvertently disclosed along with his report, on the ground that if the defendants were going to call that expert, they were in any event obliged to disclose all his evidence, warts and all. Where defendants had no reason to suspect a mistake when certain documents had been included by the claimants in the trial bundle, they were entitled to assume that they were documents on which the claimants intended to rely, whether privileged or not, and that any privilege had been waived (*Derby & Co* v *Weldon (No 10)* [1991] 1 WLR 660).

Where the defendant's solicitor in a claim for industrial injury reasonably believed that the claimant's advisers had waived privilege in sending him a copy of a medical report, the claimant was entitled to make use of it at the trial (*Pizzey* v *Ford Motor Co Ltd* [1994] PIQR P15, CA).

In *IBM Corpn* v *Phoenix International* [1995] 1 All ER 413, Aldous J held that the question whether the disclosure was understood by the solicitor for the other party to be a mistake should be adjudged according to the likely reaction of the reasonable solicitor.

The rules remain the same despite the new CPR: *Breeze* v *John Stacey & Sons* (1999) Times, 8 July, CA (where the mistake was not obvious there was no duty on the receiving party to inquire further).[14]

---

14 Where a *prima facie* case of fraud against a party has been made out the court may overrule an otherwise properly made claim to privilege (*Derby & Co* v *Weldon (No 7)* [1990] 1 WLR 1156).

In *Fayed* v *Commissioner of Police for the Metropolis* [2002] EWCA Civ 780, the Court of Appeal, reviewing the principles involved, said that an injunction to prevent the use of documents that were subject to legal professional privilege or public interest immunity but had been voluntarily, though mistakenly, sent to the other side for inspection, should only be granted where the mistake would have been obvious to a reasonable solicitor.

CONTENTS OF THE RECORDS[15]

The medical records are likely to contain some or all of the following:

- accident and emergency department record card;
- GP's referral letter;
- admitting doctor's notes on examination;
- ward doctor's clinical notes;
- operating record;
- anesthetic record;
- daily nursing notes;
- laboratory reports on blood and other bodily samples;
- radiographs and reports on radiographs;
- electrocardiograms (ECG) and reports;
- electroencephalograms (EEG) and reports;
- temperature, pulse and respiration charts;
- fluid balance charts;
- head injury charts;
- partogram (midwifery only);
- fetal heart trace (maternity only);
- correspondence to and from other hospitals involved in treatment and with the GP.

A GP's notes will include medical record cards, correspondence from hospitals and the results of tests.

NHS records belong to the Secretary of State. Records maintained by private hospitals do not include doctors' notes, which are their own property, and may often be kept separately by the treating doctor. Unlike NHS hospitals, private hospitals may not be responsible for the default of consultants, as opposed to nursing staff (see Chapter 21).

GP RECORDS

The notes kept by GPs are highly variable in quality. Before the advent of the computer, or, more accurately, before it was recognised by GPs as a useful adjunct to their practice, most records were (as many still are) contained in an envelope, the design of which scarcely changed in seven decades, on which is recorded the patient's name, date of birth and

---

15   The sections that follow were written by Dr David Kirby. They explain content for non-computerised records, still by far the majority of records.

successive addresses, with the name of each GP with whom he has been registered. Inside the envelope there are cards which have the patient's name at the top, dates of consultations in the margin, with a second margin to give a column in which is recorded whether the consultation is on a visit or at the practice, and opposite each date a brief and often scarcely legible summary of the consultation. A few practices changed their records to A4 folders, but the contents are essentially the same.

A GP who is trying to create systems which enable him to make any effective use of the records envelope will have arranged the cards in chronological order. There may also be a card at the front, usually in a different colour, on which is recorded a summary of the main health events in the patient's life; similarly there may be a treatment card, which is a list of the drugs which at any one time a patient is receiving on a regular basis so that repeat prescriptions are being made.

Even where records are to an extent computerised, reliance will still be placed on hard copy, eg the Lloyd George sheets and correspondence received.

Entries in GP records, both hard copy and computerised, can be so brief as to be incomprehensible, and often they contain abbreviations which are idiosyncratic, as well as the more generally used abbreviations which appear in hospital notes. Only a minority of GPs use any discernible system in their note-making, and these systems vary. Some GPs write a short diagnostic summary – a word or a phrase – in capitals or underlined, at the top of the notes of each consultation. However, it is not really possible after many typical consultations in general practice to make a 'diagnosis' that can be encapsulated in a few words; this is first because GP consultations are often about symptoms which can be managed and resolved – either by prescribed drugs or by the passage of a short period of rest – without the steps being taken by the GP which would allow an accurate diagnosis to be made. Second, illnesses as they are presented to GPs have several aspects – there may be a pathological process going on in the patient's body, but there is also an emotional state, a desire to use or abuse the services of the GP, a social situation for the patient's family; the 'diagnosis' can reasonably be expressed in any of these contexts, but as the consultation will have taken a particular direction (a direction which should be determined by the patient, but which all too often is in fact largely determined by the doctor), it is neither possible nor appropriate for the doctor to record more than one or two of them.

When things are written down in a patient's notes, the writer should bear in mind the possibilities that the future holds for that information to be read by many other people than himself, and this provides another powerful constraint on what a GP may write in a patient's record, because of the need to respect the confidentiality of the consultation. For all these reasons, as well as because of the fact that most GPs do not have the time to write thorough reports about each consultation, medical records in general practice are inherently inadequate.

It follows that it is not the case that there is a correlation between the quality of a GP's practice and the quality of his records. Nevertheless, there are certain minimal pieces of information that should be recorded – the date of each consultation and any prescribed drug treatment. It is in the nature of general practice that there will be occasional lapses even in these minimal requirements, but a consistent pattern of failure to record these fundamentals is highly suggestive of a low standard of medical care.

System of recording

Some GPs, especially those involved in the training of aspiring GPs, or those who have been recently trained, may use a system of recording the consultation called the 'SOAP' system:

*S*x (subjective) – what the patient says is the problem.
*O*x (objective) – what the doctor finds on examination.
*A*n (analysis) – formulation of what may be the essence of the problem.
Plan – what is to be done.

As well as the handwritten records of a GP's consultations, the records envelope will contain letters about the patient which the GP has received: these are mostly from hospitals, and are either letters written by consultants after the patient has been seen as an outpatient, or discharge summaries sent after the patient has been in hospital for a period. In poorly-organised practices these letters are often to be found folded and stuffed willy-nilly into the envelope, but in a practice where efforts have been made to actually make effective use of the patients' records they will have been sorted into date order. As these letters and summaries are typed, and are in comprehensible syntactically organised English, they constitute a much more readily assimilable source of information about the patient's medical history than the cryptic abbreviated scrawlings of the GP. Copies of the same letters will also be kept in the hospital records folders of each patient at every hospital they have attended.

The GP record folder may contain a variety of other bits of paper: there may be forms which contain information as to the results of investigations which the GP has ordered, such as blood tests or cervical smears.

An effective GP in an urban practice today will be working closely with a number of other workers in the primary health care team, including health visitors, district nurses, community psychiatric nurses, psychologists, counsellors, social workers and others. These workers in general keep their own separate records, and the meetings between the different professions at which many important decisions are taken about a patient's care are often not well minuted: it is rarely clear from a GP's records which other members of the practice team are actively involved in the treatment at any one time, nor what treatment they are providing.

(Although one expects a more modern and efficient method of keeping records to gradually emerge with the development of the new forms of primary care (groups and trusts), most GP claims currently under investigation do not disclose any such improvement.)

HOSPITAL RECORDS

National Health Service hospital records are more ordered and more consistent in their quality than are the records kept by GPs. They are usually in A4 size folders and are divided into sections: there is some variation in the nature of these sections and their order, but the usual principles are as follows: the folder contains records kept by nurses as well as those kept by doctors, but these are usually arranged in separate bundles, each in chronological order. In the medical notes each admission to hospital is filed as a complete unit which usually opens with an 'admission sheet' on which various particulars are recorded by a clerk as soon as possible after the patient enters the hospital: these include name, address, date of birth, next of kin and consultant responsible.

There should follow a thorough record of the patient's complaints and an appraisal of their current clinical state made by the house officer, the most junior of the team of doctors that is to care for the patient during his admission: this is called the 'clerking' and it constitutes a most important and valuable record, both because it is done at a most crucial time in a patient's care, especially in the case of emergency admissions, and because custom dictates that it is carried out with a great degree of thoroughness and in a certain order. Thus, this record should allow readers, if it has been done properly, to have a full understanding of the patient's clinical state at that time, if they can 'read' the traditional system of layout and abbreviation which medical students are taught to use.

In the next section an example with a glossary is presented to help 'translate' records. It is possible to attempt this because house doctors throughout the UK are taught to use much the same system: the clarity and thoroughness of their clerkings of patients is one of the chief ways in which a consultant, who is responsible for their training, will assess the competence of the house officer, so the junior will wish to make his records comprehensible and useful to the consultant. In contrast to general practice notes, therefore, the adequacy of the hospital records is some indication of the quality of care patients have received: a junior doctor who is neglectful or overworked will keep less thorough and comprehensible records, and if his seniors, the registrar or consultant, are also neglectful, this failure will not be corrected.

After the house officer has thus recorded the admission of the patient to the hospital, the doctor who is immediately responsible for supervising the house officer's work may write in the notes, usually using the same format, but more briefly. Thus, frequently in hospital records the same clinical findings are recorded again under the same date, in a different handwriting, which may be that of a senior house officer or a registrar.

There follows a sequential series of entries by one or other of the team members, the frequency of which is, in general, a reflection of how acutely ill the patient is: in an intensive care unit, the house officer or more senior colleagues may write in the notes several times a day, recording the hour at which they have assessed the patient; as well as the team of doctors responsible for the patient's care, other consultants whose opinion has been sought may write in the notes. On the other hand, the medical records kept in a long-stay ward, in a psychiatric hospital for example, may be written in only a few times a year.

Next will be filed the results of investigations carried out during that hospital admission, which are generally arrayed by sticking them in date sequence on a card, each card representing a different department – histology (the microscopic examination of tissues), biochemistry (blood levels of hormones and drugs, and of compounds the levels of which are indices of the function of the liver and kidneys), hematology (the characteristics of the cells in the blood), or X-ray. If electrocardiograms have been done these too should be arranged, in a pattern which enables the trace to be interpreted, and kept in the notes.

If an operation is performed while a patient is in hospital, this will be recorded by the house officer, but there will also be a separate sheet which has been filled in immediately after the operation by the surgeon and the anesthetist.

The admission notes are ended by the house officer, who should write a list of the drugs which a patient has been given to take at home. There will also be a typed discharge summary, which is usually written to the patient's GP by the registrar or the consultant; this document is often not written until several weeks or even months after the patient has been sent home.

In between hospital admission notes, but occasionally filed separately, there will be handwritten notes made in the out-patient clinic by the consultant, registrar or senior house officer (SHO) who has seen the patient in the clinic; also there will usually be a letter sent to the GP after each clinic visit, and copies of these letters will be kept in sequence in the patient's hospital notes.

Hospital records will contain many records kept by nurses, which may be of medico-legal importance: chief among these is the patient's 'Kardex' record: this is a system of notes kept in a single folder in the sister's office on the ward, each patient having a card which is folded into a specially designed folder which allows the patients' names to be displayed in the same sequence as their beds are arranged on the ward. When the patient leaves the hospital, the card is removed and kept in the patient's hospital records folder. The nursing staff make an entry in the Kardex for each patient every day, noting the basic observations (temperature, pulse rate and blood pressure) and commenting briefly on the patient's progress.

Also filed with the nursing records will be all the charts which have been kept at the end of the patient's bed during the admission: these will include a chart of recordings made of the patient's temperature, pulse rate and blood pressure, which may be measured hourly, four-hourly or daily, according to how acutely ill the patient is. There may also be fluid balance charts which record the volumes of fluid which the patient has been given, orally or intravenously, and the volumes they have excreted.

With these charts will be found a 'treatment card', a new one of which is made out for each hospital admission: this is kept by the patient's bed, and is written on by one of the doctors whenever he wishes to prescribe a drug; the name of the drug should be written clearly, with instructions as to dose and frequency and route of administration, with the doctor's signature; then the nurse in charge of the ward, whenever she administers the drug, will sign the card again in a column which gives the date and time.

Most patients require the services of some other professional workers, whether they be social workers, physiotherapists or occupational therapists, while they are in hospital. However, the notes of their activities kept by these other professionals are not usually assembled to be kept with the other records in the patient's hospital record folder, for reasons that are historical rather than logical.

FORM AND ABBREVIATION IN MEDICAL RECORDS

Medicine has its own language: in the past, when the knowledge and skill of physicians and surgeons were relatively limited, the dignity of their profession was enhanced and their distance above the patient increased by the use of terms the meaning of which was apparent only to their fellow trained doctors. To what extent that is no longer true today is a moot point.

However, there are other important factors as well as the plethora of 'medical' words – many derived from Latin and Greek – which are still used in notes and make them difficult to understand. NHS doctors making records, whether GPs in the community or junior doctors in hospitals, often work in situations of pressure in which it is inappropriate to spend a high proportion of time in writing: this leads not only to poor legibility,[16] but also to the proliferation of a large number of abbreviations. In using these abbreviations, doctors assume that their colleagues will be able to interpret them, and they sacrifice the possibility of non-doctors being able to understand. This follows from the prevailing attitude to records throughout the medical profession, which is that they are written for the benefit of other doctors who may be treating the same patient in future; they are certainly not written for the patient to be able to understand them.

In recent decades, advances in diagnostic methods and in treatment have led to a vast proliferation of specialities and of kinds of data that can be assembled about a particular patient; these are often presented using new codes and new words, which are hard to understand unless you have a thorough knowledge of the particular techniques.

To read medical records, one needs a medical dictionary which is up-to-date. Even if the technical words are translated, however, there remains the problem of abbreviations. In the section which follows, one may see what a house surgeon might typically write in the notes when clerking a previously fit woman with acute appendicitis; the purpose is to give an example, not only of commonly used abbreviations, but also of the way in which a doctor's notes are generally laid out and organised in a certain sequence.[17]

---

16 In *Prendergast* v *Sam & Dee Ltd* [1989] 1 Med LR 36, MLC 0018, CA, a GP was held 25% liable for injury caused when the pharmacist (held 75% liable) misread his prescription and dispensed Daonil instead of Amoxil.
17 Further hieroglyphs may be found set out in Appendix IV.

FORM AND ABBREVIATION IN HOSPITAL RECORDS
AN ANNOTATED EXAMPLE

	DATE	NAME
	TIME	ADDRESS
		DATE OF BIRTH

Complains of. . . C.O. Abdominal pain   3 days
(Presenting complaint)
(duration)

History of presenting H.P.C. Off food with central abdo. pain
  complaint 3 days ago, then pain moved to
R.I.F. = right lower quadrant R.I.F., and became more severe
  of the abdomen with nausea and anorexia. Some
1/52 = 1 week diarrhoea, 1/52
(1/12 = 1 month,
  1/7 = 1 day)

Previous medical history P.M.H. Tonsillectomy age 12

Previous obstetric history P.O.H. P 1 + 1 (T.O.P. 1980)
P = Parity (number of
  pregnancies). Figures
  represent no. of births
  followed by no. of
  miscarriages or abortions
  (= T.O.P.s)
L.S.C.S. = cesarean section L.S.C.S. (elective) 1983 for
  pre-eclampsia

Social history S.H. Mother and part-time worker
  Non-smoker
  Drinks socially

Family history F.H. Mother A & W, age 67
A & W = alive and well Father died age 68 Ca. lung
Ca. = cancer 2 sibs A & W
  Daughter aged 4 well

Systematic enquiry S.E.
Gastro-intestinal system G.I.T. Appetite normal until 3 days ago
  (tract)
B.O. = bowels open B.O. regular
° Diarrhoea = no diarrhoea ° Diarrhoea previous few months
° Melaena = no blood in ° Melaena
  motions that is black
P.R. = per rectum ° Fresh blood P.R.
Weight = weight constant Weight →

Genito-urinary tract G.U. ° Haematuria
Dysuria = pain on urinating ° Dysuria
Nocturia = arising from sleep to ° Frequency
  urinate ° Nocturia

Gynaecological Gynae. K 5/27–32
K = menstrual cycle –
  no. of days of bleeding
  no. of days of whole cycle

Cardiovascular system C.V.S. ° Palpitations
S.O.B.O.E = short of breath ° S.O.B.O.E.
  on exertion

	DATE TIME	NAME ADDRESS DATE OF BIRTH

Orthopnoea = short of breath
  on lying flat ° Orthopnoea

P.N.D = paroxysmal nocturnal
  dyspnoea (attacks of waking up
  very breathless) ° P.N.D.

Oedema = swelling with fluid
  esp. of ankles ° Oedema

Respiratory system   R.S.   ° Cough

° Haemoptysis = coughing
  blood ° Haemoptysis
                      ° Wheezing

Neurological system   Neuro.   ° Headaches – occasional
                      ° Fits

L.O.C. = episode of loss of
  consciousness ° L.O.C.

Vision ✔ = no problem with visions   Vision ✔
                      Hearing ✔

List of regular medication   *Drugs*   nil

List of drugs to which the   *Allergy*   Penicillin
  patient thinks she is allergic

ON EXAMINATION   O/E

General description   Distressed

Not anaemic, cyanosed or
  jaundiced °An, °Cy, °J

No clubbing (deformity of nails)   ° CI

No palpable lymph nodes   ° L.N.s
                      Temp 37.8°C

Cardiovascular system   C.V.S.

Pulse rate and rhythm   p 90 reg.

Blood pressure (arterial)   B.P. 120/70

J.V.P. = venous pressure
  estimated by observing
  jugular vein J.V.P. →

H.S. = heart sounds (diagram
  used as visual representation
  of the sounds) H.S.

(R)=(L) = findings same on both
  sides, ie normal ° Oedema
                      Pulses in fee (R)=(L)

Respiratory system   R.S.

T⊙ = trachea in centre
  (normal) T⊙

                      Expansion (R)=(L)

P.N. = findings on percussion of
  chest P.N. resonant (R)=(L)

B.S. = breath sounds, heard
  with stethoscope. (Added
  sounds may be crackles B.S. vesicular, nil added
  (= creps, crepitations)
  or wheezes)

	DATE	NAME
	TIME	ADDRESS
		DATE OF BIRTH

Abdominal examination   Abdo.   L.S.K.K.°

L.S.K.K.° = liver, spleen and
   kidneys no. palpable (ie not
   enlarged)

° Masses = no lumps in abdomen   ° Masses

tender, with
guarding & rebound

Guarding = reflex muscle spasm

Rebound = pain on removal of
   pressure

B.S. = bowel sounds   B.S. ✔

P.R. = rectal examination   P.R.   N.A.D.

N.A.D. = nothing abnormal
   detected

P.V. = per vaginam   P.V.
   examination of the pelvis   Uterus N/S A/V

N/S = normal size (if abnormal,   Adnexae N.A.D.
   uterine size is often expressed as
   equivalent of a certain gestational
   age in pregnancy, eg 14/40   Cervix N.A.D.
   meaning the same as the size   V/V – N.A.D.
   of a normal pregnant uterus at
   14 weeks after the last period
   began)

A/V = anteverted (alternative
   uterine positions are axial or retroverted)

V/V = vulva and vagina

Adnexae = areas at either side of uterus

Central nervous system   C.N.S.

Examination (this part of the
   examination is often highly   Cranial nerves
   abbreviated or omitted)

P.E.R.L.A. = pupils are equal   P.E.R.L.A.
   and react to light and
   accommodation

Fundi = contents of the eyeballs   Fundi N.A.D.
   are seen by the
   ophthalmoscope

Motor = examination of the   Motor   Power
   motor aspect of the nervous   Tone   (R)=(L)
   system in each limb   Co-ordination N.A.D.
                                       Reflexes

Sensory = examination of the   Sensory   Pain
   different modalities of   Light touch (R)=(L)
   sensation in the limbs and   Temperature N.A.D.
   trunk   Position sense
                                       Vibration

	DATE	NAME
	TIME	ADDRESS
		DATE OF BIRTH

SUMMARY	ANALYSIS	Previously fit mother aged – years with acute abdominal pain and fever

Δ = diagnosis		Δ appendicitis
N.B.M. = nil by mouth	Plan	N.B.M.
hourly obs. = instructions to nursing staff to record pulse, temp. and b.p. every hour		hourly obs.

| I.V.I. = intravenous drip | I.V.I. | N. saline 1L in 6 hours |
| N. saline = salt solution of similar concentration to that of plasma. (Other fluids are Dextrose saline, or 5% dextrose, which contain a sugar for energy) | | |

F.B.C. = full blood count (haematology)	F.B.C.	
U&E = urea and electrolytes (biochemistry)	U&E	
L.F.T. = liver function tests (biochemistry)	L.F.T.s	

Abbreviations and hieroglyphs

For a list of common abbreviations and hieroglyphs, see Appendix IV.

Chapter 9

Experts

I suspect that in this field of litigation it is not uncommon for the forensic experts to take relatively extreme positions in the hope of securing an outcome for the party by whom they are instructed (*per* Thorpe LJ in *Lakey* v *Merton, Sutton and Wandsworth Health Authority* [1999] Lloyd's Rep Med 119, [1999] MLC 0075).

For whatever reason, and whether consciously or unconsciously, the fact is that expert witnesses instructed on behalf of parties to litigation often tend ... to espouse the cause of those instructing them to a greater or lesser extent, on occasion becoming more partisan than the parties (*Abbey National Mortgages plc* v *Key Surveyors Nationwide Ltd* [1996] 1 WLR 1534 at 1542 *per* Lord Bingham giving the judgment of the court – quoted by Lord Woolf in *Access to Justice* Chapter 13, para 26).

THE EXPERT IS THE BACKBONE OF THE MEDICAL NEGLIGENCE ACTION

Expert evidence is needed to prove liability and causation. Very often causation requires a different specialty from liability. An expert for GP liability, for example, will never be able to give evidence on causation. An expert for A&E liability is unlikely to have the specialism necessary for speaking to causation. An expert who can speak on the management of a disease may well not be the appropriate person to speak on the likely outcome had the management been different. In a claim for obstetric injury to the fetus, the obstetrician is never used to prove causation, ie to establish that appropriate obstetric management would have avoided the injury. That is left to a neuro-pediatrican or neonatologist. On the other hand, in, for example, a claim for inadequate orthopedic management, the orthopedic consultant may be able to speak to both liability and causation.

Experts will also be needed on quantum, as for any personal injury action.

SELECTING AN EXPERT

This is not the problem it used to be. The lawyers on both sides will be experienced in the field. They will by now have their own lists of experts, many of whom they will know personally. And they will know where to seek help if stuck for an expert.[1] Because experts are so vital to a claim, one of the distinguishing characteristics of the experienced lawyer is that he will home in on precisely the right specialty and the right man within that specialty. He will study the CV of the proposed expert to ensure that he can be authoritative on the particular issue that falls to be decided and that he will not be outgunned by some world authority found by the defendants (eg not every orthopedic consultant is an expert on hand surgery; not every pediatrician is an expert on meningitis; not every anesthetist is expert on anaphylactic reactions). He may also want an expert who constitutes a balance between hands-on experience and academic stature.[2] He will do his best to instruct an expert who will not waver either in the months leading up to trial or under cross-examination. Defendants, with all the resources of the NHS Litigation Authority at their disposal, are notorious for identifying, and producing, the top expert for the precise matter in issue (a perfectly proper procedure, of course). It is at that point one glances at the claimant's expert who has brought the case thus far to see if he is showing any sign of strain.[3]

JUDICIAL INTERVENTION

It is not always easy to get permission from the court for all the necessary experts. The combination of the current governmental obsession with cutting costs and with pre-trial judicial intervention can result in courts, at the interlocutory stages, denying the claimant the ability to prepare his case properly. Some courts are sensible about it, either because they are one of the few that understand how a medical negligence action needs to be prepared (most have had little experience of that), or because they have the good sense to trust the lawyers for the claimant. After all, those lawyers would not be allowed to act in any legal aid medical negligence cases if they had not proved themselves expert in the field and obtained entry to one of the accredited panels. It is a paradox to create an expert panel and then tell judges, many of them less experienced than the lawyers, to supervise their work. Some judges still impose impossible deadlines and refuse apparently reasonable requests for necessary experts. The Court of Appeal is unlikely to interfere, as it prefers to leave all such decisions up to the lower courts, particularly if there has already been one hearing (although, when it does interfere, it almost always

---

1   An extensive database of medical experts is kept by Action against Medical Accidents (AvMA).
2   In *Hutton* v *East Dyfed Health Authority* [1998] Lloyds Rep Med 335, Bell J criticised the claimant's presentation of specialist evidence to assess the management of a generalist (at 349, 352). See also the Chinese herbalist case of *Shakoor* v *Situ* [2000] 4 All ER 181, where the claimant did not call an expert in Chinese medicine (see Chapter 16 under 'Alternative medicine').
3   It is a general rule that there is no property in a witness. This is why a party can see to interview and call the other side's witness, if he wishes. In *Lilly Icos LLC* v *Pfizer Ltd* (17 August 2000, unreported), Ch D, Jacob J held that an alleged contract with a party under which an expert was said to have bound himself not to act for the other party was unenforceable as contrary to public policy.

demonstrates a good understanding of the particular requirements of a medical negligence suit). Although one has to deplore the by now almost ubiquitous unfocussed resort to a human rights plea in virtually every lawsuit, there are appropriate contexts for such a plea, and where decisions of the lower court prevent the necessary preparation of the patient's case, the right to fair trial can reasonably be invoked (see the next section and the section on Article 6 in Chapter 27).

CUTTING DOWN ON EXPERTS

Woolf was critical of the over-use and the high expense of experts. Now, a basic ploy of the courts is to allow, even in high value cases, only one expert for each specialty. This means, for example, that the outcome of an obstetric claim for perinatal brain damage worth well over £1m will be even more of a lottery than it has been in recent years, when the norm was two experts on liability and two, or even three, on causation. The judge will have to choose, ie to prefer, one of only two experts. One does not need to have studied the writings of the American school of realist jurisprudence to understand how this works. The reports of medical negligence cases (particularly those in *Medical Litigation*, as judicial comment on experts are highlighted there) are full of examples of judges 'preferring' the evidence of one expert to that of another. Sometimes detailed reasons are given; sometimes no more is said than that the witness did not impress the judge. But, whatever is said, it is never any more than an educated guess on the part of the judge, a dollop of intuition with a dash of analysis. If the judge has two experts each side on the main issue, he will have a much wider platform on which to reach his conclusions and the fact that one of the experts irritates him will not necessarily result in that party losing the case.

In *Aleyan* v *Northwick Park NHS Trust* [1999] MLC 0150, Buckley J noted that the High Court Masters appeared to have agreed that 'wholly exceptional circumstances are needed in medical negligence situations' before more than one expert in the same discipline would be permitted. Although he was not convinced that in this particular case a second expert was needed, he said that he was not attracted to the words 'wholly exceptional circumstances' and would prefer to say that good reason should be shown why the justice of the case demanded another expert.

ES v *Chesterfield and North Derbyshire Royal NHS Trust* MLC 1051, [2004] Lloyds Rep Med 90, CA was a claim for cerebral palsy as a result of perinatal asphyxia – a fairly common claim, unfortunately. A junior doctor (by then a consultant) and a consultant were in the frame, both obstetricians. The claimant wanted two obstetric experts on the basis that it would not be a level playing field if their single expert was faced not only with a single independent expert for the defence but also with two consultants who would naturally be giving their opinions on the course followed even though they were, strictly speaking, witnesses of fact. The district judge took the unimaginative view, but the appeal succeeded. The court said the case was very important, complex and of high value. The parties would not be on an equal footing if the order of the district judge prevailed. The court said one could not isolate the evidence of the two hospital doctors from the vital question concerning appropriate professional standards. Not only was it not disproportionate to allow the claimant to call two obstetric experts; it was actually necessary for the achievement of justice.

The Woolf report identified a satellite industry of allegedly unnecessary 'experts', as a result of which one is unlikely to be allowed, *inter alios*, an employment expert or a forensic accountant, unless, in the case of the first, one needs evidence about what work an injured person might still be able to find and perform, and, in the second case, one can show that genuine expert accounting evidence is needed, eg to work out the likely profits and losses of a business. One will not be permitted an employment expert where the only issue of what work the claimant could have done can be established by a combination of judicial good sense and the New Earnings Survey. One will not be permitted an accountant merely to prepare a schedule, even though what she produces will be far clearer and more useful to the court than the efforts of a lawyer, and, if the right accountant is selected, hardly more expensive.[4] Still, this sort of reduction of experts is not wholly objectionable, provided it is not extended in a flush of enthusiasm to more necessary specialities.[5] And, taken with a judicious use of the opportunities for a joint expert report, laudable savings in costs can be achieved.

The CPR

The CPR provides by r 35.4 that all expert evidence, written or oral, requires the court's permission, and that the specialty and, if possible, the name of the desired expert should be identified.[6] This should be read with r 32.1, which gives the court an overriding and comprehensive power with regard to evidence generally. The court may give directions as to the issues on which it requires evidence, the nature of that evidence and its form of presentation. It may also exclude evidence which would otherwise be admissible (and may limit cross-examination).

JOINT EXPERT

As the quotations from the Court of Appeal at the top of this chapter acknowledge, and as acknowledged by Lord Woolf, it is sad but true that an expert will usually trim his report to the needs of those who instruct him. Occasionally an expert will give a completely impartial view, but, by and large, whether reporting on liability, causation or quantum, the report will lean slightly, or even heavily, to the side of the paymasters. Sometimes, especially with liability reports, one suspects lack of good faith. For example, defendants seem able to find experts, particularly in the field of obstetrics and GP practice, to write a report exonerating even

---

4   Actually, such work by an accountant should not be considered expert evidence, but merely a subcontracting of the work to an outside agent.

5   McKinnon J would not allow the usual cost of living expert in an unplanned pregnancy claim (*Nwoko* v *Guy's and St Thomas' NHS Trust* (8 December 1998, unreported)).

6   The court makes a clear distinction these days between permission to put in an expert report and permission to call its maker.

obvious substandard management – some time after service of which they admit liability, or at least make a substantial offer of settlement. One can feel sure that if the patient had instructed those defence experts, their report would have been very different. Patients' lawyers, too, need to beware of the expert who may be giving them a case which can in due course be demolished without much difficulty by the defendants' expert. Such an expert may, for example, be keen for his own reasons to show a centre of excellence that they have got this one wrong, or he may be too interested in the fee.

Quantum experts also seem to suffer from the same disease. Why do the initial reports of the rehabilitation costs consultant and of the architect, and most of the other specialisms, recommend more support for the injured party when instructed by the claimant and less when instructed by the defence? One never sees it the other way round, though one suspects that if the defence expert had been instructed by the claimant, he or she would have found the need, without any impropriety, for considerably more care or higher accommodation costs. The answer is that, though not acting improperly, the expert is trying to get the most, or recommend the least, depending on whom they act for. There is almost always a range of options that can be recommended and so each goes for the option that will suit his client best. It is interesting how often these experts can reach a consensus when they meet their opposite number!

With this in mind, it is easy to support the movement toward joint reports, as long as it does not get to the point where we have trial by expert instead of by the judge. Support can usually be given to joint reports on almost all quantum issues. It should not be hard to find a quantum expert acceptable to both sides,[7] and there is no reason to think that such an expert would be unconsciously motivated in favour of one side or the other. One welcome result of going for a joint report is that one does not then have to go through the time-consuming business of comparing the reports in every detail, getting your expert's comments on their report, arranging a meeting between the experts, conferring with your expert on what concessions to make on what heads of claim (Do we really need three straps a year for the hoist or will two do? Can we concede a less expensive car? Shall we split the hours of care/physio/speech therapy for the sake of agreement? etc), assessing the chances of establishing any disputed contentions, and coming to a bottom line for the purpose of settlement. The parties simply (one hopes) accept what the various joint reports recommend.

The same sort of unconscious partiality affects causation experts, assisted sometimes by pressure from the lawyers. There is more often than not scope for a difference of opinion on the usually speculative question whether, for example, earlier treatment would have avoided the injury or death. If instructed by the defence, an expert is likely to form the view that earlier treatment would have made no difference. If instructed for the patient his view might well have been different. For this reason there is also some argument for moving carefully towards

---

7   However, this writer's first effort in that direction was singularly unsuccessful. I offered a well known defence firm four rehabilitation costs consultants. They refused them all and suggested one of their own choosing, who was unknown to me!

joint reports on causation, always dependent on agreement between the parties on such a course and on the choice of expert. An expert instructed by one party without objection by the other party does not thereby become a joint expert (*Carlson* v *Townsend* [2001] 3 All ER 663).[8]

A working party has looked at the practicalities of instructing joint experts. The Clinical Disputes Forum have reported as follows:

> A second major innovation of Part 35 of the CPR was the idea of the single joint expert (SJE). Instead of each party instructing its own experts, 35.7 set out the Court's power to direct that evidence on an issue be given by one expert only, instructed by all the parties. In clinical disputes this was an entirely novel idea. It was not envisaged that single joint experts would often be instructed in relation to breach of duty although there have been one or two examples. In some of the less controversial aspects of causation the idea was less controversial; the most productive area for the single joint expert was in quantum. The Clinical Disputes Forum (CDF) has not expressed a view on the issue of single joint experts and whether they should be used at all in clinical litigation; there would probably be a wide divergence of views within the forum. The CDF was nevertheless aware of the use and success of such experts, particularly in relation to quantum issues, and set up a second working party to provide guidance for SJEs and those who instruct them. The working party began to meet in the spring of 2001 and produced its draft guidelines later the same year.

The new Protocol for the Instruction of Experts from the Civil Justice Council incorporates much of the work of the Clinical Disputes Forum in this as in other contexts.

Liability and causation

However, the courts fortunately recognise that we are not ready for joint reports on liability in medical negligence cases. The issues are too vital and too sensitive. Experts are often associated with giving evidence for one side rather than for the other. It is most unlikely that the parties would ever agree on nomination of a joint expert. The patient would want an expert known to be sympathetic to claims, ie one who, though fair, would examine every aspect of the potential claim and not shrink from identifying aspects of substandard management; the defendants would not want such an expert. After all, it took years of striving by patients' lawyers before the 'closing ranks' syndrome was overcome, and even now it is only overcome by the careful selection of experts for the claimant.

The same goes for most issues on causation. If the expert proposed by the defence is not someone who is known to the patients' lawyers to be both zealous and impartial, he will not be acceptable. Even the analysis of what might be a 'scientific' issue (eg the progress of a disease if the management had been different or the avoidance of a damaging period of hypoxia) can be influenced by a subconscious bias against (or, I suppose, in favour of) such claims.

Occasionally, a judge who does not understand medical negligence claims will make a wholly unreasonable order which the Court of Appeal roundly condemns. For example, in *Oxley* v *Penwarden* [2000] MLC 0250;

---

8   This case also makes the point that a medical report is privileged from disclosure and that the pre-action protocol for personal injury claims has not affected that privilege.

[2001] Lloyds Rep Med 347, Judge Overend, contrary to the wishes of both parties, ordered a joint report on a highly contentious, fundamental issue of causation involving a disputed allegation that proper treatment would have avoided a leg amputation. He even stated that he could see no reason why medical negligence claims should be treated in any way differently from other claims. Fortunately, the Court of Appeal understood what was necessary in such a context. Mantell LJ, having drawn attention to the note attached to r 35.7 of the CPR which stated that 'there is no presumption in favour of the appointment of a single joint expert', said:

> This was eminently a case where it was necessary for the parties to have the opportunity of investigating causation through an expert of their own choice and, further, to have the opportunity of calling that evidence before the court. It is inevitable in a case of this class that parties will find the greatest difficulty in agreeing on the appointment of a single expert. The burden would then be cast upon the court and would, in turn, lead to the judge selecting an expert, if there be more than one school of thought on this issue, from one particular school of thought and that would effectively decide an essential question in the case without the opportunity for challenge.

And Kennedy LJ said:

> We have been helpfully reminded this morning that the practice the parties wished the judge to follow in this particular case was not only one which, on the face of it, would appear to be appropriate in the circumstances of this case but was also in line with what had clearly been envisaged when the Access to Justice proposals were brought into existence and is shown to be in line with the practice which is adopted by the Masters in this building. In my judgment, it is a proper practice and should have been followed here.[9]

CPR and the joint expert

CPR 35.7, introducing the concept of the court-directed joint expert, gives the court power to direct a joint report on disputed issues and, if the parties who wish to submit evidence on those issues (termed 'the instructing parties') cannot agree on a nomination, to make one itself or make other arrangements for a nomination. The court will not insist on joint instructions, but if instructions are given separately to the joint expert by the instructing parties they must be disclosed (r 35.8).

The notes to r 35.7 say that the parties can agree that the joint report will not after all be put in evidence. If it is accepted, the instructing parties, say the notes to r 35.7, can examine him in chief. But what if one only of them disagrees with the report? Justice demands that a party who has not been allowed to call his own expert on an issue can cross-examine a joint expert imposed by the court – see the next paragraph. Note also r 35.6, which provides that a party may put written questions about his report to an expert, whether joint or not (once only, within 28 days of the report, and for the purpose of clarifying the report – unless court or the other party permits otherwise). In *Mutch v Allen* [2001] PIQR P364, CA,

---

9   See also *Simms* v *Birmingham Health Authority* [2001] Lloyds Rep Med 382, where Curtis J reversed a similarly inappropriate order by a district judge.

the court said that points not included in the report could be ventilated by this procedure if within the expert's expertise, and that questioning a party's expert in this way rendered him akin to a court expert.

Challenging a report from a joint expert

Subject to financial considerations, a single expert joint report can be challenged even if it was obtained by consent. The challenge may have to be made first by directing questions to the expert pre-trial; but one may then get permission to obtain one's own report, and in suitable (ie high value) cases, and after a meeting of the experts, one may get permission to call the new expert. Careful, and helpful, treatment of the position may be found in Lord Woolf's judgment in *Daniels* v *Walker* [2000] 1 WLR 1382, CA. In that case, the defendants wanted to instruct a care expert because they thought that the joint expert had estimated for far too much care in the joint report that they had agreed should be obtained. The other side maintained that the defendants were effectively bound by it. Lord Woolf, emphasising that the overriding objective was to deal with cases justly, disagreed. He said that, although in small value cases the objecting party might have to be restricted to asking the joint expert questions, in cases of substantial value it might well be appropriate to permit the objecting party to put his own report in evidence, provided that the issues could not be resolved simply by the experts' meeting. It is not entirely clear to what extent Lord Woolf's observations in *Peet* v *Mid-Kent Healthcare Trust* [2002] 1 WLR 210 suggesting that the evidence of the joint expert should not normally be subject to cross-examination, are consistent with the view he expressed in *Daniels* v *Walker*. *Peet* also tells us that it is not acceptable for one party, without the consent of the other(s), to have access to the single joint expert. In *Popek* v *Natwest* [2002] EWCA Civ 42 the Court of Appeal said that it was not generally open to parties to cross-examine the single joint expert, particularly where written questions had been asked and answered after the expert's report was made. In *Yorke* v *Katra* [2003] EWCA Civ 867 the Court of Appeal said that there was no rule that a party should be bound by the instruction given to a joint expert by the other side.

In *Cosgrove* v *Pattison* (2001) Times, 13 February, Neuberger J allowed a party to call a further expert in a boundary dispute following a report of a joint expert. He said relevant factors on such an application were the nature, number and importance of the relevant issues, the amount at stake, the reasons for seeking another expert, the effect on the timetable and the trial process, and the overall justice of the matter as between the parties.

DISCUSSIONS

By r 35.12, the court may direct experts' discussions for identifying relevant issues and, if possible, reaching agreement, and may direct a written report of the meeting identifying what was and what was not agreed, and why. The content of the discussion between the experts is not disclosable without agreement (ie is privileged), and – which is surely very odd – any agreement by the experts does not bind a party unless he agrees. Presumably, this means that even an expert's signed agreement to certain issues cannot be put to him at the trial without the consent of the party who instructed him. Under the old rules, meetings between experts were 'without prejudice', but one would have hoped for something more forceful under the new rules. In a pre-Woolf case, *Robin Ellis Ltd* v *Malwright Ltd* (1 February 1999, *Supreme Court Practice News* Issue 2/99 p 6), Judge Bowsher QC held that the discussions between the experts were privileged but their joint statement, though not binding on the parties, was not privileged (see also the discussion on the immunity of expert witnesses below). This would also seem to have been the firm view of Chadwick LJ in *Stanton* v *Callaghan* [1999] 2 WLR 745 at 756A, CA.[10]

It was originally intended that lawyers should not be present at these discussions. It was thought that experts could be left to come to a proper agreement or disagreement on the issue without one expert being overborne by an opposing senior, and without lawyers poking their noses in, trying to get their man to say what they needed him to say and not to say – even to unsay – what they did not want him to say, the whole degenerating into a long wrangle at substantially increased cost. Experience (including this writer's) showed in time that this was only a pious hope. Too many cases were handed away behind the patient's back by private agreement between the experts. The Clinical Disputes Forum proposed that lawyers should be present at experts' meetings (unless agreed or ordered otherwise) but not normally intervening, save to answer questions put to them by the experts or to advise them on the law. An explanation for this view is to be found in *Clinical Risk* July 2000, p 149. The case of *Hubbard* (below) shows that lawyers are not normally expected to be present at experts' meetings.[11] Whatever the outcome, it is clear that the provisions, now followed in virtually every case, for getting experts to discuss the relevant issues before trial and produce a joint report, and the facility to ask experts questions about their reports, is a substantial aid to narrowing the issues and so saving costs and leading to a trial that concentrates on what are really the relevant disputes. Appendix II contains the guidance for experts' discussions drafted by the Clinical Disputes Forum, as well as the new Protocol for the Instruction of

---

10 In the soap opera of *Unilever plc* v *Procter & Gamble Co* [2000] 1 WLR 2436, the Court of Appeal struck out an action that was based on what had allegedly been said at a 'without prejudice' meeting. For a case where the Court of Appeal held that a party had waived his right to rely on the privilege attaching to 'without prejudice' meetings by seeking to base later contentions on what had been said at such meetings, see *Somatra Ltd* v *Sinclair Roche & Temperley* [2000] 1 WLR 2453, CA.

11 In *Woodall* v *BUPA Hospitals Ltd*, MLC 0340 Judge Hindley QC, sitting as a High Court judge, allowed an appeal by which he gave permission for lawyers to attend a complex series of expert meetings in a relatively high value case. He said: 'It seems to me that in a complex case such as this involving different specialities it is extremely important for all of the lawyers concerned to have an understanding as to why measures of agreement have been achieved and, more importantly, why there has not been agreement on certain issues, so that the lawyers themselves have an opportunity of considering the cogency of arguments, because only on that basis can they properly advise their clients in terms of either narrowing issues or compromising the case.' He added that the costs of the lawyers' attendance would not be disproportionate to the issues and values of the particular claim.

Experts from the Civil Justice Council which incorporates much of the work of the Clinical Disputes Forum in this as in other contexts.

In *Hubbard* v *Lambeth Southwark and Lewisham Health Authority* MLC 0503, [2002] Lloyds Rep Med 8 claimants unsuccessfully objected to a meeting of experts on the highly original basis that their own experts, overawed by the high standing of the defence expert, would feel unable to contradict him. The Court of Appeal, pointing out that the claimants' experts had already committed their views to paper in the knowledge that they might have to go to court to support those views, dismissed the argument, adding that there was no issue under Article 6 of the Convention. The court also said that lawyers would not normally attend such a meeting: a well drafted agenda and a recording would suffice.[12]

Agendas

Tight guidelines are proposed for agendas. Not too tight, one hopes. Experience suggests to me that the provisions for not merely letting the experts have some sort of agenda, but for getting it circulated a month in advance of the meeting so that it can be agreed in meticulous detail by all relevant parties is likely, knowing lawyers, to end in the sort of to-ing and fro-ing that goes on with commercial agreements before the final draft is agreed, accompanied by a variety of coloured highlighters and conse- quent increased expense. I do not believe that such sanctification of the 'agenda' is necessary. All the experts need is some tolerably precise guid- ance as to what they should be looking at, and then let them get on with it. The agenda should not be seen as a means of cross-examining the other expert, and thus requiring many pages of subtly worded questions (and consequent increased expenditure of time and money). Unfortunately, these wise words, written for the last edition, have not been properly heeded, and so it is not unusual to see agendas containing 50 and more questions. The effect of this is confusion, often involving inconsistent responses at some point, each side always having tried, by questions sly and subtle, to winkle some useful response out of the oppos- ing expert, and then to put an interpretation on the answers that assists their cause.

WHAT THE COURT EXPECTS OF THE EXPERT

In *Loveday* v *Renton* [1990] 1 Med LR 117, Stuart-Smith LJ identified ten attributes of an expert which assist the court in assessing the weight to be attributed to his opinion: eminence; soundness of opinion; internal consistency and logic; precision and accuracy of thought; response to searching and informed cross-examination; ability to face up to logic and make concessions; flexibility of mind and willingness to modify opinions; freedom from bias; independence of thought; and demeanour. It is advis- able for the patient's advisers to explore thoroughly the profiles of all the

---

12 An Australian court declined to order a meeting of experts in a medical suit on the ground that there was no reason to think it would prove useful (*Spasovic* v *Sydney Adventist Hospital* MLC 0822).

experts, on both sides, to cover background, training experience, extent of any original research, qualifications, publications, and experience, if any, of court work, and for the purpose of evaluating comparative stature.

In *The Ikarian Reefer* [1993] 2 Lloyd's Rep 68 at 81 Cresswell J said that the expert witness had a duty to give independent evidence, uninfluenced as to form or content by the exigencies of litigation, and to provide objective unbiased opinion to the court on matters within his expertise, never assuming the role of advocate.

In *Sharpe* v *Southend Health Authority* [1997] 8 Med LR 299, Cresswell J said:

> An expert witness should make it clear in his or her report that, although the expert would have adopted a different approach or practice, he or she accepted that the approach or practice adopted by the defendant was in accordance with an approach or practice accepted as proper by a responsible body of practitioners skilled in the relevant fields.

And Thorpe LJ said in *Vernon* v *Bosley* [1997] 1 All ER 577, CA:

> The area of expertise in any case may be likened to a broad street with the plaintiff walking on one pavement and the defendant on the opposite one. Somehow the expert must be ever mindful of the need to walk straight down the middle of the road and to resist the temptation to join the party from whom his instructions come on the pavement.

The judge went on to wonder whether the practising clinician might find it easier to maintain that detachment than the professional expert witness who has retired and may spend his life doing medico-legal reports. In the same case, Stuart-Smith LJ said that the judge had not been assisted, as he should have been, by disinterested evidence from the medical professional witnesses who were allowed to range unchecked into almost every aspect of the case, and he added with a degree of prescience:

> In my opinion in this type of case in particular there is much to be said for the practice sometimes adopted in the Family Division of there being a psychiatrist appointed by the court. In the field of psychiatry it may be more difficult for those who have treated the plaintiff to approach the case with true objectivity. That was certainly the case here ... Certain it is that the case would have been much shorter and would have been kept in more manageable bounds. But at present the rules of court do not permit this course. Unless the parties agree on a psychiatrist – these parties never would have – the court has no power to make such an order.

THE CIVIL PROCEDURE RULES (CPR)

The Civil Procedure Rules now provide that it is the duty of an expert to help the court on the matters within his expertise, and that that duty overrides any obligation to the person from whom he has received instructions or by whom he is paid (r 35.3). But it should be noted that 'expert' is defined by r 35.2 as an expert 'who has been instructed to give or prepare evidence for the purpose of court proceedings'. A preliminary report for a potential claimant at the investigative stage is never intended for disclosure, and so should not be considered to have been prepared for the purpose of court proceedings. The notes to r 35.2 say that the duty 'clearly arises when he is instructed to prepare a report which might be used in the case'. But that is not what the rule says. It is a question of the 'purpose' of the report. Is it to be deemed to be 'for court proceedings' or for the enlightenment of the patient and his advisers? Surely the latter.[13] The notes do at least go on to recognise that a report may be prepared 'other than as evidence' and that, if so, it is not governed by the same considerations as regards duty to the court.

By r 35.10, the report must contain a declaration that the expert understands his duty to the court and has complied with that duty. The expert is also required to state the substance of all material instructions, written or oral, on the basis of which the report has been written, and if, but only if, the court has grounds for believing that his statement about those instructions is incomplete or inaccurate, it may order disclosure of the instructions (the rule specifically states that instructions are not privileged![14]). If an order for disclosure is made, the court may permit cross-examination on the instructions (35PD, para 3).[15]

Practice Direction 35 contains detailed instructions for the content of the report. We may note here that it is to be addressed to the court and not to the instructing party, and that where there is a range of possible opinion that range must be summarised and reasons given for the experts' preference. It should contain a summary of all relevant instructions received, both written and oral, and a statement of truth, and should comply with any approved experts' protocol. The Practice Direction is set out in Appendix I (as are the relevant parts of rule 35).

CODES OF GUIDANCE

Two codes were designed to guide experts, and those who instruct them, when working under the CPR. The first was produced by the Academy of Experts in 2000, while the other appeared in December 2001, having been prepared by a working party under the chairmanship of Sir Louis Blom-Cooper QC. This later code is published under the aegis of the Expert Witness Institute.

The Practice Direction accompanying Pt 35 of the CPR originally required, at paragraph 1.6, that an expert's report comply with the requirements of any approved experts' protocol. Neither code is or was an approved protocol. The inability of those involved to work together must have been in the mind of the Rules committee when it quietly dropped PD 1.6 in the spring of 2003. However, both codes offered guidance that many experts saw as sensible and worth following. They were, moreover, complementary to a considerable extent.

Recently the Civil Justice Council produced a very detailed authoritative code, which can be found at Appendix II. Its provisions should be

---

13 As the Code of Guidance, below, seems to acknowledge.
14 *Quaere*: can the Rules Committee abrogate settled law? Toulson J said not, in *General Mediterranean Holding SA* v *Patel* [2000] 1 WLR 272 (where the issue was legal professional privilege).
15 In *Morris* v *Bank of India* (15 November 2001), Ch D, Hart J ordered disclosure of an expert's instructions on the ground (under CPR, r 35.10) that the expert report was patently defective in failing to reveal all material instruction.

carefully studied, as it attempts to cover all aspects of expert involvement in litigation. The only point to note here in the main body of the text is that (under para 18.8) the parties' lawyers may only be present at discussions between experts if all the parties agree or the court so orders. If lawyers do attend, they should not normally intervene except to answer questions put to them by the experts or to advise about the law.

As stated earlier, there are also draft Guidelines from the Clinical Disputes Forum directed to discussions between experts. These can also be found at Appendix II.

WHAT THE LAWYER EXPECTS OF THE EXPERT

We have seen what the court requires of an expert. What does the patient's lawyer require? The following advice applied before all these new rules and guidances were produced, and is neither replaced nor contradicted by them. Let us look first at 'attitude'. An expert needs to appreciate that if he accepts instructions he must review the treatment the patient has received carefully, thoughtfully and in full detail. A quick skim through the records and a short declaration that he finds nothing to suggest negligence will not do. He must also beware of the attitude that he is doing the patient a favour in agreeing to act. Not so. He is providing a service, like all of us, and this means that he needs a degree of humility and not a touch of arrogance (the same applies to the lawyers in respect of the services they provide). He must understand that in agreeing to act he is committed to the case. This does not mean that he is required to support the claim. Not at all. He needs, as previously mentioned, to look carefully to see if the patient has received appropriate treatment and, if it appears that the treatment has been substandard, he needs to say so. But not otherwise. What is meant by 'committed' is that he will prepare his report in a reasonable time, say not more than three months, or he will pre-arrange a longer period with the solicitor. He will respond promptly to the inevitable further letters he will receive from the lawyers as the case progresses, and he will attend conferences at the lawyers' chambers or offices, ie he will not arrogantly require the lawyers to come to him. That is what is entailed in accepting instructions to act.

Many reports are inadequate. Some do not address the right questions or discover the right answers. One cannot do much about that, except determine to use tried and trusted experts. But many reports are deficient in their presentation, and that defect is amenable to correction (provided the expert is). First, it is essential to set out the *history* of the matter. History may be as per the records or as per the patient's account. The two are not always consistent. The expert needs to set out both, and he must draw attention to any important discrepancies without assuming either source to be right (unless there is good argument for so doing, in which case he must explain the argument). Some experts will set out the patient's statement more or less in full, which is not objectionable (although it is not actually telling you anything, as you naturally have a copy of the statement in your files). What is essential is that they set out the relevant extracts from the records, always giving the page number (an expert would be entitled to reject instructions if the records have not been properly sorted and paginated, and, one would hope, indexed). In other words, telling the story in their own words, however accurately, is not nearly as helpful as relating it through the records, and, where it can usefully be supplemented by the patient's account, bringing that in. The commentary can take the form of observations appended after each section of the records has been set out, or it can simply be by way of an opinion section at the end. Any significant reference in the opinion section to the history should clearly identify it; that is to say, it should not contain expressions such as 'action should have been taken when the patient first began to show signs of infection' or 'the GP should have become concerned when the headaches grew more serious'. Quite apart from the lack of precision about what action should in fact have been taken, this sort of writing normally has one searching in the earlier parts of the report in an attempt to discover what point in the medical history is being referred to. Conclusions need to be supported by appropriate reasoning and, where relevant, texts (texts published later than the incident will normally only help on causation, not on liability). Copies of relevant texts should be supplied and the significant passages highlighted.

An expert will be expected to write *clearly* and as succinctly as possible. The report will be expected to read consistently. The conclusions will be expected to tally with the observations and argument in the main body of the report. Correct English is preferable; eg 'would of' is unacceptable; so is 'if he had have been ...' (and they are expected to know that the past tense of *lead* is *led*).

It is worth emphasising that claimants' lawyers do not want to be given a case simply to please them, whether out of sympathy, or a natural inclination to oblige, or because that is perceived as the way to more cases and more fees. It is easy enough to offer a finding of substandard treatment at a distance and in writing; but it is quite another matter to defend it under cross-examination. It does the patient no favours if a case initially supported by the expert has to be discontinued at a later stage when he realises what he is up against.

JUDICIAL PREFERENCE OF EXPERTS

The law reports are full of medical (and other) cases decided simply on the ground of the judge 'preferring' one side's expert to the other. He may give detailed reasons for such preference, based on the evidence, or he may restrict himself to one or two general criticisms, or he may simply state that he prefers the evidence of X to Y. This last may be appealable (see Chapter 22). Full explanations of why he considers that an expert has got it wrong and another has got it right are infrequent. More common is the general denigration. Here are some examples.

In one of the Lloyd's Names cases (*Deeny v Gooda Walker Ltd* [1996] LRLR 183) Philips J said of an expert witness: 'He showed a keen appreciation of his own abilities and a contempt for any challenge to his views ... He adopted, throughout, a vigorously partisan approach and could scarcely ever be induced ... to make a concession, however clear it might be that a concession was due.' This was not a medical witness. Such harsh criticisms are not common. Even less common is it to find the judge in effect accusing an expert witness of lying, as he did in *Rhodes v West Surrey and North East Hampshire Health Authority* [1998] Lloyd's Rep

Med 246. More usually, the criticism is for being partisan, 'more of an advocate than an expert', and so forth. In *El-Morssy* v *Bristol and District Health Authority* [1996] 7 Med LR 232, Turner J spoke of a medical witness losing 'a proper sense of objectivity about the evidence which he was giving', and he expressed concern 'to find an expert, however distinguished a surgeon he may be, seeking to "rubbish" the sincerely held, and reasonably expressed, beliefs of those who happen to disagree with him'. And in the case that follows *El-Morssy* in the Medical Law Reports, *Wiszniewski* v *Central Manchester Health Authority* [1996] 7 Med LR 248, Thomas J said he regretted to find that a distinguished medical expert was reluctant to criticise any conduct on the part of the defendants, even where criticism was plainly merited. He said the witness was not as prepared to give straight answers to questions as, for example, in his fencing in cross-examination over what was normal practice. In *Murphy* v *Wirral Health Authority* [1996] 7 Med LR 99, Kay J described the evidence of the defence obstetric expert as 'less than satisfactory' and 'increasingly partial to the defendant'. In *Hutchinson* v *Leeds Health Authority* [2000] MLC 0287, Bennett J said of an expert hematologist: 'I find Dr R's evidence to be illogical and unsustainable ... Regrettably I did not have the same confidence in Dr R [as in the other experts]. I gained the impression of an expert witness who was clearly allied to Dr C [the impugned doctor] probably because of a shared speciality in medicine ...'

In just one issue of *Medical Litigation* (January 2000), judicial criticisms in no fewer than four different cases appear along the lines of 'spend an undue amount of their time in medico-legal work', 'not entirely detached in their analysis of the evidence', 'a degree of inflexibility which is not entirely becoming', 'unwillingness to make concessions', 'changes in the course of his evidence ... do not give me confidence', 'his evidence starts on a precarious basis', 'forensic considerations had overridden those of objectivity', 'serious allegations placed before the court on a casual and flimsy basis'. Clearly, experts need to bear in mind that anything other than a courteous, moderated and seemingly impartial response to questioning in court will damage their credibility.

Must a judge give reasons for his preference?

This important question, often vital to appeals, is not easy to answer definitively. It is fully treated in Chapter 22 in the section headed 'Must a judge give reasons for his conclusions?'

REFERENCE TO OTHER DOCUMENTS

Defendants' solicitors have frequently demanded to see statements of witnesses and any other documents referred to in the expert report. In *B* v *John Wyeth & Brother Ltd* [1992] 1 WLR 168, a judgment given within the benzodiazepine group litigation, the Court of Appeal said that waiver of privilege in respect of such material should not be inferred. Two months earlier (October 1991), Tucker J had reached a similar conclusion in *Booth* v *Warrington Health Authority* [1992] PIQR P137. But in *Clough* v *Tameside and Glossop Health Authority* [1998] 1 WLR 1478, Bracewell J, having held that service of a witness statement waives any privilege previously enjoyed by that statement, ordered disclosure by the defendants of a statement by a treating doctor referred to in an expert report served by the defendants. She said that a party should not be forced to meet an expert opinion based on documents he could not see. See also the report of an interlocutory appeal in *Forbes* v *Wandsworth Health Authority* in [1995] *Clinical Risk* (vol 1, p 153), where it was held that privilege was not lost merely because the pleadings had referred to receipt of a document in support of the argument on limitation. In *Bourns* v *Raychem* [1999] 3 All ER 154, the Court of Appeal said that in order for privilege to be waived there had to be something more than bare reference to a document in the report, or there had to be reliance by the expert in his report on that document. This would seem to be in tune with the CPR referred to above (Lord Woolf had advocated total disclosure of all documents and all instructions, but, wisely, that was thought a bridge too far).

However, one must also bear in mind CPR 31.14 which provides that a party may inspect a document mentioned in a statement of case, a witness statement, a witness summary, an affidavit, or, subject to r 35.10(4), an expert's report (r 35.10(4), as explained above, relates to the power to order disclosure of instructions given to an expert for the preparation of his report). It is not clear to what extent this rule is intended to go further than the previous RSC Ord 24, r 10, which gave the court a discretion to order or not to order disclosure.

In *Lucas* v *Barking, Havering and Redbridge Hospitals NHS Trust*, MLC 1037, [2003] Lloyds Rep Med 57, CA, the court considered the interplay between the different rules. R 31.14, as amended, states a party 'may inspect' a document mentioned in a statement of case, a witness statement or summary, or an affidavit, but, in respect to a document mentioned in an expert report, it says a party 'may apply for an order for inspection' **but** subject to CPR 35.10(4). Rule 35.10(3) requires the expert to 'state the substance of all material instructions, whether written or oral, on the basis of which the report was written, and 35.10(4), having dramatically declared that the instructions shall not be privileged against disclosure, states that the court will not, in relation to those instructions [these last five words are unnecessarily vague] order disclosure of a document unless it is satisfied that the expert's statement of instructions under 35.10(3) are 'inaccurate or incomplete'. It has never been easy to see what this means. What would amount to an inaccurate or incomplete statement of instructions?

Anyway, in this important case, the first time this troublesome rule has come before the Court of Appeal, the defendants sought sight of documents mentioned in an expert's report on the basis not that the statement of instructions from the expert was inaccurate or incomplete, but on the basis the documents in question did not form part of his instructions and therefore they had an unfettered right to see it under 31.14(2) – because the words 'subject to rule 35.10(4)' did not apply. The Master acceded to their application, but the Court of Appeal disagreed, holding that the documents did form a part of the instructions and there was no ground for thinking the expert's statement of instructions was inaccurate or incomplete. Waller J said the appeal raised a quite fundamental question as to what effect the new CPR were intended to have on the issue of privilege. It is important to note first that there are very strong indications in the judgments, albeit *obiter*, that the judges did not think that 31.14(1) gave an unfettered right to inspect a document mentioned in a statement of case, witness statement or summary, or affidavit. Waller LJ said it was unlikely that the rule had intended to abolish privilege in such cases at a stroke and without saying so. However, the main issue in the case was whether the documents referred to in the expert's report were part of his instructions. As the court found that they were, 31.14(1) was not relevant, only 31.14(2), and as there was no suggestion from the defendants that the expert's statement of instructions was inaccurate or incomplete, they were not entitled to disclosure. Waller LJ made the clear observation that 'material supplied by the instructing party to the expert as the basis on which the expert is being asked to advise should be considered as part of the instructions and thus subject to CPR 35.10(4)'. Further, the judge said there was no need to set out all the information contained in a statement referred to or all the material that had been supplied to an expert; the only obligation on the expert was to set out 'material instructions' (the judge's emphasis). Laws LJ said that the purpose of the rule was to ensure that the factual basis on which the expert had prepared his report was patent. In the ordinary way the expert was to be trusted to comply with this obligation.

So we see that the other party does not have an unfettered right to see documents referred to in pleadings, affidavits or witness statements. The other party will only be entitled to see documents referred to in an expert report if the court finds that the statement of his instructions given by the expert is inaccurate or incomplete.

In *Morris* v *Bank of India*, Ch D, 15 November 2001, Hart J ordered disclosure of an expert's instructions on the ground (under CPR r 35.10) that the expert report was patently defective in failing to reveal all material instructions.

AN EXPERT'S IMMUNITY

What if the expert's report is shown later to have been compiled negligently? In *Landall* v *Dennis Faulkner & Alsop* [1994] 5 Med LR 268, an orthopedic surgeon was sued in respect of advice given in a personal injury action to the effect that the claimant's condition could be ameliorated by a spinal fusion. The action was settled on that basis. The claimant contended that the advice was negligent and that the operation had damaged him further. Holland J held that the expert was immune from suit as the report in question had been given for the purpose of assisting the lawyers to conduct the claimant's case, and not for the purpose of advising the claimant about medical treatment. But in similar circumstances, the Court of Appeal expressed a contrary view (*Hughes* v *Lloyds Bank plc* [1998] PIQR P98). Following a road traffic accident, the injured party's GP wrote a letter for her detailing her injuries, to be sent to the third party's insurers. As the letter was provided before proceedings had been issued and purely for negotiation purposes, the GP was not covered by the immunity of a witness in respect of the allegation that he had not taken reasonable care in describing the injuries.

In *Stanton* v *Callaghan* [2000] 1 QB 75, the Court of Appeal, in a comprehensive review of the ambit of expert witness immunity, held that witness immunity attached to the joint statement produced after discussions between experts, so that no claim could be made against an expert for negligence in agreeing issues or backtracking on his original report.

Lawyers who should not have relied on an expert's report or should have known that the case was not strong enough to bring can be held liable for wasted costs (a full understanding of this important issue can be obtained by study of the following cases: *Locke* v *Camberwell Health Authority* [1990] 1 Med LR 253; revsd [1991] 2 Med LR 249, CA; *Scott* v *Bloomsbury Health Authority* [1990] 1 Med LR 214; *Ridehalgh* v *Horsefield* [1994] Ch 205, CA; *Tolstoy-Miloslavsky* v *Aldington* [1996] 1 WLR 736, CA; *Medcalf* v *Mardell* [2001] 05 LS Gaz R 36, CA; and note *Jones* v *Chief Constable of Bedfordshire Police* (30 July 1999), where the Court of Appeal said that a hopeless case does not necessarily mean that the lawyers have been negligent, because properly conducted and apparently reasonable cases can turn out to be hopeless.[16]

DO THE LAWYERS NEED MEDICAL KNOWLEDGE?

The answer is yes, to an extent. That is why one of the criteria for admission to the specialist panels is attendance at medical and medico-legal courses. The lawyer is not expected to be medically trained, but a general understanding of the medical issues in a case is essential. To this end, medical courses for lawyers are of great use.

The medically trained lawyer needs to be careful not to set up his own knowledge by way of challenge to the expert, at least where the field in question is not his own medical speciality. But more necessary than a general medical training is familiarity with medico-legal litigation. This embraces a number of aspects. The lawyer needs to be familiar with the way this litigation is practised and the way in which different defendants (trusts, health authorities, different firms of solicitors, the medical protection societies) respond to different stimuli and he needs to be familiar with the various ploys they practise. However, most importantly, he needs to be familiar with the medical focuses of different claims. This is not the same thing as saying that he needs to understand the medicine. Most medical claims fall within one or other of perhaps a dozen types of claim. Within each type, the issues are not very different. The lawyer needs to be familiar with the medical focus of each type of claim and the medical issues and arguments that usually arise. Take one example. If he is processing a claim for perinatal brain damage leading to cerebral palsy, it is obviously useful if he has a general grounding in obstetrics. But it will be enough, and in fact more relevant, if he understands the likely medical issues in the *forensic* context. So he needs to understand concepts and

---

16 In *Moran* v *Heathcote*, MLC 0344 a claimant's orthopedic expert gave a negative opinion which resulted in the discharge of the legal aid certificate. The patient continued on his own and lost at trial. He then told the expert he was going to publish an account of his dealing with the expert on the internet. The expert, fearing he would be defamed, sought an injunction against publication. Eady J declined to grant one, being satisfied that the limited ambit of the patient's commentary, as explained to him by the patient, would not attack the expert's integrity.

issues such as ultrasound scan, estimated date of delivery, absolute and relative disproportion, engagement, early and late deceleration, induction, Syntocinon, lie, presentation, descent of head, partogram, fetal distress, relative duties of midwives, SHOs, registrar and consultant, and a lot more besides. After a number of such cases, the lawyer will know what issues to focus on and he will understand without further instruction what his obstetric experts are saying. When we come to the issue of causation, the situation becomes even more technical. It is not enough for the lawyer to understand that his causation expert is saying that the child would or would not have been uninjured if delivered at a certain time. The lawyer needs to be familiar with the medical arguments on causation, including the recent efforts in the medical literature to declare causation virtually unprovable, and with the general medical consensus as to what factors need to be established if the damage is to be deemed to have been caused by perinatal asphyxia. A lawyer who is not familiar with the interpretation of CTG (cardiotocograph) traces, Apgar scores, hypoxic ischemic encephalopathy, the different types of cerebral palsy and their possible etiologies, and so forth, is going to be at a very substantial disadvantage, and therefore so also is the patient. After doing two or three cases of the same sort (eg cerebral palsy or shoulder dystocia) the lawyer is likely to know enough about the relevant issues to be able quickly to assess the strength of the proposed case and the direction in which it can proceed.

THE EXPERT WITNESS INSTITUTE (EWI)

This body, set up in 1996 as a direct result of encouragement from Lord Woolf, exists to support, encourage and improve the quality of expert evidence. It is first and foremost an educational body. It should not be confused with the Academy of Experts, of earlier provenance and concerned principally with the construction industry. There is now a fair degree of amicable interbreeding between the two bodies.

CLINICAL DISPUTES FORUM

Also distinct from the EWI is the Clinical Disputes Forum, Lord Woolf being again the progenitor of this organisation. As its name suggests, it is concerned with all aspects of medical disputes (clinical being the new, less immediately intelligible, buzzword replacement for 'medical'). The purpose of setting up the Forum was to enable all those with an interest in medical negligence claims to work together on any relevant area of concern, with the objective of improving the system. It created the Pre-action Protocol for Clinical Disputes, which is now part of the CPR, and it has also produced very detailed Guidelines for Experts' Discussions in the context of Clinical Disputes. The new Protocol for the Instruction of Experts from the Civil Justice Council incorporates much of the work of the Clinical Disputes Forum in this as in other contexts.

RECENT CASES ON PROCEDURE RELATING TO EXPERTS

In *Matthews* v *Tarmac Bricks and Tiles Ltd* (1999) 54 BMLR 139, the Court of Appeal upheld the order of the judge who had fixed the case for a date when the defendant's expert was unavailable. The court took the view that the defendant's representatives had been the authors of their own misfortune in not seeking to fix a date in good time and in not giving the court full disclosure about their difficulties.

In *Rollinson* v *Kimberley Clark Ltd* (1999) Times, 22 June, the Court of Appeal upheld the judge's refusal to adjourn a quantum-only trial for the unavailability of a defence expert witness, saying that it was unacceptable for a party to instruct a new expert close to trial without checking his availability.

In *Newton* v *Dorset Travel Service* (5 May 1999, unreported), CA, however, the court granted a short extension of time to serve a salient psychiatric report, even though there had been an unless order. The court said there had not been deliberate flouting of the order and that, although careful compliance with time orders was required, a degree of proportionality was also needed in coming to any decision in a particular case.

In *Stevens* v *Gullis* [2000] 1 All ER 527, CA, the court refused, despite the claimant's consent, to interfere with the judge's order refusing to permit the defence building expert to give evidence, on the ground that the expert had shown a wholesale disregard for his obligations under the rules.

Baron v *Lovell* (1999) Times, 14 September, CA. Where a party fails to disclose an expert report within the time specified, and so falls foul of r 32.10, the court is likely to refuse to allow him to be called if the trial can be conducted fairly on the available evidence.

Beck v *Ministry of Defence* [2004] PIQR P1, CA. At a late stage the defendant in this case wanted to change its psychiatric expert as it had, it said, lost all confidence in its original expert as having proper knowledge of the relevant psychiatric issues in the case. Naturally the claimant's solicitors refused access for a new psychiatric examination. The defendant succeeded in the two lower courts in gaining permission to start again. The single judge then gave leave for a further appeal in this interlocutory matter, a most unusual event. In the Court of Appeal Simon Brown LJ had some sympathy with the defendant's position, in that this was a high value case, involving allegations against their psychiatric personnel, and without a further report they would be proceeding with an expert in whom they had no confidence. He said that, though it would be unfair to require a defendant upon such an application to argue in detail as to why the original report and the original expert were now deemed to be unsatisfactory because that would give the claimant unfair ammunition for cross-examination of their expert if the application were refused, nevertheless, once it had been decided that the defendant should be permitted to instruct another expert, there were very good reasons why the original report should be disclosed. Ward LJ agreed, saying that expert shopping was to be discouraged and requiring the report to be disclosed was a check against possible abuse. The Master of the Rolls, agreeing, said that a claimant can properly object in any personal injury case to submitting to a second examination without good reason being shown for it. No second examination should be permitted if it appears to be 'a possibility' that the reason a defendant wants a fresh expert is that the first expert has reached a conclusion more favourable to the claimant than the defendant expected.[17]

Wardlaw v *Farrar* [2004] Lloyds Rep Med 98. The Court of Appeal, refusing an application to use further medical texts on appeal, gave guidance on the orderly deployment of the literature on which experts sought to rely. The best practice, as found on the standard form of directions used by the specialist Masters of the High Court, should be followed throughout the country.

---

17 See also *Hajigeorgiou* v *Vassiliou* [2005] EWCA Civ 236, CA.

Chapter 10

Issue of proceedings

PRIOR TO ISSUE

The Pre-Action Protocol

The Pre-Action Protocol for the Resolution of Clinical Disputes, which came into force on 26 April 1999, was the first major initiative of the Clinical Disputes Forum, one of whose aims is to find less adversarial and more cost-effective ways of resolving disputes about health care and medical treatment. The protocol, the full text of which is set out at Appendix I, tells us it is intended to encourage a climate of openness when something has 'gone wrong' with a patient's treatment, or the patient is dissatisfied with the treatment or its outcome. Proudly brandishing one of the new buzzwords in health care, it says this reflects the new and developing requirements for 'clinical governance' within 'healthcare' [sic]. The protocol is intended to be sufficiently broadly based, and flexible, to apply to all aspects of the health service: primary and secondary; public and private sectors. The introductory sections to the protocol should be read in full at least once. They explain why the protocol has been produced and what its aims are. The courts are expected to treat the standards set in the protocol as the normal reasonable approach to pre-action conduct. Any decision about sanctions is left to the courts. The protocol is not intended to be a comprehensive code governing all the steps in clinical disputes, but rather a code of good practice which parties should follow when litigation might be a possibility.[1]

Within the protocol itself, one finds a 'commitments' section, summarising the guiding principles which both sides are invited to endorse in the context of patient dissatisfaction, complaints and claims; and a 'steps' section which sets out in a more prescriptive form a recommended sequence of actions to be followed if litigation is a prospect. Suffice it here to point out that one of the health care provider's commitments is to advise patients of any adverse outcome and to provide on request an explanation and, if appropriate, an offer of remedial treatment, an apology and/or compensation. One of the patient's commitments is to consider

---

1   The court may take into account (non)-compliance with a protocol when giving directions (rr 3.1(4), (5), 3.9(1)(e)), and when making orders for costs (r 44.3(5)(a)).

the full range of options available following an adverse outcome, including a request for information, a meeting, a complaint, mediation and negotiation. The protocol explicitly abjures any intention to be prescriptive about alternative approaches to settling disputes (or about issues in relation to expert evidence).

The prescribed steps include obtaining the medical records, writing a letter of claim, and the response to it.

Obtaining the medical records

Standard forms for the request should be used (as in Annex B to the protocol). The request should contain sufficient information to alert the health care provider where the adverse outcome has been serious. Copy records should be provided within 40 days for a cost within the limits provided by the Data Protection Act 1998 (the relevant provisions used to be found in the now repealed Access to Health Records Act 1990). The health care provider is not expected to investigate every case where records are requested, but it is expected to have a policy on what cases will be investigated. In the rare event of failure to provide the records within the 40 days, an application to the court can be made. Third-party record holders are expected to co-operate. For further details see Chapter 8.

AFTER ISSUE

Serving proceedings

Claim form and particulars of claim

The claim form must be served within four months of issue (r 7.5).[2] The particulars of claim, if not served with or in the claim form, must be served within 14 days of service of the claim form, but in any event no later than the last day permitted for service of the claim form (r 7.4). Any pleading may now be termed a 'statement of case' (see the glossary at r 2.3).[3]

Rule 16.2 and 16.3 state what the claim form must contain (principally, a concise statement of the nature of the claim and the remedy sought). Rule 16.4 states what the particulars of claim must contain (principally, a concise statement of the facts on which the claimant relies).[4] For personal injury and fatal accident cases, 16PD, paras 4 and 5, contain important additional requirements – including the need, where the claimant is relying on the evidence of a medical practitioner, for a medical report

---

2   Note that by virtue of r 6.5(4)(d) where a party has specified an address for service, eg his solicitors, serving the claim form on the party will not be proper service (*Nanglegan* v *Royal Free Hampstead NHS Trust* (2001) Times, 14 February, CA). See also *Elmes* v *Hygrade Food Products* (24 January, 2001, unreported), CA.

3   The term 'statement of claim' is no longer used. A claim document in the High Court is now a 'particulars of claim', as it was, and remains, in the county court.

4   In *IBC Vehicles* v *Durr Ltd* (12 January 2000, unreported), Tugendhat QC said that there was a tendency for the court to accept that a case might be adequately notified to the other party in an expert's report or witness statement, even if it had not been adequately pleaded in the statement of case. I doubt the Court of Appeal would agree, even allowing for a degree of flexibility in the present climate.

'about the personal injuries which he alleges in his claim', and 'a schedule of details of any past and future expenses and losses which he claims'.[5] Note that the words of these two requirements are not the same as those appearing in the Rules of the Supreme Court – the medical report is not required specifically to 'substantiate' the injuries alleged, and the schedule requirement does not speak of an 'estimate' of future losses. The loss of the word 'substantiate' is to be welcomed, as it is now impossible for defendants to argue, as some have done unconvincingly in the past, that the report has to confirm causation as well as clarifying current condition and prognosis. (The now defunct draft Clinical Negligence Practice Direction provided that a schedule of loss would not be required unless the court so ordered on the application of the defendant, a very sensible provision as it is pointless and uneconomical to require a schedule of loss at the outset in a high value medical negligence claim.)

Venue

If the claim includes a claim for damages for personal injury (as most, but not all, medical negligence claims do), it can only be started in the High Court if its value, as assessed under the High Court and County Courts Jurisdiction Order 1991, is over £50,000. There are provisions in the Order for starting a low value claim in the High Court if it is particularly complex or important and needs a High Court judge. However, as a matter of practical strategy, all claims *outside* London would do well to be heard in the County Court as the High Court listing is usually fraught with administrative difficulties and the circuit judge allocated the case will probably be accredited to try High Court actions anyway. One of the very experienced High Court Masters in charge of medical negligence claims recently indicated unofficially that he would find it acceptable for a multi-track medical claim to be started in the High Court even if worth less than £50,000.

Extending time

The court has a general discretion to extend the time for serving a claim form, provided that the application is made before the last date for service. After that time, the claimant has to show that he has acted promptly in applying and that, despite taking all reasonable steps, has been unable to serve the form (or that the court has been unable to serve it). It is not clear to what, if any, extent the many authorities under the RSC on renewal of writs are still relevant.[6] In *The Hai Hing* [2000] 1 Lloyd's Rep

---

5　It is not mandatory to serve a medical report or a schedule, though without them it will not be possible to claim special damages, and any injury alleged may well be hard to prove without medical support (see *Saunders* v *Gwent Community NHS Trust* [2000] MLC 0251, CA – this was an application for permission to appeal; so one needs to bear in mind that Lord Woolf has said that judgments on such applications should not be relied on as authorities (*Clark* v *University of Lincolnshire and Humberside* [2000] 1 WLR 1988, CA)).

6　Such as *Waddon* v *Whitecroft-Scovell* [1988] 1 WLR 309, HL, *Kleinwort Benson Ltd* v *Barbrak Ltd* [1987] AC 597, HL, *Goldenglow Nut Food Co* v *Commodin (Produce) Ltd* [1987] 2 Lloyd's Rep 569, CA, *Dagnell* v *JL Freedman & Co* [1993] 1 WLR 388, HL.

300, Rix J said that the old authorities on applications for extending the validity of a writ are now illuminating, but not binding.

The court has no power to extend time for service of a claim form where the period prescribed for service in r 7.6(2) has expired and the claimant cannot bring himself within the provisions of r 7.6(3) (*Vinos* v *Marks and Spencer plc* [2000] MLC 0243, CA – the claimant's solicitors had not taken all reasonable steps to serve the form). The general discretion given by r 3.1(2)(a) (the court's general powers of management) to extend time limits did not apply (as the provisions of r 7.6 'provided otherwise' within the meaning of r 3.1(2));[7] nor did the general power to correct 'an error of procedure such as a failure to comply with a rule or practice direction' under r 3.10.

Similarly, in *Kaur* v *CTP Coil Ltd* (9 July 2000, unreported), CA (where, in addition, the form was served outside the limitation period), it had not been reasonable for the claimant's solicitors to have left the preparation of the schedule of loss until the last minute. The claimant was not entitled to rely on the general powers given to the court by r 3.10 (as per the *Vinos* case). Nor, for the same reasons, could he rely on r 3.9 (which gives the court another general power, namely the power to give relief from sanctions imposed for a failure to comply with any rule, practice direction or court order). Note that the time within which a *defence* must be filed (14 days after service of the particulars of claim, or 28 if an acknowledgment of service has been filed (r 15.4), can be extended by agreement between the parties for a further period up to 28 days (r 15.5).

The court has power to dispense with service but the Court of Appeal has shown reluctance to dispense where service out of time has been due to the claimant's fault (*Anderton* v *Clwyd* [2002] EWCA Civ 933).[8] This issue of extending time remains uncertain as one decision succeeds another and a body of case law on the new rules is laboriously constructed. As yet, the situation remains somewhat confused. For further reading, enjoy *Cranfield* v *Bridgerove Ltd* [2003] EWCA Civ 656; *Lakah Group* v *Al Jazeera Satellite Channel* [2003] EWHC 1297 (and the associated hearing at 1231); and *Mersey Docks Property*

---

7   Note that, provided the rules do not 'provide otherwise', an application for an extension of time can be granted under the general power given to the court by r 3.1(2)(a) even after the time for compliance has expired. In *Keith* v *CPM Field Marketing Ltd* (2000) Times, 29 August, the Court of Appeal said that, where an application for an extension was made under r 3.2(1)(a), an application for relief from any relevant sanction under r 3.9 should be inferred and the court should therefore systematically consider all the factors set out in r 3.9 before reaching its decision.

8   For a slight relaxation of this principle see *Wilkey* v *BBC* [2002] EWCA Civ 1561. The group of separate cases at [2002] EWCA Civ 933 raise various other points on service, including deemed day of service under CPR 6.7, non-exclusion of Saturdays and Sundays from the calculation of deemed day of service, the suggestion that CPR 6.7 could need amendment, and the distinction between a case where no service had even been attempted (so an extension of time would have to be sought) and one where a reasonable but unsuccessful attempt to serve had been made (here an order dispensing with service could be sought). These cases serve to prove what I, and others, have said from the beginning, namely that it was all very well to jettison the body of case law laboriously built up under the old rules but these bright new rules, so pristine and unburdened at their inception, would simply with the passage of time accrue their own not dissimilar body of precedent (complicated in their case by the infusion of human rights considerations).

Holdings v *Kilgour* [2004] EWHC 1638. In *Hashtroodi* v *Hancock* [2004] EWCA Civ 652, the Court of Appeal said that the power to extend time retrospectively must be exercised in accordance with the overriding objective (under r 1) and the extension should not have been granted below where the delay was due to the solicitor's incompetence. As in so many aspects of the law today, the issue of due service is now bedevilled by human rights considerations, and so will remain uncertain, as inventive lawyers find new pegs on which to hang a HR plea for a 'fair trial'.

The contents of the particulars of claim

It is now permissible, but of course not obligatory, for any party to refer in his pleading to any relevant point of law, to the name of any of his witnesses, and to attach any document he deems necessary to his case (16PD, para 14.3).

But the rules for good pleading remain the same; they are even confirmed by the requirement in r 16(4) for including 'a concise statement of the facts on which the claimant relies'. Long, inflated pleadings are not more impressive than short ones. A pleader who is thinking clearly and has confidence in his ability to express that thinking clearly will not omit anything that needs to be included. This writer would advise pleaders, and those who instruct them, as follows. Do not believe that the more prolix you are, the more effective or impressive your pleading becomes. For example, it is not necessary to set out the whole medical history. Be clear in your own mind what events you are relying on in support of your allegation of negligence, and plead only them.

On the other hand, be precise, not vague. Do not leave the field open for the defendants to serve a long and tedious request for further information, which wastes time and money as the questions are sent to your expert and his answers then sent on to you for you to copy them out in your draft. Tell the defendants in your statement of case exactly what action or omission you say was negligent, when it occurred, why you say it was negligent, what you say should have been done instead and what you say was the result to the claimant of that negligent act or omission. And do not put under your Particulars of Negligence sweeping allegations in the hope that you will in that way cover all possibilities, eg 'The defendants failed properly or at all to monitor the progress of the claimant's labour', or 'The defendants failed to provide an adequate system of anesthetic/obstetric cover', or 'The defendants failed properly to train and/or instruct their staff/trainees in such and such', or 'The defendants failed to observe and/or heed and/or act upon the signs of fetal distress'. These are all much too general and are just asking for the said tedious request for particulars. Be specific: eg 'The defendants failed properly to monitor the progress of the claimant's labour, in that at such and such a time they did such and such whereas they should have done such and such'. Sometimes the error lies simply in not adding to the general allegation words to the effect 'The facts and matters to be relied on in connection with this allegation are set out above at paras ...'. Of course, to get this sort of clarity and particularity, you have to ensure that your expert has answered the appropriate questions with sufficient precision (and that you actually understand what your case is). But nothing less will do.

Staughton LJ wrote in *Counsel:*

> A good rule for drafting documents is to sit back at the end and ask of every phrase that one has written, whether it was necessary to write it at all.

He also said:

> Unthinking copy of precedents, when nothing is ever left out as antiquated or obsolete, produces many documents which are too long, too old-fashioned and too obscure.

In *Ashmore* v *Corpn of Lloyd's* [1992] 1 WLR 446, HL, Lord Templeman said that pleadings should define the issues, be brief, chronological and consistent, and that counsel should not advance a multitude of ingenious arguments in the hope that out of ten bad points, the judge would be able to fashion a winner. He was expressly critical of the tendency in some cases for legal advisers to make every point, conceivable and inconceivable, without judgment or discrimination. And we would do well to bear in mind the words of Rose LJ In *Re Freudiana Holdings Ltd* (1995) Times, 4 December, CA:

> The legal profession must re-learn, or re-apply, the skill which was the historic hallmark of the profession but which appears to be fast vanishing: to present to the court the few crucial determinative points and to discard as immaterial dross the minor points and excessive detail.

Despite the new rules for pleading described above, this former guidance remains a useful point of reference, as does the judgment in *Hockaday* v *South West Durham Health Authority* [1994] PIQR P275, where the Court of Appeal offered a highly technical analysis of the requirements for pleading a defence:

(1)   The fundamental rule of pleading is that both a statement of claim and a defence must set out the material facts upon which the party pleading intends to rely.

(2)   As to a bare traverse: a denial or a refusal to admit is a perfectly good plea, provided that all that is thereby intended is to put the plaintiff to proof of his case, but it may be that concealed in a traverse is an affirmative case, and that may well be so where the traverse is of a negative averment.

(3)   If it is clear, either from the nature of the case or from the admission of counsel or otherwise, that it is intended to set up an affirmative case, particulars of the affirmative case ought to be delivered; otherwise the other party and the court will be in doubt as to what the issues are to be determined at the trial.

We should also bear in mind that pleadings are not a game to be played at the expense of litigants, nor an end in themselves, but a means to an end, and that end is to give each party a fair hearing (*Trust Security Holdings* v *Sir Robert McAlpine & Sons* (1994) Times, 21 December, CA, *per* Saville LJ).

Finally, the experts must vet the draft before it is served. It is they who will have to support the allegations of negligence (and the other medical aspects of the claim) in court.

Late service of particulars of claim

It is worth noting that here the court is far more relaxed about the matter than it is in respect of late service of the claim form.[9] In *Price* v *Price* [2003] 3 All ER 911 the conduct of the claimant's case had been disgraceful in a number of respects; yet the Court of Appeal said that it would be a disproportionate response to stop the case by refusing an extension altogether, and so it granted an extension on conditions (see also the Annual Practice at 7.6.4 for a useful summary of the current position).

The medical report

Now that cases are being progressed by expert solicitors, it is unlikely that anyone will make the fundamental, and previously not uncommon, mistake of serving a report on liability or causation with the pleading. Sometimes however the report on condition refers to other documents, provoking a knee-jerk reaction in the defendants by way of demanding to see those other documents, whatever they might be and however clearly they might be privileged. On this, see 'Reference to other documents' in Chapter 9.

The medical report does not always have to be a full report from an independent expert to comply with the rule. In the personal injury case of *Edwards* v *Peter Black Healthcare (Southern) Ltd* [2000] ICR 120, CA, a letter from the hospital was held to be sufficient in the circumstances; and in *Knight* v *Sage Group plc* (28 April 1999, unreported), CA, where a claimant in person served only a GP report, the court said that, although it did not satisfy the rules requirement, it was sufficient 'for the initial period of proceedings'.

The medical report should not be treated as if it were a pleading. In *Sion* v *Hampstead Health Authority* [1994] 5 Med LR 170, CA, Staughton LJ said that the claimant was not wholly and rigidly confined to what was said in the medical report; it should be treated only as a general outline of the claimant's case.[10]

The defence

A defence must be served within 14 days of receipt of the particulars of claim, or 28 days if an acknowledgment of service has been filed (r 15.4). The parties can agree to an extra 28 days (in which case the defendant must inform the court in writing).

By r 16.5 the defence must state which of the claimant's allegations he admits or denies, and which he requires the claimant to prove. Where he denies an allegation, he must give his reasons for so doing and if he intends to put forward a different version of the events from the

---

9   This was explicitly explained by the Court of Appeal in *Totty* v *Snowden* [2002] PIQR P189 and *Hewitt* v *Wirral and West Cheshire Community NHS Trust* (ib).

10 In *Woods* v *West Dorset General Hospital NHS Trust* (17 February 1998, unreported), the Court of Appeal, not surprisingly, confirmed the striking out of a medical negligence claim where the only report served with the pleading was one that exonerated the defendants!

claimant, he must set it out. A specific denial may be implied from the nature of the defence case. But if an allegation is not dealt with explicitly or implicitly, an admission will be inferred. These provisions thankfully put an end to the blanket denials favoured by many medical negligence defendants in the past.

Practice Direction 16, para 13 adds that the defendant must state in the defence whether he agrees, disputes or has no knowledge of the matters contained in the claimant's medical report; and if the defendant disputes any part of the report, he must give his reasons. If he has already obtained his own report on which he intends to rely, he must attach it to the defence (this is presumably limited to any report on condition and prognosis). He must be similarly explicit in respect of any schedule served (however he is only likely to be able to serve a useful counter-schedule) in the simpler cases.

Chapter 11

Striking out

Needless to say, striking out is a matter of great concern to a party, as default in pleading, conduct of the case, adherence to the rules or specific orders, or general inattention, can cost him a good claim (or defence). Small wonder the reports are full of cases on the subject with much refined argumentation, and that that bids fair to continue to be the situation despite the attempt by the new rules to create simplicity.

Formerly

Before the advent of the CPR there was a mass of complex and indigestible authority on striking out (whether for want of prosecution, or abuse of process or any other reason) garnered over many years. It was a thesaurus for subtle argument from the lawyers. Lengthy chapters had to be devoted to it in any book on civil practice. Now that has all been swept away, apparently. Any decision is simply to be made in accordance with the justice of the case as perceived by the trial judge, and the appeal court will be reluctant to interfere unless the decision appears to them to be clearly wrong, in which case, as ever, they will find some reason to declare the exercise of the judge's discretion flawed.[1]

The teething process

There have already been a number of appeal judgments, though. This is due to the nature of English jurisprudence, which thrives on precedent and legal quibbles. The English lawyer is not content to argue every case on the 'just' solution in the particular dispute. He is bound to refer to previous decisions. That is how the previous body of authority was built up. That is how a new body of authority will be – is being – built up. In the initial stage, as differently constituted appeal courts reflect in their particular judgments what they think is the just solution in each particular

---

1   See the May 2000 judgment of Brooke LJ in *Tanfern* v *Cameron-MacDonald* [2000] 1 WLR 1311 (and, a few months earlier, in *Copeland* v *Smith* [2000] 1 WLR 1371 at 1375, CA). Note that no second tier appeals will be entertained by the Court of Appeal unless raising an important point of principle or practice or there is some other compelling reason for the court to hear it (Access to Justice Act 1999, s 55(1)).

case, there are bound to be inconsistent decisions. So for a time, during the lengthy teething process, the law is unclear and the judicial solution to a dispute unpredictable. This is good for the lawyer, but not for the litigant. Already, the initial enthusiastically draconian approach of the appeal court to any failure to observe time limits or other infractions of the new rules has mellowed to a better wisdom[2] – largely because they foresaw the emergence of a satellite litigation challenging harsh decisions invoking, of course, a human rights plea for a fair trial (Article 6). Perhaps fearing what the lawyers, unchecked, might do with the human rights possibilities, Lord Woolf delivered a sharp rebuke to those who would have recourse in every available context to such a plea.[3]

The rules

Rule 3.4 provides that the court may strike out a statement of case (this by r 2.3(1) in effect embraces any pleading) if it discloses no reasonable ground for bringing or defending the claim, or is an abuse of the court's process or is otherwise likely to obstruct the just disposal of the proceedings, or there has been a failure to comply with a rule, practice direction or court order. The instances in the rule are not exhaustive; thus, there is still power to strike out in respect of a vexatious litigant.

Rule 3.8 provides that any sanction specified to come into effect by the rules on a certain event shall do so unless the party affected applies for relief (to be supported by evidence – r 3.9(2)). This means that parties cannot any longer of themselves agree to waive such a sanction. Rule 3.9 provides that the court must on any such application have regard to all the circumstances, including the parties' conduct, prejudice, the administration of justice and whether the errors have been that of the party or his lawyer.

Considerations relevant to the overriding objective of r 1.1 include ensuring that a case is dealt with expeditiously (and fairly) and allotting to a case an appropriate share of the court's resources, while taking in to account the need to allot resources to other cases.

Summary judgment

CPR Part 24 deals with summary judgment, which, if it is the defendant who is asking for it, is in effect a striking out application. This coinciding was expressly recognised in *Taylor* v *Midland Bank Trust Co Ltd (No 2)* [2002] WTLR 95, and *S* v *Gloucestershire County Council* [2000] 3 All ER 346, CA, at p 372 *per* May LJ. The court can give summary judgment against a party on the claim or on a particular issue if it considers that a party has no real prospect of succeeding on the claim/the defence or on the particular issue, and that there is no other compelling reason why the

---

2   One illustration of the wisdom of Draco is *Lownes* v *Babcock Power Ltd* [1998] PIQR P253, CA, where Lord Woolf said: 'The message to the profession, which should be heard and learned as a result of this case, is that the standards of diligence displayed in this case are totally unacceptable'. The claim was struck out because a schedule was not served in time under an unless order.

3   *Daniels* v *Walker* [2000] 1 WLR 1382, CA (see Chapter 27 on human rights).

case or issue should be disposed of at a trial. Practice Direction 3, para 1.6 states that a defence may fall within r 3.4(2) if it consists of a bare denial or otherwise sets out no coherent statement of facts, or the facts it sets out, while coherent, would not, even if true, amount in law to a defence to the claim.

Rules cannot displace substantive law

The rule committee is not omnipotent. In *General Mediterranean Holdings SA* v *Patel* [1999] 3 All ER 673, Toulson J held that r 48.7(3), which deals with the disclosure of privileged documents in relation to wasted costs orders, was *ultra vires* and invalid because a rule could not curtail the substantive right at common law to legal confidentiality.

This is consistent with the Court of Appeal decision in *Breeze* v *John Stacey & Sons* (1999) Times, 8 July, where it was said that the requirement to give effect to the overriding objective when exercising any power under the CPR did not affect substantive law as established by the authorities (the point at issue was whether the old law about documents disclosed by mistake still applied).

Jettisoning the old law

In one breath we are told that the old cases are no longer in point, in the next that they are helpful. We should bear in mind what Professor Scott writes in *Civil Procedure News* Issue 9/99:

> The CPR are not and cannot be a self-contained code. The rules therein are cast against the backdrop of a mass of legislation and case law, the survival of much of which is vital to the operation of the CPR in the manner that Lord Woolf would most wish them to operate ... The rules themselves acknowledge the survival of the inherent jurisdiction (see rule 3.1(1)). However lawyers may well have to tolerate the fact that the judges of the Court of Appeal will call the CPR a self-contained code when it suits them to do so.

And in Issue 10/99 he wrote:

> ... the CPR is an unhappy mixture of old and new, with the old being tinkered with in a manner which takes no, or insufficient, account of the new. This is particularly true where Lord Woolf was tempted to recommend changes, based on procedural developments that seemed to be working well in foreign jurisdictions, without fully appreciating the consequences of transplanting them to a substantially reformed English procedural context, significantly different from that in which they were wrought.

In *Bansal* v *Cheema* [2000] MLC 0380, CA, Brooke LJ said :

> In my judgment there is no value in going back to look at cases decided under the old rules. The new Civil Procedure Rules set out in a clear form the matters which a judge should take into account in exercising his discretion on an occasion like this. One of the virtues of the new rules is that he does not have to go back again and again to substantial authorities decided under the old rules.

That may be – but the growing body of precedent on the CPR bids fair to create in time a similar situation to what went before!

Cases

Biguzzi v *Rank Leisure plc* [1999] 1 WLR 1926. In this important case, the Court of Appeal, Lord Woolf presiding, recognised for the first time that draconian sanctions were not the automatic response to infringements of the new rules. One cannot in this instance do better than quote the summary in the headnote:

> Held, dismissing the appeal, that under the Civil Procedure Rules 1998 the keeping of time limits was very important and the court had an unqualified discretion under rule 3.4(2)(c) to strike out a case where a litigant failed to comply with the Rules or an order of the court; but that under the Rules the court had broad powers and, in many cases, there would be alternatives to the draconian step of striking out the claim that would make clear that the court would not tolerate delay but would also, in accord with the overriding objective in Part 1 of the Rules, enable the case to be dealt with justly; that judges had to be trusted to exercise their wide discretion fairly and justly in all the circumstances, while recognising their responsibility to litigants in general not to allow the same defaults to occur as had occurred in the past, and the Court of Appeal would not interfere unless relevant principles had been contravened; and that, accordingly, since the judge had applied the relevant principles in exercising his discretion, the court would not interfere with his decision.[4]

Mealey Horgan plc v *Horgan* (1999) Times, 6 July, Buckley J. On an application by the defendant to extend the time for service of witness statements, the court said it would be unjust to exclude a party from giving evidence at trial save in very rare circumstances, eg where there had been deliberate flouting of court orders, or inexcusable delay such that the only way the court could fairly entertain the evidence would be by adjourning the trial.

How reluctant the court can be to interfere with the judge's discretion can be illustrated by *Woodward* v *Finch* (8 December 1999, unreported), CA, where repeated failures by the claimant to comply with orders would surely under the old regime have resulted in a strike out. Yet the appeal court, Lord Woolf presiding, refused to interfere with the judge's exercise of his discretion in favour of the claimant, saying that it had not been shown that he had contravened any recognised principle.

AXA Insurance Co v *Swire Fraser* (2000) Times, 19 January, CA. Rule 3.4(2)(c) gave the court a wide discretion which did not require the proof of prejudice to party if the action were to proceed, though the question of prejudice would still be relevant to the court's decision. The new rules simply enabled the court to adopt a more flexible approach. Further, the discretion enabled the court to strike out actions where there had been deliberate default or a failure to comply with a court order without resort to the court's inherent jurisdiction to strike out actions for abuse of process.

In *Walsh* v *Misseldine* (29 February 2000, unreported), CA, the court, exercising its own discretion by consent of the parties, emphasised that a flexible approach should be taken in every case suited to the instant facts, and demonstrated how an order could be framed to meet the justice of the

---

4   Reference may also be made to the judgment of May LJ in *Co-operative Retail Services Ltd* v *Guardian Assurance plc* (28 July 1999, unreported), CA.

particular case (no strike out, but no enlargement of claimant's pleading or schedule allowed).

Keith v *CPM Field Marketing Ltd* (2000) Times, 29 August, CA. The strike out of a defence for non-contumelious failure to comply with an unless order to produce equipment was held to be totally disproportionate. The request for further time to comply had been made in good time. The circuit judge should have deemed the request to include an application for relief from the sanction if the request was refused and he should then have considered all the matters set out in r 3.9(1) (3.9 is the rule giving the court a general power to give relief from sanctions).

On the other hand ...

Strike out remains the appropriate remedy in the more serious case (*UCB Corporate Services Ltd* v *Halifax (SW) Ltd* (1999) Times, 23 December, CA). *Biguzzi* was not intended to give greater leniency to a claimant than he would have had under the old regime.

Shikari v *Malik* (1999) Times, 20 May, CA. Wholesale disregard of the setting down obligations led the court to uphold the striking out order. It was said that litigants cannot rely on the court tolerating what had been tolerated previously under the old rules. The court also said that the exercise of discretion was not limited by the decision in *Hytec Information Systems* v *Coventry City Council* [1997] 1 WLR 1666, where the Court of Appeal, presided over by Lord Woolf himself, had said that a party was generally bound by the conduct, ie the errors, of his legal representative.

Cheltenham Laminating Co v *Polyfibre Ltd* (12 October 1999, unreported), CA. With both parties in substantial default, the court nevertheless upheld the refusal to extend the time for service of statements and the consequent striking out of the claim, stating that under the new regime, fairness did not depend solely on the basis of fairness to the parties themselves, but also to other litigants and any delay would affect other proceedings (a mantra that had been used frequently in the early days leading up to the introduction of the new regime).

In *Cank* v *Broadyard Associates Ltd* [2000] MLC 0382, CA, the court criticised the decisions of two County Court judges in making and confirming a strike out of the defence for failure to comply with an order made in the proceedings. The judges had relied on a technical breach (the claimant received the required material only two or three days late); there was no merit in striking out an adequately particularised defence; and the second judge had failed to go through the checklist of matters in rule 3.9, especially para (g), (h), and (i).

In *Godden* v *Kent and Medway Strategic Health Authority* [2004] EWHC 1629 Gray J declined to strike out an action by patients against their GP where, he said, it was arguable that a health authority could be held liable vicariously for the acts of a GP who had indecently assaulted and possibly negligently treated his patients.

In *Sutradhar* v *Natural Environment Research Council* (8 May 2003), QBD Simon J the judge declined to strike out a claim arising out of the well known report of the British Geological Survey assessing the hydrochemical charter of the main aquifer units of central and north-eastern Bangladesh and possible toxicity of groundwater to fish and humans, on the ground that the concept of proximity in the context of duty of care could not be determined in isolation from the concepts of foreseeability of harm and fairness. However the Court of Appeal [2004] EWCA Civ 175 allowed the defendant's appeal by a majority and struck the claim out, saying that there was clearly insufficient proximity between the parties for a duty of care to arise.

In *McLoughlin* v *Grovers* [2001] EWCA Civ 1743 the Court of Appeal said that a claim for damages for psychiatric illness caused by solicitors' negligent preparation of the claimant's criminal defence should not have been struck out as not being reasonably foreseeable in tort or too remote in contract. Preliminary issues should usually be questions of law decided on the basis of a schedule of agreed or assumed facts.

Situations analogous to strike outs

In *Bheroo* v *Camden and Islington NHS Trust* (29 June 2000, unreported), CA, the court reversed an extraordinary decision whereby the judge had refused to allow a short extension for the service of the schedule of loss. The court said there had been no irregularity in issuing the claim (ie as opposed to serving it) without a schedule, or a medical report for that matter, but that, even if there had been, there was no reason to refuse a short extension, particularly as that would have the effect of dismissing the claim.

Bansal v *Cheema* [2000] MLC 0380, CA. On an application under r 3.9 for relief from an automatic sanction, a judge must consider systematically the matters set out in that rule. There is no need to refer to earlier authorities under the old rules.

The old authorities on applications for extending the validity of a writ are now illuminating but not binding, *per* Rix J in *The Hai Hing* [2000] 1 Lloyd's Rep 300. (See Chapter 10 for extending the time for service of claim form or particulars of claim.)

Here, however, is a decision where the old law was said to be totally relevant – *MacDonald* v *Thorn plc* (1999) Times, 15 October, CA. On an application to set aside judgment for default of defence, the court said that the confused position as to whether it was essential or merely advisable that an explanation be given by the defendant had been clarified (advisable) by *Finnegan* v *Parkside Health Authority* [1998] 1 WLR 411 at 420–421, CA, and that that remained the law.[5]

Swain v *Hillman* [2000] PIQR P51, CA. On an appeal by the defendant from the refusal of summary judgment under CPR 24.2, the court, Lord Woolf presiding, said that 'no real prospect of succeeding' meant no realistic, as opposed to fanciful, prospect of success. Where there were issues which should be considered at trial, it would not be appropriate to – in effect – strike out the claim, or for that matter the defence.

---

5   Reference may also be made to *Hamblin* v *Field* (2000) Times, 26 April, CA, where the judge had struck the claim out for delay. The appeal court discouraged the numerous citation of authorities (particularly in summary form).

Limitation

In *Securum Finance Ltd* v *Ashton* [2000] 3 WLR 1400, CA, the court said that there was no longer a principle that a second action begun within the limitation period after the first action had been struck out for inordinate and inexcusable delay should not be struck out, save in exceptional circumstances. The pursuit of the new action had to be weighed against the overriding objective of dealing with cases justly and, in particular, the court's need to allot its limited resources to other cases (r 1.1(2)(e) is in point here). The court echoed the words of the earlier proceedings in this claim, *Arbuthnot Latham Bank Ltd* v *Trafalgar Holdings Ltd* [1998] 1 WLR 1426, which offered us one of the earliest New Age brimstone and thunder utterances from the Court of Appeal, to the effect that wholesale disregard of the rules would now be regarded as an abuse of process justifying a striking out order.[6]

Factors limiting strike out

There are currently two factors limiting the use of strike out. The first is that the House of Lords is taking an innovative approach to negligence. The second is the human rights issue of a fair trial. The two factors often overlap: human rights can lead to a developing jurisprudence as well as demanding that any interlocutory or final decision in litigation be consistent with the fair trial requirement of the Convention. It has been clear for some time that the courts are aware of the possibility, even the likelihood, of a challenge along those lines. In *S* v *Gloucestershire County Council* [2001] 2 WLR 909, CA, the court said that a summary trial could be a fair hearing within the meaning of Article 6(2) (it added that a claim for damages for sexual abuse by foster parents would only be struck out in the clearest case). Generally, the court would have to be satisfied, before it struck out a claim, that all substantial facts relevant to the allegations of negligence were before the court and that there was no real prospect of their being disputed or of oral evidence affecting the court's assessment of them. In *Swain* v *Hillman* [2000] PIQR P51, CA, an appeal by the defendant from the refusal of summary judgment under r 24.2, the court, Lord Woolf presiding, said that 'no real prospect of succeeding' meant no realistic, as opposed to fanciful, prospect of success. Where there were issues which should be considered at trial it would not be appropriate to – in effect – strike out the claim, or for that matter the defence. He said the court was not to conduct a mini-trial at this stage.

As to the first factor, one may have in mind, as an example, the recent èducation cases – four of which are reported at [2000] 3 WLR 776 (*Phelps* v *Hillingdon London Borough Council* was the only one that had been tried – the others were at an interlocutory stage). The wide-ranging effect of the decisions of the House of Lords is that an educational psychologist

---

6   For a particularly unattractive decision from the Court of Appeal, refusing to interfere with a strike out ordered by the district judge and confirmed by the Recorder, see *Nascimento* v *Kerrigan* (1999) Times, 23 June. In this personal injury claim there had been a mere failure to provide a translation of the Portuguese medical report. The court emphasised that after one appeal the test for success in a further appeal was more stringent.

employed by a local education authority will, or is likely to, owe a duty to a pupil on whom she reports for her employer, and that a local education authority owes a general duty through its teachers to provide a suitable education for its pupils, particularly if they have special needs (in *G (a minor)* v *Bromley London Borough Council* [2000] 3 WLR 776, the claimant suffered from muscular dystrophy; in the other cases the disability was or was claimed to be dyslexia). In only one of the four cases under consideration had the Court of Appeal favoured the pupil. It is unthinkable that twenty or so years ago, the House of Lords would have opened up the area of education in this way, so that, in effect, pupils can sue for damages resulting from an education below the standard they could reasonably expect. One may also have in mind the jurisprudence relevant to the new claim for stress at work, as well as developments in the area of industrial claims, such as the new variations of vibration white finger.

Barrett v *Enfield London Borough Council* [1999] 3 WLR 79, HL, was a claim, struck out by the Court of Appeal and restored by the House of Lords, for negligent care of a child who had been placed in their charge under a care order (all aspects of their care were impugned, including general, domestic, educational, emotional and medical), and severe psychological and psychiatric problems were alleged to have resulted. Although the House acknowledged the likely difficulty of succeeding on such a claim, it was not willing to decide the issue of whether a duty was owed in law on the basis of assumed hypothetical facts. That should be decided on the facts as actually proved at trial. It has been said that an application to strike out should not be granted unless the court is sure the claim is bound to fail (*Hughes* v *Colin Richards and Co* [2004] EWCA Civ 266). The court cannot be sure of this in an area of developing jurisprudence since in such cases decisions as to novel points of law should be based on actual findings of fact (*Farrah* v *British Airways* (2000) Times, 26 January, CA).

In *W* v *Essex County Council* [2000] 2 WLR 601, the House of Lords once again reversed the Court of Appeal, permitting to proceed an action in which foster parents were suing the local authority for negligence in placing a known sexual abuser with them who then abused their children. They said that the question whether or not the claim was justiciable depended upon a full investigation of the facts.

Another example: in *Darker* v *Chief Constable of the West Midlands Police* [2000] 3 WLR 747, the House of Lords, reversing the Court of Appeal, held that a claim by persons acquitted of criminal offences alleging that the police had fabricated evidence should not have been struck out. Overruling *Silcott* v *Metropolitan Police Comr* [1996] 8 Admin LR 633, CA, it was held that immunity of witnesses did not extend to cover the fabrication of false evidence. And the highly significant comment was made that public policy required in principle that those who suffered a wrong should have a right to a remedy.

As to human rights: Ten years ago we had a firm, unanimous and fully reasoned decision from the House of Lords in the two cases of *X (minors)* v *Bedfordshire County Council* and *M (a minor)* v *Newham London Borough Council* [1995] 2 AC 633 to the effect that the professionals (we need not distinguish between doctors, psychologists or social workers for present purposes) involved in investigating suspected abuse cases in exercise of a statutory duty did not also owe a duty of care at common law to the children concerned, let alone to the parents. However, several years later the Strasbourg court decided that the five children in the Bedfordshire case had had their welfare neglected to such an extent by the local authority that it amounted to a violation of Article 3 of the Convention (inhuman and degrading treatment), and they awarded the very large (for Strasbourg) sum of compensation of £320,000 (*Z* v *United Kingdom* (2001) 34 EHRR 97). Both child and mother succeeded in Strasbourg in the *Newham* case in establishing a violation of Article 8 (respect for family life) (*TP and KM* v *United Kingdom* (2001) 34 EHRR 42). The negligence in this latter case lay in the failure of the health professional to listen to the child's account with proper attention, as a result of which the mother's partner was suspected of abuse and the child was removed from the mother's care for almost a year. The Strasbourg decision was based not on the decision to remove the child but on the failure to disclose their 'evidence' to the mother immediately after the removal, an action which would apparently have led to them revising their decision. Since then it has been generally accepted that, given the view of Strasbourg, a duty to act with appropriate care is in fact owed to the child in these cases. For otherwise English law would be in contravention of human rights. This change in the law was declared by the Court of Appeal in the case recently heard on appeal in the House of Lords (judgment was given by their Lordships in *JD (FC)* v *East Berkshire Community Health NHS Trust* and two other actions on 21 April 2005). Note that the events on which this East Berkshire case was based happened before the Human Rights Act came into force. Small wonder that this combination of developing jurisprudence and human rights has, generally speaking, made our courts chary about striking out. Nevertheless, strike out is what the House of Lords did in the East Berkshire case. The claimants were parents who were wrongly suspected of child abuse through the misdiagnosis of their children by doctors. Each in consequence suffered psychiatric disorder. In each case the true explanation for the child's condition was not discovered until regrettably late. The question was whether the doctors investigating the possibility of abuse against a child owed a duty not merely to the child but also to the parents. Only one Law Lord, Lord Bingham, considered the matter to be arguable and that therefore the claim should not be struck out. The other judges, not surprisingly, I would suggest, considered the arguments for the claimants to be clearly unsustainable and so the actions were struck out. Perhaps the issue will be taken to Strasbourg.[7]

---

7   We may note that in *E* v *Dorset County Council* [1995] 2 AC 633, Lord Browne-Wilkinson had said long ago that the position of psychologists in the education cases was quite different from that of the doctor and social worker in the child abuse cases.

Chapter 12

Between issue and trial

JUDICIAL DIRECTIONS

Following the service by the court on the parties of the allocation questionnaire (after a defence has been filed and pursuant to Pt 23) and its filing at court, a clinical negligence claim will be assigned to the
multi-track. The court is then directed by r 29.2 to fix a case management
conference for the purpose of giving relevant directions on every aspect of
the future progress of the case. This is the point where one can expect
unreasonable deadlines to be set and the case to be theoretically brought
to trial before it can reasonably be made ready.[1] The court may approve
directions agreed by the parties without requiring them to attend, but
that does not happen often, as the judges like to exercise their power and
impose their own idiosyncratic views. It is expressly provided that the
parties may not vary any date fixed by the court without making an
application for that purpose.

The Masters of the High Court who are assigned to medical negligence
claims have developed a useful set of standard directions, a sort of proforma (see Appendix III). This is not binding on other courts, but in at
least one respect, the direction relating to medical texts, the Court of
Appeal has said it is the exemplar that should be followed. Whatever
form directions take, it is essential that exchange of witness statements
takes place two or three months before exchange of expert reports.[2] The

---

1 The judges have target dates to meet, to conform to Woolfian principles, no matter how
   unrealistic and unreasonable the demands thus made on the lawyers. The situation is
   reminiscent of the targets for harvests to be sent to the Party proposed in the days of
   Mao. Every cadre, to curry favour, proposed a more astonishing (and unrealistic) figure
   than the neighbouring village, thus starving the peasants; and every form of trickery,
   statistical, photographic or whatever, was perpetrated to fudge the figures and show a
   harvest wildly beyond the actual crop. This last cantankerous observation from the
   previous edition is considerably less true now, fortunately. It could well be applied,
   however, to the ludicrous targets scenario that the Government tried to impose on the
   NHS, only abandoning it when it eventually perceived the catastrophic results.
2 In *Rayment* v *Ministry of Defence* (1998) 47 BMLR 92, Harrison J, drawing a clear distinction between reports on liability and causation and reports on quantum, held that
   the Master's order for sequential disclosure of the latter was appropriate. He said there
   was the significant potentiality for duplication and waste of costs if there were simultaneous exchange of experts' reports on quantum.

Court of Appeal has said more than once that the expert report must take aboard the witness statements served by the other party (see *Johnson* v *John and Waltham Forest Health Authority* [1998] MLC 0224, CA.[3]

The judicial directions are likely to lay down a detailed timetable for every report, every exchange, every agenda, every meeting and of which experts, and every joint report, as well as for the service of schedules and counter-schedules, chronologies, summaries, skeleton arguments, and so forth – in fact everything the judge can think of. This is known as case management.

FURTHER INFORMATION

What used to be called a request for further and better particulars is now termed a preliminary request for further information or clarification. Practice Direction 18 (18PD) provides that before any application is made to the court, the party desiring the information must first write to the other side asking for it. A request should be concise and strictly confined to matters which are reasonably necessary and proportionate to enable him to prepare his own case or to understand the case he has to meet. Requests may be made in a letter rather than a separate document if they are brief. They should not be made piecemeal if they can be made in a single comprehensive document.

Although there is no authority on the point yet, requests must surely arise out of the pleading (as was the case for further and better particulars). I have recently seen a several-page request (from a solicitor, not counsel) which amounted to a detailed cross-examination on every issue, of evidence, of law and of argument (a similar lengthy cross-examination was posted to the expert). The shrift these documents received was short in the extreme.

MEDICAL REPORTS ON CONDITION AND PROGNOSIS

Reports on the claimant's present medical condition, and his prognosis for the future, will be exchanged in the usual way, and agreed if possible. A claimant who unreasonably refuses to allow an examination by the defendants' expert is likely to have his action stayed (*Edmeades* v *Thames Board Mills Ltd* [1969] 2 QB 67, CA); but the onus of showing unreasonableness is on the defendants, who need to show, if they are to get a stay, that their case cannot properly be prepared without such an examination (*Lane* v *Willis* [1972] 1 WLR 326, CA). The court is unlikely to require the claimant to submit to an examination which is unpleasant, painful or risky, unless the interests of justice demand it (cf *Aspinall* v *Sterling Mansell Ltd* [1981] 3 All ER 866 with *Prescott* v *Bulldog Tools Ltd* [1981] 3 All ER 869).

---

3   In *Yousif* v *Jordan* [2003] MLC 1085 the Court of Appeal adverted to the difficulty a judge might find himself in a contested case if the experts were not to give oral evidence. It is fair to say that usually the district judge (or Master) will accede to requests for oral evidence from relevant experts

In *Smith* v *Ealing, Hammersmith and Hounslow Health Authority* [1997] 8 Med LR 290, the Court of Appeal refused an application to stay the action until the claimant submitted to a psychiatric examination, where he was claiming damages for a botched cosmetic operation on his face but was not claiming psychiatric injury. Conflict over a request for a medical examination of the claimant is not uncommon in claims for birth asphyxia leading to brain damage and cerebral palsy. Defendants will ask for a magnetic resonance (MR) scan because the result can sometimes demonstrate, by locating the site of the injury, that it must have occurred much earlier in the pregnancy, thus exonerating them from liability. Objection may be taken by the parents on the ground that a general anesthetic would be required for the procedure and that that carries a small risk of serious harm. In *Hill* v *West Lancashire Health Authority* [1997] 8 Med LR 196, Gage J held that in such circumstances it was a question of carrying out the exercise of balancing the reasonableness of the request against the reasonableness of the refusal, and he found that the balance in the end came down in favour of the claimant because of the risk of harm. In *Laycock* v *Lagoe* [1997] PIQR 518, the Court of Appeal reached a similar conclusion where the defendant was applying for an action for damages following a whiplash injury to be stayed until the claimant underwent an MR scan (there was an issue about the cause of cerebral atrophy, which the defendant said might be resolved by such a procedure).

The claimant may be allowed a friend to be present at the examination if he is nervous or if the doctor has a reputation for roughness, but he does not have a legal right to insist in every case that his own doctor be present when he is examined by the defendants' doctor (*Hall* v *Avon Area Health Authority (Teaching)* [1980] 1 WLR 481, CA; and see *Whitehead* v *Avon County Council* (1995) 29 BMLR 152, where the Court of Appeal refused an application by a nervous patient to have a friend present at a psychiatric examination. However, it is hard to see why a claimant, obviously nervous and possibly unwell, should have to walk alone into the enemy camp; and the impartiality of defendants' doctors is not sufficiently universal to warrant the judge's confidence.

If the claimant shows good reason for objecting to a particular doctor, the court is likely to be sympathetic (*Starr* v *National Coal Board* [1977] 1 WLR 63, CA).

In exceptional cases, where, for example, the liability of the *defendant* depends largely upon his medical condition, the court has power to stay proceedings if he does not submit to a medical examination (*Lacey* v *Harrison* [1993] PIQR P10).

Then there arises the question whether a claimant who submits to an examination by the defendants' doctor is entitled to see the report. The short answer is no. Of course, if the claimant's solicitors made it a condition of their agreeing to the examination that the report should be disclosed, the court will order disclosure, and if the defendants want to rely in court on this report as to condition and prognosis, they will have to disclose it in good time, but it is a privileged document and they cannot be obliged to disclose it if they do not intend to rely on it. The court will not be quick to spell out an implied agreement to disclose even where the claimant has submitted to a medical examination by the defendants' doctor and shown his own doctor's reports to the defendants and they have been agreed (see *Causton* v *Mann Egerton (Johnsons) Ltd* [1974] 1 WLR 162, CA). In *Megarity* v *D J Ryan & Sons Ltd* [1980] 2 All ER 832, the Court of Appeal refused to endorse the practice that had from time to time been followed previously of requiring the claimant to submit to medical examination only upon the condition that the ensuing report be disclosed to him. The Court of Appeal reached a similar conclusion in *Hookham* v *Wiggins Teape Fine Papers Ltd* [1995] PIQR P392. Although it appears that at one time Lord Woolf was suggesting that every report obtained by a party should be disclosed, this has not become law.

In *Beck* v *Ministry of Defence* [2004] PIQR P1, CA, the defendant at a late stage in the case wanted to change its psychiatric expert as it had, it said, lost all confidence in its original expert as having proper knowledge of the relevant psychiatric issues in the case. Naturally the claimant's solicitors refused access for a new psychiatric examination. The defendant succeeded in the two lower courts in gaining permission to start again. The single judge then gave leave for a further appeal in this interlocutory matter, a most unusual event. In the Court of Appeal Simon Brown LJ had some sympathy with the defendant's position, in that this was a high value case, involving allegations against their psychiatric personnel, and without a further report they would be proceeding with an expert in whom they had no confidence. He said that, though it would be unfair to require a defendant upon such an application to argue in detail as to why the original report and the original expert were now deemed to be unsatisfactory because that would give the claimant unfair ammunition for cross-examination of their expert if the application were refused, nevertheless, once it had been decided that the defendant should be permitted to instruct another expert, there were very good reasons why the original report should be disclosed. One reason was that otherwise the claimant would be left wondering if the original expert had decided the claim was a good one! He added that there might be a case where such a condition of disclosure should not be attached to the permission, but it was not easy to envisage one. Ward LJ agreed, saying that expert shopping was to be discouraged and requiring the report to be disclosed was a check against possible abuse. The Master of the Rolls, agreeing, said that a claimant can properly object in any personal injury case to submitting to a second examination without good reason being shown for it. No second examination should be permitted if it appears to be 'a possibility' that the reason a defendant wants a fresh expert is that the first expert has reached a conclusion more favourable to the claimant than the defendant expected. Expert shopping was to be discouraged.

WITNESS STATEMENTS

The witness statement served from a witness called to give evidence stands as his evidence unless the court orders otherwise (r 32.2). With the permission of the court, he may amplify his statement at the trial and give evidence of new matters which have arisen since his statement was served on the other side. But permission will only be given where the judge considers that there is good reason not to confine his evidence to the contents of his statement (r 32.3). Note that if a party does not call a witness in respect of whom a statement has been served and does not put in the statement as hearsay evidence, the other party may put it in as hearsay evidence (r 32.5).[4] This clarifies the conflict between earlier authorities. In *Youell* v *Bland Welch & Co Ltd* (No 3) [1991] 1 WLR 122, Phillips J decided that not only did a statement of a witness lose its privileged status when served, but also that the court had a discretion to admit it in evidence on the application of the party on whom it had been served if its maker was not called to give evidence by the serving party (see also *Black & Decker Inc* v *Flymo Ltd* [1991] 1 WLR 753 (Hoffmann J). But in *Balkanbank* v *Taher* (1994) Times, 19 February, Clarke J, as well as holding that service of witness statements did not waive privilege in respect of connected documents, said that the party serving the statement retained an absolute right whether or not to call the witness or to put in as evidence all or part of the statement (see also *Booth* v *Warrington Health Authority* [1992] PIQR P137). A witness statement may be used only for the purpose for which it is served (r 32.12). If a witness statement is not served within the time specified by the court, the permission of the court is required if the witness is to be called. Practice Direction 32 sets out detailed rules for the preparation of witness statements.

SUBMISSION OF NO CASE TO ANSWER

This is a useful tool for the defence and may properly be employed at the trial at the end of the claimant's evidence (in order to save costs) where the defendant genuinely believes that the claimant's evidence has not got over the initial evidential hurdle of making out a *prima facie* case. It should not be used, as it is so often by criminal defenders, to have a go at the end of the prosecution case on the basis that they have nothing to lose by trying it on. This used not to be a good idea in civil cases as the defendant could then be put to his election, ie he would not be allowed to call any evidence if is submission failed. However, in two recent cases at first instance it has been held that under the CPR a defendant need not be put to his election. Following *Mullan* v *Birmingham City Council* (1999) Times, 29 July, Ebsworth J held in *Worsley* v *Tambrands Ltd (No 2)* [2000] MLC 0280, without putting the defence to their election, that a submission of no case succeeded because the claimant had not made out even a *prima facie* case that the defendants had failed to give proper warnings regarding the possible connection between their product and toxic shock syndrome and what to do in the event of certain symptoms arising.

In *Saed* v *Ealing Hospital NHS Trust* MLC 0511, [2002] Lloyds Rep Med 121, a claim for failure to diagnose tuberculous meningitis and consequent severe injury, the defendant submitted no case to answer at the close of the claimant's case. Mackay J said that normally a defendant should be put to his election as to calling evidence, following *Boyce* v *Wyatt Engineering Ltd* [2001] EWCA Civ 692; but in this case, where it was clear that the claimant had no chance of proving negligence, then, consistently with the overriding objective of litigation pursuant to CPR, r 3.1(2)(m), it was neither right nor necessary to put the defendant to its election.

---

4   A party who has served a witness statement cannot be compelled to call that witness (*Society of Lloyd's* v *Jaffray* (2000) Times, 3 August).

Chapter 13

Costs issues

A NEW REGIME

This chapter focuses on specific aspects of costs likely, sooner or later, to prove troublesome in a medical negligence claim. Under the CPR, apportionment or division of costs among issues and defendants is encouraged. Part 36 offers may specify each admission and the value put upon each head of claim.[1] It is not easy to know how far a successful claimant will be denied costs where he fails on one particular issue, whether by way of failing to establish an allegation of negligence or by failing to beat the Part 36 offer in respect of a head of claim. We may expect a deal of authority to accumulate on these issues. The Court of Appeal said in *Winter* v *Winter* (10 November 2000, unreported), that, whereas before the coming into force of the CPR a party who met with 'substantial' success was entitled to 'all' his costs, the provisions of r 44(3) now enabled the court to do greater justice in a case where a successful party has caused an unsuccessful party to incur costs on an issue which later failed.

The general rule

Rule 44.3 affirms the general rule that a successful party gets his costs, but then requires the court to have regard to many other matters, including the conduct of the parties in every nice particular and the precise result of the case on each of the various issues raised. In *Antonelli* v *Allen* [2000] NLJR 1825, Neuberger J said that, where the successful litigant was unsuccessful on some of the issues, the following factors were relevant when considering costs: the reasonableness of the successful party taking the point on which he was unsuccessful; the manner in which the successful party took the point and conducted his case generally; whether it was reasonable for the successful party to have taken the point in the circumstances; the extra costs in terms of preparing for the trial and

---

1   *Amber* v *Stacey* [2001] 2 All ER 88, CA, told us that a written offer to settle was unlikely to afford protection against an order for costs where a Part 36 payment could have been made. This is perhaps still largely true but, as explained in the text of the chapter, that rule does not apply to the NHS (see below under 'Part 36 offers'). Note, incidentally, that Part 36 offers may be withdrawn at any time, ie the offeror does not have to leave the offer open for 21 days: *Scammell* v *Dicker* [2001] 07 LS Gaz R 41, CA.

preparing witness statements, documents and so on; the extra time taken up in court over the particular issue; the extent to which the unsuccessful point was interrelated, in terms of evidence and argument, with the points on which the successful party succeeded; the extent to which it was just in all the circumstances to deprive the successful party of all or any of its costs.

WHAT IF THE CLAIMANT DOES NOT SUCCEED AGAINST ALL THE DEFENDANTS?

Succeeding against the hospital but not against the GP

It is often difficult for the claimant to decide whether to put all his eggs in one basket, or to sue more than one of the medical attendants involved in a proposed claim. One has to consider the increased complexity if there are two or more defendants and, especially, the costs issues. On the other hand, to stake all on one throw of the dice may be unwise.

In *Johnson* v *John and Waltham Forest Health Authority* (1998) MLC 0244, the Court of Appeal adjudicated on the problem of the incidence of costs where a patient succeeds against only one or more of the defendants. The issue arose within the common scenario whereby the GP is sued for not getting the patient to hospital soon enough and the hospital is sued for its own negligence in its management of the patient.

The variant in this case was as follows. The claim concerned the sudden death of a young mother from bacterial endocarditis. The admitted negligence of the health authority lay in not informing the GP's surgery on 18 June 1987 of abnormal blood test results (the judge found that if they had, the deceased would have been urgently referred to hospital and her life probably saved); and the negligence unsuccessfully alleged against the GP lay in failing to refer the deceased to hospital the next day. The deceased died some 15 hours after being taken to hospital that night.

The case against the GP

In order to establish the allegation against the GP in respect of 19 June, the claimant needed first to persuade the court to prefer the evidence of the deceased's mother over that of the GP. The vital piece of information that the claimant needed to establish was that what the GP was told was that the deceased had seen his partner the previous day and been sent for blood tests (that would probably have been enough to have led within a short space of time to an urgent referral). For reasons that are not clear from the judgment, the judge at first instance concluded that the deceased had deliberately withheld that information from the GP. That was enough to preclude success on the claim against the GP, ie without the need for a finding on causation (which was also strongly contested).

The case against the hospital

The hospital eventually (only six weeks before trial and some 16 weeks after exchange of expert evidence) admitted negligence in not urgently communicating the results of the blood tests to the surgery on 18 June. So the only dispute between the claimant and the hospital was whether causation could be established for this date (ie some 24 hours before the 'causation' date on the GP claim). The judge held that it could, and in the event the claimant was awarded some £221,000 against the health authority.

At first instance

The judge at first instance ordered that the claimant pay all the costs of the claim against the GP. He declined to make an order that the hospital pay those costs. He was not even willing to make no order as to costs. The result of that order was that out of the award of damages against the hospital would come some £70,000 in respect of the GP's costs and a similar amount for the legal aid costs of the claimants in pursuing the claim. As was warned by the Lord Justice who gave leave to appeal, the costs of this unsuccessful appeal will probably have swallowed up what remained of the damages award (and so the deceased's child, aged two at the time of her mother's death, gets nothing).

The judge, having preferred the evidence of the GP about the meeting of 19 June to that of the deceased's mother, said that he would have made a different order for costs if the claim against the GP had failed only on causation, but, as it was, the case against him had failed at all stages. He said it had not been reasonable to make the allegations of negligence against the GP at the time they were made, in that they had no factual substance.

It was in these circumstances that this important appeal was brought.

Processing the claim

The conduct of the claim was hampered by both loss and late disclosure of records. These matters were vital to the claim, as was the fact that a misleading hematology result was disclosed, misleading in that the hole made by a puncher had obliterated the first digit of the results, so that the results appeared normal at 8 instead of abnormal at 18. But the court had scant sympathy for such matters. Brooke LJ said the claimant could have inspected the records (as if they would be on the lookout for every digit on every sheet!). His main point was that all had eventually become clear before the matter came to trial.

The GP claim should have been abandoned

The fundamental fact on which the court based its conclusion that the case against the GP should have been abandoned was that it was 'apparent' from the health authority's own expert report that the allegation of negligence against them would succeed, and therefore, given that that negligence resulted in the non-referral by the GP's surgery on 18 June, there was no point in further litigating a claim against the GP which involved a naturally more difficult contention about causation some 24 hours later.

This seems extremely harsh (and benefits from hindsight). Claims are not progressed on the basis of what 'appears' from a defence expert report. Either the defendants make a clear admission of breach of duty or they do not. There are plenty of ways and means for a defendant to argue round what 'appears' from an expert report. What is more, the defendants had in their pleading specifically denied the negligent conduct that was 'apparent' from their expert report. And what if the claim against the health authority had failed? The claimant's lawyers would then have been liable to criticism, or worse, for having dropped the GP from the frame when they still had a chance of succeeding against him. One knows how unpredictable a case is once it comes to trial. Something could have gone wrong with the case against the hospital at court. The claimant was still entitled to hope to establish the evidence of the mother of the deceased as against the evidence of the GP. And he was still entitled to hope to prove, upon his expert evidence, that referral on the latter of the two relevant days would on the balance of probability still have saved the life of the deceased.

The attitude of the Court of Appeal

All that the Court of Appeal were in fact saying was that the case against the GP was difficult. But so are many cases that succeed. It is clear that the court were influenced by a desire to discourage medical actions. They made a number of references to Lord Woolf and the 'level of public concern about the high failure rate of publicly funded medical negligence litigation' which was 'even higher than it was when Lord Woolf reported'.

Brooke LJ said:

> In order to succeed against [the GP] they would have had not only to hope that their clients' witnesses, who could be seen to have embellished their version of events as time went on, would be found to be more credible than [the GP], but also that somehow or other they would be able to surmount the formidable difficulties on causation which were posed by [the defence experts] in their reports.

Of course, the case against the GP posed difficulties, certainly more than the case against the hospital. In the first place, the GP was disputing liability but the hospital were not. In the second place, causation against the hospital had a 24-hour advantage on causation against the GP. Nevertheless, in my view it was unfair of the Court of Appeal to criticise the claimant's advisers for continuing with the case. If one dropped every case that posed such difficulties, many patients who have gone on to achieve substantial awards would have been ended up with nothing.

However ...

It is, nevertheless, a little difficult to see why in circumstances of this sort a hospital, who have never blamed the GP, should pay all the costs even where the court is not criticising the claimant's advisers for suing the GP. Normally, costs would follow the event. The only useful argument would be to the effect that the claim was being made in respect of NHS treatment as a whole, and the fact that both GP and hospital were being sued, and were funded from different sources, should be irrelevant. One might conclude that a fair order in this case would have been 'no order as to costs'.

Of further interest are the following observations of the court, from which it may be discerned without too much difficulty where their sympathies lay:

> It would be no bad thing if other judges were as robust as [the judge below] showed himself to be in the present case when making orders against an unsuccessful plaintiff at the end of a long and expensive trial which no private litigant would ever have dared to venture, given the odds against success.

And:

> Everyone knows that medical negligence actions are not to be enterprised lightly, and that they have their own peculiar difficulties.

He might have added 'including unsympathetic judges'.

And, commenting on the fact that the GP was 'not only' a GP of 12 years' experience in 1987, but that his expertise had led him to become a GP trainer and a tutor in general practice to two major London hospitals, as well as being chairman of his local medical committee:

> Lawyers advising a private litigant contesting issues of fact with a GP of that experience when there were no documents which favoured their client's version of events, and when that version had become visibly embellished over the years, would have been bound to have warned her of the risks she would run in continuing the action if the result depended on the way the court determined those contested issues.

And, commenting on the extent of the costs involved in the GP action:

> The mention of these vast sums casts a vivid light on the risks that plaintiffs are running in litigation as complex as this if their advisers do not maintain rigid control over expenditure ... and if they do not weigh up carefully the risks of proceeding (or continuing with) an action against more than one defendant.

An earlier case to contrary effect

In an earlier case, *Gerdes-Hardy* v *Wessex Regional Health Authority and Allan* [1994] PIQR P368, the Court of Appeal ordered the unsuccessful GP defendant to pay the claimant's costs of her two claims against the health authority even though one of those claims had not succeeded. The court said that the claimant's conduct had been reasonable, and that the fact that the GP had not sought to blame the hospital in respect of that one claim was not a conclusive factor against requiring the GP to pay those costs. The court emphasised that costs were very much a matter for the trial judge, but said that in this case he had misdirected himself, as he had taken the view that the lack of blaming was a conclusive factor against the award of costs. The court cited with approval the words of Nourse LJ in *Re Elgindata Ltd (No 2)* [1993] 1 All ER 232, CA:

> (1) Costs were in the discretion of the court. (2) They should follow the event, except when it appears to the court that in the circumstances of the case some other order should be made. (3) The general rule does not cease to apply simply because the successful party raises issues or made allegations on which he fails, but where that has caused a significant increase in the length or cost of the proceedings he may be deprived of the whole or part of his own costs. (4) Where the successful party raises issues or makes allegations improperly or unreasonably, the court may not only deprive him of his costs but order him to pay the whole or a part of the unsuccessful party's costs.

WHAT IF THE CLAIMANT RECOVERS ONLY A PART OF THE DAMAGES CLAIMED?

The *Oksuzoglu* case

In *Oksuzoglu* v *Kay* [1998] Lloyd's Rep Med 129, the claimant claimed for negligence by GPs for delay in diagnosis of a leg tumour, resulting, it was alleged, in an amputation that would not otherwise have been necessary (the 'large' claim). Following a nine-day trial in December 1994, the claimant established breach of duty but only limited causation, restricted to damages for a few months pain, discomfort and distress (the 'tiny' claim). Damages were to be assessed at a later date. Some two years after the judgment on liability, the claimant obtained leave to amend his claim to widen the scope of damages, particularly to include substantial psychiatric damage.

In a further hearing on costs, the judge ordered the defendants to pay all the costs, expressing criticism of the defendants as they could have protected their position by a payment in or a *Calderbank*[2] letter.

The Court of Appeal's criticisms, however, focused on the way in which the claimant's solicitors had processed the claim. Having said that, they were at fault for not serving a medical report with the pleading; the court stated that the substantive issue between the parties related to the large claim and on that the claimant had wholly failed. The defendants had made it clear in their *Calderbank* letter that they would be happy to negotiate a settlement of the tiny claim. The amount they paid into court in relation to the size of the tiny claim was reasonably evaluated by the defendants' solicitors on the information then before them. The defendants were essentially the winners on the issues of liability and causation. The late amendment of the claimant's case to include specific allegations of psychiatric damage completely transformed it as compared with his case on the tiny claim, to which he had, some two years earlier, been restricted by the judgment. So the appropriate order was that the defendants should pay the claimant his costs of the action up to the end of the trial on liability and causation, save that the claimant should pay the defendants 90% of their costs arising out of that trial in respect of the issues on liability and causation.

Brooke LJ said that on a preliminary issue a court may ask itself 'who essentially was the winner?' and make an appropriate order as to costs. Defendants' solicitors should be aware that, where a payment into court was not appropriate or possible, a notice admitting facts may be a more effective device for limiting their clients' liability for costs than a *Calderbank* letter.

Knight v *Bradley*

In *Knight* v *Bradley* [2000] MLC 0167, David Foskett QC, the claimant established delay in operating but could not prove any long-term

---

2   A *Calderbank* letter, a term which arose from the divorce proceedings of that name, is simply a letter, written without prejudice save as to costs (ie it will not be mentioned to the judge except at the end of the case when the issue of costs arises) that makes an offer to settle (compromise) the claim on stated terms.

consequences, nor any enduring effect upon her overall level of disability. That derived from the pre-existing degenerate disc. The defendants argued upon costs that they were the substantial winner. However, the judge said that the difference between the original realistic value of the claim and what was actually achieved was not nearly so great as in the *Oksuzoglu* case, and he said he could not see why the defendant could not have protected his position by making a suitable *Calderbank* offer (as the solicitors in the *Oksuzoglu* case had sought to do). The judge did not think that litigating the issue on which the claimant had lost had caused a significant increase in the length or cost of the trial. He would have had considerably more sympathy with the defendants' submissions on costs if they had at any time attempted to limit the issues either by a *Calderbank* letter or by way of admissions. In those circumstances the judge made the usual order as to costs.

Larkins v Davies

In *Larkins* v *Davies* [2000] MLC 0124, the claimant established delay in diagnosing tuberculosis as a result of substandard attention from a number of medical practitioners. However, seeing that he recovered from the disease relatively quickly and the enduring consequence was only the loss of some 10% of his lung function, his general damages were limited to some £26,000. However, his claim had been for £11.5m (thought to be the largest claim ever made in a personal injury action) on the basis that the tuberculosis he had contracted through substandard treatment had cost him his international business, which would otherwise have made vast profits. The evidence on that issue was long and complex (the whole trial took a month). Suffice it to say that the judge rejected the claimant's contentions. The claimant's long history of severe alcoholism clearly put him at a disadvantage in the credibility stakes. The defendants had paid a large sum of money into court, far more than the damages awarded, though, understandably, far less than the sum claimed. Consequently, the judge ordered the claimant to pay the costs of the trial out of the award of damages, and the claimant ended up with nothing.

The *Tampax* case

In *Worsley* v *Tambrands Ltd (No 2)* [2000] MLC 0280 (the defendant having succeeded in the main trial on a submission of no case ([2000] MLC 0186)), Ebsworth J, having found no reason to deny the defendants their costs, effectively ordered disclosure by the claimant's legal expenses insurers of all documentation in their possession relating to their support of the case, including advices received from the claimant's lawyers (subject to later contrary argument from the insurers if they so desired). See r 48.2 and the notes thereunder (*White Book* 48.2.1).

Other cases under this head: In *E Ivor Hughes Education Foundation* v *Leach* [2005] EWHC 1317 (Ch) Peter Smith J, the claimant recovered only £5,000 in a claim for over £610,000, each side having incurred costs of over £140,000. The claimant was ordered to pay most of the defendant's costs. See also *Devine* v *Franklin* (2002) EWHC 1846 (QB).

In *Cornelius* v *de Taranto* [2000] MLC 0218, Morland J awarded £3,000 for breach of contract where, in breach of an implied term of confidentiality, a psychiatrist who wrote a medical report for the claimant for the purposes of her action for constructive dismissal, sent that report, which contained material defamatory of the claimant, to her GP and to another psychiatrist (even though his actions had been well intentioned, in that he wanted to arrange for the claimant to have treatment). The Court of Appeal ([2000] MLC 0218) upheld the finding on liability on the ground that a client's express consent was required before a medico-legal report was transmitted to a third party. However, as the claimant had lost a substantial part of her claim the court said there should be no order as to costs (rather than the judge's order that the psychiatrist pay £45,000, which was equal to about one third of the patient's costs).

CASES

Part 36 offers

These should be made by way of payment into court. However, in *Crouch* v *King's Healthcare NHS Trust* [2004] MLC 1172 the Court of Appeal considered the effect of the NHS practice of purporting to make a part 36 offer by letter. The Trusts gave their reasons in their standard letter for not paying in as follows:

1. The defendant is an NHS public authority. You should therefore be in no doubt that its offer is a genuine one that it will pay promptly if the claimant accepts it in accordance with the terms on which we make the offer; and

2. As an NHS public authority the defendant respectfully submits that rather than paying NHS funds into court, it is preferable for the amount of its offer (which would be paid out of NHS funds) to continue to be available for provision of patient services pending resolution of this case either by agreed terms of settlement or court order;

3. As an NHS body, there is no doubt that the defendant will be able to pay the amount of its offer ...

You will appreciate that the court has power to exercise discretion on the master of costs in these circumstances and we respectfully refer you to ... *The MV Maersk Colombo* (2001) 2 Lloyd's Rep 275 ... [reference was also made to *Amber* v *Stacey* [2001] 2 All ER 88].

The court said that the court should have regard to a *Calderbank* offer to settle made by letter if it was a serious offer and that should normally have the same result as if the money had been paid into court. But the court should have regard to all the circumstances and ask whether it was right to apply that presumption or make a different order depending on the circumstances of the case, thus giving proper effect to the fact that a payment in had not been made. The presumption would not therefore automatically apply. The offer in this case from the Trust, which was bound to be good for the money, was as good as a payment into court. The successful claimant, who had however failed to beat the offer, must pay the trust's costs from 21 days after the offer had been made. This would have been the proper exercise of the judge's discretion below whether under r 36.1(2) or r 44.3.

In *Stokes Pension* v *Western Power* [2005] EWCA Civ 854 the Court of Appeal said that an offer to settle a money claim should usually be treated as having the same effect as a payment in to court if the offer was expressed in clear terms, was open for acceptance for at least 21 days and otherwise accorded with the substance of a *Calderbank* offer, was a genuine offer and the defendant was good for the money when the offer was made.

In *Dugmore* v *Swansea NHS Trust* (16 June 2004, unreported), Cardiff County Court, the claimant had already succeeded before the Court of Appeal in the first latex sensitisation claim to reach the courts ((2002) MLC 0875) and had then agreed damages of £240,000 to be paid to her by the defendants. She had earlier offered to settle for £110,000 in a letter written pursuant to Pt 36. Now in the county court she sought to enforce various financial penalties against the defendants under r 36.21 (enhanced interest on her award at up to 10% over base rate of 4.5%, costs on an indemnity basis and interest on those costs at up to 10% over base rate). Judge Masterman said that the rule was an incentive to encourage settlements. Where a defendant ignored a claimant's part 36 offer, then, if the court did not impose the sanction provided by the rule, there would be no incentive for defendants to take such offers seriously. Interest as sought was awarded.

In *Alli* v *Luton and Dunstable NHS Trust* [2005] MLC 1251, CA, a claim by a nurse for injury caused by inadequate lighting of a stairwell, the court allowed her appeal on costs and awarded her indemnity costs from the date of her part 36 offer. The defendants' lame argument that she had changed the thrust of her case during the trial was rejected.[3]

In *Daniels* v *Commissioner of Police for the Metropolis* (2005) Times, 25 October, the claimant, who had lost her case at trial with costs awarded in the usual way to the defendant, unsuccessfully advanced the extraordinary contention in the Court of Appeal that the defendant should not have its costs as it had refused to negotiate with a view to a settlement.

Mediation

The mediation lobby is strong. Judges have been threatening all sorts of dire financial penalties if a party declines to mediate. But as soon as it is the NHS that is that party, they change their tune – which is good, because, as explained in Chapter 2, mediation is a total waste of time for any substantial medical claim where compensation is the objective. In *Halsey* v *Milton Keynes General NHS Trust* MLC 1115, [2004] 1 WLR 302 a widow was suing for the death in hospital of her 83 year-old husband. It was clearly a very small claim. Her solicitors wrote a number of letters, including one to the Secretary of State for Health, asking for mediation.

---

3   In the highly complex case of *R* v *Secretary of State for Transport, ex parte Factortame Ltd* [2002] EWCA Civ 22 the Court of Appeal emphasised that there were no hard and fast rules on costs in Part 36 situations. The judge should try to assess in each case who really was the successful party and who the unsuccessful. The court held that there was no general principle that the claimant would be the successful party in terms of costs where he accepted a Part 36 payment after the expiry of the time limit for acceptance following a significant amendment to the defence case on the basis of information that had always been available to the defendant.

At all times the defendants, in reality the NHSLA, refused to accept liability, refused to offer any money at all, and refused to mediate. In due course the trial took place and the judge found for the defendants. Given how the virtues of mediation in medical cases (as well as in all other cases, about which I am not qualified to speak) have been trumpeted around one might have thought the Court of Appeal would have been critical of the obduracy of these defendants to the point of imposing some sort of costs penalty. But not a bit of it. The court accepted that active case management included 'encouraging the parties to use an alternative dispute resolution procedure if the court considers that appropriate and facilitating the use of such a procedure' (r 1.4(2)(e)), and said it was in no doubt that it should proceed on the basis that there were many disputes which were suitable for mediation. The court also said it was well aware of the ADR pledge, announced by the Lord Chancellor in March 2001, which led to the NHSLA proclaiming that it would encourage greater use of mediation. Apparently since May 2000 the NHSLA has been requiring solicitors representing NHS bodies in medical claims to offer mediation in appropriate cases and to provide clear reasons to the authority if a case is considered inappropriate. It may therefore be thought somewhat surprising that the defence solicitors in this case took the attitude that they did. Nevertheless the court fully supported their attitude and made no criticism of them at all. Rather, it criticised the claimant's solicitors for what it saw as a tactical use of their many requests in the case for mediation.

The court said, first, that there was no power to force parties into mediation: 'it seems to us that to oblige truly unwilling parties to refer their disputes to mediation would be to impose an unacceptable obstruction on the right of access to the court', ie it would contravene Article 6 of the European Convention on Human Rights. The Court of Appeal also said that, even if there were such power, it found it difficult to conceive of circumstances in which it would be appropriate to exercise it, though the court could encourage parties to mediate in as strong terms as the court might think appropriate.

Next, as to costs, the court said that one must bear in mind that depriving a successful party of his costs would be an exception to the general rule and it should only be done where that party had acted unreasonably in refusing to agree to mediation. There could, incidentally, be no criticism of any position that a party chose to adopt in the actual mediation. The court also said – which has always been my main contention – that most cases were settled by negotiation in the ordinary way. Mediation provided litigants with a wider range of solutions than those that were available in litigation, for example, an apology and an explanation. The court said that mediation and other alternative dispute resolution processes did not offer a panacea and could have disadvantages as well as advantages; they were not appropriate for every case. Those who stand to gain by mediation, that is to say the mediators' organisation, whose costs are by no means low, presumptuously tried but failed to get the court to accept that there should be a presumption in favour of mediation. The court said that factors to consider in deciding whether the refusal to mediate had been reasonable would include the nature of the dispute, the merits of the case, the extent to which other settlement methods had been attempted, whether the costs of the mediation would be disproportionately high, whether any delay in setting up and attending the mediation would have been prejudicial, and whether it had had a reasonable prospect of success.

Turning to the facts of the case, the court said that the defendants had been justified in refusing to mediate, despite the ADR pledge mentioned above. The pledge was no more than an undertaking that ADR would be considered and used in all suitable cases. The reasons justifying the defendants' refusal to mediate in this case were that they were entitled to defend the claim and to have no intention of settling it, so that this was not a case where mediation would be likely to be successful, and they were entitled to take the view that, compared to the value of the claim and the likely costs of a short trial, the costs of mediation would be disproportionately high. The claimant had the burden of proving there was a reasonable prospect that the mediation would have been successful and that the defendant had behaved unreasonably and she got nowhere near doing that. So her appeal was dismissed.

In some ways this is a remarkable judgment from the Court of Appeal. When mediation was being trumpeted, largely by mediators but also by a number of judges, as the panacea for the expense and delay of litigation, I pointed out in no uncertain terms in the journal *Medical Litigation* on more than one occasion that the NHSLA knew perfectly well whether they wanted to make an offer in a case or not and what that offer should be, and nothing would be served by having a third party trotting between the parties to try and persuade them to offer something that they would not otherwise have been willing to do. The short fact of the matter is that in the larger medical negligence claims compensation is almost 100% of the claimant's purpose, the parties almost always will be able to confer amicably and reasonably with each other, and a round table meeting between the experienced lawyers in the case is going to be at least as productive as, and probably more productive than, a mediation.

CFA

Ocloo v *Royal Brompton & Harefield NHS Trust* [2001] MLC 0539 is a sad story and proof, if any were wanted (which none is) of the perils of this sort of funding. Mother, who proved breach of duty by way of system negligence, failed to prove causation in her claim in respect of the death of her teenage daughter from heart failure. The case had been run on a CFA but, unhappily, without any insurance for the claimant against costs in the event of the claim failing. Apparently the premium had been too high – which is not difficult to believe as they almost always are (presumably there was no facility available, such as one firm of experienced solicitors apparently enjoys, of funding the premium by way of bank loan not called in if the claim fails). So Mrs Ocloo was being pressed for defence costs of over £100,000 (which seems a lot when you read the judgment and learn the details of the case). The short fact of the matter is, of course, that CFAs are impossibly dangerous in substantive medical claims, except those very few cases where liability appears well nigh incontestable. Even the LSC might have, I think much to their chagrin, got that message by now.

Proportionality of costs

In *Secretary of State for Home Department* v *Lownds* MLC 0772, [2002] 1 WLR 2450, the Court of Appeal gave guidance on this issue. Whether the costs incurred in a case were proportionate should be decided having regard to what it was reasonable for the party in question to believe might be recovered. Therefore (a) the proportionality of costs recovered by the claimant should be determined having regard to the sum that it was reasonable for him to believe he might recover at the time he made his claim; and (b) the proportionality of the costs incurred by the defendant should be determined having regard to the sum that it was reasonable for him to believe that the claimant might recover, should his claim succeed. In the case the claimant, suing for medical negligence while a prisoner, recovered £3,000 but his assessed costs amounted to £16,784. As these costs were incurred before the CPR came into force, the Court of Appeal was prepared to let the judge's order stand whereby he allowed the assessment, but they said that, had the costs been incurred after the rules came into force, they would have taken a significantly different view.

Costs capping

In *Smart* v *East Cheshire NHS Trust* [2003] MLC 1078, Gage J was asked to cap the claimant's costs. He said that:

> The court did have jurisdiction to make cost capping orders. When an application for a costs cap order is made in cases other than Group Litigation Orders (GLOs) there must be a real and substantial risk that without such an order costs would be disproportionately or unreasonably incurred; that that risk might not be managed by conventional case management and a detailed assessment of costs after a trial; and that it was just to make such an order. Low value claims would inevitably mean a higher proportion of costs to value than high-value claims. Some high-value claims would involve greater factual and legal complexities than others. Clinical negligence cases, for example, would involve more complicated issues on liability than personal injury cases arising out of road traffic accidents. Accordingly, it seemed very unlikely that it would be appropriate for the court to adopt a practice of capping costs in the majority of clinical negligence cases.

The judge added that:

> His observations were confined to actions other than those where group litigation was involved. The latter raised entirely different factors and problems. Past experience showed that the costs in group actions had a tendency to spiral out of control. The generic issues were usually managed by one firm of solicitors acting for all potential claimants whether specifically instructed by those claimants or instructed by solicitors acting on behalf of other claimants. In such cases the court had a clear duty to manage the litigation from an early stage in such a way that one or other party did not allow costs to spiral out of control.

In the instant case the judge declined to cap the claimant's costs.

> On a worst case basis the claimant's estimates of costs was very high; however, solicitors acting for claimants in such cases would inevitably have more work to do in preparing and presenting the case than defendants' solicitors. Further, there was a dispute as to what the claimant's costs would actually be. The

claimant's solicitor's estimate had been prepared taking account of a number of contingencies and unknown factors in order to cater for the inevitable uncertainties in this type of litigation. That estimate, on a realistic basis, was much less than the estimate calculated by the defence. Bearing in mind that the claimant's solicitors were experienced solicitors in this field the court was not prepared to hold that there was a real and substantial risk that costs would be disproportionately or unreasonably incurred. The discipline imposed by the prospect of a detailed assessment post trial was sufficient in this case to ensure that costs did not become disproportionate.[4]

In *Sheppard* v *Essex Strategic Health Authority* MLC 1282, Hallett J upheld the order of the Master who had made a costs capping order whereby a Costs Judge was to prescribe the allowable costs before the case went any further. The claimants' solicitors had estimated their total costs (including the costs of the claimants' previous solicitors), in a highly complex action involving two injured children, at more than £500,000. The defendants estimated their own costs at about £160,000 and their costs draftsman estimated the claimants' costs at about £240,000. The judge said that there was a strong movement towards keeping the costs of clinical negligence actions within reasonable bounds and that included pre-emptive strikes. She was sure that the Costs Judge would impose a realistic budget.

Other cases

Where a medical negligence claim was brought for protective purposes and protocol and pre-action costs were incurred by both parties but the claimant decided not to pursue her claim, HH Judge Mackay held (Liverpool County Court) that the district judge had erred in ordering the claimant to pay the costs of the defence (*Jesson* v *Glossop Acute Service NHS Trust* [2003] MLC 1136).

Where a Part 36 payment into court was made after the 21-day period for acceptance the claimant was the losing party and only exceptionally would it be a permissible exercise of discretion to refuse a defendant an order that the claimant should pay the defendant's costs thereafter (*per* Morland J in *Plymouth and Torbay Health Authority* v *Glanfield* [2002] MLC 0759).

In exercising discretion on costs the general rule is that the unsuccessful party should be ordered to pay the costs of the successful party. The court must always explain why it departed from that rule. The reasons which a judge had given for an order which he made as to costs on a wasted costs order application disclosed that the exercise of his discretion was flawed (*Bellamy* v *Sheffield Teaching Hospitals NHS Trust* (2003) MLC 0727, CA).

In *Goodson* v *HM Coroner for Bedfordshire and Luton* MLC 128, a widow sought (under Supreme Court Act 1981, s 51 as substituted by Courts and Legal Services Act 1990, s 4) a protective costs order, ie a

---

4   The substantive claim in the case was by a child alleging that the hospital should have diagnosed that the injury he was suffering from on admission was not accidental and should therefore have taken steps to have him removed from parental care, thus avoiding further injury.

pre-emptive order declaring that there would be no order as to costs in the Court of Appeal in respect of her coming challenge to the order of the judge below in relation to the conduct of the inquest. Refusing the application, the Court of Appeal said that the matter was not such that the public interest required it to be resolved in the appeal court.

GROUP LITIGATION

The courts are entitled to devise new procedures adapted to the circumstances of particular group litigation (*Horrocks* v *Ford Motor Co Ltd* (1990) Times, 15 February, CA. In *Sayers* v *SmithKline Beecham (No 3)* [2000] MLC 0281, within the MMR litigation, Bell J considered a costs-sharing order that had been made by the Master (previous case management issues are reported at [1999] MLC 0117 and [2000] MLC 0253). Further reference may be made to Professor Mildred's invaluable analysis of the disordered, not to say chaotic, scene in the UK for group litigation in Powers and Harris *Clinical Negligence* (3rd edn, 2000) Chapter 19, particularly paras 148 and 223. For a recent case management hearing in group litigation, see *Sayers* v *Smithkline Beecham plc* [2005] EWHC 539, QB (the MMR litigation).

Capping costs in group litigation

In *Various Ledward Claimants* v *Kent and Medway Health Authority* [2003] EWHC 2551, Hallett J, sitting with Master Hurst, made an order capping the costs of claimants and defendants to the end of the trial. The court said that their power derived from s 51 of the Supreme Court Act 1981 and CPR, Pt 1 (the 'overriding objective'). This was litigation in which there was a real risk that costs had been and would be incurred unnecessarily and unreasonably. The tests for costs that appeared possibly disproportionate was the test of reasonableness in addition to the test of necessity (following *Home Office* v *Lownds* (above)). The court looked askance at the analysis of work to be done offered by the claimant's solicitor.

In the organ retention cases Gage J ordered a cap on the generic costs, referring to the 'clear risk that costs might become disproportionate and excessive given the large sums already spent and the estimate of future costs' (*AB* v *Leeds Teaching Hospital NHS Trust* [2003] Lloyds Rep Med 355).

Reference to costs capping was also made in *Sayers* v *Smithkline Beecham plc* [2004] EWHC 1899, QB. See the paragraph above for cost capping in non-group litigation.

Costs-sharing orders in relation to claimants who discontinued or settled were discussed by the Court of Appeal on a generally successful appeal by the claimants in the MMR litigation at [2001] EWCA Civ 2017.

Law

Chapter 14

Negligence and the duty of care

INTRODUCTION TO NEGLIGENCE

Negligence in the medical field is no different in law from negligence in any other field. The criteria and the rules are the same, whether for liability, for causation or for compensation. At one time, Lord Denning suggested that there is a higher burden of proof where a professional man is being sued, but that proposition was clearly wrong and never got anywhere. It follows therefore that, if one is going to have to ask questions about medical negligence, one needs to know the general law of negligence.

The concept of legal negligence is difficult to analyse. Negligence in law always relates to a particular fact-situation, and what is decided in one case is usually little help in deciding later disputes. The incidents of life are mercurial, protean, amorphous. That, we may suppose, is what makes it so endlessly fascinating. But it also makes it hard for the lawyer to predict the outcome of a negligence suit, quite apart from uncertainties about the evidence and the likely findings of fact. The ingredients of negligence are a duty to take care owed in a particular situation by the defendant to the claimant, a failure to discharge the standard of care required by that duty, and a loss occasioned thereby to the claimant that is recognised by the law as a proper head of loss, of the same type as, if not identical to, loss that was foreseeable at the time of the wrongful act, and deemed by the law to have been caused by that act. The courts have an arbitrary power to decide whether a duty of care is owed in a given fact-situation; their decision depends on whether they consider it right and fair that such a duty should exist.

Meaning of the word 'negligence'

The word 'negligence' is used in different ways. For our purposes, when we ask 'has there been negligence in the handling of this case, whether by acts of commission or omission?', or 'has the doctor been negligent?', we are asking whether he has been in breach of a duty to take reasonable care with regard to his patient. It is no help to a claim if he has been in breach of a duty to take care if that duty was not owed to the patient, nor that he has been negligent in the ordinary sense of careless, unless that amounted to a breach of duty; nor does it avail if he has indeed been in breach of a duty of care to the patient but the patient cannot prove any loss that a court will take cognisance of.

'Negligence' can mean carelessness, which is not a legal term. One has to be careful to distinguish the two meanings. When, years ago, Baron Alderson said:[1]

> Negligence is the omission to do something which a reasonable man, guided upon those considerations which ordinarily regulate the conduct of human affairs, would do, or doing something which a prudent and reasonable man would not do,

He was using 'negligence' in its ordinary non-legal sense without reference to a duty of care. This is the way the word is used when we speak of 'contributory negligence', which goes to reduce the damages awarded to a claimant where he has been, in a general sense, careless of his own safety. It can also serve as a useful definition of the standard of care that has to be shown, eg by a doctor, once a duty to take care has been established.

Mere negligence in itself is not a cause of action. To give a cause of action there must be negligence which amounts to a breach of duty towards the person claiming. There are many cases where there has been clear negligence, in the absence of which damage would not have happened, and yet there is no liability under English law (*per* Greer LJ in *Farr* v *Butters Bros & Co* [1932] 2 KB 606 at 618, CA).

The ingredients

What the civil wrong, or tort, of negligence involves, insofar as it is susceptible to analysis, is a duty of care, a breach of that duty, and loss occasioned by that breach. But these ingredients do not exist separately or *in vacuo*. They will always be related to the particular facts of the case; they overlap and interact, and, moreover, they need to be considerably further defined before the analysis is of any practical use.

Thus, actionable negligence must involve a duty to act with reasonable care towards the claimant, a failure, by act or omission, to discharge that duty (proof is called for that the standard of care required in the particular case was not met), and loss occasioned by that failure, which is both reasonably proximate to the breach (proximity is measured by what should have been reasonably foreseeable at the time of the breach) and of a type recognised by the law. Sometimes the law does not recognise the loss (eg loss of the companionship of a lover or grown-up child, loss of the services of a servant, mere economic loss in some situations); so one can define the duty to take care even further: a duty towards the claimant to take care not to act in such a way as to cause the loss of which he complains. The breach must be a failure to discharge the duty, measured by the degree of care which the particular duty involves. The loss must come within the area of risk that was reasonably foreseeable from the defendant's acts. That sounds involved, but the point is that any attempt to keep separate and distinct the three factors – duty, breach, and loss – is bound to fail (however convenient it might seem for the purposes of jurisprudence):

---

1   *Blyth* v *Birmingham Waterworks Co* (1856) 11 Exch 781.

... you will find that the three questions, duty, causation, and remoteness, [run] continually into one another. It seems to me that they are really three different ways of looking at one and the same problem (*per* Lord Denning in *Roe* v *Minister of Health* [1954] 2 QB 66 at 85, CA, and *Lamb* v *Camden London Borough Council* [1981] QB 625 at 634, CA).

Negligence does not exist in a vacuum as some sort of clearly defined legal concept. It must always be related to a particular fact/situation. This is true of all law, but particularly so of the law of negligence. It is for that reason that judicial decisions in this field only infrequently create any precedent that will necessarily dictate the conclusion in a later case.

The ideas of negligence and duty are strictly correlative, and there is no such thing as negligence in the abstract; negligence is simply neglect of some care which we are bound by law to exercise towards somebody (*per* Bowen LJ in *Thomas* v *Quartermaine* (1887) 18 QBD 685 at 694, CA).

The law takes no cognisance of carelessness in the abstract. It concerns itself with carelessness only where there is a duty to take care and where failure in that duty has caused damage. In such circumstances carelessness assumes the legal quality of negligence and entails the consequences in law of negligence ... The cardinal principle of liability is that the party complained of should owe to the party complaining a duty to take care, and that the party complaining should be able to prove that he has suffered damage in consequence of a breach of that duty (*per* Lord Macmillan in *Donoghue* v *Stevenson* [1932] AC 562 at 618 at 619, HL).

In strict legal analysis, negligence means more than heedless or careless conduct, whether in omission or commission: it properly connotes the complex concept of duty, breach and damage thereby suffered by the person to whom the duty was owing (*per* Lord Wright in *Lochgelly Iron and Coal Co* v *M'Mullan* [1934] AC 1 at 25, HL).

We will therefore consider over the next chapters the three components of the tort of negligence: the establishing of a duty of care owed by the defendants to the claimant; the breach of that duty by failure to attain the standard of care the law requires for the discharge of that particular duty; and damage occasioned by that failure, which is (a) caused by it, ie not too remote (reasonably foreseeable), (b) of a sort recognised by the law and (c) of the same type as, if not identical with, the damage that was foreseeable.

THE DUTY TO TAKE CARE

No formula for testing whether in a given situation a duty of care arises has proved satisfactory. There are guidelines, of which the foreseeability of harm is the most important, for it indicates a *prima facie* duty of care. However, that duty may be negatived by any number of considerations, prime among which is the general consideration of policy as it appears to the tribunal trying the case. As is the wont of the common law, the ambit of the duty of care is continually being gradually extended by *ad hoc* judicial decisions. In that way the scope of recovery for, *inter alia*, nervous shock, economic loss, negligent misstatement, injury suffered by a rescuer, and, more recently, undiagnosed dyslexia and stress-related psychiatric injury at work (a useful new field for personal injury lawyers) has been widened.

When does a duty of care arise?

When does a duty of care arise? Unfortunately, the only sure, albeit unhelpful, general answer to this question is 'when a court decides that a defendant ought to compensate a claimant for his loss'. Sometimes the existence of a duty arises unarguably from the relationship between the parties, such as doctor and patient. In our particular context, the duty is usually no problem. But not always. Is a doctor under a duty to treat when the man next to him in the theatre is taken ill? An English court would say not. What if he is your own doctor, whom you are out with for the evening? That is not so easy. What if a compassionate bystander tries to help the sick man? Must he show some, and if so what, degree of skill? Does that depend on the gravity of the situation and the availability of professional help? What are the duties on a hospital to receive an injured man who staggers in one evening? Of course, if they accept him, a duty arises to look after him, but can they turn him away or have they a duty to succour him? What if the hospital has/hasn't a casualty department, which is shut/open? (see *Barnett* v *Chelsea and Kensington Hospital Management Committee* [1969] 1 QB 428, MLC 0005).

Even if a duty exists, to whom is it owed? In the case of the patient himself there is no problem, but what if a relative or third party suffers as a result of the doctor's negligence, either physically by way of nervous shock (see *McLoughlin* v *O'Brian* [1983] 1 AC 410, HL), or is injured by the patient (see *Tarasoff* v *Regents of the University of California* 551 P 2d 334 (Cal 1976)), or suffers financial loss? (see *Evans* v *Liverpool Corpn* [1906] 1 KB 160).

So it can be seen that, even in the medical negligence context, difficult questions as to the existence of a duty of care may arise.

There are, unfortunately, no clear rules to tell us when a duty of care will be implied. It is remarkable how difficult it is to find in the English authorities statements of general application defining the relations between parties that give rise to the duty.

> The courts are concerned with the particular relations which come before them in actual litigation and it is sufficient to say whether the duty exists in those circumstances (*per* Lord Atkin in *Donoghue* v *Stevenson* [1932] AC 562, HL).

The passage of 70 years has done little to invalidate that statement, reflective as it is of the *ad hoc* growth of the common law. We know that the categories of negligence are never closed (*per* Lord Macmillan in *Donoghue* v *Stevenson* – 'the criterion of judgment must adjust and adapt itself to the changing circumstances of life'), and that precedents can be used with some effect to show that in a similar previous situation the law has recognised a duty of care, but in a novel situation – and there are forever arising from the diverse and protean vicissitudes of life novel situations – we cannot be sure if a duty will be recognised. It depends, as I mentioned above, on the judicial hunch, almost a gut reaction – whether the judge thinks it appropriate to impose liability in a particular situation.

> How wide the sphere of the duty of care in negligence is to be laid depends ultimately upon the court's assessment of the demands of society for protection from the carelessness of others (*per* Lord Pearce in *Hedley Byrne* [1964] AC 465).

The result of the essentially non-academic and pragmatic approach of the English judiciary is that it is made more difficult both to present a coherent analysis for jurisprudential purposes and to predict the legal conclusions that will be reached on any given set of facts. The law governing the duty owed in the tort of negligence, said Lord Asquith in *Candler* v *Crane Christmas & Co* [1951] 2 KB 164 at 188, CA, seems to have been built up in disconnected slabs, exhibiting no organic unity or structure.

Foreseeability as the test of duty

It has been thought at times that if there was a foreseeable risk of the claimant suffering harm from the defendant's activities, that was enough in the normal case to create a duty of care, but that is too wide a proposition. Foreseeability has an important part to play in deciding for what damage the claimant can recover once a duty and a breach of that duty have been established, but it is not a *sine qua non* (see Chapter 18). In the context of establishing a duty, foreseeability of harm is a *sine qua non* (except where there is a duty to act arising simply out of the existing relationship between the parties – see below), but it is not conclusive of the existence of a duty; it is one of the several factors which the court takes into account when deciding whether or not to imply a duty.

A New Zealand judge summed up the position neatly when he said that where a case does not fall clearly within the ambit of previous decisions the proper approach:

> ... is to look at all the material facts in combination, in order to decide as a question of mixed law and fact whether or not liability should be imposed ... it is more than Chancellor's foot justice. The courts have evolved signposts or guidelines or relevant considerations – involving such notions as neighbours, control, foresight, proximity, opportunity for intermediate examinations, deeds or words, the degree and kind of risk to be guarded against – and these are all available to be used as aids to the end result (*Rutherford* v *A-G* [1976] 1 NZLR 403 at 411).

Judicial attempts to formulate a criterion for establishing a duty of care, though giving an impetus to the creation, extension and refinement of the tort, particularly in earlier days, have been expressed too widely and too generally to be acceptable as accurate reflections of what the law actually is. The two seminal formulations are, first, that of Brett MR in *Heaven* v *Pender* (1883) 11 QBD 503 at 509, CA:

> Whenever one person is by circumstances placed in such a position with regard to another that everyone of ordinary sense who did think would at once recognise that if he did not use ordinary care and skill in his own conduct with regard to those circumstances he would cause danger of injury to the person or property of the other, a duty arises to use ordinary care and skill to avoid such danger.

And second, that of Lord Atkin in *Donoghue* v *Stevenson* [1932] AC 562, HL – the snail in the ginger-beer bottle case – when he said that you must take reasonable care to avoid acts or omissions which you could reasonably foresee would be likely to injure your neighbour, ie a person so closely and directly affected by your act that you ought reasonably to have him in contemplation as being so affected when directing your mind to the acts or omissions concerned.

Clearly, there are many situations where you can see you may injure your neighbour but you are under no duty to desist, eg opening a cut-price supermarket next to a small store, actions taken in sport (within the rules), one of two men dying of thirst in the desert grabs the last ounce of water first. One can, with a little imagination, add to the list at will. The formulation is particularly unsatisfactory where it suggests that one is to be liable for omissions which can foreseeably injure one's neighbour. Quite the reverse: one is not liable for any omission unless there is a pre-existing duty to act. Even a doctor is not necessarily under a duty to act, where, for example, the injured party is not his patient.

The judgment of the House of Lords in *Caparo Industries plc* v *Dickman* [1990] 2 AC 605, is one of a number of important decisions on negligence from the last 15 years.

Lord Bridge said:

> Whilst recognising, of course, the importance of the underlying general principles common to the whole field of negligence, I think the law has now moved in the direction of attaching greater significance to the more traditional categorisation of distinct and recognisable situations as guides to the existence, the scope and the limits of the varied duties of care which the law imposes.

Lord Roskill said:

> ... it has now to be accepted that there is no simple formula or touchstone to which recourse can be had in order to provide in every case a ready answer to the questions whether, given certain facts, the law will or will not impose liability for negligence or, in cases where such liability can be shown to exist, determine the extent of that liability. Phrases such as 'foreseeability', 'proximity', 'neighbourhood', 'just and reasonable', 'fairness', 'voluntary acceptance of risk', or 'voluntary assumption of risk' will be found used from time to time in the different cases. But ... such phrases are not precise definitions. At best they are but labels or phrases descriptive of the very different factual situations which can exist in particular cases and which must be carefully examined in each case before it can be pragmatically determined whether a duty of care exists, and, if so, what is the scope and extent of that duty. If this conclusion involves a return to the traditional categorisation of cases as pointing to the existence and scope of any duty of care ... I think this is infinitely preferable to recourse to somewhat wide generalisations which leave their practical application matters of difficulty and uncertainty.

And Lord Oliver said:

> ... to search for any single formula which will serve as a general test of liability is to pursue a will-o'-the-wisp. The fact is that once one discards, as it is now clear that one must, the concept of foreseeability of harm as the single exclusive test – even a *prima facie* test – of the existence of the duty of care, the attempt to state some general principle which will determine liability in an infinite variety of circumstances serves not to clarify the law but merely to bedevil its development in a way which corresponds with practicality and common sense ...
>
> Perhaps therefore the most that can be attempted is a broad categorisation of the decided cases according to the type of situation in which liability has been established in the past in order to found an argument by analogy.

In *White* v *Jones* [1995] 2 AC 207, the Court of Appeal, holding that a duty of care was owed to prospective beneficiaries by solicitors instructed by a testator to change his will so as to reinstate the beneficiaries, stated that the *Caparo* case had established that for the imposition of a duty to avoid particular damage to a particular person or class of persons there had to be foreseeability of damage, proximity of relationship, and a context where it was fair, just and reasonable to impose such a duty.[2] This last requirement gives the court *carte blanche* to admit or reject a duty where there has been no previous decision on similar facts. These requirements are applicable equally where the damage is physical, to person or property (*Marc Rich & Co* v *Bishop Rock Marine Co* [1996] AC 211, HL, *X (minors)* v *Bedfordshire County Council* [1995] 2 AC 633, HL). The House of Lords upheld the Court of Appeal in *White* v *Jones*, but only by a bare majority ([1995] 2 AC 207). The majority took the view that, on the *Hedley Byrne* principle (see below, 'The duty not to make careless statements'), the solicitor had assumed responsibility not only to the testator but also to the beneficiaries to carry out his instructions; the powerful dissenting, and jurisprudentially more convincing, judgments held that there was no principle of law upon which a duty of care could be imposed in the instant circumstances. Lord Mustill said that it did not conduce to the orderly development of the law or to the certainty which practical convenience demanded if duties were simply conjured up as a matter of positive law to answer the apparent justice of an individual case. In other words, there was a complete division of opinion among our most senior judges, and it was a sheer fluke that the claimants won. If the fifth judge had been more concerned with *elegantia juris* than the apparent justice of the claim, the claimants would not have won.

As of now ...

It is virtually impossible to predict whether, in any of the manifold relationships in the outside world, the courts will find a duty of care owed to an injured party. Appeal courts often disagree with lower courts. Different formulae are proposed at different times; current buzzwords are subject to change (eg the early tests of 'who is my neighbour?' and 'foreseeability' are refined into 'did the defendant assume responsibility towards the claimant?', which in time becomes 'was there a relationship of sufficient proximity between the parties?', which then yields precedence to 'is it fair and just to impose liability?'). The progress of time brings changes in judicial thinking on social issues, particularly with the introduction of human rights law. One could list recent cases debating the duties owed by auditors, solicitors, insurers, firemen, rescuers, the police, schools, sportsmen, education authorities, and countless others, to demonstrate the truth of the above remarks. But that is more appropriate to a book devoted to negligence generally (recent *medical* cases, eg involving the ambulance service, educational psychologists, and others, are explicitly dealt with in the next chapter). Suffice it to say that these examples are all to be found in the various legal reports. Lord Slynn has said that the general test is whether the damage relied on is foreseeable

---

2   This case was recently followed in *Gorham* v *British Telecommunications plc* [2000] 1 WLR 2129, where the Court of Appeal imposed on an insurance company advising a client on pension provisions a duty of care to his dependants on the ground that they knew that he was particularly concerned about the effect of any policy on his dependants' interests.

and proximate and whether it is just and reasonable to recognise a duty of care (*Phelps* v *Hillingdon London Borough Council* [2000] 3 WLR 776 at 790, HL). Lord Clyde said that the question whether a duty of care *can* exist in a particular case is a different question from the question whether a duty of care *does* exist. The first question is resolved by considerations of policy, and in particular whether it is fair, just and reasonable to admit such a duty. The second question requires a consideration of the facts of the case and may be susceptible to different answers in different circumstances ([2000] 3 WLR 776 at 808, HL).

Islington Borough Council v *University College London Hospital NHS Trust* [2005] MLC 1254 is an interesting case. The local authority had a statutory duty to provide care for a patient negligently injured by the trust. The local authority could not get payment from her as she had no money (rather, what she did have once her claim against the trust was settled was protected). The payment, in the sum of over £81,000, represented care costs in the period up to the time when, settlement with the trust having been agreed, the patient went into private care. Naturally the patient had not sued the trust for the costs of local authority care as she was not herself under an obligation to reimburse the trust. The local authority sued the trust on the basis that the trust had owed a duty to them not to cause them economic loss by, as it were, dumping an injured patient for whom the trust were liable in their laps. They argued that it was demonstrably unfair that they should bear the cost of caring for a person whose need for care arose out of admitted negligence on the part of the trust. The Court of Appeal made clear that *Caparo* was still the basic test for a duty of care. Surprisingly, they disagreed with the judge and held that the loss to the local authority was not too remote, in other words it was foreseeable as a result of any negligence on the part of the trust. However, even though it could well be said that, as between the present parties, it would be fair, just and reasonable to impose a duty of care on the trust, they were not prepared to do so. There were wider issues and policy implications to be considered, something which, where relevant, was always to be factored into the *Caparo* test. They concluded that no duty of care existed. To declare such a duty would have far-reaching implications for the NHS and for other, non-NHS providers of care, implications that could not be fully envisaged in the ambit of this single piece of litigation. It was rather a matter for Parliament. The judgments contain many interesting observations on the elements of the *Caparo* test, and also on the rights, or rather the lack of rights, of carers to sue the tortfeasor direct.

In the commercial case of *Precis (521)* v *William M Mercer Ltd* [2005] EWCA Civ 114, the court said that the precise limits of the concept of assumption of responsibility were still in a state of development and there was no comprehensive list of guiding principles to help the court determine when an assumption of responsibility could be said to arise. The courts had therefore to look at all the relevant circumstances and determine whether they fell within the situations in which an assumption of liability had previously been held to exist or whether the circumstances were closely analogous to and consistent with the situations in which liability had been imposed in previous cases.

In *Sutradhar* v *Natural Environment Research Council* [2004] EWCA Civ 175, the Court of Appeal allowed the defendant's appeal by a majority and struck the claim out, saying that there was clearly insufficient proximity between the parties for a duty of care to arise (for further details see Chapter 11). The court said that the case of *Watson v British Boxing Board of Control* [2001] QB 1134 and the line of authorities discussed in its text approved the incremental approach to the development of the law of negligence and provided a valuable guide against which to test the assumed facts of the instant case. In the case of the brain-damaged boxer, Michael Watson, the defendants, who had provided regulations by which other parties were required to provide specified medical facilities in the event of injury, were thereby in sufficient proximity and owed a duty of care to the boxers to ensure that proper advice was taken as to what facilities should be provided and then to have ensured that they were provided. They should have known that serious brain injury was one of the injuries that could be suffered in a fight and should therefore have ensured that an appropriate resuscitative facility was available at or close to the ringside.

In *Attorney-General v Hartwell* [2004] PIQR P442 the Privy Council considered a claim against the Government of the British Virgin Islands as being vicariously liable for the injuries accidentally received by the claimant, a British holidaymaker, who was unfortunately in the line of fire when a policeman employed by the Government discharged a loaded firearm in a bar in pursuance of a personal vendetta against his wife and her suspected lover. The court said that the defendants were in breach of a duty of care in issuing the policeman with a firearm when they had failed to investigate two complaints that had earlier been made against him of violent behaviour.

For the duty of care in the medical context, see Chapter 15.

THE DUTY NOT TO MAKE CARELESS STATEMENTS

There is no logical reason why the law should have distinguished between the duty to take care in respect of acts or omissions to act and the duty in respect of statements, but it has. Or at any rate, it has where the statement inflicts, as it usually does, financial loss only; in the rare case where a careless statement leads to physical injury, the court is far quicker to find a duty to take care in speaking (see eg *Clayton v Woodman & Son (Builders) Ltd* [1962] 2 QB 533).

But the law was for many years that, in the absence of actual deceit, financial loss caused by careless statements was not actionable. However, the law was changed by the unanimous decision of the House of Lords in *Hedley Byrne & Co Ltd v Heller & Partners Ltd* [1964] AC 465, where a merchant bank was held to be *prima facie* liable to another bank's customer for negligently representing one of its own customers as creditworthy. The claimants were customers of the second bank who, relying on the defendants' representations about their customer, entered into a commercial relationship with the customer. The customer soon went into liquidation.

The merchant bank were held on the facts not to be liable by virtue of a specific disclaimer of responsibility, but the principle was established by the House of Lords that if in the ordinary course of business one person seeks advice or information from another in circumstances where that other would reasonably know that his advice is to be relied on, he is under a legal duty to take such care in giving his reply as the circumstances reasonably require. But for that duty to arise that particular relationship has to exist between the parties. It need not of course be contractual; it need not be fiduciary in the strict sense, but there does need to be a sufficient degree of proximity (that word again!) between the parties, so that the element of reasonable reliance is present.

This aspect of the duty of care was exhaustively examined by the House of Lords in *Caparo Industries plc* v *Dickman* [1990] 2 AC 605. The reasoning behind the decision that auditors of a company are under no duty of care in preparing the company's accounts to non-shareholding potential investors, nor to shareholders as potential further investors, may be summarised by saying that they had no reason to suppose that their audit would be communicated to the claimants, let alone relied on in deciding whether to invest (further) in the company (the auditor's statutory duty to shareholders was said to be imposed to enable them to exercise their class rights in a general meeting and not to extend to assist them in making investment decisions).

Compare the House of Lords' decisions in *Smith* v *Eric S Bush* and *Harris* v *Wyre Forest District Council* [1990] 1 AC 831, where a surveyor preparing a report for a mortgagee was held to be under a duty of care to the prospective purchaser, principally because he knew or should have known that the purchaser would see the report and would probably act, ie complete the purchase, in reliance on it.[3] We may also see here the vital role of policy in reaching a decision: it is one thing to hold a bank or building society responsible in a limited financial context to an individual house purchaser, quite another to hold auditors responsible in a commercial context to any potential investor in the company.

In the surveyor cases, Lord Griffiths said that what was required to impose liability was foreseeability of harm from any negligent advice, a sufficiently proximate relationship between the parties, and that it was just and reasonable to impose the liability (this, of course, gives the courts a wide (virtually unfettered) discretion to impose or not impose liability). In *Caparo* Lord Bridge said that the salient features of the cases where liability for negligent misstatement resulting in economic loss had been imposed were that the defendant was fully aware of the nature of the transaction that the claimant had in contemplation, knew that the advice or information would be communicated to him directly or indirectly, and knew that it was very likely that the claimant would rely on it in deciding whether or not to engage in the transaction.

In a claim against actuaries in respect of a report prepared on certain pension funds, the claimant alleging that it had relied on that report, the court said the salient issue was whether, when the defendants provided their report, did they do so in circumstances which, viewed objectively, meant that they were responsible to the ultimate recipient if the information was negligently prepared. The answer in this case was no (the *Precis (521)* case – see the preceding section for further details). A strange claim was made in *Legal and General Assurance Society* v *Kirk*

---

3   See also *Merrett* v *Babb* [2001] 3 WLR 1, CA.

[2001] EWCA Civ 1803. A financial consultant was sued by his employer for repayment of commission. In his defence the consultant counter-claimed for negligent misstatement consisting of the mere assertion that he owed them money. He contended that for the cause of action to be complete it was not necessary that the statement should have been communicated to an enquirer, such as someone in connection with a job application submitted by the consultant. The Court of Appeal, not surprisingly dismissing the appeal, said that it was impermissible to extend the basic principle that for the claim to come into being it was necessary that there should have been 'reliance by somebody upon the accuracy of that which the word communicates and the loss or damage consequential upon that person having adopted a course of action upon the faith of it' (Lord Oliver in *Caparo* v *Dickman* (1990) 2 AC 605). The claimant would have to prove damage through reliance by a third party on the employer's statement. In this case no reference had been given, therefore no reliance had been placed by a third party, hence no damage had been sustained.

In *McCunn* v *Riola* [2001] EWCA Civ 1502 the issue was whether the defendant had assumed responsibility in law for his statements to the claimant about the progress being made in replacing the claimant as guarantor of a lease. Dismissing the defendant's appeal, the Court of Appeal said that a single request for information might well not have founded a claim, but in all the circumstances of the party's dealings the importance to the claimant of the issue must have been clear to the defendant. Hence a duty of care arose.

The doctor/patient relationship

For the doctor's duty not to make misleading statements to the patient, see Chapter 15.

Chapter 15

The duty of care in the medical context

The doctor's duty to take all due care of the patient arises from the relationship of doctor and patient and involves not merely a duty to take care once activity (treatment) is commenced, but also a duty to initiate action, ie to take all steps necessary for the health of the patient. It is, however, confined to times when and places where the doctor can properly be expected to be 'on duty'. The cry of 'Is there a doctor in the house?' does not impose legal liability on the medical theatre-goer. The duty is also confined to medical matters. It may extend, on the modern developments in the general law of negligence, to other people than the patient.

THE DUTY ARISING

In most medical negligence contexts, the duty of care is not a problem, because it is obvious that the doctor owes a duty of care to the patient. This duty arises out of the relationship. It is not based on foreseeability of harm. There would still be a duty to take care of the patient in a particular situation where as it so happened harm was not reasonably foreseeable. It is not a duty that arises from an activity undertaken, as in so many negligence situations, eg undertaking building works, sporting activities, care of prisoners, driving a motor vehicle, etc. It arises simply from the relationship, regardless of activity undertaken. This is why there is a duty to act, and not merely a duty to take care once activity is undertaken. Such a case, where there is a duty to act, is not the same, and requires different consideration from the activity situation. Without a 'relationship' based on the status of the parties, ie here a doctor-patient status, there is no duty, as we have seen, to act. One is permitted to do nothing. If a bleeding man comes to my door needing help, I am not legally obliged to give it. Once there is a duty to act, the obligee will be in breach if he does not commence all necessary activity, quite apart from being in breach if he does not use due care in carrying out the activity (the treatment). Negligent omissions can be the failure to commence activity where there is a duty to act, as well as the failure to take some appropriate step in the course of the activity once commenced (see, on the doctor's duty, *Pippin* v *Sheppard* (1822) 11 Price 400, where an averment that the defendant had been employed to 'treat, attend to and cure divers grievous hurts, cuts etc' and as a result of his treatment 'the said wound became and was grievously aggravated and made worse', was held to be a good plea; see also *Edgar* v *Lamont* 1914 SC 277).

When then is a doctor under a duty of care? Is that duty owed only to the patient? Is that duty owed only in respect of strictly medical activities? Is he liable only for losses coming within the scope of his medical activities?

A doctor is not legally obliged to assist, eg at a car accident (there is no duty to act where the claimant is not a patient or required to be accepted as a patient, as at a casualty department; see *Thompson* v *Schmidt* (1891) 8 TLR 120, CA). If he chooses to, as no doubt he would, he must exercise all proper skill. If he is a GP and the injured party just happens to be his patient, he might be held to be under a legal duty to act, for the court might well say that his duty to look after the patient's health was not limited to the location of surgery or home. If he happened to be the consultant who had recently operated on the now injured party, the court would be unlikely to say that his duty extended to further assistance on the highway, even if the patient was still under his care as an out-patient.[1]

A non-medical bystander is under no duty to give succour (we do not have 'good Samaritans' legislation, as in France), but if he does he must act with the care that is reasonably to be expected from someone who undertakes to help. If he makes the victim worse, he will be liable (there is no duty on a non-medical man who is asked to act, *Shiells* v *Blackburne* (1789) 1 Hy Bl 158; but if he has made representations of prowess a duty of care arises, *Ruddock* v *Lowe* (1865) 4 F & F 519; *Brogan* v *Bennett* [1955] IR 119). In a 1988 case, a motorcycle scrambler unsuccessfully sued the St John Ambulance Brigade on the ground that the volunteers who came to his aid when he fell from his motorcycle failed to spot a back injury and made it worse by getting him to stand.

In *Capital and Counties plc* v *Hampshire County Council* [1997] QB 1004, CA, a fire brigade case, Stuart-Smith LJ said:

> ... a doctor who happened to witness a road accident will very likely go to the assistance of anyone injured, but he is not under any legal obligation to do so, save in certain limited circumstances which are not relevant, and the relationship of doctor and patient does not arise. If he volunteers his assistance, his only duty as a matter of law is not to make the victim's condition worse. Moreover, it is clear that no such duty of care exists, even though there may be close physical proximity, simply because one party is a doctor and the other has a medical problem, which may be of interest to both.

In *Powell* v *Boldaz* [1998] Lloyd's Rep Med 116, CA, the court struck out a claim by parents for psychiatric damage alleged to have been caused to them by a conspiracy to conceal vital medical records, following negligent failure to treat their son which led to his death. The court said there was no basis for the claim in unlawful conspiracy because it was not shown that any conspiracy that might have taken place was aimed at the claimants, and neither reasonable possibility of harm nor causation was

---

1   Ethical guidance (dated 16 May 1988) from the GMC on HIV infection and AIDS stated that refusal to treat on the ground of personal risk to the treating doctor might amount to serious professional misconduct.

established. On the doctor-patient relationship, the court said that a doctor who had been treating a patient who had died, and who then told relatives what had happened, did not thereby undertake the doctor-patient relationship towards the relatives.

In *Barnett* v *Chelsea and Kensington Hospital Management Committee* [1969] 1 QB 428, MLC 0005, Nield J held that a hospital owed a duty to act *vis-à-vis* a person who presented himself at the casualty department, notwithstanding that he had not yet been received into the hospital in any way. The failure to act when he so presented himself was negligent (although on the facts it was found not to have contributed to his subsequent death). Nield J said that, although there could be cases where the casualty officer was not required to see the caller (eg if he already has his own doctor whom he can attend and is merely seeking a second opinion), in general, the duty of the casualty officer is to see and examine all patients who come to the casualty department. Once he has started the activity of treatment and care, by examination in the first instance, it is his duty to take all reasonable steps, which in this particular case would have required the admission of the caller to the wards.

The doctor's duty in child abuse cases

This question has come to the fore recently, by virtue of our signing up to the human rights bandwagon and the scope these vaguely expressed entitlements give for inventive lawyers to argue for extending the traditional principles of common law – all on legal aid, of course. Ten years ago we had a firm, unanimous and fully reasoned decision from the House of Lords in the two cases of *X (Minors)* v *Bedfordshire County Council* and *M (a minor)* v *Newham London Borough Council* [1995] 2 AC 633 to the effect that the professionals (we need not distinguish between doctors, psychologists or social workers for present purposes) involved in investigating suspected abuse cases in exercise of a statutory duty did not also owe a duty of care at common law to the children concerned, let alone to the parents. However, several years later the Strasbourg court decided that the five children in the Bedfordshire case had had their welfare neglected to such an extent by the local authority that it amounted to a violation of Article 3 of the Convention (inhuman and degrading treatment), and they awarded the very large (for Strasbourg) sum of compensation of £320,000 (*Z* v *United Kingdom* (2001) 34 EHRR 97). Both child and mother succeeded in Strasbourg in the Newham case in establishing a violation of Article 8 (respect for family life) (*TP and KM* v *United Kingdom* (2001) 34 EHRR 42). The negligence in this latter case lay in the failure of the health professional to listen to the child's account with proper attention, as a result of which the mother's partner was suspected of abuse and the child was removed from the mother's care for almost a year. The Strasbourg decision was based not on the decision to remove the child but on the failure to disclose their 'evidence' to the mother immediately after the removal, an action which would apparently have led to their revising their decision.

It has since then been generally accepted that, given the view of Strasbourg, a duty to act with appropriate care is in fact owed to the child in these cases, for otherwise English law would be in contravention of human rights and that would never do. This change in the law was declared by the Court of Appeal in the case recently heard on appeal in the House of Lords (judgment was given by their Lordships in *JD (FC)* v *East Berkshire Community Health NHS Trust* and two other actions on 21 April 2005 [2005] 2 WLR 993, MLC 1242). Note that the events on which this East Berkshire case was based happened before the Human Rights Act came into force).

The issue in these associated cases was whether a duty was owed to the parents. The facts can be stated as follows. The claimants were parents who were wrongly suspected of child abuse through the misdiagnosis of their children by doctors. Each in consequence suffered psychiatric disorder. In each case the true explanation for the child's condition was not discovered until regrettably late. In each case it was assumed for the purposes of the appeals against striking out orders that the respective doctors failed in their investigation and diagnosis of the child's condition to exercise reasonable and proper professional care, failures which would render them liable in damages for injuries suffered by anyone to whom they owed a duty of care. It was also assumed that the respective parents had suffered foreseeable psychiatric injury.

Lord Bingham, the lone dissenting voice among their Lordships, considered the matter to be arguable and therefore the claim should not be struck out. However it would seem that if a doctor investigating the question of abuse should be liable to the parents if he acted without due care, thus causing a parent to be accused and/or the child to be taken away from the family, thus causing foreseeable psychiatric harm to one or both parents, then there was no reason why a negligent surgeon, for example, should not be liable for psychiatric harm suffered by a parent if his negligence injures or kills the child. What floodgates would open if a doctor with the medical charge of a child also owed a duty of care to the parents!

Lord Nicholson said that the duty towards the parent went no further than to act in good faith. That had long been the criteria in this area of law concerning the reporting and investigation of suspected crime. Note the claimant had not gone as far as to argue for a general duty to all who might fall under suspicion, but only to a parent or other primary carer, not for example to a teacher or childminder. The claimant argued that the potential for disruption of family life (a human right, of course) tilted the balance in favour of such a duty being owed to a primary carer (the test as per *Caparo Industries plc* v *Dickman* [1990] 2 AC 605, 618 being whether it is 'fair, just and reasonable that the law should impose [such] a duty'). There was some support for this proposition to be found in the Strasbourg decision in *Venema* v *Netherlands* (2002) 39 EHRR 102, where the court held that there had been a breach of Article 8 because the parents had not been sufficiently involved in the decision-making process. However, Lord Nicholson saw an insuperable obstacle to the claim in the context of 'conflict of interest'. The doctor was charged with the protection of the child, not the parent. The interests of the child in that situation were not identical with those of the parent; indeed they could be diametrically opposed. The duty they owed to the child in making these decisions should not be clouded by imposing a conflicting duty in favour of parents or others suspected of having abused the child. This was the conclusion already reached by the High Court of Australia in *Sullivan* v *Moody* (2001) 207 CLR 562. (Note also that the Privy

Council reached the same conclusion in the New Zealand appeal of *B* v *Attorney-General of New Zealand* [2003] 4 All ER 833.)

Lord Rodger said there were many situations where the infliction of foreseeable harm did not of itself give rise to a duty of care. Apart from the context of commercial competition, he gave an example of the woman who leaves her husband for another man. No-one suggests the distraught husband can sue for having been caused foreseeable psychiatric injury. And, of course, there is no common law right to compensation by way of general damages for the negligent killing of a close relation. Lord Rodger said that for the most part the settled policy of the law is opposed to granting remedies to third parties for the effects of injuries to other people. He said the claimants were seeking to introduce an exception to that approach. In carrying out their duty of investigation the doctors had regard only to the interests of the children. If they had also to have regard to a duty not to injure the parents by coming carelessly to the conclusion that they might have abused their child, they would have to consider two sets of interests which were inconsistent with each other. The duty to the parents might lead them to act differently from how they would have acted if there were no such duty. In other words, they might not act in a way that was wholly influenced by their concern for the child.

Lord Brown said it was easy to sympathise with the parents, their plight and their grievances. But that did not mean that a right to redress must necessarily follow. He said there had been a constant stream of authority against the proposition that a parent was owed a duty in these contexts. Among other cases he cited the words of Hale LJ (now Baroness Hale) in the adoption case of *A* v *Essex County Council* [2004] 1 WLR 1881, 1900, where she said that the child's interests in an adoption case might well conflict with those of the parents and the prospective adopters. Lord Brown said he failed to see how a duty to the parent could fail to impact upon the doctor's approach to his task and thus create a conflict of interest. It was vital that doctors should have only the child's interests to consider when dealing with the sadly all too prevalent issue of abuse. Only in that way could one hope for successful management of the general problem. Further:

> The law has always placed strict limitations upon the right to recover for psychiatric injury and it is not easy to see why, if no such right exists in a father whose child is negligently allowed to die, it should be given to a father wrongly suspected of child abuse. In the first case the child is lost for ever; in the second for a comparatively short time.

And he expressed the difficulties he foresaw in this way:

> First, the insidious effect that the doctors' awareness of the proposed duty would have upon the mind and conduct of the doctor (subtly tending to the suppression of doubts and instincts which in the child's interests ought rather to be encouraged), and second, the consideration inevitably bound up with the first, the need to protect himself against the risk of costly and vexing litigation, by no means invariably soundly based. This would seem to me a very real risk in the case of disgruntled parents wrongly suspected of abuse; all too readily they might suppose proceedings necessary to vindicate their reputation.

He added:

> I acknowledge it is the parents who are paying the price of the law's denial of a duty of care. But it is the price they pay in the interests of children generally.

The well-being of innumerable children up and down the land depends cru-
cially upon doctors and social workers concerned with their safety being subjected by the law to but a single duty: that of safeguarding the child's own
welfare. It is that imperative which in my judgment must determine the outcome of these appeals.

The education cases

In *E* v *Dorset County Council* [1995] 2 AC 633, the House of Lords refused
to strike out claims based on a specific duty of care owed by a local education authority for acts or omissions of its individual psychologists,
teachers or officials in failing to ascertain learning problems and provide
appropriate advice and assistance to the claimant and his parents pursuant to the statutory code dealing with special educational needs
enacted by the Education Acts. Explaining the difference between that
case and *X (minors)* v *Bedfordshire County Council* (above), which at that
time was still good law, Lord Browne-Wilkinson, with great prescience,
said:

> The position of the psychologists in the education cases is quite different from
> that of the doctor and social worker in the child abuse cases. There is no poten-
> tial conflict of duty between the professional's duties to the claimant and his
> duty to the educational authority. Nor is there any obvious conflict between the
> professional being under a duty of care to the claimant and the discharge by
> the authority of its statutory duties.

Four conjoined cases can be found at MLC 0228, [2001] 2 AC 619. *Phelps*
v *Hillingdon London Borough Council* was the only one that had been
tried – the others were at an interlocutory stage. The wide-ranging effect
of the decisions of the House of Lords is that an educational psychologist
employed by a local education authority will, or is likely to, owe a duty to
a pupil on whom she reports for her employer, and that a local education
authority owes a general duty through its teachers to provide a suitable
education for its pupils, particularly if they have special needs. In *G (a
minor)* v *Bromley London Borough Council* [2000] 3 WLR 776, the
claimant suffered from muscular dystrophy; in the other cases the disability was or was claimed to be dyslexia. However the Court of Appeal,
misliking the Pandora's box thus opened, said in *Devon County Council* v
Clarke [2005] EWCA Civ 266 that it was wrong to characterise all educational negligence cases as being single claims for a failed education over
a period of time as if special rules applied to them and that the jurisdiction to award damages in cases of this sort was not to be seen as a charter for claimants to make allegations against all the professionals who
had been involved in a child's education, secure in the knowledge that,
provided they succeeded in one allegation against one professional, they
would recover all their costs from the local education authority. The
interests of professionals needed to be considered as well as the right of a
child to claim damages in negligence.

In *DN* v *Greenwich London Borough Council* [2004] EWCA Civ 1659
the Court of Appeal held that a local education authority was liable for
the negligence of an educational psychologist who had failed, among
other things, to identify the claimant's complex social and communication
needs, but, where expert evidence was uncertain on the issue of the outcome for the claimant if he had been placed in an appropriate school, the

measure of damages would be small. The extent to which lawyers are prepared to propose and support claims of this sort can be gauged by the fact that damages were unsuccessfully sought on the basis that, by reason of his poorly served educational needs, the claimant had become an arsonist. The law reports are beginning to fill with these hopeful education claims. One unsuccessful appeal by a claimant can be found in *Carty* v *Croydon London Borough Council* [2005] EWCA Civ 19. In that case can be found guidance as to the relevant issues where the allegation was that a public authority had been negligent in the performance of its functions. The court said there were two areas of potential enquiry in such a case. The first was whether the issue was justiciable at all, the second was the application of the three-stage *Caparo* test – foreseeability of damage, proximity, and whether it was fair, just and reasonable that the law should impose a duty of care.

Duty owed to others

If negligent medical treatment causes the death of a patient, liability may extend, on the 'aftermath' principle of *McLoughlin* v *O'Brian* [1983] 1 AC 410, HL, to a member of the deceased's immediate family (see Chapter 19). In *Goodwill* v *British Pregnancy Advisory Service* [1996] 1 WLR 1397, CA, a claim, not surprisingly, failed where it necessarily involved establishing that a doctor carrying out a vasectomy owed a duty not merely to the patient, but to all the women the patient might in the future have sexual intercourse with.

Medical examination with a view to employment

In *Roy* v *Croydon Health Authority* [1997] PIQR P444, CA (appealed on other issues sub nom *R* v *Croydon Health Authority* [1998] Lloyd's Rep Med 44, CA), the defendant health authority required the claimant to undergo an occupational health medical examination as a prospective employee. The defendants' radiologist carelessly failed to note that an X-ray disclosed a serious pathology. It was admitted that the defendants owed a duty of care in these circumstances (the case was fought at first instance and upon appeal on quantum only). So, although the claimant was not the patient of the radiologist or the health authority, there was no dispute about his duty not only to his employers but also to the claimant to interpret the X-ray competently.

This case should be distinguished from *Kapfunde* v *Abbey National plc* [1999] Lloyd's Rep Med 48, CA. Although in *Baker* v *Kaye* [1997] IRLR 219, 39 BMLR 12, a judge at first instance held that a doctor retained by a company for the purpose of examining a potential employee for his medical fitness to do a job was held to owe a duty of care to the potential employees in carrying out his examination and in interpreting the results of that examination when reporting to the company, the Court of Appeal in *Kapfunde* overruled that decision. The salient facts were that a GP had a contract with Abbey National whereby she assessed the health of any prospective employee. In this case she had, upon written material, not an examination, declared that the claimant was unsuitable to be employed as she had sickle cell disease and so was at risk of having a lot of time off work for illness. Having unsuccessfully sued for racial discrimination, the claimant went on to allege in this action that the GP owed her a duty of care, which she had breached. The Court of Appeal, having declined to interfere with the judge's findings that the GP was on a contract for services and not a contract of service and therefore Abbey National would not in any event be vicariously liable for any breach of duty by her, and that anyway she had not been negligent, held on the main issue, whether a duty was owed, that the claim fell to be decided as a claim for economic loss for negligent misstatement. They applied the law as stated by the House of Lords in the *Caparo* case [1990] 2 AC 605, said that the situation was analogous to that of the social workers and the doctors in *X* v *Bedfordshire County Council* and *M* v *Newham London Borough Council* [1995] 2 AC 633, HL (no duty of care owed to a child or her mother by a psychiatrist or social worker examining or inquiring for evidence of sexual abuse on behalf of the local authority in the exercise of their statutory child care functions), and that therefore there was no sufficient proximity or special relationship between the GP and the claimant for a duty to arise. She was acting for Abbey National, who had instructed her, not for the claimant.[2] In view of later developments in the House of Lords, as exemplified in the cases reported under the leading title of *Phelps* v *Hillingdon London Borough Council* [2000] 3 WLR 776, HL (see above) and the ground-breaking decision of the House of Lords in *JD* v *East Berkshire Community Health NHS Trust* (see above), the *Kapfunde* case might now have had a different outcome.

The medical report and witness immunity

In *Landall* v *Dennis Faulkner & Alsop* [1994] 5 Med LR 268 an orthopedic surgeon was sued for advice given in a personal injury action to the effect that the claimant's condition could be helped by a spinal fusion. The action was settled on that basis. The claimant contended that the advice was negligent and that the operation had damaged him further. It was held at first instance that the expert was immune from suit as the report in question had been given for the purpose of assisting the lawyers to conduct the claimant's case, and not for the purpose of advising the claimant about medical treatment. The report constituted 'pre-trial work so intimately connected with the conduct of the case in court that it could fairly be said to be a preliminary decision affecting the way the case was to be conducted when it came to a hearing'.[3]

Contra, in *Hughes* v *Lloyds Bank plc* [1998] PIQR P98, the claimant in a proposed personal injury action settled her claim with the third party insurers consequent upon letters she obtained from her GP about her

---

2   In *Cameron* v *Merton, Sutton and Wandsworth Health Authority* [2000] MLC 0192, an applicant in person on a second tier appeal unsuccessfully argued that her claim should not have been struck out where it alleged that a doctor examining her fitness to take up a teaching employment should have found her to be unfit and that as a result of that breach of duty she had become ill in the job.

3   Where a negligent medical report for the purposes of litigation has resulted in an under-estimate of the injury and the case has been settled for too little, the medical defence societies have in the past been ready to settle claims (see also *Pimm* v *Roper* (1862) 2 F & F 783; and, to a contrary intent to the *Stevens* case (see below), *McGrath* v *Kiely and Powell* [1965] IR 497).

condition without there having been a medical examination (the bank represented the deceased GP). The claimant contended that in those letters the GP had negligently under-stated her injuries. The action was struck out below both as an abuse and on the ground that the GP was immune from suit. The Court of Appeal disagreed, saying that at the time the doctor provided the claimant with the letters proceedings had not been issued and so could not be said to be preliminary to his giving evidence as an expert. The documents were not supplied for disclosure to the other side in the context of proceedings, but purely in the context of negotiation. As a result, the doctor was not covered by the immunity of a witness (*Landall* was not considered by the court). However, Lord Bingham acknowledged the 'extreme difficulty' of drawing the line between the public policy rule of immunity for witnesses and the right of a litigant to sue for negligent professional advice.

In *M* v *Newham London Borough Council* [1995] 2 AC 633, HL, Lord Browne-Wilkinson said that a psychiatrist would have witness immunity where, having been instructed by the local authority to examine a child by way of an inquiry into sexual abuse and its possible perpetrators, she would naturally know that her report might found proceedings (see above for later developments in this case).

A full analysis of expert witness immunity was recently undertaken by the Court of Appeal in *Stanton* v *Callaghan* [2000] 1 QB 75, which concerned a claim against a surveyor for alleged negligence when reporting on methods of remedying subsidence with a view to the sale of a house.

In *N* v *Agrawal* [1999] MLC 0100, the claimant's hopeless contention was that the accredited medical examiner who examined her following her complaint of rape and buggery, and made a report upon her examination, owed her, the victim, a duty to attend court and give evidence at the trial of her alleged assailant, and that her failure to do so had resulted in foreseeable exacerbation of the victim's psychological trauma. The Court of Appeal struck out the claim on the ground, *inter alia*, that it was clear law that a witness was not under a duty to any person to give evidence, apart from her civic duty.

The ambulance case saga

In February 1991, an ambulance was called for a young married woman suffering severe asthma. Despite a number of calls, it took 38 minutes to arrive. The young woman suffered respiratory arrest and brain damage. At first instance it was held that the allegation of negligence by way of failure to respond promptly to the call had no prospect of success and should be struck out. The Court of Appeal disagreed, stating that it was arguable that once a 999 call requesting the dispatch of an ambulance was accepted sufficient proximity existed between the parties as to give rise to a duty of care ([1999] Lloyd's Rep Med 58, [1998] MLC 0065). At the trial, Turner J held that there was a duty on the ambulance service to respond with appropriate speed once an ambulance had been allocated and the service informed that time was of the essence, and that the service was in breach of that duty ([1999] Lloyd's Rep Med 424, [1999] MLC 0112). The matter went again to appeal, where the Court of Appeal upheld the judge (*Kent* v *Griffiths, Roberts and London Ambulance Service* [2000] 2 WLR 1158, [2000] MLC 0164). The court said that the ambulance service should be regarded as part of the health service, where a duty of care to patients normally existed, rather than as providing services equivalent to those rendered by the police or the fire service when responding to a 999 telephone call. (Note that various recent cases have limited the liability of police and fire services for damage caused by neglect of their duty, on public policy grounds for the most part – the defendants in this ambulance case were trying to put themselves under the same umbrella.) The ambulance had been allocated to this particular patient; there were no alternative demands on it and no reasonable explanation why it failed to attend within a proper time; and therefore there were no circumstances which made it unfair, unreasonable or unjust that a duty of care to the patient should exist once the 999 call had been accepted.

WHERE A DOCTOR IS NOT REQUIRED TO FORESEE LITIGATION

In *Stevens* v *Bermondsey and Southwark Group Hospital Management Committee* (1963) 107 Sol Jo 478, it was held at first instance that the doctor was not required to foresee the legal consequences of his advice. A casualty officer who negligently diagnosed a minor injury was not liable for the financial loss to the patient, when, not knowing therefore that he had suffered a serious injury, he settled his claim against the tortfeasor for a smaller sum than it was worth.

DANGEROUS PATIENTS

Earlier cases suggested that the doctor was under a duty of care to potential victims of a dangerous patient who was not properly contained (*Holgate* v *Lancashire Mental Hospitals Board* [1937] 4 All ER 19; *Ellis* v *Home Office* [1953] 2 All ER 149, CA). The principle was explained by the House of Lords in *Home Office* v *Dorset Yacht Co Ltd* [1970] AC 1004, the case about the escaped Borstal boys. A Californian court has taken the matter further. In *Tarasoff* v *Regents of the University of California* (1976) 551 P 2d 334 (Cal), a duty was recognised upon a psychiatrist to warn the intended victim if his patient uttered death threats in session. In *Osman* v *Ferguson* [1993] 4 All ER 344, the Court of Appeal held that the police owed no duty to act where a teacher obsessed with a pupil warned them he might do something criminally insane (but the European Court allowed an appeal against this decision [1999] 1 FLR 193 – see Chapter 27).

In *Palmer* v *Tees Health Authority* [1998] Lloyd's Rep Med 447, where a mother claimed for nervous shock sustained in and about the death of her daughter at the hands of a mentally disordered patient, Gage J held that a health authority owed no duty of care to the public generally (as opposed to person who might be specifically at risk) in respect of its care of such patients. His decision was upheld by the Court of Appeal ([1999] Lloyd's Rep Med 351, [2000] PIQR P1). The court expressly disapproved of the decision in *Holgate*.

In *Clunis* v *Camden and Islington Health Authority* [1998] QB 978, CA, the unusual allegation by the mentally disordered claimant was that there had been a negligent failure to provide him with appropriate after-care so that he had killed an innocent passer-by after being discharged from hospital, which had so upset him (the killer, not the victim) that he wanted damages for his mental trauma. The Court of Appeal struck out his claim on the ground of *ex turpi causa non oritur actio*,[4] and further held that the statutory provisions requiring after-care to be provided did not give rise to any private law cause of action (the court based their decision on the House of Lords judgments in the *X (minors)* v *Bedfordshire County Council* case (see above for the chequered later history of that decision)). The court took the view that the statutory duty to provide after-care was 'different in nature from that normally owed by a doctor to a patient'. Modern jurisprudence might well now, on the back of human rights, give a different answer. In *Worrall* v *British Railways Board* (29 April 1999, unreported), CA, the court, following *Clunis*, refused damages flowing from sexual offences committed by the claimant due to personality change after an accident. The court said it would not lend its aid to the recovery of damages based upon the commission of criminal offences.

Further cases on the duty owed in and around medical evaluations

Earlier cases seemed to establish a duty of care on a doctor when recommending the admission of a patient to hospital for mental disorder (*Everett* v *Griffiths* [1920] 3 KB 163, CA; *de Freville* v *Dill* (1927) 96 LJKB 1056). However, in *M* v *Newham London Borough Council* [1995] 2 AC 633, the House of Lords held that no duty of care was owed to a child or a mother by a psychiatrist or social worker examining or inquiring for evidence of sexual abuse on behalf of the local authority in the exercise of their statutory child care functions.

> ... the social workers and the psychiatrist did not, by accepting the instructions of the local authority, assume any general professional duty of care to the plaintiff children. The professionals were employed or retained to advise the local authority in relation to the well being of the plaintiffs but not to advise or treat the plaintiffs.

As we saw above, this is no longer the law, and so the earlier cases need to be treated with care.[5]

Handwriting

The doctor's duty of care extends, contrary to what has been popularly believed, to his handwriting, so that if he writes a prescription the illegibility of which contributes to the pharmacist dispensing the wrong medicine, he will be liable for any injury suffered by the patient (*Prendergast* v *Sam and Dee Ltd* [1989] 1 Med LR 36, CA).

4 　As there is no useful translation of the now proscribed lingua latina, there would presumably be no pleadable ground on which such a case could now be struck out.

5 　As early as December 1987, Eastham J had awarded £10,000 to a six-year-old Cleveland girl and her mother after the child had been (admittedly) negligently diagnosed as sexually abused (the vaginal swab had been contaminated by a sperm sample placed on the same laboratory slide!) (*G* v *North Tees Health Authority* [1989] FCR 53).

Non-medical matters

The duty of care is a duty to take all reasonable steps, including the duty to commence activity, where appropriate, for the proper medical care of the patient. The duty does not extend to other fields. If a doctor gives advice on investments to a patient he is clearly not under the same duty of care as he is when he gives medical advice. Where a factory doctor advises on non-medical matters, such as administration and economy, the high standard of care demanded of a physician in medical matters does not apply to the non-medical matters (*Stokes* v *Guest Keen and Nettlefold (Bolts and Nuts) Ltd* [1968] 1 WLR 1776 at 1784, *per* Swanwick J).

THE DUTY NOT TO MAKE CARELESS STATEMENTS

For the general duty, see the previous chapter. In the doctor-patient relationship, there will always be a duty upon the doctor to take care when he speaks. This is part and parcel of the relationship. The patient is clearly going to be relying on what he is told. Diagnosis and advice are as important as treatment. But one can envisage situations where the doctor will not be under a duty. If he is unwise enough to give a spot diagnosis at a cocktail party to a man who is not his patient but who is forcing his ailment on the doctor's attention, it is hardly likely that a court will hold him liable, unless the circumstances are very special – perhaps the doctor gave the appearance of considering the matter seriously and then told the man he must surely have cancer, as a result of which the man killed himself. Such a statement could be held to be so unwise as to attract liability. But if all he says is 'you probably need to get back to work and forget your problem' and the man then returns to work and collapses, it is likely that a court would say that the special relationship needed for the imposition of a duty to take care in respect of careless statements had not arisen. Lord Oliver gave examples in the *Caparo* case of medical misstatements that would attract liability: the doctor who gives negligent advice over the telephone to the parent of a sick child, and the chemist's assistant who mislabels a dangerous medicine.

In *Allin* v *City and Hackney Health Authority* [1996] 7 Med LR 167, the county court judge awarded £10,000 to a mother who suffered post-traumatic shock on being wrongly and negligently informed that her new-born child had died.

In *AB* v *Tameside and Glossop Health Authority* [1997] 8 Med LR 91, CA, a claim, not surprisingly, failed where it was alleged that the manner in which information was given to patients was negligent. It was alleged that they should not have been told by letter, but face to face, that there was a very remote risk they had been infected by a health worker who had been found to be HIV positive (remarkably, the trial judge had found for the claimants).

A 'statement' by a doctor to a pharmacist (ie a prescription) needs to be legibly written (see *Prendergast* v *Sam & Dee Ltd* [1989] 1 Med LR 36).[6]

---

6   This passage was cited with approval by the Court of Appeal in the medical negligence claim of *R* v *Croydon Health Authority* [1998] Lloyd's Rep Med 44.

THE DUTY OF CONFIDENTIALITY

> ... in common with other professional men ... the doctor is under a duty not to
> disclose [voluntarily] without the consent of his patient information which he,
> the doctor, has gained in his professional capacity, save ... in very exceptional
> circumstances ... [*Hunter* v *Mann* [1974] QB 767 at 772].

The doctor is under a legal as well as a moral duty not to divulge confidential information about a patient without his consent. Until 1989,
there were no English reported cases on this aspect of his duty (the best
one could do was to refer to the report of *Kitson* v *Playfair* (1896) Times,
28 March); but it was clear that a court would be prepared to restrain the
dissemination or use of such information in an appropriate case. The
judgments of the House of Lords in *Gillick* v *West Norfolk and Wisbech
Area Health Authority and the DHSS* [1986] AC 112 (concerning contraceptive advice and treatment to minors) affirmed the duty of confidentiality.[7] Then came the Court of Appeal decision in *W* v *Egdell* [1990] Ch
359, where a psychiatric patient, confined for having committed multiple
killings under the disability of serious mental illness, complained that
the psychiatrist who prepared an (unfavourable) report on him at his own
request with a view to his using it in support of his application to the
mental health review tribunal to secure a transfer to a regional secure
unit had, contrary to the patient's express instructions, disclosed it to the
medical officer in charge of his detention, and also to the Home Office.
The patient had withdrawn his application to the tribunal and, in effect,
now wanted the report suppressed. The court stressed the importance of
the duty of confidentiality, particularly to a member of the public in this
claimant's position. But where, as so often, there was a competing interest, a balancing exercise had to be carried out: in this particular case the
court concluded without doubt that the public interest in being protected
from those who were suffering from a mental illness that might constitute a threat to the safety of others overrode the duty of confidentiality.
This was because the psychiatrist was concerned to put before those
responsible for making decisions about the patient's care, transfer and
discharge relevant information and opinion of which they were either not
aware or not heedful; and any such decision reached upon inadequate
information could give rise to a real risk to the public at large.[8,9]
    However, the doctor, unlike the lawyer, has no professional privilege
which would excuse him from divulging confidential information when
questioned in legal proceedings. Doctors are compellable witnesses in

---

7   Reference may be made to the Scottish cases of *AB* v *CD* (1851) 14 D 177 and *AB* v *CD*
     (1904) 7 F 72.
8   Reference may also be made to *X* v *Y* [1988] 2 All ER 648, where a health authority
     sought to restrain a newspaper from publishing the names of doctors who were alleged
     to have contracted AIDS (the paper had paid someone to reveal the names that
     appeared in the hospital records). Rose J held that the public interest in the preserva-
     tion of the confidentiality of hospital records identifying actual or potential AIDS suf-
     ferers outweighed the public interest in the freedom of the press to publish such
     information, because victims of the disease ought not to be deterred by fear of discov-
     ery from going to hospital for treatment. (See also *R* v *Crozier* (1990) 8 BMLR 128, CA.)
9   In a very early case, action was taken to prevent publication of a diary kept by a physi-
     cian to George III (*Wyatt* v *Wilson*, see (1849) 41 ER at 1179).

relation to matters within their professional knowledge, but, as Lord Denning said in *A-G* v *Mulholland and Foster* [1963] 1 All ER 767 at 771, CA, the judge will respect the confidences received by a doctor in the course of his profession and will not direct him to answer unless it is not only relevant but is also a proper and necessary question in the course of justice to be put and answered. As a corollary, the doctor's immunity from action for breach of confidence when so answering is 'settled in law and cannot be doubted' (*Watson* v *McEwan* [1905] AC 480 at 486, HL).

The ethical duty was recognised at least as early as the fifth century BC: 'Whatsoever in connection with my professional practice I see or hear in the life of men which ought not to be spoken of abroad I will not divulge as reckoning that all such should be kept secret' (a modern translation of the relevant part of the Hippocratic Oath – see Appendix V for the full text). The BMA, in its *Handbook of Medical Ethics*, states that a doctor must preserve secrecy on all he knows. However, in certain contexts the duty of confidentiality is overridden by other considerations. The *Handbook* gives five exceptions:

- the patient gives consent;
- when it is undesirable on medical grounds to seek a patient's consent but it is in the patient's own interest that confidentiality should be broken;
- the doctor's overriding duty to society [a doctor should surely reveal information which would show his patient to have been guilty of a serious crime, for he is under the ordinary duty imposed on every citizen not to protect offenders];
- for the purposes of medical research when approved by a local clinical research ethical committee; and
- when the information is required by due legal process.[10]

Does the patient lose the right to insist on confidentiality once he sues?

English law would answer that question in the affirmative. In *Hay* v *University of Alberta Hospital* [1991] 2 Med LR 204, a court of first instance held that by bringing a medical negligence action, a patient was to be taken to have given an implied waiver of his right to confidentiality. A similar view was taken by Buckley J in *Shaw* v *Skeet Aung Sooriakumavan* [1996] 7 Med LR 371.[11] In *Nicholson* v *Halton General Hospital NHS Trust* [1999] MLC 0189, the Court of Appeal stayed the action until the claimant waived confidentiality. However, in *MS* v *Sweden* (1997) 3 BHRC 248 para 41, the European Court acknowledged that the protection of personal data, particularly medical data, is of fundamental importance to a person's enjoyment of his or her right to respect for private and family life.[12] Any state measures which compelled

---

10 The GMC's *Blue Book* on 'Professional Conduct and Discipline' gives similar, detailed guidance at paras 79–82.

11 Claimants in medical negligence actions are currently normally required to disclose all their medical records. This may sometimes also be the case for an ordinary accident claimant (see *Dunn* v *British Coal Corpn* [1993] PIQR P275, CA).

12 See Chapter 27, where Article 8 of the European Convention is considered in detail.

disclosure of such information without the consent of the patient called for the 'most careful scrutiny'. Whether interference could be justified would depend upon the reason for disclosure and the safeguards surrounding its use. Although parties were only required to disclose evidence which was relevant, a defendant might not be entitled to inspect all of a claimant's medical/personal records as this might be unjustified and disproportionate. The court indicated that the right to privacy was not automatically waived by the mere fact of commencing proceedings, and observed that the disclosure required in that case was limited to the extent that the evidence was material (see also *Z* v *Finland* (1997) 25 EHHR 371). So this European decision appears to be in conflict with the normal rule under our law (see also *Dunn* v *British Coal Corpn* [1993] PIQR P275, CA).

The collection of medical data and the maintenance of medical records fall within the sphere of 'private life' (*Chare née Jullien* v *France No 14461/88*, 71 DR 141 at 155 (1991)). Unjustified collection, and, one would suppose, dissemination of medical information on an individual will be a breach of the Article (but note that there are widely based exceptions justifying what would otherwise be a breach). In *R* v *Department of Health, ex p Source Informatics Ltd* [2000] 2 WLR 940, CA, the wholly reputable applicants were in the business of obtaining information on patients from GPs and pharmacists about prescribed drugs, the information coming from prescription forms. All information passed on was anonymised. Nevertheless, the Department of Health had advised that the transmission of such information was in breach of the doctor's duty of confidence. However, the Court of Appeal said that a patient had no proprietorial claim to the prescription form or to the information it contained, and had no right to control the way the information was used, provided only that his privacy was not put at risk; that where his identity was protected, it would not be a breach of confidence for GPs and pharmacists to disclose to a third party, without the patient's consent, the information contained in the patient's prescription form.

Damages for breach of confidence

In *Cornelius* v *de Taranto* [2000] MLC 0218, Morland J awarded £3,000 for breach of contract where, in breach of an implied term of confidentiality, a psychiatrist who wrote a medical report for the claimant for the purposes of her action for constructive dismissal, sent that report, which contained material defamatory of the claimant, to her GP and to another psychiatrist (even though his actions had been well intentioned, in that he wanted to arrange for the claimant to have treatment). The Court of Appeal upheld the finding on liability on the ground that a client's express consent was required before a medico-legal report was transmitted to a third party ([2001] EWCA Civ 1511).

The Pinochet case

In *R* v *Secretary of State for the Home Department, ex p Kingdom of Belgium* [2000] MLC 0271, the Court of Appeal ordered disclosure, limited to four named states who had unsuccessfully sought General Pinochet's extradition, of the medical reports which had led the Home

Secretary to refuse extradition. The court, while confirming the basic right to confidentiality, said that in the circumstances, the integrity of the international criminal justice system needed to be demonstrated, and that the governing interest was the public interest in operating a procedure which would be perceived and accepted by the great majority to be fair, an imperative which outweighed any private interest. Further, the disclosure fell within the exceptions of Article 8 of the Convention as being both 'in accordance with the law' and 'necessary in a democratic society ... for the prevention of disorder or crime'.

Statutory exemptions to the rule of confidentiality

In certain contexts, legislation specifically requires the doctor to transmit medical information to the authorities. He must inform of notifiable diseases (the nature of the disease and name and location of the patient), currently cholera, plague, relapsing fever, smallpox, typhus and AIDS (Public Health (Control of Disease) Act 1984 and SI 1985/434).[13] The Abortion Act 1967 and associated regulations (SIs 1968/390, 1969/636, 1976/15 and 1980/1724) require doctors to deposit with the Chief Medical Officer at the DHSS (now the Department of Health) detailed information relating to pregnancies terminated under the Act. Under the Misuse of Drugs Act 1971 and associated regulations a doctor must get in touch with the Drugs Branch of the Home Office in relation to any patient whom he attends who appears to the doctor to be drug-dependent. A doctor may also be required to disclose the identity of a patient whom he has treated after a road accident, by virtue of s 168(2) of the Road Traffic Act 1972, which requires any person to 'give any information which it is in his power to give [which] may lead to the identification of the driver'. Refusal to disclose such information has led to the conviction of a doctor of an offence under the section (see *Hunter* v *Mann* [1974] RTR 338). It has been an offence for anyone with certain information about terrorists to fail without reasonable excuse to give it to the police (Prevention of Terrorism (Temporary Provisions) Act 1984).

Further reading

Further material on confidentiality can be found in Chapter 8, under 'Confidentiality of medical records' and 'Privilege'.

---

13   Health authorities must provide reports under the AIDS (Control) Act 1987, but these do not need to reveal identities.

Chapter 16

The standard of care

INTRODUCTION

The degree or standard of care required by the law for the discharge of a duty of care depends on a number of factors, including: how likely it is that harm will arise from the activity undertaken, how serious the harm might be, the cost of avoiding the risk and the interference that would cause to the activity, the usefulness of the activity, and a pot-pourri of prevailing social and economic conditions.

A professional is required to exercise the ordinary skill of a competent practitioner in his field. A doctor will not be adjudged to have failed to come up to the required standard if a responsible body of medical opinion, albeit a minority one, would find his actions acceptable. However, the court is entitled to consider whether the reasons given by a body for defending the management stand up to logical analysis.

Errors of judgment may or may not amount to negligence; there is no magic in that expression. Where lack of funds prevent the acquisition of staff adequate in number and experience to provide the best care, it is not entirely clear to what extent a patient can maintain that an inexperienced doctor doing his best in a specialised post is nevertheless negligent if he does not come up to the standard of an experienced doctor, or whether the health authority is nevertheless negligent in its own right for not providing, through appropriately qualified staff, the proper standard of care. There may be a human rights issue in this context (see the Chapter 27 and 'The right to life').

There is no breach of duty unless the defendant has failed to meet the standard of care required by the law in the context of the duty that exists to take all reasonable care. Two questions arise: what is the standard of care in a particular case, and how is the claimant to prove that the defendant has failed to come up to that standard? We consider the first question in this chapter, and the second in Chapter 22.

THE STANDARD

The care that is required of a person undertaking an activity, that is the standard of reasonable care that he has to display, depends on a number of factors: the nature and value of the activity he is undertaking; the risk that he is creating; the seriousness of the likely consequences if he does not exercise due care or if something untoward happens; the expense and difficulty of taking precautions; and the overall view of the court as to the suitability of recovery in the particular case (this last is a mixture of the court's views on policy and justice – see Chapter 14).

> It is the duty [of an employer] in considering whether some precaution should be taken against a foreseeable risk, to weigh, on the one hand the magnitude of the risk, the likelihood of an accident happening [this seems tautological!], and the possible seriousness of the consequences if an accident does happen, and, on the other hand, the difficulty and expense and any other disadvantage of taking the precaution (*per* Lord Reid in *Morris* v *West Hartlepool Steam Navigation Co* [1956] AC 552, HL).
>
> It is well settled that in measuring due care you must balance the risk against the measures necessary to eliminate the risk. To that proposition there ought to be added this: you must balance the risk against the end to be achieved (*per* Denning LJ in *Watt* v *Hertfordshire County Council* [1954] 1 WLR 835 at 838, CA).

The standard of care, in its basic form, is that care which a reasonable person would take in the circumstances. That, of course, does not get one very far. It is the court that will decide what a reasonable person would have done. In *Bolton* v *Stone* [1951] AC 850, HL, cricketers who could foresee the possibility of a ball hitting a passer-by outside the ground were nevertheless under no duty of care to take precautions, as the risk was not great enough. If they had been playing baseball, no doubt the decision would have been different. Cricket is too valuable an activity in the eyes of the English judges to be hampered by pettifogging considerations about the possibility of hitting a child on the head with a ball as it walks down the road outside.

> People must guard against reasonable probabilities but they are not bound to guard against fantastic possibilities (*Fardon* v *Harcourt-Rivington* (1932) 146 LT 391 at 392, HL, *per* Lord Dunedin).

The consequences of injury from flying fragments of metal to a one-eyed workman is greater than to a two-eyed workman; so the standard of care and the precautions to be taken, eg the provision of goggles, may well be higher (*Paris* v *Stepney Borough Council* [1951] AC 367, HL).

> In every case of a foreseeable risk it is a matter of balancing the risk against the measures necessary to eliminate it (*per* Denning LJ in *Latimer* v *AEC Ltd* [1953] AC 643, HL). [We may well add: 'and the importance, in the eyes of the court, of the activity being undertaken.']
>
> But it does not follow that, no matter what the circumstances may be, it is justifiable to neglect a risk of such a small magnitude. A reasonable man would only neglect such a risk if he had some valid reason for doing so, eg that it would involve considerable expense to eliminate the risk. He would weigh the risk against the difficulty of eliminating it (*per* Lord Reid in *Overseas Tankship (UK) Ltd* v *Miller Steamship Co Pty* [1967] 1 AC 617 at 642, PC).
>
> A relevant circumstance to be taken into account may be the importance of the end to be served by behaving in this way or that. As has often been pointed out, if all the trains in this country were restricted to a speed of five miles an hour, there would be fewer accidents, but our national life would be intolerably slowed down. The purpose to be served, if sufficiently important, justifies the assumption of abnormal risk (*per* Asquith LJ in *Daborn* v *Bath Tramways Motor Co Ltd* [1946] 2 All ER 333 at 336, HL).

Even a small risk is sufficient to be foreseeable if a reasonable man would not disregard it (*Gerrard* v *Staffordshire Potteries* [1995] PIQR P169, CA).

In *Page* v *Smith* [1996] AC 155, HL, Lord Ackner said in relation to a claim that a road traffic accident had caused psychiatric, though not physical, injury:

> Assuming in favour of the respondent that the circumstances of the accident were such that (1) the risk of injury by nervous shock was remote; and (2) such a risk, although a possibility, would become an actuality only in very exceptional circumstances, nevertheless, the risk could not be said to be so far-fetched or fantastic as to be 'a mere possibility which would never occur to the mind of a reasonable man': *per* Lord Dunedin in *Fardon* v *Harcourt-Rivington* (1932) 146 LT 391. The risk was a real risk in the sense that it was justifiable not to take steps to eliminate it only if the circumstances were such that a reasonable man, careful of the safety of his neighbours, would think it right to neglect it. A reasonable man would only neglect such a risk if he had some valid reason for doing so, eg if it would involve considerable expense to eliminate the risk. He would weigh the risk against the difficulty of eliminating it.

The court will always pay regard to evidence of the approved common practices of the trade in deciding whether there has been lack of reasonable care; but for learned professions, as opposed to trades, the court is slow to conclude that any practice approved by some part of the profession involves a breach of the duty of care, and this is particularly so where a medical practice that has the sanction of a body, even a minority, of practitioners, is alleged to have been negligent (see below).

A note on the Compensation Bill

This was announced in November 2005. I doubt it will have any significant bearing on the standard of care in medical situations, but you never know. Under the exciting head of 'Background and useful information' we are told in respect of clause 1 (which forms the entirety of Pt I, which itself is the only bit of the Bill that need concern us):

> The provision on negligence makes clear that when considering a claim in negligence, in deciding what is required to meet the standard of care in particular circumstances, a court is able to consider the wider social value of the activity in the context of which the injury or damage occurred.

The clause itself reads at the moment:

Deterrent effect of potential liability

> A court considering a claim in negligence may, in determining whether the defendant should have taken particular steps to meet the standard of care (whether by taking precautions against a risk or otherwise), have regard to whether a requirement to take those steps might—
>
> (a) prevent a desirable activity from being undertaken at all, to a particular extent or in a particular way, or
>
> (b) discourage persons from undertaking functions in connection with a desirable activity.

Managing illness is, of course, a desirable activity. Would a court perhaps consider that doctors might in certain circumstances be discouraged from undertaking functions in connection with curing the sick and the disabled if required to take too many or too arduous steps or precautions?

SKILLED PROFESSIONS

Every person who enters into a learned profession undertakes to bring to the exercise of it a reasonable degree of care and skill. He does not undertake, if he is an attorney, that at all events you shall gain your case, nor does a surgeon undertake that he will perform a cure; nor does he undertake to use the highest possible degree of skill. There may be persons who have higher education and greater advantages than he has, but he undertakes to bring a fair, reasonable and competent degree of skill (*per* Tindal CJ in *Lanphier* v *Phipos* (1838) 8 C & P 475).

If a smith prick my horse with a nail etc, I shall have my action upon the case against him, without any warranty by the smith to do it well ... for it is the duty of every artificer to exercise his art rightly and truly as he ought (FNB 94 D).

The public profession of an art is a representation and undertaking to all the world that the professor possesses the requisite ability and skill (*per* Willes LJ in *Harmer* v *Cornelius* (1858) 5 CBNS 236, an action against a professed artisan painter).

And the seminal case for the modern law, in particular for medical negligence claims:

Where you get a situation which involves the use of some special skill or competence, then the test as to whether there has been negligence or not is not the test of the man on the top of a Clapham omnibus, because he has not got this special skill. The test is the standard of the ordinary skilled man exercising and professing to have that special skill ... A man need not possess the highest expert skill; it is well established law that it is sufficient if he exercises the ordinary skill of an ordinary competent man exercising that particular art (*per* McNair J in *Bolam* v *Friern Hospital Management Committee* [1957] 1 WLR 582 at 586, MLC 0004).

MEDICAL CASES

In *R* v *Bateman* (1925) 94 LJKB 791, CCA, it was said that the physician:

... owes a duty to the patient to use diligence, care, knowledge, skill and caution in administering the treatment. No contractual relation is necessary, nor is it necessary that the service be rendered for reward ... The law requires a fair and reasonable standard of care and competence.

If he is following generally approved practice, the doctor will not be held to be negligent. 'A defendant charged with negligence can clear himself if he shows that he acted in accordance with general and approved practice' (*Marshall* v *Lindsey County Council* [1935] 1 KB 516 at 540, CA, *per* Maugham LJ). This statement was approved by the House of Lords in *Whiteford* v *Hunter* [1950] WN 553.

A court cannot choose between two approved practices, ie between two schools of thought. If a respectable[1] body of medical opinion, albeit a minority one, would at the time of the alleged negligence have approved of the course taken by the defendant, then he has cleared himself of the allegation of negligence (*Maynard* v *West Midlands Regional Health Authority* [1984] 1 WLR 634, MLC 0009, HL).

> In the realm of diagnosis and treatment there is ample scope for genuine difference of opinion and one man clearly is not negligent merely because his conclusion differs from that of other professional men ... The true test for establishing negligence in diagnosis or treatment on the part of a doctor is whether he has been proved to be guilty of such failure as no doctor of ordinary skill would be guilty of if acting with ordinary care ... (*per* Lord President Clyde in *Hunter* v *Hanley* 1955 SLT 213 at 217, MLC 0002).

This statement has often been approved in the English courts – see the *Bolam* case (above), *Whitehouse* v *Jordan* (above), *Maynard*'s case (above), the *Sidaway* case (below).

In the *Maynard* case Lord Scarman said:

> A case which is based on an allegation that a fully considered decision of two consultants in the field of their special skill was negligent clearly presents certain difficulties of proof. It is not enough to show that there is a body of competent professional opinion which considers that theirs was a wrong decision, if there also exists a body of professional opinion, equally competent, which supports the decision as reasonable in the circumstances. It is not enough to show that subsequent events show that the operation need never have been performed if at the time the decision to operate was taken it was reasonable in the sense that a responsible body of medical opinion would have accepted it as proper.

And Lord Scarman went on to commend the words of Lord President Clyde (cited above).

> A doctor's duty is to exercise ordinary skill and care according to the ordinary and reasonable standards of those who practise in the same field of medicine. The standard for the specialist is the standard of the specialists. A doctor is not negligent if he has acted in accordance with a practice accepted as proper by a responsible body of medical men skilled in that particular art (*per* Sellers LJ in *Landau* v *Werner* (1961) 105 Sol Jo 1008, CA).
>
> The *Bolam* principle may be formulated as a rule that a doctor is not negligent if he acts in accordance with a practice accepted at the time as proper by a responsible body of medical opinion even though other doctors adopt a different practice. In short, the law imposes the duty of care: but the standard of care is a matter of medical judgment (*per* Lord Scarman in *Sidaway* v *Board of Governors of the Bethlem Royal Hospital and the Maudsley Hospital* [1985] AC 871 at 881, MLC 0010, HL).

---

1   The word 'responsible' appears to be interchangeable with 'respectable' (see Lord Scarman's words, cited below, in the *Maynard* case). It has been argued in a case that the body of medical opinion established by the defendants' evidence is not 'responsible' because it irresponsibly supports the complained of treatment, but it seems clear that the epithet refers to the general standing of the doctors comprising the body and cannot refer simply, or at all, to their attitude to the complained of treatment. If it could be understood in that limited sense, it would, in the proper sense of the phrase, be begging the question. These epithets pre-dated the case of *Bolitho* (see below). Nowadays we could, if we wished, equate the responsible and reasonable medical view with one that stands up to logical analysis.

An example of a 'two schools of thought' situation is *Pargeter* v *Kensington and Chelsea and Westminster Health Authority* [1979] 2 Lancet 1030, where the defendants avoided liability by showing that there was a respectable body of medical opinion that took the view that papaveretum should be administered after an open eye operation, even though there was an opposing school of thought.

In *Hughes* v *Waltham Forest Health Authority* [1991] 2 Med LR 155, the Court of Appeal annulled the judge's award of £220,000 in favour of the claimant, saying that the fact that two distinguished surgeons in a particular speciality were critical of the decision of two of their colleagues did not prove that the action of the latter was negligent, even if it had turned out to be a mistake. The proper test of negligence was said to be whether the surgeons, in reaching their decision, had displayed such a lack of clinical judgment that no surgeon exercising proper care and skill could have reached the same decision. In *Taylor* v *Worcester and District Health Authority* [1991] 2 Med LR 215, the claimant's claim for damages for awareness during a Cesarian section failed because the judge concluded that the anesthetist had followed a procedure that was acceptable at the time of the operation (1985). In *Adderley* v *North Manchester Health Authority* (1995) 25 BMLR 42, CA, it was held that a diagnosis of schizophrenia, though wrong, was not negligent on the *Bolam* principle, the appeal court being bound by the judge's finding that it was a 'two schools of thought' case.

In *Ashcroft* v *Mersey Regional Health Authority* [1983] 2 All ER 245, Kilner Brown J said that the question was whether it had been established on a balance of probabilities that the doctor had failed to exercise the care required of a man possessing and professing special skill in circumstances which required the exercise of that special skill. No added burden of proof rested on the claimant. The more skilled a person was the more care which was expected of him. That test should be applied without gloss either way.

In *Burgess* v *Newcastle Health Authority* [1992] 3 Med LR 224, a neurosurgeon avoided liability in respect of his management of a right frontal craniotomy by showing that a 'widely respected body of neuro-surgeons' (*per* Turner J) would have acted in the same way. And in *Defreitas* v *O'Brien* [1993] 4 Med LR 281, both orthopedic surgeon and neuro-surgeon avoided liability by showing that their management was acceptable to a responsible body of medical opinion (see below for the Court of Appeal decision).

Although the *Bolam* principle has often been represented as nothing more than the general principle that applies to all skilled callings (see, for example, Lord Diplock's treatment of it in the *Sidaway* case), it was always unlikely that a court would be so willing to treat evidence of professional practice as conclusive in any other than the medical context. In all other professions, the court was (and is) likely to be willing to declare that a practice followed by responsible members of a profession attracts legal liability if it feels strongly enough about it. And in the medical context, even before the House of Lords judgments in the very important case of *Bolitho* (see below), there was the odd case where the court overruled the practice of responsible doctors.

In *Clarke* v *Adams* (1950) 94 Sol Jo 599, the judge rejected the standard warning given by radiologists before giving heat treatment, saying that it amounted to negligence because it did not give the patient a clear enough indication as to when the danger point in the treatment might be reached. In *Hucks* v *Cole,* a 1968 case reported at [1993] 4 Med LR 393, CA, a doctor who failed to treat a patient with penicillin was held negligent even though responsible doctors testified that they would have acted as the defendant had. Sachs LJ said that if the court was satisfied that a lacuna existed in professional practice whereby the patient was exposed to unnecessary risks, the court would so declare and would expect the professional practice to be altered accordingly. It was not conclusive of proper practice that other practitioners would have acted as the defendant did; the judge was not satisfied that their reasons for so doing stood up to analysis. It was not clear for a long time how that decision (from a very strong court – Lord Denning, Diplock and Sachs LJJ) could be reconciled with the *Bolam* principle, though some help might be gleaned from Sachs LJ's observation that it was not a 'two schools of thought' case, but now see the *Bolitho* case below.

An example of the court's willingness to impose its own view of what is reasonable and what is not upon the practices of professions other than the medical is *Nye Saunders & Partners* v *Bristow* (1987) 37 BLR 92, CA. The trial judge found on the evidence that at the relevant time there was no body of responsible professional opinion among architects that would have failed to give a warning as to inflation when estimating building costs, but that, even if he was wrong there, he was prepared to hold that no prudent architect would have omitted such a warning. He thus applied the *Bolam* test as endorsed by the House of Lords in the *Sidaway* case [1985] AC 871, MLC 0010 but went on to apply the proviso stated by Lord Bridge, to the effect that the court could overrule (medical) practice as to non-disclosure of risk where the risk was so obvious that no prudent doctor would fail to disclose it. The Court of Appeal refused to interfere with either of those findings. Reference may also be made to the Privy Council case of *Edward Wong Finance Co Ltd* v *Johnson Stokes & Master* [1984] AC 296, where the court was not at all reluctant to find an established conveyancing practice among Hong Kong solicitors to be unacceptable. Consider also the words of Phillips J in the Lloyd's Names litigation (*Deeny* v *Gooda Walker Ltd* [1996] LRLR 183):

> Suppose a profession collectively adopted extremely lax standards in some aspect of its work. The court would not acquit practitioners of negligence simply because they had complied with those standards.

However, this was a commercial case. The learned judge may not have been so quick at that period to thus express himself if he had been sitting on a medical negligence trial. The court is likely to be slower to find unacceptable a practice acceptable to some part of the medical profession.[2]

Further discussion of the *Bolam* test

The comprehensive application of the *Bolam* test in the field of medical law, ie to every question of diagnosis, treatment and disclosure of risks,

---

2   For further discussion of the duty of disclosure see Chapter 23 under 'Duty of disclosure: general'.

has occasioned concern among those who act for patients, because it has seemed at times as if all that is needed for a successful defence is for one or two doctors to state on oath that they would have acted as the accused doctor acted, or, even less than that, that they find his actions to have been acceptable. However, the following material shows that that is too facile an approach to the question.

In the first place, it should be recognised that the test was originally directed to situations where there could be shown to be an accepted practice which the accused doctor had followed. It was then, without any real analysis, extended to cover single instances of a clinical decision or clinical judgment, receiving in this context the House of Lords imprimatur in the *Maynard* case (see the passage cited above). However, the judgments of the House of Lords some 25 years before in *Chapman* v *Rix*, a 1960 decision reported in [1994] 5 Med LR 239, had given one to understand that a doctor could not necessarily escape liability merely by calling colleagues to say they would have done the same as he had done – although it could be argued that, as the case concerned the failure of a hospital doctor to give full information to the patient's GP on discharge, it was, as Lord Keith said, 'hardly a medical question at all'. But the fact remains that Lord Goddard clearly stated that he could not agree with what Romer LJ had said in the Court of Appeal if that judge had meant that 'if a doctor charged with negligence could find two other doctors to say they would have acted as he did, that of itself entitled him to a verdict'.

Next, as already noted, the Court of Appeal in 1968, in *Hucks* v *Cole* (above), clearly was not reduced to powerlessness by the evidence from other doctors that they would have acted as the defendant had. Mustill LJ put an interesting gloss on this case in his judgment in *Bolitho* v *City and Hackney Health Authority* [1993] 4 Med LR 381, CA, when he said (at 393):

> In my judgment the court could only adopt the approach of Sachs LJ and reject medical opinion on the ground that the reasons of one group of doctors do not really stand up to analysis, if the court, fully conscious of its own lack of medical knowledge and clinical experience, was none the less clearly satisfied that the views of that group of doctors were *Wednesbury* unreasonable, ie views such as no reasonable body of doctors could have held. But, in my view, that would be an impossibly strong thing to say of the honest views of experts of the distinction of Dr Dinwiddie and Dr Robertson in the present case.[3]

In a case which can be seen as the harbinger of the modern law, *Joyce* v *Merton Sutton and Wandsworth Health Authority* [1996] 7 Med LR 1, the Court of Appeal said, significantly, that the test was not simply whether what was done was in accordance with accepted general practice, but also involved the question whether that clinical practice stood up to analysis. Roch LJ said that it would have been a misdirection to himself if the judge below had simply stated that a defendant was not guilty of negligence if his acts or omissions were in accordance with accepted clinical practice, because he would have needed to add 'provided that that general practice stood up to analysis and was not unreasonable in the light of the state of the medical knowledge at the time'. Roch LJ said that addition

---

3 The phrase '*Wednesbury* unreasonable' is a reference to the well-known case of *Associated Provincial Picture Houses* v *Wednesbury Corpn* [1948] 1 KB 223, CA.

was very important because without it, the decision of negligence or no negligence was left in the hands of the doctors, whereas that question must at the end of the day be one for the courts. In *Newell* v *Goldenberg* [1995] 6 Med LR 371, Mantell J had already disregarded the evidence that 'some doctors' would not warn of the risks of vasectomy as not being a responsible or reasonable practice, because 'common sense and prudence dictated that such a warning be given'.

Then came the extremely significant observations of Lord Browne-Wilkinson in *Bolitho* v *City and Hackney Health Authority* [1997] 4 All ER 771, HL:[4]

> ... the court is not bound to hold that a defendant doctor escapes liability for negligent treatment or diagnosis just because he leads evidence from a number of medical experts who are genuinely of opinion that the defendant's treatment or diagnosis accorded with sound medical practice. In the *Bolam* case itself, McNair J stated that the defendant had to have acted in accordance with the practice accepted as proper by a 'responsible body of medical men'. Later he referred to 'a standard of practice recognised as proper by a competent reasonable body of opinion'. Again, in the passage which I have cited from the *Maynard* case, Lord Scarman refers to a 'respectable' body of professional opinion. The use of these adjectives – responsible, reasonable and respectable – all show that the court has to be satisfied that the exponents of the body of opinion relied upon can demonstrate that such opinion has a logical basis. In particular in cases involving, as they so often do, the weighing of risks against benefits, the judge before accepting a body of opinion as being responsible, reasonable or respectable, will need to be satisfied that, in forming their views, the experts have directed their minds to the question of comparative risks and benefits and have reached a defensible conclusion on the matter.

It is interesting that, as well as citing *Hucks* v *Cole* [1993] 4 Med LR 393, CA, with approval, the learned Law Lord cited the case of *Edward Wong Finance Co Ltd* v *Johnson Stokes & Master* [1984] AC 296, PC, thus confirming that the *Bolam* test applies equally to all professional activities, whether involving doctors, solicitors or others.

Lord Browne-Wilkinson went on to say:

> These decisions demonstrate that in cases of diagnosis and treatment there are cases where, despite a body of professional opinion sanctioning the defendant's conduct, the defendant can properly be held liable for negligence (I am not here considering questions of disclosure of risk). In my judgment that is because, in some cases, it cannot be demonstrated to the judge's satisfaction that the body of opinion relied upon is reasonable or responsible. In the vast majority of cases the fact that distinguished experts in the field are of a particular opinion will demonstrate the reasonableness of that opinion. In particular, where there are questions of assessment of the relative risks and benefits of adopting a particular medical practice, a reasonable view necessarily discloses that the relative risks and benefits have been weighed by the experts in forming their opinions. But if, in a rare case, it can be demonstrated that the professional opinion is not capable of withstanding logical analysis, the judge is entitled to hold that the body of opinion is not reasonable or responsible.
>
> I emphasise that in my view it will very seldom be right for a judge to reach the conclusion that views genuinely held by a competent medical expert are unreasonable. The assessment of medical risks and benefits is a matter of clinical judgment which a judge would not normally be able to make without

---

4   The facts of this case are set out in Chapter 17.

expert evidence. As the quotation from Lord Scarman makes clear, it would be wrong to allow such assessment to deteriorate into seeking to persuade the judge to prefer one of two views both of which are capable of being logically supported. It is only where a judge can be satisfied that the body of expert opinion cannot be logically supported at all that such opinion will not provide the bench mark by reference to which the defendant's conduct falls to be assessed.

But two points still remain to be made.

First, the judge has to be satisfied that the defence evidence does indeed establish that a responsible body of medical opinion would have found the conduct of the accused doctor to be acceptable. He is permitted to take the view that the defence expert is simply wrong, perhaps because he has not considered all the factors, or that he does not speak for a responsible body but only for himself. In other words, the judge can simply reject his evidence.[5] So one of the objectives of cross-examination is likely to be to show the defence expert as unreliable or partisan. Recent examples of such rejection can be found in *Parry v North West Surrey Health Authority* [1994] 5 Med LR 259 and *Bowers v Harrow Health Authority* [1995] 6 Med LR 16; *Hepworth v Kerr* [1995] 6 Med LR 139; *Early v Newham Health Authority* [1994] 5 Med LR 214; *Murphy v Wirral Health Authority* [1996] 7 Med LR 99; *El-Morssy v Bristol and District Health Authority* [1996] 7 Med LR 232; *Wisziewski v Central Manchester Health Authority* [1996] 7 Med LR 248; *Le Page v Kingston and Richmond Health Authority* [1997] 8 Med LR 229; *Kennedy v Liverpool Women's Hospital NHS Trust* MLC 1285 paras 43, 47, 57.[6] And one may recall at this point the words of Oliver J in *Midland Bank Trust Co Ltd v Hett Stubbs & Kemp* [1979] Ch 384 at 402:

> Clearly, if there is some practice in a particular profession, some accepted standard of conduct which is laid down by a professional institute or sanctioned by common usage, evidence of that can and ought to be received. But evidence which really amounts to no more than an expression of opinion of a particular practitioner of what he thinks he would have done had he been placed, hypothetically and without the benefit of hindsight, in the position of the defendants, is of little assistance to the court.

Note may be taken here of *Ratty v Haringey Health Authority* [1994] 5 Med LR 413, where the Court of Appeal reversed the judge's finding in favour of the patient on the ground that, given that he accepted the evidence and the standing of the defendants' experts, he was not entitled to hold that no responsible practitioner would have acted as the accused surgeon did. This case shows that to be immune from appeal the judge needs to state that he does not accept that the defence evidence establishes that a responsible body of medical opinion would have found the impugned actions to be acceptable. Even if the appeal court is anxious to

---

5 See, eg, the observations of Kay J in *Dowdie v Camberwell Health Authority* [1997] Med LR 368.

6 The judge ought to give reasons for preferring one expert to another because, otherwise, the Court of Appeal will find it easy to invalidate his judgment. An example of unreasoned, though no doubt not unreasonable, preference can be found in the judgment of Tudor Evans J in *Djemal v Bexley Health Authority* [1995] 6 Med LR 269 (however, the decision was not appealed). See Chapter 22 under 'Must a judge give reasons for his conclusions?'

support the doctor it will find it hard, if not impossible, to justify reversing the judge's rejection of the defence evidence.

Note, also, *Knight* v *Home Office* [1990] 3 All ER 237, in which Pill J rejected a claim that a mentally disordered prisoner who committed suicide had not been properly looked after by the prison hospital staff, on the ground that the decision to observe him at 15-minute intervals had been a decision that ordinary skilled medical staff in their position could have made. However, in the course of his judgment he said, with a degree of prescience:

> The reasons given by the doctors for their decision should, however, be examined by the court to see if they stand up to analysis: see *Hucks* v *Cole*, *per* Sachs J.[7]

Reference should also be made to the Court of Appeal decision in *Defreitas* v *O'Brien* [1995] 6 Med LR 108, where the Court of Appeal said that it was not a question of counting heads to determine whether a body of doctors constituted a responsible body for the purposes of the *Bolam* test; in appropriate circumstances the judge could find that a small number constituted the necessary defence.

Second, the judge may take the view that, whatever the defence experts say about what they would have done at the time, they are wrong, ie faced with the actual situation, they would not have acted as the accused doctor did. An example of this can be found in the judgment of Simon Brown LJ in *Bolitho* (above) (his was a dissenting judgment, but it nevertheless illustrates the point).

Logical analysis

In *Marriott* v *West Midlands Regional Health Authority* [1999] Lloyd's Rep Med 23, the trial judge had found that, if the defence GP expert's evidence did in fact establish that there was a body of GPs who would not have referred the patient to hospital, 'then such approach is not reasonably prudent'. The Court of Appeal said that the judge was entitled, following *Bolitho,* to subject a body of opinion to analysis to see whether it could properly be regarded as reasonable, and she had been entitled to conclude that it could not be reasonable to fail to refer the patient in such a condition as supported by the defence GP expert (however, Pill LJ said that the defence expert's conclusion had not been based on the facts as found by the judge and therefore the 'logical analysis' test did not arise).

In *Penney, Palmer and Cannon* v *East Kent Health Authority* [1999] Lloyd's Rep Med 123; affd [2000] Lloyd's Rep Med 41, CA, the Canterbury cervical smears case, the judge found that the *Bolam* principle did not apply because there was no dispute about acceptable or unacceptable

---

7   In *Brooks* v *Home Office* (1999) 48 BMLR 109 Garland J said that the standard by which the defendant's provision of care was to be judged was according to the standard of obstetric care which the plaintiff could have expected outside prison, subject to the constraints of having to be transported and having her freedom restricted. As the consultant in charge of the obstetric unit at Holloway was away, and, as the doctor left in charge had no expertise on which to base any conclusion from the scan, the only prudent course was to have referred the plaintiff to a specialist. To acquiesce in a delay of five days was a failure to have made expertise available when it should have been.

practice, only a factual dispute about whether the cyto-screeners had given the wrong classification to smears; but, even if the principle had applied, he was satisfied that the evidence of the three experts called by the defence did not stand up to logical analysis because the cyto-screeners did not have the ability to draw a distinction between benign and pre-cancerous cells, and so should have classified the smears as borderline. On the defendants' unsuccessful appeal, the court said that the *Bolam* test did apply as the cyto-screeners were exercising skill and judgment in determining what report they should make, but they agreed with the judge that the logical analysis test was applicable, and that it led to the conclusion that the exonerating opinion of the defence experts did not stand up to such analysis.

In *Walsh* v *Gwynedd Health Authority* ML 5/98 p 9, the county court judge at Llangefni rejected a consultant psychiatrist's expert evidence about lack of suicidal intention on the part of a patient when seen by the registrar and consequently his exoneration of the registrar's management, on the ground that his expert opinion did not stand up to analysis (and also probably did not represent a 'body' of medical opinion).

In *Newbury* v *Bath District Health Authority* (1998) 47 BMLR 138, where the patient unsuccessfully claimed damages for an improperly performed lumbar fusion, Ebsworth J said, with regard to the choice of surgery, that neither the claimant's nor the defendant's expert witnesses would have carried out the surgery using the technique employed by Mr Bliss. His choice of that technique was unwise, but that was not the correct legal basis for assessment of liability. The question was whether, on a logical analysis of the decision, it was one a reasonably competent consultant could, at that time, have made. A competent consultant would keep abreast of his field and adjust his procedures appropriately in the light of information he received thereby, but he would be entitled to keep an old, tried method in his armoury for use where properly judged to be suitable. That other surgeons might use other methods with success did not render the use of well-tried methods negligent. Mr Bliss had been entitled to make the judgment which he had made and was not negligent in so doing, nor had the surgery been carried out negligently. In *Calver* v *Westwood Veterinary Group* [2001] PIQR P168, MLC 0350 the Court of Appeal held that there had been no justification for the judge's condemning as illogical the defence expert's exoneration of the defendant vet's management of a sick mare. The judgment of Simon Brown J repays study.

In *Reynolds* v *North Tyneside Health Authority* [2002] Lloyds Rep Med 459 Gross J said that, even if there was a body of opinion which would support not performing a vaginal examination immediately upon the admission of a pregnant woman following spontaneous rupture of the membranes, the only justification offered for that view, the increased risk of infection, could not withstand scrutiny, was illogical and indefensible. Therefore this was a rare case in which it was appropriate to conclude that there was no proper basis for such a body of opinion.

A hope for the future

One may hope that, as the significance and effect of the logical analysis test is properly appreciated by defendants and their experts, the hired-hack syndrome, whereby reports are written defending clearly unreasonable management, will gradually become a thing of the past.

Where Bolam *not applicable*

The principle is not applicable to questions of fact, hypothetical or otherwise. This is really too obvious to need stating, but it does. Where there is an issue of causation, such as whether treatment which was not given would have cured the patient or otherwise reduced or avoided injury, a dispute between the experts does not involve the *Bolam* test. The judge will simply have to decide whose evidence he accepts. But, as already suggested, he should give reasons for his preference, for otherwise the Court of Appeal will find it relatively easy to disagree. In *Fallows* v *Randle* [1997] 8 Med LR 160, CA, Stuart-Smith LJ said:

> In my judgment that principle has really no application where what the judge has to decide is, on balance, which of two explanations – for something which has undoubtedly occurred which shows that the operation has been unsuccessful – is to be preferred. That is a question of fact which the judge has to determine on the ordinary basis on a balance of probability. It is not a question of saying whether there was a respectable body of medical opinion here which says that this can happen by chance without any evidence, it is a question for the judge to weigh up the evidence on both sides, and he is, in my judgment, entitled in a situation like this, to prefer the evidence of one expert witness to that of the other. It seems to me that the judge, faced with the alternative theories in this case as to why the [contraceptive] ring was not in position, was entitled on the balance of probabilities to prefer the evidence of Dr Sharp ... to the somewhat remote theories of the defendant and Professor Tindall. I do not think that the *Bolam* principle should be applied in a situation like this at all ... I find it impossible to say that the learned judge was not entitled to come to the conclusion which he did on the facts of the case. He based them on the evidence of Dr Sharp, a fully qualified and responsible expert, as to what was the most likely explanation of what had happened as a matter of fact.

It should not have been thought, though it was, and by those who should have known better, that the decision in *Bolitho* v *City and Hackney Health Authority* [1993] 4 Med LR 381, CA, was inconsistent with this statement. For further discussion of this case and the judgments of the Court of Appeal and the House of Lords, see below in Chapter 17.

ALTERNATIVE THERAPIES

The problem

Claims against alternative practitioners have always created something of a difficulty when it comes to assessing the standard of care given. Is it the standard that others practising in the same field consider to be appropriate, or is it to be judged by a more orthodox standard? If the management is to be judged by others practising in the field, the level of care acceptable to those practitioners might outrage orthodox practitioners. If it is to be judged by orthodox practitioners, there would be no scope for alternative practitioners. Cases have been brought against physiotherapists, osteopaths, chiropractors and other practitioners of robust massage and manipulation. Some of the 'disciplines' have regulatory bodies, and it may be possible to prepare a claim based on the opinion of an expert well-versed in that field with the support also of an orthodox expert, such as an orthopedic consultant. Such a case was *O'Loughlin* v *Greig* [1999] MLC 0131. The patient unsuccessfully sued her chiropractor alleging dangerous procedures. The judge preferred the evidence of the defence expert, who was a solicitor as well as a senior chiropractor, to the patient's expert, a professor of complementary medicine from Exeter University. Even where the practitioner can only offer qualifications which are not generally recognised (eg, to invent one, the Diploma of the School of Physical Well-being), it is usually possible to contend success-fully that he must at least demonstrate an understanding of anatomy and the basics of physiotherapy, so that if the patient is exhibiting signs which to a qualified practitioner would suggest a prolapsed disc or incip-ient cauda equina syndrome, the practitioner will know enough not to proceed with manipulation. Where there appears to be no discipline to which one can refer the treatment given, the practitioner may appear to be a maverick, even if an entirely honest one, and will then be judged by more or less orthodox standards. Bear in mind that anyone can set them-selves up to offer advice and treatment of a medical nature (particularly in the area of mental health). Licences are not required. But where the practice is unorthodox in this country but well recognised and properly regulated in another part of the world, such as shiatsu massage (com-plete with back-walking) or, as in the case below, Chinese herbal medi-cine, the court will need to hear, as a first step at any rate, from an expert versed in the foreign practice. But that still leaves open the question whether the *Bolam* test is satisfied merely by experts in that foreign art agreeing that what was done was within the reasonable management. What if the practice appears to English doctors to be useless, dangerous or little more than superstition?

A judicial approach

The issue arose for judicial decision, probably for the first time, in *Shakoor* v *Situ* [2000] 1 WLR 410. The defendant was a properly trained, well-qualified and experienced practitioner of Chinese herbal medicine. He prescribed a classic remedy to a patient who then suffered a fatal idio-syncratic reaction by way of acute liver failure. It was alleged that the defendant had been negligent because papers in orthodox medical jour-nals (which he did not take – though he did read Chinese publications) warned of such a risk. The widow did not adduce any evidence from an expert in Chinese herbal medicine, but relied only on the published mat-ter (and on evidence from orthodox consultants that they had no reason to believe that the treatment was effective). One may perhaps assume that such inquiries as she had made of other Chinese herbalists did not result in any condemnation of the defendant's management. The defen-dant himself had a supportive opinion from a fellow practitioner.

Clearly, the judge had a difficult task. Views in the West on Chinese herbal medicine vary, despite its age-old acceptance in the East and its long practical and academic tradition, from the admiring to the dismis-sive. The judge (Bernard Livesey QC) took a middle course, and one which is easy to applaud. He said that, even if practitioners in the rele-vant art agreed that the care was proper, a claimant could still succeed by showing that the prevailing standard of skill in that art was deficient in the UK, having regard to risks which were not (but should have been) taken into account. It was not enough that orthodox practitioners might condemn the management. It was an important consideration that the patient had chosen to go to an alternative practitioner. 'Why should the patient later be able to complain that the alternative practitioner has not provided him with skill and care in accordance with the standards of those orthodox practitioners whom he has rejected?' Neither assessment was conclusive – neither that afforded by orthodox practitioners, nor that from practitioners in the impugned art. The judge said that an alternative practitioner practising his art alongside that of orthodox medicine must take account of the implications of that fact. The defendant had a duty to ensure that the remedy prescribed was not merely believed within the art to be beneficial, but he had also a duty to ensure that it was not harmful. He had, in one way or another (perhaps by subscribing to a news service that would do most of the work for him), to keep abreast of relevant publications in the orthodox field as well, to the extent that a similar practitioner in the orthodox field would be expected to keep abreast. A similar practitioner would be a GP.

So, thus far, the claimant had proved her point and validated the way in which the action had been prepared. But the judge went on to conclude that the published material relied on by the claimant was in fact not sufficiently unambiguous to have deterred a competent GP from prescribing such a remedy (had he been so inclined). In the result, therefore, the defendant was found to have acted in accordance with the standard of care appropriate to traditional Chinese herbal medicine as properly practised in accordance with the standards required in the UK. Nevertheless, the claimant established an important point, namely that alternative practitioners need to keep abreast of orthodox opinion and research such as might reasonably affect their clinical judgment. Had the published material in this case more clearly shown that the decoction posed a real and serious risk, the claimant would have won the case.

Finally, these words of the judge are worth quoting, said in response to the claimant's orthodox experts who did not 'believe in' the treatment afforded:

> I note in passing that it seems only to have been in about 1992 that British dermatologists, in despair at the dependence of orthodox practitioners on steroid medication for chronic eczema, turned to traditional Chinese herbal medicine and discovered to their great surprise and delight that what the Chinese had been prescribing for hundreds perhaps thousands of years was in fact an effective treatment in many intractable cases.

Other scenarios

How the court would judge a claim against a shiatsu practitioner, or even a Rolfer, remains to be seen. How far would the likely condemnation by orthodox practitioners of shiatsu techniques take the claim? What about unlicensed and apparently unqualified psychotherapeutic techniques? By what standards are they to be judged (assuming that injury can be proved – which is not easy in 'psychological' claims)? Judging by the almost complete absence of any such reported cases, it may be a long time before these questions receive any sort of authoritative response.

STANDARD OF CARE AND DISCLOSURE OF RISKS

The principle that in medical negligence actions the defendant has only to show that at the time of the alleged negligence there was a body, albeit a minority one, of responsible medical opinion that would have approved his actions, has been applied to the duty of disclosure as to the risks of treatment, in the cases of *Sidaway* v *Bethlem Royal Hospital* [1985] AC 871, MLC 0010, HL, and *Gold* v *Haringey Health Authority* [1988] QB 481, CA. This situation is considered below in Chapter 23, under 'Duty of disclosure: general'.

ERRORS OF JUDGMENT

One particular aspect of the standard of care is the question whether an error of judgment amounts to negligence. In *Hucks* v *Cole* (above), Lord Denning MR said:

> With the best will in the world, things sometimes go amiss in surgical operations or medical treatment. A doctor is not to be held negligent simply because something has gone wrong. He is not liable for mischance or misadventure; or for an error of judgment. He is not liable for taking one choice out of two or favouring one school rather than another. He is only liable when he falls below the standard of a reasonably competent practitioner in his field so much that his conduct may be deserving of censure or inexcusable.

And in *Whitehouse* v *Jordan* [1980] 1 All ER 650; MLC 0008, Lord Denning said in the Court of Appeal:

> We must say, and say firmly, that, in a professional man, an error of judgment is not negligent.

But in the House of Lords, Lord Edmund-Davies said ([1981] 1 WLR 246 at 257):

> To say that a surgeon committed an error of clinical judgment is wholly ambiguous, for, while some such errors may be completely consistent with the due exercise of professional skill, other acts or omissions in the course of exercising 'clinical judgment' may be so glaringly below proper standards as to make a finding of negligence inevitable.
>
> ... doctors and surgeons fall into no special legal category ... the true doctrine was enunciated ... in *Bolam* v *Friern Hospital Management Committee* [1957] 1 WLR 582, 586, ... applied in *Chin Keow* v *Government of Malaysia* [1967] 1 WLR 813 ... If a surgeon fails to measure up to that standard [namely the standard of the ordinary skilled man exercising and professing to have the special skill in any respect] ('clinical judgment' or otherwise), he has been negligent and should be so adjudged.

And Lord Fraser said (at 263):

> ... I think that the learned Master of the Rolls must have meant to say that an error of judgment 'is not necessarily negligent'. But in my respectful opinion the statement as it stands is not an accurate statement of the law. Merely to describe something as an error of judgment tells us nothing about whether it is negligent or not. The true position is that an error of judgment may, or may not, be negligent; it depends on the nature of the error. If it is one that would not have been made by a reasonably competent professional man professing to have the standard and type of skill that the defendant held himself out as

having, and acting with ordinary care, then it is negligent. If, on the other hand, it is an error that such a man, acting with ordinary care, might have made then it is not negligent.

The question, therefore, is: would a doctor acting with reasonable care have done what the defendant did? It was pointed out earlier that it is not advisable to ask your expert whether there is evidence of negligence, for that may well put him off. Much better to ask whether a want of reasonable care is evident. Everyone makes mistakes. Even Homer nods. A surgeon may have been exemplary in all his work, save that on one occasion, perhaps through overwork or just human fallibility, he fell below the standard of care required. This may or may not be characterised by the expression 'error of judgment', but it is probably better not to use it as it seems to have created confusion.[8] The doctor is not to be vilified for one slip in a distinguished career, but he cannot on that account escape liability to compensate the patient for a mistake that the exercise of reasonable care would have avoided.

> Counsel for the defendants referred to Professor's status as 'Olympian'. My recollection of classical mythology is that the gods on Olympus were no strangers to error ...
> ... [but] I hope Professor will take comfort in the thought that even Apollo, the god of healing and the father of Aesculapius, had his moments of weakness (*per* Pain J in *Clark* v *MacLennan* [1983] 1 All ER 416).

There are, of course, situations where even while exercising due care the surgeon can damage the patient. One dramatic example is the risk of damaging the spinal cord or the adjoining nerves when performing a laminectomy. This is a dangerous operation; the instruments can go too far even though the surgeon is using all possible care. Provided he has told the patient of the risks in accordance with the prevailing practice at the time, he is not legally liable for his damaging act.

The claimant in *Ashton* v *Alexander and Trent Regional Health Authority* (29 January 1988, unreported), CA sustained a displaced fracture of the lower left jaw when, under general anesthetic, an unerupted molar tooth was removed by hammer and chisel. The surgeon accepted that the most likely cause was either excessive force on the chisel or insufficient removal of bone from the jaw, and that would mean that he had fallen below his usual standard. On that the Recorder found negligence. However, the Court of Appeal ordered a new trial, saying that an error of judgment might or might not be negligent, the admission of a mistake does not equate with an admission of negligence, and the Recorder should have gone on to ask whether the error was one that would not have been made by a reasonably competent professional person professing to have the standard and type of skill that the defendant held himself out as having, and acting with ordinary care.

---

8   In the Scottish case of *Phillips* v *Grampian Health Board (No 2)* [1991] 3 Med LR 16, Lord Clyde said that it was not enough for the claimant to show there had been an error in clinical judgment; she had to prove an error that no doctor of ordinary skill would be guilty of if he were acting with reasonable care.

DEPARTING FROM USUAL PRACTICE

This is not of itself proof of negligence. That principle is given statutory force in the context of actions for pre-natal injury by s 1(5) of the Congenital Disabilities (Civil Liability) Act 1976 (see Chapter 25). A doctor is entitled to use his common sense, experience and judgment in the way he decides to treat any patient; a slight departure from the textbook does not establish negligence (*per* Streatfeild J in *Holland* v *Devitt & Moore Nautical College* (1960) Times, 4 March). It has to be shown that the defendant took a course which no physician of ordinary skill would have taken if acting with reasonable care.

It was alleged in *Slater* v *Baker and Stapleton* (1767) 2 Wils 359 that the defendant, an apothecary and chief surgeon at Bart's, had been negligent in treating a broken leg, in that he had re-broken it and then attempted to straighten it through extension rather than compression, using some new-fangled machine. The jury found for the claimant, and, affirming the verdict, the court said:

> For anything that appears to this court, this was the first experiment made with this new instrument; and if it was, it was a rash action, and he who acts rashly acts ignorantly: and although the defendants in general may be as skilful in their respective professions as any two gentlemen in England, yet the court cannot help saying, that in this particular case they have acted ignorantly and unskilfully, contrary to the known rule and usage of surgeons.

In *Cooper* v *Nevill* (1961) Times, 24 March, where a surgeon had left an abdominal pack in the patient's body, the Privy Council said there was no justification for any departure from the normal routine.

A psychiatrist had social contacts with his female patient. He was found negligent by the trial judge. In the Court of Appeal Sellers LJ said:

> ... a doctor might not be negligent if he tried a new technique, but if he did he must justify it before the court. If his novel or exceptional treatment had failed disastrously he could not complain if it was held that he went beyond the bounds of due care and skill as recognised generally. Success was the best justification for unusual and unestablished treatment. Here the medical evidence was all one way in condemning social contacts and the doctor had failed to convince the judge that his departure from accepted practice was justified (*Landau* v *Werner* (1961) 105 Sol Jo 257; affd 105 Sol Jo 1008, CA).

Where there was a departure from normal practice in performing a colporrhaphy operation (to remedy stress incontinence) within three months of birth, which proved to be unsuccessful, it was held that such a departure had not been shown to have been justified and therefore constituted a breach of the duty of care owed to the patient (*Clark* v *MacLennan* [1983] 1 All ER 416).

In *Wilsher* v *Essex Area Health Authority* [1987] QB 730, CA, Mustill LJ said:

> ... where the doctor embarks on a form of treatment which is still comparatively untried, with techniques and safeguards which are still in the course of development, or where the treatment is of particular technical difficulty ... if the decision to embark on the treatment at all was justifiable and was taken with the informed consent of the patient, the court should ... be particularly careful not to impute negligence simply because something has gone wrong.

In *Hepworth* v *Kerr* [1995] 6 Med LR 139, the judge was satisfied that the defendant anesthetist had been negligent in adopting a new hypotensive anesthetic technique which, as he knew, had never been attempted routinely before by anyone else. Although he had practised the technique previously on some 1,500 patients to a greater or lesser extent, he had never attempted to make any proper scientific validation of it, and without that validation he was not justified in involving the patient in such a fundamental departure from conventional wisdom.

LITERATURE

It is a doctor's duty to keep reasonably abreast of medical knowledge, and for that purpose he needs to be aware of recent developments published in the medical press. But the doctor is not expected to read and ingest every available item. Thus in *Crawford* v *Charing Cross Hospital* (1953) Times, 8 December, CA, a surgeon was not expected to know that a particular placing of a patient's arm during a blood transfusion was dangerous, as the only publicisation of that fact had been one article in a recent medical journal. In *Groom* v *Selby* (above), the court held that a practitioner in traditional Chinese herbal medicine was required to keep himself informed, if only by employing a reading service, of relevant developments in traditional medicine (see above under 'Alternative therapies').

In *Robb and Unitt* v *East London and City Health Authority* [1999] MLC 0102 (the breast radiation litigation), Ebsworth J said that the issue was raised as to the degree to which the claimants' cases were based upon US research and international practice. Medicine was a science as well as an art, and the knowledge upon which its practice was founded was not confined within national boundaries. Historically, different practices had tended to develop in different countries; it did not follow from that that a particular technique was negligent simply because it could be shown that things were done differently elsewhere. It would be a matter of degree and common sense. Practices adopted in another country were not necessarily evidence of the appropriate standard in the UK, but information as to the hazards in a particular treatment carried out elsewhere and the extent to which they could be reduced or avoided might well be relevant to the cost (in the sense of risk/benefit analysis of a practitioner here). With regard to the allegations of the patients based on the professional literature, the judge expressed a need for caution. Pointing out that standard textbooks at the relevant times did not necessarily reflect many of the contemporary publications relied upon, Mrs Justice Ebsworth said that a doctor might well need to be cautious before changing an established technique recognised and not condemned by the standard textbooks on the basis of individual articles. He might have to do so, because textbooks can become outdated by the growth of knowledge between editions, but before changing he would need to be confident that the message of the literature was clear and, in his clinical judgment, appropriate for his patients. The judge added that the literature in the case served two essential purposes: (1) in relation to the inherent risks of radiotherapy and the need for a cost-benefit analysis in treatment and the prevailing standards of treatment; (2) in relation to the knowledge of the specific risks in issue in the cases and in particular the technical aspects of the claim (ie dosimetry and the radio sensitivity of the brachial plexus).

In an industrial case, *Thompson* v *Smiths Shiprepairers (North Shields)* [1984] 1 All ER 881 at 894, Mustill J said:

> One must be careful when considering documents culled for the purpose of a trial, and studied by reference to a single isolated issue, not to forget that they once formed part of a flood of print on numerous aspects of industrial life, in which many items were bound to be overlooked. However conscientious the employer, he cannot read every textbook and periodical, attend every exhibition and conference, on every technical issue which might arise in the course of his business; nor can he necessarily be expected to grasp the importance of every single item which he comes across.

For a case on the use of 'old' practices, rather than later developments, see *Newbury* v *Bath District Health Authority* (1998) 47 BMLR 138 (above).

PSYCHIATRISTS AND SELF-INFLICTED INJURY

Psychiatrists are very hard to sue successfully, because, however detrimental their attentions may be, lack of precise medical knowledge in this area of medicine usually prevents any causal connection being established between the treatment and the deterioration of the patient.

Furthermore, as psychiatry is not a science, and so little is known by the medical profession about the workings of the human mind, anything goes in the way of treatment, including drugging the patient, and, not so long ago, lobotomies and electro-convulsive therapy; so it is virtually impossible to get expert evidence to prove the treatment ill-advised. However, in *Landau* v *Werner* (1961) 105 Sol Jo 257; affd 105 Sol Jo 1008, CA,[9] a psychiatrist who had social intercourse with a female patient was held to have acted in such a way as would be considered undesirable by the profession, especially as he knew that she had already fallen in love with him. She later suffered a general deterioration in her mental condition and attempted suicide.

There was no liability when a mental patient who was receiving electro-convulsive therapy, a form of treatment which had at that time the approval of a considerable body of medical opinion, suffered a pelvic fracture on each side when the head of the femur was driven through the acetabulum: *Bolam* v *Friern Barnet Hospital Management Committee* [1957] 1 WLR 582, MLC 0004.

A practitioner recommending the admission to hospital of a mentally disordered patient under what is now the Mental Health Act 1983 owes a duty to the patient to exercise proper care and skill and is liable in damages for loss or injury arising from the failure to exercise that care (*de Freville* v *Dill* (1927) 96 LJKB 1056). His duty 'is not merely a duty to take reasonable care in making inquiries, that is, in ascertaining the necessary data, but includes a duty to exercise reasonable professional skill

---

9   Note that a detailed summary of virtually all of the older cases can be found in Nelson-Jones and Burton *Medical Negligence Case Law* (2nd edn, 1995) – if a copy of that useful tome can be unearthed.

in forming a conclusion from such data': *Everett* v *Griffiths* [1920] 3 KB 163 at 216, CA, *per* Atkin LJ.

If a practitioner signs a certificate of insanity without making proper examination or inquiries and damage ensues to the patient, it was said as long ago as 1862 that an action lies (*Hall* v *Semple* (1862) 3 F & F 337). A recent case where it was clearly stated that recommendations by doctors for compulsory detention for medical treatment which were made without proper care could found an action for damages is *Routley* v *Worthing Health Authority* [1983] (Nelson-Jones and Burton *Medical Negligence Case Law* 536).

A wrongful regime imposed on a psychiatric patient could be the subject of a claim for damages (*Furber* v *Kratter* (1988) Times, 21 July).

One area, however, where psychiatrists have not infrequently been successfully sued is in relation to their care of mentally disordered patients. In a leading case leaving a suicide-risk patient unobserved and with an open window behind his bed was held to constitute a lack of proper care, so that the hospital was liable when the patient got out of the window and threw himself off a roof. A high degree of surveillance was required in the case of patients with suicidal tendencies; the duty of care extended to a duty to protect the patient from the risk of self-inflicted injuries: *Selfe* v *Ilford and District Hospital Management Committee* (1970) 114 Sol Jo 935.

In *Lepine* v *University Hospital Board* (1964) 50 DLR (2d) 225; affd (1965) 54 DLR (2d) 340, a hospital was held negligent for not having a constant watch on a patient suffering from a dangerous condition of post-epileptic automatism, who jumped from a window.

A patient of suspected suicidal tendencies managed to elude the nurses, went home and killed herself. The hospital was found not to have been negligent: *Thorne* v *Northern Group Hospital Management Committee* (1964) 108 Sol Jo 484.

There was no liability where a patient had attempted suicide after treatment and severely crippled himself. Lord Denning said that such actions ought to be discouraged as a matter of public policy: *Hyde* v *Tameside Area Health Authority* (1981) 2 PN 26, CA.

Children require a specially watchful eye. Where a seven-year-old boy was left without supervision near an open window and fell out, the hospital was liable: *Newnham* v *Rochester and Chatham Joint Hospital Board* (1936) Times, 28 February.

But where the injury occurs in a non-medical context, ie it does not give rise to considerations about care and treatment, the conclusion may be different. Thus a hospital was not negligent where a girl of nine injured herself when she ran into glass swing doors in the hospital, at a time when the orderly was momentarily absent. The hospital's duty in the non-medical context was said to be that of an ordinary prudent parent (*Gravestock* v *Lewisham Group Hospital Management Committee* (1955) Times, 27 May).

It was not negligent to leave a partially disabled child to manage a jug of hot inhalant in bed on her own: *Cox* v *Carshalton Hospital Management Committee* (1955) Times, 29 March.

There was no evidence, said the appeal court, to substantiate a finding of negligence where a psychiatric patient set herself alight with a box of matches (*Gauntlett* v *Northampton Health Authority* (12 December 1985, unreported), CA, Nelson-Jones and Burton p 349). See also *Hay* v *Grampian Health Board* [1995] 6 Med LR 128 (preventable suicide attempt).

In *Mahmood* v *Siggins* [1996] 7 Med LR 76, a GP was held to have been negligent for not referring a manic depressive to the local community mental health team. The patient later jumped from a third floor balcony.

This line of authority becomes somewhat bizarre where killers sue for not having been prevented from killing. In July 1995, Leicestershire Health Authority paid £30,000 plus £15,000 costs to David Hoare, a paranoid schizophrenic who, one week after his release back into the community, which he alleged had been premature, stabbed a woman to death. In *Clunis* v *Camden and Islington Health Authority* (1996) Times, 27 December, Mawrey QC refused to strike out as disclosing no cause of action a claim by the mental patient who had killed a complete stranger, Jonathan Zito, at Finsbury Park tube station in December 1992. The judge said there was no rule of public policy whereby a party who could recover damages for self-inflicted personal injury was precluded from seeking indemnity for damages he himself had to pay to others as a result of the activities (criminal or otherwise) which constituted that self-injury. Therefore, the claimant was not precluded from recovering damages if he could show that his mental condition had deteriorated as a consequence of the murder, or damages flowing from his future as a potentially life-long secure mental patient, or damages representing such sums as he might be liable to pay to his victim's dependants. The Court of Appeal reversed this decision on both breach of duty and causation ([1998] QB 978, petition dismissed [1998] 1 WLR 1093), and doubted the conclusions of Woolf J in *Meah* v *McCreamer* [1985] 1 All ER 367 and *Meah* v *McCreamer (No 2)* [1986] 1 All ER 943 (there the claimant had suffered injuries from the negligent driving of the defendant, including a person-ality change that had led him to attack women as a result of which he was sent to prison. Woolf J held that the imprisonment was within the area of causation of the original negligence but that the damages the claimant had to pay to his victims were not).

In *Walsh* v *Gwynedd Health Authority* ML 5/98 p 9, the county court judge held that defendants should have appreciated there was a suicide risk, the defendant's psychiatric experts' reasons did not stand up to analysis, and the risk of suicide was increased by 'nominal observation only'; therefore causation was established.

In *D* v *South Tyneside Healthcare NHS Trust* [2004] PIQR P150 the Court of Appeal dismissed a claimant's appeal where a patient, put on hourly observation, had left the hospital, swallowed medication and suf-fered brain injury. The court said that there was a reasonable body of pro-fessional opinion that supported the contention that hourly observation was sufficient and that observation every 15 minutes was not called for.

LACK OF FUNDS

What if it is difficult for a hospital to deliver as high a standard of care as it would wish or as normal standards would dictate because it does not have the equipment or doctors, and the staff it does have are overworked and tired, or lack experience? Hardly an unusual situation! We saw earlier (Chapter 5) that challenges to health authority or Minister over the allocation of resources are unlikely to succeed in the absence of special circumstances, but if there is a failure in care is it any defence for the hospital to say that the staff worked as hard and as long, and with as much expertise, as they could, but economies prevented further care or more experienced doctors from being provided?

The hours worked by junior doctors have at times been extreme, despite repeated governmental pledges over the years to reduce them to a reasonable level. In late 2000, Government figures showed that 38% of England's 30,000 junior doctors were still working more than the 56-hour limit that hospitals were supposed to have introduced in 1994. A few years ago, the Court of Appeal on an interlocutory application refused to strike out a former junior hospital doctor's claim against his employer health authority for forcing him to work 88 or more hours a week, and held that health authorities could not lawfully require junior doctors to work for so many hours that there was a foreseeable risk of injury to their health: the Vice-Chancellor said that in any sphere of employment other than that of junior doctors an obligation to work up to 88 hours in any one week would be rightly regarded as oppressive and intolerable (*Johnstone* v *Bloomsbury Health Authority* [1992] QB 333, CA).[10]

The BMA's representative for junior doctors said in June 1994 that nothing in the television series *Cardiac Arrest* struck him as unrealistic. He had in mind the actual death of a doctor who collapsed in January 1994 after an 86-hour week.

The same standard of care is expected from the learner driver as from any other driver on the road (*Nettleship* v *Weston* [1971] 2 QB 691, CA).[11] However, a learner driver chooses to drive on the highway; it is not a matter of necessity. The learner doctor goes where he is put, and the health authority usually has no option, if it is to provide a service pursuant to its statutory duty, but to put him there.[12] This question was considered in the medical context at the Court of Appeal stage in *Wilsher* v *Essex Area Health Authority* [1987] QB 730. A baby suffered from lack of oxygen after birth. Over a period of some weeks, devoted care from the medical staff saved it from permanent damage other than an incurable condition of the retina, which caused permanent near-blindness. The trial judge found that there had been negligence and the Court of Appeal upheld the decision.

The claim was apparently pursued only on the basis of vicarious liability and not on the basis of a primary non-delegable duty of care resting on the health authority. During their judgments the judges of the Court of Appeal made various pronouncements on the standard of care owed by young doctors in positions of considerable responsibility. Mustill LJ said that he did not accept the notion of a duty tailored to the actor rather than the act which he elects to perform, whereby the patient's right to

---

10　This claim was settled for £5,000.
11　The position is different if a driver is not aware he is suffering from a disability which renders him unfit to drive (*Mansfield* v *Weetabix Ltd* [1998] 1 WLR 1263, CA).
12　In *Collins* v *Hertfordshire County Council* [1947] 1 All ER 633, it was said that it would be no excuse that the doctor was a student; nor (*Jones* v *Manchester Corpn* [1952] 2 All ER 125, CA) that he was inexperienced; nor that he was unwell (*Nickolls* v *Ministry of Health* (1955) Times, 4 February).

complain is more limited where he happens to be in the hands of a doctor who is a novice in the particular field than if he is in the hands of one who has already spent months on the ward. The judge accepted that if hospitals abstained from using inexperienced personnel they could not staff their wards and theatres and the junior staff could never learn, but:

> ... to my mind it would be a false step to subordinate the legitimate expectation of the patient that he will receive from each person concerned with his care a degree of skill appropriate to the task which he undertakes, to an understandable wish to minimise the psychological and financial pressures on hard-pressed young doctors ...
>
> For my part I prefer the third of the propositions which have been canvassed. This relates the duty of care not to the individual but to the post which he occupies. I would differentiate 'post' from 'rank' or 'status'. In a case such as the present the standard is not just that of the averagely competent and well-informed junior houseman (or whatever the position of the doctor), but of such a person who fills a post in a unit offering a highly specialised service.

Glidewell LJ said that the law required the trainee or learner to be judged by the same standard as his more experienced colleagues. If it did not, inexperience would frequently be urged as a defence to an action for professional negligence.

But the Vice-Chancellor disagreed. He said that he could not accept that the standard of care required of an individual doctor holding a post in a hospital is an objective standard to be determined irrespective of his experience or the reason why he is occupying the post in question. A doctor learning specialist skills could not be said to be at fault if, at the beginning, he lacked the very skills which he was seeking to acquire. A learner need only come up to the standards of a careful doctor with his limited qualifications, notwithstanding that the post he held required greater experience than he in fact possessed. The law was not to be distorted by making findings of negligence personally against young doctors who had done their best in the position in which they had been put.[13]

The Court of Appeal judgments in *Bull and Wakeham* v *Devon Area Health Authority* [1993] 4 Med LR 117, MLC 0022 repay study. There was a medically unacceptable delay of one hour in securing the attendance of a suitably qualified doctor to deal with an emergency arising in the delivery of a second twin, as a result of which he suffered brain damage. On the question whether the defendants should have had in place a system which guaranteed prompt attendance, Slade LJ said the evidence pointed strongly either to inefficiency in the system for summoning the assistance of the registrar or consultant or to negligence by some individual in the working of that system. Dillon LJ said that any hospital which provided a maternity service for expectant mothers ought to be able to cope properly with premature delivery of twins, and there should have been at the hospital a staff reasonably sufficient for the foreseeable requirements of the patient. He described the hospital's system for providing senior attendance where the need arose as 'unreliable and essentially unsatisfactory'. Mustill LJ said that the system fell short of the required standard, which demanded at the least that a doctor of suitable experience be

---

13 The Court of Appeal decision was reversed in the House of Lords on grounds not relevant to this discussion (see below, Chapter 17).

available within 20 minutes to handle any emergency. It was not a question of an 'ideal' solution appropriate to 'centres of excellence', nor a question of highly specialist techniques or advanced new instrumentation which it would be unrealistic to expect in provincial hospitals, but just a question of getting the right people together in the right place at the right time.

Although it does not seem to have been expressly argued in either case on behalf of the defendants that lack of funds prevented a better system and as therefore one should perhaps assume that there were sufficient funds to ensure a proper system, the question of deployment of limited resources can surely not have been far from the defendants' mind. One still waits to see what the court's reaction would be to a plea from defendants that their funding did not permit a better system even though the care they provided placed the patient at risk. Could the Government be held in breach of human rights for not making the funds available to provide a good level of care and staffing (eg the right to life, the right not to be subjected to inhuman or degrading treatment)? Some commentators have promised all sorts of exciting developments along those lines but I regard all that as part of the general hype over human rights. Provided the court cannot fault the decision-making process by which the funds are allocated (whether by the Treasury or the Department of Health or the NHS Executive or a health authority) it is unlikely to uphold a claim. To do so would stultify the whole system (see also Chapter 5 on suing for policy matters and Chapter 27 on human rights).

In *Robertson* v *Nottingham Health Authority* [1997] 8 Med LR 1, CA, where significant breakdowns in the defendants' systems of communication in respect of obstetric care were proved and shown to constitute breaches of proper practice, Brooke LJ said that a health authority had a non-delegable duty to establish a proper system of care just as much as it had a duty to engage competent staff and a duty to provide proper and safe equipment, safe premises and a reasonable regime of care, ie a regime of a standard that could reasonably be expected of a hospital of the size and type in question – in the present case a large teaching centre of excellence. It mattered not whether those at fault could be individually identified. If they could, the hospital would be vicariously liable for their negligence, but, if not, the hospital would be in breach of its own duty of care for failing to provide a proper system.[14] But what the judge did not say is that those obligations were regardless of whether sufficient funds had been made available.

In *Ball* v *Wirral Health Authority* [2003] Lloyds Rep Med 165, where the claim (in part) was that the health authority failed to have adequate facilities for the care of babies suffering from respiratory distress syndrome, Simon J said that the fact that an area of medicine might be underfunded or that a particular hospital might not have the same

---

14   One would like to think that successful claims could be brought against hospitals based on the current unacceptable standards of hygiene (and that the defence would not have the chutzpah to plead lack of funds); but such claims are hard to prove in terms of causation, not so much in the sense of showing that the patient contracted a specific infection while in hospital but in the sense of showing that it was contracted from a hospital source that would not have been infective given proper management.

facilities as another might give rise to public concern but did not necessarily provide the basis for a successful claim in negligence, as English public and private law in general left decisions on funding and facilities to those who had legal responsibility for making them.

In *Hardaker* v *Newcastle Health Authority* MLC 0395, [2001] Lloyds Rep Med 512, where a diver claimant contended that he had suffered injury because the hospital had failed to keep its decompression chamber manned adequately and at all proper times, Burnton J said that the court was not competent to adjudicate upon a health authority's system for dealing with such a rare medical event as decompression illness, where the issue was one of allocation of resources; and it was not, in any event, enough for the claimant to criticise the system without suggesting a more suitable alternative.

See also Chapter 5 for further commentary of allocation of funds.

PREVAILING CONDITIONS

The standard of care to be expected may vary with the specific circumstances prevailing at the time. One can hardly expect the same meticulous attention in a hospital that is coping with a rail disaster or an epidemic as at normal times:

> ... in what may be called 'battle conditions' ... an emergency may overburden the available resources, and if an individual is forced by circumstances to do too many things at once, the fact that he does one of them incorrectly should not lightly be taken as negligence (*Wilsher*'s case (above) *per* Mustill LJ).

In *Wooldridge* v *Sumner* [1963] 2 QB 43, the Court of Appeal said that an error of judgment committed by a horseman at the National Horse Show which resulted in injury to a spectator committed 'in the agony of the moment' did not amount to negligence. In such circumstances there had to be something in the nature of a reckless disregard of the spectator's safety. Like *Bolton* v *Stone*, the cricket ball case (see Chapter 14), the court's view was perhaps influenced by the fact that riding is an establishment diversion.

Chapter 17

Loss/injury: damage and causation

INTRODUCTION

The claimant in a negligence action has to show that as a result of the defendant's negligence, ie breach of a duty of care owed to him, he has suffered damage. The damage may be physical (to person or property), mental or financial, but it must be:

- caused by the breach of duty: a patient who cannot show that an admitted act of negligence contributed to his present condition has not proved a causative link between the negligence and his injury;[1]
- a type of damage which is recognised by the law: certain types of damage are not recognised by the law, at any rate if they stand alone, eg distress and disappointment, mental strain or nervous shock not amounting to a psychiatric disorder or illness. Mere financial loss is not recoverable if it stands alone, ie not accompanied by any physical injury to person or property and did not arise in the context of a fiduciary or proximate relationship between the parties; and
- it must come within the foreseeable area of risk created by the breach of duty. The damage will not be the subject of compensation, even if directly caused by the breach of duty, if it is of a completely different type or caused in a completely different way than that which was foreseeable.

All these matters are considered in detail below.

The different factors in negligence are not clearly separate from one another. They shade off into and overlap each other. A woman who loses wages looking after a lover who has gone to bed because the doctor wrongly and negligently told him he was ill and needed bed-rest may be told by the court that her claim cannot succeed because the doctor owed her no duty of care, or that she cannot recover for mere economic loss, or

---

1   That is why some defendants in medical negligence actions concentrate, often *faute de mieux*, on causation, casting around with increasing desperation for any argument they, or, more often, the expert they instruct can find, to support a contention that the result would not have been improved even with proper care.

that the damage she suffered was too remote, or not foreseeable, or that it was not caused by the breach of duty because her decision to look after her friend broke the chain of causation; or the court may even, as a last resort, pray in aid public policy.[2] In the final analysis, a claim that does not clearly come within the body of case law created by the courts in the past, ie a claim that presents a novel quality, will be accepted or rejected by the courts according to the judge's overall view as to whether it is appropriate that it should succeed or not (what has been called 'the judicial hunch'); and if the judge feels that the claim should not succeed he will hang his decision on one or other of the legal pegs that are available. Judicial hunches are influenced by social considerations which vary with the era; they are currently being influenced by awareness of human rights.

ACTUAL DAMAGE

The claimant has, of course, to show that he has suffered some damage (negligence is not actionable without proof of damage). What amounts to injury in the context of the personal injury action was considered in *Church* v *Ministry of Defence* (1984) 134 NLJ 623, where a worker in the Chatham docks sustained from the inhalation of asbestos dust symptomless pleural plaques in his lungs together with symptomless incipient fibrosis that could possibly develop into asbestosis and consequent anxiety when he realised what had happened. Pain J said that there was a small risk that the claimant might go on to suffer further incapacity and it would be wrong in the light of current knowledge about the disease to disregard the plaques as not amounting to an injury in law.[3]

In *Sykes* v *Ministry of Defence* (1984) Times, 23 March, Otton J found that such plaques, involving definite structural changes, even without the incipient fibrosis that Mr Church suffered, plus the risk of the onset of separate lung complaints amounted to actionable damage. (In any event increased vulnerability must surely amount to damage, for it gives rise to the chance of injury developing.)

Asymptomatic pleural changes in the form of pleural plaques and thickening plus anxiety about his condition falling short of nervous shock were 'actionable damage' for the purposes of an award to a claimant of provisional damages under s 32A of the Supreme Court Act 1981 (*Patterson* v *Ministry of Defence* [1987] CLY 1194, *per* Simon Brown J). A worsened prognosis, eg where there is a delay in diagnosing cancer, can constitute compensatable injury (see, for example, *Judge* v *Huntingdon Health Authority* [1995] 6 Med LR 223). But see below, *Gregg* v *Scott*, under 'Loss of a chance'.

---

2   A current buzzword that means much the same thing, used by Lord Steyn in *McFarlane* v *Tayside Health Board* [2000] 2 AC 59, HL, is 'distributive justice'.

3   He also said that anxiety alone was an actionable injury, but this must be wrong in view of the clear authority that mental states not amounting to psychiatric disorder and not accompanied by other actionable injury give no cause of action (see Chapter 21).

PROOF OF CAUSATION

The claimant has to prove that the breach of duty caused his injury. The issue of causation can raise notoriously difficult intellectual issues, eg as to what was the cause or an operative or significant cause of an accident, and in what circumstances the chain is broken, but on the whole the courts give pragmatic answers depending on their assessment of the factual situation.

> Causation is to be understood as the man in the street, and not as either the scientist or the metaphysician would understand it. Cause here means what a ... man would take to be the cause without too microscopic analysis but on a broad view (*per* Lord Wright in *Yorkshire Dale Steamship Co* v *Minister of War Transport* [1942] AC 691 at 706, HL).

And Lord Denning once said:

> ... it is not every consequence of a wrongful act which is the subject of compensation. The law has to draw a line somewhere. Sometimes it is done by limiting the range of persons to whom duty is owed, sometimes it is done by saying there is break in the chain of causation. At other times it is done by saying that the consequence is too remote to be a head of damages. All these devices are useful in their way. But ultimately it is a question of policy for the judges to decide ...

However, what is the common sense answer in any situation often admits of divergent views (see, for example, the varying views of the Law Lords about the cause of an accident when an unsafe roof fell on a miner in *Stapley* v *Gypsum Mines Ltd* [1953] AC 663, HL).

One example where there is no causative link between breach of duty and damage is when an employer, who is in breach of his duty to his employees in not providing safety helmets, is held not liable for head injuries suffered by one of them when it is shown that the employee would not have worn a helmet even if it had been provided for him (*Cummings (or McWilliams)* v *Sir William Arrol & Co Ltd* [1962] 1 WLR 295, HL; *Wigley* v *British Vinegars Ltd* [1964] AC 307, HL; *Homer* v *Sandwell Castings Ltd* [1995] PIQR P318, CA).

MEDICAL CASES

Causation is tremendously important in medical cases, and always needs careful consideration. This is because the etiology of medical conditions is often unclear and because the situation will often be complicated by the presence of an underlying illness or other pre-existing vulnerabilities.

In every case, the chain of causation, whether only one link long or more, must be carefully considered. For example, it is all very well to prove that a GP should have visited, but one is likely also to need to consider what he would have found, what action he would or should have taken, and what result that would probably have had. One probably needs to ask a specialist what the GP would have found if he had conducted such examination as the GP expert says he should. One then has to ask the GP expert whether finding what the specialist says would have been found at that time required immediate hospital referral or whether a review in a few hours or advice to the patient or parents to call if the situation deteriorated would do. One then asks the specialist whether, assuming the GP had taken the least urgent action which would have remained within the bounds of reasonable management, the outcome would probably have been different. This may involve further links in the chain of causation by way of analysing what the hospital or specialist to which the patient should have been referred would probably have done and when. In a cancer case, one may find the expert unable to say whether earlier diagnosis and treatment would have produced a better outcome.[4] If that is so, one cannot establish causation. In an obstetric case it is not infrequently possible without too much difficulty to establish a failure of care. But it is a quite different matter to prove that proper care, usually involving earlier delivery (often by Cesarian section), would have avoided the injury. The expert evidence on that issue may well be extremely technical and speculative. One may be unable to show that the injury was not sustained considerably earlier in the pregnancy, or, at the other end of the spectrum, one may be unable to show that the period of perinatal hypoxia would have been sufficiently curtailed by earlier delivery to avoid damage.[5] In this context, a recent attempt was made on behalf of defendants generally to establish that causation could not be proved in such a case unless there was evidence, from a sample of the child's blood, of metabolic acidosis beyond a stated level. As such a measurement is rarely made, this cunning approach, if accepted, could have prevented causation being established in most cerebral palsy claims. However, the authority and content of the paper were soundly demolished soon after (see *Clinical Risk* July 2000).

The possible scenarios on causation in medical negligence claims are legion, as the cases show. All one can do is make a careful analysis of what probably would have happened, step by step, if proper management, as certified by the appropriate experts, had taken place. Many and varied are the possible defences on causation. It is an unusual case that does not offer some opportunity for such a defence. Hence the fascination of the subject for defendants. The reports are full of cases where the defence has succeeded on some causation argument or other. One surprising example is *Pearman* v *North Essex Health Authority* [2000] Lloyd's Rep Med 174, where the defence expert convinced the judge, contrary to common sense (as the judge admitted), that the claimant could not prove that earlier treatment of cauda equina syndrome would have produced a better outcome. And there are plenty of cerebral palsy claims that have failed on causation (an example is *Matthews* v *East Suffolk Health Authority* [1999] MLC 0170 – and a further defendant in that case succeeded in a different causation defence in respect of a failure to administer antibiotics). The same goes for most orthopedic claims (along the lines of proper treatment would not have made any difference to the outcome). Where damage appears post-operatively, other causes can often be postulated

---

4   An award of provisional damages may be appropriate (see *Thurman* v *Wiltshire and Bath Health Authority* [1997] PIQR Q115).

5   An unfortunate example is *De Martell* v *Merton and Sutton Health Authority,* where the patient had already won an important preliminary hearing establishing the right at common law to sue for pre-natal injury ([1993] QB 204, CA).

(for example *Gray* v *Southampton and South West Hampshire Health Authority* [2000] MLC 0209). But perhaps the most distressing – one could say objectionable – causation argument was the successful defence in the *Bolitho* case, which is discussed below.

Further examples of cases on causation

The significance of causation in medical negligence cases is indicated by the number of times it has been an issue in reported cases every year, and the manifold ways in which medical claims can be contested by causation defences, whether valid or trumped up. A glance through the headnotes for any of the series of medical reports online or in hard copy will demonstrate this.

If failure to treat a patient made no difference because he would have died anyway, his death is not caused by the negligence. Thus in *Barnett* v *Chelsea and Kensington Hospital Management Committee* [1969] 1 QB 428, MLC 0005, a casualty officer was negligent in not treating a night watchman who complained of vomiting after drinking tea. He later died of arsenic poisoning. His widow's claim failed on the ground that the workman would have died even if he had received all due care, because the judge concluded on the evidence that there was no chance that the only effective antidote could have been administered in time.

In *Robinson* v *Post Office* [1974] 1 WLR 1176, CA, a doctor was found to be negligent in not administering a test dose of an anti-tetanus serum before injecting it in a patient who had cut his leg. The patient was allergic and developed encephalitis which led to brain damage and paralysis. The Court of Appeal said that the question (on this issue) was whether the negligence of the doctor had 'caused or materially contributed' to the claimant's injury, and that the onus was on the claimant of proving on the balance of probabilities that it had. The Court of Appeal said that the judge had been right to conclude on the evidence before him that even if the test dose had been administered there would have been no observable reaction in the patient and that therefore the doctor would in any event have gone on to administer the injection. So the injury would have happened anyway.[6]

In *Vernon* v *Bloomsbury Health Authority* [1995] 6 Med LR 297, the court held that, even if the defendants had been negligent in failing to monitor the patient while on Gentamicin, further assays would probably not have revealed any danger signals.

In *Hotson* v *East Berkshire Area Health Authority* [1987] AC 750, the House of Lords denied compensation to an infant claimant on the basis that his injury would not on the balance of probabilities have benefited by the treatment which the defendants negligently failed to afford him (see below for a full discussion of that case and 'loss of a chance').

---

6   The old case of *Rich* v *Pierpoint* (1862) 3 F & F 35 was to similar effect: the wrongful administration of tartaric acid made no difference to the outcome: it 'turned out to be of no consequence'.

In *Gregory* v *Pembrokeshire Health Authority* [1989] 1 Med LR 81, the claimant was delivered of a child suffering from Down's syndrome. She alleged, correctly, that the consultant had been negligent in not telling her that the sample from her amniocentesis had not produced sufficient cultures to determine whether her child would suffer from Down's syndrome. She contended that, had she been so informed, she would have had the test repeated, the result would have been positive and she would have arranged for an abortion. The judge accepted that she could have obtained a legal abortion, but he concluded that she would have discussed the matter first with the consultant and would as a result have accepted what would have been his advice, namely not to undergo a second amniocentesis (amniocentesis always carries a risk to the fetus; there was no reason to suspect at that time that something was actually amiss, and the statistical chance of chromosomal abnormality was 1 in 800). So the outcome would have been the same even had the defendants not been negligent; therefore the claim for the cost of raising the child failed. And the Court of Appeal saw no reason to criticise the judge's conclusion, arrived at on the evidence and his assessment of the witnesses, that the claimant would not have proceeded to a second amniocentesis. A claim similarly failed in *Deriche* v *Ealing Hospital NHS Trust* (2003) MLC 1083 where Buckley J held that, even if a pregnant woman had been properly counselled about the risk of fetal damage from her chicken pox, she would not have decided to terminate the pregnancy.

Compare *Rance* v *Mid-Downs Health Authority* [1991] 1 QB 587, [1990] 2 Med LR 27: here a mother of a child born suffering from spina bifida alleged that the defendants should have discovered the defect in the fetus and she would then have had an abortion. Brooke J said that, even if he were satisfied that negligence had been made out, any abortion would have had to take place when the gestational age was more than 27 weeks; this would have been a crime by virtue of the Infant Life (Preservation) Act 1929 because the child would then have been capable of being born alive; and a claim for damages which depended for its success on establishing a chain of causation which included the commission of a criminal offence could not be accepted by the court. So the situation was as if the mother had failed to prove that she would have proceeded to an abortion; so the outcome would have been the same. If the facts of this case were repeated at the present time, the judge would not find that the proposed abortion would be a crime, thanks to s 37(1)(d) of the Human Fertilisation and Embryology Act 1990, which permits the termination of a pregnancy at any stage where there is a substantial risk that if the child were born it would be seriously handicapped.

In *Smith* v *Barking, Havering and Brentwood Health Authority* [1994] 5 Med LR 285, the claimant proved that the defendants had been negligent in not warning her of the risks of a difficult operation on the cervical canal but failed in her claim for damages for serious injury suffered in the operation because the judge was satisfied that, even if warned, she would still have agreed to the operation as it was her only chance of avoiding the onset of tetraplegia.

Then there was the House of Lords decision in the *Wilsher* case, considered in detail below, where it was held that the claimant had failed to prove that his injury was due to negligence rather than to one or another of various other possible causes which did not involve negligence.[7]

Causation also proved the stumbling block for the claimants who sought to allege that the pertussis vaccine caused brain damage to their children (see *Loveday* v *Renton* [1990] 1 Med LR 117).

In the Australian case of *H* v *Royal Alexandra Hospital for Children (NSW)* [1990] 1 Med LR 297, the claimant, a boy born in May 1973, established negligence by the hospital in not warning his parents of the risk of AIDS infection from the blood product that was used to treat his hemophilia in September 1983, but the court found that he had failed to establish that, given the appropriate warning, his parents would have refused the treatment. Similarly, even if the manufacturers of the product had been negligent in not giving such a warning to the doctors and hospitals to whom they supplied it, the judge's conclusion was that such a warning would not have affected the attitude of the doctors to the use of the product on this patient (a conclusion which was reinforced by, if not solely due to, the fact that the treating doctors were aware of the risks in any event). It was for causation considerations of this type that the hugely expensive benzodiazepine group litigation in this country eventually fizzled out a few years ago.[8]

Sellers v *Cooke and East Dorset Health Authority* [1990] 2 Med LR 13 and 16, CA is interesting: although the claimant succeeded in persuading the Court of Appeal that certain fresh evidence suggesting a negligent termination of her pregnancy could not reasonably have been obtained by her for the trial (which she had lost), the court went on to hold that, even if that evidence were to establish that her pregnancy had been negligently terminated, that would not have affected the outcome, because the judge had found that the fetus would probably not in any event have survived.

In *Marsden* v *Bateman* [1993] 4 Med LR 181, the claimant failed to establish that her brain damage was due to untreated neonatal hypoglycemia rather than a congenital condition.

In *Stockdale* v *Nicholls* [1993] 4 Med LR 190, the claim failed because the judge held that earlier admission to hospital would not have affected the outcome, in that the claimant would still have been admitted for observation only, and the unavoidable and unpredictable onset of septicemia resulting in fitting and brain damage would have occurred in hospital at the same time and with the same results.

In *Robertson* v *Nottingham Health Authority* [1996] 7 Med LR 421, the trial judge held that the period of culpable delay during labour had made no difference to the outcome because the fetal brain injury had been

---

7   In *Pickford* v *Imperial Chemical Industries* [1997] 8 Med LR 270, the Court of Appeal said that where there were two alternative explanations of the cause of an injury advanced by the medical experts, the judge had simply to decide upon the evidence which was the most likely. However, it is not clear to what extent this proposition was invalidated by the House of Lords decision (which restored the decision of the trial judge in favour of the defendants on the basis that it had been for the claimant to establish the cause of her injury, not for the defendants to prove some other cause ([1998] 1 WLR 1189)).

8   See also *CJD Litigation Straddlers A and C* v *Secretary of State for Health* (22 May 1998), Morland J (the test was: if the hypothetical warning letter had been sent, would the clinicians probably have stopped the treatment?).

sustained before ever the mother had been admitted to hospital. The Court of Appeal held that the judge should have found a more extended period of delay, but, despite that and the fact that he had not dealt in his judgment with the significance of an apparently normal first CTG trace, his conclusion on causation would probably have been the same ([1997] 8 Med LR 1).

In *Brown* v *Lewisham and North Southwark Health Authority* [1999] Lloyd's Rep Med 110, [2000] MLC 0081, the trip a patient was obliged to undertake by train and taxi from Guy's Hospital in London back to his Blackpool hospital following his negligent discharge with a chest infection was not a cause of later vascular gangrene leading to amputation of a leg. An idiosyncratic reaction to Heparin at the Blackpool hospital was the cause; it would have happened in any event.

In *Brock* v *Frenchay Healthcare Trust* [1999] MLC 0101, there had been a negligent delay in administering Mannitol, but earlier administration would not have helped.

In *Windyk* v *Wigan Health Authority* [1999] MLC 0088, a claim for a negligently advised operation on a man with little sight (he then lost what little he had), the defendants failed to show that he would in any event have progressed to complete loss of vision.

In *Hossack* v *Ministry of Defence* [2000] MLC 00185, CA, no causal connection was found between a negligent failure to downgrade a soldier for training status and the development of chronic medial tibial syndrome. The court imported into the tortious context the well-known contractual principle that an event which simply provides the opportunity for something else to happen is not thereby the cause of it (the 'Galoo' principle – see [1994] 1 WLR 1360, CA).

In *C* v *A Health Authority* (3 November 1998, ML 12/98 p 7), a negligent failure to offer a booking appointment was not causative of the birth of a congenitally handicapped child because the consultant, reasonably, would not in any event have recommended the sort of scan which might have shown the defect.

In *Coffey-Martin* v *Royal Free Hampstead NHS Trust* (15 December 2000, unreported), QBD Foskett QC, the mother proved breach of duty in that the defendants did not examine her anal sphincter following the birth of her child, but failed on causation as the court concluded that examination would probably not have detected the damage, and, even if it had, repair procedures would probably not have avoided much of the injury.

Where a solicitor fails to serve a writ in a medical claim but the claim is adjudged hopeless, there will be no causation and the claim against the solicitor will be struck out (*Harris* v *Bolt Burdon* (2 February 2000, unreported), CA.

The Bolitho *case*

In *Bolitho* v *City and Hackney Health Authority* [1993] 4 Med LR 381, CA; affd [1997] 4 All ER 771, HL, the facts can be summarised in this way: a child was ill in hospital; it was agreed that it was negligent that during the night no doctor had responded to a call made by the night sister; it was agreed that, if a doctor had come and had intubated the child, the cardiac arrest and brain damage that he went on to suffer would have been avoided. One might think that the defendants would have paid up on these facts, but no. They chose to argue (successfully) that the claimant could not prove that, if a doctor had come, she would probably have intubated. The claimant's expert said that it would have been mandatory to intubate; the defendants' expert said that he would not have intubated. The doctor (Dr Horn) who should have responded to the call from the sister said that she would not have intubated. Faced with this conflict of medical opinion, the judge held that the claimant had not proved that the outcome would probably have been different if the doctor had responded to the nurse's call. By a majority the Court of Appeal upheld this decision.

Pending appeal to the House of Lords in *Bolitho,* the Court of Appeal considered a not dissimilar situation in *Joyce* v *Merton, Sutton and Wandsworth Health Authority* [1996] 7 Med LR 1. It was agreed that if a vascular surgeon had been called to the ward to review the patient following the initial operation on his arm and had operated within 48 hours, the injury (by way of thrombosis leading to brain stem infarction) would probably have been avoided. But the defendants argued successfully that, even if a vascular surgeon had been called in, the findings of the judge on causation could not be overturned. Those findings were that there was no relevant deterioration in the condition of Mr Joyce during the 48 hours following the procedure; that it was not mandatory to call for a vascular surgeon; and, most significantly, even if a vascular surgeon had monitored the condition of the patient, no vascular surgeon at that hospital would or should have seen a need to operate. In other words: (1) the course that would have ensued would in any event have been conservative treatment; and (2) it could not be said that such a conservative course was unacceptable.

In the *Bolitho* case, the claimant could not show that the doctor would have intubated, nor that it would have been mandatory to intubate. In the *Joyce* case, the claimant could not show that a vascular surgeon would have operated within the crucial 48-hour period, nor that it would have been mandatory for him to have done so.

The House of Lords upheld the decision of the Court of Appeal and for the same reasons ([1998] AC 232, [1997] 4 All ER 771). Lord Browne-Wilkinson gave the only speech (although Lord Slynn expressed a degree of anxiety at the actual result). Their conclusions can be shortly expressed. The judge had asked the right two questions:

(1) Would Dr Horn (or her junior) have intubated? Answer: the judge's acceptance of her evidence that she would not have intubated could not be interfered with.
(2) Would it have been negligent if she had not intubated? Answer: The judge was impressed with the expert evidence called for the defence. He had no grounds for rejecting it as illogical or unreasonable, nor, said the House of Lords on reviewing the evidence and pointing out that the condition of the child at the relevant time did not appear on the evidence to have deteriorated to the point where intubation would have been necessary, had they.

The trouble with this sad story is not that the approach of the courts was at any time unsatisfactory in law, but that one cannot help feeling that the defendants, in creating their defence, were just too clever by half.

Also consider

In *Sherlock* v *North Birmingham Health Authority* (24 July 1996, unreported), QBD Owen J held that, although there had been negligence in not informing the senior doctor of certain events when the child claimant was being cared for on the ward in respect of acute myocarditis, that information would not have caused the senior doctor to order the earlier transfer to the intensive therapy unit that might have avoided the subsequent brain damage (nor would such inaction have been negligent). The Court of Appeal, dismissing the appeal, said that the judge had been entitled to accept the evidence of the doctor himself on that issue ((1998) 40 BMLR 103, [1998] JPIL 230). In *Morley* v *Frohn* (28 July 1995, unreported), QBD Wright J held that it was not possible to say with certainty what would have happened if a prostate tumour had been diagnosed earlier, and, as conservative management would have been a reasonable and responsible option, the patient could not establish that earlier diagnosis would have altered the outcome.

Failure to warn: The duty of disclosure of risks is dealt with compendiously in Chapter 23. As far as causation only is concerned, an interesting application of the principles of causation is found in the cases concerning a surgeon's failure to warn of the risks of an operation or disclose other information. Even if he was in breach of his duty in not making a certain disclosure, the patient, generally speaking, has still to show that she suffered loss thereby. If the court concludes that the claimant has not proved on the balance of probabilities that she would have declined the operation, and so avoided the injury, she has not made out a case (*Smith's* case (above) is an example of this). In the specific context of failed sterilisation followed by pregnancy, the woman has to show that she would have declined to be sterilised and taken some other prophylactic measure, perhaps a vasectomy for her husband. In one case, the court accepted, after a failed vasectomy, that the couple would have realised earlier that the woman was pregnant and would have had an abortion, but by the time they did in fact realise she was pregnant, it was too late for a termination (*Thake* v *Maurice* [1986] QB 644, CA; see also *Buchan* v *Ortho Pharmaceutical* (1984) 8 DLR (4th) 373; and Chapter 24 below). In the Scottish case of *Goorkani* v *Tayside Health Board* [1991] 3 Med LR 33, the court said the doctor should have disclosed the risk of sterility from long-term ingestion of Chlorambucil, but that the patient would in any event have accepted the risk as it was the only hope of saving his sight. It is, however, important to factor in to any analysis of causation in this context the rather surprising decision of the House of Lords in *Chester* v *Afshar*, which is dealt with in detail in Chapter 23.

'Material contribution'

It is trite law that any contribution to the injury which is not negligible (ie does not fall within the *de minimis* principle) may be taken to have 'materially contributed' to the injury (see *Bonnington Castings Ltd* v *Wardlaw* [1956] AC 613, MLC 0003, *per* Lord Reid, and *Clarkson* v *Modern Foundries Ltd* [1958] 1 All ER 33). It is, or should be, also hornbook law that if you prove that a cause made a material contribution to your injury, you can recover for the whole of the injury, leaving the tortfeasors (if more than one) to sue each other for contribution. The first of these principles is dealt with in this section, the second (though they overlap, of course) in the later section, under 'Divisible injury'.

In *Hotson* v *East Berkshire Area Health Authority* [1987] AC 750, HL, Lord Bridge said that the claimant had to prove that the delay in treatment was 'at least a material contributory cause' of his injury.

In *Murray* v *Kensington and Chelsea and Westminster Area Health Authority* (11 May 1981, unreported), CA, a baby's sight was lost due to excessive oxygen. The trial judge had found one incident only of negligence on the part of the doctors, namely in administering extra oxygen in the first 36 hours of life, but had found for the defendants nevertheless on the basis that it was not proved that it was that particular quantity of oxygen that had caused the injury, for it could have been caused by later doses, in respect of which no negligence was found. The Court of Appeal upheld his decision. It seems hard on the claimant that the judges were not prepared to conclude on the evidence that the initial excess had probably made a material contribution to the injury.

In the Scottish case of *Kay* v *Ayrshire and Arran Health Board* [1987] 2 All ER 417, HL, a child suffering from pneumococcal meningitis was negligently given three times the proper dose of penicillin. Liability was admitted for the short-term effects of convulsion and temporary paralysis, but denied in respect of the permanent deafness that later occurred. The House of Lords, confirming the appeal court's reversal of the trial judge's award of damages for the deafness, said that there was no evidence which would support a finding that the overdose caused the deafness or even materially increased the risk of its occurring. On the evidence the probability was that it was the original meningitis that caused the deafness.

In *Hutchinson* v *Epsom and St Hellier's NHS Trust* [2002] MLC 1072 the defendants' failure to carry out liver function tests on the deceased and their consequent failure to advise him to stop drinking made a material contribution to his death. The deputy High Court judge held that the widow was entitled to recover in full.

In *King* v *Samsung Heavy Industries Ltd* (10 April 2002, unreported), the Court of Appeal said that, where the finding had been that an employer's breach of duty, though not necessarily the main or sole cause of the claimant's carpal tunnel syndrome, had been a material cause contributing to the injury, that was sufficient for a finding of liability against the employer.

In *Wilsher* v *Essex Area Health Authority* [1988] AC 1074, HL, where it was alleged that administration of excessive oxygen had caused neonatal blindness, the House of Lords was unanimously of the view that there had to be a retrial for the simple enough reason that on the evidence there were a number of possible causes for the injury to the child and the judge had not at any time made any finding that excess oxygen was the actual cause, the effective cause or even the most likely cause (that omission seems to have been due to the judge's misunderstanding of part of the expert evidence). Had he made that finding, his conclusion would have been unassailable. But he did not and so a retrial before another judge on the issue of causation was unavoidable (the attempt by the majority of the Court of Appeal to shore up the trial judgment was unacceptable to the House of Lords).[9]

In *Simmons* v *British Steel plc 2002* [2004] PIQR P33, the House of Lords held that the defendant employer was liable for the claimant's psychiatric illness where one of the causes had been the claimant's anger following an accident at work for which the employer was liable.

Materially increasing the risk: Pursuant to the *McGhee* case (below), it had been thought that even if the claimant could not show that what was done materially contributed to his injury (because the state of medical knowledge at the time was not sufficiently advanced to demonstrate the connection), it was nevertheless enough if he showed that what was done materially increased the risk of injury. In those circumstances, the court would be entitled to infer, as a matter of fact, that what was done did play a part in the causing of the injury:

> It has often been said that the legal concept of causation is not based on logic or philosophy. It is based on the practical way in which the ordinary man's mind works in the everyday affairs of life. From a broad and practical viewpoint I can see no substantial difference between saying that what the defendant did materially increased the risk of injury to the plaintiff and saying that what the defendant did made a material contribution to his injury (*per* Lord Reid in *McGhee* v *National Coal Board* [1973] 1 WLR 1 at 5, MLC 0007, HL).

This principle was extended by a majority of the Court of Appeal in *Wilsher* v *Essex Area Health Authority* [1987] QB 730, where the fact that the administering of an excess of oxygen was only one of the possible causes of loss of sight in a neonate did not preclude the court from attributing the injury to that cause. The principle was also applied in *Bryce* v *Swan Hunter Group plc* [1988] 1 All ER 659 and *Fitzgerald* v *Lane* [1987] QB 781, CA. But we then learnt from the judgment of the House of Lords in the *Wilsher* case that the interpretation put upon Lord Reid's words in the *McGhee* case was misconceived, and that that case added nothing to the traditional rules on causation: it was up to the claimant to show on the balance of probabilities that the act or omission complained of caused or materially contributed to his injury (see below for further discussion of *Wilsher*). So the matter stood until the very important House of Lords decision in *Fairchild* v *Glenhaven Funeral Services Ltd* (see the section below for a discussion about that case).

The 'but for' test: It is not always easy to be confident about applying the 'material contribution' test. It may feel more logical to ask the question: would the injury have been sustained if the alleged negligence had not taken place? In some circumstances, the tests may give different answers. That is because injury may be caused by more than one factor. Where a patient suffers brain damage from an underlying illness and also as a result of wrong medication, the 'but for' test might yield the result that the patient had not shown causation because the underlying illness would probably have resulted in the injury in any event, while

---

9   There was in fact no retrial as an amicable settlement was reached about the end of
     1990, under which a proportion of the total damages claimed was paid to the claimant.

the 'material contribution' test would establish causation. In other cases, the inability to satisfy the 'but for' test might also lead to the conclusion that the other factor did not play a material part in the injury. The 'but for' test could obviously not be applied in the case of joint tortfeasors, because each defendant could escape liability by pleading that even if he had not been negligent the injury would nevertheless have been sustained. It is also important to bear in mind the rule that joint tortfeasors are individually liable for the whole of the relevant damages in the context where there is a negligent late referral to hospital or specialist, and hospital or specialist is also negligent in the management of the patient. In those circumstances, it should not be open to the first defendant to plead that the injury was caused only by the second failure of management (but see below under 'Divisible injury' and 'Breaking the chain of causation').

In *Page* v *Smith (No 2)* [1996] 1 WLR 855, CA, the Master of the Rolls said:

> Secondly, it was argued that the judge had erred in asking whether on the balance of probabilities the defendants' negligence had materially contributed to the recrudescence of the plaintiffs' symptoms. He should, it was said, have asked himself whether on the balance of probabilities the plaintiff would have suffered the injury for which he was claiming compensation but for the defendant's negligence. I do not for my part accept these criticisms. In a case in which other causes could have played a part in the causation of the defendant's exacerbated symptoms, it was in my view entirely appropriate for the judge to direct himself in the way that he did, reminding himself that a cause was only to be regarded as material if it was more than minimal or trivial or insignificant. I cannot in any event see that in a case such as this the outcome would be different whichever test is formulated. The judge had already accepted the view expressed by one of the medical experts that the plaintiffs' recovery would probably have continued but for the accident. The judge adopted a straightforward, pragmatic approach which was in my judgment entirely appropriate in the circumstances.

This was a claim for the exacerbation of a psychiatric injury (chronic fatigue syndrome) caused by a road traffic accident. The issue whether a psychiatric injury had to be foreseeable in the context of a road traffic accident had already gone to the House of Lords, where it had received a negative response ([1996] AC 155).

In *Vernon* v *Bosley* [1997] 1 All ER 577, CA, the issue was to what extent, if any, the claimant, who had suffered the unimaginably traumatic experience of watching his two daughters drown when the car driven by their nanny crashed into a river, could recover for nervous shock, seeing that (a) bereavement had in itself been a cause of his illness, and (b) damages for bereavement and the consequent grief reaction were not recoverable beyond the bereavement award. The 'but for' test would probably have yielded the result that his illness would have been suffered in any event as a result of 'mere' bereavement, ie even if he had not been present at the tragedy. Nevertheless, he recovered in full. The Court of Appeal, in long and complex judgments, refused to discount the injury and the relevant compensation merely because some part of it was referable to and caused by grief and the consequences of bereavement. As Evans LJ said:

> I would hold that damages are recoverable for mental illness caused or at least contributed to by actionable negligence of the defendant ie in breach of a duty

of care, notwithstanding that the illness may also be regarded as a pathological consequence of the bereavement which the plaintiff, where the primary victim was killed, must inevitably have suffered.[10]

The 'but for' test gives a wrong answer also in the context of a loss-causing event where the negligent act had no more synergistic connection with the event than that it afforded it an opportunity to occur (see *Hossack* v *Ministry of Defence* (above)).[11]

There is a discussion of the interplay between 'material contribution', 'material increase in risk' and the 'but for' test in the interesting case of *Donachie* v *Chief Constable of the Greater Manchester Police* [2004] EWCA Civ 405.

The *Fairchild* case

The decision of the House of Lords in *Fairchild* v *Glenhaven Funeral Services Ltd* [2002] 3 WLR 89, MLC 0786 may be summarised in this way. Where two (or more) employers have been similarly negligent in failing to protect an employee from the risk of contracting a disease (meosthelioma in this instance) and the employee contracts that disease but it is not possible in the current state of medical and scientific knowledge to show during which employment the disease was probably contracted, both employers are to be held to have caused the disease and so both are liable to the employee. The disease in this case is apparently not cumulative and is contracted once for all at a single moment when a fibre enters the respiratory system. It was not possible to tell under whose employment that fibre was ingested.

An analogy may posit two independent hunters each negligently discharging identical bullets in the direction of a jogger with the result that one only of the bullets cripples the jogger. It is impossible to show whose bullet caused the damage. No sensible person, I venture to think, would deny the jogger his claim, but would say that, as both the hunters had negligently created the identical risk of an injury which in fact materialised, they should both be liable. That is the effect of the House of Lords judgments. Incidentally, it is worth noting on the side that neither counsel nor the court suggested that each individual employer should only be liable for part of the compensation due to the injured employee; in other words the doctrine of material contribution was given its proper effect in this case. It must next be noted that, though the House of Lords pronounced a new rule on causation, they were careful to limit it for the time being to the specific circumstances of the instant case.

---

10 In a minority judgment, Stuart-Smith LJ came to the 'clear conclusion that the claimant did not discharge the onus that was upon him of proving that the shock of witnessing the accident caused or substantially contributed to the illness from which he was suffering'. He said that to reach a contrary conclusion was speculation and guesswork.

11 The Court of Appeal case of *Chapman* v *Tangmere Airfield Nurseries Ltd* (4 December 1998; see JPIL (1999) p 65) provides useful matter on 'material contribution', the 'but for' test, and contributory negligence. Evans LJ said that for liability it was sufficient for the defendant's negligence to have been, put colloquially, *a* cause. It did not have to be *the* cause. He also deprecated the judge's resort to a 'but for' test.

To explain the function of the new rule on causation we need first to look more closely at the House of Lords judgment in the case of *McGhee* v *National Coal Board* [1973] 1 WLR 1, MLC 0007, HL. One recalls that all that the plaintiff could prove in that case by his expert medical evidence was that the employer's failure to provide showers had increased the risk of his contracting dermatitis; he could not prove that the provision of showers would probably have prevented the disease, ie that he probably would not have contracted it if there had been no negligence. The speeches of the House of Lords giving judgment in his favour were understood at the time to be pronouncing a rule of causation to the effect that there was 'no substantial difference between saying that what the defendant did materially increased the risk of injury to the plaintiff and saying that what the defendant did made a material contribution to his injury' (*per* Lord Reid at page 5). However, Lord Bridge said in *Wilsher* v *Essex Area Health Authority* [1988] AC 1074 that *McGhee* did not introduce any new principle of causation because the conclusion of the House of Lords was merely based on a factual inference that they drew in the circumstances of the case to the effect that the evidence established to their satisfaction that the failure to provide showers had in fact made a material contribution to the plaintiff contracting the dermatitis. However, a large part of the speeches of the House in *Fairchild* was devoted to a minute analysis of what the judges in *McGhee* had and what they had not said. Their conclusion (by a clear majority of four to one) was that the *McGhee* decision was not based on any inference from the evidence but did indeed propose a new principle of causation, albeit in the limited circumstances that the House was now prepared to endorse.

What then are those limited circumstances?

Lord Bingham said that such injustice as there might be in imposing liability on a duty-breaking employer, who might not in fact have been the one responsible for injuring the claimant, was heavily outweighed by the injustice of denying redress to a victim (and all his brethren went on to agree with him). However, this attribution of liability to a defendant where he had not on traditional legal principles been proved to have caused the claimant's injury was limited, for the present time at any rate, to a scenario where certain conditions were satisfied. The conditions specified by Lord Bingham are tightly based around the facts of the instant case, and require that an employee should have contracted meosthelioma from inhaling asbestos dust at some time while working for one or other of a number of different employers, all of whom had been negligent in relation to the risk of contracting such an injury, and that because of the current limits of human science the claimant should be unable to prove within whose employment he had in fact contracted the injury. Clearly the rule as so defined is of no use in medical negligence claims. However, Lord Bingham said that it would be unrealistic to suppose that the principle that he was affirming would not over time be the subject of incremental and analogical development, but he did not suggest more specific possibilities.

Lord Nicholls, agreeing in effect with the full tenor of Lord Bingham's judgment, said that the principle must be closely confined in its application or it could become a source of injustice to defendants. There must be good reason for departing from the normal threshold 'but for' test, and the reason must be sufficiently weighty to justify depriving the defendant of the protection that test normally and rightly afforded him. Policy questions would loom large. It was not possible to be more specific.

Lord Hoffman said that it was open to the House to formulate a special rule of causal relationship in the type of case with which they were dealing. Otherwise guilty employers would escape all liability and negligently injured claimants would never achieve compensation. He, too, made it clear that this exceptional rule was being limited to the salient facts of the instant case. But he, like the House of Lords in *Wilsher,* rejected the reasoning of the Court of Appeal in that case, which was based on their belief that *McGhee* established a general principle that, where a defendant had materially increased the risk of a claimant sustaining a particular injury, that was enough to prove that he had made a material contribution to the injury. He said that, unlike the instant case, it could not be said that the duty to take reasonable care in treating patients would be virtually drained of content unless the creation of a material risk of injury were accepted as sufficient to satisfy the causal requirements for liability. The political and economic arguments involved in the massive increase in liability of the NHS which would have been a consequence of the broad rule favoured by the Court of Appeal in *Wilsher*'s case were far more complicated than the reasons given in *McGhee* for imposing liability upon an employer who failed to take simple precautions. Nevertheless he too indicated that the rule might well be capable of development and application in new situations.

Lord Rodger concluded that the claimants should be taken in law to have proved a material contribution to their injury by defendants who had been shown to have by their negligence materially increased the risk of them contracting meosthelioma. Then he, alone of the judges, went on to suggest the more general conditions within which the new principle should apply. This is useful because the new rule obviously has to be definable in terms not restricted to an employee developing meosthelioma from being exposed to asbestos while in more than one employment. There must be a more general rule underlying that specific instance of it.

Lord Rodgers suggested that:

- the necessary causation must be unprovable by current science;
- the defendant's conduct must have materially increased the risk of injury to the claimant and must have been capable of causing the injury;
- significantly, the claimant must prove that his injury was in fact caused by the sort of risk that the defendant had negligently created. So if other risks of a different nature could have caused the injury the principle would not apply. *Wilsher* is an example of this. The agencies implicated in creating the risks must operate in substantially the same way. He said that the principle applied where the other source(s) of the injury involved lawful conduct by the same defendant but *quaere* if the conduct was that of another person or a natural occurrence.

The reason the principle would not apply in a case like *Wilsher* is that there were a number of different agents that could have caused the RLF (retrolental fibroplasia, an ophthalmic disease) and excess oxygen was only one of them. The other possible causes were of a completely different nature. The defendants were only implicated in respect of the excess oxygen risk. Had the trial judge made a finding of fact that excess oxygen was the most likely cause the plaintiff would have succeeded. But he did not – probably because there was no evidence on which such a finding could properly be based. He merely applied the *McGhee* principle, as did the Court of Appeal. The House of Lords said, as they have also done in the *Fairchild* case, that such an application is not permissible. As Lord Rodger said:

> The principle does not apply where the claimant has merely proved that his injury could have been caused by a number of different events, only one of which is the eventuation of the risk created by the defendant's wrongful act or omission. This will usually mean that the claimant must prove that his injury was caused, if not by exactly the same agency as was involved in the defendant's wrongdoing, at least by an agent that operated in substantially the same way.

In speaking to the Personal Injury Bar Association in 2002 Lord Hope said:

> It is clear that the law will not soften its demands without a clear and compelling reason. So it must be demonstrated by evidence that there was only one possible cause, that in subjecting the claimant to that cause the defendant was in breach of its duty of care and that by doing so it materially increased the risk of injury. But it must also be demonstrated that it is not possible to go further and establish the causal link which the law normally requires. If that is the case, a material increase in the risk will be sufficient to satisfy the causal requirements for liability.

Despite the clearly limited boundaries of this new rule of causation, it appears that the courts may be regarding the rule as of more general application. For example, in *Brown* v *Corus (UK) Ltd* [2004] PIQR P476 the Court of Appeal held an employer liable for causing a vibration syndrome where it had materially increased the risk of the claimant contracting the disease, even though the precise reduction in the exposure that proper management would have brought about could not be known. Note that there was no question of more than one possible cause here. There was only the proof that the employer was in breach for not having taken steps to reduce the exposure.

Relevance to medical cases

There are many scenarios where proof that proper management would have avoided the injury is lacking. Up till now such a claim has been lost for failure to prove causation. Strictly interpreted, it seems to me that for a *Fairchild* argument to succeed, there would have to be more than one possible cause, proof that the defendant materially increased the risk of the injury, and that the limits of science made it impossible to establish causation in the normal way. However, if we allow ourselves a broader base for the new rule, it does not take much imagination to envisage how the more usual claim where, simply, causation is weak could have a chance now of succeeding with the aid of a cleverly formulated argument based on 'material increase in risk'. One awaits such an event with eager anticipation.

An example: In *Gray* v *Southampton Health Authority* (2001) MLC

0209, CA severe post-operative brain damage occurred in a context of hypotension or hypoxia. None of the experts was able to say with confidence what the cause of the brain damage was. Could a *Fairchild* cum *McGhee* argument have now won the case for the claimant?

Divisible injury

Old law overturned?

The Court of Appeal decision in *Holtby* v *Brigham & Cowan (Hull) Ltd* [2000] Lloyd's Rep Med 254, [2000] PIQR Q293 is not easy to reconcile with the established law on material contribution in causation (ie that if you prove a material contribution to your injury as against one tortfeasor, he is liable to compensate you for the whole of the injury). It might be taken to mean that where two separate agencies (hospitals, doctors, etc) are responsible for a patient's injury, he can only recover a percentage of his damages from each, the total still to be 100% but the contribution to be made by each defendant to be decided by the judge.

However, the case need not and should not be interpreted so widely. The key to its proper interpretation (if there is one) lies in the concept of a *divisible injury*, ie one where it is clear that the defendant could not have been responsible for more than a part of the injury *and* it is just that he should not pay for the whole of the injury. The facts were that in this claim for injury from exposure to asbestos dust, the claimant had only spent half the period of exposure at the defendant's site. It appeared from the medical evidence that the claimant's condition would have been better if he had only been exposed while working for the defendant. It was therefore successfully argued that a part of the injury had not been caused by the defendant. Obviously, apportioning the injury could only be a matter of impression (the trial judge was said to have been generous when he applied a discount of only 25%). But this concept of apportionment of injury (and hence of compensation) is ripe for abuse. If applied at all, it should only be applied in cases where (a) it is reasonable to discern different injuries or at any rate different levels of injury as having been caused by different tortfeasors (or a tortfeasor and a non-tortfeasor) and (b) it is reasonable to deny the injured party full compensation from a particular defendant.

Settled law

The settled law of cases such as *Bonnington* [1956] AC 613, MLC 0003, HL, and *Wilsher* [1988] AC 1074, MLC 0016, HL cannot be, and has not been, disturbed by this decision of the Court of Appeal. The issue of divisibility of the injury was not raised in those cases. It looks as if it could have been raised in *Bonnington*, but it was not. The inference from this is that no one ever thought of it before. The bare pronouncement by Stuart-Smith LJ in the *Holtby* case that, although a material contribution to an injury entitles the claimant to succeed, 'strictly speaking, the defendant is liable only to the extent of that contribution', appears to be unsupported by authority and at variance with established law.

In *Thompson* v *Smiths Shiprepairers (North Shields Ltd)* [1984] QB 405, Mustill J was faced with a situation where the claimant had *already* contracted the disease when the period of negligent exposure began. That is why he allowed recovery only in respect of an extra slice of injury. But that should not lead to piecemeal awards simply because different employers have each contributed to the injury. Sometimes a workman will have worked for a number of employers, perhaps some of them negligent and others not. Is his injury to be parcelled up into small lots?

Longmore J, in the asbestosis case of *Milner* v *Humphreys and Glasgow Ltd* (24 November 1998, unreported), said:

> ... the principle [is] that where an injury is indivisible, any tortfeasor whose act has been a proximate cause must compensate for the whole injury, leaving the tortfeasor to sort out with other possible tortfeasors any other appropriate claim for contribution ... Where there are causes concurrent in time, the likelihood is that a resulting injury will be indivisible; but where causes are sequential in time, it is not likely that an injury will be truly indivisible especially if the injury is a disease which can get worse with cumulative exposure.
>
> ... the principle is that where it is proved that a wrongful act has made a material contribution to the plaintiff's injury, the law regards this as sufficient discharge of the plaintiff's burden of proof on causation to render the defendant liable for the injury in full. That does not mean that no question of apportionment can ever arise, but it does, in my judgment, meant that, unless the defendant pleads and proves facts which *justify* [my emphasis] apportionment, the plaintiff can recover in full.

However, it is essential that the application of the divisibility concept be restricted to appropriate cases. Even where divisibility is discernible, it must be up to the good sense of the judge whether or not to apply the concept.

In *Barker* v *Saint Gobain Pipelines plc* [2004] PIQR P579 the deceased, who died from asbestos-induced meosthelioma, had been exposed to asbestos while employed by the defendant and also while self-employed. However Moses J not only held that the *Fairchild* rule applied where the target employment was accompanied by a period of self-employment, but also declined to apportion the damages between the periods of employment. He said the law imposed liability on a party who materially increased the risk of an injury which later materialised, even though others might also have been responsible. He said the injury was indivisible (it is apparently caused by a single fibre entering the respiratory system at a single time) and that it was not appropriate to apportion the damages by reference to the extent a defendant materially increased the risk, even if such a risk was capable of calculation. The Court of Appeal upheld his conclusions, saying that there was no apportionment for an indivisible injury.

In *Simmons* v *British Steel plc 2002* [2004] PIQR P33, the House of Lords held that the defendant employer was liable for the claimant's psychiatric illness where one of the causes had been the claimant's anger following an accident at work for which the employer was liable. Lord Rodger said that the usual rule, to be found in *Wardlaw* v *Bonnington Castings* (above) applied and that, in the absence of any basis for identifying and apportioning the respective roles played by the various factors in the development of the pursuer's condition, the pursuer was entitled to recover damages for all of his injuries.

This seems to be the opposite of the view the Court of Appeal took in *Allen* v *British Rail Engineering* [2001] PIQR Q101, a vibration white finger case. There they are saying that indivisibility will be the exception and apportionment will be the general rule ('in principle the amount of the employer's liability will be limited to the extent of the contribution which his tortious conduct made to the employee's disability'). The traditional rules seem to have been bent to accommodate these multiple industrial claims, and divisibility is interpreted impossibly widely, meaning no more than 'apportionability'. Any judge's guess or stab at apportioning will do.

The Rahman *case*

There was an even less convincing application of the concept of divisibility in *Rahman* v *Arearose Ltd and University College London NHS Trust* [2000] 3 WLR 1184, [2000] MLC 0223, CA (note that no reference is made in the judgment to the *Holtby* case).

The importance of the *Rahman* case is that the Court of Appeal was asked to decide on apportionment of liability in the unfortunately far too common situation where a non-medical negligent act causes a patient to present at hospital and then negligent medical treatment adds to the hitherto foreseeable adverse consequences of the original injury. Perhaps the original injury was sustained at work, or in a road traffic accident. It should have been minor, but negligent medical treatment, whether of commission or omission, has made it much worse. This scenario also raises the issue of 'breaking the chain of causation'. The two issues overlap; breaking the chain has a section to itself below. The facts can be simply stated: a manager at Burger King was viciously assaulted as a result of his employer not taking proper measures to protect him. Among his injuries was serious damage to one eye. However (this is not explicitly stated in the judgment but it must be so), he would probably not have lost the sight of that eye if he had not received admittedly negligent treatment at the hospital.

This is a type of situation that arises time and again in medico-legal practices. Is the answer to any suggestion for division of responsibility and compensation that the employer is not responsible in law for loss of the eye, as negligent medical treatment should not be deemed by the law (even though a common enough occurrence these days!) to be a foreseeable consequence, and is therefore a *novus actus*? (See below under 'Breaking the chain of causation'.) If that is the correct answer, one has to apportion both general and special damage, so that the employer pays only for the foreseeable consequences of the injury, just as, if the initial injury had been a non-negligent accident, the hospital would only be liable for the extra slice of injury that it had caused (and the consequences of that extra slice).

Or should one hold both defendants liable in full, on the doctrine of material contribution, leaving apportionment to be defined as between the defendants?

No previous authority

Although this sort of situation is common, it seems never to have been the subject of litigation before (maybe such claims are virtually always settled by amicable division of responsibility). The nearest one can get to it are the many old cases under the Workmen's Compensation Act 1925, where the injured workman had to prove that his disability had been caused by the accident rather than by the hospital's negligent treatment. Those cases are not particularly helpful as the social and policy considerations of the time would have been very different and because they were not straightforward tort cases, but involved decisions from arbitrators as to whether a disability fell within the words of the Act or not ('... results from the injury'). Nevertheless, it is worth looking briefly at one of them, *faute de mieux*, where the House of Lords by a majority concluded that negligent medical treatment broke the chain of causation so that the disability did not 'result from' the injury at work (*Hogan* v *West Hartley Bentinck Collieries (Owners) Ltd* [1949] 1 All ER 588, HL).

Hogan's case

In *Rothwell* v *Caverswall Stone Co Ltd* [1944] 2 All ER 350, CA, du Parcq LJ had said at 365 that negligent medical treatment, whether of commission or omission, 'may amount to a new cause'. In *Hogan*, Lord Simonds agreed, and said that the question whether the incapacity was due to the original accident or the intervention of a *novus actus* 'can only be answered on a consideration of all the circumstances and, in particular, of the quality of that later act or event'. Lord Normand said that it was axiomatic that additional injury caused by medical negligence should not be attributed to the original injury (though additional injury resulting from non-negligent medical treatment should).

Lord MacDermott disagreed. He saw no reason why the workman should lose the right to compensation under the Act just because he had been unfortunate enough to suffer from negligent medical treatment. Lord Reid agreed with him, saying that it was within the contemplation of the Act that the negligent treatment necessitated by the original injury might be inefficient (but he seems to have been meaning inefficiency of a lesser degree than actual negligence). More significantly, he was the only judge to ask why there should not be dual causes for the incapacity.

The Rahman case (continued)

In the *Rahman* case, the parties appear to have expected the court to divide up the injury, or perhaps only as between the defendants. The psychiatrists had been asked to prepare a joint report which attempted in particular the extraordinary task of attributing different *aspects* of the very substantial psychiatric injury to the different torts (the assault and the medical treatment). I do not know if they expected the court to attribute different aspects of the injury to the different defendants, *vis-à-vis* the claimant, both in respect of the claim for general damages and in respect of the allied manifold claims for special damages.

The salient issue in such a situation must be whether the doctrine of 'material contribution' is displaced by the doctrine of *novus actus*. However, at no point in the *Rahman* judgment (given only by Laws LJ) is there any reference to the doctrine of material contribution. In *Rahman*, the court, having declared for the purposes of apportionment under the Civil Liability (Contribution) Act 1978 that the two defendants were not concurrent tortfeasors, was then concerned to fix the proportion of liability which each defendant should bear *vis-à-vis* the claimant, there being no question of each being liable for the whole of the injury subject to apportionment among themselves.

Laws LJ said more than once that it would be wrong for a defendant to pay for any part of the injury or its consequences which, on the evidence, he clearly was not responsible for. That may sound fair on the face of it, but it ignores the principle of material contribution, and, if his approach is to be adopted, will allow for this sort of complex and highly speculative divisibility exercise, by experts and judges, in many more cases than hitherto.

In *Rahman*, the court went to infinite pains to divide up responsibility down to the last small head of special damage. This complexity could have been avoided by applying the test of material contribution, as was done in the cases (not mentioned in the judgment) of *Vernon* v *Bosley* [1997] 1 All ER 577, CA, and *Page* v *Smith (No 2)* [1996] 1 WLR 855, CA. It would still have been necessary to clarify what proportion of the total damages each defendant should bear as between themselves, but their insurers could probably have come to an agreement on that.

After complex analysis of the different aspects of what was really an indivisible injury, the Court of Appeal upheld the judge's original apportionment of 25% to the employer and 75% to the hospital. As between the two defendants, it might have been helpful to seek to divide up responsibility in this way (in the absence of agreement), but this was not a truly divisible injury, neither in its physical nor its psychiatric consequences, nor in its special damages claims. Each defendant should have been wholly liable as against the claimant.

For a sensible treatment of the divisibility question, see *Athey* v *Leonati* [1999] Lloyd's Rep Med 458: some of our judges might do well to heed the approach of the British Columbia Court of Appeal. The trial judge had awarded 25% damages on the basis that the claimant's disc herniation had been caused 25% by the negligence of the defendant drivers and 75% due to pre-existing disease. The court said there was no room to divide up the causes where one was non-tortious, and in any event 25% was a 'material contribution' and therefore rendered the defendants liable for the whole of the injury.

Negligence that increases injury

In many cases, the most that the patient is given by his causation expert is that proper treatment would probably have reduced the injury. It is then important to achieve some sort of definition of the extra slice of injury, partly in order to be able to assess general damages, and partly (and usually more significantly) in order to define what special damage (whether in the form of care, transport needs, accommodation or whatever) can be attributed to the extra slice of injury. In that particular context, it is surely necessary to establish that the aids and equipment and care claimed for would not have been necessary without the extra slice of injury. In *Tahir* v *Haringey Health Authority* [1998] Lloyd's Rep Med 104, CA, Otton LJ said that in such a context it is not sufficient to show that delay materially increased the risk of injury or that delay could cause injury, because the claimant had to go further and prove that damage was actually caused, and, more significantly, it was not sufficient to show a general increment of injury from the delay because 'some measurable damage' had to be proved. The Lord Justice went on to say that in the absence of any evidence before the trial judge which either identified or qualified additional deficit, it was not possible to assess damages. However, Sir Ralph Gibson said that:

> If it was common ground, or if the judge held upon evidence which she accepted, that in probability each hour of delay caused significant aggravation of, or addition to, the residual disability suffered by the plaintiff, then I would agree that the judge could properly assess damages as she did. The fact that the doctors could not identify any particular form of residual disability resulting from such delay, or precisely quantify any worsening of any form of residual disability as a result of that delay would not, in my judgment, deprive the plaintiff of the right to appropriate damages. I cannot accept, however, that any such common ground existed.

Leggatt LJ said that neither expert had identified any respect in which the plaintiff was actually worse off on account of the delay, and in the absence of any identification of any individual disability that occurred or was increased, and of any attempt to define the extent of any increase the plaintiffs claim failed, because there was no evidence before the judge that any damage caused by the defendants' negligence was more than minimal. He added the interesting observation that:

> When a doctor has been at fault no court wishes to send his patient away empty-handed. But where the fault is not shown to have resulted in any particular loss of amenity, there is nothing which the court can legitimately translate into money by way of compensation.

It is understandable that the claimant in this case found himself in difficulty because the case was presented on the basis that the negligence had been responsible for the whole of a substantial injury and it only became apparent during the trial that it was not going to be possible to prove more than a relatively minor increment.[12]

Breaking the chain of causation

As we have seen, an intervening act or event occurring after the original act of negligence may operate to break the chain of causation, with the result that the wrongdoer is not liable for loss caused by that event. There is no clear test or formula for deciding whether an act, which may be of a third party or of the claimant himself, and may be lawful or unlawful, voluntary or involuntary, will break the chain of causation. The most useful test is to ask whether the act was reasonably foreseeable at the time of the original negligence, but that is not conclusive of the issue. The court will in any event judge each case on its own facts and decide the question according to its own view of whether justice requires the tortfeasor to compensate the claimant for the additional damage suffered from the intervening act.

---

12   In *Taylor v West Kent Health Authority* [1997] 8 Med LR 251, Kay J found that delay in diagnosing breast cancer did not substantially alter the outcome, but that there was a degree of injury in that the claimant would probably have lived 18 months longer. Damages were left to the parties to agree.

We have already seen that the court will adjudge an effect too remote where it regards it as inappropriate that the wrongdoer should be made liable in respect of it. In such cases it may be said that the effect is not to be regarded in law as having been caused by the original negligence. This may be so even though the effect appears to be both directly and foreseeably caused by the negligence, without any intervening act that could be said to have broken the chain of causation. Where, however, there is such an intervening act, whether of human agency, lawful or unlawful, voluntary or involuntary, or whether of a third party or of the claimant himself, or whether it be an event which is not of human origination, the court is free, if it chooses, to say that the intervening act, which in the case of a third party's act and sometimes in the case of the claimant is described by the Latin tag of *novus actus interveniens* (an independent supervening act), breaks the chain of causation, so that the damage flowing from it cannot be regarded in law as having been caused by the original negligence.

However, it is by no means easy to predict when such an intervening act will be regarded as breaking the chain of causation. At times, the test applied seems to have been whether the intervening act was reasonable in the circumstances, but currently the question seems to turn on foreseeability, though that is not necessarily conclusive of the issue. Was it reasonably foreseeable that the intervening act would occur? On that basis, the courts have several times ruled on a wrongdoer's liability for the criminal acts of third parties (*Stansbie* v *Troman* [1948] 2 KB 48, CA; *Lamb* v *Camden London Borough Council* [1981] QB 625, CA; *Ward* v *Cannock Chase District Council* [1985] 3 All ER 537; *P Perl (Exporters) Ltd* v *Camden London Borough Council* [1984] QB 342, CA; *King* v *Liverpool City Council* [1986] 1 WLR 890, CA; *Smith* v *Littlewoods Organisation Ltd* [1987] AC 241, HL). Compare also *Topp* v *London Country Bus (South West) Ltd* [1993] 1 WLR 976, CA, with *Grand Metropolitan plc* v *Closed Circuit Cooling Ltd* [1997] JPIL 191 (vehicles left with keys in ignition: was an unlawful taking a *novus actus?*).

Lord Reid said in *Home Office* v *Dorset Yacht Co* [1970] AC 1004, HL, that for a *novus actus* not to break the chain of causation, it would have to be an act which was likely or probable to happen; but Lord Denning and Watkins LJ took a contrary view in *Lamb*'s case (above), where a judicious mix of 'reasonable foreseeability' and 'policy' was applied to deny recovery. Watkins LJ said that a robust and sensible approach to the question of remoteness would often produce an instinctive feeling that the event or act being weighed in the balance was too remote to sound in damages (this is the 'judicial hunch' or 'gut reaction' referred to, from time to time, above). Lord Denning said:

> ... it is not every consequence of a wrongful act which is the subject of compensation. The law has to draw a line somewhere. Sometimes it is done by limiting the range of persons to whom duty is owed. Sometimes it is done by saying that there is a break in the chain of causation. At other times it is done by saying that the consequence is too remote to be a head of damage. All these devices are useful in their way. But ultimately it is a question of policy for the judges to decide ...
>
> It seems to me that it is a question of policy which we, as judges, have to decide. The time has come when, in cases of new import, we should decide them according to the reason of the thing. In previous times, when faced with

a new problem, the judges have not openly asked themselves the question: what is the best policy for the law to adopt? But the question has always been there in the background. It has been concealed behind such questions as: Was the defendant under any duty to the plaintiff? Was the relationship between them sufficiently proximate? Was the injury direct or indirect? Was it foreseeable or not? Was it too remote? And so forth. Nowadays we direct ourselves to considerations of policy.

But the guidelines of foreseeability, remoteness etc, must still serve a purpose. Policy is an unruly and unpredictable steed. It may tip the balance in many cases, but if it is the only criterion the law becomes fearfully uncertain, and depends only on the view of the particular tribunal. It is still necessary and appropriate for cases to be argued on the lines of the law as set out in the precedents, as far as the legal principles can be gleaned therefrom, and even if that is not very far it is better than nothing.

Where an injury is subsumed into a later injury (eg a broken leg is then severed in a later accident), the original tortfeasor remains liable for the damage he did, and cannot take advantage of the later event to reduce his liability (*Baker* v *Willoughby* [1970] AC 467, HL); but a supervening serious illness which was unconnected with the accident and which was already dormant within the claimant at the time of the accident will go to reduce the damages payable (*Jobling* v *Associated Dairies Ltd* [1982] AC 794, HL). If a car is already damaged so that a wing needs respraying, a defendant who crashes into that wing cannot be held liable for the cost of the respraying, only for any extra cost he puts the owner to (*Performance Cars Ltd* v *Abraham* [1962] 1 QB 33, CA).

This issue of supervening cause, like all aspects of causation, is a fruitful source of academic disputation, and for the practitioner admits of no easy formula. Lord Wilberforce said in *Jobling's* case (above) that no general, logical, or universally fair rules could be stated, which would cover, in a manner consistent with justice, cases of supervening events, whether due to tortious, partially tortious, non-culpable or wholly accidental events. The courts could only deal with each case as best they could to provide just but not excessive compensation.

In a case we looked at above, *Hogan* v *West Bentinck Hartley Collieries (Owners) Ltd* [1949] 1 All ER 588, where an injury at work to a workman's thumb was followed by an ill-advised amputation of the thumb, it was held by a bare majority in the House of Lords that that unreasonable operation broke the chain of causation (Lord Simonds said that the question of *novus actus* could only be answered on a consideration of all the circumstances and, in particular, the quality of the later act or event). In *Roberts* v *Bettany*, (22 January 2001, unreported), CA, the court said it was a question of whether the intervening act was of so powerful a nature that the conduct of the defendants was not a cause at all but merely part of the surrounding circumstances.

In the Australian case of *Martin* v *Isbard* (1946) 48 WALR 52, where after being involved in an accident, the claimant contracted an anxiety and litigation neurosis because she was wrongly told by her doctor that she had suffered a fracture of the skull, it was held that the advice given by the doctor broke the chain of causation as it was a *novus actus*.

It was held in *Robinson* v *Post Office* [1974] 1 WLR 1176, CA, that where the Post Office had through their original negligence caused the minor leg injury of their employee, the claimant, the doctor's negligence in failing to administer a test dose before injecting with an anti-tetanus serum did not break the chain of causation. They had to take the claimant as they found him, which included his allergy to the anti-tetanus serum.

Where the act is that of the claimant himself, a number of other factors come into play. If that act is so unreasonable as to eclipse the defendant's wrongdoing, then it will have broken the chain of causation and the defendant will not be liable for the ensuing damage. An odd example of this is the South African case of *Alston* v *Marine and Trade Insurance Co Ltd* 1964 (4) SA 112, where the fact that the claimant, who had suffered brain injury in a motor accident, ate cheese while on a certain drug and as a result suffered a stroke, was held to break the chain of causation even though the claimant could not have known it was dangerous to do that.

An example of a case where the conduct of the claimant did not break the chain of causation is *Emeh* v *Kensington and Chelsea and Westminster Area Health Authority* [1985] QB 1012, where the Court of Appeal in no uncertain terms reversed the trial judge's finding that the refusal of an abortion by a woman who had become pregnant after a negligently performed sterilisation was so unreasonable an act that it eclipsed the original negligence.

There is considerable material on *novus actus* in *Reeves* v *Metropolitan Police Comr* [1998] QB 169, CA; revsd [2000] 1 AC 360, HL, where the police were found to be negligent in closing the flap on the door of a cell where they were holding a prisoner who was known to be a suicide risk (despite being sane). By a majority the Court of Appeal held that the voluntary act of the deceased in committing suicide was not a *novus actus*. The House of Lords agreed, stating that a deliberate and informed act intended to exploit a situation created by a defendant did not negative causation where the defendant was in breach of a specific duty imposed by law to guard against that very act. Neither the defence of *novus actus* nor that of *volenti non fit iniuria* (meaning that the claimant took upon himself by his deliberate and conscious act the risk of harm) could succeed. But a defence of contributory negligence did succeed to the tune of 50% of the compensation otherwise due (see the section below on contributory negligence).[13]

We may here add to our treatment of the 'divisible injury' in this way: given that a fairly common scenario in the medical context where a defendant seeks to take advantage of a plea of *novus actus* is where both GP and hospital have been negligent, the former for not making earlier referral and the latter for not treating the injury or disease competently,

---

13 In *Sabri-Tabrizi* v *Lothian Health Board* 1998 SC 373, Lord Nimmo-Smith held at first instance that a woman's decision to continue intercourse with the protection of a condom after she knew that her sterilisation had failed was a *novus actus,* so that the defendants were not liable for a pregnancy that occurred despite the condom. This seems unreasonable.

In *Gill* v *Home Office* (6 July 2000, unreported), CA, there was held to be no *novus actus* where an inadequately detained prisoner with a history of violence assaulted a prison officer when allowed to go to slop out unaccompanied. The court said that the injury sustained was the very kind of injury that was foreseeable if he were let out.

it is clear that the GP should not be heard to say that he can escape liability because the hospital should have cured the problem. That is tantamount to resurrecting the ancient doctrine of 'last opportunity' (under which only the person who had the last opportunity to avoid the accident was liable). The correct answer is that they are both tortfeasors and both responsible, in such proportion as the court directs, for the relevant compensation. A more subtle argument on the part of the GP would be to contend that it would have made no difference if he had referred earlier because the patient would have received the same incompetent and ineffective treatment from the hospital. One answer to that contention would be to satisfy the court that the patient would probably have received competent treatment (ie competent and curative treatment). Even if the GP proved that, although the patient could have been cured by competent treatment, the hospital would on earlier referral probably still have provided incompetent treatment, one would hope that the court would nevertheless find that both GP and hospital played a material part in causing the injury for which compensation is claimed, rather than finding that in the circumstances the GP's negligence was not causative of injury.

In the common dual liability situation for a patient's claim, where the original accident, whether road traffic, or employment or whatever, is mistreated at hospital, it appears from the material we have considered above under 'Divisible injury' that a court would not simply hold that the medical negligence broke the chain of causation. More likely, it would apportion the damages as between the two defendants in such proportion as it considered was merited by their respective fault.[14]

In *Webb* v *Barclays Bank plc and Portsmouth Hospitals NHS Trust* [2001] MLC 0400, [2002] PIQR P61 the claimant fell and injured herself through the negligence of the first defendant, an injury which led to amputation through the negligence of the second defendant. The Court of Appeal said that, on the point of contribution as between the defendants, the question was whether, when an employee was injured in the service and by the negligence of her employer, his liability to her is terminated by the intervening negligence of a doctor brought in to treat the original injury, but who in fact made it worse. The answer was that the chain of causation in such a case would only be broken where the medical treatment was of such a degree of negligence as to be an entirely inappropriate response to the injury. Such was not the instant case. Responsibility was assessed at 25% for the first and 75% for the second defendant. In *Panther* v *Wharton* [2001] MLC 0358 the deputy High Court judge came to a similar conclusion where the chain was from GP to hospital ('Dr Wharton's negligence [*at the hospital*] was not a *novus actus interveniens*: it did not cause the need for the amputations, he failed to act so as to prevent them. That omission did not constitute an event of such impact that it obliterated the wrongdoing of Dr Adegoko [*the GP*]').

---

14   The widow of the actor and comedian, Roy Kinnear, obtained £650,000 from the film company that was responsible for the fatal injury he sustained when he fell from a horse while filming in Spain. Some time later, Hidden J ordered the Spanish hospital to pay 60% of the damages for failing to treat the injury properly (reported in *The Times*, 22 December 1994).

Duty to mitigate

Another principle that falls to be considered in this context is the rule that a claimant is under a duty to take reasonable steps to minimise his loss; if those steps include submitting to medical examination and accepting medical treatment, then failure so to do will go to reduce the award (*Selvanayagam* v *University of West Indies* [1983] 1 WLR 585, PC). In *Geest plc* v *Lansiquot* [2002] Lloyds Rep Med 482 the Privy Council said that, if a defendant intends to contend that a claimant has failed to act reasonably to mitigate his loss, notice of such contention should be clearly given long enough before the hearing to enable the claimant properly to prepare to meet it, and the onus of proving unreasonable refusal of medical treatment is on the defendant.

CONTRIBUTORY NEGLIGENCE

Where some blameworthiness attaches to the claimant's conduct, in that he has shown a failure to take proper care for his own safety, the matter can be dealt with by a proportionate reduction in the award on the principle of contributory negligence. That is not very likely to arise in medical negligence cases, but an example is *Brushett* v *Cowan* [1991] 2 Med LR 271, where the Newfoundland Court of Appeal held that the claimant, who was a registered nursing assistant with some experience in orthopedics, was 50% to blame for her injury when she fell while using crutches and broke her leg, because she had failed to seek instructions regarding the proper use of the crutches. Or a patient may be held negligent for failing to report to his GP when the hospital had advised him to do so or for failing to attend review appointments. In the end, it is simply a matter of common sense whether the patient has been irresponsible in regard to his own health and safety.

We noted above a recent case where the House of Lords found contributory negligence by virtue of a deliberate act of self-harm by a rational prisoner in police custody (*Reeves* v *Metropolitan Police Comr*).

In *Fraser* v *Winchester Health Authority* (1999) 55 BMLR 122, CA, a young support worker who was injured in an explosion when she changed a gas cooker cylinder in a tent lit by candle was held to have been one-third contributorily negligent for her own safety (the defendants had given no instructions on the manoeuvre, but the claimant agreed that she should have known better).

In *Jebson* v *Ministry of Defence* [2000] PIQR P201, the Court of Appeal, reversing the judge, found that where an intoxicated off-duty soldier, travelling with his mates in the back of an inadequately supervised army lorry, had injured himself by foolishly attempting to climb on to the canvas roof of the vehicle from the tailgate, the way in the which the injury had been caused fell within the area of foreseeability for which the failure of the defendants to provide proper supervision was referable. The Court then upheld the judge's finding of 75% contributory negligence.

In *Marshall* v *Lincolnshire Roadcar Co* (7 December 2000, unreported), CA, a woman aged 20 was injured when she stepped off a bus before it had completely stopped at the bus stop. The driver was at fault in opening the doors early, but, strangely, the court upheld, but only by a majority, the judges finding that this was not a case of contributory negligence because the claimant was 100% to blame for her accident. For good measure, the majority added that her action was also a *novus actus*.

In *Pidgeon* v *Doncaster Health Authority* [2002] Lloyds Rep Med 130, the County Court judge at Sheffield held that the health authority was liable for the negligent evaluation of a cervical smear test which failed to reveal a pre-cancerous condition, but the claimant was two-thirds responsible (contributorily negligent) for the development of cervical cancer as she had failed to attend screenings in the following nine years. The case of *Sabri-Tabrizi* (see footnote 13 above) was distinguished as the claimant's failure in *Pidgeon* was not so utterly unreasonable as to break the chain of causation entirely.

Where a claim is pursued for professional negligence for loss of the chance of suing, any contributory negligence likely to have been found at the original trial must be factored in when assessing the percentage of total damages to be awarded (*Sharpe* v *Addison* [2003] EWCA Civ 1189, CA). See the following section for further explanation.

LOSS OF A CHANCE

This section considers what a patient has to prove where the admitted breach of duty involves a failure to treat. This limited aspect of causation deserves special consideration because the complaint arises time and again: 'I was denied the proper treatment for my condition. They admit negligence. I might have been cured.' (Or, in the appropriate case, 'My wife/husband/child might have lived'.)

What is the problem?

The problem is that, according to traditional jurisprudence, one has to prove that, on the balance of probabilities – ie more likely than not or at least a 51% chance, the outcome would have been better. Why should it not be enough, it is often asked (especially by the patient or his family), given that proper treatment was neglected, to show a chance (let us say, a more than minimal chance) that the treatment would have been successful, and so to award a proportion of total damages dependent upon the percentage chance of the treatment being successful?

What is the modern origin of the rule that the likelihood of a successful outcome must be shown to have been more than evens? For that we turn to the seminal case of *Hotson* v *Fitzgerald* [1987] AC 750, CA, MLC 0012, HL.

Hotson v *Fitzgerald*

The facts can be simply stated. The defendants' doctor failed to treat the young claimant at the proper time and so he developed a permanent disability of the hip. The evidence established that, even if he had been properly treated, he would still probably (a 75% chance) have contracted the disability. The defendant said that therefore the claimant had not proved on the balance of probabilities that he had suffered an injury. The claimant argued that he had been deprived of the chance of recovery and should therefore receive one-quarter of full compensation for his injury. The defendants' argument was in accord with traditional jurisprudence, but both at first instance and in the Court of Appeal the claimant's contention was accepted. The Master of the Rolls said:

> ... it is unjust that there should be no liability for failure to treat a patient, simply because the chances of a successful cure by that treatment were less than 50%. Nor by the same token can it be just that if the chances of a successful cure only marginally exceed 50%, the doctor or his employer should be liable to the same extent as if the treatment could be guaranteed to cure. If this is the law, it is high time that it was changed, assuming that this court has power to do so ... the essence of the plaintiff's claim is that he has lost any benefit which he would have derived from timely treatment.

The court said that this benefit sounded in damages, subject to proper evaluation. The categories of loss were never closed, and it was not only financial or physical injury that were fit subjects for compensation.

In the House of Lords

But the House of Lords unanimously decided that the finding by the trial judge that there had been only a 25% chance that any treatment would have been beneficial, ie would have prevented the necrosis, was equivalent to a finding that the claimant had not proved on the balance of probabilities that the admitted negligence had caused the necrosis, and so the claim could not succeed. The correct approach was to decide first as a matter of fact and in the usual way what was the condition of the claimant when he arrived at the hospital. In this particular case the question could be framed as: 'Had the blood vessels running along the claimant's leg been injured to such an extent that necrosis was in any event inevitable?'. The court said that the finding of only a one in four chance of benefit meant that the claimant would not have benefited from treatment, ie they applied the traditional rule that a court can only conclude that something would have happened if it is more likely than not that it would have happened.

Lord Bridge said that unless the claimant proved on the balance of probabilities that the delayed treatment was at least a material contributory cause of the avascular necrosis, he failed on the issue of causation and no question of quantification could arise.

Lord Ackner said that to follow the principle of proportionate deduction for the chance of benefit was 'a wholly new doctrine which has no support in principle or authority and would give rise to many complications in the search for mathematical or statistical exactitude'.

In this way the House of Lords affirmed the traditional jurisprudence.

Let us assume that we can prove that treatment should have been given at a certain (earlier) time. As we have seen, we are constrained by the *Hotson* decision to prove that, more likely than not, that treatment would have produced a substantially better outcome (we use the word 'substantially' in order to give the claim sufficient financial expectations to justify proceedings).

Do not confuse

We should not confuse the question of showing a percentage chance of there having been a better outcome with the question of by what percentage an assuredly better outcome would have been better. If one can show that the outcome would probably have been better, it does not matter that the degree of betterment can only be expressed as a percentage and that that percentage may itself be less than 50%. In many cases involving a failure to give timely treatment for cancer the most the experts can do is suggest statistics for survival, ie as it would have been and as it now is, given the delay in diagnosis and treatment. Provided one can achieve some clarity on the degree of worsened outcome, given that the experts are satisfied that on the balance of probability the prognosis would have been better, the case on causation is proved, and all one has to do (although this may not be easy) is to evaluate for the purposes of quantum the difference between the two prognoses.

In *Judge* v *Huntingdon Health Authority* [1995] 6 Med LR 223, a breast cancer case, Titheridge QC, sitting as a High Court judge, found that on the balance of probability breast nodes had not been involved in the cancer at the time when diagnosis and treatment should have taken place, and that therefore there had been, on the statistics, an 80% chance of a cure at that time. However, he went on, wrongly in my view, to indicate that the claimant was entitled to 80% of full damages. An 80% probability of survival should have been taken as proof of survival and therefore full damages awarded.

This section needs to be read now in the light of the House of Lords decision in *Gregg* v *Scott* [2005] MLC 1202.

Gregg v *Scott* and the loss of a prognosis

Introduction

The basic facts of this case are capable of fairly short summary, though also capable of well nigh endless legal argument. The judges of the House of Lords took months to reflect and research and finalise their views. Even then, the result in this extremely important case comes to us only by a bare majority.

Diagnosis of cancer (lymphoma in the left axilla) was delayed by GP negligence for nine months. In that time it made further progress (invading the pectoral muscles) causing the patient additional pain and suffering, requiring more intensive treatment, and possibly affecting the prognosis.

Two things need to be made clear at this point. The first is that the original claim was based on the assertion that the patient would probably have survived (ie survived ten years, which is taken by the medical profession, and accepted by the lawyers, to equate with a cure) but now, as a result of the negligent delay, would not. This had to be changed as it was discovered shortly before trial that his cancer was particularly malignant, so that instead of the hitherto claimed probability of survival he had in fact had from the outset, even if treated timeously, a less than even chance of survival. Undeterred, his advisers amended his claim to what was in effect loss of a chance, or – more precisely – injury by way of a diminished chance of survival. Note that each time the case was tried the outlook for the patient, by reason of his survival up to the respective time, had grown better, so that by the time the matter came before the Lords one had to wonder if he would have done any better anyway!

The second point, commented upon by their Lordships, is that, although there was clearly a (relatively small) claim for the additional physical suffering caused by the spread of the cancer during the period of delay, that was not a head of claim being pursued by the claimant. He put all his eggs in the basket of loss of prognosis, ie reduced chance of survival.

One further preliminary note: the whole case was done on statistics, by way of evidence from medical experts. By the time of the trial at first instance the original statistic (above 50%) for likely cure if treated timeously had fallen to 42%, whereas the actual prospect of cure, given the delay in diagnosis, was only 25%. Bear in mind again that it does not necessarily follow that the chances of survival would have suffered that reduction if there had been no delay. *Post hoc* is not the same as *propter hoc*.[15]

Approaches

If one accepts this statistical basis for judging a claim (artificial in so many ways), there are two possible approaches. The first is the traditional one: to succeed the claimant need prove that he would have been cured but now will not be, issues which are to be decided on the balance of probabilities. The 45% statistic means that probably he would not have survived ten years (would not have been cured) anyway; so he has suffered no injury. This was the basis of the *Hotson* decision in the Lords. However, as we have seen, that decision, that the child's leg would not have been 'cured' in any event, was based on a finding of fact by the trial judge that so many blood vessels had been lost by the time he came to hospital that the failure to treat him properly at the hospital caused no loss as the leg was doomed in any event. The statistics offered a 25% chance of survival for the leg if properly treated, but the judge did not base his finding that the leg would have been lost on that (at any rate not on that alone). He had this physical fact on which to base his finding, ie the physical fact that the condition of the leg, which was vitally relevant to its prospect of survival, was such that there could be no prospect of survival. In the case of *Gregg* the evidence of statistical chance was paramount, making it more purely a claim for loss of a chance. There was no evidence to allow the sort of physical finding that was possible in *Hotson*. The only relevant evidence was what the experts gave by way of statistics culled from this or that series in the literature. Very unsatisfactory, but *faute de mieux*!

On the traditional approach (and ignoring the unreliability of statistics when applied to a specific case) the only response could be that the claimant had lost nothing as he would not on the balance of probability have been cured in any event.

The second approach would be to admit in circumstances of this sort an exception to the traditional legal test, as was done twice in recent years,

---

15 Let the dumbers-down put that into a neat English translation, if they can!

in the *Fairchild* case (see the section so titled earlier in this chapter) and in *Chester* v *Afshar* [2005] 1 AC 134, MLC 1170 (see Chapter 23 under 'Duty of disclosure'). Two of the judges supported this approach, but three were not prepared to modify the traditional approach. (The trial judge had dismissed the claim; so had the Court of Appeal but only by a majority.)

So the House, which had showed such imagination in carving out new paths to yield the just result in *Fairchild* and in *Chester* v *Afshar*, baulked at the final fence in this third recent test of their judicial creativity.

Lord Nicholls

Lord Nicholls, for allowing the claimant's appeal, said that a remedy for a claimant in this situation was essential. The loss of a 45% prospect of recovery was just as much a real loss for the patient as the loss of a 55% prospect of recovery. In both cases the patient was worse off. He lost something of importance and value. I would interpose here to say that formulation seems to me to beg the question, the question being whether a diminished prospect is in fact an 'injury'. This gets perilously close to the clearly inadmissible claim of persons who, living in the neighbourhood of a factory when a noxious emission negligently occurs, claim for their reduced prospects of survival, at a time when there is no reason to believe they have suffered anything at all apart from now being at risk where they were not at risk before.

So the question is not whether a chance has been lost – clearly it has – but whether such a 'loss' is cognisable by the law as a claimable head of damages. In some circumstances, of course, loss of a chance is recognised as a claimable loss. Loss of a chance to try for job or role or whatever, loss of a chance of bringing a successful claim, loss of a chance where the loss would hinge on what a third party might have done; but note that these claims are all for loss of a chance involving financial loss, not physical injury. As already remarked, the law has for years recognised a consequential or parasitic loss of chance of physical integrity, as when something is added to general damages for the chance of osteo-arthritis or epilepsy developing. But none of these scenarios are much similar to an isolated (standalone) medical claim for loss of a chance of surviving (wholly or in relation to a part of the body). Nevertheless, Lord Nicholls said that, where there is substantial uncertainty about whether the desired outcome would have been achieved (and there surely is uncertainty, I would add, where the whole question turns on what statistic the experts manage to derive from a study of what reports are available about what may have happened to a limited number of other patients whose situation may have been in some respects similar to that of the claimant), the law would do better to define the claimant's actionable damage more narrowly by reference to the opportunity the claimant lost. The judge said that medical science would often be uncertain what the outcome would have been, and so loss of a chance of favourable outcome should be the basis for damages. The doctor's duty, here breached, was to promote the patient's prospects of recovery (not to reduce them, I would add). He went on to point to the inherently limited usefulness of statistics (about other patients) when used to predict what would have happened to a particular patient. But 'in the present context use of statistics for the purpose of evaluating a lost chance makes good sense'. Lord Nicholls also emphasised the difference between a *Hotson* case, where a finding of fact about the physical condition of the patient at the time of the negligence determined in itself a certain enough conclusion about the likely outcome, and a *Gregg* case where there was no such prior finding of fact possible. It is interesting to note that as long ago as 1987 (in *Hotson*) Lord Bridge had recognised the distinction between these two sorts of cases.

Lord Nicholls argued strongly for the recognition of a lost chance as a head of damage in cases where medical opinion could only assess the patient's original prospects of recovery on a statistical basis ('fraught with a significant degree of medical uncertainty').

Clearly there is much force in this argument. A law which permits recovery when the chance of survival has gone from 60% to 45% but not when it has gone from 45% to virtually nil does not command respect. The problem, of course, lies in the introduction into these cases of statistics. That is what gives the whole argument of the majority such an unrealistic flavour. Once you say that the statistics show that this particular patient had only a less than 50% chance of recovery, the case is lost, as the traditional approach moves to dominate the debate. But if you allow that the statistics cannot reasonably be used in that way and that they only show various possibilities, it becomes easier to accept that the traditional approach should not be followed.

Lord Hope

Lord Hope agreed that the claimant's appeal should be allowed. He was not the only judge to comment in some surprise on the fact that the claimant was not pursuing any injury claim except the loss of a chance of recovery. But he used the fact of the unclaimed physical injury to support his view that the significant reduction in the prospects of recovery which the claimant had suffered could and should be claimable in damages. He said that the physical injury, in addition to pain and suffering, caused a reduction in the prospects of a successful outcome and this loss of prospects was consequential on the physical injury and so was a proper subject for damages. Not quite the way Lord Nicholls put it, but yielding the same overall conclusion.

Clearly, the question of recognising loss of prospects as a stand-alone claim is one of policy. In *Fairchild* and in *Chester* v *Afshar* the House was prepared on policy grounds to declare for the patient. Here they were not.

The majority:

Lord Phillips

Lord Phillips, in a detailed study, argued that the statistics had been misinterpreted by all except him. He said the position had been complicated by the better than expected progress of the patient during the long course of the litigation. Nor was he convinced that the progress of the cancer during the nine months delay was due to the negligence of the defendant doctor. He said, surely rightly, that the expert's model was a very inadequate tool for assessing the effect of delay in treatment on the claimant's

progress and that his subsequent clinical progress was of critical significance in re-assessing the issue. He said that the closer the claimant
became with the passage of time to being a survivor (ie surviving ten
years) the smaller the likelihood that the delay in commencing his treatment had had any effect on his expectation of life. Analysis of statistics
was very difficult in medical cases. That was a reason for adopting the
easier and more robust method of traditional valuation. [But that was
being based on 'unreliable' statistics too!] Lord Phillips said he was well
aware of the need for justice but he was not persuaded that justice
demanded that this sort of statistical loss should sound in damages. As he
had already explained, the difficulties in evaluating such a case on the
chance basis rather than the traditional probability basis ('the complications of this case') had persuaded him that the traditional basis should
not be abandoned for any sort of special rule. 'Awarding damages for the
reduction in the prospect of a cure where the result of treatment is still
uncertain is not a satisfactory exercise.'

Lord Hoffman

Lord Hoffman did not see any clear way in which a new rule for cases of
this sort could be formulated. He did not favour the 'consequential' hook
proposed by Lord Hope. He said that the various control mechanisms proposed to confine liability for loss of a chance within artificial limits were
not attractive. A wholesale adoption of possible rather than probable causation as the criterion of liability would be so radical a change in our law
as to amount to a legislative act, which would have enormous consequences for insurance companies and the NHS.

Baroness Hale

Baroness Hale said that she was for a long time attracted by the principal argument submitted for the claimant, namely that the loss of prognosis was simply consequential on the physical damage, ie the spread of the
cancer during the period of delay. But, she said, on a proper interpretation of what the trial judge had written, he did not find that the delay
caused the spread. She agreed that the instant case was not covered by
Hotson as the outcome in *Hotson* was determined inevitably by the poor
condition of the leg on arrival at hospital whereas the outcome for the
cancer could not be so determined but remained uncertain, capable of
expression only on a statistical basis. It was, as accepted by the claimant,
a question of policy whether the traditional approach should be modified
in cases of this sort by allowing a claim for loss of or reduction in the
chance of a successful outcome. There were attractions in allowing an
award of damages for loss of such a chance where physiological changes
were provable, but such an approach would be difficult to apply, particularly in showing that the delay had caused the loss of chance.

I think that we have to see the strongest objections of Baroness Hale in
the following passages. She was particularly affected by the prospect that
any claim for personal injury could be drafted as a claim for loss of chance
of a better outcome, and she did not see how the two bases for a claim –
loss of chance and balance of probability – could co-exist. It would not
make sense if the claimant could at more than 50% go for probability and

so get 100% damages and at 49% go for loss of a chance and so get substantial damages. Defendants would lose out either way. But if loss of a chance was adopted and probability had to be dropped, claimants who would now get 100% damages would in future be limited to a proportion unless they showed 100% probability (ie certainty). Expert evidence and trials would be far more complex and costly, and recovery far less predictable. Further, there would be no reason to limit the change in the basis of recovery to medical claims.

Baroness Hale summarised her view by saying that 'the complexities of attempting to introduce liability for the loss of a chance of a more favourable outcome in personal injury claims have driven me, not without regret, to conclude that it should not be done'.

Comment

I can see no reason why loss of chance, in appropriate cases, should not go to swell general damages where it is shown that it arises from physiological changes which are due to the negligence. In other words it is a consequential loss, consequential on negligence causing physical injury. The courts, as we well know, have no problem in saying in effect to a claimant: 'You have suffered a physical injury which has meant (*inter alia*) that you are now at a 15% risk of developing epilepsy whereas before the negligence the risk was minute or non-existent. Your chance of remaining free of epilepsy has therefore been reduced from close to 100% to 85%. You may never contract epilepsy but there is that risk now due to the negligence. We will take that factor into account when assessing general damages.' Why then should a court not say in the appropriate case: 'It is proved that if your cancer had been treated timeously you would have had a 45% chance of no relapse and so of keeping your breast/womb (or whatever). It is also proved that the negligent delay has impaired that prospect, to the extent that now there is virtually no chance (or only a 20% chance). The risk of your suffering that injury has been appreciably increased [just as the risk of possible epilepsy is increased in the earlier example]. We will take that factor into account in assessing general damages.'

The court might find it hard to assess quantum, particularly in cases where potential loss of working years is involved, but plenty of quantum assessments are difficult without causing the court to throw up its hands in despair (or the towel in). I cannot see anything in the *Gregg* speeches which could outlaw that approach, which is consistent with the traditional law. Indeed Baroness Hale, given proper causation, would seem to accept it.

Further examples

Many further examples could be given of a patient failing on causation because he could not prove on the balance of probabilities that proper treatment would have resulted, in one way or another, in a better outcome. In *Gregory v Pembrokeshire Health Authority* [1989] 1 Med LR 81, the judge said there was no question of assessing the chances that the claimant, had she been properly advised, would have proceeded via a second amniocentesis to an abortion – he had simply to decide on the evidence whether on the balance of probabilities she would or would not.

In *Hardaker* v *Newcastle Health Authority* MLC 0395, [2001] Lloyds Rep Med 512, Burnton J held that the claimant failed on causation as the expert evidence as to whether immediate decompression would have produced a better outcome for the claimant diver proved only an unquantified chance of a better but unidentified outcome. Therefore the claimant had failed to prove he had suffered any damage, as a chance of a better recovery below 50% did not sound in damages. It is interesting to note that Burnton J (rightly) viewed the observations of Andrew Smith J in *Smith* v *NHS Litigation Authority* [2001] Lloyds Rep Med 90, as made *per incuriam*. Andrew Smith J had said that, even if the congenital displacement of the hip, which was the subject of the action he was trying, would probably not have been discovered by a competent examination, the claimant would have been able to claim percentage damages.

However, the situation is different in Australia. The Court of Appeal of Victoria allowed damages for loss of a chance of a better outcome on earlier diagnosis in the case of *Gavalas* v *Singh* [2001] MLC 0388, saying that the precise boundaries of such a claim awaited future determination. A similar view had been taken the year before by the New South Wales Court of Appeal in *Rufo* v *Hoskin* [2004] MLC 1119, where the court said the judge did not err in not being satisfied, on the balance of probabilities, that the breaches of duty by the respondent, which he found to have occurred, caused the fractures suffered by the appellant and it was open to the judge not to be satisfied that (a) but for the negligence, the injury (by way of fractures) would not have occurred; or (b) that the negligence materially contributed to the occurrence of the fractures; or (c) that the fractures were the realisation of a risk created by the negligence. However, the evidence strongly supported a conclusion that the negligence materially increased a risk, which was otherwise very substantial, that fractures would occur; and that the occurrence of the fractures was a realisation of that total risk – as distinct from the increment to the risk created by the negligence. The appellant was entitled to be compensated for the loss of the chance that, but for the negligence, the fractures would not have occurred (or would not have occurred at the time or with the severity of their actual occurrence). Accordingly, it was an error for the judge to hold that the increased risk was too speculative to justify an award of damages: so long as such an increase was material, the court was required to do its best to assess it. Well!

Where chance is assessed

However, there are many situations where the courts assess the chance of an event and award proportionate damages. On one occasion proportionate damages were awarded in a medical case (though in reverse, as it were, and so to the patient's disadvantage). In *Clark* v *MacLennan* [1983] 1 All ER 416, Pain J found that the defendants were in breach of their duty in performing a certain operation prematurely and that if it had been performed at the right time the patient would have stood a two in three chance of avoiding the injury. But instead of saying that she had proved on the balance of probabilities that her injury was caused by the breach of duty, he awarded her two-thirds of full damages. However, this acceptance of the 'chance' approach in a personal injury action is very much a one-off phenomenon.

One further medical case that appears on the face of it to be an illustration of the percentage approach is *Bagley* v *North Herts Health Authority* [1986] NLJ Rep 1014, where Simon Brown J, true to his reasoning in the Court of Appeal in the *Hotson* case, having found that a hospital had been negligent in not carrying out blood tests on a mother, as a result of which she gave birth to a stillborn child, knocked 5% off the damages awarded because, even had the hospital acted properly, there would still have been a 5% chance that the child would not have lived. However, it is understood that the parties had already agreed a 5% discount, so that the judge was merely implementing their agreement rather than endorsing of his own accord a percentage approach.[16]

Scenarios involving 'chance'

The question arises whether there is any reasonable distinction between the scenarios where the 'chance' approach has been accepted and the medical negligence context. Claims, in contract or in tort, for being prevented from auditioning for a role have long involved compensation for the loss of the ability to compete and so, expressly or implicitly, of the chance of competing successfully.

The most obvious 'chance' scenario for our purposes is where a solicitor is sued for not having properly processed a claim. It is clear law that in such a context the court will award damages in proportion to the chance of success of the original action (the right to sue is regarded, quaintly, as a chose in action and it is that asset which falls to be valued). The seminal case is *Kitchen* v *Royal Air Forces Association* [1958] 1 WLR 563, CA; and a medical example is *Gascoigne* v *Ian Sheridan & Co and Latham* [1994] 5 Med LR 437, where 60% of the total damages relevant to the original medical claim was awarded.

In *Harrison* v *Bloom Camillin* [1999] 45 LS Gaz R 32, a claim against solicitors for failing to process an action against accountants for negligent advice, Neuberger J carefully assessed every aspect of the mooted claim against the accountants to arrive at an estimate of the chances of success and the likely damages. He ended with a deduction of 35% for the risk of losing on negligence and a further 20% for the risk of losing on causation.[17]

In *O'Shea* v *Weedon & Co* ML 8/98 p 8, Alliott J found that the original claim for a failed sterilisation that the defendant solicitor had failed to progress had not stood a 'real and substantial rather than merely a negligible prospect of success', and so the claim against the solicitor failed. In *Hatswell* v *Goldsbergs (a firm of solicitors)* [2001] EWCA Civ 2084, the Court of Appeal endorsed the judge's conclusion that the claimant's chances of success in his original medical negligence claim were nil. He

---

16 In *Ata-Amonoo* v *Grant* (26 January 2001, unreported), CA, the court said that in assessing damages for loss of a chance it was legitimate for the judge to deal with the sums involved in general terms and not to specify the actual percentage discounts.

17 In *Hanif* v *Middleweeks* (19 July 2000, unreported), CA, the court said that a purely mathematical approach to assessing an overall loss of the chance to pursue proceedings was not appropriate.

would have been seeking to prove by his own recollection some 14 years after the event that he had made complaints to his GP which were completely inconsistent with the contemporaneous medical notes.

In *Sharpe* v *Addison* [2003] EWCA Civ 1189, the Court of Appeal, holding that the claim of a victim of a road traffic accident would not have been 'of no real value', said the test as to whether a claim was worthless was very similar to the test for striking out.

Another example is that a widow in a Fatal Accidents Act claim will be awarded compensation in proportion to the chances she had of financial support from the deceased.

It is also relevant that in a normal personal injury action a percentage chance (often as little as 10%) of some further injury arising in the future (eg osteo-arthritis developing in an injured joint) will be assessed and a suitable addition made to the award.

But, as mentioned above, the traditional jurisprudence is that a probability has to be shown. In *Sykes* v *Midland Bank Executor and Trustee Co Ltd* [1971] 1 QB 113, the Court of Appeal would not accept that clients who entered into an underlease after negligent advice from their solicitors could recover damages in proportion to the chance, as assessed by the court, that they would not have signed the underlease had they been properly advised. The court's task was to decide whether or not on the balance of probabilities the claimants had shown that they would not have signed if properly advised. Salmon LJ said that the argument for damages proportionate to the chance the claimants would have executed the underlease if properly advised would lead to the strange result that, unless the defendants could prove with certainty that they had not caused damage, they would be liable for the remote chance that they had done so. This is unconvincing, because the same argument could be applied to all the contexts where loss of a chance is accepted as the basis for compensation.

The insurance cases

In *Dunbar* v *A and B Painters Ltd* [1986] 2 Lloyd's Rep 38, the insured party sued his brokers, whose negligent misrepresentation to the insurers had voided the policy. On a quite different ground (because the employee had fallen from a height above the 40-foot maximum covered by the policy) the insurers would have been entitled to refuse to indemnify the insured in any event. The employee recovered against the employer (the insured party). The question was whether the negligent brokers should reimburse the employer in full. The brokers argued that if there was, say, a 30% chance that the insurers would have repudiated the policy in any event, they should be relieved of liability *pro tanto*. The employers said that the correct approach was to ascertain whether on the balance of probabilities the insurers would have repudiated the contract and, if the answer was in the negative, the brokers should reimburse them, the employers, in full. The Court of Appeal disagreed: the correct approach was not to ask if on the balance of probabilities the insurers would in fact have refused to indemnify on the 'height' ground, but to assess the chance that they would have refused and award proportionate damages. They said the judge had wrongly adopted the 'probability' test, but in the event it did not make any difference because he had in any case effectively assessed that chance at nil. Therefore, his decision to award full damages against the brokers, whether on a 'probability' basis or an 'assessment of chance' basis was appropriate. The court cited the similar earlier case of *Fraser* v *B N Furman (Productions) Ltd* [1967] 1 WLR 898, CA, though on a careful reading of that case it does not offer support for a 'chance' approach in this context. Further, it is not easy to reconcile the *Dunbar* decision with the *Sykes* case referred to above.

Further cases

In *Spring* v *Guardian Assurance plc* [1995] 2 AC 296, the House of Lords held that an employer who negligently gave a bad reference for the claimant, their ex-employee, might be liable to him in damages. Lord Lowry said that the claimant did not have to prove that the prospective employer would probably have employed him, merely that he had lost a reasonable chance of employment (which would have to be evaluated).

In *Allied Maples Group* v *Simmons & Simmons* [1995] 1 WLR 1602, the Court of Appeal held that, where the claimant purchasers had shown that the defendants, their solicitors, should have given them further information about the proposed sale which would *on the balance of probability* have caused them to seek to renegotiate the terms of the sale, they did not have to prove that they would probably have achieved a renegotiation; it was enough that they could *establish a more than minimal chance* of that (and it was that chance which fell to be assessed for damages). The basis for this distinction between proof on a balance of probability and proof of a chance appears from the judgments to depend upon whether the necessary inquiry concerns what the claimants themselves would have done or what an independent third party would have done. However, in that event it is not easy to see why the 'loss of a chance' approach should not apply in a *Bolitho* situation (*Bolitho* v *City and Hackney Health Authority* (above)). The chain of causation in that case depended on what the defendants' doctor would have done if she had responded to the nurse's nocturnal call to come to the ward. The fact that she happened to be an agent of the defendants is neither here nor there. It might have been, for example, a negligent failure to refer to a different hospital that constituted the proven allegation of negligence. Are we to conclude that in such a context the question what the doctors at that other hospital would have done should be resolved on a 'chance' basis, whereas in the fortuitous event of the hospitals being managed by the same health authority the question of causation should be resolved on a probability basis? That would be absurd.

The Court of Appeal followed the reasoning of the *Allied Maples* case in *First Interstate Bank of California* v *Cohen Arnold & Co* [1996] 5 Bank LR 150, CA.

In *Rosling King* v *Shaw* (7 December 1995, unreported), QBD, the defendant proved upon his counter-claim that the negligence of the claimants had deprived his Danish lawyer of the opportunity of levying execution against a debtor of the defendant while that debtor was still in funds. Nicholas Strauss QC assessed the chances of the Danish lawyer acting successfully in that way at 30%.

In *Stovold* v *Barlows* [1996] PNLR 91, CA, Stuart-Smith LJ (who seems to have been responsible for the genesis of this 'third party' rule in his judgment in the *Allied Maples* case) affirmed this approach to causation where the question was what an independent third party might have done. In that case the negligence of the defence solicitors was alleged to have cost the claimant vendor the completion of the sale of his home. The Court of Appeal said that the approach of the trial judge was wrong when he took the view that the claimant had to satisfy the court on the balance of probabilities that the prospective purchaser would have completed the sale. The proper approach was to evaluate the loss of the claimants' chance that, if the documents that should have arrived had arrived, the sale would had gone ahead. The court themselves assessed that chance at 50%, thus reducing the judge's award of total damages by half.

In *Doyle* v *Wallace* [1998] PIQR Q146, the Court of Appeal assessed the chance that the claimant would have become a teacher, not the probability, as it depended on what a third party might have done. The defendant had argued that the chances of the claimant becoming a teacher would have been less than 50% and therefore she could not recover any damages for loss of earnings as a teacher.[18]

There is an interesting gloss on the subject in an informative article on the Human Growth Hormone litigation by Mark Mildred at [1998] JPIL 262. The defendants argued that the question whether treatment would have been stopped if the clinicians had been given certain information fell to be evaluated on percentage terms. Morland J rejected that argument (judgment 22 May 1998), saying that once a claimant had proved on the balance of probabilities that treatment would have been stopped, he or she was entitled to succeed. A discount was appropriate only in relation to quantification of uncertain damages, for example the likelihood of promotion to a higher paid job or the like. However, it might be thought that, as the clinicians were not the defendants, the issue involved what a third party would have done, and therefore, if there is any principle at all flowing from the *Allied Maples* case, loss of a chance would apply in this context.[19]

In *Normans Bay Ltd* v *Coudert Brothers* [2003] EWCA Civ 215, a complex commercial case, solicitors were sued for negligent advice in relation to a bid for shares in a Russian company. Though the bid appeared to be successful, it was later declared invalid by the Moscow Arbitration Court. The claimant contended that proper advice would have meant that the bid would have been made in a form that would have been safe from invalidation. The court below and on appeal declared that the prospect that the bid would not have been invalidated must be assessed on chance, not probability. In the event the Court of Appeal reviewed the chance and reduced it from 70% to 40%.

---

18   See also *Anderson* v *Davis* [1993] PIQR Q87.
19   In *Smith* v *National Health Service Litigation Authority* [2001] Lloyd's Rep Med 90, [2001] MLC 0286, Andrew Smith J rejected the claim that, as a baby in 1973, the claimant had not been properly examined for signs of congenital displacement of the hip, but added, *obiter,* that, had he found that she had not been properly examined, he would have assessed the *chance* that examination would have led to detection and successful treatment of the condition. However, it is not possible to understand his reasons for distinguishing the issue before him from the similar issue before the House of Lords in the *Hotson* case and for stating that the 'chance' principle of the *Allied Maples* case applied rather than the 'balance of probabilities' principle of the *Hotson* case.

The most recent case in this context of chance generally (not 'third party' chance) is *Gregg* v *Scott*, which has its own section above.

Conclusion

The short fact of the matter is that there is no logical explanation, at least as far as the 'third party' rule is concerned, for the distinction drawn by the courts between situations where damages are assessed on a percentage basis and those where damages are assessed on a probability basis. In the first place it cannot be of any intrinsic significance whether the chance of an action being taken had the situation been different relates to an action to be taken by the claimant, by a party to the action, or by a third party. Further, as indicated above, there will be situations where it is simply fortuitous whether or not the hypothetical action under investigation is an action that would have been taken by an agent of the defendants or of some other body, and therefore it makes little sense to have two different tests of causation depending on that meaningless distinction.

The solution?

In the last edition I wrote, hopefully, under the above section heading:

> There is no reason at all why loss of a chance (ie an appreciable chance, something more than a minimal chance) should not be the basis for assessment of damages where the chance relates to a real possibility of benefiting from medical treatment. The scenarios where loss of a chance is agreed on the authorities to be a proper basis for compensation cannot reasonably be distinguished from this medical context. Where, as in *Hotson*, experts agree that there was a one in four chance that injury or death would have been avoided by timely treatment, this means, presumably, that one in four of such patients would gain that benefit. In those circumstances it is very hard on a patient, and certainly does not sound just, that he be told that his chance of being that one in four patient is worth nothing.

But now, given the House of Lords decision in *Gregg* v *Scott*, loss of a chance of a better outcome is dead in the water for the normal medical claims, unless it can be joined as parasitic or consequential damage to another head of claim, probably general damages, in which case there is still hope it might succeed. As to the 'third party' rule, that is unlikely to become any clearer, as it is a flimsy construct.

Chapter 18

Loss/injury: foreseeability and remoteness

Damages are recoverable only in respect of injury of a type that was foreseeable (though no definition of 'type' is available). But this must be read subject to the important rule that the wrongdoer must take the claimant as he finds him, so that the fact that the injury develops unexpected complications or, through hypersensitivity, more harm is suffered than was to be expected is no bar to recovery. Nor is the fact that the injury did not arise in the precisely foreseeable manner.

Strictly, injuries which are of an unforeseeable type and do not come within the rule that the wrongdoer must take the claimant as he finds him are not subjects for compensation (an example would be where a brick is thrown from a window and there is a foreseeable risk from it striking someone, but in fact it hits an electricity cable and in a manner not to be foreseen causes a person in the vicinity to be electrocuted – injury from impact would seem of a different kind from injury by electrocution). A judge would be entitled to hold the wrongdoer not liable for the injury suffered, but in practice he might well find a way to implement his 'gut reaction' to the situation and award compensation, eg by 'finding' that there was in fact some slight degree of foreseeability of electrocution.

TOO REMOTE

Even if the claimant has established a duty of care, a breach of that duty, and loss of a type recognised by the law and caused by the breach, the defendants will only be liable to compensate for that loss if it was reasonably foreseeable at the time of the breach that it could arise. In other words, the basic principle (though subject, as we shall see, to substantial exceptions) is that you cannot recover for an injury that was not foreseeable.

This is sometimes expressed as a statement that the loss must not be too remote. But that catch-all expression is also used to mean that no duty was owed to the particular claimant (the claimant was too remote, not being within the area of foreseeable risk created by the defendant's actions, and therefore so was the damage he suffered); or that no duty was owed to take care not to inflict the particular sort of harm suffered, or not to inflict it in that particular way; or that the chain of causation was broken; or that policy militates against recovery. Thus a mother who suffers nervous shock on being told of the death of her son and is denied damages on the basis that she does not come within the 'aftermath' principle (see Chapter 19) may be told that the damage she suffered was too remote. This may mean that no duty was owed to her by the tortfeasor, or that the intervening act of her informant broke the chain of causation, or that the law or policy forbids recovery in the particular circumstances.

To assist clarity of thought on this issue, it is better therefore to avoid the expression 'too remote' (it is in fact unhelpful in any context), and say simply that the loss must be reasonably foreseeable. As we have seen, foreseeability of harm, though a prerequisite for a duty of care does not of itself prove the existence of a duty. It is a prerequisite for a duty of care because, if there is no reasonable foreseeability of harm arising from an act there can be no duty of care in relation to it. Here, however, we consider the essential requirement of foreseeability in the context of recoverability of loss. We assume therefore in the discussion that follows that duty and breach have been proved.

The basic principle is that a tortfeasor is liable only for the natural and probable consequences of his actions, those that he, as a reasonable man, could have foreseen as likely to occur, and which should therefore have caused him to hold his hand. Damage which occurs directly from the breach is not the subject of compensation, as a general rule, unless it was also foreseeable. This is the result of the Privy Council decision in *Overseas Tankship (UK) Ltd* v *Morts Dock and Engineering Co Ltd* (also known as *The Wagon Mound*) [1961] AC 388, which overruled the long-standing decision to the contrary of the Court of Appeal in *Re Polemis* [1921] 3 KB 560.

A fairly recent medical case provides a good example of the operation of the principles of remoteness and foreseeability. In *R* v *Croydon Health Authority* MLC 0019, [1998] Lloyd's Rep Med 44, CA, the claimant, a trained nurse, married and of child-bearing age, had to undergo a medical check with a view to taking employment with the defendants. The defendants' radiologist who interpreted her X-rays was admittedly negligent in not referring her for specialist opinion. It was admitted that, had that been done, the serious pathology of primary pulmonary hypertension would have been diagnosed, she would have been warned of the serious risk to her health if she were to become pregnant, and she would have chosen not to become pregnant, particularly as pregnancy might shorten her life and therefore leave her child without a mother. As it was, the negligence of the radiologist deprived her of that warning and therefore a few months later she became pregnant, giving birth in due course to a healthy child. It was understandable that she claimed compensation for, among other things, the trauma of the pregnancy and the cost of upkeep of her daughter. She succeeded at first instance ([1997] PIQR P444), but on appeal the court held that, as far as the radiologist was concerned, a decision to become pregnant fell outside the area of foreseeability. In other words, it was too remote. The court said that the radiologist never actually saw the claimant and knew very little about her except her age (this in itself is unconvincing, as the defendants would have had detailed knowledge of her and they should be taken in this context to stand in the shoes of their radiologist). Kennedy LJ said that the claimant's domestic life fell outside the scope of the radiologist's duty. The damage was too remote. 'The express obligations assumed by the radiologist did not, as it seems to me, extend to the plaintiff's private life'. Chadwick LJ said:

> ... a proper examination of the facts in the present case leads to the conclusion that, whatever duty of care was owed to the plaintiff by the health authority as a prospective employer, the scope and extent of that duty stopped short of responsibility for the consequences of the decision by the plaintiff and her husband that she should become pregnant. I think it essential to keep in mind that the relationship between the plaintiff and the health authority was that of prospective employee and employer. There was nothing in the evidence before the trial judge to suggest the relationship between the plaintiff and her prospective employer had anything to do with whatever plans the plaintiff and her husband may have had for starting a family.

Whatever semantic analysis one likes to construct, the reality of the matter is that the trial judge thought the employers should pay for the child because without their negligence the child would not have been born, whereas the Court of Appeal thought otherwise. However one dresses one's reasons up in the terminology of remoteness or foreseeability, this sort of decision turns on a question of policy, or, less elegantly, gut reaction.[1] (The issue of liability for the cost of upkeep of a child born in such circumstances is dealt with in Chapter 24.)

DEGREE OF FORESEEABILITY

It is not clear how foreseeable a consequence has to be, ie what chance of its happening is sufficient. In *The Wagon Mound (No 2)* [1967] 1 AC 617, the Privy Council's view was that once *some* foreseeability of fire was proved that was sufficient, however remote that possibility. It was said in the Australian case of *Commonwealth of Australia* v *Introvigne* (1982) 150 CLR 258, that 'a risk of injury is foreseeable so long as it is not far-fetched or fanciful, notwithstanding that it is more probable than not that it will not occur'. These propositions, however, are hardly consistent with what is generally understood to be the law, that the loss has to be reasonably foreseeable – unless we are being told that reasonable foreseeability of harm is appropriate for establishing a duty of care but any degree of foreseeability short of the far-fetched is enough in the context of compensation. We can well do without yet another subtle refinement in the law of negligence! (For a discussion on the degree of *risk*, see Chapter 16 under 'The standard'.)

---

1   It is of interest to note the principle applicable in contract, that it is not enough for a claimant to show that 'but for' the breach something would not have happened; he must go further and show that the breach did not merely give the occasion for the further events (see eg *Galoo Ltd* v *Bright, Grahame, Murray* [1994] 1 WLR 1360, CA). In other words, he must satisfy the court of a sufficient connection between the breach and the later events for which compensation is claimed for the court to be satisfied that the defendants should pay.

EXCEPTIONS

Policy

To the basic rule that the wrongdoer is liable for the natural and probable consequences of his wrongful act, and for no other consequences, there are a number of very substantial exceptions. In the first place, the law will draw a line at some point as a matter of policy to prevent over-extensive recovery.

> The law cannot take account of everything that follows a wrongful act; it regards some subsequent matters as outside the scope of its selection, because 'it were infinite for the law to judge the cause of causes' or consequence of consequences ... In the varied web of affairs the law must abstract some consequences as relevant, not perhaps on grounds of pure logic but simply for practical reasons (*per* Lord Wright in *Liesbosch, Dredger (Owners)* v *SS Edison (Owners)* [1933] AC 449 at 460, HL).

It is always difficult to predict and impossible to define the line where liability stops. It is left to the good sense of the judge in each particular case to decide where practical convenience and policy dictate that it be drawn.

> It is something like having to draw a line between night and day; there is a great duration of twilight when it is neither night nor day; but ... though you cannot draw the precise line, you can say on which side of the line the case is (*per* Blackburn J in *Hobbs* v *London and South Western Rly Co* (1875) LR 10 QB 111 at 121).

The legal basis for drawing the line is variously expressed:

> In order to limit liability ... the courts sometimes say either that the damage claimed was 'too remote' or that it was not 'caused' by the defendant's carelessness or that the defendant did not 'owe a duty of care' to the plaintiff (*per* Thesiger J in *SCM (UK)* v *Whittall* [1970] 1 WLR 1017 at 1031).

Or it may simply be said that justice or social convenience demands that a limit be placed upon the defendant's liability. For a good example of policy invalidating a claim where logic would allow it, see *McFarlane* v *Tayside Health Board* [2000] 2 AC 59, HL, which is treated in detail in Chapter 24.

'You must take the plaintiff as you find him'

The most comprehensive exception to the foreseeability principle that goes to extend a defendant's liability is the rule that a tortfeasor must take the claimant as he finds him, in relation both to his physical condition and to his financial circumstances. If you carelessly knock a man over in circumstances where you could reasonably expect a slight injury and a claim for average earnings lost over a relatively short period, you will nevertheless be liable for full damages if he turns out, through an inherently weak physical condition, to suffer far greater damage and for a longer period, and also to be a very high earner, perhaps with several extremely lucrative contracts lined up which he cannot now fulfil.

> One who is guilty of negligence to another must put up with idiosyncrasies of his victim that increase the likelihood or extent of damage to him; it is no answer to a claim for a fractured skull that its owner had an unusually fragile one (*per* Mackinnon LJ in *Owens* v *Liverpool Corpn* [1939] 1 KB 394 at 400–1, CA).

It is not only if the foreseeable injury proves more serious than could have been anticipated that the tortfeasor must pay, but also if a different type of injury arises out of the foreseeable injury. Thus, in *Robinson v Post Office* [1974] 1 WLR 1176, CA, where a claimant developed encephalitis as a result of an allergic reaction to an anti-tetanus injection, the defendants, whose negligence was responsible for the original slight injury that led to the need for an injection, were held liable to compensate him for the full extent of his injury.[2]

There have been very many cases where unforeseeable complications involving a different type of physical injury from that which could have been foreseen have been the subject of compensation. For example, in *Warren v Scruttons* [1962] 1 Lloyd's Rep 497, a defendant had to compensate for the unforeseeable aggravation of an existing eye condition that developed after the claimant had hurt his finger on a frayed rope. A cancer which unforeseeably developed from a foreseeable burn on the lip was held to be a proper subject for compensation in *Smith v Leech Brain* [1962] 2 QB 405. Where a woman had to wear a cervical collar as a result of a foreseeable physical injury she was able also to recover compensation for injury suffered when she fell down stairs due to the fact that she could not see so well with the collar on (*Wieland v Cyril Lord Carpets Ltd* [1969] 3 All ER 1006). Eveleigh J said:

> ... in determining liability for ... possible consequences of personal injury, it is not necessary to show that each was within the foreseeable extent or foreseeable scope of the original injury in the same way that the possibility of injury must be foreseen when determining whether or not the defendant's conduct gives a claim in negligence.[3]

In the road traffic case of *Giblett v P & NE Murray Ltd* [1999] 22 LS Gaz R 34, CA, the court said that the claimant did not have to prove that her psychiatric injury in the form that it took or its sequelae were reasonably foreseeable by the defendants. Even in the context of nervous shock, or any other attributable psychiatric condition, the defendant had to take the primary victim as he found him: it would avail the defendant nothing that the victim had a psychologically vulnerable 'eggshell' personality.

'TYPE' OF INJURY SUFFERED

Of course, if no injury could be foreseen then the fact that an abnormally susceptible claimant suffered some injury does not give rise to a claim; there would probably be neither a duty nor a breach in those circumstances, but even if there were, there would be no liability where no injury could reasonably be foreseen from the acts in question. For an injury to be claimable, it must, if it does not accompany a foreseeable injury, at least be of the same type as the foreseeable

---

2   See also *Brice v Brown* [1984] 1 All ER 997 where the nervous shock sustained was particularly severe due to a basic mental instability. There is also relevant material in the judgments of the Court of Appeal in *Vernon v Bosley* [1997] 1 All ER 577.

3   Where a second injurious condition does *not* flow from the original injury, causation has to be established on the balance of the probabilities in respect of the second condition (see Lord Bridge's judgment in *Hotson v East Berkshire Area Health Authority* [1987] AC 750, HL).

injury (although, as we see below, it is quite unclear what is meant by 'type'). Thus, in *Bradford* v *Robinson Rentals Ltd* [1967] 1 WLR 337, a driver was negligently exposed to freezing conditions in an unheated vehicle as a result of which he developed the unforeseeable injury of frostbite. Rees J made it clear that recovery was permissible in respect of the frostbite as the foreseeable injury, ie common cold, pneumonia, chilblains, was of the same type as that which was in fact suffered. In *Ogwo* v *Taylor* [1988] AC 431, the House of Lords held that injury caused to a firefighter from the steam that arose when he sprayed water on to a fire was not different in kind from injury caused directly by the flames.

The apparent necessity for a connection between the type of damage that was foreseeable and the type of damage that was suffered arises from the decision of the Privy Council in *The Wagon Mound* (above). That case arose out of the careless spillage of oil on the waters of Sydney harbour. Damage to slipways by pollution was foreseeable, but the damage by fire that occurred was not. The Privy Council said that as the damage that occurred was of a different type from what was foreseeable (ie damage by fire and not damage by pollution), recovery was not permitted. Ironically, in *The Wagon Mound (No 2)* [1967] 1 AC 617, which concerned the same facts, a contrary decision was reached as to liability, but that was because the evidence given in that trial established, as we saw above, that there was a slight possibility to be foreseen of damage by fire.

What is completely unclear is what is meant by 'type' of damage in the context of physical injury. A claimant is assisted by the rules that the defendant must take him as he finds him, and that neither the extent of the damage has to be foreseeable nor the precise manner in which it arose, and it is hard to see what practical scope is left for a rule that restricts liability by providing that the injury suffered has to be of a type that was foreseeable. In *Thurogood* v *Van den Berghs and Jurgens* [1951] 2 KB 537, the Court of Appeal permitted recovery by an injured workman when he caught his fingers in a fan even though the foreseeable injury was by catching his necktie in it (a decision that seems good sense); but that was upon an application of the principle derived from *Re Polemis* [1921] 3 KB 560, CA, that all damage directly caused was claimable for, and that principle was rejected by the Privy Council in *The Wagon Mound* (above). In *Tremain* v *Pike* [1969] 1 WLR 1556, Payne J refused relief to a herdsman who contracted a rare disease from rats' urine because the only foreseeable consequence from exposure to rats was rat-bite or food-poisoning, which was said to be 'entirely different in kind'. This decision must surely have been wrong (see, to an apparently contrary intent, *H Parsons Livestock Ltd* v *Uttley Ingham & Co Ltd* [1978] QB 791, CA).

In *Woodhouse* v *Yorkshire Regional Authority* [1984] 1 The Lancet 1306, the claimant suffered foreseeable digital contracture deformity from a carelessly performed operation. The defendants were held liable also for a hysterical condition that developed because they had damaged a claimant with a hysterical personality and they had to take her as they found her. In *H* v *Royal Alexandra Hospital* [1990] 1 Med LR 297, the fact that a hemophiliac given AIDS-contaminated blood products was infected with a retro-virus and not with a virus (which alone was foreseeable when the negligent act took place) was of no assistance to the defendants as the damage was of the same kind as what was foreseeable.

In *Doe* v *USA* [1990] 2 Med LR 131, the US Rhode Island District Court held that it was foreseeable in 1983 that if a patient required through negligence an extensive blood transfusion he might contract AIDS from it.

In *Aswan Engineering Establishment Co* v *Lupdine Ltd* [1987] 1 WLR 1, the Court of Appeal held that, where material packed in pails was exposed for hours to the Arabian sun so that the pails collapsed, the manufacturers of the pails were not liable to the users because the damage suffered was of an unforeseeable type. However, it would seem better to say that the manufacturers had not been negligent in the way they manufactured and marketed the pails because no loss was reasonably foreseeable from their use. It does not seem an appropriate situation to bring in the rule as to type of damage, which only applies when there has been a breach of duty resulting in some loss.

In *Wood* v *Bentall Simplex Ltd* [1992] PIQR P332, a farmer was held not to have contributed to his own death by building a grid of a non-approved pattern across the entrance to his slurry tank because the consequence of death by asphyxiation after he entered the tank to clear a blockage resulting from the unorthodox construction was not foreseeable. All that was foreseeable was that a person entering the tank to cure the (foreseeable) blockage might slip and fall. The Court of Appeal said that the test of liability for injury by asphyxiation was foreseeability of injury by asphyxiation.

In *Page* v *Smith* [1996] AC 155, the House of Lords was principally concerned with the question of whether a claimant involved in a road traffic accident could recover damages for psychiatric injury where only physical injury was foreseeable. The Court of Appeal had held that possibility of psychiatric injury was essential and that in the instant case it had not been foreseeable. The House of Lords by a bare majority restored the decision of the trial judge. Lord Lloyd held that psychiatric injury in a road traffic accident was foreseeable. But he went further than that. He said that, whereas possibility of psychiatric injury was a crucial ingredient where the claimant was the secondary victim [for discussion of primary and secondary victims see Chapter 19], it would not be sensible in the case of a primary victim, in an age when medical knowledge is expanding fast and psychiatric knowledge with it, to commit the law to a distinction between physical and psychiatric injury which might already seem somewhat artificial, and might soon be altogether outmoded. 'Nothing will be gained by treating them as different "kinds" of personal injury, so as to require the application of different tests in law.' Lord Browne-Wilkinson held that in the instant circumstances psychiatric injury was foreseeable, and, further, expressly endorsed Lord Lloyd's remarks about the dangers of seeking to draw hard and fast lines between physical and psychiatric illness. He said that for the courts to impose different criteria for liability depending on whether the injury was physical or psychiatric was likely to lead to a growing complication in straightforward personal injury cases. The law would be more effective if it accepted that the results of being involved in a collision might include both physical and psychiatric damage. Lord Ackner was for allowing the appeal on the basis that psychiatric injury was foreseeable. He did not go further than that. On the other hand, Lord Jauncey, in a long and carefully reasoned judgment, concluded that for recovery for psychiatric injury foreseeability of psychiatric injury was essential, and he was not satisfied that in the circumstances of this accident there was such foreseeability. Lord Keith supported that view. It therefore appears that not only were the *dicta* to the effect that foreseeability of personal injury would suffice for a claim for 'mere' psychiatric injury arising out of a road traffic accident *obiter* but, further, such a view was endorsed by only two of the judges. Two were of a contrary view and one was silent on the issue.[4] Nevertheless it is now accepted law that this decision established the following principles (*per* the Court of Appeal in *Donachie* v *Chief Constable of the Greater Manchester Police* [2004] EWCA Civ 405):

- A defendant owes a duty of care to a person where he can reasonably foresee that his conduct will expose that person to a risk of personal injury.
- For this purpose the test of reasonable foreseeability is the same whether the foreseeable injury is physical or psychiatric or both.
- However, its application to the facts differs according to whether the foreseeable injury is physical or psychiatric; in the latter case, if the claimant is not involved in some sort of 'event' caused by the negligence, he is a 'secondary' victim and liability is more difficult to establish.
- If the reasonably foreseeable injury is of a physical nature but such injury in fact causes psychiatric injury it is immaterial whether the psychiatric injury was itself reasonably foreseeable. Equally if, as in the instant case, the breach of duty causes psychiatric injury causing in turn physical injury, it is immaterial that neither the psychiatric injury nor the particular form of the physical injury caused was reasonably foreseeable.[5]

In *Hepworth* v *Kerr* [1995] 6 Med LR 139, the judge was satisfied that, although the specific risk of anterior spinal artery syndrome from the deliberately induced anesthetic hypotension was not one which could reasonably have been foreseen, it was enough that risk of major organ under-perfusion was reasonably foreseeable and it mattered not that that source of danger acted in an unpredictable way. The mechanism and the source of danger were the same, and the defendant had run the unnecessary and foreseeable risk of causing injury to the claimant by under-perfusion of major organs of the body. What happened was 'but a variant of the foreseeable' and 'within the risk created by the negligence'.

---

4   We may note here that it was held in *Walker* v *Northumberland County Council* [1995] ICR 702, that psychiatric damage was foreseeable where employees were put under excessive strain by their workload. In *Schofield* v *Chief Constable of West Yorkshire* [1999] ICR 193, where a policewoman suffered psychiatric injury, but not physical, when a sergeant negligently discharged a firearm, the Court of Appeal said that the case was similar to *Page* v *Smith*: it was enough that there was a foreseeable risk of physical injury.

5   For an interesting slant on how the appeal judges are currently viewing the distinction, if any, between physical and mental injury, see the aviation case of *King* v *British Helicopters* [2002] 2 WLR 578, HL, and in the Court of Appeal *sub nomine Morris* v *KLM* [2001] 3 WLR 351, where the correct interpretation of 'bodily injury' in the Carriage by Air Act 1981 was under review.

THE 'PRECISE MANNER'

We have already adverted to the rule that it does not help a defendant to argue that, although the type of damage could be foreseen, the precise manner in which it arose could not. In *Hughes* v *Lord Advocate* [1963] AC 837, where a child picked up a lighted Post Office paraffin lamp and entered an unguarded manhole, damage by burning was foreseeable, so that although the manner in which that damage arose was not foreseeable (the child was burned not by the oversetting of the lamp but by an explosion), that did not prevent recovery. In *Stewart* v *West African Terminals* (1964) 108 Sol Jo 838, the Court of Appeal said that as long as a result is within the general sphere of contemplation, and not of an entirely different kind, the precise chain of events need not be foreseeable.

> It is not necessary that the precise concatenation of circumstances should be envisaged. If the consequence was one which was within the general range which any reasonable person might foresee (and was not of an entirely different kind which no-one would anticipate) then it is within the rule that a person who has been guilty of negligence, is liable for its consequences (*per* Lord Denning).
> ... the precise mechanics of the way in which the negligent act results in the original injury do not have to be foreseen (*per* Eveleigh J in *Wieland* v *Cyril Lord Carpets* [1969] 3 All ER 1006).

The question of the manner in which the damage arose overlaps with the question whether the damage was of a type that was foreseeable. The difficulties that can arise over these subtle distinctions when injury occurs in an unforeseen manner and one has then to ask whether it still remains within the type of injury foreseeable is illustrated by *Doughty* v *Turner Manufacturing Co Ltd* [1964] 1 QB 518, CA, where it appears that the fact that there was a foreseeable risk only of damage from splashing when a cover was carelessly let slip from a height of a few inches into molten liquid prevented recovery for injury caused when the liquid erupted due to an unforeseeable chemical reaction a few moments later. Such subtle distinctions were eschewed in *H Parsons Livestock Ltd* v *Uttley Ingham & Co Ltd* [1978] QB 791, where the Court of Appeal said that as long as some illness to the claimant's pigs was foreseeable as a result of the defendant's negligence, they were liable for the unforeseen illness that did in fact develop, the consequence being of the same type as that which was foreseeable (this was a claim in contract but the court said that the law as to the amount of damages recoverable was the same in contract as in tort).

In *Jolley* v *Sutton London Borough Council* [2000] 1 WLR 1082, the House of Lords reversed the wholly unreasonable conclusion of the Court of Appeal. A boat was left abandoned on land by the defendants. Children played with it. They propped it up; it fell of the prop; the claimant was injured. The defendants admitted they should not have left it there and that some injury was foreseeable from children playing on it and falling through rotten planking. The Court of Appeal decided that injury from the boat falling over after having being propped up was not foreseeable and was of a different type and kind from an injury caused by simply falling through rotten planking. The House of Lords, pointing out that the wider risk could have been eliminated without any more expense than that involved in eliminating the narrower risk (ie by removing the boat), restored the judgment of the trial judge in favour of the claimant.

In *Jebson* v *Ministry of Defence* [2000] PIQR 201, the Court of Appeal, reversing the judge, found that where an intoxicated off-duty soldier, travelling with his mates in the back of an inadequately supervised army lorry, had injured himself by foolishly attempting to climb on to the canvas roof of the vehicle from the tailgate, the way in the which the injury had been caused fell within the area of foreseeability for which the failure of the defendants to provide proper supervision was referable. The Court then upheld the judge's finding of 75% contributory negligence.

In *London Borough of Islington* v *UCL Hosptial NHS Trust* [2005] EWCA Civ 596, MLC 1254, where the local authority who had to provide care for a patient negligently injured by the hospital sought to recover the cost of that care from the hospital, the Court of Appeal said that the defendant must be taken to have known that the range of patients whom it treated would have a range of care requirements and financial needs. Care by a local authority in a case in which it could not recover the cost of the care could not be seen as so unusual as to fall outside that range. The precise manner in which the injury would occur did not have to be foreseeable, so the defendant did not have to know that Mrs J would require local authority care and would not be able to pay for it; but only to have institutional knowledge that some patients with Mrs J's disability would fall into that category.

CONCLUSION

For the purposes of the medical negligence action, we may sum up (remembering that we are here only dealing with the question what damage may be compensated for, given a breach of duty, and also bearing in mind that the law is far from clear in this area) as follows.

If there was no foreseeability of harm on the facts that the defendants knew or ought to have known, then recovery for any injury occasioned will not be permitted.

If there was foreseeability of physical damage, however slight the chance and however slight the injury to be foreseen, then compensation may be got for all physical injury resulting from the breach of duty that is of the same type as the injury to be foreseen, plus any injury, however unforeseeable, that is consequent upon the foreseeable injury. Unforeseeable injury not consequent upon a foreseeable injury is not compensatable, but this is subject to the rule that the tortfeasor must take the claimant as he finds him.

Subject to that rule, some injury must actually be suffered that falls within the type of injury to be foreseen, ie within the area of risk created (in *The Wagon Mound* (above) the Privy Council said that foreseeability must be of 'the damage that happened – the damage in suit'). Whether a court these days is likely in practice to say that the injury suffered was of a different type or kind from the injury that could have been foreseen and thus deny recovery to a person injured through another's admitted negligence may be doubted. If a man carelessly tosses a brick out of an upper window and it falls on to an electric cable which causes a passer-by to be electrocuted through an unforeseeable chemical reaction, it may well go against the judicial grain to hold that the injured party cannot recover because the only foreseeable injury was from being struck by the brick and electrocution was a different type of damage. Probably in such a case the court would 'find' that there was a slight degree of foreseeability of electrocution.

When all is said and done, on this aspect of negligence as on every other, the determining factor will be the judge's view as to whether justice dictates recovery. He will then find a legal peg on which to hang his decision. That is particularly easy in the field of negligence, where so much is uncertain and lacks precision. As Lord Wright said in *Hay (or Bourhill)* v *Young* [1943] AC 92 at 107, HL: '... negligence is a fluid principle, which has to be applied to the most diverse conditions and problems of human life.' It may well be that, as RWM Dias has said, 'the principles of the future will be that a negligent person shall be liable according as the court thinks reasonable in the circumstances'. The progress of law within a society is always from formalism to flexibility, albeit that in the common law tradition judicial activism is usually disguised by an artfully contrived appearance of deference to authority.[6]

---

6   'In previous times, when faced with a new problem, the judges have not openly asked themselves the question: what is the best policy for the law to adopt? But the question has always been there in the background. It has been concealed behind such questions as: Was the defendant under any duty to the plaintiff? Was the relationship between them sufficiently proximate? Was the injury direct or indirect? Was it foreseeable or not? Was it too remote? and so forth' (*per* Lord Denning).

Chapter 19

Loss/injury: nervous shock[1]

Shock, anxiety, depression, disappointment or grief, not amounting to psychiatric disorder, is not compensatable when it stands alone, but it may be taken into account to increase the award when it accompanies other, recognised injuries. Nervous shock amounting to psychiatric disorder is as much a head of damage as physical injury. To recover, the claimant has to be within the range of persons likely to be harmed by nervous shock; but even then the law permits recovery in the case of one who suffers nervous shock as a result of a person's death only where the shock is suffered by a close relative who either witnesses the death or its immediate aftermath.

PRIMARY AND SECONDARY VICTIMS

It is important first to distinguish between primary and secondary victims. This was made abundantly clear by the House of Lords in *Page* v *Smith* [1996] AC 155. Lord Keith pointed out that the cases divided broadly into two categories, those in which the claimant was involved as a participant in the incident which gave rise to the action, and those in which the claimant was a witness to injury caused to others, or to the immediate aftermath of an accident to others. Lord Lloyd said that in the instant case the claimant was not in the secondary position of a spectator or bystander (he was alleging psychiatric, but not personal, injury as a result of a minor traffic accident), but was a participant, directly involved in the accident and well within the range of foreseeable physical injury, and so a primary victim. The judge pointed out that the factual distinction between primary and secondary victims of an accident was obvious

---

1 Nervous shock claims can be worth a great deal of money, at any rate where the injury precludes employment. Mr Tredget, who could not return to work as a result of nervous injury sustained when he was present at the stillbirth of his child, received in the region of £300,000 by way of settlement (his case on liability is considered in detail below). Mr Peter Vernon, a successful businessman who could no longer work after seeing his daughters drown in a car accident, was awarded £1m by Sedley J for loss of earnings (plus £37,500 for general damages and £152,000 for future care): (1995) 28 BMLR 1 (liability had been admitted) – see below.

and of long-standing. He said that none of the control mechanisms, by way of tests of proximity and ties of affection (as to which, see below), were required in the case of a primary victim. Although foreseeability of psychiatric injury remained a crucial ingredient when the claimant was the secondary victim, for the very reason that the secondary victim was almost always outside the area of physical impact and therefore outside the range of foreseeable physical injury, foreseeability of physical injury was sufficient to found a claim based solely upon psychiatric injury.

This chapter is concerned principally with the claim by a secondary victim.[2]

WHAT IS SHOCK?

Nervous shock is more than the normal emotions of distress, disappointment, unhappiness, grief, anxiety or depression: these do not constitute a head of damages in themselves but can serve to increase an award for a recognised loss, whether physical or financial (eg the 'spoilt holiday' cases where disappointment over a spoilt holiday can increase the award beyond the mere financial cost of the holiday). Nervous shock means an actual mental disorder, a 'positive psychiatric illness' (*per* Lord Bridge in *McLoughlin* v *O'Brian* [1983] 1 AC 410, HL).

In *Nicholls* v *Rushton* (1992) Times, 19 June, the Court of Appeal restated in the clearest terms the rule that nervous reaction falling short of actual psychological illness cannot be the subject of compensation unless it is parasitic to physical injury. And in *Hicks* v *Chief Constable of South Yorkshire Police* [1992] PIQR P433, the House of Lords said that horror and fear for one's own safety (as the Hillsborough stadium collapsed), not amounting to recognisable psychiatric damage, do not sound in damages.

In *Reilly* v *Merseyside Health Authority* [1995] 6 Med LR 246, an unsuccessful claim for damages for extreme claustrophobia suffered by an elderly couple trapped in a lift for over an hour, the Court of Appeal said that that was not a nervous disorder but nothing more than 'excitement of normal human emotion'. Presumably the medical report failed to identify an actual psychiatric disorder consequent upon the frightening experience.

In *Page* v *Smith* [1996] AC 155, HL, Lord Keith said that the decided cases indicated that 'nervous shock' meant a reaction to an immediate and horrifying impact, resulting in some recognisable psychiatric illness. There had to be some serious mental disturbance outside the range of normal human experience, not merely the ordinary emotions of anxiety, grief or fear. And Lord Jauncey said that the ordinary emotions of anxiety, fear, grief or transient shock were not conditions for which the law gave compensation.

---

2   For further enlightenment on the distinction between primary and secondary victims, see *Schofield* v *Chief Constable of West Yorkshire Police* (1998) 43 BMLR 28 CA, in which post traumatic stress disorder was sustained by a woman police officer when her sergeant discharged a loaded firearm in the confines of a bedroom where they were making inquiries of the family.

Contra, in *M (a minor)* v *Newham London Borough Council* [1995] 2 AC 633, CA, the Master of the Rolls rejected the claim that the psychiatric damage said to have been suffered by a child as a result of allegedly incompetent diagnosis of sexual abuse was not damage which the law recognised as compensatable injury.[3] He pointed to Lord Ackner's words in the Hillsborough stadium case (*Alcock* v *Chief Constable of South Yorkshire Police* [1992] 1 AC 310), where the Law Lord had acknowledged that future development of the law was to be expected, and to the warning given by Lord Bridge in *McLoughlin* v *O'Brian* (above) against the temptation of seeking to freeze the law in a rigid posture.

At first instance in *RK and MK* v *Oldham NHS Trust* [2003] Lloyds Rep Med 1, Simon J said that emotional responses of even the most serious type did not found a claim in damages and the court should not infer an injury where experts in the field did not.

In the dyslexia case of *Robinson* v *St Helens Metropolitan Council* MLC 0835, the Court of Appeal said that emotional and psychological damage resulting in failure by appropriate teaching to ameliorate the congenital condition of dyslexia was a personal injury, although it fell short of psychiatric injury in the recognised form. This would seem to run counter to all other authority on the subject. We may also note that in a lecture to the Personal Injuries Bar Association (PIBA) in 2005 Lord Phillips MR said: 'Where there is no physical injury, however, no claim will lie unless the claimant is suffering from a recognised psychiatric illness. Emotional distress that falls short of this does not attract compensation.'[4]

The older cases

Where the nervous shock is allied to a more apparent physical injury there has been no problem with recovery. But where it stands alone the courts have been reluctant to permit recovery, both, in the older cases, because knowledge of mental trauma was scanty, and also because of a feeling that public policy should draw the line at recovery for mental shock.

Thus, where a level crossing attendant negligently allowed a pregnant woman to cross the railway lines in her carriage in front of an oncoming train and she suffered nervous shock and a miscarriage, the Privy Council would not permit her to succeed. But that was in 1888 (*Victorian Railways Comrs* v *Coultas* (1888) 13 App Cas 222). A pregnant barmaid suffered nervous shock when a negligently driven van crashed into the pub. She succeeded, but only because her shock arose 'from a reasonable fear of immediate personal injury to [herself]' (*Dulieu* v *White & Sons* [1901] 2 KB 669). The scope of the claim was extended by the majority decision in *Hambrook* v *Stokes Bros* [1925] 1 KB 141, CA: a mother

---

3   This aspect of the case does not seem to have been relevant to the appeal to the House of Lords ([1995] 2 AC 633, HL).

4   For an interesting slant on how the appeal judges are currently viewing the distinction, if any, between physical and mental injury, see the aviation case of *King* v *British Helicopters* [2002] 2 WLR 578, HL, and in the Court of Appeal *sub nomine Morris* v *KLM* [2001] 3 WLR 351, where the correct interpretation of 'bodily injury' in the Carriage by Air Act 1981 was under review.

suffered shock through fear that her children had been injured when she saw a runaway lorry careering down a hill from the bend round which her children had just gone out of sight (her apprehension was unhappily justified). The significance of this decision was twofold: first, it severed the link between nervous shock and fear of impact to oneself; second, it suggested extension of the claim to cases where the disaster had already occurred and the fear of what might be about to occur was no longer relevant.

The only case in which the House of Lords had considered the matter before *McLoughlin* v *O'Brian* (above) was *Hay (or Bourhill)* v *Young* [1943] AC 92. The claimant heard the noise of a road accident as she alighted from a bus, went of her own volition to the scene and, seeing upon the road the blood of the dead motorcyclist (who was not known to her), suffered shock. Understandably, her claim was rejected. It could be said she as passer-by was owed no duty by the negligent driver, at least no duty as far as the infliction of injury by shock was concerned, or that the actual injury suffered was too remote, or unforeseeable.

In *Hinz* v *Berry* [1970] 2 QB 40, CA, it was agreed without dispute that a mother could recover for psychiatric illness caused by her witnessing a ghastly accident to her family on the other side of the road. Lord Denning MR said that it was settled law that 'damages can be given for nervous shock caused by the sight of an accident, at any rate to a close relative'.

But recovery had not always been limited to a 'close relative'. In *Chadwick* v *British Railways Board* [1967] 1 WLR 912, the estate of a rescuer at the Lewisham rail disaster recovered in respect of a psychiatric disorder caused by his work amid the dead and dying that night. (See also *Galt* v *British Railways Board* (1983) 133 NLJ 870, where a train driver recovered for nervous shock occasioned by his seeing in front of him two men on the track whom he then thought he went on to strike and kill.) In *Wigg* v *British Railways Board* [1986] NLJ Rep 446n, (1986) Times, 4 February, Tucker J held that it was reasonably foreseeable that a train driver who stopped the train and got down to help a passenger, who had in fact been killed due to the negligence of the guard in giving the starting signal, might suffer nervous shock thereby.[5]

Recovery for nervous shock was extended by the House of Lords in *McLoughlin* v *O'Brian* [1983] 1 AC 410, where a mother was told at home by a witness that her family had just been involved in a serious road accident. She rushed to the hospital to find one child dead, two others seriously injured, and her husband in a state of shock. She herself suffered nervous shock, organic depression and a change of personality. She lost her claim at first instance and in the Court of Appeal, on the ground that her injury was not foreseeable and she herself was owed no duty of care, but the House of Lords reversed the decision. Lord Wilberforce promulgated the 'aftermath' principle. Recovery was

---

5   For an example of an unsuccessful claim for shock suffered by a rescuer, see the Piper Alpha case of *McFarlane* v *EE Caledonia Ltd* [1994] PIQR P154, where the Court of Appeal held that there had been insufficient involvement or risk of involvement by the claimant in the tragedy (the fire-fighting vessel he was in was never in danger). Similarly, *Hegarty* v *EE Caledonia Ltd* (1997) Times, 13 February, CA.

permitted, but only where the shock came through sight or hearing of the event or its immediate aftermath. This is an example of judicial law-making – but none the worse for that. If therefore a relative visits the hospital to find a patient dying because of negligent treatment and suffers himself some psychiatric disorder as a result of nervous shock, he could recover damages. Probably also if he sees the corpse soon after, provided the relationship is sufficiently close; but not if the shock is occasioned merely by being told of the death and its circumstances, however horrible, and however close the relationship. In *Schneider* v *Eisovitch* [1960] 2 QB 430, recovery for shock on being so informed was permitted as an additional item of damages, where a wife, injured along with her husband in a road accident, learned that he had died. (It is of interest to note that the New South Wales legislature intervened as early as 1944 to permit recovery for this sort of injury suffered by a close relative of a person 'killed, injured or put in peril', irrespective of any spatial or temporal nexus with the accident.)

So we can summarise by saying that claims for nervous shock by witnesses, or secondary victims as they are now called, have had only slow and restricted acceptance in English law. The claim was first recognised where the claimant had been put in fear of imminent physical harm (this context should really be seen as one of primary victim, just as if the harm had materialised), then extended to shock caused by fear that imminent harm was about to befall others, to the witnessing of a shocking event (also to shock caused to a rescuer by actually participating in a horrific event), then, by the House of Lords decision in *McLoughlin* v *O'Brian* (above) to shock caused by coming upon the aftermath of a horrific event. Recent developments have done nothing to extend the ambit of the claim for the secondary victim.

Further developments

In the Hillsborough stadium case (*Alcock* v *Chief Constable of South Yorkshire* [1992] 1 AC 310), the House of Lords held that a claimant claiming for nervous shock over the death or injury of another must satisfy the test of proximity, in that it must have been foreseeable that this particular claimant might suffer nervous shock over the death of that particular relative or friend. The law would not define a class of qualifying relationships. The required proximity (to be based upon close ties of love and affection) was to be proved by evidence; it could in the case of obviously close familial ties be presumed (a presumption that could, however, be rebutted by appropriate evidence). The court was prepared to make the presumption in the case of claimants who had lost a son or a fiancé but not, in the absence of evidence of closeness, in the case of a brother, brother-in-law or grandson. Second, the court reaffirmed Lord Wilberforce's limited extension of the right of recovery to the 'aftermath' principle, ie the witnessing of the traumatic event or its immediate aftermath. It was not possible to bring within that principle the viewing of the distressing scenes on television, emphasis being laid on the fact that the television code of ethics meant that the suffering of recognisable individuals was not broadcast. Although it was not impossible that a television viewer might be sufficiently proximate in appropriate circumstances (probably where the telecast was horrifyingly graphic), the viewing of the television scenes in this case did not create the necessary degree of proximity and could not be 'equiparated' with the position of a claimant at the ground. Thus, there are two tests of proximity for the claimant to satisfy, the first relating to the victim, the second to the event – the second can be further divided into the proximity of the claimant to the accident and the means by which the shock has been caused. Lord Ackner said that 'shock' involved the sudden appreciation by sight or sound of a horrifying event which violently agitated the mind; as the law presently stood, it did not include psychiatric illness caused by the accumulation over a period of time of more gradual assaults on the nervous system. So illness caused by the stress of caring for an injured relative over a period of time would not be compensatable.

The court's decision was that none of the claimants could succeed – those at the ground failed the test of proximity of relationship, those elsewhere failed the test of proximity in time and space (those who came to the hospital or mortuary later were said not to be within the 'immediate' aftermath as they did not get there for some eight hours – the mother in *McLoughlin* v *O'Brian* (above) had arrived at the hospital within one hour).[6]

A disappointing example of the restrictions that the Court of Appeal has placed on the ambit of the nervous shock claim can be seen in *Taylorson* v *Shieldness Produce Ltd* [1994] PIQR P329, CA. Parents went immediately one morning to the hospital to which their 14-year-old son, their only child, had been admitted after being crushed under a reversing vehicle. They did not see him at the hospital, but they followed the ambulance that transferred him to another hospital, the father glimpsing him in the ambulance, the mother seeing him briefly as he was being rushed into the intensive care unit on a trolley. They did not see him then for a few hours while he was being treated. The father saw him that evening, when he had black eyes, blood on his face and a tube attached to the top of his head to relieve pressure on the brain. The mother saw him the next day in a similar state. The boy remained unconscious for two days. Then the life support machine was switched off. The parents were with him throughout that time.

The court said that the shocking events were not sufficiently proximate and that the involvement of the parents did not come within the aftermath principle. It seems that the first conclusion was based on the lack of close contact in the first few hours and the second on the refusal of the court to adopt the reasoning in the Australian case of *Jaensch* v *Coffey* (1984) 155 CLR 549 and extend the aftermath period to include the two days waiting at the bedside of the dying child.

It is also to be noted that the court found that causation was not proved, in that it took the view that the real cause of the psychiatric injury was the loss of their child and that the injury would have been

6   *Contra, McCarthy* v *Chief Constable of South Yorkshire* (11 December 1996, unreported), QBD Toulson J, where a claimant had had a good view from his stand of the horrific events of the day in which his half-brother died.

sustained even if there had been no question of any participation in any aftermath.[7]

In *Page* v *Smith* [1996] AC 155, where a claimant who had been involved in a minor traffic accident and had suffered no physical injury alleged that he had suffered a psychiatric injury, in that his pre-existing pathology of chronic fatigue syndrome had become chronic and permanent, the House of Lords held by a bare majority that, as the claimant was the primary victim and not a mere witness or bystander, the rules of proximity did not apply, and therefore, as some injury, albeit physical if not actually psychiatric, was foreseeable from the accident, he was entitled to recover damages.[8]

In *Vernon* v *Bosley* [1997] 1 All ER 577, CA where the claimant had witnessed the drowning of his two children (than which a more dreadful experience could hardly be imagined),[9] the Court of Appeal held that the legal test determining recoverability was whether the claimant had suffered mental injury caused by the negligence of the defendant and not whether he had suffered post-traumatic stress disorder rather than pathological grief disorder. Accordingly, the secondary victim could recover damages for mental illness caused or at least contributed to by the actionable negligence of the defendant, notwithstanding that the illness could also be regarded as a pathological consequence of the bereavement which the claimant had inevitably suffered. It followed that damages payable to a claimant who was a secondary victim of a breach of a duty of care owed by the defendants and who suffered mental illness, which was properly regarded as a consequence both of his experience as a bystander and of an intense and abnormal grief reaction to the bereavement which he suffered, should not be discounted for his grief and the consequences of bereavement, even though his illness was partly so caused. This decision appears to be inconsistent with the judgment of the Court of Appeal in *Calascione* v *Dixon* (1993) 19 BMLR 97, where they held that the trial judge had been right to distinguish between post-traumatic stress disorder suffered by a mother on seeing the corpse of her son mangled after a road traffic accident and pathological grief reaction which was not due to the accident or its aftermath.

---

7   In the Canadian case of *Beecham* v *Hughes* [1988] 6 WWR 33, the husband of a woman brain-damaged in a car crash was unable to recover damages for his own nervous shock as the evidence indicated that it had been caused not by his presence at the accident and its immediate aftermath but by his ongoing distress at the condition of his wife.

8   Followed by Garland J in *Zammit* v *Stena Offshore Ltd* [1997] CLY 1857, where a diver suffered psychiatric but not physical injury in a diving accident (which left him suspended and helpless at the end of an umbilical for half an hour) caused by his employer's negligence. However, the Court of Appeal held, surprisingly, in *Gifford* v *Halifax Building Society* [1995] JPIL 323 that psychiatric injury was not reasonably foreseeable upon the giving of negligent financial advice that led to the loss of the claimant's home. Why not? (The fact that judgment was given a few days before the decision of the House of Lords in *Page* v *Smith* was published is irrelevant.) We may also briefly note *Abada* v *Gray* (1997) 40 BMLR 116, CA, where the rejection by the trial judge of a claim that a traffic accident had led to schizophrenia and epilepsy was upheld.

9   The judgment of Sedley J at first instance can be found at (1995) 28 BMLR 1. The initial huge award, including £1m for loss of earnings, £37,500 for general damages and £152,000 for future care, was reduced on a separate appeal upon the admission of fresh evidence indicating a better prognosis (*Vernon* v *Bosley (No 2)* [1997] 1 All ER 614, CA).

In *Frost* v *Chief Constable of South Yorkshire Police* [1998] QB 254, CA; revsd [1999] 2 AC 455, HL, the House of Lords, reversing the decision of the Court of Appeal, held that police officers, who had suffered psychiatric injury when performing rescue duties in the aftermath of the Hillsborough football stadium disaster, could not recover damages. They were secondary victims and had to satisfy the tests for secondary victims. The fact that they were employed by the defendant did not affect that requirement. Noting that many relatives who were secondary victims had failed in earlier claims, the court said it would be unfair if police officers could recover in similar circumstances. Lord Steyn said that the law in this field was 'a patchwork quilt of distinctions which are hard to justify'; and Lord Hoffmann said that the search for principle had been called off in the *Alcock* case, that it was too late to go back on the control mechanisms stated in *Alcock*, and until there was legislative change the courts must live with them and judicial developments must take them into account.

In *Young* v *Charles Church (Southern) Ltd* (1997) 33 BMLR 146, [1997] JPIL 291, the Court of Appeal permitted recovery for psychiatric illness sustained through witnessing the electrocution of a workmate as a result of the defendants' negligence (the Scottish Court of Session had reached a contrary conclusion in *Robertson* v *Forth Road Bridge Joint Board* [1995] IRLR 251, but that was before the House of Lords decision in *Page* v *Smith* [1996] AC 155, HL).

In *Hunter* v *British Coal Corpn* [1999] QB 140, CA, the claimant had suffered psychiatric injury by way of 'surviving guilt' after a pit explosion which killed his mate. As he had left the actual scene of the accident some minutes before to look for equipment (though he was still fairly close, heard the explosion and saw the cloud of dust rising), and as he was not in any danger himself, the court said his claim could not succeed. He could not be treated as a secondary victim because he had not witnessed the accident; he had (merely) suffered an abnormal grief reaction on hearing of the death, triggered by an irrational feeling of responsibility; his 'survivor's guilt' was too remote an injury. This case is an excellent illustration of how artificial and generally unsatisfactory is the current state of the law in relation to nervous shock claims.

In the highly distressing case of *Galli-Atkinson* v *Seghal* [2003] Lloyds Rep Med 285, the Court of Appeal sensibly and fairly held that the immediate aftermath of a fatal road accident in which the claimant's daughter was killed extended from the moment of the accident until the moment the claimant left the mortuary. The visit to the mortuary, not long after the claimant had arrived at the police cordon at the site of the accident, was not merely to identify the body, which still bore the horrifying marks of the fatal injury, but also to complete the story as far as the claimant was concerned. An 'event' for the purposes of establishing a claim by a secondary victim might be made up from a number of components, as had been said in *North Glamorgan NHS Trust* v *Walters* (see below).

Psychiatric injury, though not in the area of nervous shock, and the relevant principles to a proper adjudication was considered in the new money-earner for lawyers, stress at work cases. The relevant authorities are *Sutherland* v *Hatton* [2002] PIQR P221, CA, and *Barber* v *Somerset County Council* (2004) 2 All ER, HL.

An unusual case

In *Attia* v *British Gas plc* [1988] QB 304, a woman had allegedly suffered positive psychiatric illness (as opposed to 'normal' grief and distress) through seeing her home burnt down before her eyes as a result of the defendants' negligence. The Court of Appeal refused to strike out the claim for nervous shock (the claim for damage to property had been settled), saying that there was in principle no reason to preclude recovery if the injury and foreseeability were proved in the usual way. In other words, nervous shock arising out of damage to property rather than damage to the person is not for that reason alone to be irrecoverable. Scott J has doubted whether shock caused by the disclosure of confidential medical information could properly be reflected in an award of damages (*W* v *Egdell* [1990] Ch 359). See also the sharp rejection by the Court of Appeal in *Powell* v *Boldaz* [1998] Lloyd's Rep Med 116 of the claim for nervous shock sustained as a result of getting certain upsetting written information in A4 rather than A5 form.

Also unusual, not so much for the law as for the facts, is *Donachie* v *Chief Constable of Greater London Police* [2004] EWCA Civ 405. The claimant police officer was, without proper thought for his safety, given a task by his superior officer of placing a tracking device under a suspect's car while the suspect was in the pub. Due to the defective nature of the device he had to try nine times before succeeding. All the while his fear for his own safety grew in case the suspect and friends should emerge from their drinking. As a result he developed a clinical psychiatric state, leading to an acute rise in blood pressure, which caused a stroke. The Court of Appeal, summarising the principles to be derived from *Page* v *Smith* [1996] 1 AC 155, HL (these are set out in the preceding chapter), said that there was a reasonable foreseeability that the employer's breach of duty would cause physical injury to the officer, though not of the kind he actually suffered and via the unforeseeable psychiatric injury actually caused by the employer's negligence. So he was a primary victim in respect of whom there was a reasonable foreseeability of physical injury and, in consequence, in respect of whom it was not necessary to prove involvement in an 'event' in the form of an assault or otherwise. If A put B in a position, said the court, whereby A can reasonably foresee that B would fear physical injury, and B, as a result, suffers psychiatric injury and/or physical injury, B was then a primary victim.

Still within the realm of the unusual, we find *Froggatt* v *Chesterfield and North Derbyshire Royal Hospital NHS Trust* [2002] MLC 0887, Forbes J. A young wife had undergone a mastectomy followed by radiotherapy and chemotherapy, only to be told the following month that the diagnosis of cancer had been an error. She then underwent extensive reconstruction surgery, which left her cosmetically and physically impaired and with substantial psychiatric symptoms, for which she obtained appropriate damages. What was unusual is that her husband succeeded in obtaining damages as a secondary victim having suffered psychiatric injury by way of sudden shock and horror on seeing his wife undressed for the first time, and her son obtained a small amount of damages as a secondary victim for psychiatric damage suffered when he overheard a telephone conversation in which his mother discussed the fact that she had cancer and was likely to die. This is surely the far boundary of the nervous shock claim. Could the defendants have foreseen the telephone conversation or injury arising therefrom? Or the arising of the husband's psychiatric illness? The claims of husband and son were dealt with in very short measure at the end of an extensive judgment on the patient's claim. I am not at all sure these claims would stand up to a lengthier analysis.

THE MEDICAL ACCIDENT

What if a close relative suffers psychiatric damage through being present at and around the death and/or terminal illness in hospital (or elsewhere) of a loved one, the injury being due to medical negligence? There is no reason in principle why the tests of proximity (or the 'aftermath' test) should not be satisfied in this context. Until recently, there was no English authority on the point, but several settlements of such claims had been achieved. In the Australian case of *Jaensch* v *Coffey* (1984) 155 CLR 549 (not a medical accident case), Deane J permitted recovery for nervous shock where a wife came to her injured husband's bedside in hospital, and through her constant attendance upon him and her fear that he was going to die suffered severe anxiety and depression.[10] The judge said:

> The aftermath of the accident extended to the hospital to which the injured person was taken and persisted for so long as he remained in the state produced by the accident up to and including immediate post-accident treatment ... Her psychiatric injuries were the result of the impact upon her of the facts of the accident itself and its aftermath while she was present at the aftermath of the accident at the hospital.

In principle there is no difference between claims for shock due to horrific scenes at the hospital after a road accident and the same after a medical accident, so the case of *Taylorson* (above) is also in point. However, the difficulty with the medical accident context is that horrific scenes are less likely, and so the question that immediately springs to mind is how the element of shock can be satisfied in such a case (assuming that there is no such shocking element as the relative finding the loved one dying or dead at home). In the Hillsborough case Lord Ackner said:

> 'Shock', in the context of this cause of action, involves the sudden appreciation by sight or sound of a horrifying event, which violently agitates the mind. It has yet to include psychiatric illness caused by the accumulation over a period of time or more gradual assaults on the nervous system.

In *Jaensch* v *Coffey* (above) Brennan J said:

> I understand 'shock' in this context to mean the sudden sensory perception – that is, by seeing, hearing or touching – of a person, thing or event, which is so distressing that the perception of the phenomenon affronts or insults the claimant's mind and causes a recognizable psychiatric illness.

---

10   Note, incidentally, that the claimant's predisposition to such injury was no defence; similarly in *Brice* v *Brown* [1984] 1 All ER 997, Stuart-Smith LJ held that, once nervous shock was a foreseeable consequence of a breach of duty, it made no difference that the precise nature and extent of the injury were not foreseeable (the claimant had suffered particularly severely due to a basic mental instability) – see Chapter 23 under 'You must take the claimant as you find him'.

There are now, besides the judgment in *Taylorson* (set out above), recent decisions in medical negligence actions, including one from the Court of Appeal, which make it more difficult for a claim of this sort to succeed.

In *Taylor* v *Somerset Health Authority* [1993] 4 Med LR 34, MLC 0025, Auld J rejected a claim by a widow who had come to the hospital after her husband had suffered a fatal heart attack at work (due to earlier medical mismanagement). She had not believed that he had died, not even when she was so informed by a doctor. She then saw him lying peacefully behind curtains in the basement of the hospital. The judge said that this did not fulfil the test of temporal proximity (in other words, she was too late on the scene). He also said that there had to be an external traumatic event; however, in the *Sion* case (see below) Peter Gibson LJ made it clear that an external horrific event was not a prerequisite as the crucial element in this sort of claim was a sudden awareness, violently agitating the mind, of what was occurring or what had occurred. It could, nevertheless, be argued that in the *Taylor* case what was absent was the necessary element of horror or sudden shock. One has to remember that one cannot claim merely for psychiatric injury caused by the death of a loved one. The claim is a claim for *shock*.

In *Sion* v *Hampstead Health Authority* [1994] 5 Med LR 170, MLC 0027, the Court of Appeal struck out as doomed to fail a claim by a father who suffered psychiatric injury through attending for some two weeks by the bedside of his 23-year-old son who had been injured in a traffic accident and fatally deteriorated in hospital due, allegedly, to negligent medical treatment. The court took the view on the pleadings, having regard principally to the psychiatric report that was served with the particulars of claim, that there was no evidence of 'shock', no sudden appreciation by sight or sound of a horrifying event, but rather a continuous process that ran from the father's first arrival at the hospital to a death two weeks later that was by then not unexpected – and on then to his realisation after the inquest of the possibility of medical negligence.

This seems odd. In the first place, does it make any sort of sense that there would probably have been a good claim if the father had still been hoping for recovery when death occurred and had therefore been 'shocked' when there was a sudden fatal deterioration? Second, there do in fact appear to have been discrete 'shocking' events during the two-week period, such as a sudden (though not immediately fatal) deterioration, sudden respiratory difficulties, cardiac arrest and transfer to the intensive care unit.

A more imaginative judgment (in the best sense) was given in the Central London County Court by Judge White on 4 February 1994 in the case of *Tredget and Tredget* v *Bexley Health Authority* [1994] 5 Med LR 178, MLC 0024. Although this was before the Court of Appeal judgment, it was after Brooke J had struck out Mr Sion's claim at first instance, and nothing that was said in the Court of Appeal invalidates Judge White's approach.

In the first place, this case concerned claims for nervous shock sustained by both parents as a result of a traumatic and frightening delivery of their fatally injured child, following negligent failure to go for an earlier Cesarian section, and as a result of attending upon their son during his short life of some two days. So the case was rather different from the usual 'attending by the bedside' case.

Judge White accepted, as did the Court of Appeal in the *Sion* case, the following requisites for a successful claim:

> The plaintiff must show he has suffered an actual psychiatric illness caused by shock (ie the sudden and direct appreciation by sight or sound of a horrifying event or events, rather than from stress, strain, grief or sorrow or from gradual or retrospective realisation of events); that there was propinquity in time or space for the causative event or its immediate aftermath; that such injury was reasonably foreseeable; and that the relationship between plaintiff and defendant was sufficiently proximate.

It is surprising that the health authority sought to argue that there had been no element of shock in the events that the parents had experienced, and quite amazing that they should have chosen to contest the mother's claim on that basis. Fortunately, the judge sensibly declined to see the two-day period as lacking the element of shock. He saw the traumatic birth (in which the husband had been involved, and which had been complicated by shoulder dystocia – an obstetric emergency) and the delivery of a clearly traumatised baby and the ensuing harrowing hours as a single event ('frightening and harrowing') which satisfied the requisite of a sudden shock to the nervous system. He said:

> Of course, it was not in the nature of an immediate catastrophe which lasts only a few seconds – panic in a stadium or a motor accident – but one just as traumatic, for those immediately involved as participants, as each of the parents was ...
>
> In my judgment, if this is a new step in the development of the law, it is not only ... within the principles that have been set out, but has its own in-built limits, being founded on the special relationship, with all that follows, of the parent with the child at the unique human moment of birth.[11]

In *Palmer* v *Tees Health Authority* [1998] Lloyd's Rep Med 447, the mother of a child murdered by a released psychiatric patient could not recover damages for nervous shock when she saw the child's body three days later, a decision upheld by the Court of Appeal ([1999] Lloyd's Rep Med 351, [2000] PIQR P1).[12] In *Farrell* v *Merton Sutton and Wandsworth Health Authority* [2000] MLC 0236, ML 8/00, Steel J held that where a mother sustained psychiatric damage through being aware during a Cesarian section under inadequate anesthetic and also through learning of her child's brain damage when she saw him for the

---

11   We may note here that in *Allin* v *City and Hackney Health Authority* [1996] 7 Med LR 167, a mother recovered damages for psychiatric injury sustained on being informed wrongly (and negligently) that her new-born child had died.

12   In *Tranmore* v *TE Scudder Ltd* [1998] JPIL 336, visiting the mortuary 24 hours after his son had been killed by falling rubble took the father outside the 'aftermath' principle, even though he had visited the accident site at the time (he had not seen his son there, though).

first time the next day, throughout all those events she remained a primary victim.[13]

In *North Glamorgan NHS Trust* v *Walters* [2002] MLC 0876, [2003] PIQR P316, the mother attended the last two days of her infant son's life after he had suffered a fatal injury due to the defendant's negligence. She was first told that brain damage was unlikely, later that he had in fact suffered severe brain injury and needed life support. The child later died in his mother's arms when the support was withdrawn. *Sunt lacrimae rerum.* The Court of Appeal, dismissing the defendant's appeal, and declaring that the only issue in the case was whether the mother's illness 'arose from the sudden appreciation by sight or sound of a horrifying event or its immediate aftermath', said that the law permitted a realistic view to be taken of what constituted an 'event'. 'Event' was for secondary victims a convenient description for the series of events which made up the entire event beginning with the negligent infliction of damage to the conclusion of the immediate aftermath, whenever that might be. Its identification was a matter of judgment from case to case depending on the facts and circumstances of each case. On the facts of this case the court said that there was an inexorable progression from the moment when the fit causing the brain damage occurred which shortly thereafter made the child's death inevitable and the dreadful climax when he died in his mother's arms. It was a seamless tale lasting for a period of 36 hours which for the mother was undoubtedly one drawn-out experience. The entire event was undoubtedly a 'horrifying' event. The assault on the mother's nervous system began when she was woken by her child's convulsion and she reeled under successive blows as each was delivered. In other words the blows were each of them a sudden assault; the picture was not of a gradual assault (some distinction!). Clarke LJ said that although the court's decision did not actually involve taking the step forward of allowing a claim for a secondary victim for psychiatric illness caused by the accumulation over a period of time of more gradual assaults on the nervous system (as opposed to a sudden assault on same), he for his part would have been willing to take that step forward on the facts of the instant case if that had been necessary.

A lamentable step backward, however, was taken by a deputy High Court judge in *Ward* v *Leeds Teaching Hospital NHS Trust* MLC 1265, [2004] Lloyds Rep Med 530, CA where the defendants succeeded in their

---

13 In *Toth* v *Ledger* [2000] MLC 0521, CA, a father claimed damages from an allegedly negligent GP for nervous shock sustained through attending his five-year-old son's terminal hours in hospital following untreated hypoglycemia (due to glycogen storage disease). Despite having earlier settled his claim for bereavement, the father was allowed to pursue a second action for damages for nervous shock, the court taking the view that the well-known principle of *Henderson* v *Henderson* did not operate to make the second action an abuse of court. The question of abuse had to be decided on a broad merits-based assessment. The claim for nervous shock had been delayed by legal aid problems. Had there been none, it would have been included in the first action. The defendants had not been led to believe at the time of settlement that it would not be pursued. It was not an abuse of court. (Readers interested in this litigation could go to the GMC issue reported as *R* v *General Medical Council, ex p Toth* MLC 0270, [2000] Lloyd's Rep Med 368, wherein Mr Toth successfully obtained an order from Lightman J requiring the GMC, who were not in fact opposing the claimant on any substantive issue, to continue to investigate his complaint against the GP.)

wretched argument that the psychiatric injury suffered by a mother at the death of her daughter due to a negligently handled anesthetic was not due to the events in hospital but due to the bereavement *simpliciter*. The judge took the view that there was no shock or horrifying event for the mother as she sat by her daughter's bedside (on and off) for two days awaiting her death. The death of a loved one in hospital, he said, did not meet that description unless also accompanied by circumstances that were wholly exceptional in some way so as to shock and horrify. No wonder the law in this field, and the odd judge, is so often considered an ass.

At this point we may glance at *Farrell* v *Avon Health Authority* [2001] Lloyds Rep Med 458 where a father who, arriving at hospital, was told his newborn child had died but then that that had been a mistake and he lived, obtained damages as a primary victim for foreseeable psychiatric damage. One might have thought he would have been overjoyed to learn of the hospital's mistake, but apparently not.

WHAT NEEDS TO BE PROVED?

What, then, does the claimant need to establish to succeed in this sort of claim (assuming he cannot show himself to have been a primary victim)?

- In the first place the psychiatric report must certify clearly that the claimant has suffered an actual psychiatric injury, ie going beyond the normal ambit of a bereavement reaction, grief, fear or distress.
- Next, one has to show that the circumstances were such that nervous shock was foreseeable.
- Next, the claimant needs to satisfy the test of familial proximity, ie to show that nervous shock to this relative or close friend was foreseeable. Note the arbitrary treatment of this requirement by the House of Lords in the Hillsborough case.
- Next, the claimant needs to satisfy the test of temporal and spatial proximity, ie show that the claimant was sufficiently close in time and space to the events that are alleged to have caused the injury.
- Next the report must identify a discrete shocking event (or events) that constituted a sudden assault upon the nervous system of the claimant and was responsible wholly or at any rate materially for the injury. It may be unwise to rely on any protracted period of time as being the horrifying event unless the sights and sounds during that period were more or less continuously horrifying, although recent cases (see above) indicate that the courts are applying a less severe test in this context.
- The psychiatric report should make it clear that the injury would probably not have been sustained simply through the loss of the loved one, ie in the absence of the identified shocking event(s).

A FINAL NOTE

Before one criticises the policy, whether consciously formed or not, of restricting the ambit of the claim, one should bear in mind that nervous shock means just that, and that the claim began life as a reaction to a horrifying event, usually a motor accident or the threat of one on the part of those involved in it, at the time or in the direct aftermath when the immediate marks and traces of the shocking event were still observable and capable of evincing nervous shock in a relevant witness, eg victims of a motor accident at hospital but still displaying the immediate signs of their trauma.

How far these stringent conditions can be satisfied in a claim arising out of medical mismanagement remains unclear. It must depend on the precise events. If the claimant was present when a shocking emergency or a shocking deterioration in the patient occurred, or comes to the hospital and finds the patient in a state that reasonably shocks, or perhaps is present at an unexpected, and therefore in itself shocking, death, the claim might well be successful. But if there is a slow process of decline leading to a death that was not really unexpected at the time, or at any rate was on the cards, and the death did not involve any particularly shocking factors beyond the actual dying, the claim may fail. It would have failed a little while ago, but now, as I have said, a more generous judicial interpretation of the factors necessary for such a claim to succeed may prevail. In the PIBA lecture (see above) Lord Phillips said that 'the aftermath principle is one of considerable elasticity'.[14]

A knee-jerk reaction?

Generally speaking, the oft heard criticism that the patient body has now become a group of acquisitive compensation seekers, ready, with ever helpful lawyers, to spring into litigious action (in both senses) at the drop of a scalpel is misconceived. However, in the context of proposed nervous shock claims there may be some truth in it. One can easily enough get the impression that as soon as any health body makes any insensitive move or fails to treat patients with consideration, the cry for compensation is heard, a lawyer arises to represent the aggrieved, and other members of the family (for good measure), and litigation is proposed, often with apparently little regard to the legal basis for a claim. The body organs 'scandal' is an example of this. However regrettable the hospitals' behaviour may have been, it was very difficult to see how a court would hold that, in disposing of a child's (or an adult's) remains, a hospital owed a common law duty to the family not to treat the body in such a way as to cause foreseeable and proven psychiatric illness to them if and when their actions were discovered.[15] For the way Gage J dealt with the issue see *AB* v *Leeds Teaching Hospital NHS Trust* [2004] MLC 1101.

---

14 It is worth noting that the Australian High Court has rejected our control mechanisms. In *Annetts* v *Australian Stations Pty Ltd* [2002] HCA 35 a 16-year-old died of exhaustion alone in the outback when working as a jackaroo. His parents joined the unsuccessful search for him, finding only his blood-stained hat. Three months later his body was found. The parents recovered for psychiatric damage sustained over this period. In *Gifford* v *Strang Patrick Stevedoring Pty Ltd* [2003] HCA 33, children who suffered psychiatric injury on being told of their father's death recovered damages. Now there is a move afoot to introduce some sort of control mechanism. Some states have already done this by legislation.

15 See *Dobson* v *North Tyneside Health Authority* [1997] 1 WLR 596, CA. Maybe recourse can be had to the 'human right' to family life (though in such circumstances 'life' would not appear to be the right word).

FATAL ACCIDENT AND BEREAVEMENT

On behalf of the deceased himself, that is to say the estate of the deceased, a claim lies only for funeral expenses. The claim for loss of expectation of life, which used to be set at a formal figure of about £1,250, was abolished by the Administration of Justice Act 1982. The deceased also has no claim for loss of earnings during the lost years, ie the years when he would have earned had he been alive. There may be a small claim for his suffering in the interval, if there was one, between the injury and his death. Apart from that, nothing. So one can see how truer than ever is the common law saying 'It is cheaper to kill than to maim'. Had he been maimed, the deceased could have claimed a substantial sum for pain and suffering and loss of amenity, all his lost earnings and the cost of all necessary care for the rest of his life.

The tortfeasor, or his insurance company, will not, however, escape scot-free if the deceased had dependants (by virtue of the Fatal Accidents Act 1976, as amended). For full details of the fatal accidents legislation the reader is referred to the standard textbooks. The important points to note here are as follows.

First, by virtue of the amendment made to the Act by the Administration of Justice Act 1982, the spouse of the deceased or a parent of an unmarried minor deceased (note: a child cannot claim for loss of a parent) killed by negligence can claim from the tortfeasor (regardless of any dependency) the statutory bereavement award of £10,000.[16] This is, of course, a minimal amount and is no sort of compensation for the loss of a loved one. But it has to be remembered that at common law the general rule is that no person has a financial or indeed a legal interest in the life of another person, so that no duty of care is owed by A to B not to kill B's relative (or employee, for that matter) by negligence. So the statutory award represents a legislative exception to the common law rule in a context where no duty of care was owed to the claimant. The 'aftermath' principle represents, as we have seen, another limited exception to the rule.

Second, the general effect of the long-standing and important statutory exception to the common law rule effected by the fatal accidents legislation is that those who were or had an expectation of being financially supported by the deceased may claim their loss from the tortfeasor over the whole of the period during which they could have expected to be supported by him. Again, for the details of this legislation, the reader is referred to the standard textbooks.

DEATH OF AN INFANT AND NERVOUS SHOCK

It is not easy to know how to assess damages for a stillbirth or a miscarriage. They will, of course, vary according to the time at which the miscarriage takes place and according to the degree of nervous shock (ie

---

16 A deceased child must have died, not merely sustained the lethal injury, before his eighteenth birthday for the parents' entitlement to arise (*Doleman* v *Deakin* (1990) Times, 30 January, CA).

actual psychiatric injury) suffered by the mother. But there is little in the way of precedent.

One must first bear in mind that mental trauma unaccompanied by physical injury will not found a claim in negligence unless the mental trauma amounts to actual psychiatric damage (to be proved by a medical report). It should be possible in most cases of miscarriage or stillbirth to identify a physical injury, eg the pain of the abortion or the prolongation of labour beyond the appropriate point.[17] It may well be that damaging the child *en ventre*[18] constitutes in itself a physical injury to the mother.

For an early miscarriage, up to a few weeks, say, the award is likely to be about £2,500 – of course, if any sequelae are proved, eg substantive psychiatric injury, or difficulty or impossibility of conception, gestation or parturition in the future, damages will be substantially increased. The estimate above applies to a miscarriage that leaves no substantive sequelae.

After the early days, the award will increase as the pregnancy advances until you have the stillbirth. The real question on assessing for a stillbirth (again, assume no substantive nervous shock, only the normal sorrow, distress and disappointment, with some identifiable physical injury on which to hang that) is whether one takes the bereavement award as a guide. However, as explained above, that is an award under the fatal accident legislation and presupposes no common law duty of care owed to the relative (the spouse or parent). So it can be viewed as a bonus added by the legislation. In the case of the stillbirth, there is of course a duty of care owed to the mother. Nevertheless, the old principle of the common law that no person has an interest in the life of another means that traditional learning would say that the mother cannot be compensated for the death of her child as such (apart from the bereavement award, which presumably cannot apply where the child is not born alive and so is never a 'person' within the meaning of the legislation).

Cases

There are a few reported cases on damages for stillbirth. In *Bagley* v *North Herts Health Authority* [1986] NLJ Rep 1014, Simon Brown J acknowledged that damages could not be awarded to the mother for grief and distress as such (Lord Wilberforce had made that clear in *McLoughlin* v *O'Brian* (above)) or for loss of society, or for the statutory bereavement award, but he found other means of compensating her. He awarded damages for loss of satisfaction in bringing the pregnancy to a successful end, for disappointment at the shattering of her plans for a family and for being deprived of the joy of bringing up an ordinary healthy child, and he said that those damages would amount to not less than the statutory sum. In fact, the mother received some £18,000, but a lot of that was for other heads of claim such as actual physical sequelae

---

17　In some other contexts it will be essential to prove nervous shock, eg where cancer is negligently diagnosed and, although the patient does not accept treatment and is therefore not physically harmed by the misdiagnosis, they suffer very great anxiety for a period of time until the diagnosis is corrected.

18　The medics prefer us to say '*in utero*'.

(she suffered a substantial nervous illness as a result). Counsel in the case has said that one could probably think in terms of about £6,000 for the actual stillbirth.

In *Kralj v McGrath and St Theresa's Hospital* [1986] 1 All ER 54, where £10,000 general damages were awarded after a horrendous and agonising piece of obstetric mismanagement had caused the stillbirth of one of a pair of twins, Woolf J said that not only was the mother entitled to damages for shock at what had happened, but, if her injury was aggravated by the grief she was suffering, that could be reflected in the award. Having stated that it would be wholly inappropriate to introduce into the medical context the concept of aggravated damages, the judge awarded compensation also for the financial loss that would arise if the parents went on to implement their desire for a larger family; if they decided not to, then that award would be appropriate nevertheless to cover disappointment over the loss of their objective; £10,000 was awarded for pain and suffering, and £18,000 for loss of the mother's earnings. It is not possible to know how much of the total award was for the stillbirth pure and simple (if one may use that expression) – indeed it is probable that the judge did not assess that aspect separately in his own mind.

In *Grieve* v *Salford Health Authority* [1991] 2 Med LR 295, Rose J awarded a woman with a pre-existing vulnerable personality £12,500 in respect of initial prolongation of labour, some additional pain, loss of her stillborn child and of the satisfaction of a successful conclusion to the pregnancy, plus psychological damage likely to endure for some four years from the date of the stillbirth. This could possibly be seen as about £6,000 for the stillbirth in itself and about £6,000 for the four-year nervous illness.

In *Kerby* v *Redbridge Health Authority* [1993] 4 Med LR 178, a twin was fatally injured before birth in 1988 by admitted negligence, and survived only three days. Ognall J said, with reference to the dicta in *Bagley* (above), that damages for 'dashed hopes' would duplicate the bereavement award, but he awarded, nevertheless, in addition to the bereavement award, £10,000 for the Cesarian section and consequent scar, a depressive illness of moderate severity lasting some six months, and the constant reminder of what might have been by the presence of the surviving twin.

If the matter were put to the test, it is likely that a court would award close to the bereavement award for a stillbirth pure and simple. One line of argument that might suggest that damages should not greatly exceed the bereavement award is as follows: what if the child dies shortly after birth, let us say through poor neonatal care? How does one justify any award other than the bereavement award in that case? In which event, why should the situation be radically different if the child died just before birth? No duty of care is owed by the pediatricians to the mother in respect of their care of the neonate. Probably the only way of increasing the award substantively beyond the bereavement level of £7,500 in such a context is to show that the mother suffered substantial nervous shock – ie an actual psychiatric injury – that comes within the 'aftermath' principle of *McLoughlin* v *O'Brian* (above).

A final note: In earlier editions of this book it was suggested that, regardless of whether 'normal' grief and distress at loss of a loved one will attract the bereavement award or no compensation at all in a given situation, the award for nervous shock should only reflect that element of suffering which is additional to 'normal' grief and distress (see the report on the Zeebrugge Ferry awards in Kemp & Kemp *Quantum of Damages*, C4-350). However, the Court of Appeal judgments in *Vernon* v *Bosley* [1997] 1 All ER 577 (see the section above on 'Further developments') may have given the lie to that observation.

Chapter 20

Loss/injury: economic loss

INTRODUCTION

Mere economic loss, ie economic loss that is not consequent upon physical damage to person or property or the threat of it, is as a general rule not recoverable in tort, as opposed to contract. It is, however, recoverable when it arises from careless statements, provided there is a duty in the circumstances on the person making the statement to take care; that duty will arise in the context of a fiduciary relationship. Recent years have seen the formulation by the courts that recovery is also permitted where there is a sufficient relationship of proximity between the parties to permit the court to infer that the defendant voluntarily assumed a duty of care in respect of the alleged negligent activity; but it is hard to know in any particular case whether or not the court will discern such a relationship. Apart from these contexts, a line will be drawn by the court as a matter of policy to prevent recovery for economic loss that does not flow from, ie is not consequent upon, some physical damage or the threat of it.

There has never been any problem in compensating for financial loss where it accompanies injury to person or property. If your car is damaged, you can hire another pending repair; if you are injured, you can recover lost earnings. Nor has there been any difficulty in permitting recovery for economic loss consequent upon breach of contract. But, as regards liability in tort, carelessness, whether in act or word, which gives rise to foreseeable economic loss only is a different matter. 'The reluctance to grant a remedy for the careless invasion of financial or pecuniary interests is long-standing, deep-rooted and not unreasonable' (*per* Professor Heuston). The court might declare that there was no duty of care, as where a large supermarket setting up next door to a small competitor puts the latter out of business, or that the damage was too remote, or that public policy drew the line at recovery in respect of the loss claimed, or simply that mere economic loss was not recoverable.

As with so many aspects of the law of negligence, the question of recovering economic loss is one of policy. Whenever the courts draw a line to mark out the bounds of 'duty', they do it as a matter of policy so as to limit the responsibility of the defendant. Whenever the courts set bounds to the 'damages' recoverable – saying that they are, or are not, too remote – they do it as a matter of policy so as to limit the liability of the defendants (*per* Lord Denning MR in *Spartan Steel and Alloys Ltd* v *Martin & Co (Contractors) Ltd* [1973] QB 27 at 36, CA).

The 'electricity' cases

However, when the economic loss is consequent upon physical injury, it is usually recoverable. Thus, in *SCM (United Kingdom) Ltd* v *W J Whittall & Son Ltd* [1971] 1 QB 337, defendants who negligently cut off the electricity supply to the claimants' factory were held liable by the Court of Appeal for the loss of profit which resulted from the solidifying in the furnaces of molten metals, because it stemmed from the damage to furnace and metal, but not for further economic loss which was said to be too remote. Lord Denning said that recovery for mere economic loss was not usually permitted by the law, on the ground of public policy, rather than by the operation of any logical principle; and Winn LJ said that, apart from the special case of liability for negligently uttered false statements, there was no liability for negligent unintentional infliction of any form of economic loss which was not itself consequential upon foreseeable physical injury or damage to property.

In the similar *Spartan Steels* case (above) the defendants negligently damaged the electric cable supplying the claimants' factory, who had therefore to pour molten metal out of their furnaces, for otherwise it would have solidified and damaged the furnaces. They lost part of the value of the metal and their profit on its resale. In addition, they claimed for loss of profit on the four further melts they could have performed in the time the power was off. Though they succeeded at first instance, the Court of Appeal would not permit recovery in respect of the four melts, on the basis that whereas loss of profit on the metal that was poured out was consequential on the physical damage to that metal and the risk of damage to the furnaces, loss of profit on the four hypothetical melts was mere economic damage not consequent upon the physical damage or the risk of physical damage. Lord Denning said that the more he thought about the subject of recovery for economic loss, the more difficult he found it to put each case into its proper pigeonhole:

> Sometimes I say: 'There was no duty.' In others I say: 'The damage was too remote.' So much so that I think the time has come to discard those tests which have proved so elusive. It seems to me better to consider the particular relationship in hand, and see whether or not, as a matter of policy, economic loss should be recoverable or not.

In truth, as Edmund Davies LJ pointed out in a strong dissenting judgment, there was no logical distinction between the two losses. It must simply be seen as a matter of policy that the court insisted on drawing a line to the defendants' liability.[1]

Development

For a time, beginning with the decision of the House of Lords in *Anns* v *Merton London Borough Council* [1978] AC 728, it seemed that economic

---

1   Economic loss can be recovered where it is claimed as part of a claim which originates in a claim for physical damage (*The Kapetan Georgis* [1988] FTLR 180).

loss which was foreseeable should be recoverable, as any other loss, unless there were policy considerations in the particular case militating against such recovery. This general formulation was later whittled down by the courts; the context in which it was proposed, the liability of local authority inspectors for certifying defective foundations, was itself reduced to the situation where physical damage was created or threatened; and then the very decision itself, imposing liability for economic loss in these circumstances, was declared misconceived because the court in 1978 had failed to recognise that the damage for which it was permitting compensation was mere economic loss and to do that was to introduce a wholly new and unsuitable extension to the law (see further below on this).

In *Junior Books* v *Veitchi* [1983] 1 AC 520, the House of Lords held that, assuming the facts pleaded were true, subcontractors who laid a defective floor would be liable to the claimant occupiers of the building for the cost of repair and certain financial loss flowing therefrom. This was despite the fact that there was neither a contractual nexus between the parties nor any physical damage or threat of it to the building. It was said that where there was a sufficient relationship of proximity between the parties the duty of care extended to the duty not to inflict carelessly economic loss (Lord Roskill said that the defendants, as subcontractors, were in almost as close a commercial relationship with the plaintiff as it was possible to envisage, short of privity of contract).

Lord Brandon dissented, saying that to impose liability would be to create obligations appropriate only to a contractual relationship, and that the authorities made it clear that in the absence of physical damage or the threat of it mere economic loss was not recoverable.

Retrenchment

Recovery for mere economic loss was denied in shipping contexts – by the Court of Appeal in *Leigh and Sillavan Ltd* v *Aliakmon Shipping Co* [1985] QB 350, where buyers sued shipowners in contract and tort for damage to goods caused by bad stowage; and by the House of Lords in *Candlewood Navigation Corpn* v *Mitsui OSK Lines Ltd* [1986] AC 1, involving a time charterer's claim for financial loss. In *Muirhead* v *Industrial Tank Specialities* [1986] QB 507, the Court of Appeal rejected a claim for mere economic loss by the user against the manufacturer of lobster tanks. It was said that there was not a sufficiently close relationship between the two for such a duty to arise; there had to be such a very close proximity of relationship between the parties and reliance by the claimant on the defendant that the defendant was to be taken voluntarily to have assumed direct responsibility to the claimant.[2]

Then came the highly significant House of Lords' decision in *Caparo Industries plc* v *Dickman* [1990] 2 AC 605, where it was held that auditors of a company owed no duty of care not to inflict economic loss on shareholders or potential investors who relied on the audit in deciding whether to invest (further) in the company. The court said that liability for economic loss due to negligent misstatement was confined to cases

---

2   See also *Virgo Steamship Co* v *Skaarup Shipping Corpn* [1988] 1 Lloyd's Rep 352.

where the statement or advice had been given to a known recipient for a specific purpose of which the maker was aware, and on which the recipient had relied and on which he had acted to his detriment. As the auditors had no reason to think that their report would go to the claimant, let alone that it would be relied on by them in deciding whether to invest (further) in the company, there was no sufficient proximity between them and the claimants to found a duty of care (see also Chapter 14 under 'The duty not to make careless statements' for further cases).

The decisions of the House of Lords in July 1990 in *Murphy* v *Brentwood District Council* [1991] 1 AC 398, and *Department of the Environment* v *Thomas Bates & Son* [1991] 1 AC 499 concerned liability for economic loss caused not by misstatement but by negligent conduct. The House of Lords made it clear that, as presently constituted, they shared the disquiet that had been voiced increasingly in the last five years or so about the wholesale extension of the law of negligence, in cases where no physical injury had been sustained, that was inherent in and threatening to develop as a logical outcome from the 1978 decision of the House of Lords (as then constituted) in *Anns* v *Merton London Borough Council* [1978] AC 728. In our present context, the point to note is that the court made it clear that there can be no general formula for establishing when mere economic loss is recoverable – one can only look to decided cases and see if one's own case falls more or less within the factual matrix of any case where liability has been imposed.

There is, of course, scope for the court to admit a new situation, for the categories of negligence are never closed, but it would need careful argument and the court would need to be convinced that policy and justice required that liability be imposed. One recent example of the court being so convinced is *Spring* v *Guardian Assurance plc* [1995] 2 AC 296, where the House of Lords held that an insurance company owed a duty of care to a former representative when providing him or prospective employers with a reference (the breach of duty was by way of careless statement and the damage purely economic). Another is *Welton* v *North Cornwall District Council* [1997] 1 WLR 570, where the Court of Appeal permitted recovery for economic loss in respect of building works required, quite wrongly, to be done to a restaurant by an incompetent environmental health officer. The court said:

- that the officer had 'assumed a responsibility' to take care in respect of what he said to or required of the restaurant owner; and
- that it was fair, just and reasonable, and in accordance with public policy, that a duty of care should be imposed.

In *Hamble Fisheries Ltd* v *L Gardner & Sons Ltd* [1999] 2 Lloyd's Rep 1, where damages for economic loss occasioned by the failure of marine engines was claimed in tort against the manufacturer (for not warning of that possibility), the Court of Appeal, dismissing the purchaser's appeal, said that the general rule was as set out in the *Murphy* case (above): there was no duty on a manufacturer towards a consumer for economic loss. The pertinent question was whether in a given situation there was a special relationship of proximity on the manufacturer to safeguard the consumer from economic loss. *Contra*, in *Bailey* v *HSS Alarms* (2000) Times, 20 June, the Court of Appeal discerned the requisite special relationship between a property owner and a company who provided security services to the property (the two parties not being in direct contractual relationship). The company were held liable to the owner for economic loss when thieves broke in and stole.

In *Commissioner of Police of the Metropolis* v *Lennon* [2004] 1 WLR 2594, the claimant police officer had asked for advice from an employee of the Commissioner who had held herself out as familiar with the ins and outs pertaining to the claimant's transfer to a new force, in particular in connection with the preservation of his housing allowance. That advice was wrong and caused the claimant economic loss. The Court of Appeal dismissed the Commissioner's appeal, saying it was irrelevant that the employee was not a professional adviser as she had expressly assumed responsibility for giving the claimant the advice in relation to possible loss of housing allowance. She had led the claimant to believe that he could leave it to her and could rely on her, and had not told him to seek advice elsewhere. No new category of duty situation had been created by the judge. It was well established that liability in tort for pure economic loss could arise from the negligent carrying out of a task undertaken pursuant to an express voluntary assumption of responsibility, given appropriate reliance by the relevant party.

The 'wrongful birth' cases (dealt with in detail in Chapter 24) have usually raised issues about the right to claim for economic loss, and the decisions of the courts have been influenced strongly by policy considerations, of which the case of *McFarlane* v *Tayside Health Board* MLC 0127, [2000] 2 AC 59, HL is the most egregious example.

COMMENT

In the absence of a special relationship of proximity and/or a voluntary assumption of risk (it is not clear what terminology to use – see eg *Reid* v *Rush & Tompkins Group* [1990] 1 WLR 212, CA), there is no duty of care not to inflict mere economic loss. It remains very difficult to predict if in a given situation the court will or will not discern the requisite special relationship. The position is, of course, clear enough if a product causes *physical* injury, as the ginger beer with the decomposing snail in it taught us many years ago (*Donoghue* v *Stevenson* [1932] AC 562)).

Junior Books v *Veitchi* [1983] 1 AC 520 must be seen now as a flash in the pan: if that case recurred today, Lord Brandon's dissenting judgment would be followed – no court is going now to hold that a subcontractor is under a duty of care in his work not to inflict mere economic loss on the building owner with whom he is not in a contractual relationship.[3]

MEDICAL CONTEXT

Most, but not all, medical negligence actions are in respect of personal injury. Within the doctor-patient relationship there is normally a sufficient proximity and reliance by the patient on the doctor to give rise to a

---

3   The House of Lords made it clear enough in *D & F Estates* v *Church Comrs for England* [1989] AC 177 what they thought of the *Junior Books* decision.

duty not to inflict mere economic loss, so that, for example, a careless diagnosis that leads to the patient taking time off work will give rise to compensation for lost wages. Where a negligently premature discharge from hospital of an infected child causes his siblings to contract the infection, resulting in financial loss to the parents, a court would probably hold the hospital liable (see on these facts *Evans* v *Liverpool Corpn* [1906] 1 KB 160, where the father failed in his action against the hospital, but on the basis that as the law then stood the hospital was not liable for the negligence of the discharging physician). Claims for the cost of upkeep of an unplanned child may be for economic loss only, ie where there is no claim made for any personal injury (see Chapter 24, where it is explained that, although such claims are no longer possible in the case of a healthy child, they appear to be possible to a limited extent if the unplanned child is born handicapped).

Chapter 21

Who to sue[1]

An employer is vicariously responsible for the negligent acts or omissions of his servant committed within the scope of the employment, but, as a general rule, not for the negligence of an independent contractor, provided he showed due care in selecting the contractor.

The correct defendant in respect of allegations of negligence at a hospital is the body in charge at the time of the negligence (ie health authority for older claims, NHS trust for more recent ones). The trust or health authority is liable for the negligence of any of its staff, including all medical personnel it engages to carry out the necessary treatment upon the patients, because it is under a primary non-delegable duty of care to see that the patient receives proper treatment. It is therefore unnecessary to pray in aid the principle of vicarious liability. A health authority is not responsible for the negligence of a doctor who has been selected and employed by a private patient (or his GP).

A private clinic is probably responsible only for the negligence of its resident staff, though where it selects and engages the surgeon itself a court is these days likely to find a primary duty of care, just as with a NHS hospital.

The GP is alone liable for his own negligent acts. He is also liable for the acts of anyone he employs, and may possibly be liable for outside services he engages to look after patients in his absence.

GENERAL PRINCIPLES

The general principles of vicarious liability, that is the liability of one person for the negligence of another, are as follows (they are stated in summary form as the topic is too complex to be discussed here in detail, and our concern is with the medical negligence context; so I give merely the outline of the law and one or two useful references).[2] In the complex

---

1 The solecism is deliberate, in the interests of euphony.
2 The House of Lords had occasion to consider the whole issue of vicarious responsibility in the context of a complex international banking dispute (*Crédit Lyonnais Bank Nederland NV* v *Exports Credits Guarantee Department* [2000] 1 AC 486, [1999] 1 All ER 929). See *Lister* v *Hesley Hall Ltd* in the main text below.

partnership contribution lawsuit of *Dubai Aluminium Co Ltd* v *Salaam* [2002] 3 WLR 1913 the House of Lords said that vicarious liability meant that, with regard to third parties, the employer, although personally blameless, stood in the shoes of the wrongdoer employee for the purpose of liability to the claimant. This vicarious liability was substitutional, not personal.

The claimant has first to show that the negligence complained of was due to the act or omission of an employee of the defendant. An employee is one who is engaged upon a contract of service.

The test of employment has varied through the years. Basically, a man is not an employee if the person who engaged him has no say in how he does his work, but only in what work he is to do. If the person engaged is subject to the control and directions of the other in respect of the manner in which the work is to be done, he will be an employee (the leading case is *Mersey Docks and Harbour Board* v *Coggins and Griffith (Liverpool) Ltd* [1947] AC 1, HL). It is often not easy to decide on applying this test whether there is a situation of employment. A good reference point is the judgment of Mackenna J in *Ready Mixed Concrete (South East) Ltd* v *Minister of Pensions and National Insurance* [1968] 2 QB 497.[3] In *Kapfunde* v *Abbey National plc* [1999] Lloyd's Rep Med 48, a GP had a contract with Abbey National whereby she assessed the health of any prospective employee. She had, upon written material, not an examination, declared that the claimant was unsuitable to be employed as she had sickle cell disease and so was at risk of having a lot of time off work for illness. Having unsuccessfully sued for racial discrimination, the claimant went on to allege in this action that the GP owed her a duty of care, which she had breached. The Court of Appeal upheld, *inter alia*, the judge's findings that the GP was on a contract for services and not a contract of service and therefore Abbey National would not in any event be vicariously liable for any breach of duty by her.[4] In *North Essex Health Authority* v *Dr David-John* [2003] Lloyds Rep Med 586, the Employment Appeal Tribunal held that the GP was not in any contractual relationship with the health authority, but that, if he was, it was as an independent contractor.

Second, the claimant has to show that the negligence complained of was committed within and not outside the course or scope of the employee's employment. Is the unauthorised and wrongful act of the employee one way, albeit an improper way, of discharging his obligations under the contract of employment, or is it an independent act unconnected with his employment (a useful point of reference on this question is *Century Insurance Co* v *Northern Ireland Road Transport Board* [1942]

---

3   Reference may also be made in this context to the House of Lords' judgment in *McDermid* v *Nash Dredging and Reclamation Co* [1987] AC 906.

4   For another analysis of the distinction between a contract for services and a contract of service, see *Thames Water Utilities* v *King* (23 July 1998, unreported), CA.

AC 509).[5] An employee may be acting within the scope of his employment even if he acts in express disregard of instructions or prohibitions from his employer (compare *Limpus* v *London General Omnibus Co* (1862) 1 H & C 526 with *Twine* v *Beans Express Ltd* [1946] 1 All ER 202, and observe the difficulties which those conflicting lines of authority gave the Court of Appeal in *Rose* v *Plenty* [1976] 1 WLR 141.

A master may be liable for the dishonest acts of his servant, eg where he approbates the act or it is committed in the furtherance of his purpose; but where the act is quite outside the purpose for which the servant is employed the master will not be liable. Compare *Morris* v *CW Martin & Sons Ltd* [1966] 1 QB 716, CA, where an employer was liable when his employee stole the fur that it was his job to clean, with *Heasmans* v *Clarity Cleaning Co* [1987] ICR 949, CA, where the dishonest use of the telephone in an office by an employee employed only to clean that office was not something for which the employer was liable. However, one must now consider the approach of the House of Lords in the *Lister* case (below).

Assaults: In *Lister* v *Hesley Hall Ltd* [2002] 1 AC 15, HL, claimants, who had been resident some years earlier at the defendant's school for boys with emotional and behavioural difficulties, sued for personal injury in respect of sexual abuse by the warden employed by the defendants. The House of Lords said that it was important to avoid becoming involved in the simplistic and erroneous task of trying to determine whether the acts for which an employer was sought to be held vicariously liable were modes of doing authorised acts. The proper approach was to adopt a broad assessment of the nature of the employee's employment. The defendant had undertaken to care for the boys in its charge through the services of the warden. The warden's torts were sufficiently closely connected with his employment that it would be fair, just and reasonable [that ubiquitous phrase again!] to hold the defendant vicariously liable.

In *Mattis* v *Pollock* [2004] PIQR P21 a nightclub was held vicariously responsible for the stabbing of a customer by its doorman, where the fight

---

5   Other cases illustrating the test of 'was it a mode, albeit an improper mode, of performing his duties under the contract of employment' are *Irving* v *Post Office* [1987] IRLR 289, [1987] ICR 949, CA (the Post Office was not vicariously liable for the spiteful act of a postman scrawling a racist slur on an envelope before delivering it to the home of the victim of his malice, because his act was unconnected with the performance of his duties). A policeman's employer was not vicariously liable for his tort of blackmailing a woman he was investigating into yielding her body to him, as he was clearly on an adventure of his own (*Makanjuola* v *Metropolitan Police Comr* (1989) Times, 8 August). Members of a fire brigade who, while operating a 'go-slow' policy, took so long to reach a fire that the building and its contents were substantially destroyed, were not acting in the course of their employment, and so their employer was not liable for their default (*General Engineering Services* v *Kingston and St Andrew Corpn* [1989] 1 WLR 69, PC). An assault by bouncers was an unauthorised act but nevertheless within the course of their employment ('within the province of their proper duty generally to preserve the integrity of the club') (*Vasey* v *Surrey Free Inns plc* [1996] PIQR P373, CA). See the main text for other 'bouncer'-type cases. In *T* v *North Yorkshire County Council* (1998) 49 BMLR 150, the Court of Appeal held that where a teacher sexually abused a mentally disabled schoolboy entrusted to his care, that did not amount to the performance of his duties in an unauthorised manner, and therefore the local authority were not liable for the offence. But see also the *Lister* judgment from the House of Lords, detailed in the main body of the text.

began in the club but the stabbing took place later after the doorman had got home, armed himself with a knife and found his enemy on the street. The Court of Appeal said that the doorman was employed to keep order and to act in an aggressive and intimidatory manner, and it would be fair and just to hold the club vicariously responsible for the assault. It is in fact hardly surprising the club were held liable, given that the doorman had not been registered for doorman work by the licensing authority. Still in the salubrious realm of nightclubs, in *Naylor* v *Payling* [2004] PIQR P615 a customer was assaulted by a doorman. The doorman was employed by a security agent. That agent had a contract with the club to provide security. The agent had failed to take out any public liability insurance. So the customer sued the club instead of the agent. The customer did not seek to argue that the agent was an employee rather than an independent contractor, but that the club owed customers a duty to ensure that the agent was properly insured. The Court of Appeal rejected his claim, saying that the agent had reasonably appeared competent to the club, both originally and over the period of some 18 months prior to the assault, and it was not incumbent on the club to ensure that he was properly insured. This situation has arisen in the medical context also, for example, where a culpable locum GP has no insurance. He is not employed by anyone; he is an independent contractor, and it seems that the resident GP need do no more than book his locum (much more scope for that now that GPs do not need to be on night duty themselves!) through a reputable agency.

In *Attorney-General* v *Hartwell* [2004] PIQR P442, the Privy Council considered a claim against the Government of the British Virgin Islands as being vicariously liable for the injuries accidentally received by the claimant, a British holiday-maker, who was unfortunately in the line of fire when a policeman employed by the Government discharged a loaded firearm in a bar in pursuance of a personal vendetta against his wife and her suspected lover. The claimant succeeded in that the court said that the defendants were in breach of a duty of care in issuing the policeman with a firearm when they had failed to investigate two complaints that had earlier been made against him of violent behaviour. However, the point here is that they held the Government *not* to be vicariously liable for the assault, saying that the acts of the employee (he had travelled to a neighbouring island, not on duty, but with the express intent of seeking his wife out) were not sufficiently closely connected with those acts which he was authorised to do.

The 'scope of employment' principle could assume significance in a medical negligence context, in that, even though, as we shall see, there is a primary non-delegable duty of care imposed upon a trust or health authority, negligence by medical personnel falling outside the scope of their employment would not render the health authority or trust liable (for example, staff playing a game of cricket on the lawns and carelessly hitting the ball at a patient sitting in the sun, or an off-duty nurse running down a patient as she drives out of the grounds). In *Rosen* v *Edgar* (1986) 293 BMJ 552, the claimant, acting in person, sued a consultant for acts done by his senior registrar. It was held, as one would expect, that a senior employee was not answerable for the fault of a junior employee, for he did not employ him, albeit he had overall supervision of him. In *Godden* v *Kent and Medway Strategic Health Authority* MLC 1263, [2004]

Lloyds Rep Med P521, patients of a GP who had been convicted of assaulting them sued the health authority for breach of a duty of care at common law and deriving from s 29 of the National Health Service Act 1977, and as vicariously liable for the GP's torts. On an application by the defendant to strike out the claim, Gray J held that the contention of a duty of care failed (the health authority was not responsible under the Act for the provision of the relevant medical services – general practitioners were) except in so far as it was arguable that the defendant had a duty to act upon information it had earlier received about the GP's conduct. He was unwilling to strike out what would seem to be an impossible allegation that the health authority was liable vicariously for the GP's torts. It does not employ GPs. They are on contracts for services: in other words they are independent contractors. We await the trial with interest!

Whether an act falls within the course of employment is a question of fact in each case, and a broad view must be taken of all the surrounding circumstances.

It is, of course, always necessary to establish who is the employer. This used to be fairly easy in the medical field. The GP was responsible for the surgery and GP visits, the health authority for everything else. Then NHS trusts arose. They now proliferate, so that all sorts of medical care are in the control of different types of trust, whether a hospital trust or a community trust, or, now, primary care trusts. A health visitor, for example, may be employed by a GP, by a community trust, by a primary care trust or by a health authority. A GP may even be employed by a trust. Clinics may be run as part of a GP practice, or by a trust or a health authority. Who will be responsible for walk-in centres? Who is responsible for telephonic advice given by NHS Direct? The possibilities are legion. A claimant has to be careful, far more than before, to identify the source of the alleged negligence and ascertain who, if anyone, is the relevant employer. See below under 'Suing the wrong defendant'.

INDEPENDENT CONTRACTOR

As we have seen, there is in general no liability for the acts of an independent contractor, ie one who is free to perform the work contracted for in his own way. Sometimes, the factual matrix within which the question of 'independence' and control arises is complex. In *P v Harrow London Borough Council* [1993] 2 FCR 341, [1993] IFLR 723, a local education authority which, in furtherance of its duty under the Education Act 1981 to make provision for children with special educational needs, sent boys with emotional behavioural difficulties to an independent school approved by the Secretary of State for Education and Science, was held by Potter J not liable in negligence for sexual abuse committed on the boys by the headmaster of the school while the boys were in his charge. The contact between the local authority and the boys was said by the court to have been wholly in the context of assessment and place provision and not in the context of physical control or direction, which was at all times in the charge of the parents and the staff of the school. Compare *Lister* v *Hesley Hall Ltd* (above).

However, if the employer has a primary duty to perform an act, he will be liable if his agent in the performance of that act, whether independent contractor or not, performs the act negligently.[6] It is not generally clear to what extent a person has, apart from a contractual or statutory duty, a primary duty of care in respect of an activity,[7] although fortunately it is now beyond argument that under English law a health authority is under a primary non-delegable duty of care in respect of the treatment that is afforded the patient under its auspices.

It may be that the scope of the primary duty in law cannot as a general rule be extended beyond acts which create a source of danger. In respect of hazardous activities, the employer is liable for the negligence of an independent contractor. Liability is, however, restricted in all cases to acts which fall within the duty of care of the employer: he is not liable for the collateral negligence of the independent contractor, ie for acts which are not in fulfilment of the activity in respect of which the primary duty of care is imposed on the employer (a leading case is *Padbury* v *Holliday and Greenwood Ltd* (1912) 28 TLR 494, CA). The liability of the employer for the acts of the independent contractor should not be seen as an example of vicarious liability, that is to say liability assumed by one person on behalf of another, but rather as an example of the situation where a person is himself under a primary duty of care which he cannot delegate to another (see below under 'The primary duty of care').

HEALTH AUTHORITY OR TRUST AS DEFENDANT

The appropriate defendant when the action arises out of NHS treatment in hospital is the health authority or NHS trust (whichever was in charge of the hospital at the time of the alleged negligence).[8] A few hospitals have for years had special constitutions, so that the hospital itself or its board of governors is the appropriate defendant, but, usually, in the past a NHS hospital came within the jurisdiction of a health authority at district level, and it was that authority which had to be made the defendant. Now that virtually all hospitals have opted out of health authority control under the National Health Service and Community Care Act 1990 (though remaining, of course, within the NHS), the appropriate defendant if one is suing in respect of treatment at a hospital will be the new body. The hospital administrator will always provide the correct name of the body that runs the hospital.

However, it should always be borne in mind that the body responsible for any negligent conduct in NHS treatment is the body in charge of the

---

6   A primary duty can often be construed in a contractual context (see eg *Wong Mee Wan* v *Kwan Kin Travel Services Ltd* [1996] 1 WLR 38, PC, the case of the negligently driven speedboat on a Chinese package holiday).

7   A claim for a non-delegable duty of care as between a Lloyd's Name and his members' agent failed in *Aiken* v *Stewart Wrightson Members' Agency* [1995] 1 WLR 1281, Potter J.

8   The National Health Service Act 1977 provides by Sch 5, para 15: 'An authority shall, notwithstanding that it is exercising any function on behalf of the Secretary of State or another authority ... be liable in respect of any liabilities incurred (including liabilities in tort) in the exercise of that function in all respects as if it were acting as a principal. Proceedings for the enforcement of such ... liabilities shall be brought, and brought only ... against the authority in question in its own name.'

hospital at the time of the alleged negligence. This body may have changed its name or even disappeared as a separate body. It may simply have a new name. Or it may have merged. Or it may have been subsumed into an existing body or into a new body entirely. Although the legislature will always have provided for some body to have taken over the pre-existing liabilities of the old body (the NHS Litigation Authority if all else fails), it will *not* be the NHS trust that may now be running the hospital (a trust would not exactly be delighted to hear that its limited funds are going to be targeted to settle the health authority's liabilities!). Again, it is not difficult to find out the name of the body running the hospital at the time of the alleged negligence, and it is just as easy to find out, if that body is no longer extant under the same name, what body is now responsible for the pre-existing liabilities of the original body.

Action may be brought for an act or omission that is directly the responsibility of the authority, such as a failure to provide appropriate medical facilities (see, for example, *Bull and Wakeham* v *Devon Health Authority* [1993] 4 Med LR 117, CA, where the court found that the system of obstetric cover provided was not acceptable in that it gave rise to a real inherent risk that an obstetrician might not attend reasonably promptly); or for an act or omission that is directly the responsibility of the hospital, such as a failure to take appropriate general anti-infection measures (*Lindsey County Council* v *Marshall* [1937] AC 97, HL); or for specific acts of negligence by its staff.[9] By and large, all medical personnel working at the hospital may be regarded as employed by health authority or trust. Obviously, the nursing staff are and the resident doctors and technicians, but, even though, strictly speaking, senior staff and consultants are probably not 'employed', the point is, rightly, not taken (except in the case of private hospitals).

There is no point in adding the particular doctor as defendant where the health authority or trust is in any event clearly liable for any negligence on the doctor's part. It increases costs, delays the trial, and it may be unfair on a young doctor unnecessarily to turn the spotlight and put the pressure on him when he may have been doing his overworked best, perhaps also when he had been, for lack of better qualified staff, required to discharge a responsibility for which he was not yet properly trained (this is not just a matter of being gentlemanly, for it is not in anyone's interest to discourage or even destroy a young doctor in such circumstances).

SUING TWO DEFENDANTS

The situation often arises that there appear to be two different parties potentially liable, for example, GP and hospital, or two different hospitals run by different health authorities. Liability may be in the alternative or both may be severally liable. One is then anxious about costs in the event of succeeding against one only. This topic is considered in Chapter 13.

---

9   See *Robertson* v *Nottingham Health Authority* [1997] 8 Med LR 1 at 13, CA, *per* Brooke LJ.

SUING THE WRONG DEFENDANT

It is, of course, better to sue the correct defendant from the outset. In appropriate cases, the correct defendant may properly raise a plea of limitation where the claimant seeks to add or substitute him at a later stage. The rules on adding a new defendant in the context of limitation are not easy to understand (see Chapter 26 under 'Amending the claim'). However, it may not be necessary to enter the treacherous waters of limitation simply because you seek to change the name of the defendant. For example, a health authority is not going to object if you get the wrong title when you are clearly intending to sue that body. Perhaps that body now has a new name or has been subsumed into another already existing, or newly created, body. If, however, you have named a completely different health authority instead of the body that was in charge of the hospital at the relevant time, there may be a little more difficulty. On the other hand, it would be surprising if a health authority raised a plea of limitation where the mistake was to have sued the NHS trust in respect of negligence occurring at a time when the health authority was still in charge of the hospital.

If the wrong defendant has been sued, the mistake could probably be corrected pursuant to CPR, r 19.2, 19.5 or 17.4. In *Gregson* v *Channel Four Television Corporation* (2000) Times, 11 August, CA, the court said, echoing the previous law, that CPR 19.5 applied where the application was to substitute a new party for a party who was named in the claim form in mistake for the new party, and CPR 17.4(3) applied where the intended party was named in the claim form but there was a genuine mistake as to the name of the party and no-one was misled. The court said there was no significant conflict between the two rules. In this case CPR 17.4 applied: it was not a question of substituting a new party, and the judge's discretion in favour of the claimant had been correctly exercised. Sometimes it is not clear which GP in the practice saw the patient at the relevant time. Best then to sue the practice as a whole, or to plead liability on the ordinary principles of partnership.

Cases under the old rules (RSC)

Although the rules as such no longer exist, the approach of the court is not likely to differ fundamentally under the new rules. The old rule which permitted an amendment to correct the name of the party when there had been a mistake, provided the mistake did not cause any reasonable doubt as to the identity of the person intending to sue, was RSC, Ord 20, r 3, and the seminal case in recent years has been *Evans Construction Co Ltd* v *Charrington & Co Ltd* [1983] 1 QB 810, CA. In *Ritz Casino Ltd* v *Khashoggi* (29 March 1996, unreported), an amendment was permitted where the claimant had sued in the wrong company name upon two dishonoured cheques. In *Hibernian Dance Club* v *Murray* [1997] PIQR P46, CA, the court held that a mistake in suing the members and/or proprietors of the club under a collective title apt to describe them but devoid of personality at English law, as opposed to suing individually named defendants, was not such as to cause any reasonable doubt that the claim was being asserted against the membership as a whole. The provisions of RSC, Ord 20, r 5 were apt to cover such a case where the action had been hitherto a nullity because the claimant had sued an entity which did not exist in law.[10]

THE PRIVATE PATIENT

The private claimant has to be careful. Though a private clinic is responsible for its resident staff, on the basis that they are employed by the clinic, a consultant may be an independent contractor, engaged on a contract for services rather than a contract of service. If he is not employed by the clinic, the clinic will not be vicariously liable for his actions; and, furthermore, it is doubtful if a court would accept the argument that he was engaged to perform hazardous activities and for that reason the clinic must be held vicariously responsible if he is negligent in the course of performing them (one of the exceptions to the rule that a person who engages an independent contractor is not liable for his negligence, provided that due care was taken in the selection of the contractor). So the private patient will probably have to sue the consultant concerned if it is his acts or omissions that are alleged to be negligent. It is, however, arguable that, provided it was the clinic and not the patient that engaged the surgeon, albeit upon a contract for services, the clinic is under the same primary duty of care as an NHS hospital (there seems no reason to limit Lord Denning's words (see below) as to the primary duty of care to NHS institutions). Where a clinic, specialising in a particular form of treatment, eg liposuction or ophthalmic laser treatment, contracts with a patient to provide medical treatment, it is highly likely that the court would find that the clinic had a primary non-delegable duty of care in tort, or a similar duty on a proper construction of the contract.

In *Ellis* v *Wallsend District Hospital* [1990] 2 Med LR 103, the New South Wales Court of Appeal held that a public hospital was not vicariously liable for the acts of an 'honorary medical officer', a neuro-surgeon, who was treating a patient pursuant to a direct engagement between him and the patient. This case needs to be studied by anyone seeking to impose liability outside the NHS framework on a health authority or hospital for a doctor's negligence.

The Queen's Bench case of *Loft* v *Gilliat* [2003] MLC 1084 is of interest. A couple claimed damages for negligent advice given to the wife when she was awaiting implantation of her eggs (to be fertilised by a donor) with a view to conceiving a second child (the same way as her first had been conceived), her medical charge being in the hands of a private unit, the Infertility Advisory Centre. She was undergoing this treatment because her husband's sperm could transfer to the child his disease of Huntington's chorea. Mrs Loft claimed that prior to implantation of the eggs someone at the clinic (but not the defendant) advised her, amazingly, to have intercourse with her husband as that would make the uterus more receptive to the eggs. She then conceived a second daughter, but by her husband's sperm, not through the IVF treatment. The child was sadly suffering from the disease (her birth was in 1989 but the diagnosis was not made for some nine years, so there was no limitation problem for the

---

10   See also *Signet Group plc* v *Hammerson UK Properties Ltd* [1998] 03 LS Gaz R 25, CA.

mother's claim). Mrs Loft claimed financial compensation for her daughter's disability, but she did not claim against the company that owned the Centre at the relevant time because it was in liquidation. She sought to hold the medical director, Dr Gilliat, liable, on the basis that he was in charge of the clinic and that she had made the contract with him (he having represented the Centre at the contractual stages). At the relevant time he was not an employee of the company, he was an independent contractor, and he was not personally treating Mrs Loft at the time. The case was difficult. Dr Gilliat denied that he was liable to Mrs Loft by reason of his being in charge of the centre and he denied that he was vicariously liable for acts of the staff at the centre. His case was that the company was trading as the advisory centre. The contract was between the company and Mr and Mrs Loft. His contentions were accepted by the judge.

Contract

The private patient's relationship with her doctors and hospitals will depend from the contracts she makes with them. The NHS patient has no contract. An attempt to establish a general principle that an NHS patient has a contract with her GP failed in *Reynolds* v *Health First Medical Group* [2000] Lloyd's Rep Med 240 (this ploy was an endeavour in an unplanned pregnancy case to avoid being caught by the *McFarlane* decision – as to which see Chapter 24).

Charlesworth on Negligence (7th edn) at p 542 stated:

> The duty in contract is only owed to the parties to the contract, but it would seem that there is in most cases a contract between patient and medical practitioner, even if the patient himself is not liable for payment of the services rendered, such payment being made by someone else;

but no authority was given for that proposition. In *Emeh* v *Kensington and Chelsea and Westminster Area Health Authority* [1985] QB 1012, CA, Slade LJ spoke of the claimant 'contracting' with the health authority (though he was not concerned with this particular point). On the other hand, the Master of the Rolls appears to have assumed in *Hotson* v *East Berkshire Health Authority* [1987] AC 750, CA, *obiter* that an NHS patient is not in contractual relation with the NHS or its staff. It is in any event clear that, given a contract, the duty of care is owed both in contract and in tort (see *Midland Bank Trust Co* v *Hett Stubbs & Kemp* [1979] Ch 384), and that the claimant can elect which remedy to pursue.[11]

---

11 In *Lancashire and Cheshire Association of Baptist Churches Inc* v *Howard & Seddon Partnership* [1993] 3 All ER 467, it was held that there was no reason in principle why a duty of care in tort should not exist, and be sued upon, in the context of a contractual professional relationship. In *Henderson* v *Merrett Syndicates Ltd* (and associated cases) [1995] 2 AC 145, the House of Lords held that Lloyd's underwriting agents owed to various Lloyd's Names a concurrent duty of care in contract and in tort to carry out their underwriting functions with reasonable care and skill, and that the claimants could elect which remedy to pursue. In *Holt* v *Payne Skillington* [1996] 02 LS Gaz R 29, 77 BLR 51, CA, it was said that a duty in tort could in appropriate circumstances be wider than the concurrent duty in contract.

THE GP

If negligence is alleged against a GP or anyone employed by him (eg nurses, receptionists, secretaries), including any locum he engages, it is the GP who is the appropriate defendant (a physician was held liable for his apprentice's negligence in *Hancke* v *Hooper* (1835) 7 C & P 81).[12] It has to date seemed unlikely that he would be held to have a primary non-delegable duty towards the patient to ensure that any alternative care he arranges for when he is 'off' comes up to appropriate professional standards.[13] But with the development of primary care groups and primary care trusts and the transfer to them of so many of the previous functions of the health authority it would make sense, logical as well as practical, if the concept of non-delegable duty of care was extended to cover primary care (see below). The locum or doctor concerned in the alternative service is, of course, liable for any negligent act or omission on his part. But at the moment it is not easy to take the GP's liability for an independent locum further than to say that he must be reasonably satisfied of the competence of the deputising service he engages. GPs are engaged, on contracts for services, formerly by the Family Health Services Authority (more formerly the Family Practitioner Committee) acting for the health authority, but now FHSAs have been replaced by primary care trusts.[14] While the duty to provide GP care is in the hands of the local health authority, it may be possible to contend that the health authority is under a primary non-delegable duty to provide GP care, similar to its duty in respect of hospital care, and that therefore the health authority is liable for the GPs negligence (see below under 'The primary duty of care'). But this is the argument, it would seem, that was not accepted by Gray J in *Godden* v *Kent and Medway Strategic Health Authority*, at any rate as to a primary duty of care (see above). Probably, the GP does not have a contract with his patient, unless the patient is a private patient (see above under 'Contract'). A GP is not permitted to act privately for a patient who is on his NHS list (as one knows, the GP may refer the patient to a consultant who may treat privately). It might occasionally be the case that certain services carried out upon the premises of a general practice are performed by agents of the health authority or of some trust, rather than employees of the doctor, for example, immunisation services or, if it should come to this, AIDS screening and inoculation. Care always needs to be taken in identifying the employer. For example, the health visitor, the community nurse and the community midwife, though working closely with the GP, are usually employed by the health authority or

---

12   There can be rare cases where the GP was at the relevant time employed by an NHS trust pursuant to the National Health Service (Primary Care) Act 1997.

13   In *Lobley* v *Going* [1985] N–J & B 431, it was stated that if it was brought to a GP receptionist's attention that a small child had been brought to the surgery in an ill condition, with respiratory difficulties about which the parents were concerned, it was her duty to inform the doctor immediately and if she did not do so she would be guilty of negligence. It would follow that the employer GP, or GP practice, would be vicariously answerable for that negligence (on the facts it was held that she had not been negligent).

14   See *Roy* v *Kensington and Chelsea and Westminster Family Practitioner Committee* [1992] 1 AC 624, HL.

nowadays by some trust or other, and although they may be acting at times under the direction of the GP, it is the health authority (or trust) in such cases and not the GP who will be responsible for any mistakes they personally make. However, as stated above, the situation may well be getting more complex with the changes currently under way in primary care. Where the practice is a primary care trust, as opposed to a primary care group, the trust should be recognised as having legal personality, like any other NHS trust.

GPs are not obliged to insure, although it is likely to be a condition of any partnership agreement that participating doctors do insure. There is apparently no obligation on a consultant in private practice to insure, either, though he would be wise to![15]

THE PRIMARY DUTY OF CARE

The most important point about NHS hospital treatment is that it is not necessary to prove the facts that would give rise to vicarious liability, because the hospital has a primary non-delegable duty of care to provide proper treatment.

While the courts were still applying the distinction between employer and independent contractor for the purpose of establishing liability on the part of a hospital for the negligence of medical personnel, the nice distinctions of the common law mentioned above (eg as to whether the employer could control the manner in which the work was done) were important. So in *Hillyer* v *St Bartholomew's Hospital* [1909] 2 KB 820, CA, Kennedy LJ expressed the view that a hospital, though responsible for the exercise of due care in selecting its professional staff, whether surgeons, doctors or nurses, was not responsible if they or any of them acted negligently in matters of professional care or skill.

> I see no ground for holding it to be a right legal inference from the circumstances of the relation of hospital and patient that the hospital authority makes itself liable in damages if members of the professional staff, of whose competence there is no question, act negligently towards the patient in some matter of professional care or skill, or neglect to use or use negligently in his treatment the apparatus or appliances which are at their disposal (*per* Kennedy LJ).

It was even said that as soon as the nurses enter the operating theatre, the health authority was no longer liable for any errors they may make because they were then under the control of the surgeon, for whose errors the health authority was not responsible.

In *Davis* v *LCC* (1914) 30 TLR 275, a local education authority could not be held liable for a medical practitioner's negligence in carrying out an operation upon a school pupil if he had engaged a competent practitioner and if that practitioner was not in his employment.

In *Gold* v *Essex County Council* [1942] 2 KB 293, the Court of Appeal was concerned to distinguish between different types of staff: the hospital would not be responsible for the acts of a consulting surgeon or

---

15 An employee held out as a partner was held liable with the partners for negligence by any of them (*Nationwide Building Society* v *Lewis* [1997] 1 WLR 1181; revsd [1998] Ch 482, CA.

physician, but the position of a house physician or surgeon was left open. Goddard LJ said that responsibility for the position of doctors on the permanent staff would depend on whether the doctor was engaged on a contract for services or a contract of service. On the facts the defendants were responsible for the negligence of a radiographer who was a full-time employee.

In *Collins* v *Hertfordshire County Council* [1947] KB 598, Hilbery J considered that a hospital was responsible for the acts of a house surgeon but not for the acts of a part-time surgeon.

In *Cassidy* v *Ministry of Health* [1951] 2 KB 343, MLC 0001, CA, it was left to Lord Denning, as ever, to direct the law onto a path more appropriate to modern social needs. In that case, Somervell LJ was prepared to hold a hospital liable for the acts of permanent medical staff, those who were employed to provide the patient with nursing and medical treatment, but not for the acts of a visiting or consulting surgeon or physician. Both he and Singleton LJ decided for the claimant on the basis that, even though the claimant could not pinpoint the employee who had been negligent, there had clearly been negligence by one or more employees of the hospital.

Denning LJ said that the hospital was under a duty to take reasonable care of all patients, whether private or not. They would be discharging that duty through their staff, and it was no answer for the hospital to say that the staff concerned were professionals who would not tolerate any interference with the way they did their work. When hospitals undertook to treat a patient, and themselves selected and appointed and employed the professionals who were to give the treatment (as opposed to the patient himself selecting and employing the staff – which he would be doing if he were to ask a consultant to operate on him privately), the hospital was responsible for any negligence, no matter whether of doctors, surgeons, nurses or anyone else; and 'it does not depend on the fine distinction whether the medical man was engaged under a contract of service or a contract for services'.

> I take it to be clear law as well as good sense that where a person is himself under a duty to use care, he cannot get rid of his responsibility by delegating the performance of it to someone else, no matter whether the delegation be to a servant under a contract of service or to an independent contractor under a contract for services.

In *Roe* v *Minister of Health* [1954] 2 QB 66, McNair J at first instance held himself bound by the majority in *Cassidy*'s case to find that a specialist anesthetist who carried on a private anesthetic practice but was under an obligation to provide a regular service to the hospital concerned, and on the occasion in question had been assisting the theatre staff of the hospital, was not a person for whose acts the hospital could be held liable. On appeal, Somervell LJ said that he regarded the anesthetist as on the permanent staff of the hospital and therefore it would be liable for his errors. Morris LJ said that the hospital had undertaken to provide all the necessary facilities and equipment for the operation and the obligations of nursing and anesthetising. This was going some way towards Denning LJ's concept of a primary non-delegable duty of care, but Morris LJ was still basing himself on the maxim of vicarious liability, *respondent superior.*

Once again, it was Denning LJ who brushed aside nice distinctions with a robust and lucid exposition:

> I think that the hospital authorities are responsible for the whole of their staff, not only for the nurses and doctors, but also for the anesthetists and surgeons. It does not matter whether they are permanent or temporary, resident or visiting, whole-time or part-time. The hospital authorities are responsible for all of them. The reason is because, even if they are not servants, they are the agents of the hospital to give the treatment. The only exception is the case of consultants or anesthetists selected and employed by the patient himself.

Early cases, before the acceptance of the primary duty of care, are worth a glance.

Evans v *Liverpool Corpn* [1906] 1 KB 160, where a hospital was not liable for the negligent discharge by a physician of a boy still infectious from scarlet fever; *Hillyer*'s case (above), where the hospital was not liable for the burning of a patient's arms in the operating theatre; *Strangways-Lesmere* v *Clayton* [1936] 2 KB 11, no liability for the negligence of nurses in administering the wrong dosage (overruled by *Gold*'s case (above)); *Dryden* v *Surrey County Council and Stewart* [1936] 2 All ER 535, no liability for the discharge home after an operation of a patient with a wad of surgical gauze still inside her. *Junor* v *McNicol* (1959) Times, 26 March, HL, where a house surgeon was declared not liable for the negligent treatment of a child because he was acting under the instructions of the consultant. Surgeons were not liable for negligent bathing of a patient by nurses: *Perionowsky* v *Freeman* (1866) 4 F & F 977. A surgeon was not liable when a tube was found in the patient's body three months after surgery as it could have been put or left there by the nurses and house doctors any time since the operation: *Morris* v *Winsbury-White* [1937] 4 All ER 494.

These cases were important in the context of vicarious liability, when it mattered on whom the claimant could fix liability. Vicarious liability in the context of medical negligence may well still assume significance for the private patient, eg in the case of a private clinic, where the clinic may be able to avoid liability for the mistakes of a visiting consultant, though probably only where the patient has chosen and privately contracted with him, or, if the consultant is being sued himself, he may be able to avoid responsibility for the mistakes of others not under his direct control at the time.

The interaction between vicarious responsibility and the non-delegable duty of care, and the significance of the distinction between these two bases of liability, was considered by the Court of Appeal in the case of *Wilsher* v *Essex Area Health Authority* [1987] QB 730 (reversed on another ground by the House of Lords).[16]

In *X (minors)* v *Bedfordshire County Council* [1995] 2 AC 633, HL, Lord Browne-Wilkinson said:

> This allegation of a direct duty of care owed by the authority to the plaintiff is to be contrasted with those claims which are based on the vicarious liability of

---

16 Sir Nicholas Browne-Wilkinson V-C said: '... a health authority which so conducts its hospital that it fails to provide doctors of sufficient skill and experience to give the treatment offered at the hospital may be directly liable in negligence to the patient.'

the local authority for the negligence of its servants, ie for the breach of a duty of care owed by the servant to the plaintiff, the authority itself not being under any relevant duty of care to the plaintiff ...

This distinction between direct and vicarious liability can be important since the authority may not be under a direct duty of care at all or the extent of the duty of care owed directly by the authority to the plaintiff may well differ from that owed by a professional to the patient. However, it is important not to lose sight of the fact that, even in the absence of a claim based on vicarious liability, an authority under a direct duty of care to the plaintiff will be liable for the negligent acts or omissions of its servant which constitute a breach of that direct duty. The authority can only act through its servants.

The position can be illustrated by reference to the hospital cases. It is established that those conducting a hospital are under a direct duty of care to those admitted as patients to the hospital (I express no view as to the extent of that duty). They are liable for the negligent acts of a member of the hospital staff which constitute a breach of that duty, whether or not the member of the staff is himself in breach of a separate duty of care owed by him to the plaintiff.[17]

M v *Calderdale and Kirklees Health Authority* [1998] Lloyd's Rep Med 157 was, before being overruled, a case of great interest. A girl of 17, an NHS patient, was sent by her NHS consultant to a private clinic for a termination. She did not choose the clinic. She simply went where she was told to go. She remained pregnant, gave birth to a child, and obtained judgment for the negligence of clinic and surgeon. The surgeon was not insured and the clinic was being wound up. Naturally, she looked to the NHS for her damages. It is no credit to the defendants to report that they maintained that they had no liability for the errors of the private clinic and surgeon as they were independent contractors who had been chosen with all due care. The judge rejected their argument, holding that, both by virtue of s 1 of the National Health Service Act 1977 and at common law, they had a continuing primary non-delegable duty of care to the patient which was not discharged by their selection of a private clinic to perform the operation (he also found that they had not used due care in their selection of a clinic). He approved of the passage in *Clerk and Lindsell on Torts* (17th edn, 1995) para 5.16, to the effect that the hospital authority itself is under a duty to its patients which it does not discharge simply by delegating its performance to someone else, no matter whether the delegation be to an employee or an independent contractor. But now we have the Court of Appeal decision in *A* v *Ministry of Defence* [2004] Lloyds Rep Med 351 which expressly disapproves (of) the *Calderdale* decision. Negligence in a German hospital caused brain injury at birth to the child of a serving British soldier. Guy's and St Thomas' Hospital had undertaken to the MOD in 1996 to procure secondary medical care for servicemen in Germany and their dependants. The German medical units were called Designated German Providers (DGPs). The Court of Appeal held that there was no basis in law for

---

17   The Ontario Court of Appeal has reviewed the concept of the non-delegable duty of care and by a majority declined to follow the English cases (*Yepremian* v *Scarborough General Hospital* (1980) 110 DLR (3d) 513). Arnup JA said that great care had to be taken when considering the English cases as the interrelationship of the state, the medical profession, the hospitals and their patients had developed in England along different lines from those it had followed in Ontario.

imposing on the MOD a non-delegable duty of care in this context, ie a duty to ensure proper skill and care by the German hospital. The duty, as with the engagement of any independent contractor, was confined to an obligation to provide access to an appropriate system of hospital care provided by another, which duty was fulfilled by the exercise of reasonable care by the MOD in its selection of an agent (here Guy's and St Thomas') to procure DGPs.

Chapter 22

The proof of negligence

INTRODUCTION

There are a number of difficulties a claimant faces in proving negligence. They include the problem of ascertaining exactly what was done in the course of treatment, of securing expert evidence which will allege and substantiate a want of due care, of proving a causative link between the treatment and the injury, and of overcoming any possible pro-doctor prejudice in the mind of the judge, and, if the matter goes further, the appeal court.

The burden of proving negligent conduct resulting in injury is upon the claimant. Where there is no direct or circumstantial evidence which permits a conclusion to be drawn as to how the accident happened, the claimant may pray in aid the maxim *res ipsa loquitur* (the matter speaks for itself). This applies where what happened is not the sort of thing that would normally happen in the absence of negligence in some form or another. The court may then find that there was negligence even though it is not known what form that negligence took. If the defendants give a reasonable explanation as to how the accident might have happened without negligence, or show that they had in fact taken every possible care of the patient, the court will not be entitled to rely on the maxim.

CLOSING RANKS

It is common knowledge that it has in the past been extremely difficult to prove that a doctor has been negligent. The usual reason given for this is that you could not find an expert who is willing to accuse a colleague. This is known as the 'closing ranks' syndrome, and it no doubt has contributed to patients' difficulties, particularly where the specialty concerned is a narrow one, for its practitioners will almost certainly all know each other, so that the reluctance to accuse of negligence is all the more pronounced. Fortunately it is easier these days to get a fair assessment of a patient's treatment than it was, due largely to greater expertise in choosing experts.

JUDICIAL PREJUDICE

But there are other reasons why it is hard to prove medical negligence. One reason is, or at any rate has been, the anti-patient, or generally anti-claimant, prejudice of some judges. To read some of the older cases, one would think that the patient was virtually guilty of *lèse-majesté* in bringing an action. Up till recently the track record of some judges, often those who made a good living at the Bar defending personal injury claims, afforded depressing evidence of their prejudice. Even in the Court of Appeal, practitioners were able to identify a senior judge of that persuasion (identification is possible merely by perusing his judgments over the years). The retirement of these judges has ameliorated the position, though they can unfortunately be recalled for the odd case. Though an appeal judge does not make findings of fact, he can usually find an excuse, if he wants one, to reverse the court of first instance, whether on law, on fact (even the verdicts of libel juries can now, apparently, be overturned), or on discretion. This matter of judicial bias is one of the reasons why medical negligence claims are always unpredictable and why it is always best to get some sort of more or less reasonable settlement rather than risk an anti-claimant tribunal.

Another problem, though not one of bias, is judicial ignorance or inexperience. No attempt is made by the listing officers to give medical claims to a judge who has had some experience, at the Bar or in office, of such cases. Perhaps that would for the most part be logistically impossible. But the result is that complex claims are often heard by a judge who has no background knowledge of medical matters, and, though no doubt his (or her) acumen is acute, he (or she) can be misled by a smooth talking expert (for the defence usually) or can simply grab hold of the one issue he (or she) actually understands and decide the case on that basis. For some unfortunate consequences see the cases below under 'Must a judge give reasons for his conclusions?'.

DIFFICULTIES IN CAUSATION

Another obstacle to proving a claim for compensation is that, even if one knows what specific acts or omissions were alleged to have been negligent, one has to prove that not only did they constitute a less than reasonable standard of care, but also that they were the cause of injury or loss to the patient. Negligence is not actionable without proof of loss or injury arising from the negligent acts or omissions. But the etiology of medical conditions is notoriously complex and obscure. Would the correct or timely treatment have prevented death or resulted in the patient being better off than he actually is? How to prove that a particular act or omission caused any part of the claimant's present condition? Can one give, and is it relevant to give, an estimation of the chances of proper treatment having saved or helped him? The problem of causation, of showing that what was done or omitted was not only negligent by professional standards but also caused or may have caused a deterioration in the condition of the patient that would not otherwise have occurred, is considered above in Chapter 17.

BURDEN OF PROOF

The burden of proving what needs to be proved to establish a case rests on the claimant. It has been said that there are no special rules about the burden or standard of proof in cases involving professional negligence, but that it must necessarily be harder to prove negligence where a case concerns the 'complicated and sophisticated professional activities of a doctor, lawyer or architect' (*Dwyer* v *Roderick* (1983) 80 LS Gaz R 3003, 127 Sol Jo 805, CA).

In *Hucks* v *Cole* MLC 0604, [1993] 4 Med LR 393, CA, Lord Denning had said that:

> A charge of negligence against a professional man was serious. It stood on a different footing to a charge of negligence against the driver of a motor car. The consequences were far more serious. It affected his professional status and reputation. The burden of proof was correspondingly greater. As the charge was so grave, so should the proof be clear.

It is clear that that does not represent the modern law.[1]

In *Ashcroft* v *Mersey Regional Health Authority* MLC 0337, [1983] 2 All ER 245, the judge said that the question was whether it had been established on a balance of probabilities that the physician had failed to exercise the care required of a man possessing and professing special skill in circumstances which required the exercise of that special skill. No added burden of proof rested on the claimant. The more skilled a person was the more care which was expected of him. That test should be applied without gloss either way (Kilner Brown J).

The claimant has to persuade the court that the only explanation for the injury that can reasonably be accepted is one that involves negligence. If the court cannot select between two explanations for complications following treatment, only one of which involves negligence, then the claimant has not proved his case (*per* Beldam J in *Harrington* v *Essex Area Health Authority* (1984) Times, 14 November).[2]

In *Clark* v *MacLennan* [1983] 1 All ER 416, Pain J said that where in the context of a general duty of care there had been a failure to take a generally recognised precaution which had been followed by damage of the kind that that precaution was designed to prevent, the burden of proof shifted to the defendant to show either that he was not in breach of duty or that the damage was not caused by the breach. In that case there had been a departure from the usual practice of not performing a certain operation for stress incontinence within three months of delivery; that departure was found to have been unjustified and therefore constituted a

---

1   The same thing may be said for the odd pronouncement from Lord Denning in *Bater* v *Bater* [1950] 2 All ER 458, CA (approved by the Court of Appeal in *Hornal* v *Neuberger Products Ltd* [1956] 3 All ER 970, Lord Denning being a party thereto) to the effect that the degree of probability required to establish proof could vary with the gravity of the allegation. Are we supposed to think, for example, that 51% probability is enough to prove negligence against a shopkeeper or builder, but 75% is required against a doctor? Hardly!

2   A judge is entitled to conclude that he simply does not know what happened, in which case, if *res ipsa loquitur* does not apply, the claim fails (*Ratcliffe* v *Plymouth and Torbay Health Authority* [1998] Lloyd's Rep Med 162, CA).

breach of the duty of care. It was followed by a consequence that that precaution was designed to prevent, ie breakdown of the repair effected in
the operation, and it was therefore up to the defendants to satisfy the
court that that damage had not flowed from their breach of duty to the
patient. However, it was expressly denied by the House of Lords in
Wilsher v *Essex Area Health Authority* MLC 0016, [1988] AC 1074 that
the burden shifted in such circumstances. In *Gregory* v *Pembrokeshire
Health Authority* MLC 0596, [1989] 1 Med LR 81 at 85, Rougier J rejected
the suggestion that whenever the fault complained of was a fault in omission the burden of proving causation shifted to the defendants: 'the burden of proof on the balance of probabilities remains on the plaintiff
throughout'.

In *Defreitas* v *O'Brien* [1995] 6 Med LR 108, CA, Otton LJ said the
Bolam test did not impose any burden of proof on the defendant to establish that his diagnosis or treatment would be acceptable to a responsible
body of medical opinion. The burden of proof was on the claimant.

Lost records

It is a sad fact of life that if, as not uncommonly transpires, vital records
are 'missing' a claim that could otherwise be proved may fail. However,
Latin may help here. In *Malhotra* v *Dhawan* [1997] 8 Med LR 319, the
Court of Appeal, considering the maxim *omnia praesumuntur contra spoliatorem*, indicated that inferences could be drawn against a party who
had destroyed relevant evidence (although the court said the maxim only
applied where that had been done to stop the other party showing how
much of his property had been taken).[3] In *Le Page* v *Kingston and
Richmond Health Authority* MLC 0610, [1997] 8 Med LR 229, John
Samuels QC, sitting as a deputy judge of the Queen's Bench Division,
said that the defendants could not properly complain if he drew inferences from surviving documentation which might have been contradicted
by other records which they had improperly destroyed.

In *Skelton* v *Lewisham and North Southwark Health Authority* MLC
0662, [1998] Lloyd's Rep Med 324, the inadequacy of the anesthetic notes
(brief, unsigned, without a record of key events and pressures), although
not causative of the damage, was said by the judge to be indicative of an
unexplained carelessness. In *Rhodes* v *Spokes and Farbridge* MLC 0640,
[1996] 7 Med LR 135, Smith J said:

> A doctor's contemporaneous record of a consultation should form a reliable evi-
> dential base in a case such as this. I regret to say that Dr Farbridge's notes of
> the plaintiff's attendances do not provide any such firm foundation. They are
> scanty in the extreme. He rarely recorded her complaints or symptoms; he
> rarely recorded any observations; usually he noted only the drug he prescribed
> ... The failure to take a proper note is not evidence of a doctor's negligence or of
> the inadequacy of treatment. But a doctor who fails to keep an adequate note
> of a consultation lays himself open to a finding that his recollection is faulty

---

3   In *Dobson* v *North Tyneside Health Authority* [1997] 1 WLR 596, the Court of Appeal
said that for the maxim to apply it had to be shown that the spoliator was a 'wrongdoer'.

and someone else's is correct. After all, a patient has only to remember his or her own case, whereas the doctor has to remember one case out of hundreds which occupied his mind at the material time.

RES IPSA LOQUITUR

What we consider here is a situation that often arises, where not merely is it unclear why the patient's condition has deteriorated or what the cause must have been of the injury he suffered, but where he cannot even point to any act or omission and say that that was wrong, and in all probability caused his present condition, because the only acts or omissions he knows to have taken place are unimpugnable. Therefore, all he can say is that something must have been done which should not have been done, because his injury could not have arisen without something having been done wrong. This is the principle of evidence known as *res ipsa loquitur*, 'the matter speaks for itself'.

There must be reasonable evidence of negligence. But where the thing is shown to be under the management of the defendant or his servants, and the accident is such as in the ordinary course of things does not happen if those who have the management use proper care, it affords reasonable evidence, in the absence of explanation by the defendant, that the accident arose from want of care (*per* Erle CJ in *Scott* v *London and St Katherine Docks Co* (1865) 3 H & C 596, Ex Ch).

The maxim applies where 'the circumstances are more consistent, reasonably interpreted without further explanation, with ... negligence than with any other cause of the accident happening' (*per* Kennedy LJ in *Russell* v *London and South-western Rly Co* (1908) 24 TLR 548 at 551, CA).

The court is in any event entitled to make an inference as to how an accident happened upon the evidence before it. It may be that no one can give direct evidence of how it happened, but, if the evidence that is given permits a reasonable inference to be drawn as to the cause, the court in drawing such an inference is not applying the principle of *res ipsa loquitur*, for that principle only applies where the cause cannot be specified, whether upon direct evidence or by inference.

> If the facts are sufficiently known the question ceases to be one where the facts speak for themselves, and the solution is to be found by determining whether on the facts as established negligence is to be inferred or not (*per* Lord Porter in *Barkway* v *South Wales Transport Co Ltd* [1950] 1 All ER 392 at 395, HL).

An example of this type of inference is found in the case *Clowes* v *National Coal Board* (1987) Times, 23 April, in which the Court of Appeal said that, where there is no clear evidence of an accident but the court knows of habitual careless behaviour which could have caused it, the court may assume that to be the cause in the absence of any other explanation.

The maxim is also misapplied if it is sought to be used where it is known what the doctor did and the dispute is as to whether that constituted negligence. A surgeon performing a laminectomy may penetrate too far and injure the nerve or the spinal cord. One cannot say indignantly: 'Of course it was negligent; the matter speaks for itself.' That is simply a misunderstanding of what the maxim means in law. It would be up to expert evidence to establish whether or not any surgeon exercising due care could make that mistake.

The statement of claim usually pleads that the claimant will pray in aid the principle of *res ipsa loquitur*, but that would appear to be unnecessary if the pleading is otherwise complete as to the facts alleged (see *Bennett* v *Chemical Construction (GB) Ltd* [1971] 3 All ER 822, CA).

The maxim has often been applied where a defendant is carrying out lifting or building operations and the claimant is injured by a falling article. It is not known what made it fall, but the court declares that it would be unlikely to have happened without negligence.

In *Howard* v *Wessex Regional Health Authority* MLC 0603, [1994] 5 Med LR 57, Morland J said that *res ipsa* could not help the patient where she had sustained tetraplegia following maxillo-facial surgery by way of a sagittal split osteotomy, because her injury was most likely due to a fibro-cartilaginous embolism, which would not connote negligence. As the helpful note by Margaret Puxon QC at the end of the report of *Howard* shows, it appears that the defendants, as not infrequently happens in medical cases, advanced their explanation for the injury very late in the day. It seems surprising that the judge accepted it.

In *Delaney* v *Southmead Health Authority* MLC 0582, [1995] 6 Med LR 355, the patient alleged that she had sustained damage to her arm as a result of negligent placing during surgery. The Court of Appeal upheld the finding of the judge in favour of the defendants. They said that, even if *res ipsa* applied, it was always open to a defendant to rebut a case of *res ipsa* either by giving an explanation of what happened which was inconsistent with negligence or by showing that he had exercised all reasonable care. Stuart-Smith LJ doubted that the principle was useful in medical negligence actions, at least not where 'all the evidence in the case has been adduced',[4] and Dillon LJ said:

> I cannot for my part accept that medical science is such a precise science that there cannot in any particular field be any room for the wholly unexpected result occurring in the human body from the carrying out of a well-recognised procedure.[5]

In *Jacobs* v *Great Yarmouth and Waverney Health Authority* MLC 0710, [1995] 6 Med LR 192, a case of anesthetic awareness, the Court of Appeal said (in 1984) that *res ipsa loquitur* meant no more than that on the facts that a claimant was able to prove, although he might not be able to point to a particular negligent act or omission on the part of the defendants, the fair inference to draw was that there had been negligence of some sort on the part of the defendants; but if there were further evidence presented

---

4   Judge Thompson QC commented on this observation in *Ritchie* v *Chichester Health Authority* [1994] 5 Med LR 187 at 206.

5   Stuart-Smith LJ offered further thoughts on the principle of *res ipsa* in *Fallows* v *Randle* [1997] 8 Med LR 160 at 163, CA, where he cited a passage from Megaw LJ in *Lloyde* v *West Midlands Gas Board* [1971] 1 WLR 749 at 755, CA. The Court of Appeal decision in *Ratcliffe* v *Plymouth and Torbay Health Authority* [1998] Lloyd's Rep Med 162 repays study. It shows that a judge is entitled to conclude that he simply does not know what happened, and that in such circumstances there is no presumption that *res ipsa* applies.

by the defendants, those facts might be shown in an entirely different light so that it would not be possible to draw the inference of negligence.

In *Hooper* v *Young* MLC 0602, [1998] 2 Lloyd's Rep Med 61, CA, Otton LJ said that it was a pity *res ipsa* had ever entered the case because it had no place where the event that caused the injury (damage to a ureter by kinking of the suture) could have happened without negligence.

In *Girard* v *Royal Columbian Hospital* (1976) 66 DLR (3d) 676, where the patient had suffered permanent paralysis of both legs after a spinal anesthetic, the Canadian judge, Andrews J, exonerating the anesthetist, used words similar to Dillon LJ in the *Delaney* case (above):

> The human body is not a container filled with a material whose performance can be predictably charted and analysed. It cannot be equated with a box of chewing tobacco or a soft drink. Thus, while permissible inferences may be drawn as to the normal behaviour of these types of commodities, the same type of reasoning does not necessarily apply to a human being. Because of this, medical science has not yet reached the stage where the law ought to presume that a patient must come out of an operation as well as or better than he went into it.

In *Bull and Wakeham* v *Devon Area Health Authority* MLC 0022, [1993] 4 Med LR 117, CA, two of the judges differed on the question whether *res ipsa* applied to the failure of the hospital to have an obstetrician attend the mother at the vital time, Mustill LJ taking the view (at 142) that as the facts of the 'accident' were largely known the principle did not apply.

Despite the sporadic judicial observations disapproving of a plea of *res ipsa*,[6] the maxim serves a purpose when properly used. How did an eight-year-old mentally retarded child come to be on a main road when she should have been in the care of her school? No one knew. But the application of *res ipsa* led to the conclusion that in some way or another there must have been a want of care on the part of the school staff (*J* v *North Lincolnshire County Council* [2000] PIQR P84, CA).

Rebuttal

The defendant may rebut the presumption of negligence, but not merely by showing the general precautions he had taken. It is not entirely clear on the authorities how far the defendant must go to shift the onus of proof back to the claimant, in particular, whether he has to show a possible or a likely cause of the accident that would not involve negligence. It was said in *Moore* v *R Fox & Sons* [1956] 1 QB 596, CA, that it was not sufficient for the defendants to show several hypothetical causes consistent with the absence of negligence and that the accident might have occurred without negligence on their part; to discharge the onus they had to go further and either show that they had not been negligent (it would seem to be enough in this connection if the defendants satisfied the court that all possible precautions had been taken) or give a reasonable explanation of the cause of the accident which did not connote negligence.

---

6   'There is substantial doubt whether *res ipsa loquitur* is ever susceptible to refined arguments and detailed analysis of authority, *per* Judge LJ (*Carroll* v *Fearon, Bent and Dunlop Ltd* [1998] PIQR P416, CA – a claim for injury caused by a defective tyre).

It was said in *Ng Chun Pui* v *Lee Chuen Tat* [1988] RTR 298, PC, that the burden of proving negligence remains upon the claimant, despite the applicability of the doctrine of *res ipsa loquitur*.

The cases make it clear that one must draw a distinction between the situation where there is more than one possible cause for the injury and the situation where the precise cause is unknown. In the second situation one may be able to take advantage of the maxim. In the first situation it is simply a matter for the judge to decide what was the operative cause, and, in doing this, he is entitled to prefer the evidence of one expert to another (*Fallows* v *Randle* [1996] MLC 0591 is an example of this; reference may also be made to *Betts* v *Berkshire Health Authority* [1997] 8 Med LR 87). He may also draw inferences from the evidence. In *Skelton* v *Lewisham and North Southwark Health Authority* MLC 0662, [1998] Lloyd's Rep Med 324, Kay J decided that the only possible explanation on the facts for the administration of certain drugs preoperatively was an episode of hypotension causing brain injury. In *Bull* v *Devon Area Health Authority* MLC 0022, [1993] 4 Med LR 117, CA, Slade LJ said that the trial judge had gone further than he needed when he found that the claimant had excluded all possible causes of his injury other than that for which he contended, because it would have been sufficient to make the less unqualified finding that the cause for which he contended was established on the balance of probabilities.

Whose negligence?

In some of the older cases, the issue has been whether it can be shown that the negligence the court is asked to infer must have been that of the defendant himself or one of his agents and not that of someone for whom the defendant was not responsible. One would, therefore, encounter the problem as to who was the servant or agent of the surgeon and who was the servant or agent of the hospital (see Chapter 21). Now that most cases are brought against the NHS trust or health authority, which is responsible for all the medical personnel involved in the treatment of the patient, this particular issue is not likely often to arise (it could still be relevant in the field of private practice and in cases against a GP). Suffice it to say that the claimant must show that the accident could not reasonably have happened without some want of care on the part of the defendant himself or his agents.

Examples

When one considers the number of times the maxim has been accepted by a court as an aid to its decision, one can only wonder why it has come in for such bad press recently. Probably the answer is that it is due to unnecessary and inapposite recourse to it by claimant's lawyers in many cases.

Whether or not the accident is one which the court will find would not usually happen without some negligence somewhere will depend on expert evidence. Things can go wrong in operations without there being any negligence. Denning LJ had this to say in *Cassidy* v *Ministry of Health* [1951] 2 KB 343 at 365, MLC 0001:

If the plaintiff had to prove that some particular doctor or nurse was negligent he would not be able to do it. But he was not put to that impossible task: he says, 'I went into the hospital to be cured of two stiff fingers. I have come out with four stiff fingers, and my hand is useless. That should not have happened if due care had been used. Explain it if you can.' I am quite clearly of the opinion that that raises a *prima facie* case against the hospital authorities: see *per* Goddard LJ in *Mahon* v *Osborne* [1939] 2 KB 14, 50. They have nowhere explained how it could happen without negligence. They have busied themselves in saying that this or that member of their staff was not negligent. But they have not called a single person to say that the injuries were consistent with due care on the part of all the members of their staff. They called some of the people who actually treated the man ... but they did not call any expert at all to say that this might happen despite all care. They have not therefore displaced the *prima facie* case against them ...

Both Somervell LJ and Singleton LJ agreed that the facts disclosed a *prima facie* case of negligence on the basis of *res ipsa loquitur* ([1951] 2 KB 343 at 348, 353).

In *Roe* v *Minister of Health* [1954] 2 QB 66, patients in hospital for minor operations were paralysed by the spinal anesthetic each was given:

The judge has said that those facts do not speak for themselves, but I think that they do. They certainly call for an explanation. Each of these men is entitled to say to the hospital: 'While I was in your hands something has been done to me which has wrecked my life. Please explain how it has come to pass' (*per* Denning LJ at 81).

Morris LJ said:

When [the claimants] proved all that they were in a position to prove they then said *res ipsa loquitur*. But this convenient and succinct formula possesses no magic qualities: nor has it any added virtue, other than that of brevity, merely because it is expressed in Latin. There are certain happenings that do not normally occur in the absence of negligence, and upon proof of these a court will probably hold that there is a case to answer.

However, in this case, the hospital gave an explanation of the accident which was accepted by the court as absolving them from any negligence (the ampoules of anesthetic had been kept in a solution of phenol, which seeped into the anesthetic after the ampoules had developed in some way or another tiny, undetectable cracks or molecular flaws. At that time such a possibility and the danger arising therefrom were totally unknown).

In this case Lord Denning also referred to the position where both hospital and private doctor deny negligence but give no explanation for the patient's injury. He said:

I do not think that the hospital authorities and [the doctor] can both avoid giving an explanation by the simple expedient of throwing responsibility on to the other. If an injured person shows that one or other or both of two persons injured him, but cannot say which of them it was, then he is not defeated altogether. He can call on each of them for an explanation.

In *Saunders* v *Leeds Western Health Authority and Robinson* MLC 0657, [1993] 4 Med LR 355, the heart of a four-year-old girl stopped for some 30 minutes during an operation under anesthetic to remedy a congenitally deformed hip. The defendants agreed that did not normally happen without a want of care somewhere but they offered an explanation as to how the accident might have happened. Mann J rejected their explanation and said:

> The plaintiff's reliance on *res ipsa loquitur* makes it unnecessary for her to suggest a specific cause for the cardiac arrest. It is plain from evidence called on her behalf that the heart of a fit child does not arrest under anaesthesia if proper care is taken in the anesthetic and surgical processes.

This decision has been thought to constitute a helpful departure for claimants in the court's willingness to infer negligence, at any rate in the context of injury under or from anesthetic; but, though the case is certainly not without significance as a precedent, it is important to note that the defendants admitted here that the principle of *res ipsa* applied to the facts. See also *Glass* v *Cambridge Health Authority* [1995] 6 Med LR 91.

In *Moore* v *Worthing District Health Authority* MLC 0981, [1992] 3 Med LR 431, Owen J rejected a plea of *res ipsa* where a patient was left with bilateral ulnar nerve palsy following a mastoidectomy. He absolved the defendants from failing to protect the arms properly while the patient was under anesthetic by accepting their contention that the patient had been abnormally vulnerable to such an injury, despite the absence of any real evidence of such a condition. One wonders if this is an example of a contrived explanation of an injury by the defence being accepted by a judge who is reluctant to find doctors guilty of mismanagement.

Other examples

In *Mahon* v *Osborne* [1939] 2 KB 14, where the surgeon was sued when a swab was left inside the patient, the majority of the Court of Appeal was of the view that the principle did not apply in the case of a complex operation where a number of medical staff took part, but it is now clear that the correct view was that taken by Goddard LJ when he said:

> There can be no possible question but that neither swabs nor instruments are ordinarily left in the patient's body ... If therefore a swab is left in the patient's body, it seems clear that the surgeon is called upon for an explanation. That is, he is called upon to show, not necessarily why he missed it but that he exercised due care to prevent its being left there.

This view was endorsed by the Court of Appeal in *Urry* v *Bierer* (1955) Times, 15 July, where there was a dispute as to which of the two, surgeon or nurse, had the responsibility for seeing all the swabs were removed after an abdominal operation. As mentioned above, now that the hospital will be liable in almost all cases for the negligence of any of those who treat the patient, this sort of tedious analysis of who had what responsibility and who was whose agent is unlikely to arise.

Reference may also be made to *Cavan* v *Wilcox* (1973) 44 DLR (3d) 42, where the maxim was applied to the situation of a patient who developed gangrene after he had been given an injection in his arm; and to *Fish* v *Kapur* [1948] 2 All ER 176, where it was held that the maxim did not apply where a dentist's patient's jaw was broken during an extraction.

In *Clarke* v *Worboys* (1952) Times, 18 March, where the patient's buttock was burnt in electro-coagulation treatment, the Court of Appeal reversed the judge's finding and held that the evidence showed that such an accident would not happen if reasonable care were used.

The maxim was successfully invoked by the widow of a man who was asphyxiated when he swallowed a dental throat pack (*Garner* v *Morrell* (1953) Times, 31 October).

In *Ludlow* v *Swindon Health Authority* MLC 0611, [1989] 1 Med LR 104, where the claimant alleged she had been awake during a Cesarian section as a result of what must have been the negligent administration of the anesthetic, the judge said that for the doctrine of *res ipsa loquitur* to apply, the claimant had first to establish that she had indeed been awake during the operation. As he was not satisfied of that the doctrine could not help her.

In *Leckie* v *Brent and Harrow Area Health Authority* [1982] 1 Lancet 634, it was held that a 1.5 cm cut on the cheek of a baby delivered by Cesarian section would not happen without some lack of care. The matter spoke for itself.

Reasonable traction could have caused the claimant's lesion of the musculocutaneous nerve, as could also excessive traction, and so the maxim could not help him, in the case of *Levenkind* v *Churchill-Davidson* [1983] 1 Lancet 1452.

The claimant was successful in *Woodhouse* v *Yorkshire Regional Health Authority* [1984] 1 Lancet 1306. She was a pianist whose ulnar nerves were severely damaged in an operation for a subphrenic abscess. The judge said that the evidence established that this sort of injury would not occur if the standard precautions to avoid this recognised hazard had been taken. The Court of Appeal upheld his decision. *Contra O'Malley-Williams* v *Governors of National Hospital for Nervous Diseases* (1975) 1 BMJ 635, where it was held that the maxim did not apply where partial paralysis was sustained by the claimant (who was also an accomplished pianist) because the injury sustained was recognised as an inherent risk of the treatment undergone, namely an aortagram for recurrent episodes of loss of vision in the right eye.

In *Brazier* v *Ministry of Defence* [1965] 1 Lloyd's Rep 26, the defendants satisfied the judge that he should not infer negligence on the part of a person giving an injection to the claimant as the cause of the needle breaking, because the actual cause could properly be inferred to be a latent defect in the shaft of the needle (similarly in *Corner* v *Murray* [1954] 2 BMJ 1555).

In the Scottish case of *Fowler* v *Greater Glasgow Health Board* 1990 SLT 303n, a court of first instance was unable to infer negligence in treatment from the fact that the doctors had failed later to give the parents of a dead child an explanation of what had happened.

In *Coyne* v *Wigan Health Authority* MLC 0573, [1991] 2 Med LR 301, the defendants agreed that *res ipsa* applied when hypoxia leading to brain damage occurred during recovery from a routine operation, but they failed to satisfy the judge that it was due to the (non-negligent) cause of silent regurgitation of gastric content. Therefore the matter did 'speak for itself' and the claimant succeeded.

For another application of the maxim, see the final part of the judgment of Waterhouse J in *Bentley* v *Bristol and Weston Health Authority (No 2)* MLC 0339, [1991] 3 Med LR 1 (damage to the sciatic nerve during a total hip replacement).

APPEALS AND THE BURDEN OF PROOF

The principles of appeal

The two most significant principles of law affecting appeals are: (a) the trial judge had the great advantage of seeing and hearing the witnesses, whether lay or expert, and so the appeal tribunal must be very slow to interfere with those findings (as opposed to the *inferences* which the judge drew from his findings or from facts not in dispute); and (b) the exercise of a discretion by the judge should not be invalidated merely because the appeal tribunal would have exercised their discretion differently. The second principle comes to the fore in medical negligence claims upon the issue of discretion under s 33 of the Limitation Act 1980, which is treated at length in Chapter 26. What we consider here is the extent to which the Court of Appeal has on occasions interfered with the findings and conclusions of the trial judge and how it has justified such interference. In *Pickford* v *ICI* [1997] 8 Med LR 270, CA, Stuart-Smith LJ said:[7]

> I am well aware of the inhibitions laid upon this court in interfering with and reversing the trial judge's findings of fact, especially primary findings. The law is succinctly summarised in the Annual Practice at paragraph 59/1/55 and is very familiar to any member of this court. I do not propose to set it out *in extenso*. We were also referred by Mr Hytner to a passage in the speech of Lord Bridge of Harwich in *Wilsher* v *Essex Area Health Authority* [1988] AC 1074 where he reminded the court that similar principles apply in relation to the evaluation of disputed medical evidence. But it is our duty to reconsider the matter, paying great weight to the opinion of the trial judge, especially where there is a conflict of evidence and the demeanour and bearing of the witness plays a significant part in the judge's decision.

And Ward LJ said in *Briody* v *St Helens and Knowsley Health Authority* MLC 0099, [1999] Lloyd's Rep Med 185:

> Although this court is well able to consider the medical records as they stand, the case depended on more than drawing inevitable inferences from those statements and the judge had the unenviable task of assessing the witnesses and deciding, if there were a conflict, which evidence he preferred. Although I do not shrink from overruling him if, on full consideration, I come to the conclusion that he was wrong, nonetheless, due weight is to be given to the decision of the judge at first instance and I need to be satisfied that his overall conclusion was *plainly* wrong. That requires a close look at the whole of the evidence.

The advantage enjoyed by the trial judge extends to the hearing of expert witnesses. In *Wilsher* v *Essex Area Health Authority* MLC 0016, [1988] AC 1074, HL, Lord Bridge said (at 1091):

> Where expert witnesses are radically at issue about complex technical questions within their own field and are examined and cross-examined at length about their conflicting theories, I believe that the judge's advantage in seeing them and hearing them is scarcely less important than when he has to resolve some conflict of primary fact between lay witnesses in purely mundane matters.

---

7   The actual decision of the Court of Appeal in this claim for repetitive strain injury was reversed by the House of Lords ([1998] 1 WLR 1189), but not so as to invalidate the above cited remarks of Stuart-Smith LJ.

In *Wardlaw* v *Farrar* MLC 1079, [2004] Lloyds Rep Med 98, a fatal accident claim over the death of the defendant GP's patient arising out of a failure to consider a diagnosis of pulmonary embolism and so arrange hospital admission, the Court of Appeal said that the judge had evidently been much more impressed by the expert cardiological evidence called for the defendant and there was clear authority that an appellate court should be very slow to interfere with a trial judge's views on the quality of the evidence of expert witnesses whom he had had the advantage of seeing and hearing; so the court would not interfere with the judge's assessment and the appeal was dismissed.

In *Gray* v *Southampton & South West Hampshire Health Authority* [2001] MLC 0662, a claim for brain damage sustained in or around a surgical procedure, the Court of Appeal said that where the trial judge had not rejected the evidence of the attending anesthetist it was not open to them to reach conclusions of primary fact the effect of which would be to reject such evidence.

Must a judge give reasons for his conclusions?

A judge does not always have to spell out his reasons for every conclusion to which he comes (*Abada* v *Gray* (1997) 40 BMLR 116, CA, a personal injury claim where the trial judge was held to have been entitled to prefer the defendant's medical evidence, even though he had made no express findings of fact). But where no inference as to the judge's reasoning can reasonably be drawn from a judgment that did not make express findings on relevant issues, a retrial will be ordered (*Sewell* v *Electrolux Ltd* (1997) Times, 7 November, CA).

In *Eckersley* v *Binnie* (1988) 18 Con LR 1 at 77, CA, Bingham LJ said:

> In resolving conflicts of expert evidence the judge remains the judge; he is not obliged to accept evidence simply because it comes from an illustrious source; he can take account of demonstrated partisanship and lack of objectivity. But, save where an expert is guilty of a deliberate attempt to mislead (as happens only very rarely), a coherent reasoned opinion expressed by a suitably qualified expert should be the subject of a coherent reasoned rebuttal, unless it can be discounted for other good reason.

Many, if not most, medical negligence trials are decided by the judge's preference for the evidence of one expert rather than another. So important is the quality of expert and the evidence he gives, and the manner in which he gives it, that judicial comments on experts in all medical negligence cases are now collected on the database of *Medical Litigation* (at www.medneg.com). Of course, it does not follow that an expert is not a good expert simply because a judge does not accept his evidence. He may have failed to impress the judge for any number of peripheral reasons. But if he is explicitly criticised by the judge, as is not uncommon, perhaps for being partial or lacking independence, or 'going too far', or it is said that he vacillated or changed his tune, there is usually a good reason for such criticism.

In *Stefan* v *General Medical Council* (1999) 49 BMLR 161, the Privy Council said that, although at common law there was no general duty to give reasons universally imposed on all decision-makers, the trend of the law had been towards an increased recognition of the duty upon decision-makers of many kinds (the case involved a challenge to a decision of the health committee of the GMC that the appellant's fitness to practice was seriously impaired due to mental condition and the consequent indefinite suspension of his registration).

In *English* v *Emery Reimbold & Strick* [2002] 1 WLR 2409, a personal injury claim where the critical issue was whether a disabling dislocation of the claimant's spine was attributable to an injury for which the defendant was responsible, the Court of Appeal gave guidelines on how and when to appeal on the ground that the trial judge's reasons for his decision were inadequate. The court said: (1) it was the judge's duty to produce a judgment that gave a clear explanation for his order. (2) An unsuccessful party should not seek to upset a judgment on the ground of inadequacy of reasons unless, despite the advantage of considering the judgment with knowledge of the evidence given and submissions made at trial, that party was unable to understand why it was that the judge had reached an adverse decision. (3) The effect of the human rights legislation and Strasbourg jurisprudence [yes, it crept in here, too] was that a decision should be reasoned; however the extent of the reasoning did not go further than that required under domestic law. (4) The practice of giving no reasons for a decision as to costs could only comply with Article 6 of the European Convention on Human Rights if the reason for the decision was implicit from the circumstances in which the award was made. (5) The following course was recommended to deal with cases where inadequacy of reasons was at issue. When an application for permission to appeal on the ground of lack of reasons was made to the trial judge, the judge should consider whether his judgment was defective. If he concluded that it was, he should set out to remedy the defect by the provision of additional reasons, refusing permission to appeal on the basis that he has adopted that course. If he concluded that the reasons were adequate he should refuse permission to appeal. If an appellate court found an application for permission to appeal well founded, it should consider adjourning the application and remitting the case to the trial judge with an invitation to provide additional reasons for his decision or, where appropriate, his reasons for a specific finding. Where the appellate court was doubtful as to the adequacy of the reasons it was appropriate to adjourn to an oral hearing on notice. Where permission to appeal was granted the appellate court should review the judgment in the context of the evidence and submissions at trial in order to determine whether it was apparent why the judge reached his decision. If satisfied that the reason was apparent then the appeal should be dismissed. If the reason for the decision was not apparent then the appeal court should decide whether itself to proceed to a new hearing or to direct a new trial.

Examples

In the professional negligence (surveyors, not medical) case of *Flannery* v *Halifax Estate Agencies* [2000] 1 WLR 377, CA, Henry LJ said that the professional judge today owed a duty to give reasons, although there were some exceptions (not relevant for our purposes). He said it was not a useful task to attempt to make absolute rules as to the requirement for the judge to give reasons, because issues were so infinitely various. But with expert evidence it should usually be possible to be more explicit in giving reasons (he cited *Eckersley* v *Binnie* (above)). The parties should be left in no doubt why they had won or lost. Further, a requirement to give reasons concentrated the mind of the judge, so that his deliberations would probably be more soundly based on the evidence. The extent of the duty depended on the subject matter. Where the dispute involves something in the nature of an intellectual exchange, with reasons and analysis advanced on either side, the judge must enter into the issues canvassed before him and explain why he preferred one case over the other. This was likely to apply particularly in litigation where, as in the instant case, there was disputed expert evidence. The court said that in the instant case the judge's preference for the defendants' expert, which was decisive, should have enabled him to give his reasons in the form of the 'coherent reasoned rebuttal' referred to by Bingham LJ in the *Eckersley* case. So the judge had been under a duty to give reasons but had not done so. The court could not know whether he had had adequate or inadequate reasons for his conclusion. In the circumstances the appeal by the claimants was allowed.

On the other hand, consider the medical case of *Polson* v *de Silva* [1999] MLC 0076, CA. This had been a successful claim against a GP for failing to respond to a mother's request to visit her sick child at home, with the result that the child sustained hearing loss from meningitis. The court said that the judge had carefully considered the evidence and had been fully entitled to prefer the expert evidence of the two consultant physicians for the claimant over that of the defendant's expert witness. There was an ample basis for the judge to conclude that earlier treatment would have avoided the deafness. Clearly, in this case the court was satisfied that the judge had properly considered the evidence and had had valid reasons for preferring the evidence of the claimants' experts.

In *Lakey* v *Merton, Sutton and Wandsworth Health Authority* [1999] MLC 0075, the patient appealed against a finding that a decision by the hospital not to X-ray the patient's leg had not been negligent. The argument was that the judge had failed to evaluate the evidence of the two experts and to make clear findings as to what part of the evidence of each he accepted and what part he rejected. The Court of Appeal gave this issue careful consideration, stating that in order to weigh the submissions *it was necessary to analyse the manner in which the judge expressed his conclusions* (my emphasis). The court concluded that in fact the judge had explained his reasoning very fully and had 'explained himself at considerable length', relying on at least six specific reasons. It is interesting to note that towards the end of his judgment, Thorpe LJ said:

> I suspect that in this field of litigation it is not uncommon for the forensic experts to take relatively extreme positions in the hope of securing an outcome for the party by whom each is instructed. I suspect also that in this case the judge found that each was guilty of some error in presentation.

It is also important to note that the learned Lord Justice said:

> So it seems to me that it is not incumbent on a judge to explain at great length why he has found the expert contribution perhaps partisan and perhaps unhelpful. His function is to explain clearly the conclusions which he has reached, and Mr Justice Holland certainly did that in this case with exemplary clarity and logic.

In the cervical smears case (*Penney, Palmer and Cannon* v *East Kent Health Authority* MLC 0068, [1999] Lloyd's Rep Med 123; affd MLC 0126, [2000] Lloyd's Rep Med 41 CA), the claimants had two histopathologists, the defendants three. The two sides were in total disagreement over what the smears disclosed (the evidence about interpreting smears was immensely technical), but even more significantly over what the average screener, exercising due care, should have written in his or her report. By and large, the claimants' experts said the warning of 'borderline' changes should have been signalled. The defendants' experts said that writing up the reports as 'negative' was not unreasonable (the claimants had gone on to suffer invasive cancer).

The judge concluded that a proper standard of care had not been shown. He based his conclusion on the fact that at almost every point he *preferred the evidence of the claimants' experts*. Using the words of *Bolitho* (see Chapter 14), he said he did not consider the evidence of the defendants' experts stood up to logical analysis.

The Court of Appeal dismissed the defendants' appeal.

In *Ludlow* v *National Power plc* (17 July 2000, unreported), CA, the court said that a judge was required to give reasons for a decision so that a party was in no doubt as to why he had lost and could assess whether the decision was properly appealable. However, the particular judgment left no doubt as to why the claimant had failed to satisfy the judge that an accident at work had caused psychiatric illness. The judge had preferred the evidence of the defence psychiatrist on the issue, and this he had been entitled to do as he had taken the view that that expert had had a wider range of relevant experience than the claimant's expert.

Compare *Coleman* v *Dunlop Ltd* [1998] PIQR P398, CA, in which a new trial was ordered where, in a claim for repetitive strain injury sustained at work, the judge had simply stated a preference for the defence consultant on the basis of wider relevant experience without making appropriate findings of primary fact and explaining her inferences therefrom. Henry LJ said:

> In my opinion, on trial of the action it is the duty of the judge first to resolve the issues before him and to give reasons. It is true that, in relation to matters in these courts, there is no statutory duty on the judge to give reasons. It is also true that for a long time it has been contended that the common law imposed no such duty. But the common law is a living thing, and it seems to me that the point has now come where the common law has evolved to the point that the judge, on trial of the action must give sufficient reasons to make clear his findings of primary fact and the inferences that he draws from those primary facts sufficient to resolve the live issues before him, explaining why he has drawn those inferences.

In an industrial liability case it was said that the judge should have given intellectual reasons for his preference (*Dyson* v *Leeds City Council* (22 November 1999, unreported)). In *Smyth* v *Greenhouse Stirton & Co* (4 October 1999, unreported), it was said that explicit reasons for preferences were not necessary where they could be inferred from the judgment. In *Matthews* v *East Sussex Health Authority* [1999] MLC 0170, the judge had been entitled to give particular weight to the evidence of the defence pathologist. In *Carr* v *Stockport Health Authority* [1999] MLC 0082, the judge had been entitled to prefer the evidence of one lay witness to another without referring specifically to their demeanour.

In *SmithKline Beecham Biologics SA* v *Connaught Laboratories Inc* (1999) 51 BMLR 91, the Court of Appeal said that in all cases the judge's judgment ought to provide a coherent summary of the issues, the evidence and the reasons for the decision, whether the judgment is delivered orally in open court, or handed down in open court in written form with copies available for the press and public.

In *Temple* v *South Manchester Health Authority* [2002] MLC 0846, a claim for alleged mismanagement in the treatment in hospital of a child's diabetic ketoacidosis, the Court of Appeal, dismissing the claimant's appeal, said that although the reasons the judge gave for accepting the views of an expert pediatrician called for the defence were open to some criticism, such criticisms could not by themselves outweigh or undermine the positive impression made by her oral testimony, supported in substantial measure by the published material. Similarly, in *Clifford* v *Grimley* [2001] EWCA Civ 1658 (not a medical case) the Court of Appeal said that the extent of the trial judge's duty to give sufficient reasons for his conclusions was dependent on the subject matter in each individual case. A short analysis of the evidence in this case was held to be sufficient.

In *Montanaro* v *Home Office* [2002] MLC 0777, Sedley LJ said the giving of reasons was a key judicial function and there was little use in giving reasons if a full and accurate record of them was not made (see below for further details).

In *Gow* v *Harker* [2003] MLC 1035, a claim for injury caused through mismanagement of a blood test, the Court of Appeal said that, when on the evidence there were so many improbabilities and at least one apparent impossibility, and the judge did not address the issues in his judgment adequately or at all, his judgment could not be upheld, the defendant's appeal succeeded and a new trial was ordered in front of a different judge. Similarly, in *Glicksman* v *Redbridge Health Care NHS Trust* [2001] MLC 0219, a claim for alleged negligent performance of the repair of a suspected incisional hernia, the Court of Appeal, discerning in the judgment below no reasoned rebuttal of any expert's view in circumstances which called out for definition of the issues, marshalling of the evidence and for reasons to be stated, ordered a new trial in front of a judge experienced in medical negligence.

See also *Baird* v *Thurrock Borough Council* (7 November 2005, unreported), CA, where the court invalidated a finding of liability by the judge as he had given no reasons for preferring the claimant's evidence to the contrary evidence of two other lay witnesses.

Practice Direction

A relevant *Practice Direction* ([1999] 1 WLR 2) tells us that the court which has just reached a decision is often in the best position to judge whether the case is or is not one where there should be an appeal. The appeal court will rarely interfere with a decision based on the judge's evaluation of oral evidence as to the primary facts or if an appeal would involve examining the fine detail of the judge's factual investigation. Leave is more likely to be appropriate where what is being challenged is the inference which the judge has drawn from the primary facts, or where the judge has not received any particular benefit from having actually seen the witnesses, and it is properly arguable that materially different inferences should be drawn from the evidence. The appeal court will not interfere with the exercise of discretion of a judge unless the court is satisfied the judge was wrong. The burden on an appellant is a heavy one.

Recent appeals

The following brief survey of appeals and their outcome may help to give some further indication of the approach of the Court of Appeal in medical cases and, most significantly, their treatment of a judge's findings of fact. Appeals turning on points of substantive law are not considered here as they feature in other parts of the book.

Successful appeals by the defendant

Marwan Nawaf Nayef Raji-Abu-Shkara v *Hillingdon Health Authority* MLC 0617, [1997] 8 Med LR 114 (Waite, Roch, Auld LJJ): the court allowed the defendants' appeal from the judge's finding that the respiratory arrest that had caused the claimant's brain damage had been due to a failure of medical and nursing care. This is a good example of the court's willingness to make its own assessment of the evidence given below, form its own conclusions about its effect, and reverse the judge on the ground that he had no reason to reject the defence evidence and no good reason to reach the conclusions that he did.

Robertson v *Nottingham Health Authority* MLC 0644, [1997] 8 Med LR 1 (Sir Stephen Brown P, Roch, Brooke LJJ): this claim alleged perinatal brain damage due to hypoxia that should have been avoided. The judge found negligence but no causation. On appeal by both parties the court was prepared on the evidence to enlarge the period of culpable delay in delivering the child, but said that, even given the longer period, the judge would still have found that the injury had been sustained before the period of culpable delay began.

Tahir v *Haringey Health Authority* MLC 0632, [1998] Lloyd's Rep Med 104, CA (Leggatt, Otton LJJ, Sir Ralph Gibson): the trial judge found negligent delay in attending to the claimant's symptoms but rejected the claimant's case that the delay had caused his serious neurological injury, and she awarded modest compensation for a small increment in the extent of the injury. The defendants succeeded on appeal on the ground that there had been no evidence before the judge on which she could properly find that the delay had caused any additional injury.

Hooper v *Young* MLC 0602, [1998] Lloyd's Rep Med 61, CA (Stuart-Smith, Waite, Otton LJJ): the defendants succeeded on appeal on the ground that the evidence did not permit the judge to conclude that pre-operative injury to a ureter by kinking of the suture had happened through negligence, seeing that it could equally have happened without negligence and there was nothing in the evidence making the former more likely. Stuart-Smith LJ offered the observation that it was important that the court did not make facile findings of negligence against doctors.

Ratty v *Haringey Health Authority* MLC 0638, [1994] 5 Med LR 413 (Balcombe, Kennedy, Evans LJJ): the court, having made yet another careful analysis of medical evidence adduced at first instance, found themselves persuaded to set aside a finding by the judge of negligence in undertaking and performing colorectal surgery consequent upon a diagnosis of cancer. The court upheld only a minor aspect of the claim, and so reduced the award from nearly £130,000 to £5,000.

Hughes v *Waltham Forest Health Authority* MLC 0605, [1991] 2 Med LR 155, CA (Fox, Butler-Sloss, Beldam LJJ): the court reversed the judge's finding that there had been negligence in the management of the deceased's gastric pathology, on the basis that the evidence called by the defendants established that a body of responsible opinion would find the management to have been acceptable. And the court (*obiter*) reversed the judge's finding on causation, saying that the evidence did not establish that the management, whether negligent or not, had been an effective cause of death.

Knight v *West Kent Health Authority* MLC 0057, [1998] Lloyd's Rep Med 18 (Kennedy, Morritt, Chadwick LJJ) is a good example of how carefully the Court of Appeal will scrutinise the evidence to see whether the judge's findings of negligence can be supported. In this case a critical issue was whether the baby's head was higher in the vaginal canal at the time when it was admitted and whether the consultant should have intervened. This was important because two hours later the mother suffered substantial injury from a strenuous forceps delivery, and it was alleged that at the earlier time the head would have been higher and so a Cesarian section and not a forceps delivery would have been indicated. The court concluded that there was insufficient evidence for the judge's finding that the baby's head would have been too high for a forceps delivery. They also said that the judge's other determinative finding, that the forceps delivery was not performed to a proper standard of care, depended upon her conclusion that the obstetrician had encountered resistance when starting to pull, which was not supported by the evidence.

Dunn v *Bradford Hospital NHS Trust* [1999] MLC 0084 (Beldam, Chadwick LJJ): there was no proper evidence on which the judge could base his conclusion that it was through negligence that the claimant had fallen from a hospital trolley. The Court of Appeal also strongly criticised the judge for his disparaging remarks about the defence lawyers, which it said were quite without foundation.

In *Burke* v *Leeds Health Authority* [2001] MLC 0314, CA, where the judge had found that the oncologists recommending treatment by intense chemotherapy for a child's leukemia were negligent not to have told the parents that it would be possible, though not optimum, to delay treatment for a while, the defendant's appeal succeeded on the basis that the judge's finding of breach of duty could not be sustained in the absence of any expert evidence supporting such a conclusion. The treatment had led to spastic quadriplegia.

Unsuccessful appeals by the claimant

Scott v *Wakefield Area Health Authority* MLC 0659, [1997] 8 Med LR 341, CA (Beldam, Ward, Schiemann LJJ): the claimant unsuccessfully contended that the judge's conclusion that the defendants had not negligently managed his visual disability was not supported by the evidence.

Jacobs v *Great Yarmouth and Waverney Health Authority* MLC 0710, [1995] 6 Med LR 192 (Stephenson, O'Connor, Griffiths LJJ – judgment given in 1984): the claimant unsuccessfully contended that the judge had not been entitled to find on the evidence that her 'anesthetic awareness' had been post-operative, not preoperative.

Delaney v *Southmead Health Authority* MLC 0582, [1995] 6 Med LR 355 (Dillon, Butler-Sloss, Stuart-Smith LJJ – judgment 1992): the claimant unsuccessfully argued that the finding of the trial judge was against the weight of the evidence when he concluded that her brachial plexus lesion had not been caused by improper placing of her arm during her cholecystectomy.

Sellers v *Cooke* MLC 0660, [1990] 2 Med LR 16, CA (Slade, Balcombe, Butler-Sloss LJJ): the trial judge found that neither negligence nor causation had been established in this claim for negligent obstetric attention resulting in the death of the fetus. The Court of Appeal dealt only with causation (because there had been a successful application to admit fresh evidence on appeal relating to negligence), and concluded that in any event, ie regardless of whether the fresh evidence might have persuaded them that the judge's finding on negligence could not stand, his negative conclusion on causation (that the child would have died anyway) could not be successfully challenged.

Gregory v *Pembrokeshire Health Authority* MLC 0596, [1989] 1 Med LR 81 (O'Connor, Nicholls, Taylor LJJ): the judge found that the claimant mother should have been told that the amniocentesis sample had been inadequate, but that she would have accepted what would have been the consultant's advice, namely not to risk another amniocentesis; so she failed on causation because her Down's syndrome child would have been born in any event. The Court of Appeal felt unable to interfere with this negative finding on causation, emphasising, as it always does except where it wants a different result, that the judge, who had heard and seen the witnesses, was in the best position to assess the evidence, and to draw inferences from and reach conclusions upon it.

Sherlock v *North Birmingham Health Authority* ((1997) 40 BMLR 103, [1998] JPIL 230) (Pill, Henry, Chadwick LJJ): the Court of Appeal refused to interfere with the judge's findings that, even though the advice of the paediatric senior registrar should have been sought, he would not have advised transfer to the intensive care unit (the procedure that would probably have avoided respiratory collapse of the patient) and that it would not have been mandatory to effect such transfer.

Lavelle v *Hammersmith and Queen Charlotte's Special Health Authority* (16 January 1998, unreported) (Hirst, Henry, Auld LJJ): where the new-born claimant was disastrously injured during a balloon atrial sepostomy (to correct his congenital heart condition) and there were two possible ways the injury could have been caused, only one of which involved negligence, the trial judge was held to have been entitled to conclude on the evidence that it had not been proved that the injury had been caused in the negligent manner.

Brock v *Frenchay Healthcare Trust* MLC 0101, [1999] MLC 0101 (Simon Brown, Auld, Thorpe LJJ): the judge's finding could not be faulted where he concluded that the delay in administering Mannitol after a head injury had not affected the outcome.

Brown v *Lewisham and North Southwark Health Authority* MLC 0081, [1999] Lloyd's Rep Med 110 (Beldam, Morritt, Mantell LJJ): the judge had been entitled to conclude that there was no evidence to support the claimant's contention that the journey by way of transfer between a London and a Blackpool hospital had been an effective cause of the deep vein thrombosis that led to loss of a leg.

Hallatt v *North West Anglia Health Authority* MLC 0055, [1998] Lloyd's Rep Med 197 (Hobhouse, Swinton Thomas, Buxton LJJ): the judge had been entitled to find that a single and isolated observation of mild glycosuria during pregnancy at 29 to 30 weeks did not mandate a glucose tolerance test.

Matthews v *East Suffolk Health Authority* [1999] MLC 0170 (Henry, Robert Walker LJJ, Alliott J): the finding by the judge that prompt treatment with antibiotics would not have lessened the brain damage sustained by the appellant, because it had already occurred, was upheld.

Carew v *Bexley and Greenwich District Health Authority* [1999] MLC 0125 (Peter Gibson, Pill, Chadwick LJJ): the judge had fairly concluded that there were no warning signs of a mother's pre-eclampsia and that the single failure to take a urine sample was not causative of the child's brain damage as it would probably not have yielded a significant result.

Lakey v *Merton, Sutton and Wandsworth Health Authority* [1999] MLC 0075 (Nourse, Thorpe, Potter LLJ): the judge had been entitled to conclude that the A & E decision not to X-ray a patient presenting with gross pain in the right hip was reasonable.

Vadera v *Shaw* [1998] MLC 0335 (Henry, Otton, Buxton LJJ): the judge had been entitled to find on the evidence that a single high reading was not a basis for a finding of hypertension, and that there was no substantive history of headaches in this patient, who alleged that the contraceptive pill, Logynon, had caused her to have a stroke.

Morris v *Blackpool Victoria Hospital NHS Trust* [2004] MLC 1169, CA: this was an obstetric case where it was agreed all round that a further scan would have revealed IUGR (inter-uterine growth retardation) and the child would then have been delivered promptly so as to avoid his brain injury. The judge's finding that the child had not been suffering from IUGR went wholly against the weight of the evidence and the Court of Appeal were bemused by it. But the appeal by the claimant failed notwithstanding, because the judge's other important finding that there had been no mandatory indication to perform another scan, and therefore no breach of duty (and so, of course, no causation), was reasonable, said the appeal court, and was not affected by his substandard performance on the wholly distinct IUGR issue.

Successful appeals by the claimant

Arkless v *Leicestershire Health Authority* (22 October 1998, unreported), Medical Litigation 11/98 p 6 (Stuart-Smith, Otton, Tuckey LJJ): given the findings of fact of the Recorder as to the presence of clinical signs of congenital displacement of the hip at the 6–9 months check and the view of the defence expert that examination should have detected such signs, the only conclusion open to the judge should have been that the health visitor had not conducted a competent examination.

In a claim by a prisoner that a prison doctor had negligently failed to diagnose his scaphoid fracture, the court allowed his appeal on the ground that the trial judge's interventions had been made largely against the claimant and the judge had had no warrant for finding that no fracture had been sustained by the time the doctor saw the prisoner and the claimant had therefore not had a fair trial (human rights featured prominently) – *Montantaro* v *Home Office* [2002] MLC 0777.

Starcevic v *West Hertfordshire Health Authority* [2001] MLC 0428, is an interesting case. The main issue in this appeal from Kennedy J was whether the deceased had complained of pain and swelling in his calf and on that issue whether the widow's account or the medical staff's account should be preferred. On consideration of all the evidence the appeal court concluded that the only possible conclusion was that the widow's evidence should have been accepted by the judge, her appeal was allowed and agreed damages awarded.

Webb v *Barclays Bank plc and Portsmouth Hospitals NHS Trust* MLC 0400, [2002] PIQR P61, was not strictly a successful appeal by claimant though it resembled one; it occurred in the following circumstances. Mrs Webb sustained a fall while employed by Barclays. Upon advice from a doctor at the hospital she underwent an amputation. She sued both employer and hospital, the former for failing to provide a safe environment for work, and the latter for negligent advice causing her to have an amputation which she did not need. The bank settled the totality of her claim and served a contribution notice on the hospital alleging that the advice to accept an amputation had been negligent and that Mrs Webb would have declined an amputation had she been given proper advice. Mrs Webb did not give evidence at the trial of the contribution issue. The judge was not satisfied that causation was proved. But The Court of Appeal said that there was ample evidence to show that if she had been given proper advice she would have declined the amputation. Therefore the contribution notice was valid and the appeal was allowed.

Unsuccessful appeals by the defendant

Fallows v *Randle* MLC 0591, [1997] 8 Med LR 160, (Stuart-Smith, Peter Gibson, Ward LJJ): a failed sterilisation case, where the court dismissed the defendants' appeal, saying that it had been open to the judge to prefer the evidence of the claimant's expert as to the probable reason why the clip was found not to be on the Fallopian tube.

Lybert v *Warrington Health Authority* MLC 0712, [1996] 7 Med LR 71 (Nourse, Millett, Otton LJJ): the court refused to interfere with the judge's finding that no proper warning of the failure rate had been given before a sterilisation, or that in the particular circumstances of the case where the couple were awaiting the claimant's hysterectomy they would have taken the added (and admittedly unusual) precaution of using a condom while waiting for the hysterectomy. Comment: it was certainly open to the appeal court on the evidence to have come to directly contrary conclusions; so this has to be seen as a sympathetic decision (see further Chapter 24).

Bull and Wakeham v *Devon Area Health Authority* MLC 0022, [1993] 4 Med LR 117, CA (Slade, Dillon, Mustill LJJ): the defendants failed to persuade the court to reverse the judge's findings that they did not have in place an adequate system of obstetric care and that that had caused or contributed to perinatal injury. This case offers useful material on the (theoretically) limited scope for the appeal court to interfere with findings based on a judge's assessment of the oral evidence.

O'Keefe v *Harvey-Kemble* (1998) 45 BMLR 74 (Swinton Thomas, Potter LJJ): the Recorder had been entitled to find that insufficient information had been given to the patient before a breast reduction operation and that she would have declined the procedure if properly informed of the risks. Reading between the lines of the judgments, one gets the impression that the judges were a little surprised at the Recorder's dismissal of the defence evidence, but nevertheless felt unable to interfere with his conclusions.

Briody v *St Helens and Knowsley Health Authority* MLC 0099, [1999] Lloyd's Rep Med 185 (Simon Brown, Ward, Walker LJJ): the court would not interfere with the vital finding that the obstetrician had failed to satisfy himself that the head was likely to be a good fit for the pelvis.

Burrows v *Forest Healthcare NHS Trust* [1999] MLC 00149: the judge had been entitled to find that it had been negligent not to open a third port when performing a laparoscopy and that, had that been done, the small bowel would probably not have been cut.

Penney, Palmer and Cannon v *East Kent Health Authority* [2000] Lloyd's Rep Med 41, [1999] MLC 0126, (Lord Woolf, May and Hale LJJ) the Canterbury cervical smears case: the judge found that the *Bolam* principle did not apply because there was no dispute about acceptable or unacceptable practice, only a factual dispute about whether the cytoscreeners had given the wrong classification to smears; but, even if the principle had applied, he was satisfied that the evidence of the three experts called by the defence did not stand up to logical analysis because the cytoscreeners did not have the ability to draw a distinction between benign and pre-cancerous cells, and so should have classified the smears as borderline. On the defendants' unsuccessful appeal the court said that the *Bolam* test did apply as the cytoscreeners were exercising skill and judgment in determining what report they should make, but they agreed with the judge that the logical analysis test was applicable and that it led to the conclusion that the exonerating opinion of the defence experts did not stand up to such analysis.

Polson v *de Silva* [1999] MLC 0076, CA (Simon Brown, Waller LLJ): the defendants failed in their attempt to invalidate the judge's conclusion that treatment some 48 hours after the symptoms of bacterial meningitis had appeared would probably have avoided deafness.

Note that other examples can be found in the various preceding sections dealing with appeals, particularly the section headed 'Must a judge give reasons for his conclusions?'.

Chapter 23

Consent[1]

Any operation or treatment which involves an invasion of the patient's bodily integrity requires his consent, or that of his guardian. Without consent the operation is a battery, and damages can be recovered without proof of fault. If the patient would have consented if asked, and the operation has benefited him, damages are likely to be nominal. The patient must be in a fit condition, ie *compos mentis*, to give consent. Consent to treatment is not valid if the nature and purpose of the proposed treatment have not been explained in broad terms to the patient. Once that has been done, however, the consent will not be invalid merely because the risks of the operation were not explained, but an action in negligence may lie, provided the patient would not have accepted the treatment if he had known the risks, and no responsible body of medical opinion would have approved of the failure to disclose them.

ASSAULT AND BATTERY

We start from the premise that any contact by the physician with the patient's body, whether by laying hands on it, eg for an operation, for an injection, for massage or, less directly, by the use of a machine directing electro-magnetic or other waves at the body, eg radiotherapy, chemotherapy, X-rays, sound or heat treatment, is *prima facie* or potentially a trespass to the person, as involving an invasion of the patient's bodily integrity.[2]

It is not significant whether the conduct complained of is termed a trespass, an assault or a battery. The nub of it is the unlawful, intentional application of force to the person of another.

> If a man intentionally applies force direct to another, the plaintiff has a cause of action in assault and battery, or, if you so please to describe it, in trespass to the person ... (*per* Lord Denning, in *Letang* v *Cooper* [1965] 1 QB 232, CA).

---

1   The Department of Health has issued detailed guidance on consent (see Appendix VII for the full text).
2   Every human being of adult years and sound mind has a right to determine what shall be done with his own body; and a surgeon who performs an operation without the patient's consent commits an assault (*per* Cardozo J in *Schloendorff* v *Society of New York Hospital* 105 NE 92 (NY, 1914)).

It is generally thought that the interference with the claimant's bodily integrity has to be by way of an intentional act; otherwise the cause of action lies in negligence (see *Fowler* v *Lanning* [1959] 1 QB 426). An intention to injure is not essential, but the act that violates the bodily integrity of the claimant, ie the contact, must be intentional. In *Wilson* v *Pringle* [1987] QB 237, the Court of Appeal said, in the context of the horseplay that goes on between schoolboys, that the contact must be proved to be a hostile contact. Hostility was not to be equated with ill-will or malevolence, and would be a question of fact. Clearly, one cannot require any sort of hostility to be proved when a surgeon operates without consent. Yet it is a battery. The 'hostility' factor must surely be limited to situations where the contact could otherwise be one of the incidents of friendly intercourse (eg slapping a batsman on the back after a good innings or part of accepted horseplay among friends). One would do best to adopt the formulation of Goff LJ in *Collins* v *Wilcock* [1984] 1 WLR 1172, when he said that there was a general exception to the illegality of intentional physical contact which embraced all physical contact generally acceptable in the ordinary conduct of daily life. Goff LJ expressly disassociated himself from the antic notion that a battery is only committed where the action is 'angry, revengeful, rude or insolent' (Hawkins *Pleas of the Crown* (8th edn, 1824) vol 1, ch 15, s 2) – words hardly apt to describe a surgical intervention! Wood J took this view in *T* v *T* [1988] Fam 52, when he said that, as the law stood, a surgeon who performed a termination of pregnancy on a mentally handicapped adult would be liable for trespass (assuming it was not a medical emergency) despite the absence of hostile intent (see below under 'Mentally disordered persons').

Another example of a 'friendly' (non-hostile) assault is the hairdresser who, without getting proper consent, applies a 'tone rinse' to a customer's hair (*Nash* v *Sheen* [1953] CLY 3726).

In *Appleton* v *Garrett* MLC 0045, [1997] 8 Med LR 75, Dyson J awarded aggravated damages for trespass where the defendant had prescribed and carried out unnecessary dental treatment for the sole purpose of getting himself more work.[3]

CONSENT OF THE PATIENT

What prevents an operation, or any other invasion by the physician of the patient's bodily integrity, from being an assault is the consent of the patient.

Consent may be express or implied, oral or written. For surgical procedures a written consent is usually taken. This will refer in short form to the operation to be undertaken, and is likely to authorise 'such further or

---

3   In *R* v *Richardson* (1998) 43 BMLR 21, a criminal conviction was overturned on appeal where a dentist who had been struck off continued to treat her patients with their apparent consent but without telling them of her disqualification. The Court of Appeal said that only a mistake about the nature of the act alleged to constitute an assault or the identity of the assailant vitiated consent in criminal law, and for this purpose a person's professional status or qualifications did not constitute part of their identity. Consequently, the appeal would be allowed. The court said the civil law concept of informed consent had no place in the criminal law.

alternative operative measures as may be found to be necessary during the course of the operation'. This should probably be understood to authorise only operative measures connected with the specific treatment, ie it should be read, as we say, *ejusdem generis*.[4] Measures of a different nature would have to be justified by the physician's right to act in an emergency to protect the patient's health (see below).

For treatment involving little risk the consent may be oral; in appropriate cases it may be implied from the fact that the patient has consulted the doctor. It has been said that consent to such surgical and medical treatment as the doctors might think necessary is not to be implied simply from the fact of entering hospital (*Stoffberg* v *Elliott* (1923) CPD 148). An apparent consent, oral or written, will not be valid if the physician should have seen that the patient did not realise the significance of what he was giving his consent to (*Chatterton* v *Gerson* [1981] QB 432; *Kelly* v *Hazlett* (1976) 75 DLR (3d) 536).

If the patient has not given his consent to the treatment and it involves an invasion of his bodily integrity the treatment constitutes an assault and the cause of action lies in assault and battery.

In *Re C* [1994] 1 WLR 290, Thorpe J held that a 68-year-old schizophrenic was entitled to an injunction preventing the hospital from amputating his leg because it had not been established that the patient's general capacity was so impaired by his illness as to render him incapable of understanding the nature, purpose and effects of the treatment advised and so his right of self-determination had not been displaced.

In *Allan* v *New Mount Sinai Hospital* (1980) 109 DLR (3d) 634, an anesthetist who acted without negligence was held liable in battery for unforeseeable injury suffered by the patient because he administered the injection that led to the injury into the patient's left arm, the patient having expressly told him not to inject into that limb. The defendant acted in accordance with normal medical procedure, but he had ignored the claimant's instructions. He was accordingly liable for trespass to the person, and for all the damage that flowed directly from that trespass (see below under 'Assault v negligence').

In *Secretary of State for the Home Department* v *Robb* [1995] Fam 127, Thorpe J authorised prison staff to accept the decision of an adult prisoner of sound mind to refuse all nutrition. The judge said that a prisoner of sound mind, just like any other adult, had a specific right of self-determination. It was not absolute, requiring to be balanced against potentially countervailing state interests in preserving life, preventing suicide and protecting innocent third parties, but in this case there were no such countervailing considerations.[5]

---

4   For examples of 'unrelated procedures' see *Mulloy* v *Hop Sang* [1935] 1 WWR 714 (amputation of hand); *Allan* v *New Mount Sinai Hospital* (1980) 109 DLR (3d) 634 (see below); and *Schweizer* v *Central Hospital* (1974) 53 DLR (3d) 494 (operation on back not justified by consent to one on toe).

5   According to guidelines for the medical profession issued August 1997 by the Mental Health Commission, patients suffering from anorexia can legally be force-fed to save their lives. Doctors had previously understood from a decision in January 1996 from the European Court of Human Rights that they were not entitled to force-feed an adult woman who had been progressively starving herself to death since she was 16. (For a case on a minor's anorexia, see *Re W (a minor: medical treatment)* [1993] Fam 64, CA.)

In *Davis* v *Barking, Havering and Brentwood Health Authority* [1993] 4 Med LR 85, McCullough J said that a separate consent was not required where, within proper medical practice, a caudal anesthetic (about which the patient had not been told) was added to her general anesthetic during an operation for marsupialisation of a Bartholian cyst. He said that sectionalising consent for every step in a procedure would lead to the 'deplorable' prospect of this type of action being brought in trespass rather than in negligence ('deplored' to a greater or lesser extent by Bristow J in *Chatterton* v *Gerson* [1981] QB 432; Hirst J in *Hills* v *Potter* [1984] 1 WLR 641n at 653; and Lord Scarman in the *Sidaway* case [1985] AC 871 at 883, MLC 0010, HL).

In *Newbury* v *Bath District Health Authority* (1998) 47 BMLR 138, the patient unsuccessfully claimed injury for an improperly performed lumbar decompression and fusion. The issue of consent was whether the patient was entitled to more information than she was given. Ebsworth J said that there might be circumstances in which a patient would be entitled to be told that a proposed operation was not in the mainstream of treatment. That would obviously be so if the treatment involved a method which was either entirely new, or relatively untried, or if it was one that had fallen out of use because it had been shown to be defective and was no longer accepted by a responsible body of medical opinion. The evidence in this case did not reach that state, there being no evidence that the technique used had been condemned at the date it was employed. Whilst it would have been preferable for the claimant to have been told that the proposed use of Harrington rods was unusual and for her to be given the alternative, there was no duty on the consultant to tell her. There had been no negligence in obtaining consent.

In *Burke* v *Leeds Health Authority* [2001] MLC 0314, CA, where the judge had found that the oncologists recommending treatment by intense chemotherapy for a child's leukemia were negligent not to have told the parents that it would be possible, though not optimum, to delay treatment for a while, the defendant's appeal succeeded on the basis that the judge's finding of breach of duty could not be sustained in the absence of any expert evidence supporting such a conclusion. The treatment had led to spastic quadriplegia.

The *St George's Healthcare Trust* case

In *St George's Healthcare NHS Trust* v *S* [1999] Fam 26, [1998] 3 All ER 673, CA, a 36-year-old mother, suffering from pre-eclampsia, refused medical advice to have a Cesarian section, despite being told of the risk to her and her child from natural birth. She was then consigned to a mental hospital against her will. Transferred to a labour ward, she continued to refuse consent to a section. A judge at first instance authorised the section dispensing with her consent. A baby girl was duly born. The mother then appealed to the Court of Appeal. The court upheld her complaints. It declared that, even when his or her own life depended on receiving medical treatment, an adult of sound mind was entitled to refuse; that, although pregnancy increased the personal responsibilities of the woman, it did not diminish her entitlement to decide whether to undergo medical treatment; and an unborn child was not a separate person from his mother and its need for medical assistance did not prevail over her right not to be forced to submit to an invasion of her body against her will, whether her own life or that of her unborn child depended on it, and that right was not reduced or diminished merely because her decision to exercise it might appear morally repugnant; and that, unless lawfully justified, the removal of the baby from within the mother's body under physical compulsion constituted an infringement of her autonomy and amounted to a trespass, and the perceived needs of the fetus did not provide the necessary justification. Further, the detention under the Mental Health 1983 was declared unlawful because detention against the will of the party was not justified merely because his thinking process was unusual and contrary to the use of the overwhelming majority of the community at large. In any event a patient detained pursuant to the Act could not be forced into medical procedures unconnected with his mental condition unless his capacity to consent to such treatment was diminished.

It is impossible to read the report of this case without seeing parallels, not too far-fetched, albeit in reverse form, between the treatment this woman received until the time the Court of Appeal took charge of the matter and the way in which Chinese officials, particularly away from the big cities, enforced the one child policy on mothers who had gone one pregnancy too far.

A few weeks after giving their May 1998 judgment, the court formulated guidelines for all medical practitioners applying to any case involving capacity when surgical or invasive treatment might be needed. These guidelines are sufficiently important and comprehensive to require setting out in full at this point:

The guidelines depend on basic legal principles which we summarise:

1. They have no application where the patient is competent to accept or refuse treatment. In principle a patient may remain competent notwithstanding detention under the Mental Health Act 1983.

2. If the patient is competent and refuses consent to the treatment, an application to the High Court for a declaration would be pointless. In this situation the advice given to the patient should be recorded. For their own protection, hospital authorities should seek unequivocal assurances from the patient (to be recorded in writing) that the refusal represents an informed decision, that is, that she understands the nature of and reasons for the proposed treatment, and the risks and likely prognosis involved in the decision to refuse or accept it. If the patient is unwilling to sign a written indication of this refusal, this too should be noted in writing. Such a written indication is merely a record for evidential purposes. It should not be confused with or regarded as a disclaimer.

3. If the patient is incapable of giving or refusing consent, either in the long term or temporarily (eg due to unconsciousness), the patient must be cared for according to the authority's judgment of the patient's best interests. Where the patient has given an advance directive, before becoming incapable, treatment and care should normally be subject to the advance directive. However, if there is reason to doubt the reliability of the advance directive (for example, it may sensibly be thought not to apply to the circumstances which have arisen), then an application for a declaration may be made.

Concern over capacity

4. The authority should identify as soon as possible whether there is concern about a patient's competence to consent to or refuse treatment.

5. If the capacity of the patient is seriously in doubt, it should be assessed as

a matter of priority. In many such cases the patient's GP or other responsible doctor may be sufficiently qualified to make the necessary assessment, but in serious or complex cases involving difficult issues about the future health and well being or even the life of the patient, the issue of capacity should be examined by an independent psychiatrist, ideally one approved under s 12(2) of the Mental Health Act 1983. If following this assessment there remains a serious doubt about the patient's competence, and the seriousness or complexity of the issues in the particular case may require the involvement of the court, the psychiatrist should further consider whether the patient is incapable by reason of mental disorder of managing her property or affairs. If so the patient may be unable to instruct a solicitor and will require a guardian ad litem in any court proceedings. The authority should seek legal advice as quickly as possible. If a declaration is to be sought, the patient's solicitors should be informed immediately and if practicable they should have a proper opportunity to take instructions and apply for legal aid where necessary. Potential witnesses for the authority should be made aware of the criteria laid down in in *Re MB (an adult: medical treatment)* [1997] 2 FCR 541, CA and this case, together with any guidance issued by the Department of Health and the British Medical Association.

6. If the patient is unable to instruct solicitors, or is believed to be incapable of doing so, the authority or its legal advisers must notify the Official Solicitor and invite him to act as guardian ad litem. If the Official Solicitor agrees he will no doubt wish, if possible, to arrange for the patient to be interviewed to ascertain her wishes and to explore the reasons for any refusal of treatment. The Official Solicitor can be contacted through the Urgent Court Business Officer out of office hours on [020 7936 6000].

The hearing
7. The hearing before the judge should be inter partes. As the order made in her absence will not be binding on the patient unless she is represented either by a guardian ad litem (if incapable of giving instructions) or (if capable) by counsel or solicitor, a declaration granted ex parte is of no assistance to the authority. Although the Official Solicitor will not act for a patient if she is capable of instructing a solicitor, the court may in any event call on the Official Solicitor (who has considerable expertise in these matters) to assist as an amicus curiae.

8. It is axiomatic that the judge must be provided with accurate and all the relevant information. This should include the reasons for the proposed treatment, the risks involved in the proposed treatment, and in not proceeding with it, whether any alternative treatment exists, and the reason, if ascertainable, why the patient is refusing the proposed treatment. The judge will need sufficient information to reach an informed conclusion about the patient's capacity, and, where it arises, the issue of best interest.

9. The precise terms of any order should be recorded and approved by the judge before its terms are transmitted to the authority. The patient should be accurately informed of the precise terms.

10. Applicants for emergency orders from the High Court made without first issuing and serving the relevant applications and evidence in support have a duty to comply with the procedural requirements (and pay the court fees) as soon as possible after the urgency hearing.

Conclusion
There may be occasions when, assuming a serious question arises about the competence of the patient, the situation facing the authority may be so urgent and the consequences so desperate that it is impracticable to attempt to comply with these guidelines. The guidelines should be approached for what they are, that is, guidelines. Where delay may itself cause serious damage to the patient's health or put her life at risk then formulaic compliance with these guidelines would be inappropriate.

In *Ms B* v *A NHS Hospital Trust* [2002] EWHC 429 (Fam), Dame Elizabeth Butler-Sloss held that a seriously physically disabled patient but one with the mental capacity to make decisions about treatment, even when a consequence of such decisions could be death, had the right to decide to refuse treatment. Autonomy was a fundamental principle in English law, as was the sanctity of life.

On the other hand, in *R* v *Feggetter, ex p Wooder* [2002] EWCA Civ 554, the Court of Appeal sanctioned treatment against the will of a competent patient. It said that decisions to give a psychiatric patient treatment against his will (in this case a decision made by a second opinion appointed doctor) had, by virtue of the Human Rights Act, and by virtue of the fact that medical treatment was to be given which would violate the autonomy of a competent non-consenting adult, to be accompanied by reasons given.

Blood transfusion cases

In *Re T (adult: refusal of treatment)* [1993] Fam 95, CA, where a 20-year-old woman was refusing a blood transfusion after a road accident, Lord Donaldson said that the right of a rational adult patient to refuse treatment was paramount and had to prevail over society's conflicting interest in upholding the concept that all human life was sacred and should be preserved if at all possible. However, the court found reasons for holding that the patient had not given a properly informed refusal which applied to the present situation, due to her inherently weakened condition, the continually changing circumstances of her medical condition, and to the degree of pressure that appeared to have been put upon her by her Jehovah's Witness mother shortly before she had refused the transfusion. Butler-Sloss LJ said that there was abundant evidence to justify the court in concluding that the young woman was subjected to her mother's influence so as to vitiate her refusal to the transfusion.[6]

Provided that the patient is adult and rational, the court cannot over-rule her wishes. If the doctor nevertheless proceeds in the face of a refusal of treatment, he will be committing an assault. In *Malette* v *Shulman* [1991] 2 Med LR 162, a Canadian court ordered a doctor who gave a blood transfusion in the face of clear objection from the patient to pay $20,000 for assault, saying: 'A conscious rational patient is entitled to refuse any medical treatment and the doctor must comply, no matter how ill-advised he may believe that instruction to be.'

In *NHS Trust* v *Ms T* [2004] EWHC 1279 (Fam), where the patient lacked mental capacity to decide on her future medical treatment and where her condition was unlikely to change, Charles J made an interim declaration that the health authority could administer to the patient an emergency life-saving blood transfusion contrary to her wishes.

Cesarean sections

In a number of cases at first instance emergency orders were made at short notice authorising Cesarean sections upon women who had not

---

6 Further blood transfusion cases are considered below in the section headed 'Children'.

consented. The mother was not always represented and the medical evidence was often scanty. In one case the woman refused only because she had a needle phobia (*Re L* [1997] 2 FLR 837). The issues arising in this context have now been extensively considered and ruled upon twice by the Court of Appeal.

In *Re MB* (1997) 38 BMLR 175, the court held an emergency hearing in February 1997 that was not completed until the early hours of the morning.[7] The mother was 23. The child was presenting by the breech. Cesarean section was obviously desirable; otherwise there was a 50% risk to the child (though none to the mother). The mother wanted a Cesarean section and consented to it, but each time she saw the anesthetic needle, or the mask, she changed her mind. So the problem was purely one of needle phobia. Her mental state was that she was a naive, not very bright, frightened young woman, but was not exhibiting any psychiatric disorder. At first instance the judge authorised the use of reasonable force for the purpose of performing a Cesarean section.

The Court of Appeal first set out *basic principles*:

(1) In general it was a criminal and tortious assault to perform physically invasive medical treatment, however minimal the invasion might be, without the patient's consent.

(2) A mentally competent patient had an absolute right to refuse to consent to medical treatment for any reason, rational or irrational, or for no reason at all, even where that decision might lead to his or her own death.

(3) Emergency medical treatment could be given, provided the treatment was a necessity and did no more than was reasonably required in the best interests of the patient.

The court reviewed the various Cesarean section cases at first instance, and said that, with the exception of *Re S (adult: surgical treatment)* [1993] 1 FLR 26, the court had expressly decided that the mother did not have the capacity to make the decision. The Court of Appeal was alive to the objections that had been made to these orders, principally that no woman should be compelled to undergo such an invasive surgical procedure against her will, not even if it was necessary to save the life of her child.

On the issue of *capacity to consent* the court offered the following guidelines:

(1) Every person is presumed to have the capacity to consent to or to refuse medical treatment unless and until the presumption is reported.

(2) A competent woman who has the capacity to decide may for religious reasons, other reasons, for rational or irrational reasons or for no reason at all, choose not to have medical intervention, even though the consequence may be the death or serious handicap of the child she bears, or her own death. In that event the courts do not have the jurisdiction to declare medical intervention lawful and the question of her own best interests objectively considered does not arise.

---

7   In view of the comprehensive and authoritative judgment in this case, the earlier cases at first instance are not detailed here. They can be found within the judgment.

(3) Panic, indecisiveness and irrationality in themselves do not as such amount to incompetence, but they may be symptoms or evidence of incompetence.

(4) A person lacks capacity if some impairment or disturbance of mental functioning renders him or her unable to make a decision whether to consent to or to refuse treatment. A patient will be unable to make a decision on consent when he cannot understand and retain the relevant information, or cannot assess it properly, or through confusion, shock, fatigue, pain or drugs may temporarily lose the capacity. Panic and fear may also destroy capacity.

In the particular case the court concluded that the mother's needle phobia rendered her incapable at the relevant time of making a decision at all.

The court then decided that the *best interests* of the mother required the Cesarean section to be carried out. There was medical evidence that she was likely to suffer significant long-term damage if her child sustained injury or died, but, on the other hand, would suffer no lasting harm if the anesthetic were given.[8]

The court went on to consider the important issue of whether the *interests of the unborn child* were relevant. The court firmly stated that there was no jurisdiction to consider the unborn child as a person whose interests needed protecting. That would need the intervention of Parliament. Finally, the court advised on the *procedure* to be adopted where the capacity of the patient to consent to or refuse the medical intervention was in issue.

The other case is *St George's Healthcare NHS Trust* v *S* (above). The guidelines formulated by the court in that case have been set out above.

Note that it appears still to be open to the court to hold, if the circumstances are appropriate and the court so desires, that the mother is (ie must be) suffering from some impairment or disturbance of mental functioning and so unable to understand and assess the information given her by the doctors.

Prisoners

The Court of Appeal said in *Freeman* v *Home Office (No 2)* [1984] QB 524, that a prisoner was able to give a valid consent to the administering of drugs, and whether he had actually done so was a question of fact for the trial judge, and a court had to be alive to the risk that in a prison setting an apparent consent might not be a real one. A prisoner who has not given consent to treatment may of course maintain an action for assault (*Barbara* v *Home Office* (1984) 134 NLJ 888).

---

8 Consideration of what is in the patient's best interests is appropriate to the context of withdrawal of treatment, but it should not be used to give a doctor a licence to proceed in the absence of consent other than in an emergency. In *Frenchay Healthcare NHS Trust* v *S* [1994] 1 WLR 601, CA, Lord Donaldson MR said: 'It is, I think, important that there should not be a belief that what the doctor says is the patient's best interest *is* the patient's best interest. For my part I would certainly reserve to the court the ultimate power and duty to review the doctor's decision in the light of all the facts.'

ASSAULT v NEGLIGENCE

A number of factors distinguish the action for assault from that for negligence.

(1) Fault, as we have seen, is irrelevant. If the patient can show he did not consent to the treatment he will be able to recover damages without proof of negligence.

(2) Whereas in the action for negligence the defendant is only liable for loss and injury which was foreseeable at the time of the negligent act (see Chapter 16), the tortfeasor in trespass is liable for all damage flowing directly from the assault, whether foreseeable or not. The wrongful act consists in laying hands on the claimant, and for that the defendant is liable in respect of all loss and injury flowing directly from the assault, however unforeseeable (see *Allan* v *New Mount Sinai Hospital* (above) *per* Linden J). Nevertheless the injury or loss must be of a type which the law recognises, and within the rules as to remoteness of damage in the sense that it must be directly caused by the assault.

(3) Whereas negligence is not actionable without proof of actual damage or loss, trespass has no such requirement. Even if no injury is suffered, damages may be awarded to compensate for the fact of the assault (these are likely to be nominal in such a case, though one can envisage an award for, eg the indignity suffered). The limitation period will therefore start to run, in the absence of special factors (see Chapter 25), when the assault takes place and not when injury is suffered, as the cause of action is complete at the time of the assault. In negligence the cause of action is not complete until damage has been suffered.

(4) The limitation period for a claim for assault is six years, not three, as it has been held, oddly enough, that the provisions of s 11 (and consequently s 14) do not apply to such a claim (*Stubbings* v *Webb* [1993] AC 498, HL).

(5) The fact that the patient would have consented if asked does not absolve the defendant from liability, but it would seem sensible to take that fact into account in reducing damages, for otherwise a person might recover damages for an operation, carried out without consent, but which benefited him and which he would have agreed to if asked. If the cause of action is in negligence the defendant is entitled to contend that the patient has suffered no injury because, even if he had not been negligent, eg even if he had explained the nature of the operation properly, the patient would still have agreed to it. It was probably with reference only to liability that Bristow J said in *Chatterton* v *Gerson* [1981] QB 432:

> Where the claim is based on trespass to the person, once it is shown that the consent is unreal, then what the plaintiff would have decided if she had been given the information which would have prevented vitiation of the reality of her consent is irrelevant.[9]

---

9   And see *Davis* v *Barking etc Health Authority* (above).

It may be that the fact that no action will lie for assault in respect of emergency treatment reasonably and carefully carried out upon a patient without his consent may be based on this principle. The patient would have consented if it had been possible to ask him.

EMERGENCY TREATMENT

There is no English reported case directly on the right or duty of a doctor to carry out emergency treatment on a patient when consent cannot be obtained, but commentators generally agree that, where such treatment is necessary to preserve the life or the health of the patient, no action lies for assault. Another possible basis for this immunity, beside that of implied consent, is the duty of the physician, albeit a moral rather than a legal one, to take all reasonable steps to preserve life.

In *Wilson* v *Pringle* [1987] QB 237, the Court of Appeal, speaking of the 'legal rule [that] allows a casualty surgeon to perform an urgent operation on an unconscious patient who is brought into hospital' said:

> The patient cannot consent, and there may be no next-of-kin available. Hitherto it has been customary to say in such cases that consent is to be implied for what would otherwise be a battery on the unconscious body. It is better simply to say that the surgeon's action is acceptable in the ordinary conduct of everyday life, and not a battery.

And see the observation of Wood J in *T* v *T* (above). In *Re MB* [1997] 8 Med LR 217, the Court of Appeal said, *obiter*, that emergency medical treatment could be given, provided it was a necessity and did no more than was necessary in the best interests of the patient.

In *Marshall* v *Curry* [1933] 3 DLR 260, a case decided in the Supreme Court of Nova Scotia, a surgeon who found and removed a grossly diseased testicle during an operation for a hernia was found when sued for trespass to have acted properly.

> Where a great emergency which could not be anticipated arises' a doctor is justified in acting 'in order to save the life or preserve the health of the patient' (*per* Chisholm CJ).

But the fact that it is convenient to perform the operation at the time is not sufficient to give the doctor immunity from an action for trespass; it must actually be necessary. In *Murray* v *McMurchy* [1949] 2 DLR 442, the Supreme Court of British Columbia imposed liability on a surgeon who, while performing a Cesarian section, discovered fibroid tumours on the uterus of the patient and, concerned for the hazards of any future pregnancy, tied her tubes. Here the action of the doctor, though undertaken from the best of motives, was not a necessity at that particular time (for a suitably academic treatment of this topic, see P D G Skegg 'A justification for medical procedures performed without consent' (1974) 90 LQR 512).

In *R* v *Bournewood Community and Mental Health NHS Trust, ex p L* [1999] 1 AC 458, [1998] 3 All ER 289, HL, the court held that the common law doctrine of necessity allowed informal detention of mental patients, ie without actual consent or formal detention under the Mental Health Act. The general principle of necessity was said to apply where there was a necessity to act when it was not practicable to communicate with the assisted person, and the action taken must be such as a reasonable person would in all the circumstances take, acting in the best interests of the assisted person (as *per* Lord Goff in *Re F* [1990] 2 AC 1, HL).

CHILDREN

In this and the following sections we consider the context where a valid consent cannot be given because the patient is under a clear disability. Note that the guidelines offered by the Court of Appeal in *St George's Healthcare NHS Trust* v *S* (above) relate to all cases of incapacity and, as it appears, all invasive procedures.

In *Re S (hospital patient: court's jurisdiction)* [1996] Fam 1, the Court of Appeal, assuming jurisdiction in a dispute between carer and family over the issue in which country a patient who was too ill to make his own views known should be cared for, made it clear that the court was ready, without raising technical objections about the *locus standi* of an applicant and even where, as here, the issue in question was not particularly momentous, to give declaratory judgments to ensure that the patient's best interests were protected in cases where the patient was unable for one reason or another to express any or any reliable preference.

An infant can give a valid consent to treatment if he is old enough and sufficiently intelligent to understand what is proposed and the risks involved. If he is not so capable, then, under the age of 16, consent lies with his parents or guardian. For children over 16, the Family Law Reform Act 1969 provides, by s 8:

> Section 8(1): The consent of a minor who has attained the age of sixteen years to any surgical, medical or dental treatment which, in the absence of consent, would constitute a trespass to his person, shall be as effective as it would be if he were of full age; and where a minor has by virtue of this section given an effective consent to any treatment it shall not be necessary to obtain any consent for it from his parent or guardian.
>
> (2) In this section 'surgical, medical or dental treatment' includes any procedures undertaken for the purposes of diagnosis, and this section applies to any procedure (including, in particular, the administration of an anesthetic) which is ancillary to any treatment as it applies to that treatment.
>
> (3) Nothing in this section shall be construed as making ineffective any consent which would have been effective if this section had not been enacted.

In *Gillick* v *West Norfolk and Wisbech Area Health Authority* [1986] AC 112, HL, an action by a parent to get declared unlawful DHSS advice permitting a doctor to prescribe the pill to children without telling their parents, the court said that the parental right to determine whether or not a child should receive medical treatment terminated when the child achieved a significant understanding and intelligence to enable him or her to understand fully what was proposed; but it was also said that parental rights clearly existed and did not wholly disappear until majority. Lord Scarman said:

> ... the parental right yields to the child's right to make his own decisions when he reaches a sufficient understanding and intelligence to be capable of making up his own mind on the matters requiring decision.

In *W v Official Solicitor* [1972] AC 24, HL, the court was prepared to countenance the ordering of a blood test upon a minor to determine paternity if it was in the public interest that it should be so ordered. And, on the other side of the coin, a judge authorised an abortion upon a 15-year-old girl against the wishes of her parents because the court was satisfied that the girl both wanted and understood the implications of the operation (*Re P (a minor)* (1982) 80 LGR 301).

In *Re R (a minor) (wardship: consent to treatment)* [1992] Fam 11, CA, the issue was whether a psychiatrically disturbed girl of 15 in the care of the local authority could effectively refuse consent to the administration of the anti-psychotic drugs that the treating doctors thought were essential to her condition. Waite J had taken the view, which had been the generally understood view, that the *Gillick* decision meant that neither parent nor court could override the decision of a *Gillick*-competent child to accept or refuse treatment. However he also concluded that in fact the child was not *Gillick*-competent and so could not give a valid refusal.

In the Court of Appeal Lord Donaldson took a much wider view of the court's powers and a much narrower view of the child's. He said that the court in the exercise of its wardship jurisdiction, which was wider than, independent of, and not derived from the parental powers (and had, of course, not been in issue in the *Gillick* case), was entitled to override the wishes of a ward, and indeed also of the parents, whether consenting to or refusing treatment, and whether the child was *Gillick*-competent or not. He also said that parents could give a valid consent to treatment in the face of the child's refusal, and that if Lord Scarman in *Gillick* had meant otherwise his words were *obiter*. The farthest Lord Donaldson went was to accord the child a right to insist on such treatment as the doctors advised even if the parents objected. However, these far-reaching observations were in themselves *obiter* as the court held that this particular patient, even though she had lucid intervals when according to the medical evidence she was in her rational mind, could not be regarded in the context of her fluctuating disease as being generally of sufficient understanding to meet the criteria for *Gillick*-competence.

There is certainly ground for concern at the assumption by the court of overriding powers in the case of a *Gillick*-competent child; it can be strongly argued that the court's powers in this context should be no greater than that of a natural parent. Furthermore, what power has the court to deprive the competent child over 16 years of age of the right to consent that he has been given by Parliament?

A year later Lord Donaldson had occasion to repeat his assertion that, although a minor over the age of 16 has a right to consent to medical treatment in defiance of his parents' wishes, that does not include an absolute right to refuse treatment. In *Re W (a minor) (medical treatment)* [1993] Fam 64, the Court of Appeal, in the exercise of its inherent jurisdiction to protect minors, overrode the refusal of a girl aged 16 to consent to necessary treatment for anorexia nervosa. Thorpe J had held that the child was *Gillick*-competent but that the court would exercise an overriding right to order the treatment necessary to save her life. In the Court of Appeal Lord Donaldson said that the court's inherent powers under the *parens patriae* jurisdiction were theoretically limitless and certainly extended beyond the powers of a natural parent, and it was clear beyond doubt that the court could override the wishes of a *Gillick*-competent minor, not by ordering the doctors to treat, but by authorising them to treat according to their clinical judgment of what was in the best interests of the patient.

However, in this case, too, the court doubted that the minor was able to give a valid or informed refusal because the nature of her disease would impair her judgment, in that it created a compulsion to refuse treatment or to accept only treatment that was unlikely to be effective.

Note here a disquieting decision reached by Douglas Brown J in *South Glamorgan County Council* v *W and B* (1992) 11 BMLR 162: the court authorised psychiatric treatment against the wishes of a competent 15-year-old girl.

Reference may also be made to *Re K, W and H (minors) (consent to treatment)* [1993] 1 FCR 240, where Thorpe J said that parents' wishes could override refusal of *Gillick*-competent minors (though all three minors in the case were in fact held not to be competent).

In *Re M (child: refusal of medical treatment)* (1999) 52 BMLR 124, Johnson J authorised a heart transplant operation on a 15-year-old girl against her wishes but in accordance with her mother's wishes. He said that, although there were risks attached to the surgery and thereafter, including the risk that she would carry resentment for the rest of her life at what would be done to her, those risks had to be matched against the certainty of death if the transplant was not carried out. M's refusal to consent was important but not decisive and, while there was great gravity in the decision to override M's wishes, it was necessary to do so in order to achieve what was, on balance, best for her.

In *R* v *Portsmouth Hospitals NHS Trust, ex p Glass* (1999) 50 BMLR 269, CA, a child, considered to be in a terminal state by the hospital, was treated with diamorphine contrary to his mother's wishes. Violent scenes ensued at the hospital. After the child had been discharged from the hospital, the trust suggested to the parents that it would be better if any further treatment took place elsewhere. A misconceived claim for judicial review of the hospital's actions was then commenced. Obviously the court was not going to give directions on clinical management, particularly when the critical period was long over. However, for present purpose it is worth noting what Scott Baker J said at first instance (the Court of Appeal agreed):

> Life and death cases, like the present one, often raise incredibly difficult issues to which there is no right answer. Anyone who doubts the potential difficulties of the issues in this case should read three documents which have been exhibited with the applicant's bundle of authorities and literature. They are: *Seeking Patients' Consent: The Ethical Considerations* by the General Medical Council; *Withdrawing and Withholding Treatment*: A consultation paper from the BMA's Medical Ethics Committee; and *Withholding and Withdrawing Life Saving Treatment in Children – a Framework for Practice* from the Royal College of Pediatric and Child Health, September 1987.

And Lord Woolf said:

> There are questions of judgment involved. There can be no doubt that the best course is for a parent of a child to agree on the course which the doctors are proposing to take, having fully consulted the parent and for the parent to fully understand what is involved. That is the course which should always be adopted in a case of this nature. If that is not possible and there is a conflict, and if the conflict is of a grave nature, the matter must then be brought before

the court so the court can decide what is in the best interests of the child concerned. Faced with a particular problem, the courts will answer that problem.

In my judgment that is the desirable way forward. Of course it does involve expense; it involves coming to the courts to obtain a ruling. The courts will do their best to reduce that expense. But the answer which will be given in relation to a particular problem dealing with a particular set of circumstances, is a much better answer than an answer given in advance. The difficulty in this area is that there are conflicting principles involved. The principles of law are clearly established, but how you apply those principles to particular facts is often very difficult to anticipate. It is only when the court is faced with that task that it gives an answer which reflects the view of the court as to what is in the best interests of the child. In doing so it takes into account the natural concerns and the responsibilities of the parent. It also takes into account the views of the doctors, and it considers what is the most desirable answer taking the best advice it can obtain from, among others, the Official Solicitor. That is the way, in my judgment, that the courts must react in this very sensitive and difficult area.

Blood transfusion cases

In *Re O (a minor) (medical treatment)* [1993] 4 Med LR 272, Johnson J authorised a blood transfusion for a two-month-old girl born 12 weeks prematurely, despite the objections of her Jehovah's Witness parents. Booth J acted similarly to overrule the wishes of the parents of a ten-month-old girl suffering from leukemia in the case of *Camden London Borough Council v R (a minor) (blood transfusion)* (1993) 15 BMLR 72, stating that the court could grant a specific order to permit a transfusion under s 8 of the Children Act 1989, and that it was not necessary to invoke the inherent jurisdiction of the court.

Similarly, in *Devon County Council v S* (1992) 11 BMLR 105, Thorpe J authorised a non-urgent transfusion to enable chemotherapy upon a boy aged four-and-a-half where there was only an even chance of success and his Jehovah's Witness parents objected.

Reference may also be made to in *Re E* [1993] 1 FLR 386, in which Ward J authorised a life-saving blood transfusion for a leukemic boy of 15 from a family of Jehovah's Witnesses.[10]

In *Re L (a minor)* (1998) 51 BMLR 137, the President authorised blood transfusions for a Jehovah's Witness, a girl of 16, who had sustained severe burns, on the basis that her sheltered lifestyle as a Witness limited her understanding of her condition and the need for treatment, and that the treatment sought was in her best interests.

See also *Re T (a minor) (wardship: medical treatment)* [1997] 1 WLR 242, CA, discussed below under 'The quality of life and terminally ill patients'.

In *Re B (a child)* [2003] EWCA Civ 1148, the Court of Appeal upheld the judge's decision when he granted the father's applications under s 8 of the Children Act 1989 that, contrary to the mother's wishes, the

---

10 In *Re W (a minor) (HIV test)* [1995] 2 FCR 184, Kirkwood J authorised a blood test on a child whose mother had died of an AIDS-related illness as being in the best interests of the child. Wilson J authorised a blood test on a baby for HIV detection despite the parents' opposition (*Re C (a child)* also *sub nom Camden London Borough Council v A, B and C*) (1999) 50 BMLR 283).

children's best interests required that they receive the full MMR vaccination.

Sterilisation and termination

The rules for seeking a declaration that a sterilisation procedure upon a minor (or a mentally handicapped person) might lawfully be carried out were set out at [1993] 3 All ER 222, dated May 1993. It has been held that a declaration is not required for a medically indicated hysterectomy on a minor (*Re E (a minor)* [1991] 2 FLR 585). These principles must be read subject to the recent guidance from the Court of Appeal in *St George's Healthcare NHS Trust* v *S* (above).

Reference may also usefully be made to ss 1–4 of the Children Act 1989.

Circumcision

The Court of Appeal upheld an order of Wall J refusing permission for circumcision to be carried out on a child where the Muslim father wanted it and the mother did not (*Re J (child's religious upbringing and circumcision)* (1999) 52 BMLR 82.

MENTALLY DISORDERED PERSONS

Part IV of the Mental Health Act 1983, besides providing by s 62 that urgent treatment may be given to a patient without his consent, permits treatments for the mental disorder from which the patient is suffering (other than the more serious treatments) to be given without his consent.[11] The most serious treatment, involving interference with brain tissue or other serious treatments specified in regulations, must have the consent of the patient. For treatments of middling seriousness, as specified in regulations, consent is not required if a second medical opinion advises that the treatment be given.

What if the patient is incapable of giving consent, whether to the most serious form of treatment for mental disorder or for routine medical treatment unconnected with mental disorder? – a mentally handicapped person who is not mentally disordered within the meaning of the Act may also be in this position. In *R* v *Dr M, ex p N* [2002] EWCA Civ 1789, the Court of Appeal said that a court could be properly satisfied that it was appropriate to give permission for treatment to be given to a patient who did not consent to it only if it had been convincingly shown that the treatment was a medical necessity.

In *Re D (a minor)* [1976] Fam 185, the court was required to decide if it should authorise the sterilisation of a mentally handicapped 11-year-old girl. On the evidence Heilbron J concluded that that was not an appropriate course, the court proceeding on the assumption that a parent could

---

11   In *B* v *Croydon Health Authority* [1995] Fam 133, a declaration was obtained from the Court of Appeal that tube-feeding a mental patient who was refusing to eat did not require her consent as it constituted 'medical treatment given for the mental disorder' from which she was suffering within the meaning of s 63 of the Mental Health Act 1983.

give consent for such an operation on a child, and that, where the child was a ward of court, the court could give that consent in place of the parent.

In *Re B (a minor)* [1988] AC 199, the House of Lords upheld the order of the courts below, who had authorised a sterilisation upon a severely mentally handicapped girl of 17. It was said that sterilisation of a minor would always need the court's approval. The court expressly left undecided the question whether (apart from the limited context afforded by the Mental Health Act 1983, as set out above) any person or court could authorise or give consent to medical treatment upon an adult who was not capable of giving consent himself.

The House of Lords considered the relevant issues in *Re F* [1990] 2 AC 1. This 33-year-old patient was born in 1953 and as a result of a respiratory infection as a baby had the general mental capacity of a four- or five-year-old. She had recently formed an attachment to another patient within her hospital and ran the risk of becoming pregnant (the pill and an IUD were contra-indicated). All her carers, the judge at first instance and the Court of Appeal concluded that it was in her best interests to be sterilised. The court decided that there was a rule at common law, hitherto unknown, that a doctor was entitled, where the patient was unable to give consent, to carry out any treatment which was in the best interests of the patient; and the best interests of the patient were to be measured according to the classic *Bolam* test, namely that if there was a responsible body of medical opinion that would have supported what the doctor did, then he cannot be criticised. This is a very dangerous rule (for the patient), and a novel one – fortunately it is probably *obiter*, in that it was not necessary to the actual decision. What it would mean is that not only is a doctor exonerated in an emergency situation as long as he acts in accordance with some accepted practice or another, which is understandable, and not only can he carry out upon a mental patient any treatment that would have the approval of any minority body of medical opinion but also, during an operation, he can perform other procedures that take his fancy as long as a minority opinion would support him. It is a pity that the words of Lord Donaldson when the case was in the Court of Appeal were not heeded:

> [Consent] is a crucial factor in relation to all medical treatment. If it is necessarily absent, whether temporarily in an emergency situation or permanently in a case of mental disability, other things being equal, there must be greater caution in deciding whether to treat and, if so, how to treat.
>
> As far as the actual decision is concerned, the court said that it followed that there was no legal obligation on the doctors to seek the approval of the court before sterilising a patient whose mental condition made consent impossible to obtain, but the court strongly urged the medical profession to seek that approval first (Lord Griffiths was alone in saying that the court should insist that its approval be sought first).

In *Re LC (medical treatment: sterilisation)* [1997] 2 FLR 258, Thorpe J declined an application by the local authority, supported by the mother, for the sterilisation of a girl in her twenties with a mental age of three. She had been indecently assaulted while in the care of a specialist residential home. The judge concluded that, on balance, her current level of care and supervision was of such a high standard that it would not be in the girl's best interests to impose on her a surgical procedure which was not without its risks nor without painful consequences.

In *Re S (adult patient) (sterilisation)* [2001] Fam 15, the Court of Appeal, reversing the order of the judge below, said that it was not in the best interests of a mentally handicapped 29-year-old woman to be sterilised: a coil was a better option. It reached a similar conclusion (*mutatis mutandis*) in respect of proposed male sterilisation in *Re A (medical treatment: male sterilisation)* (1999) 53 BMLR 66, CA, saying that the concept of best interests related to the mentally incapacitated person and were not limited to best medical interests, but encompassed medical, emotional and all other welfare issues. In this case a vasectomy operation at the present time was not essential to A's future well-being.

The rules for seeking a declaration that a sterilisation procedure upon a mentally handicapped person may lawfully be carried out were set out at [1993] 3 All ER 222, in a *Practice Note* dated May 1993. They must be read subject to the Court of Appeal guidance in *St George's Healthcare NHS Trust* v *S* (above). It has been held that a declaration is not required for a medically indicated hysterectomy on a mentally handicapped adult (*Re GF* [1993] 4 Med LR 77), nor for a termination (*Re SG* [1993] 4 Med LR 75). In *Re H (a mental patient)* [1993] 4 Med LR 91, Wilson QC held that there was no call for a declaration to be given to legitimate investigations for a brain tumour in a mentally handicapped 25-year-old. The judge was clearly concerned that the medical profession should not think it must be forever seeking authorisation from the court for its procedures.

In *R* v *Kirklees Metropolitan Borough Council, ex p C (a minor)* [1993] 2 FLR 187, the Court of Appeal held that a local authority could give valid consent for a psychiatric admission in respect of a child in its care.

In *R* v *Mental Health Act Commission, ex p W* (1988) Times, 27 May, the Divisional Court reversed the refusal of the mental health commissioners to issue a certificate to a patient under s 57 of the Mental Health Act 1983 to the effect that he was capable of understanding the nature, purpose and likely effects of the treatment for pedophilia that he desired to undergo.

In *Re Y (mental patient: bone marrow donation)* [1997] Fam 110, Connell J authorised a bone marrow transplant from a mentally disordered adult to her sister, who was suffering from pre-leukemic bone marrow disorder. The donor lived in a community home, and was regularly visited by her sister and her mother. The judge said that there was evidence that the mother's life also would be prolonged by a successful transplant between her daughters, and he concluded that the donor would receive an emotional, psychological and social benefit from the operation and suffer minimal detriment. Accordingly, the blood tests and the bone marrow harvesting operation would be in her best interests.

In *Re Z (medical treatment: hysterectomy)* (1999) 53 BMLR 53, Bennett J authorised a laparoscopic sub-total hysterectomy on a mentally disordered woman of 19, saying that, since her periods brought her nothing but misery, pain and discomfort and served no useful purpose either reproductively or emotionally, it was in her best interests that her periods should cease altogether. Were she to become pregnant she would be incapable of raising a child and the trauma of pregnancy, childbirth and the inevitable removal of her child would be a catastrophe for her. Furthermore, if she had to undergo an abortion the psychological and emotional fallout would be disastrous. Therefore, the risk of pregnancy had to be removed completely. The subtotal hysterectomy would not only dramatically improve her quality of life by eliminating her menstrual periods, but also give her total protection from pregnancy. Accordingly, it was in her best interests that she undergo a laparoscopic subtotal hysterectomy and so her mother's application would be granted.

In a number of recent cases the President of the Family Division, Dame Elizabeth Butler-Sloss, has authorised an innovative form of treatment for patients lacking capacity who were suffering from variant CJD, a rare and fatal neuro-degenerative condition: see, for example, *EP* v *Trusts A, B, and C* [2004] Lloyds Rep Med 211. The court said that the treatment, though innovative, was in the best interests of the patients. The concept of best interests encompassed medical, emotional and all other welfare issues.

In *An NHS Trust* v *D* [2004] Lloyds Rep Med 107, Coleridge J, authorised the termination of pregnancy of a mental patient on the ground that the procedure was in her best interests, and he gave guidance as to when it was necessary in such a situation to apply to the court for a declaration.

THE QUALITY OF LIFE AND TERMINALLY ILL PATIENTS

Perhaps the most difficult and anxious decision the courts have ever been asked to take in this context arose in the recent conjoined twins case (*Re A (children) (conjoined twins: surgical separation)* [2000] 4 All ER 961, CA). For a variety of reasons, the court authorised the operation that would terminate the life of one twin (a child that was in any event dependent for her vital organs on her sister) but would give the other twin a fair chance of a reasonable life. The issues raised in that unique case were more a matter of medical, and general, ethics than of medical negligence, and the lengthy judgments at least as philosophical as jurisprudential, and for that reason they are not treated in detail here. Suffice it to say that there was an issue of consent, in that the parents were not consenting to the operation and the doomed twin had no say in the matter. The 'quality of life' of the two twins was a vital element in the court's decision.

Human rights considerations figure prominently in the context of 'quality of life' cases (such as fall to be decided after the Act came into force).

The factor of 'quality of life' arises most commonly where a patient is terminally ill or in a vegetative state.

In *Re B (a minor) (wardship: medical treatment)* [1981] 1 WLR 1421, heard in the Court of Appeal in August 1981, a child born suffering from Down's syndrome needed an operation to clear an intestinal blockage if she was to live. If it was carried out she stood a good chance of living 15 to 20 years. The parents refused their consent to the operation, believing that it was in the child's best interests that she be allowed to die, rather than face a short life of severe handicap. The local authority had her made a ward of court, and, when the surgeon in charge accepted the parents' decision, applied to the court. At first instance Ewbank J refused to order the operation to be performed by another willing surgeon.

On appeal Templeman LJ said that it was a very poignantly sad case.

The child would probably not be a cabbage but would certainly be very severely mentally and physically handicapped. He said it was the duty of the court to decide whether it was in the interests of the child that the operation should take place and, while the view of the parents should be given substantial weight, it was wrong to approach the matter on the basis simply that the parents' wishes should be respected. The question was, was the child's life demonstrably going to be so awful that in effect she must be condemned to die? The trial judge was clearly of the view that it was not. He said that, although there might be cases of severe proved damage where the future was so uncertain and where the life of the child was so bound to be full of pain and suffering that the court might be driven to a different conclusion (so to allow the child to die), the evidence in the instant case only went to show that if the operation took place and was successful, then the child might live the normal span of a Down's syndrome child with the handicaps and defects and life of a Down's syndrome child, and it was not for the court to say that life of that description ought to be extinguished. Dunn LJ agreed. He said that there was no evidence that the child's short life was likely to be an intolerable one. The child should be put into the same position as any other Down's syndrome child and it must be given the chance to live an existence.

These judgments show that the parents will not be granted by the courts the right to decide whether or not their baby should live in such circumstances; that the courts are willing to consider the quality of life as a valid factor influencing their decision (they may well take the view that there is no rule that life is to be preserved at all costs); and that life would need to be proved to be utterly dreadful, to the point of being intolerable, one might say unliveable, before it should be considered not worth preserving.

In *Re C (a minor) (wardship: medical treatment)* [1990] Fam 26, the Court of Appeal were concerned with a 16-week-old baby suffering from congenital hydrocephalus (she had already been made a ward of court for non-medical reasons). A pediatrician had reported on behalf of the Official Solicitor that she was irreversibly brain-damaged, that her condition was hopeless and that the objective of treatment should be to ease her suffering and not to prolong her life. The court accepted that she should be treated within the parameters of the report but declined to give specific instructions as to that treatment.

In *Re J (a minor) (wardship: medical treatment)* [1991] Fam 33, [1990] 2 Med LR 67, the Court of Appeal said that a court, acting solely on behalf of and in the best interests of a ward who was profoundly, but not terminally, ill, might in appropriate circumstances approve a medical course of action which failed to prevent death. The correct approach in determining the child's best interests was to assess the quality of life if life-prolonging treatment were given and to decide whether, in all the circumstances, such a life, judged from the child's viewpoint, would be intolerable to him. There was therefore no absolute rule that, save where a ward was terminally ill, the court should never withhold consent to treatment to prolong life regardless of its quality and of any additional suffering which the treatment itself might cause. In this case the court approved the consultant's advice that if further resuscitation by way of ventilation was required it would not be in the child's best interests unless his doctors thought so at the time.

In *Re J (a minor) (child in care: medical treatment)* [1993] Fam 15, an infant, who was born in January 1991, had suffered severe brain injury in a fall a year later. The local authority, acting under s 100 of the Children Act 1989, applied to the court to determine whether the consultants' decision was appropriate, namely that, if the baby suffered a life-threatening event, only ordinary resuscitative measures should be employed, not intensive therapeutic measures such as artificial ventilation. Waite J made an order that if a life-threatening event occurred full resuscitative measures should be employed. The Court of Appeal said that that order was inconsistent with established law. It was up to the treating doctors in the exercise of their clinical judgment to decide at any relevant time what treatment was appropriate. Leggatt LJ said the court was not depriving the doctors of the right to give life support, but was merely declining to deprive them of the power that they had always had of deciding themselves what was the appropriate treatment. Balcombe LJ said that it would put the doctors in an impossible position to order them to treat in a certain way, because if they did they might be acting contrary to what they believed was best for their patient and if they did not they would be in contempt of court. Lord Donaldson also made the distressing but valid point that doctors had to have regard day in day out to the limitation of resources when deciding what treatment to give to what patient (as we know from the decided cases, the court will not dictate the allocation of resources).

In *Airedale NHS Trust* v *Bland* [1993] AC 789, the House of Lords approved an order authorising discontinuance of life-sustaining treatment in the case of a patient who had been in a persistent vegetative state for some three years since the Hillsborough stadium tragedy. It was said that the principle of the sanctity of life, which was not absolute, was not violated by ceasing to give medical treatment and care involving invasive manipulation of the patient's body, to which he had not consented and which conferred no benefit upon him.

In *Frenchay Healthcare NHS Trust* v *S* [1994] 1 WLR 601, a young adult had been admitted to hospital following an overdose of drugs. It was clear that his condition had developed into a persistent vegetative state, with no cognitive function and no chance of recovery. His nasogastric feeding tube had become dislodged and the consultant considered that it was not in his best interests to replace it. The Court of Appeal said that, although ultimate power was reserved to the court to review a doctor's decision as to what was in the patient's best interests, there was no reason to question the consultant's conclusion, albeit the context of acute emergency did not permit leisurely investigation, and so the court endorsed the judge's decision to grant a declaration to the defendants that they might lawfully refrain from intervention. The Master of the Rolls said in the course of his judgment:

> It is, I think, important that there should not be a belief that what the doctor says is the patient's best interest *is* the patient's best interest. For my part I would certainly reserve to the court the ultimate power and duty to review the doctor's decision in the light of all the facts.

In *Re A* [1992] 3 Med LR 303, Johnson J made a declaration that a child, who was brain-stem dead, was dead for all legal and medical purposes and that disconnecting the ventilator would not be unlawful.

In *Swindon and Marlborough NHS Trust* v *S* [1995] 3 Med LR 84, Ward J declared that it was lawful for a patient in a persistent vegetative state, who was being cared for at home by her family, to be allowed to die by the discontinuance of all life-sustaining treatment.

In *Re T (a minor) (wardship: medical treatment)* [1997] 1 WLR 242, the Court of Appeal refused to authorise a liver transplant upon an 18-month-old boy against the wishes of his parents. The medical evidence was unanimous that he would otherwise die before he was three and that it was in his best interests to have the operation. Mother and child had gone to live abroad (the mother gave evidence at first instance by video link). The court said that the paramount consideration in such cases was the best interests of the child. The court stated that the judge, who had authorised the procedure, had concentrated on the clinical issues instead of taking a wider view and considering the further implications of such an order. Care of the child post-operatively would devolve upon the mother and would require her complete co-operation with the medical regime. Forcing her to play this crucial and irreplaceable part in the aftermath of major invasive surgery throughout the childhood of her son was a consideration that could not be ignored. The judge had failed to put into the balance these broader considerations. The court was not prepared to overrule the decision of the parents, and to order mother and child to return to the UK to accept the proposed surgery, and in that way to require the mother to undertake all the necessary care. The pediatrician was clearly of the view that, even assuming that the operation proved wholly successful in surgical terms, the child's subsequent development could be injuriously affected if his day-to-day care depended upon the commitment of a mother who had suffered the turmoil of having her child compelled against her will to undergo, as a result of a coercive order from the court, a major operation against which her own medical and maternal judgment wholeheartedly rebelled. To prolong life was not always the sole objective of the court and to require it at the expense of other considerations might not be in a child's best interests. The judge had wrongly regarded the parents' decision as unreasonable.

The Scottish courts have held that, where a hospital patient was permanently unconscious and insensate and it was no longer possible to suggest that the continuance of medical treatment was of any benefit to her, there were no longer any best interests to be served by continuing such treatment, and accordingly the court, pursuant to its authority as *parens patriae* would authorise the relevant medical practitioners to discontinue life-sustaining treatment (*Law Hospital NHS Trust* v *Lord Advocate* [1996] 2 FLR 407, 1996 SLT 869). In *South Buckinghamshire NHS Trust* v *R (a patient)* [1996] 7 Med LR 401, Sir Stephen Brown P validated a Do Not Resuscitate (DNR) notice in respect of a 23-year-old man who had been born with a serious malformation of the brain and cerebral palsy and was existing in a low awareness state at an NHS trust residential home. It was proposed to perform a gastrostomy. The judge said that the principle of law to be applied was that of the best interests of the patient, and the correct approach was for the court to judge the quality of life the patient would have to endure if given the treatment and to decide whether, in all the circumstances, such a life would be so afflicted as to be intolerable to that patient. In the particular case the judge concluded that it would not be in the best interests of the patient to subject him to cardio-pulmonary resuscitation in the event of his suffering a cardiac arrest. In *Re C* [1996] 2 FCR 569, 32 BMLR 44, the same judge authorised the switching off of the life-support machines in the case of a three-month-old baby who was enduring 'an almost living death' and for whom the future was 'quite hopeless'. Although the child was neither braindead nor in a coma, she could not see, hear, move or communicate, and was expected to live no more than a further two years during which time her condition would deteriorate causing further pain and distress.

In *Re C (a minor)* [1998] Lloyd's Rep Med 1, where a child of some 16 months was suffering from spinal muscular atrophy, had a life expectancy of not more than a year, and was enduring increasing distress from the procedures being taken to keep her alive, and where the parents for religious reasons could not consent to any measures which would shorten her life, Sir Stephen Brown P made an order permitting withdrawal of ventilation and non-resuscitation in the event of respiratory arrest.

The Royal College of Pediatrics and Child Health produced guidelines in September 1997 for situations in which doctors should consider withdrawing medical treatment from children and allowing them to die. The guidelines say such a decision is warranted where the child is braindead or in a permanent vegetative state; where care delays death without easing suffering; where the child survives so physically or mentally impaired that it is unreasonable to expect him to suffer further; or where the illness is so progressive and irreversible that further treatment is intolerable (the procedure for obtaining leave to withdraw resuscitative treatment in cases of vegetative state can be found at [1994] PIQR P312).[12]

In *A National Health Service Trust* v *D* [2000] Lloyd's Rep Med 411, Cazalet J held that a declaration, contrary to the wishes of the parents, permitting doctors to non-resuscitate in the event of cardiac or respiratory arrest of a 19-month-old boy with irreversible brain damage was not in breach of the right to life under the Human Rights Act as the treatment advised was in the child's best interests, and it also protected his rights under Article 3 not to be subjected to inhuman and degrading treatment, which included the right to die with dignity.

In *A NHS Trust* v *M* [2000] MLC 0272, Butler-Sloss P held that, if artificial nutrition and hydration were withdrawn from two patients who had been for years in a permanent vegetative state, there would not be a breach of the right to life. She said that the article did not impose an absolute obligation to treat if such treatment would be futile. The article only imposed a positive obligation to give life-sustaining treatment in circumstances where, according to responsible medical opinion, such treatment was in the best interests of the patient (see Chapter 27). In *NHS Trust A* v *H* (2001) 2 FLR 501 the President said that the state of the law as represented by the judgment in the *Bland* case (above) was compatible with Article 2 of the Convention and that in the instant case of a permanent vegetative state it would be lawful to discontinue all life-sustaining treatment. (In view of recent miraculous recoveries the court may perhaps in due course amend the *Bland* directions.)

---

12 Reference may be made to *R* v *Portsmouth Hospitals NHS Trust, ex p Glass* MLC 0114, (1999) 50 BMLR 269, CA, which is considered above in the section headed 'Children'.

In *B* v *An NHS Hospital Trust* [2002] MLC 0737, the President awarded nominal damages for trespass to a competent patient whose clearly expressed wishes not to be artificially ventilated were ignored for a number of months.

Contrast *R (on the application of Burke)* v *GMC* [2004] EWHC 1879 (Admin), where Munby J said that under the Convention, as at common law, if a patient was competent or, although incompetent, had made an advance directive which was valid and relevant to the treatment in question, his decision to require the provision of artificial nutrition and hydration in his dying days was determinative of the issue. The judgment of the Court of Appeal reversing the decision of the judge is dealt with in Chapter 27.

In *Re LM (a child)* [2004] EWHC 2713, Butler-Sloss P decided that it was in the best interests of a baby suffering from a life-limited genetic disorder, who had only a few weeks or months to live, not to undergo further aggressive treatment in the form of mechanical ventilation. And in *Wyatt* v *Portsmouth NHS Trust* [2005] EWHC 693 (Fam), Hedley J held that it would not be in the best interests of a child suffering from chronic respiratory disease to die in the course of futile aggressive treatment. In the event of respiratory collapse all treatment up to but not including incubation and ventilation would be in her best interests.

The Court of Appeal very recently reviewed the whole issue of 'best interests' in the case of *Wyatt and Wyatt* v *Portsmouth Hospitals NHS Trust* MLC 1284, a case involving a seriously disabled two year old girl with a complex medical history who had never left hospital. The court said the welfare of the child was paramount and the judge must look at the question from the assumed viewpoint of the patient. There was a strong presumption in favour of a course of action which would prolong life but that presumption was not irrebuttable. The term 'best interests' encompassed medical, emotional and all other welfare issues.

And in *NHS Trust* v *A* (1 September 2005, unreported), MLC 1283, CA, a case which concerned the withdrawal of support, which was naturally intrusive, for the heart, lungs and kidneys of an 86 year old man, the court said the correct question should be formulated as: was it in the best interests of the patient that the treatment which was prolonging his life should be continued; that there was no absolute rule to prevent a court declaring that doctors might no longer need to give treatment where the result of not giving the treatment would be to result in the earlier death of the patient; that it was for the court and not for a doctor to decide what was in the best interests of the patient; and that in this case the court would declare that the doctors treating the patient in the intensive care unit were not bound to continue to give invasive and uncomfortable treatment to the patient where there was no benefit to him.

DUTY OF DISCLOSURE: GENERAL

So far we have looked at situations where consent was clearly not given for the operation undertaken. But what if the patient knows something, but not everything, about the treatment proposed? How much does the doctor have to reveal? And does a failure to reveal mean that no valid consent can be given, so that the doctor is liable in assault, or should it be seen as an aspect of negligence, so that the action will lie only in negligence, with the consequent limiting factors applicable to such an action (as set out above).

In *Chatterton* v *Gerson* [1981] QB 432, Bristow J considered a claim by a woman that an operation to relieve pain in a post-operative scar area in the right groin had been carried out without consent and negligently. The operation had proved unsuccessful, and she claimed for assault, on the basis that her consent was vitiated for lack of proper explanation as to the nature of the procedure to be undertaken, and for negligence, on the basis that the defendant was in breach of his duty of care towards her because his failure to give a proper explanation of the nature and the implications of the proposed operation made it impossible for her to give an informed consent.

On the question whether there was a real consent so as to free the physician from liability for assault, and on the distinction between a claim for assault and one based on negligence, the judge said:

> It is clear law that in any context in which consent of the injured party is a defence to what would otherwise be a crime or a civil wrong, the consent must be real. Where, for example, a woman's consent to sexual intercourse is obtained by fraud, her apparent consent is no defence to a charge of rape. It is not difficult to state the principle or appreciate its good sense. As so often, the problem lies in its application ...
>
> In my judgment what the court has to do in each case is to look at all the circumstances and say 'Was there a real consent?' I think justice requires that in order to vitiate the reality of consent there must be a greater failure of communication between doctor and patient than that involved in a breach of duty if the claim is based on negligence. When the claim is based on negligence the plaintiff must prove not only the breach of duty to inform, but that had the duty not been broken she would not have chosen to have the operation. Where the claim is based on trespass to the person, once it is shown that the consent is unreal, then what the plaintiff would have decided if she had been given the information which would have prevented vitiation of the reality of her consent is irrelevant.
>
> In my judgment once the patient is informed in broad terms of the nature of the procedure which is intended, and gives her consent, that consent is real, and the cause of the action on which to base a claim for failure to go into risks and implications is negligence, not trespass ... in my judgment it would be very much against the interests of justice if actions which are really based on a failure by the doctor to perform his duty adequately to inform were pleaded in trespass.

That remains the best statement of the English law on the question when an apparent consent is invalid for lack of information, so as to afford a claim for assault.[13] Only if the physician fails to 'inform in broad terms of the nature of the procedure which is intended' will the apparent consent

---

13   In *Abbas* v *Kenney* [1996] 7 Med LR 47, where the patient claimed that she had not been told clearly enough that a pelvic clearance might be undertaken, Gage J said that a doctor has a duty to explain what he intends to do and the implications of what he is going to do. It must be explained in such a way that the patient can understand. The precise terms, however, and precise emphasis on what he intends to do is a matter for the individual doctor, based on his clinical judgment.

be vitiated and an action for assault lie.[14] Any lesser failure in giving information can give rise only to an action in negligence for breach of duty. What then is the surgeon's duty of disclosure?

The risks of the operation

Every operation is attended by its risks. So is most treatment. Every drug can produce unwanted side effects. No treatment can be guaranteed to succeed. When something goes wrong the patient first asks whether the doctor has been negligent in his treatment. Has he made a negligent diagnosis, or prescribed the wrong drugs when he should have known better? Or has he performed the operation without due care? When it appears that in the strictly medical context the doctor's performance has been unimpugnable, the patient's complaint is likely to be: 'You never told me this might happen. If you had I would have declined the treatment.' The English courts have had to consider which of two tests to adopt for assessing the duty upon a doctor to disclose the risks inherent in a particular treatment. The tests may be termed 'the medical standard' and 'informed consent'.

The medical standard

Under the medical standard the medical profession is permitted to set its own standards of disclosure without supervision by the court. The profession itself decides what disclosure is to be made in any particular case. It is enough for a defendant to avoid liability if he shows that at the time of the treatment there was a body of responsible medical opinion, albeit a minority one, that would have done what he did. This enables a defendant to succeed simply by producing one or two physicians who endorse his conduct, and it is of no avail for the claimant to produce evidence to a contrary effect. If the court accepts that there was such a body of medical opinion it will not be entitled to choose between the differing schools of thought. This is a unique advantage for the professionals. The court is forever choosing between differing expert testimonies in other fields and making up its own mind as to what constitutes negligence.

This medical standard had for a long time been accepted as the test for assessing negligence in treatment and diagnosis (see Chapter 16 above for a full discussion), but it was not clear before the decision of the House of Lords in the *Sidaway* case (see below) that it would be applicable to the question of disclosure of risks.

Informed consent

There had grown up across the Atlantic, in some US jurisdictions and also in Canada, a different test, whereby the court had the right to assess and delineate the extent of the duty of disclosure in any particular case.

---

14   In *Slater* v *Baker and Stapleton* (1767) 2 Wils 359, it was said that 'a patient should be told what is about to be done to him, that he may take courage and put himself in such a situation as to enable him to undergo the operation' – courage is what was needed in those days, one may be sure!

This was the test of 'informed consent'. If the patient was not given sufficient information upon which he could reach an informed decision whether to accept the treatment proposed or not, then he was not able to give a valid consent. It was for the court to decide whether he had been given that information, not for the doctors. The leading cases illustrating this doctrine are, in the US, *Canterbury* v *Spence* 464 F 2d 772, MLC 0006 (1972); *Scaria* v *St Paul Fire and Marine Insurance* 227 NW 2d 647; *Zelesnik* v *Jewish Chronic Disease Hospital* 336 NYS 2d 163 (1975); and in the Supreme Court of Canada, *Hopp* v *Lepp* (1980) 112 DLR (3d) 67 and *Reibl* v *Hughes* (1980) 114 DLR (3d) 1.

The courts have variously said:

> To bind the disclosure obligation to medical usage is to arrogate the decision on revelation to the physician alone. Respect for the patient's right of self-determination on particular therapy demands a standard set by law for physicians rather than one which physicians may or may not impose upon themselves.
>
> The duty to disclose or inform cannot be summarily limited to a self-created custom of the profession, to a professional standard that may be non-existent or inadequate to meet the informational needs of a patient.
>
> Risk disclosure is based on the patient's right to determine what shall be done with his body. Such right should not be at the disposal of the medical community.

According to the doctrine of informed consent, a risk is required to be disclosed when a reasonable person, in what the physician knows or should know to be the patient's position, would be likely to attach significance to the risk or cluster of risks in deciding whether or not to forgo the proposed therapy. The physician can plead therapeutic privilege, and show that there was a good clinical reason why a particular disclosure should not have been made.

Expert evidence of current medical practice remains cogent and persuasive evidence of the appropriate standard, but it is not conclusive. As it was neatly put in a Canadian case:

> No longer does the medical profession alone collectively determine, by its own practices, the amount of information a patient should have in order to decide whether to undergo an operation (*White* v *Turner* (1981) 120 DLR (3d) 269).

Anyone interested in applications of the doctrine of informed consent might wish to read some of the cases in which the Canadian reports abound: *Videto* v *Kennedy* (1981) 125 DLR (3d) 127; *Bucknam* v *Kostuik* (1983) 3 DLR (4th) 99; *Considine* v *Camp Hill Hospital* (1982) 133 DLR (3d) 11; *Ferguson* v *Hamilton Civil Hospitals* (1983) 144 DLR (3d) 214; *Casey* v *Provan* (1984) 11 DLR (4th) 708; *Grey* v *Webster* (1984) 14 DLR (4th) 706.

The Saskatchewan Court of Appeal's decision in *Haughian* v *Paine* (1987) 37 DLR (4th) 624, is interesting. Although based on the doctrine of informed consent, it makes the generally valid point that a patient is entitled to be told of non-surgical alternatives to the treatment proposed.

Kitchen v *McMullen* [1990] 1 Med LR 352, New Brunswick Court of Appeal, can be used to illuminate the difference in the law on the doctor's duty to disclose the risks of an operation or treatment between Canadian law, where the patient's rights are respected, and here, where they are not. In short, the claimant was given an anti-coagulant (Hemofil) to control bleeding after a tooth extraction. Like all blood products Hemofil carries a small risk of hepatitis, which materialised. The claimant sued for damages on the ground that he should have been warned of the risk, claiming that, if he had been warned, he would not have accepted the treatment.

Now, under the Canadian doctrine of informed consent the doctor has a duty to disclose all 'material' or 'unusual or special' risks. Those risks are (more or less) such risks as the court feels would affect the mind of a patient when deciding whether or not to accept the treatment proposed. What is important here is that it is for the court to decide the status of the risk, not for the doctors. So if the court decides the risk was 'material', then it matters not that no doctor ever discloses it. A doctor is in breach of his duty in not doing so. In this way the Canadian court protects the right of a patient to be properly informed about the treatment proposed. But under English law, as explained below, there is no duty to disclose any risk unless there is no body of responsible medical opinion, not even a minority one, that would follow the course of not disclosing it. So it is left to the medical profession to decide what the patient may or may not know about the treatment he is being offered. So much for patients' rights.

The second aspect of the Canadian test is to decide if a reasonable patient in the claimant's position would have declined or accepted the treatment if warned. This issue is similarly relevant under our law: if the court decides that the risk should have been disclosed (for example, it is likely to find that the risk of failure of a sterilisation should these days be disclosed to the woman), it still has to decide if the patient would have nevertheless accepted the operation or the treatment (thus it might well find that the woman would have taken the 1 in 500 risk of the sterilisation failing, rather than try some other, probably even less secure, method). Canadian law has a rather complex test of whether a reasonable patient would have refused the treatment: our test is simply to ask whether the claimant has satisfied the court on the balance of probabilities that he would have refused it.

The actual decision in the *Kitchen* case was that all three judges found that the risk was one that should have been disclosed to the patient, but two of them then decided that he would have accepted the risk (the third said he would have waited to see if the bleeding got worse). So his action failed.

In *Ellis* v *Wallsend District Hospital* [1990] 2 Med LR 103, the New South Wales Court of Appeal held that where the patient's evidence was that if warned of the risks of an operation she would have declined it the trial judge was not at liberty to reject that evidence unless there was contrary evidence showing the claimant's contention to be 'inherently incredible' or 'inherently improbable'.

For a recent decision of the High Court of Australia see *Chappell* v *Hart* [1999] MLC 0067. A surgeon was liable for failing to warn of a slight risk of voice damage from a throat operation in circumstances where the patient had specifically inquired.

The English test

The English test for establishing negligence in matters of treatment and diagnosis was clear. The medical standard test had been clearly set out in the direction to the jury given by McNair J in *Bolam* v *Friern Hospital Management Committee* [1957] 1 WLR 582. This direction had become a *locus classicus* and was expressly endorsed by the House of Lords in *Whitehouse* v *Jordan* [1981] 1 WLR 246 and *Maynard* v *West Midlands Regional Health Authority* [1984] 1 WLR 634. But did it apply to the duty to disclose material risks? In fact the *Bolam* case included an allegation of failure to disclose the risks inherent in the treatment undertaken, but it was generally thought that it was still arguable that the test for the duty of disclosure was not necessarily the same as the test for diagnosis and treatment. In the seminal case of *Hunter* v *Hanley* 1955 SLT 213, MLC 0002, a Scottish case upon which McNair J relied, Lord President Clyde had spoken only of diagnosis and treatment:

> In the realm of diagnosis and treatment there is ample scope for difference of opinion and one man clearly is not negligent merely because his conclusion differs from that of other professional men ... The true test for establishing negligence in diagnosis or treatment on the part of a doctor is whether he has been proved to be guilty of such failure as no doctor of ordinary skill would be guilty of if acting with ordinary care ...

In *Hills* v *Potter* [1984] 1 WLR 641n, Hirst J rejected any form of the doctrine of informed consent as having no place in English law and adopted the medical test (though he made it clear that the claimant would have failed in either event).

The Sidaway case

The most important case on this issue has been *Sidaway* v *Board of Governors of the Bethlem Royal Hospital and the Maudsley Hospital* [1985] AC 871, MLC 0010, HL. The facts were that the claimant suffered paralysis following an operation upon her cervical vertebrae. The operation carried a small risk of untoward damage, about a 2% risk of damage to nerve root or spinal cord. Damage to the cord would produce a far more serious result, and the risk of that happening was less than 1%. The surgeon warned of the risk of damage to the nerve root but not of the risk to the spinal cord. The trial judge found that the patient had not been told of all material risks so as to be able to give a fully informed consent to the operation, but, as he was satisfied that the surgeon, in giving the limited disclosure that he did, was following a practice that had the backing of a body of responsible medical opinion at the time of the operation, the claimant must fail, because the test in English law was the medical standard, not informed consent.

The Court of Appeal by a majority endorsed this view ([1984] QB 493). Dunn LJ said a contrary result would damage the doctor/patient relationship and might well have an adverse effect on the practice of medicine. Sir Nicolas Browne-Wilkinson said that the particular quality of that relationship meant that the duty of disclosure in that context should be approached on a different basis from that applicable to ordinary professional men, that the patient must have all the information he reasonably should, but that to test the reasonableness of the disclosure made one look to the standards of the profession. However, the Master of the Rolls said that, although evidence of the medical practice was important, the definition of the duty of care was not to be handed over to the medical profession. It was a matter for the law and the courts, who could not stand idly by if the profession, by an excess of paternalism, denied their patient a real choice. In other words, he said, the law will not permit the medical profession to play God.

Although the House of Lords judgments reveal different bases for their conclusions, it is tolerably clear that they, albeit by a bare majority, endorsed the medical test, though adding a proviso. Lord Diplock said that the *Bolam* test should be applied to the context of disclosure as to that of treatment and diagnosis. He pointed out that there might at any one time be a number of practices that satisfied the test, and he said:

> To decide what risks the existence of which a patient should be voluntarily warned [about] and the terms in which such warning, if any, should be given, having regard to the effect the warning may have, is as much an exercise of professional skill and judgment as any other part of the doctor's comprehensive duty of care to the individual patient, and expert medical evidence on this matter should be tested in just the same way.

On the question of informed consent, Lord Diplock said that the doctrine was jurisprudentially unsound as it sought to transfer to the sphere of negligence considerations as to consent that were only meaningful in the context of assault and battery (it is indeed true that the US courts had had difficulty in reconciling the absence of 'consent' with a cause of action not in battery but in negligence).

Lord Bridge, with whom Lord Keith agreed, rejecting the informed consent approach, said that a decision as to what degree of disclosure of risks is best calculated to assist a particular patient to make a rational choice as to whether or not to undergo a particular treatment must primarily be a matter of clinical judgment, and so the issue was to be decided primarily on the basis of expert medical evidence, applying the *Bolam* test; but he added (this is the proviso I mentioned above) that the judge might in certain circumstances come to the conclusion that disclosure of a particular risk was so obviously necessary to an informed choice on the part of a patient that no reasonably prudent medical man would fail to make it. He instanced a 10% risk of a stroke from an operation, though he pointed out that there might even there be some cogent clinical reason militating against disclosure.

Lord Templeman's approach was different: he said that neither was the patient entitled to know everything nor the doctor to decide everything. The doctor was under an obligation to provide information adequate to enable the patient to reach a balanced judgment, subject always to the doctor's own obligation to say and do nothing which he was satisfied would be harmful to the patient: the court would award damages if satisfied that the doctor blundered and that the patient was deprived of information which was necessary for that purpose. Although Lord Templeman makes it clear that in his view the patient is not entitled to know everything, particularly if he does not ask, there is in his judgment no suggestion that the court is bound by medical evidence. He says more than once that it is for the court to decide whether sufficient information was given. This puts him on the same side of the conceptual fence as Lord Scarman, who effectively adopted the doctrine of informed consent, though holding against the claimant on the facts.

In *Moyes* v *Lothian Health Board* [1990] 1 Med LR 463, a Scottish court of first instance rejected a claim that certain risks alleged to be inherent in an angiography procedure should have been disclosed to the patient, principally because it was shown that at the time of the procedure, in 1981, it was consistent with responsible medical practice to give no warning at all.

In *Heath* v *West Berkshire Health Authority* [1992] 3 Med LR 57, the claimant failed in her allegation that she should have been warned of the risk of lingual nerve damage arising from an operation to extract a wisdom tooth because the evidence accepted by the judge was that at the time of the operation there was a responsible body of medical opinion that gave no such warning.

In *Smith* v *Tunbridge Wells Health Authority* [1994] 5 Med LR 334, a surgeon failed to inform a man of 28 sufficiently clearly before a rectopexy of the risk, sadly fulfilled, that the procedure could make him impotent. The judge held that, as his condition was not particularly serious, he would probably have declined the operation. Similarly, in *McAllister* v *Lewisham and North Southwark Health Authority* [1994] 5 Med LR 343, a neurosurgeon had failed properly to warn his female patient of the relevant risks before surgery to correct arteriovascular malformation in her leg. What is particularly of note is that the judge held that she would probably have declined the operation if she had been warned even though her evidence was to the effect that she really could not answer such a hypothetical question.

In *Smith* v *Salford Health Authority* [1994] 5 Med LR 321, the patient failed on causation, ie he proved that the warnings given before surgery on his neck were inadequate but the judge concluded that proper warnings would not have put him off the operation. However, he still won the case as he succeeded in proving operative negligence.

In *Williamson* v *East London and City Health Authority* [1998] Lloyd's Rep Med 6, Butterfield J held a plastic surgeon liable for not giving sufficient information about the extent of the the breast operation she intended to perform.

In *Webb* v *Barclays Bank and Portsmouth Hospitals NHS Trust* [2001] Lloyds Rep Med 500, the Court of Appeal said that, where a doctor through ignorance brought about by his negligent failure to inform himself fully about the pathology of the patient's knee, that did not absolve him from the consequences of his negligent advice which resulted from such ignorance. Had he conducted a proper investigation and given the patient the appropriate advice, she would not then have consented to the amputation. In *Enright* v *Kwun* [2003] MLC 1017, Morland J held that the medical attendants of a 37-year-old pregnant woman had failed to tell her of the one in 250 risk of Down's syndrome and the option of an amniocentesis. If they had she would have had the amniocentesis which would have shown the defect and she would then have opted for a termination.

The Lord Bridge proviso

Little has so far been made of the proviso Lord Bridge offered in the *Sidaway* case (*above*). Would a court be willing to hold that a doctor could be liable for not disclosing a risk despite it being shown that it was not the practice of the profession at the time to do so? The relaxation of the strict *Bolam* principle afforded by the *Bolitho* decision (as explained in

Chapter 16) might suggest that the court would be willing to be the ultimate arbiter of what should be disclosed, similarly to the Canadian principle (Lord Browne-Wilkinson expressly said in *Bolitho* that he was not
considering the issue of disclosure of risks). Lord Woolf offered some support to this suggestion in the case of *Pearce v United Bristol Healthcare
NHS Trust* [1998] PIQR P53, [1999] MLC 0086, CA.

Pearce v United Bristol Healthcare NHS Trust

The claimant mother maintained an unusual contention. She had tragi-
cally given birth to a dead child in December 1991. The consultant had
advised her a few days before the birth, some two weeks after the estimated date of delivery, to wait yet longer, rather than be induced. It was
not suggested that his advice that induction would be dangerous was
negligent. But it was alleged that he should have disclosed the small
additional risk involved in waiting, and, if he had done so, the mother
would have sought and obtained a Cesarian section. Lord Woolf, who gave
the only reasoned judgment, gave detailed consideration to the *prudent
doctor* proviso. Lord Woolf described these words in the speech of Lord
Bridge (in *Sidaway*) as 'particularly apposite':

> ... even in a case where, as here, no expert witness in the relevant medical field
> condemns the non-disclosure as being in conflict with accepted and responsi-
> ble medical practice, I am of opinion that the judge might in certain circum-
> stances come to the conclusion that disclosure of a particular risk was so
> obviously necessary to an informed choice on the part of the patient that no
> reasonably prudent medical man would fail to make it. The kind of case I have
> in mind would be an operation involving a substantial risk of grave adverse
> consequences, as, for example, the 10 per cent risk of a stroke from the opera-
> tion which was the subject of the Canadian case of *Reibl* v *Hughes*. In such a
> case, in the absence of some cogent technical reason why the patient should
> not be informed, a doctor, recognising and respecting his patient's right of deci-
> sion, could hardly fail to appreciate the necessity for an appropriate warning.

Lord Woolf expressed himself in terms much more consistent with the
Canadian, American and Australian law of disclosure of material risks (ie
where, put loosely, the court is the arbiter of what needs to be disclosed
and not the medical profession), rather than the far more doctor-oriented
English law. He said:

> In a case where it is the alleged that a plaintiff has been deprived of the oppor-
> tunity to make a proper decision as to what course he or she should take in
> relation to treatment, it seems to me to be the law, as indicated in the cases to
> which I have just referred, that if there is a significant risk which would affect
> the judgment of a reasonable patient, then in the normal course it is the
> responsibility of a doctor to inform the patient of that significant risk, if the
> information is needed so that the patient can determine for him or herself as
> to what course he or she should adopt.

And he said that when one refers to a 'significant risk' it is not possible to
talk in precise percentages.
    And:

> ... where there is what can realistically be called a 'significant risk', then in the
> ordinary event, as I have already indicated, the patient is entitled to be
> informed of that risk.

The way in which Lord Woolf expressed himself offers opportunities in the future for the effective use of the prudent doctor proviso, in the sense that a patient should find it easier to argue in appropriate circumstances that a risk should have been disclosed, and the court should declare such, even though the defendants show that there is a body of medical opinion that approves of non-disclosure in the relevant circumstances.[15]

Practical difficulties

In practice, claims for failure to warn of risks are difficult. In the first place they are usually an after-thought, by solicitor or patient, where the obvious allegation, ie negligence in advising or carrying out treatment or medical care, has proved unfounded upon receipt of expert medical advice. Thoughts then turn to the possibility of claiming that information should have been given before the treatment which would have – so it has to be presumed – led to a substantially better outcome. A number of hurdles need to be overcome. First, one has to establish a duty to give specific information, ie one has to show that at the relevant time there would be no responsible body of medical opinion, not even a minority one, that would have found it acceptable not to give that information. Then one has to prove that such information was not given. The defendant may say that it was, in which case it is a matter of his word against the patient's. The patient may be helped if there is no record of such information being given. Then, usually the most difficult hurdle of all, the patient has to show that, if the information had been given, he would have avoided substantive injury. This usually means that he would have declined the procedure. Or sometimes it may mean that, having received all proper information, he would have elected for another procedure. In either event he will have to prove that one or other of those courses would have been followed. If there was no substantially better alternative, he will have to show that he would have declined the treatment. But in most cases it will be clear that he needed the treatment and unlikely that he would have continued to endure his pathology merely because he was told of a small risk of adverse effects. Even if he can show that he would have declined the operation, he still has to show that his current condition is substantially worse than it would have been. Proof of these various matters is not impossible, as the successful cases show, but causation, in this sort as in all sorts of medical claims, needs strict analysis. Parents who claim that they would have let their child die if they had known that an essential heart operation carried a small risk of brain damage are likely to have difficulty in establishing that contention. For the highly significant case of *Chester* v *Afshar* see the section so headed below.

Australia

The High Court of Australia has explicitly refused to follow *Sidaway*. In *Rogers* v *Whittaker* [1993] 4 Med LR 79, the evidence showed that a responsible body of medical practitioners would not have disclosed to the

---

15 See also in Chapter 1 Lord Woolf's observations in his recent address to University College, London.

claimant the risk to her good left eye from sympathetic ophthalmitis if her defective right eye were removed. This would have been enough to lose her the case if *Sidaway* had been applied. However, it was held that it was for the courts to adjudicate on what was the appropriate standard of care after giving weight to 'the paramount consideration that a person is entitled to make his own decision about his life', that breach of duty of care was not to be concluded on the basis of the expert medical evidence alone, that evidence of accepted medical practice was a useful (but not a conclusive) guide for the courts, and that the factors according to which a court determined whether a medical practitioner was in breach of the standard of care would vary according to whether it was a case involving diagnosis, treatment, or the provision of information and advice: the different cases raised varying difficulties which required consideration of different factors. The finding of the courts below that the defendant had been negligent in not disclosing the risk was upheld.

It is time now that the English courts reviewed their rejection of the doctrine of informed consent and their consequent refusal to acknowledge any right in the patient to be given any information beyond what the medical profession sees fit to disclose. Lord Woolf has given a lead. Let it be followed.

The duty to answer questions

The judgments of the Law Lords in the *Sidaway* case make it clear at least that, when questioned specifically by a patient of apparently sound mind about risks involved in a proposed treatment, the doctor must answer as truthfully and as fully as the questioner requires. This duty to answer has been said, though *obiter*, by Lord Donaldson MR to apply to questions asked *after* treatment, ie in an effort to find out exactly what was done and what, if anything, went wrong. This was said in the context of an application for pre-trial disclosure (*Lee* v *South West Thames Regional Health Authority* [1985] 1 WLR 845, CA).

Before absolving a doctor, therefore, who has made only a limited disclosure, the court should at the very least be satisfied that there was a responsible body of medical opinion that would at that time have made only such limited disclosure, that the patient did not (expressly or impliedly) ask for further information, and that it could not be said that any prudent doctor would have made further disclosure.

It was said at first instance in *Blyth* v *Bloomsbury Health Authority* [1993] 4 Med LR 151, that a health authority that receives a reasonable request from a patient as to the possible side effects of a drug that is prescribed for her (Depo-Provera in this case), but administers the drug without warning of possible dangers, will be liable to pay damages if it is proved that the patient would not have taken the drug had she been given the relevant information. However, allowing the authority's appeal, the Court of Appeal said that there was no evidence on which the judge could properly have found that insufficient information was given in answer to the claimant's request so as to constitute a breach of duty. The court also said, *obiter*, that even where a patient asks for information the duty to inform him is governed by the *Bolam* principle, so that in this context, too (the context of a patient actively seeking information before deciding whether or not to accept the proposed treatment), the medical standard must be applied. This reading of the observations of the Law Lords in the *Sidaway* case is, it is submitted, not only a misreading but is in itself quite unacceptable. It turns over to the medical profession the decision as to what to reveal when they are specifically asked for information, thus totally negating the right of a patient to be properly informed before deciding whether to submit to treatment.[16]

In *Wyatt* v *Dr Curtis and Central Nottingham Health Authority* [2003] MLC 1080, the GP (first defendant) admitted negligence in not warning a pregnant mother of the risk to her baby of her chicken pox. She then sought to hold the health authority at least equally liable for not ascertaining that the GP had not warned the mother, on the basis that the mother had impliedly asked the doctor at the hospital for the relevant information. But this attempt at establishing a 'constructive' request for information did not succeed. The Court of Appeal held that the hospital was entitled to assume that competent advice had already been given to the mother by her GP.

Chester v *Afshar*

The facts in this important case (MLC 1170, [2004] UKHL 41) are easy enough to summarise. The well-known neurosurgeon, Mr Afshar, was found by the trial judge to be in breach of duty in not warning the patient of the small risk of paralysis resulting from cauda equina compression during the lumbar operation. The risk materialised through no fault of the surgeon and the unfortunate patient suffered serious permanent injury. The judge, Sir Denis Henry, did not find for a fact that she would never have had the operation if warned (that would have been an open and shut case for the patient, just as it would have been a hopeless case if the finding was that the warning would not have deterred the patient). He found that she would have declined to have it at that time, but would have sought a second or even a third opinion. He made no finding one way or another as to whether she would have had it somewhere at someone's hands at some future date. The judge concluded that that was good enough to show that the surgeon was liable for the injury. The Court of Appeal agreed. One may think it was perfectly logical and sensible to state that, even if she did at some future time undergo the operation, the chances of the injury arising were the same as originally, ie a very great deal less than 50%, and therefore the appropriate conclusion was that the injury would not have occurred. Of course, if the fact that the patient suffered this injury was good evidence that she probably would have suffered it also in any later operation, which is sometimes the case, then she could not succeed. But that was not the case here.

Their Lordships, with the possible exception of Lord Walker, took the view that, as the surgeon's breach of duty had not increased the risk of the injury happening (ie the very fact that the chance of injury, though still very low, would remain precisely the same at any future operation), he had not caused the injury. As indicated above, I would prefer to argue that the chance of her suffering the injury at any future date was 1% and

---

16 On the duty to disclose risks if asked, see also *Smith* v *Auckland Hospital Board* [1965] NZLR 191; *Hatcher* v *Black* (1954) Times, 2 July.

therefore, on the balance of probabilities, she would not have suffered it. But, with the possible exception of Lord Walker, who alone made the point that the scenario might well be different at a later date (in terms of surgeon, environment and maybe other more subtle factors), the House agreed that to permit the claimant to succeed in this case there would have to be an extension to the normal rules of causation (just as there was in their decision in the *Fairchild* case (see Chapter 17)).

The claimant nevertheless succeeded, albeit by a bare majority (just as in the similar Australian case of *Chappell* v *Hart* [1999] MLC 0067). Three of the judges were for making such an extension on policy grounds, two were not. The policy is that patients' rights to disclosure have to be protected. If the surgeon fails to recognise those rights and the very injury against which he was required to give a warning materialises, it is only right and proper that he should be held liable, even if that amounts to putting him in the position of insurer.

The simplest expression of the minority view was put by Lord Hoffman, who said that the claimant had failed to prove her loss as the risk would have been the same whenever or wherever the operation might have been carried out. In other words, the purpose of warning was to enable the patient, if she so wished, to take steps to remove or minimise the risk – which it had not been proved she would or could have done. Therefore the surgeon's failure to warn had not been the cause of her injury. Nor did he see any good reason for a policy extension. Lord Bingham took a similar view on both conclusions, stating that he saw no reason to provide for potentially very large damages to be paid by a defendant whose breach of duty had not been shown to have worsened the physical condition of the claimant.

Those in favour of the claimant's case were Lords Steyn, Hope and Walker. They agreed with the minority (at any rate the first two clearly did) that the application of normal principles of causation would not permit the claimant to succeed, and then went on to allow the policy extension, saying that, just as in *Fairchild*, there was in this case too, no causation proved on ordinary legal principles, but that there was a special case for making an exception and declaring that in these particular circumstances there would be a special rule for deeming causation to have been proved, or at any rate – and this is of course the important issue shorn of legal casuistry – for imposing liability on the surgeon.

What does this decision mean in practical terms to the medical negligence practitioner? In the first place it means that if the patient would have declined an operation if given a necessary but omitted warning of a risk and the risk materialised and the relevant injury occurred, her claim is not defeated by the fact that, though declining the operation at that time, she would probably have decided thereafter to have it anyway. But are there any limits to this? What if she would have decided, after taking a second opinion, to have it a few days later with the same surgeon in the same hospital? Perhaps the court would conclude that the chance of the risk materialising in those circumstances did not remain the same, but, as it had already been seen to have happened in virtually identical circumstances, it could be inferred that it would probably happen again. On the other hand, the risk in this *Chester* case was one that materialises totally at random, and one remembers that the chance of the tossing of a coin producing, say, a sixth consecutive tails is (I believe) still 50%.

In the second place, this decision, by the very manner in which it is based on policy, indicates (a) that patients' claims may in other contexts be able to initiate new rules of law, and (b) that some members of the House of Lords clearly have empathy – I would not presume to say sympathy – with the position of the patient *vis-à-vis* the doctor.

NON-THERAPEUTIC CONTEXTS

There are various references in the argument and judgments in the *Sidaway* case to the 'healing' or 'therapeutic' context in which that case was set. Is this rule, whereby the medical profession sets its own standards for disclosure, limited to such a context? It is perhaps understandable that the decision as to what should be disclosed to the patient about the risks of the operation should be viewed as a clinical decision and part and parcel of the delicate relationship between the physician and a sick patient – there may well be therapeutic considerations. But what if there are none, or none of any great substance? What if the patient needs advice about an elective procedure and the options involved in, for example, cosmetic surgery, or birth control or diet? This question arose in *Gold v Haringey Health Authority* [1986] 1 FLR 125.

The facts were that when in 1979 Mrs Gold entered her third pregnancy, she and her husband decided to have no further children after that one. They reached a provisional decision that Mr Gold would be vasectomised. But when she informed the consultant at the ante-natal clinic that she wanted no more children, she was told that a sterilisation would be arranged for her. Nothing was said about the other contraceptive options and nothing was said about the failure rate of sterilisation. There was evidence to the effect that in 1979 there was a responsible body of medical opinion that would not have spoken of the options or the failure rate. The judge said that the *Sidaway* case was decided in a therapeutic context, and that he was concerned with a different situation, where a woman asks for advice as to methods of contraception and is told that sterilisation is right for her without being told of other options and without being given the information that there is a risk of failure. He said that in that context the adequacy of what she is told was to be determined not exclusively by reference to the prevailing medical practice but by the court's view as to whether the person giving advice – who might be a hospital doctor, a GP or a counsellor at a family planning clinic or a health visitor – acted negligently. He saw no reason to extend the exceptional test in respect of negligent advice given by a doctor to the context of contraceptive counselling. And he found that there was a duty upon the doctors concerned to have mentioned the options and the failure rate, a duty which they had not discharged.

However, the Court of Appeal took a different view ([1988] QB 481). They said that the distinction the judge drew between therapeutic contexts, where the *Bolam* principle applied, and non-therapeutic contexts, such as contraceptive counselling, was artificial and contrived, and ran counter to the intent of the *Sidaway* decision. The fact that medical practice as to warning was divided at the time of Mrs Gold's sterilisation meant *ipso facto* that a doctor who did not warn could not be held in breach of his duty. The result of this decision is that, even in the context of an adult and healthy woman wanting to know the best way to avoid having any more children, her right to information to help her decide is governed solely by what the profession is willing to tell her, and the court will not assert any other right to information on her behalf. As long as there are some doctors, sufficient to constitute a responsible body of opinion, who give only a limited or no disclosure (in this or any other context), such disclosure will be declared by the court to be consistent with the patient's rights.[17] However, this decision was given some 17 years ago, before *Bolitho* and before *Pearce*. It would be nice to think that it no longer represented the law.

Experiments

There is a more stringent need for disclosure of risks where the treatment is to any extent experimental. In *Chadwick* v *Parsons* [1971] 2 Lloyd's Rep 49; affd [1971] 2 Lloyd's Rep 322, CA, the defendant admitted liability on the basis that in his desire to find patients in need of a particular treatment, he was so enthusiastic about the prospects of success that he failed to disclose the serious risks which the operation carried.

The fact that English law allows the doctor's duty to be judged by the doctors themselves created particular difficulties in the context of the keyhole (minimally invasive) endoscopic procedures. Laparascopic sterilisation had been around for a long time, but in recent years more and more surgical procedures are carried out by keyhole techniques. Because neither the medical profession nor their disciplinary bodies took care to ensure that no practitioner jumped on to the bandwagon without proper training, many procedures were carried out by inadequately trained surgeons. The lack of accredited training made it hard to prove that a particular doctor was acting outside acceptable limits as viewed by the profession; and even more difficult to define satisfactorily, ie in a manner that would constitute legal proof pursuant to the *Sidaway* test, that more information, whether about the proposed treatment or other options, should have been given. Even now, some years down the line, it is difficult to establish that the profession has formed any consensus about what information should be given to the patient. Different practitioners, all eagerly accepting patients for the brave new forms of surgical technique, give various bits of information to their patients, no doubt according to their own lights, but in those circumstances it is not possible for the patient to prove that all responsible practitioners would give some specific information. Unless the courts adopt in that context the only sensible approach, namely to make up their own minds, upon the evidence given as to the nature and novelty of the procedure and the experience of the defendant, what he reasonably should have said to the patient, there is little chance of a successful claim, and, in the wider scene, little chance of getting the profession to get its act in order.

---

17   The various factors which go to decide what should be revealed before any particular treatment, whether the professional standard prevails or the court has an overall jurisdiction to decide whether the medical practice is appropriate, were considered in detail by Woodhouse J in the New Zealand case of *Smith* v *Auckland Hospital Board* [1964] NZLR 241 (overruled on other grounds [1965] NZLR 191, but Woodhouse J's views were specifically endorsed by the Ontario courts in *Male* v *Hopmans* (1965) 54 DLR (2d) 592, and on appeal (1967) 64 DLR (2d) 105).

Chapter 24

The failed sterilisation and similar mishaps

An unplanned pregnancy can arise as a result of a failed sterilisation, male or female. The claim is that a pregnancy has been endured and (if the pregnancy is not terminated) a child, whether handicapped or healthy, has been born who would not have been born if there had been no negligence in or around the sterilisation. A similar claim is made where a pregnancy should have been terminated but, due to negligence, was not, eg an incompetently performed termination or a failure of ante-natal screening to detect fetal defects which would have resulted in a lawful termination.

Until the surprising decision of the House of Lords in *McFarlane* v *Tayside Health Board* [2000] 2 AC 59, [1999] 4 All ER 961, MLC 0127, the cost of raising a healthy unplanned child had been allowed in innumerable cases. It formed the bulk of the claim. Such a claim usually settled within a range of £50–80,000. Following the *McFarlane* decision (as a Scottish case it is not strictly binding in England, but it is of overwhelming persuasive authority) claims for a healthy child born due to negligent medical attention are of modest value, limited to somewhere between £5,000 and £10,000 general damages for the pregnancy (depending whether it was easy or not), plus any special damage arising directly out of the pregnancy and not simply as a result of the birth. This would include, for example, time off work while pregnant and in the aftermath, clothes required for the pregnancy, and medical costs arising directly out of the pregnancy. If the pregnancy left the mother with psychological injury, this would increase general damages. An uncomplicated claim of this type may now be unable to satisfy the legal aid costs-benefit ratio.

The right to claim the cost of care for an unplanned *handicapped* child was left open by the House of Lords. Already some authority has accumulated on that issue.

No claim for wrongful life

Note that in any event the child himself has no claim as the doctors did not cause the handicap, only the birth – the claim is by the parents. Not surprisingly, the court will not assess compensation for being born handicapped as against not being born at all (*McKay* v *Essex Health Authority*

[1982] QB 1166, CA). So one needs to watch out for limitation in these cases.[1]

Sterilisation

The failure rate of sterilisation

The failure rate for female sterilisation was, until recently, accepted to be, overall, somewhere between 1 in 250 and 1 in 500, a figure which included both operator failure and natural recanalisation (no separate figures exist). On this basis, given that there are about 100,000 sterilisations each year, there would therefore be about 300 unplanned pregnancies a year. However, recent statistical evidence from the US has indicated a much higher rate of failure. The failure rate for vasectomy has usually been considered to be substantially lower, though some experts say that is not proven. The failure rate for vasectomy, once the initial period for testing the semen for sperm has been successfully concluded, is generally thought to be no more than one in several thousand. Failure of vasectomy discovered during the post-operative testing period is referred to as 'early recanalisation', thereafter 'late recanalisation'.

Lines of attack

There are two separate possible lines of attack, of which only the first is likely these days to have the potential to support a claim.

The *first* line of attack is the allegation that the operation was incompetently performed.

Proof: Where conception has taken place within a few months of a sterilisation by clips (the usual method these days) most, but not all, experts would say that the most likely inference is that one of the clips was not properly applied to the tube (different considerations may apply where the sterilisation was not by clips or rings). A few experts, particularly if instructed by the defence, would argue that a fistula could have formed soon after the procedure or the tube recanalised unusually quickly.

But how does one prove that the clip or ring was misplaced (or, for example, that the burns of diathermy were wrongly sited or otherwise incompetently applied) where pregnancy takes place a considerable time after the sterilisation? X-rays will not help. There has to be an invasive procedure. If the patient may be about to undergo a Cesarian section or a further sterilisation, one should ensure that a reliable observer (this may be the treating doctor) reports on the state of the tubes. An invasive procedure for the sole purpose of obtaining evidence would be medically unethical.

If a clip is found on the wrong structure, such as a neighbouring ligament, there can be no proper defence. The defence expert occasionally maintains that misplacing the clip can happen in the best of hands. This is untrue. The operator should ensure that the clip properly occludes the lumen of the tube. He should be able to see this. If he is in any doubt, it is his duty to advise the woman to have a hysterosalpingogram (see

---

1   See 'The action for wrongful life' at the end of this chapter.

McLennan v *Newcastle Health Authority* MLC 0615, [1992] 3 Med LR 215). It follows that if the clip is found on the tube but not properly occluding the lumen, there is no proper defence.

There may also be further evidence about the position of the clip after the relevant parts of the tubes have been sent for histological examination.

If the clip is found not to be on any structure but lying loose in the peritoneal cavity, this will indicate negligence, as, whatever defence might be offered, properly applied clips do not fall off, at least not until sufficient time has elapsed for the tube to atrophy substantially (ie several years). This sort of defence was unsuccessfully maintained in *Fallows* v *Randle* MLC 0591, [1997] 8 Med LR 160, CA.

In *Fallows* v *Randle* the defendant raised this sort of misleading defence when his patient was discovered within six months of the sterilisation to be pregnant again. Even though at the re-sterilisation the left tube was found not to be occluded and the ring was seen in the top of the broad ligament (whoever wrote the note tried to insert a possible get-out for the surgeon by adding the words 'possibly having slid off the tube'), the defendant fought the case through trial (unsuccessfully) on the basis that the ring could have been properly applied but slipped off or that a fistula could have arisen. The judge preferred the evidence of the claimant's expert, namely that the only reasonable explanation for the failure of the operation was negligence in applying the ring. Not satisfied with the deserved failure of his defence, the defendant appealed. The court declined to interfere with the judge's findings, saying that he had plainly been impressed by the evidence of the claimants' expert and they would not interfere with a finding of fact, even in relation to an expert witness, if the judge had based, in part at any rate, his assessment on seeing and hearing the witness and on his view of him. The court said the judge was entitled to prefer the evidence of the claimants' expert to the somewhat remote theories of the defendants and their expert.

For the medical and evidential complexities that can arise in a case that alleges misplacement, one may steel oneself to read the judgment of Popplewell J in *Taylor* v *Shropshire Health Authority* MLC 0048, [1998] Lloyd's Rep Med 395.

The *second* line of attack is to allege that the woman was not warned of the failure rate. This is unlikely to succeed these days as the standard consent form for sterilisation gives such a warning, and in most cases it is not reasonably open to the woman to say that she did not have time to read it. Also, most doctors will put a note in the records at some time preoperatively to the effect that they have warned. A number of cases succeeded in former years where no warning was given. One has first to show (by expert evidence to that effect) that no responsible doctor would have failed to warn at the relevant date (this criterion, ie the *Bolam* test as extended to the context of pre-operative disclosure by the House of Lords in *Sidaway* v *Board of Governors of the Bethlem Royal Hospital* MLC 0010, [1985] AC 871,[2] was held by the Court of Appeal to apply to an

---

2 Lord Woolf offered some amelioration of the strict *Sidaway* principle, perhaps influenced by the *Bolitho* decision of the House of Lords ([1998] AC 232), in *Pearce* v *United Bristol Healthcare NHS Trust* [1999] PIQR P53, CA, when he said that the patient has a right to be informed of any 'significant' risk (see Chapter 22).

elective sterilisation procedure in *Gold* v *Haringey Health Authority* [1988] QB 481). Proving a duty to warn is easy enough for an operation within the last ten or so years.

Next, one has, of course, to prove as a fact that no warning was given. This may simply be a dispute of fact between doctor and patient. These days a hospital will almost certainly use a specialised form of consent for a sterilisation (a GP doing a vasectomy may well not), which will warn of the risk. Assuming the patient signed the form well before the operation, it will not avail to say she did not read it.

However, *causation* is always a problem in claims alleging a failure to give necessary information before treatment. One has, third, to show that the warning would have made a difference to the outcome. In the context of sterilisation it has virtually never been known for a woman to refuse the procedure on being told of the small failure rate.[3] Occasionally it can be reasonably alleged that for medical reasons a further pregnancy would pose such a threat to the health of mother or child that her partner would also have been sterilised, or other additional contraceptive precautions would have been taken, if she/they had been told of the failure rate (a contention of this sort succeeded in *Gowton* v *Wolverhampton Health Authority* MLC 0959, [1994] 5 Med LR 432 and in *Lybert* v *Warrington Health Authority* MLC 0712, [1996] 7 Med LR 71, CA, where the couple were in the unusual position of awaiting in any event a hysterectomy, the Court of Appeal declined to interfere with the judge's findings that they would during the interim period have taken additional contraceptive precautions, though the court stressed the very unusual circumstances that enabled them to accept the finding that the couple would have taken double contraceptive precautions; see, *contra*, *Newell* v *Goldenburg* (below under 'Additional cases on negligence')). Occasionally one can allege that, although a warning would not have deterred the woman from accepting the operation, she would have realised she was pregnant soon enough to enable a simple termination rather than having to undergo the more complex and, to her, unacceptable option of a late termination (this last contention succeeded in the vasectomy case of *Thake* v *Maurice* [1986] QB 644, MLC 0011, CA, affirming [1984] 2 All ER 513).

The couple succeeded at first instance in *Gold* v *Haringey Health Authority* [1986] 1 FLR 125 on the ground that, if warning of the failure rate of sterilisation had been given, they would have gone for a vasectomy instead (reversed on appeal on a different ground).[4]

---

3   In *Ellis* v *Wallsend District Hospital* [1990] 2 Med LR 103, the New South Wales Court of Appeal said that a patient's evidence that she would have declined surgery if properly warned should not be rejected unless it was inherently incredible or inherently improbable.

4   Note that stressing the irreversibility of the operation does not amount to a contractual warranty that the patient will remain permanently sterile (*Eyre* v *Measday* [1986] 1 All ER 488, CA), nor to such a representation in tort (*Gold* v *Haringey Health Authority* [1988] QB 481, CA). In *Worster* v *City and Hackney Health Authority* (1987) Times, 22 June, Garland J held that a consent form which included the words 'We understand that this means that we can have no more children' did not amount to a representation that the operation was bound to be successful.

Vasectomy

It is almost always impossible to show that a vasectomy has been performed incompetently. The anatomy does not usually permit that. So any allegation has to be that the semen was improperly declared to be sperm-free. Perhaps the man's GP told the patient he was sterile when there had only been one sperm test, or perhaps the laboratory reports were misinterpreted by the GP. In these cases one would expect the patient's partner to have become pregnant fairly soon (assuming regular intercourse), for otherwise natural recanalisation is the more likely explanation.

A claim for omission to warn of the risk of late recanalisation (ie after the successful conclusion of the post-operative testing period) is subject to the same difficulties as a similar claim in respect of female sterilisation (see above). In *Stobie* v *Central Birmingham Health Authority* (1994) 22 BMLR 135, a couple unsuccessfully contended that such warnings of the failure rate as they were given in and around a vasectomy, including a warning on the consent form, did not extend to late recanalisation, or at any rate were reasonably understood as relating only to possible early failure, ie before the semen samples had been declared sperm-free.

It is, of course, necessary to prove, if the issue is disputed, that it was the claimant that impregnated the mother of the child.

For further cases on negligence in and around pregnancy see the section below headed 'Additional cases on negligence'.

What is the value of such a claim?

As already indicated, claims for the unplanned birth of a healthy child have been stripped of their value by the retrograde House of Lords decision in *McFarlane* v *Tayside Health Board* MLC 0127, [2000] 2 AC 59, which we consider below in detail.

Pre-McFarlane

McFarlane was a very surprising decision (unanimous, though based on a variety of different reasoning). In 1985, the Court of Appeal had considered the conflicting judgments at first instance on the question whether damages could be recovered for the expense of bringing up a healthy child who would not have been born had it not been for some sort of negligent mismanagement,[5] and had concluded that there was no ground, neither in law nor in policy, for denying such a claim (*Emeh* v *Kensington, Chelsea and Westminster Area Health Authority* [1985] QB 1012).

Since then, countless claims had been brought for such economic damage, and in none of them was it argued that it was not recoverable (though occasionally a judge expressed surprise that this was the law). Most of these claims for the birth of an unplanned healthy child served schedules of loss in the area of six figures and settled for somewhere between £50,000 and £80,000. The principle was that the new child had the right to be brought up in the same standard of living as the previous

---

5   *Udale* v *Bloomsbury Area Health Authority* [1983] 1 WLR 1098; *Thake* v *Maurice* [1986] QB 644, [1986] 1 All ER 497, MLC 0011, CA.

children. Therefore if the standard of living of the family had been low, the award was likely to be low. In some cases it was argued that the family had only had at their disposal state benefits for the upkeep of their previous children, and therefore the child benefit attributable to the new child was all they could expect. This argument had never found much favour, although settlements in such cases could be as low as £25,000. On the other hand, in some cases the sums recovered exceeded five figures, for example where mother had been a high earner. In one or two cases private school fees were obtained, and even in one case a dowry for the unplanned daughter.

Salih v *Enfield Health Authority* [1991] 2 Med LR 235, was a very odd decision of the Court of Appeal. The court said that, if defendants by their negligence had made it a practical impossibility for a mother to contemplate having further children in these circumstances, the financial cost of savings made (by not having the expense of any more children) must be taken into account. It should be ignored.

In one of the nearest cases in point of time before the *McFarlane* decision, *Taylor* v *Shropshire Health Authority* [2000] MLC 0226, arguments which were soon to be accepted in *McFarlane* were rejected by the High Court judge and over £1.3m was awarded for the unplanned birth of a disabled child. As we shall see, a claim (substantial, although its limits have not yet been determined) is still possible for the unplanned birth of a disabled child, but the ordinary costs of raising a child (ie had the child not been disabled) have to be discounted.

Nunnerley v *Warrington Health Authority* [2000] MLC 0128, was a pre-*McFarlane* decision by Morison J in October 1999 and *Taylor* v *Shropshire Health Authority (No 2)* MLC 0226, [2000] Lloyd's Rep Med 96, was a decision given on 25 November 1999 by Judge Nicholl sitting as a High Court judge. In neither of these cases could the court have had the benefit of the *McFarlane* judgment in the House of Lords (the judgment of the Scottish appeal court would not have been of much persuasive authority). The House of Lords decision was handed down on 25 November (by coincidence the same day as the *Taylor* decision – by a further coincidence the *Nunnerley* decision appeared in the Times law reports that same day).

Nunnerley

Liability for the birth of a child suffering from tuberous sclerosis was admitted for the purposes of this preliminary hearing; it was also agreed that a parent could claim damages for the wrongful birth of a handicapped child independent of any claim for personal injuries. The relatively narrow issue before the court was whether the parents could successfully claim for the cost of care likely to be given after the age of 18.

The judge's conclusion was that they could. This was treated as a liability issue only. Although it appears from the judgment that the judge was of the view (*obiter*) that (a) parental care could be valued and compensated for in the usual way, and (b) necessary professional care could be claimed for even though the parents would not be able to afford it from their own resources, counsel has told me that the argument never went beyond the narrow point as to whether such care as might be claimable could remain claimable into the child's majority. At a full hearing on 9

March 2000, the Court of Appeal ([2003] Lloyds Rep Med 365 sub nom *Gaynor N and Vincent N* v *Warrington Health Authority*) refused permission to appeal. They said that, even given *McFarlane*, there was no reason to impose a cut-off date at the age of 18 for such heads of claim as might be recoverable. To impose such a cut-off would run counter not only to the general principles of negligence but also to the approach of family law to the responsibilities of parents.

Taylor

In this case the defendant's counsel, Coonan QC, argued, as he was later to do (but successfully this time) in the *Rand* case (see below), that, unless an actual cost was incurred for past or future care (he would, presumably, allow that loss of a job was an actual cost), compensation under that head could only, if at all, be reflected in general damages by way of loss of amenity. The judge in *Taylor* roundly rejected that argument in respect of future care, holding that it made no difference that the claim was the parents' and not the child's and that therefore they were entitled to recover the commercial value of their services less 25%, just as if the claim had been the child's. It is impossible to think that that view will be accepted when any authoritative appeal in any case on this issue is heard.

It is of note that the judge's award for the distress of the pregnancy was as high as £15,000, to which he added the even higher award of £25,000 for the burden and anxieties of bringing up a disabled child (he deducted only £2,500 for the 'joy' that a child brings). The scale of these awards can be justified by the evidence of substantial psychiatric distress suffered by the mother over a period of years. Without that evidence it would be hard to see any proper basis for them (it was not a question of increasing the award of general damages for loss of amenity (as was later done by Newman J in *Rand* – see below) as the judge did not have that approach in mind).

The *McFarlane* case

This decision by the House of Lords signalled the end to large recoveries for the unplanned birth of a healthy child. Despite the criticism it received, it was expressly approved by the House in the *Rees* case (see below). Any *personal injury* caused by the negligence, for example the pregnancy and any stress or psychological damage as a result, will be compensatable. But such injury is unlikely to attract more than about £10,000. Special damages flowing directly from the fact of pregnancy could increase the award. The facts in the *McFarlane* case were simple. After four children, the couple decided on a vasectomy. They were given the all clear on the semen samples, which was admitted to have been incorrect information, though negligence was not admitted. The mother later became pregnant and gave birth to a healthy child. At first instance the whole of the claim was struck out (ie the personal injury claim based on the pregnancy and the economic claim for the cost of upbringing). On appeal the whole of the claim was restored.

The claim for the pregnancy

The defendants argued, astonishingly, that even the claim for the unwanted pregnancy should be disallowed on the basis that a pregnancy should not be regarded as a personal injury, not even an unwanted one. Even more surprisingly, that contention had been accepted in the Scottish court of first instance. However, on both appeals the judges had no difficulty in allowing that part of the claim (damages for that aspect of the claim had been agreed at £10,000; the economic claim was put at £100,000, a fairly usual figure for such a claim). Lord Millett suggested that about £5,000 should be allowed for the frustration of the couple's desire to restrict their family (it is not clear if this would be in addition to compensation for the pregnancy itself).

Two different approaches

As can be seen from the summary below, some of the judges favoured a policy-type approach (based on general moral and societal considerations) over a legalistic one (based on standard legal principles such as foreseeability, proximity, causation and reasonable restitution), while others vice versa. But they all agreed that the economic claim could not stand.

However, whatever the grounds they gave for their conclusions, one cannot help seeing in the outcome further evidence of a general policy decision taken at the highest level, to the effect that the amount and incidence of personal injury damages over the whole spectrum must be kept as low as possible, no doubt on the basis that that is best for society as a whole. In fact, an example of 'distributive justice' (as *per* Lord Steyn).

The judges' reasoning

Lord Slynn based his view on the standard *Caparo* rule (*Caparo Industries plc* v *Dickman* [1990] 2 AC 605, HL) that economic loss is only recoverable where there was a sufficient relationship of proximity to be able to say that the defendants had assumed responsibility for the consequences in respect of which recovery was being claimed and that it was fair, just and reasonable to impose such a duty. As one knows, this 'test' gives the court an unfettered right to impose its own view of policy. Apart from 'policy', it is not easy to see why Lord Slynn decided this question in the negative. He could just as easily have decided it in the 'logical' (his word) fashion, namely that the cost of upbringing was an obviously foreseeable consequence of the negligence and impossible to dissociate from it.

Lord Steyn decided the question as a moral issue and on the grounds of 'distributive justice', which means the just distribution of burdens and losses among members of a society. Lord Steyn said that was what lay behind the negative decisions in the various jurisdictions to which the court had been referred,[6] and said this was not a matter of public policy.

---

6   Their Lordships conducted an exhaustive investigation, a *tour d'horizon* (to adopt their phrase), into decisions in other jurisdictions. Although the English authorities were virtually all one way (positive), there have been a substantial amount of negative decisions elsewhere.

He said the real reasons for the court's conclusions should not be masked by unreal and formalistic propositions along the lines of no loss, no foreseeable loss, no causative link, only reasonable restitution, etc. Judges should give real reasons for their decisions.

> The truth is that tort law is a mosaic in which the principles of corrective justice and distributive justice are interwoven. And in situations of uncertainty and difficulty a choice sometimes has to be made between the two approaches. In my view it is legitimate in the present case to take into account considerations of distributive justice. That does not mean that I would decide the case on grounds of public policy. On the contrary, I would avoid those quick sands. Relying on principles of distributive justice I am persuaded that our tort law does not permit parents of a healthy unwanted child to claim the costs of bringing up the child from a health authority or a doctor. If it were necessary to do so, I would say that the claim does not satisfy the requirement of being fair, just and reasonable.

Like Lord Slynn, Lord Steyn did not wish to base his conclusion on the 'set-off' argument (ie allow for the 'joys' of parenthood as against the economic demands).

More reasons

However, Lord Hope took the view that the benefits or set-off principle was relevant, but then said that as it was impossible to value them as against the damage by way of the cost of upkeep and therefore the logical (*sic*) conclusion was that such recovery was not permissible. Otherwise the parents would be getting more than they had lost!

He also adopted, perhaps less unreasonably, the *Caparo* test of proximity which also led him to a negative conclusion.

Lord Clyde agreed with this approach. He said that policy considerations could be found to point either way, eg sanctity of human life as against the right of parents and benefit to society of limiting families. Therefore, the decision should not be founded on policy considerations. For him the principal relevant consideration was the legal rule of reasonable restitution.

> In such a context I would consider it appropriate to have regard to the extent of the liability which the defenders could reasonably have thought they were undertaking. It seems to me that even if a sufficient causal connection exists the cost of maintaining a child goes far beyond any liability which in the circumstances of the present case the defenders could reasonably have thought they were undertaking.

But why? Why should not a defendant understand that if a child is born through his negligence he will have to shoulder the financial burden rather than the parents?

Lord Clyde also considered that the extent of these economic claims was out of proportion to the wrongdoing.

But why? An unplanned child can not only throw the lives of the other members of the family into turmoil, thwarting their intentions and the plans they have made, but will often substantially impair earnings and careers and create a crippling financial burden.

Lord Millett was, strangely, not prepared to assume that the reason for the couple not wanting a fifth child was financial. He then made it clear that he did not accept the set-off/benefits argument, nor the strictly legalistic ones. He took what one might term the 'moral high ground':

> There is something distasteful, if not morally offensive, in treating the birth of a normal, healthy child as a matter for compensation ... I accept the thrust of both the main arguments in favour of dismissing such a claim. In my opinion the law must take the birth of a normal, healthy baby to be a blessing, not a detriment. In truth it is a mixed blessing. It brings joy and sorrow, blessing and responsibility. The advantages and the disadvantages are inseparable. Individuals may choose to regard the balance as unfavourable and take steps to forego the pleasures as well as the responsibilities of parenthood. They are entitled to decide for themselves where their own interests lie. But society itself must regard the balance as beneficial. It would be repugnant to its own sense of values to do otherwise. It is morally offensive to regard a normal, healthy baby as more trouble and expense than it is worth.

But is this sort of moralising convincing? The fact of the matter is that parents in cases of this type have responsibly done everything to limit their family and then through negligence have been lumbered with an extra child. Of course, they love the child.[7] But why should they have to pay for rearing him? The child will no doubt bring some pleasure to the parents, but that was not of their choosing. Why should that fact militate against a simple claim to be reimbursed the economic loss arising from the birth? One can, of course, create all sorts of arguments about blessings in disguise, mixed blessings, the joy of a child, the expectation of being supported by our children in our senility, etc. And, on the legalistic approach, one can similarly deploy clever arguments on each side. But it is all just window dressing. In the end, all it comes down to is a policy decision. So one asks: does 'distributive justice' suggest a negative decision on such a claim? I suggest not. There is nothing unjust about allowing these claims (they will not bankrupt the NHS) and a deal of injustice to the parents in denying it.[8]

The High Court of Australia has, by a whisker, decided a similar later case along the lines of *McFarlane*. This was by a majority of four to three, after both courts below had found in favour of the claimant! (*Cattanach* v *Melchior* [2003] MLC 0722). The lengthy judgments make interesting reading, and provide valuable material for any moot on the issue.

A *cunning ruse*

An attempt was made in the county court case of *Reynolds* v *Health First Medical Group* [2000] Lloyd's Rep Med 240 to get round the limiting effect of this decision by amending a claim by an NHS patient for the birth of a healthy child due to alleged GP negligence so as to allege a

---

7   What though, as a moot point, if it were shown that they did not love him and that his birth in fact had engendered in them only negative responses?

8   The top court in South Africa recently saw no bar to allowing recovery in such a claim along the lines of English law pre-*McFarlane*. In *Mukheiber* v *Raath* (1999) 52 BMLR 49, the Supreme Court of Appeal said that the cost of maintaining the child was a direct consequence of the misrepresentation (that the defendant had sterilised the mother) but it was not unlimited. The doctor's liability for maintenance could be no greater than that which rested on the parents to maintain the child according to their means and station in life, and lapsed when the child was reasonably able to support itself.

contract between patient and GP (and then to maintain that a claim for upkeep based on a contractual rather than a tortious relationship was not covered by *McFarlane*). Not surprisingly, the judge found that there was no contract between a NHS patient and her GP. Although he did not need to go further, it is clear that the contention that *McFarlane* would not apply to a contractual relationship (such as would exist in the case of a private patient) is quite hopeless, except in the highly unlikely event of the contract specifically providing that the defendant undertook responsibility for the extended economic losses.

So what is now the value of such a claim?

If the child is healthy

(A) GENERAL DAMAGES

An uncomplicated, unplanned pregnancy going to term has always been worth about £5,000. If there are complications the award of general damages can be increased.

In *Akintubobo* v *Lewisham Health Authority*, (reported in Butterworths Personal Injury Litigation Service at 1.109.2), Alliott J, giving judgment in 1987, said that the appropriate sum for an unwanted pregnancy was £3,000 (though Brooke J awarded only £2,500 in *Allen* v *Bloomsbury Health Authority* [1992] 3 Med LR 257). In *Fish* v *Wilcox* (9 April 1992, unreported), QBD Cardiff, Swinton Thomas J awarded £9,000 for a difficult pregnancy and delivery resulting in the birth of a handicapped child (appealed on other grounds [1994] 5 Med LR 230).

In *Chaunt* v *Hertfordshire Area Health Authority* (1982) 132 NLJ 1054, Park J awarded £2,000 for the unwanted pregnancy and the termination.

Other awards include £3,000 in 1988 in *Emeh* (below) at first instance; £2,750 for a worrying pregnancy in *Jones* v *Berkshire Health Authority* (2 July 1986, unreported), QBD; £3,000 in *Benarr* v *Kettering Health Authority* [1988] NLJR 179; and £5,000 in *Salih* v *Enfield Health Authority* [1990] 1 Med LR 333.

If the pregnancy was terminated, whether by abortion or miscarriage (there is, of course, no obligation to terminate – *Emeh* v *Kensington and Westminster and Chelsea Health Authority* [1985] QB 1012, CA), there may be psychological injury for which additional general damages can be sought (see *Taylor* v *Shropshire Health Authority* [2000] MLC 0226, where the judge awarded £15,000). There may be a claim for the wasted expenses involved in preparing for the birth. It is likely now that the uncomplicated claim will settle for about £10,000. And see other cases detailed above under the heading 'Pre-*McFarlane*'.

(B) SPECIAL DAMAGES

Pre-*McFarlane* there used to be a claim for the cost of upkeep to age 18 (or thereabouts) – perhaps in the area of £40,000 after deduction of child benefit – plus other costs, such as an extension to the home, moving house, a new car, mother's loss of wages. The schedule used to be based on the payments made to foster parents as per the National Foster Care Association rates (Brooke J endorsed such a calculation in *Allen* (above), – but see, *contra* to some extent, *Robinson* v *Salford Health Authority*

[1992] 3 Med LR 270). Some cases adduced evidence from experts on the cost of living, but, in tune with the Woolf reforms and cutting down on the cost of experts, such evidence was later declared inadmissible (*Nwoko* v *Guy's and St Thomas NHS Trust* (8 December 1998, unreported) *per* McKinnon J). None of these heads of claim are admissible any longer.[9] In *Greenfield* v *Irwin (aka Greenfield* v *Flather)* (2001) MLC 0341, CA, it was held that, following *McFarlane*, there could be no claim for the mother's loss of earnings when she had to give up employment to look after her healthy, unplanned child (human rights was pleaded here – the 'family life' Article – not surprisingly it received short shrift). Although *McFarlane* did not expressly deal with this head of claim, there could be no meaningful distinction between the costs incurred in bringing up a child and the need for the mother to cease working to look after the child (note that this is not the same head of claim as a clearly permissible claim limited to loss of earnings while pregnant and recovering therefrom).

If the child is handicapped

(A) GENERAL DAMAGES

These are much the same as for a healthy child, save that damages may be recoverable for a mother's shock on discovering she has given birth to a handicapped child (see *Hardman* v *Amin* (below)).

(B) SPECIAL DAMAGES

This is where, thanks to the House of Lords' revisionist approach, a Pandora's box was opened resulting in confusing and inconsistent decisions from the lower courts, lengthy debates about remoteness, assumption of responsibility and the distinction between claims for personal injury and claims for economic loss. As outlined above, the Lords in *McFarlane* implicitly left open the question whether the cost of care and allied expenses could be claimed where the child was born handicapped. The position is rather clearer now thanks to the *Parkinson* and *Rees* decisions (see below), although it may be necessary for the time being to refer to earlier cases at first instance for any assistance as to just what heads of loss are claimable as special damage in the case of an unplanned child born disabled.

The McLelland case

While this case was being tried the judgment on *McFarlane* was published, and so the lawyers in the case adjusted their arguments on the hoof, as it were.

In this Scottish case of *McLelland* v *Greater Glasgow Health Board* [2001] MLC 0321, the defendants had admitted liability for all

---

9   There is an interesting report of the case of *Pearson* v *Central Sheffield University Hospitals NHS Trust* in (2000) *Clinical Risk* 259, where the mother, beating a payment in of £18,000, was awarded a total of nearly £26,000, including psychological injury, loss of earnings and care provided to her as a direct result of the pregnancy.

reasonable damages flowing from the birth of a child handicapped by Down's syndrome, on the basis that they admitted a breach of duty in not offering the mother an amniocentesis (there was no argument, either, about the claimants' assertion that such a test would have disclosed the abnormality, and that she would then have requested and obtained a termination). The trial judge awarded:

(1) *Solatium* for both husband and wife. This is similar to but certainly not identical with a claim for *nervous shock*. The award for *solatium* was £15,000 (which may be thought of as 'general damages') to the mother and £5,000 to the father.

(2) An uncontroversial award of £750 was made for the *layette*.

(3) The *cost of raising the (handicapped) child* was divided into the costs of *maintenance*, themselves split between 'basic cost' and 'extra costs as a result of the handicap', and, on the other hand, the cost of providing *care*, but only *additional* care, required because of the disability (note that in these cases no claim is made for care by parents in raising a healthy child – probably because the effort of care can be balanced by the pleasure given by the child).

(4) The judge declined to follow the very odd Court of Appeal decision in *Salih* v *Enfield Health Authority* [1991] 2 Med LR 235, ie he rejected the defendants' contention that, as the couple would have had another child in any event, the costs of raising the handicapped child were not *additional* costs. It did not seem to him that spending money on bringing up a handicapped child born as a result of the defendants' negligence was in substance the same thing as spending money on bringing up a healthy child who would have been born at a somewhat later date if the negligent omission had not taken place. In those circumstances the judge declined to follow the Court of Appeal decision.

(5) *Basic maintenance costs* and *extra costs* were awarded up to age 19 without much in the way of dispute. However, the judge disallowed the cost of basic maintenance after the age of 18, not because the claim was misconceived in principle (he had already made it clear that that was not his view), but because he was satisfied that the cost would be undertaken by the state and so would not fall on the parents' shoulders. But he allowed the extra costs, ie the *additional* costs due to the handicap as he was not satisfied that the state would meet those.

(6) *Care costs*: the judge said that the parents were not entitled to compensation for the hours of care given and to be given (which the claimants had limited to *extra* care needed as a result of the disability) because they had not themselves expended any money on such care, and the claim was not a claim by an injured party to reimburse his carers, and so the appropriate way to compensate for such care was to include it in the overall award for *solatium* (which can be viewed by way, as it were, of general damages for the invasion of the parents' free time or amenity). However, the judge had no problem with reimbursing the parents for *professional* care which they had actually purchased or would reasonably purchase if they had the money to do so. This, like the claim for extra costs of maintenance, extended over the whole of the life expectancy of the child.

(7) There was little dispute about the *mother's claim for loss of wages* as a result of having to look after her child. Such a claim in the case of a healthy child would appear no longer to be possible in the light of the *McFarlane* decision. In the *McLelland* case the claim was allowed for the whole of the mother's working life.

So the claimants' lawyers achieved a very considerable victory, gaining an award, before an agreed 5% discount, of about £374,000.

On appeal to the Inner House of the Court of Session the trial judge's awards were largely upheld ([2001] MLC 0364. Two of the three judges removed that part of the award that related to the ordinary costs of upkeep, ie for a non-disabled child. That amounted to only some £50,000, being the cost of the *layette* and ordinary upkeep to age 19. The third judge saw no reason to split up the costs of maintenance and would not have interfered with the judge's award at all.

The Rand *case*

Rand and Rand v *East Dorset Health Authority* [2000] Lloyd's Rep Med 181, Newman J, was the first full post-*McFarlane* judgment from the High Court on the question what damages can be awarded for the negligently caused birth of a handicapped child. It was admitted that a failure to tell the parents of the results of a scan had deprived them of the opportunity, which they would have taken, to obtain a termination of the pregnancy, the fact or risk of a Down's syndrome child having been demonstrated on the scan. So the only question was: in respect of the birth of Katie in 1988 suffering from Down's syndrome, what heads of damage remained after *McFarlane*?

Newman J's judgment is complex, and, like the curate's egg, is good only in parts. The part that is disagreeable is his conclusion that any financial claim must be limited to monies that the parents had expended or were likely to expend from their own funds, ie there could not, for example, be a claim for the cost of employing expensive help which they would not be able to employ, or would not choose to employ, unless they recovered the cost from the defendants. So the ambit of the claim would be very different from the situation where the defendants have caused the child's injury. And it means, as the judge acknowledged, that wealthy parents will be able to claim more, provided their claim is reasonable (because they will be able to afford more from their own funds in the way of, eg help and equipment and therapies). This unsatisfactory approach was rejected by Henriques J in *Hardman* v *Amin* [2000] Lloyd's Rep Med 498 (see below), and by Turner J in *Roberts* v *Bro Taf Health Authority* [2001] MLC 0518.

Amid the complexities we may note that the judge awarded £15,000 for the shock and pain associated with the birth of Katie, and for the fact that he accepted that it was not too remote a consequence that the mother went on to have another child in order to demonstrate that she could give birth to a normal child (which seems a somewhat elastic approach to the concept of remoteness), he awarded the fairly large sum of £30,000 to the mother (and £5,000 to the father) for 'loss of amenity', which reflected the fact that they would be caught up in the care of their daughter for many years. In other words, although he was not prepared to make a straightforward award for the cost of future additional care arising out of the disability (because such a head of damages was limited by the parents' own financial means), he was prepared to compensate the parents with a general lump sum award for loss of amenity in having to give up those hours.

In the event, the parents recovered just under £120,000.

Further cases post-McFarlane

In *Hardman* v *Amin* MLC 0369, [2000] Lloyd's Rep Med 498, there should have been a termination for rubella infection. Liability was admitted for the birth of a handicapped child. Henriques J, in a judgment carefully considering all available authorities, felt unconstrained by *McFarlane* and differed substantially in his conclusions from Newman J in the *Rand* case. He allowed general damages for the pregnancy and specifically for the shock of mother realising that she had given birth to a handicapped child. He held that the continuation of a pregnancy resulting in the birth of a handicapped child was a personal injury; that the claim for upkeep was a claim for pure economic loss, but that there was sufficient proximity between the defendant GP and the patient for the birth of a handicapped child to be a consequence in law of the original negligence, and that awarding compensation for that consequence would not go beyond reasonable restitution. He held that a claim for the past and future care given by the mother as a result of the disability was permissible (either on the ordinary principles of a personal injury claim including a 25% discount for non-commercial care or by way of claim for loss of amenity – as per Newman J). And that, *pace* Newman J, the question of what the parents could afford out of their own monies was irrelevant, whether in relation to care or other needs. The judge's compassionate approach can be seen from these two observations he made:

> The claimant can get damages for the past and future cost of providing for Daniel's special needs and care related to his disability ... The claimant should be placed in a position in which she can care for her disabled child's reasonable needs during the duration of their joint life span.

The only point on which I would question the wisdom of this decision is the acceptance by the judge of the unsatisfactory reasoning of the Court of Appeal in the *Salih* case (above), whereby if defendants by their negligence have made it a practical impossibility for a mother to contemplate having further children in these circumstances, the financial cost of savings made (by not having the expense of any more children) must be taken into account.

The Parkinson *case*

Parkinson v *St James and Seacroft University Hospital NHS Trust* [2001] MLC 0360, CA was an important case. It was the first time, post-*McFarlane*, that the Court of Appeal had considered the question of what compensation could be obtained for the unplanned birth of a handicapped child.

The facts can be simply stated: a handicapped child had been born due to an admittedly negligently performed sterilisation. The birth of a fifth child had been 'catastrophic' for the family and the marriage (Brooke LJ). At first instance Longmore J had allowed only the additional costs flowing from the disability. Both sides appealed; both appeals were dismissed.

Somewhat surprisingly the court did not think it relevant to consider the earlier cases at first instance, Brooke LJ stating that the policy issues were different where the allegation was that there should have been a termination (rather than that there should never have been a conception). The logic of this is difficult to follow, but at least it had the effect of relieving the court from entering into an analysis of the complex and inconsistent arguments deployed in those judgments.

First, how disabled does the child have to be to make a claim? Hale LJ adopted the test of disability found in s 17(11) of the Children Act 1989: a child is disabled if he is blind, deaf or dumb or suffers from mental disorder of any kind or is substantially and permanently handicapped by illness, injury or congenital deformity or such other disability as may be prescribed. Brooke LJ said that 'significant disability' (the phrase used in the *McFarlane* case) would cover disabilities of the mind, including severe behavioural disabilities, but not minor defects or inconveniences. Each case would be judged on its own facts. No real difficulty there.

Next, the response to the main issue. The effect of the decision is to allow 'the extra costs of caring for and bringing up a disabled child' in that 'a disabled child needs extra care and expenditure' (*per* Hale LJ). The award should be limited to 'the extra expenses associated with the child's disability', 'the special upbringing costs associated with rearing a child with a serious disability' (*per* Brooke LJ).

What we are not told, however, is what heads of expense or loss can properly be brought within these formulae. Does it, for example, include compensation for parental care? Does it include all the heads of claim for professional care, aids and equipment, accommodation etc that are relevant where the child's injury is caused by medical mismanagement? Also unclear is whether this court was of the view that the claim went beyond majority (although at the application for leave to appeal in the case of *Nunnerley* v *Warrington Health Authority* (above) the Court of Appeal had said that it did).

Brooke LJ offered an impressive cerebral analysis of the numerous buzz-word bases currently available for admitting or rejecting a claim for compensation based on the tort of negligence (the three-fold test, proximity, assumption of responsibility, fair-just-reasonable, corrective or distributive justice, public policy, what the man on the Clapham tube train might think, and so on). He analysed the judgments in the House of Lords, saying that the task was made more difficult by the fact that the law lords had spoken 'with five different voices'. He concluded that there was no valid argument against parents being recompensed for the costs of extraordinary care in raising a deformed child.

Hale LJ's judgment demands careful study by elderly male lawyers. The judge brought into clear and inescapable focus the very substantial changes that pregnancy brings to the physical, psychological, and social life of a woman. Along with these physical and psychological consequences goes a severe curtailment of personal autonomy. Literally, one's life is no longer just one's own but also someone else's. One cannot simply rid oneself of that responsibility. ... The process of giving birth is rightly termed 'labour'. It is hard work, often painful and sometimes dangerous. ... Paternal responsibility is not simply or even primarily a financial responsibility: see Children Act 1989, s 3(1). The primary responsibility is to care for the child. The labour does not stop when the child is born. Bringing up children is hard work. ... The obligation to provide or make acceptable and safe arrangements for the child's care and supervision lasts for 24 hours a day, 7 days a week. At this point Hale LJ indicates, I feel, that she would have expected claims for any unplanned birth to have included a claim by way of valuation of parental care.

On *McFarlane* Hale LJ said:

> Their Lordships' reasons for denying what would on normal legal principles be recoverable [ie that losses flowing directly from negligence should be compensated] were variously and elegantly expressed ... In truth they all gave different reasons for arriving at ... the same result.

Like many of us, Hale LJ found it difficult to understand why, once it is agreed that the doctor assumes some responsibility for preventing conception, he is nevertheless liable for some only of the clearly foreseeable, indeed highly probable, resulting losses. At one point she suggested that a mother might be driven to have an abortion as a result of the *McFarlane* decision, presumably if she knew or learnt in time enough about the law to realise that she would have no claim for financial help in respect of all the 'dis-benefits' the child would bring her.

Note also that Hale LJ said that many would challenge the assumption that the benefits of having a new child outweighed the disadvantages so as to 'cancel out' the claim. She said that many would argue that the true cost to the primary carer of bringing up a child are so enormous that they easily outstripped any benefits. And the notion of a child bringing benefit to the parents is deeply suspect, smacking of commodification [*sic*] of the child, regarding the child as an asset to the parents. She suggested that a conventional sum could be deducted from a claim to allow for the so-called 'benefit' of having a child.

One can see, on studying the *Rees* case below (the disabled mother case), that the House of Lords (albeit *obiter*) supported this decision of the Court of Appeal but only by a majority. Two at least of the judges did not approve of it. If a *Parkinson* issue comes directly in front of the House (rather than *obiter*), one cannot guarantee that there will be a majority in favour of it among those judges who hear the case.

Groom v Selby

In *Groom* v *Selby* [2001] MLC 0483, CA (at first instance MLC 0294), a GP admitted negligence in not diagnosing a pregnancy in time for the mother to have found a termination to be acceptable, which she otherwise would have done. The additional factor in this claim was that the child, Megan, was born apparently healthy (on 26 May 1995) but, because of an infection contracted from the maternal vagina perinatally, went on to develop septicemia and brain damage. Nevertheless, the judge at trial treated her as a child born 'unhealthy' rather than healthy. 'Megan is not and never has been a healthy child.' The Court of Appeal dismissed the defendant's appeal, saying that their decision recently given in *Parkinson* disposed of the instant appeal. They saw no distinction between wrongful conception and wrongful birth cases; contracting the disease was a foreseeable consequence of birth, the defendant was deemed to have accepted responsibility for the foreseeable and disastrous consequences of her negligence, and an award of compensation limited to the special upbringing associated with rearing a child with a serious disability was fair, just and reasonable. The child was apparently to be viewed as 'born disabled' (within the meaning of expression in *McFarlane*) although there were no signs or symptoms of infection at birth, because, it was said, her exposure to the bacterium which proved her downfall occurred during the process of birth. All the causes of her meningitis were in place when the umbilical cord was severed: all that remained was for the bacterium to penetrate a weak point in the child's skin or mucous membranes and the damage was done. The fact that failure to fix the child's apparent state of health at birth as the cut-off point would be making judges' tasks unnecessarily difficult when they were invited to try future cases on the borderline should not stand in the way of doing justice in such a case, in which a child's enduring handicaps, caused by the normal incidents of intra-uterine development and birth, were triggered off within the first month of her life. A generous decision. What, though, if the pathology, though innate at birth, manifests itself much later?

The *Rees* case

In *Rees* v *Darlington Memorial Hospital NHS Trust* [2003] MLC 1053 seven judges heard the appeal in the House of Lords. The decision went by a bare majority against the claimant. The unusual fact of this case is that the unplanned child was healthy; it was the mother who was disabled. She had very little vision and for that reason expressly had asked for a sterilisation, which was negligently performed.

Counsel for the claimant sought in the first place to convince the court to reverse *McFarlane*. The court was not convinced. They declared that it had been a good decision (it had been the unanimous decision of five Lords of Appeal in extra-ordinary including Hope, Millett and Steyn who also featured in this *Rees* case), and, further, that, even if they now harboured any doubts, which was not admitted, they would not go back on it for reasons of security (of the law).

As to simple compensation under *McFarlane* for a healthy child: this was a little surprising. In *McFarlane* Lord Millett had alone of the five proposed that all a *McFarlane* mother should recover should be a nominal sum of £5,000 for the loss of her right to control the extent of her family. He had not even been willing to allow what the others had been willing to allow, namely something for the pregnancy itself (general damages which defendants have almost always been willing to pay, in the sum of about £7,500, plus all costs arising directly out of the pregnancy). In the *Rees* case the judges, four of them – Bingham, Nicholls, Millett, Scott – who considered that the *Rees* scenario fell within the *McFarlane* rule, adopted, and adapted, the Millet suggestion. They allowed the pregnancy damages, but **plus** the Millett award, which they increased (Millett agreed) to £15,000. This 'gloss' on *McFarlane*, as they called it, was heavily criticised by Lord Steyn who said that such a gloss ran counter to the views of the majority in *McFarlane*, had not been considered in the court, was a radical and most important development which should only be embarked upon after rigorous examination of competing argument, was a solution of a heterodox nature which had neither English nor foreign juridical support, was contrary to principle, that it was a novel procedure for judges to undertake the creation of such a remedy and was beyond the permissible limits of judicial creativity, that his brethren had strayed into forbidden territory, that it was a backdoor evasion of the legal policy enunciated in *McFarlane*, and could only be effected by Parliament. In other words, he didn't like it! (Nor did Lord Hope.)

Legal policy: all the judges were prepared to declare, insofar as they were supporting *McFarlane* and any of its derivatives, that (a) an orthodox application of familiar and conventional principles of the law of tort would have permitted the claimant in *McFarlane* to recover damages for the costs of bringing up her healthy child (ie negligence followed by foreseeable loss) – indeed Lord Bingham said that he did not find it surprising that that had been the law here before *McFarlane* – and (b) the denial to a *McFarlane* claimant of such otherwise clearly recoverable damages was not due to the court's view of public policy but to the court's view of legal policy. A distinction without a difference?

Ratio of the McFarlane *rule*: As we have seen, this was not clear in the *McFarlane* speeches themselves, as the judges gave a variety of reasons. In *Rees*, although Lord Steyn remarked amusingly that he was not proposing 'to undertake the gruesome task of discussing the judgments in *McFarlane*', the *McFarlane* ratio was reasonably summarised down to two principles, neither of them in the least convincing. The first is that a child is a God-given gift and, in respect of a healthy child at any rate, its birth should not be the subject of a claim; the second is that the benefit principle requires that the benefit a claimant receives from having a child must be set against the economic loss claimed and as that benefit is incalculable, no damages can be awarded for the economic loss. The first is a bit of prissy pseudo-religious nonsense, a sort of antiquated Victorianism that has no place in modern law ('morally offensive to regard a normal healthy baby as more trouble and expense than it is worth', *per* Lord Millett in *McFarlane*). A child may or may not be a benefit. Probably not much of one to a mother or a family who had most earnestly desired not to have a(nother) child. The second argument can be met in three ways. First, you can only set against the economic loss a like benefit. To suggest that the benefit of having a child should be set against such loss is a nonsense. Second, seeing that we are all agreed that you cannot value the benefit of a child – in other words the concept is a nonsense – that is a good reason for ignoring it, not a reason for going on to conclude that therefore the economic claim must fail. That is totally illogical. Third, if you really feel you have to value the benefit, give it the value the law has already put upon the life of a child, namely £10,000.

The long and the short of it is that each judge decides as a matter of *public policy* what can and what cannot – ie what should and what should not – be recovered in a negligence claim, that is to say what he considers fair, just and reasonable, and then cobbles together more or less unconvincing reasons to support his view. The judges will often pray in aid the common man, of whose mind they suppose that they have a particularly keen perception, and declare stoutly that the public at large would find any other conclusion than the one they are proposing to be unfair, unjust and unreasonable.

Does the McFarlane *rule apply to all negligent birth claims or is there an exception for the disabled child/mother?* (ie the *Parkinson* and *Rees* aspects) – *per* Lords Bingham, Nicholls, Millett, Scott: Lord Bingham said he would apply the rule, without differentiation, to *all* claims. He said it was anomalous that the defendant's liability should relate to a disability which the defendant had not caused. He also said it was undesirable that parents, in order to recover compensation, should be encouraged to portray their children or themselves as disabled. And he used the argument that it would be difficult to quantify the additional costs attributable to the handicap. Lord Nicholls took a similar view. He thought it was disproportionate for the NHS to bear all the costs of bringing up the child, and he said the birth of a child should not be treated as comparable to a parent suffering a personal injury. Lord Millett stuck by the nominal award in 'healthy' cases that he had advocated in *McFarlane,* but it is interesting, and important, to note that he explicitly kept an open mind about disabled child cases. He said that he would not find it morally offensive if additional costs could be recovered in a *Parkinson* case, but that did not have to be decided in the instant appeal. As to the disabled mother scenario, he stated, rightly surely, that it is a mistake to assume that, because the costs attributable to the disability are 'extras' whether the disabled party is the child or the parent, there is any symmetry between the two 'disabled' scenarios. He then said that just as there would be a range of varying circumstances for a non-disabled mother, so would there be for the disabled mother.

Lord Scott stressed the 'incalculable benefit' rule, and said that the mother's visual disability did not take the case out of the normal principle established by the *McFarlane* rule. All the features that justified creating an exception under the *McFarlane* rule were present, too, in the disabled mother scenario. On the *Parkinson* scenario, he, too, kept an open mind, but he did make the interesting suggestion that a disabled child claim should only succeed if the reasons for the original sterilisation or other procedure had included a fear that any child could be born disabled. In relation to a sterilisation where there had been no such fear, apart from the normal chance of that happening (one in a few hundred), he appears to be telling us that the birth of a handicapped child would not be sufficiently foreseeable to justify a claim. Then he says that on the facts existing in *Parkinson*, the decision of the Court of Appeal was not justified.

So the *obiter* **tally** so far in relation to a *Parkinson* claim from the majority of four judges who rejected the *Rees* claim, is two against, one somewhat supportive (Millett), and one supportive provided there had been an actual fear of any child born being handicapped.

The Parkinson and the Rees aspects (*per* Lords Steyn, Hope and Hutton): These were the three judges, the minority, who accepted Mrs Rees' claim. Lord Steyn said he agreed with the decision in *Parkinson*. The policy on which the *McFarlane* principle was based simply did not apply to the seriously disabled child. However, in the case of the disabled mother it was not possible to regard her as unaffected by the *McFarlane* principle. An exception would have to be made if she was to recover. He would favour such an exception.

Lord Hope agreed with the decision in *Parkinson* even though he had been a strong advocate of the 'incalculable benefit' argument in

McFarlane. Presumably the additional costs of upbringing in the context of disability are for some reason not caught by that argument. And he saw no reason not to allow the exception to apply in the case of a disabled parent, too. He agreed that in all these cases care would need to be taken in calculating the additional costs but to describe the task as one of acute difficulty seemed to him to be an over-statement. By allowing the seriously disabled parent to recover the extra costs of child-rearing which were due to her disability the law would be doing its best to enable her to perform the task of child-rearing on equal terms with those who did not have any such disability.

Lord Hutton said (a) that it was fair, just and reasonable to award damages for the extra costs of bringing up a disabled child, and (b) that the difficulties hypothesized by Waller LJ in the Court of Appeal should not deter the court from accepting a *Rees* claim. There was a clear distinction between a healthy mother and a disabled mother. Pointing to hard cases on the boundary of recoverability did not invalidate the principle of recovery by a disabled mother.

So in respect of a *Parkinson* scenario (the disabled child) the **tally** among the judges who favoured Mrs Rees' claim, three of them (as against four who did not), was, as one would expect, all in favour.

Final tally: So the net tally for the disabled mother, the *only* issue which fell to be decided in this case (apart from the unanimous approval given to the *McFarlane* decision in the case of a healthy child) was four against the claim and three for it. So the law by the barest whisker will not now permit such a claim. However, the net tally (*obiter*) for a *Parkinson* claim (disabled child) was three in favour, two against, a fourth probably in favour (Millett) and one in favour, it appears, only if there had been a real fear that any further child could suffer from a congenital handicap.

Make of all that what you will, when you come to consider the chances of your claims succeeding in similar circumstances!

Or put it another way in simple, though not I hope simplistic, terms: all healthy child claims are valid only to the tune of £15,000 plus costs arising directly out of the pregnancy and the immediate aftermath; disabled child claims in all probability continue to include the additional costs of upbringing flowing directly from the handicap.[10] What can be actually recovered under that principle remains to be determined at appellate level.

Additional cases on negligence

Scuriaga v *Powell* (24 July 1980, unreported), CA, is interesting as being, as far as one can see, the first case in an English court on the subject of failed sterilisation.

---

10 Before the *Rees* case had reached the House of Lords (but after the Court of Appeal had upheld by a majority the judgment of the trial judge in favour of the claimant) the Court of Appeal held in a preliminary ruling in *AD* v *East Kent Community NHS Trust* [2002] MLC 0879 that, assuming a sectioned female mental patient had become pregnant and given birth to a child as a result of negligence, she could not recover damages for the care of the child given by the grandmother who had assumed official responsibility for her.

In *Newell* v *Goldenberg* [1995] 6 Med LR 371, Mantell J found that, although there might have been in 1985 some surgeons who were not warning of the failure rate of a vasectomy, they would not have been acting reasonably or responsibly. However, having gone on to find that the couple would in any event have accepted the procedure, he rejected their contention that, if the warning had been given, the wife would also have been sterilised. It is not easy to see how it was ever thought that such a contention could succeed, given that, even after the birth of the unplanned child and subsequently, the couple were content to rely only on condoms.

In *Danns* v *Department of Health* [1996] PIQR P69, the claimant had been vasectomised in 1983. Presumably because his advisers could not find expert evidence to prove that no responsible body of doctors would have approved at that time of the omission tell him of the failure rate, they hit on the ploy of suing the Department for not having disseminated knowledge of the failure rate to the public generally before that date. Not surprisingly, Wright J held that the action failed as there was not sufficient proximity to establish a duty and there had been no negligence. The claimant unsuccessfully prayed in aid the Ministry of Health Act 1919, s 2, whereby a duty is laid on the Minister 'to take all such steps as may be desirable to secure ... the collection, preparation, publication and dissemination of information and statistics relating thereto' (ie to public health generally). The judge said that any decisions by the defendant as to what materials were to be disseminated were entirely a question of policy in respect of which the Minister was entitled to exercise his discretion. It is a matter of surprise for some that the decision of Wright J was appealed, but for none that the appeal was unhesitatingly dismissed, the court stating that the prospects of a successful appeal had always been slight ([1998] PIQR 226).

A case that does credit to the imagination of the claimant's advisers is *Goodwill* v *British Pregnancy Advisory Service* [1996] 1 WLR 1397, CA. Some three years before the claimant started a relationship with a man, he had been vasectomised. During their relationship the vasectomy spontaneously reversed and the claimant gave birth to a healthy daughter. She sued the doctor who carried out the vasectomy for not warning his patient at the time of the failure rate. The Court of Appeal said that the claim, involving as it did the allegation that the doctor had owed a duty of care to an indeterminately large class of females who might have sexual relations with his patient during the patient's lifetime, was manifestly unsustainable and frivolous, vexatious and an abuse of the process of the court. We may note that, quite apart from the jurisprudential difficulty that this claim posed for the claimant, the circumstances of her own position were against her. One judge said:

> It is beyond belief that in ceasing to use any contraceptive methods this mature educated woman was induced by and relied on [her lover's] bare assertion to her that he had had a vasectomy and could not have any more children, given that she only removed her contraceptive coil after taking advice from her GP on that and on the fact that [her lover] had told her that he had had a vasectomy. What the GP told her in any event alerted her to the possibility, albeit very small, that despite the vasectomy [her lover] would make her pregnant. She took that risk.

Another of the judges stated that it could not be said that the doctor performing the vasectomy knew or ought to have known that he was advising, as well as his patient, any of his patient's future sexual partners who chanced to receive his advice at second hand. He described the claim as 'far fetched'.

In *Enright* v *Kwun* [2003] MLC 1017, Morland J, a mother aged 37 succeeded in establishing liability for a failure by her medical attendants to offer her the option of an amniocentesis. If she had been given the option, she would have accepted the procedure, the Downs syndrome defect would have been discovered and she would have opted for a termination.

Marian Richardson v LRC Products Ltd [2000] Lloyds Rep Med 280

Already with two children, the Richardsons had, from 1993, used condoms for contraception. All would have been well had not, one afternoon in May 1995, the condom split during use (the teat parting from the body of the condom at about shoulder level). In due course a child was born, healthy and well loved. An action was begun (this was before the House of Lords decision in *McFarlane*) pursuant to the Consumer Protection Act, ie *not* based in negligence, alleging that the condom had been defective. This was put in two ways, contending that it had been exposed to the detrimental and weakening influence of ozone during the course of manufacture, alternatively that it must have been defective in some way or another because otherwise it would not have fractured (bear in mind that this was a radical fracture where the whole of the teat parted company with the rest of the condom).

Most of the evidence and almost all of the judgment was occupied with the scientific evidence. A summary will suffice. The judge heard evidence about the circumstances of the condom's manufacture and the environmental qualities of the factory, and also about the care that the Richardsons took to keep the broken condom in the same condition after the event (the teat was never recovered). He concluded that it had not been established that the condom had been exposed to any deleterious ozone effect before it left the factory. But he went further than that. He also concluded, on highly technical evidence, that the fracture occurred independently of any ozone involvement.

Turning to the *res ipsa* argument, he said that he was satisfied by evidence given by a defence expert that condoms occasionally failed for no known reason. This is perhaps a little harder to understand. Just because it has not been possible on occasions in the past to discover why a condom has split (for hygienic reasons it appears that the actual condoms are not subject to examination, which seems a little over-sensitive – clinicians are not slow to examine stools in the interests of their patients), that does not mean one has to conclude that it was not inherently defective. Surely it is possible to manufacture a condom so that it is bound to be able to stand up to reasonable use without fracturing. If it does fracture it should be up to the manufacturer to provide an exonerating explanation, not up to the user to provide an incriminating one.

However, the judge went on (*obiter*) to disallow the claim on quite another ground. He said that there had been a duty to mitigate the damage, and that Mrs Richardson should have sought out the 'morning-after' pill, whether by telling her GP what had happened or in some other way, which would probably have avoided the pregnancy. Failure to do this invalidated the claim. Views may differ, but it may be thought that this was unreasonable of the judge. Mrs Richardson knew there was a morning-after pill; she thought, reasonably enough, that its efficacy was limited to the morning after; it was then Saturday afternoon; she did not think it was a sufficient emergency for calling on the deputising service. Should she lose her whole claim just for that? The judge said that the least she should have done was to telephone, and that, if she had done that, she would have been told to come and pick up a prescription which could have been taken to the nearest open chemist, or she might have been given accurate information to the effect that Monday would be soon enough. True, a claimant has a duty to take reasonable steps to mitigate his damage or loss (eg he would need to provide strong evidence to excuse himself from accepting a recommended remedial operation), but the duty should not be extended beyond what is clearly a reasonable requirement. For example, we know that a pregnant woman is not obliged to accept a termination (though if she has had one or two before, she probably needs to give a reasonable explanation why she did not have a third one). Is it reasonable to require a woman in the position of Mrs Richardson to rush for the morning-after pill?

In addition, the judge stated summarily that he saw no reason why *McFarlane* should not apply to a consumer product case. This actually needs a little more thought. If the rationale of the House of Lords judgment can properly be said, on the majority view, to be a matter of distributive justice, ie that the NHS or the medical profession should not have to bear the cost of raising the unplanned child, then this argument would not apply to the profit-making manufacturer. If the true rationale is that it is odious to award damages for a healthy child (or impossible to calculate them given the need to deduct the benefit of a child), then it could be conceded that it would be just as odious (or impossible) where a manufacturer would be footing the bill.

Sabri-Tabrizi v Lothian Health Board

This was a Scottish case at first instance concerning a not uncommon situation, namely a second pregnancy after a failed sterilisation. The claimant had been sterilised in September 1991, but became pregnant again in the spring of 1992. She underwent a termination at the beginning of June 1992. However, using only condoms (as it would appear), she became pregnant again in early July 1992, the child of this pregnancy dying *in utero* (necessitating a sad procedure to remove the infant in November 1992). It appears that, somewhat unusually, a second sterilisation procedure had been carried out while she was pregnant with this second child, in August 1992. It is presumed that her pregnancy had not been known at the time. The question whether the August sterilisation damaged the second child was not canvassed at this hearing. This hearing was an application by the defendant to strike out the claim for damages in respect of the second pregnancy on the ground of *novus actus* or *volenti* or remoteness.

In his judgment (1998) 43 BMLR 190, Lord Nimmo Smith said that all the submissions of the defendants turned on the one point, namely that because the mother had had sexual intercourse with her husband when she knew she was still fertile, the consequences of that act could not be laid at the defendants' door. He based his conclusion adverse to the claimant on the fact that it was *unreasonable* of her to expose herself to the risk of becoming pregnant again. Therefore her decision to have sexual intercourse in the knowledge that she was not sterile constituted a *novus actus* and broke the chain of causation. But, even accepting the judge's test of *novus actus*, namely whether the claimant's act was unreasonable,[11] can it really be said that it was unreasonable of the couple to continue to have intercourse, using the only method of contraception that was available to them thanks to the defendants' negligence? What were they supposed to do? Abstain? The fact of the matter is that the defendants, through their negligence, made it impossible for the couple to have any safer intercourse than that provided by condoms. Even if one applies other tests of *novus actus* that have been variously promulgated in the cases, such as foreseeability or policy, the result in this case cannot be reasonably validated.

Triplets

In *Thompson* v *Sheffield Fertility Clinic* [2000] MLC 0282, Hooper J found that the implantation of three embryos in fertility treatment had been in breach of a term of the contract between the mother (who went on to give birth to healthy triplets) and the clinic, as she had made it clear to them that she could not consent to the implantation of more than two embryos. The question of damages for the breach was not decided as the claim was settled shortly after judgment for £20,000. It is understood that the compensation went to offset costs, as there had been an earlier offer in excess of that amount. It was obviously prudent not to litigate damages as one cannot see how the claimant could have escaped being caught by the *McFarlane* decision, and in the particular circumstances recovering nothing (not even for the pregnancy and associated expenses, as she would have been pregnant with twins in any event!).

Limitation

The limitation period cannot begin before the woman knows she is pregnant. Even then one can reasonably argue, in cases of operator failure, that she cannot know what the relevant act or omission is (to which her pregnancy is due) until she receives some explanatory medical input (usually in the form of an expert medical report). But it is clearly safer to work from the date she knew she was pregnant.

In *Walkin* v *South Manchester Health Authority* [1995] 1 WLR 1543, CA, the mother issued within the three-year period a writ claiming damages for personal injuries and economic loss arising from a failed sterilisation followed by the birth of a child. That writ was never served. Some two years later she issued a second writ outside the three-year limitation period, but claimed only for economic loss in an attempt to take advantage of the normal six-year period of limitation. The Court of Appeal, not surprisingly, did not endorse this ploy. They said that, whether or not she

---

11 For a discussion of *novus actus*, see Chapter 17.

was claiming damages for the unwanted pregnancy, her claim was for 'damages in respect of personal injuries' within the meaning of s 11(1) of the Limitation Act 1980. However, Roch LJ reserved the question of the proper limitation period in the case of a failed vasectomy where the woman did not know of the vasectomy and actually wanted a child. The judge said that in those circumstances a pregnancy that was not 'unwanted' by the woman would not be a personal injury to her or anyone else and the man's loss would be purely financial. So here is a clear case of sexual discrimination. A man can claim the cost of upkeep simpliciter where a vasectomy has failed and so take advantage of the six-year limitation period, but where a sterilisation has failed the woman is limited to a three-year period of limitation because she underwent the 'personal injury' of an unplanned pregnancy (whether or not she claims damages for it). We may note that in *Roy* v *Croydon Health Authority* [1997] PIQR P444, CA, Kennedy LJ said that when a mother actually wants the pregnancy and the (healthy) child 'there is simply no loss which can give rise to a claim for damages in respect of either the normal expenses and trauma of pregnancy or the costs of bringing up the child'.

In *Godfrey* v *Gloucestershire Royal Infirmary NHS Trust* [2003] MLC 1010, a wrongful birth claim for failure to give the mother proper advice about termination was held to be a personal injury action, following *Walkin*, and therefore out of time, but Leveson J exercised s 33 discretion to permit the claim to proceed nevertheless.

Loss of fertility

This is the reverse side of the coin. The amount awarded for loss of fertility will depend on the age of the woman and whether she already had the size of family she wanted. There is no clear-cut case assessing the amount, but it appears that for a young woman who is deprived of the right to have a family the award will be not less than £30,000. In *Morgan* v *Gwent Health Authority* [1988] 2 Lancet 519, the Court of Appeal increased from £8,000 to £20,000 the award to a young woman who after a negligent transfusion of Rh+ instead of Rh- blood was now at risk as to the health of any future fetus and would find it hard to find a husband with a compatible blood group. In *Biles* v *Barking and Havering and Brentwood Health Authority* [1988] CLY 1103, general damages of £45,000 were awarded to a woman of 19 who was unnecessarily sterilised. This sum included compensation for much pain and suffering involved in attempts at in vitro fertilisation. Counsel in the case have stated (NLJ, 5 February 1988, p 80) that for 'probable permanent infertility' they reckon that the award, which was not divided up by the judge, was £25,000. The award of £4,000 in *Devi* v *West Midlands Regional Health Authority* (9 December 1981, unreported), CA, was for an older woman who already had a family of four. An award of £3,000 general damages for the 'somewhat remote chance' that the claimant would have had a third child was made in *Wells* v *Surrey Area Health Authority* (1978) Times, 29 July. And a mother of three sons was awarded £750 for a sterilisation performed without her consent at the birth of the third son in *Hamilton* v *Birmingham Regional Hospital Board* [1969] 2 BMJ 456.

Where a primigravid of 22 suffered a post-natal hemorrhage after the birth of twins necessitating a hysterectomy (followed by psychological consequences and some minor gynaecological complications), Samuels QC awarded her £45,000 general damages (*Le Page* v *Kingston and Richmond Health Authority* MLC 0610, [1997] 8 Med LR 229). He drew a distinction between sterility caused by interference with the function of the Fallopian tubes and sterility consequent upon loss of the womb. In *Butters* v *Grimsby and Scunthorpe Health Authority* [1998] Lloyd's Rep Med 111, MLC 0049, the Court of Appeal endorsed an award of £50,000 general damages to a young woman who, shortly after the birth of her first child in 1992, had undergone a negligently conducted ERPC (evacuation of retained products of conception), which damaged her uterus and cervix. She had endured some four years of misery, involving a number of investigative procedures, two terminations of pregnancy, permanent scarring, and finally a hysterectomy. She and her husband had wanted another two or three children. The court had occasion to consider the Judicial Guidelines on sterility. In fact the court, having admitted fresh evidence demonstrating the recent ongoing medical problems faced by the patient, increased the award by £5,000.

In *Briody* v *St Helens and Knowsley Health Authority* [2000] PIQR Q165, Ebsworth J awarded £66,000, to include compensation for substantial psychiatric consequences, where a 19-year-old woman lost her first child and her womb (in 1973 she had previously succeeded in a hearing on limitation and one on liability (MLC 0099 [1999] Lloyd's Rep Med 185, CA)). The costs of surrogacy were not allowed, on the basis that the chances of success were slim and the arrangement would in any event be unlawful. The Court of Appeal agreed ([2001] MLC 0165).

The action for wrongful life

> Never to have lived is best, ancient writers say,
> Never to have drawn the breath of life,
> Never to have looked into the eye of day.
> The second best's a brief goodnight and quickly turn away.

A free translation of some mournful observations by a Sophoclean chorus.[12]

> An action on behalf of a child, whether born normal or handicapped, alleging that his birth (not his injuries though) only came about because the doctors were negligent, is a non-starter.

The action for wrongful life, as it has been called in the US (in contradistinction to the action for wrongful birth), is an action by the child himself, claiming that through the doctor's negligence he has been born, where if the doctor had not been negligent he would not have been born.

The metaphysical issues raised by this contention are impossible to resolve satisfactorily in a court of law, or elsewhere for that matter. The child does not complain that the physician's negligence has caused him to be born handicapped, for the physician did nothing to cause or contribute to the handicap. But, he says, if you had sterilised or aborted my mother properly (or however the claim might arise), I would not now be living. Theoretically, a healthy child could so contend, not only a handicapped

---

12   *Oedipus Colonaeus* 1225 *et seq.*

one. But if there is any claim at all to be countenanced here, it obviously is even more difficult, perhaps even ludicrous, for a healthy child to contend that he has been injured by the mere fact of being born, whereas, in the case of a severely handicapped child, there is at least some superficial attraction in the contention that his quality of life is so wretched as to amount to a continuous state of suffering, and that he should be recompensed for having to endure that. The logical fallacy is, of course, as already indicated, that the negligence, assuming there to have been negligence, is not responsible for the difference between a life of suffering and a reasonable life (this can often be recompensed under the Congenital Disabilities (Civil Liability) Act 1976 (see Chapter 25)), but between a life of suffering and a state of non-life; and how can the court possibly evaluate the state of non-being?

Transatlantic cases

The US courts have almost invariably rejected this claim. The Illinois Court of Appeal said in 1963: 'Recognition of the plaintiff's claim means the creation of a new tort, a cause of action for wrongful life. The legal implications of such a tort are vast, the social impact could be staggering ...' (*Zepeda* v *Zepeda* 41 Ill App 2d 240 (1963)). In a 1977 case (394 NYS 2d 933), a New York court, while permitting the parents of a deformed child to recover for pain and suffering over the birth, rejected the child's claim. It has been said by the Supreme Court: 'Thus, the threshold question here is not whether life with deformities, however severe, is less preferable than death, but rather whether it is less preferable than the "utter void of non-existence".'

In the Canadian case of *Cataford* v *Moreau* (above), the judge, rejecting the child's claim, said:

> La naissance d'un enfant sain ne constitue pas pour cet infant un dommage, et encore moins un dommage compensable en argent. Il est bien impossible de comparer la situation de l'enfant après sa naissance avec la situation dans laquelle il se serait trouvé s'il n'était pas né. Le seul énoncé du problème montre déjà l'illogisme qui l'habite. D'ailleurs par quelle perversion de l'esprit pourrait-on arriver à qualifier comme un dommage l'inestimable don de la vie?
>
> (The birth of a healthy baby does not constitute a loss for that child, let alone a loss that can be compensated for by money. One cannot compare the child's position after being born with what it would have been had he not been born. Merely to state the problem demonstrates its inherently illogical nature. Moreover, by what sort of warped outlook could one put under the head of loss or damage the priceless gift of life?)

There was, however, one occasion when a New York court refused to strike out the claim of a deceased child born with a fatal kidney disease after his parents had been told that the disease would not be transmitted to the fetus. It was said by the court to be 'tortious to the fundamental right of a child to be born as a whole, functional human being'. That decision was not upheld on appeal – the reasoning of the lower court seems to have fallen into the fallacy above referred to, whereby the defendant is illogically held responsible for the suffering of the child.

The McKay *case*

The first and, probably, the only action in which the claim for wrongful life has been considered in the English courts came before the Court of Appeal in February 1982. The facts in *McKay* v *Essex Area Health Authority* [1982] QB 1166, CA, were that a child was born disabled as a result of her mother having contracted German measles during the pregnancy. It was alleged, *inter alia*, that the medical staff were negligent in not giving the mother proper advice and information which, had it been forthcoming, would have led to an abortion. So the mother claimed on her own account. But there was also a claim on behalf of the child for her having 'suffered entry into a life in which her injuries are highly debilitating', in other words, for having been born, or at any rate for having been born into a life of handicap and suffering.

On a preliminary hearing, the Master struck out the child's claim as disclosing no reasonable cause of action; Lawson J restored it on the ground that it was really a claim for injuries suffered and was highly arguable; the Court of Appeal was unanimously of the view that the Master's decision was right (although, as a matter of procedure, Griffiths LJ was not prepared to interfere with the judge's exercise of his discretion).

Stephenson LJ pointed out the lack of success such a claim had met with in the US, and that the Law Commission report on injuries to unborn children (Cmnd 5709), which was followed by the Congenital Disabilities (Civil Liability) Act 1976, counselled against admitting such a claim. He said that the claim must be viewed as an allegation that the defendants were negligent in allowing the child to be born at all. To impose on the medical advisers a duty owed to the child over and above that owed to the mother to give the mother the opportunity to terminate the child's existence would constitute a further inroad on the sanctity of human life, which would be contrary to public policy. In addition, the judge adverted to the impossibility of evaluating the difference between the child's handicapped existence and the non-existence it would have had had the defendants not been negligent.

Ackner LJ said that he could not accept that the common law duty of care to a person could involve the legal obligation to that person, whether or not *in utero*, to terminate his existence. Such a proposition ran wholly contrary to the concept of the sanctity of human life. On the question of damage he said that what the doctor was blamed for was causing or permitting the child to be born at all, not for causing or contributing to her injuries; and he asked how a court could begin to evaluate non-existence. 'No comparison is possible and therefore no damage can be established which a court could recognise. This goes to the root of the whole cause of action.'

Griffiths LJ, while of the view that, procedurally, the application should fail and the matter be argued at the trial, had no doubt that the claim did not lie. 'The most compelling reason to reject this cause of action is the intolerable and insoluble problem it would create in the assessment of damages.'

All the judges expressed the view that s 4(5) of the Congenital Disabilities (Civil Liability) Act 1976, while not applying to the instant birth – which took place in 1975, before the date upon which the Act came into force (22 July 1976) – had the effect of abolishing this cause of action for births after that date. This, with respect, is clearly wrong, in the sense that it puts an interpretation upon the section which Parliament did not intend and which the words cannot bear, however desirable the result may be thought. The Act gave a child the right to sue a tortfeasor for injuries sustained in the womb; one would therefore expect that the Act would seek to abolish, *ex abundanti cautela*, any common law cause of action that might possibly exist corresponding to the new statutory cause of action, and this is exactly what it does. Section 4(5) abolishes any law in force before the passing of the Act ('whereby a person could be liable to a child in respect of disabilities with which it might be born'). The action for wrongful life is not an action in respect of the child's disabilities at birth; as the court itself said in this case (as noted above) it is a claim for having been born at all. The section is simply concerned with actions for personal injury suffered before or possibly at birth. That the section does not apply to the action for wrongful life is demonstrated not only by the context of the Act and the obvious intended scope of the subsection, but also by the reflection that this action would in theory, if it existed, be open to a healthy child, for the essence of the complaint is 'you permitted me to be born, [sc] into this dreadful world when, had it not been for your negligence, I would have remained in the tranquil and carefree land of the unborn'. The fact that the claimant may be handicapped rather than healthy is not of the essence of the action, though it would of course make it even more difficult to show that he had suffered loss, ie that he was worse off alive than unborn (see the following chapter for a discussion of the 1976 Act).

The New South Wales Court of Appeal has recently upheld the judgments dismissing three cases where a handicapped child claimed damages for 'wrongful life', declaring the claims unjusticiable (*Waller* v *James, Harriton* v *Stephens, Waller* v *Hoolahan* [2004] MLC 1104). Surprisingly, one of the three judges dissented.

In 2001 the French Parliament passed a law reversing the success that such a claim had enjoyed in the highest court (the *Perruche* case).

Chapter 25

The Congenital Disabilities Act 1976

The Act enables a child injured *en ventre sa mère* and thereby born disabled to recover damages for its disabilities from the person responsible, provided that person is in breach of duty to the parent. A doctor whose treatment, before ever conception takes place, negligently impairs the reproductive faculties of a man or a woman can be held liable by the disabled child that that man or woman later begets, provided that neither parent knew the risk they were taking when having intercourse.

THE PROBLEM

What if negligent treatment harms the fetus, so that the child is born handicapped? Perhaps drugs for the pregnant woman have been manufactured, marketed or prescribed without proper care. Or perhaps her antenatal care has been deficient. And what if, before ever conception took place, the mother's (or the father's) reproductive capacity was, unknown to her (or to him), harmed by treatment or drugs so that later she conceived a handicapped child? Or there may have been a transmission to the mother (or father) of tainted blood, years before, or tainted semen in an artificial insemination. Or a Rhesus negative mother was not given, after the birth of a Rhesus positive child, the anti-D gamma globulin injections that would immunise her, so that in her next pregnancy her blood contaminated the fetus, with the result that her second child suffered Rhesus disease.[1]

These are just a few of the possibilities where negligence towards a parent can result in the birth of a handicapped child.

---

1   Liability was admitted in the case of *Roberts* v *Johnstone* [1989] QB 878, CA, where the defendants, although knowing that a mother had in 1975 mistakenly been given a blood transfusion of Rhesus positive blood, failed, her husband being Rhesus negative, to protect her child when she later, in 1981, became pregnant, so that the claimant was born severely handicapped from hemolytic disease (she recovered some £400,000 damages (see also *Lazenvnick* v *General Hospital of Munro City Inc*, Civ Act 78-1259, Cmnd Pa, 13 August 1980)).

In the post-conception case the child is effectively saying: 'You injured me, albeit I was only a fetus then, and as a result of that injury I have been born handicapped instead of whole.' In the pre-conception case he says: 'If you had treated my mother (or my father) with proper care I would have been conceived and born hale and hearty. You are responsible for my present plight and so you must compensate me for it.'

THE COMMON LAW

Before 1990, there was no English authority which decided whether the common law recognised the right of a child injured *en ventre sa mère* to sue when born (though the Irish case of *Walker* v *Great Northern Rly Co of Ireland* (1890) 28 LR Ir 69 gave a negative answer). The thalidomide litigation, which raised this question in the most urgent form, did not provide an answer, as a settlement was reached (see *S* v *Distillers Co* [1970] 1 WLR 114), though it appears that the defendants, while hotly contesting negligence, did not deny the right of the children to recover if in fact there had been negligence. In the Canadian case of *Montreal Tramways* v *Léveillé* [1933] 4 DLR 337, the court was prepared to recognise the right of a child to recover for damages negligently inflicted upon it when in the womb, while at the same time pointing out:

> The great weight of judicial opinion in the common law courts denies the right of a child when born to maintain an action for pre-natal injuries (*per* Lamont J).

Such a claim was later recognised in the South African case of *Pinchin* v *Santam Insurance Co* 1963 (2) SA 254 (Supreme Court, Witwatersrand Local Division), in the Australian case of *Watt* v *Rama* [1972] VR 353, in the Canadian case of *Duval* v *Seguin* (1972) 26 DLR (3d) 418, and in the Australian case of *X and Y* v *Pal* [1992] 3 Med LR 195.

Recovery by the estate of a pre-viable stillborn fetus was permitted in *Presley* v *Newport Hospital* 365 A 2d 748, Rhode Island (1976) (and such a cause of action was allowed in *White* v *Yup* 458 P (2d) 617 (1969)). But under English law it was thought that a child had no rights and therefore no *locus standi* as a litigant until birth (*Paton* v *British Pregnancy Advisory Service Trustees* [1979] QB 276). This principle was not affected by the fact that, once born, the child might have under the Act of 1976 rights in respect of damage done to it in the womb or to its parent before conception. In *C* v *S* [1988] QB 135, the Court of Appeal ruled that an 18-week fetus was not a 'child capable of being born alive' within the meaning of the Infant Life (Preservation) Act 1929, so that an otherwise lawful termination of pregnancy at that stage under the Abortion Act 1967 was not a crime. The Appeal Committee of the House of Lords later that day rejected all the arguments of the young father who sought an injunction to stop his girlfriend from having the abortion. It would appear therefore that their Lordships, as well as agreeing with the issue decided by the Court of Appeal, must have been of the view that the father had no standing to interfere with the mother's proposed abortion (indeed even a husband is no better placed, as was shown by the *BPAS* case cited above), and that the fetus was not a legal person for the purposes of bringing an action through his father (or semble anyone) to restrain the act which would destroy it.[2]

Then in the cases of *Burton* v *Islington Health Authority* and *De Martell* v *Merton and Sutton Health Authority* [1993] QB 204, MLC 0927, the Court of Appeal held that children damaged *in utero* before the Act came into operation were nevertheless entitled to sue for damages at common law.[3] The decision of the Supreme Court of Canada in *Montreal Tramways* v *Léveillé* (above) was approved, namely that when a child not actually born at the time of the accident was subsequently born alive and viable, it was clothed with all the rights of action which it would have had if actually in existence at the date of the accident. The case of *Walker* (above) was held not to be the modern law of England. The reasoning of the two judges at first instance was approved. Potts J had said in *B* v *Islington Health Authority* [1991] 1 QB 638, that there was a potential duty on the defendants towards the child who might later be born and that the cause of action was complete when the birth took place. Phillips J had said in *De Martell* v *Merton and Sutton Health Authority* [1991] 2 Med LR 209, (a) that the claimant's case accorded with the legislative policy and that the Act of 1976 recognised the possibility that the claimant had a valid claim at common law, and (b) that the damage was suffered by the claimant at the moment that, in law, he achieved personality and inherited the damaged body for which the defendants, on the assumed facts (as the issue was being decided as a preliminary point), were responsible, and that the events prior to the birth in February 1967 were mere links in the chain of causation between the defendants' assumed lack of skill and care and the consequential damage to the claimant (*quaere*: does one not 'inherit' the body long before birth? Science and religion would surely say so, but maybe not the law).

The decision of the English Court of Appeal was followed by the Scottish appeal court in *Hamilton* v *Fife Health Board* [1993] 4 Med LR 201.

A claim at common law (ie before the Act) in respect of pre-conception negligence seems never to have come before the English courts. But such a claim has occasionally been recognised in the US. In *Renslow* v

---

2   The Court of Session held upon similar facts that causing a fetus to be aborted was not a civil wrong that was actionable at the instance of the father (*Kelly* v *Kelly* [1997] 2 FLR 828). The fact that the child might sustain an action after birth for pre-natal injury (see below) did not mean that it had legal personality before birth. An injured fetus has only a potential right to sue which crystallises when legal personality is achieved at birth. That is how one reconciles this 'fetal' right with the denial of protection to a child if injured or about to be injured by his mother (see, for example, the Cesarian section cases dealt with in Chapter 23 above, and the conjoined twin case referred to in the same chapter under 'The Quality of Life; and, as explained below, the 1976 Act does not render a *mother* liable for negligently injuring her unborn child – except by negligent driving. In *Christian Lawyers Association of South Africa* v *Minister of Health* (1998) 50 BMLR 241, McCreath J held in the Transvaal High Court that in the provision in the South African Constitution guaranteeing the right to life to 'everyone', the word 'everyone' did not cover a fetus and therefore legislation permitting abortion in certain circumstances was not in conflict with the constitutional guarantee. The judgment contains much useful material on the philosophical and legal issues arising out of the question whether a fetus has a legal persona before birth.

3   The *de Martell* case later failed on causation ([1995] 6 Med LR 234).

Mennonite Hospital 351 NE 2d 870, Ill 1976, the mother had at the age of 13 been given a transfusion of mismatched blood, so that the child she gave birth to eight years later was handicapped. In *Jorgensen* v *Meade Johnson Laboratories* 483 F 2d 237, CCA 10, it was held that Down's syndrome twins had the right to maintain an action for chromosome damage against the manufacturers of the contraceptive pill their mother had been taking.[4]

THE ACT

The Congenital Disabilities (Civil Liability) Act 1976 was based on the recommendations of the Law Commission contained in their *Report on Injuries to Unborn Children* (Cmnd 5709, August 1974). (The text of the Act is set out below in Appendix I.)

The right of the child to claim compensation depends on its injuries having been caused by negligence. A child born handicapped through the 'will of God' alone has no claim. Our law is based on fault; we have as yet no system, as in some other jurisdictions, notably New Zealand and Sweden, of compensation for injury without proof of fault. So the parents who manage to prove medical fault connected with the birth of their handicapped child will receive a lot of money, and the parents who cannot do that, either for lack of evidence or because there was no fault, are left to struggle.

The general principle under the statute, which applies to births after but not before 22 July 1976 (s 4(5)), is that a child injured *en ventre sa mère* by the negligence (or, of course, the deliberate assault) of any person, except his mother,[5] can maintain an action for damages for those injuries after his birth. He can also sue anyone who, before ever he was conceived, tortiously injured either of his parents with the result that when he was later conceived and born he was disabled (this includes suing his father for injuring his mother, for example by infecting her with a sexually transmitted disease).

The action can only be maintained at the suit of a child who is born alive, which means alive when it first has a life separate from its mother (ss 1(1) and 4(2)) – presumably at the moment of severance of the umbilical cord. (Section 4(4) provides that for the purpose of recovering damages for loss of expectation of life the child must live for at least 48 hours; but for deaths after 1982, the provisions of the Administration of Justice Act 1982 have now in any event abolished the right to claim under that head.)

The child has to show that he was born disabled, ie born with any deformity, disease or abnormality, including a predisposition (whether or not it is susceptible of immediate prognosis) to physical or mental defect in the future (ss 1(1) and 4(1)); that the defendant was in breach of his

---

4   Reference may also be made to the Canadian case of *Cherry* v *Borsman* [1991] 2 Med LR 396.

5   A child would have no civil claim against its mother for having injured it in the womb through drug-taking, though the mother might, under a different jurisdiction, have the child taken from her, and could in certain circumstances face prosecution under the Infant Life (Preservation) Act 1929 (see *Re D (a minor)* [1987] AC 317, HL).

duty of care to the mother (it is irrelevant that the mother herself suffered no damage from the breach); that his having been born disabled was the result of that breach of duty; and that the breach affected either parent in his or her ability to have a normal, healthy child (ie pre-conception), or affected the mother during pregnancy, or mother or child in the course of its birth, so that the child was born with disabilities which would not otherwise have been present.

These results are achieved by the legislation in the following ways:

If the child is born disabled as a result of an 'occurrence' before its birth, and someone other than the mother is 'answerable' for it, the child can sue for the disabilities as damage resulting from the wrongful act (s 1(1)).

The 'occurrence' must be one which affected either parent's ability to have a normal, healthy child, or which affected the mother during pregnancy, or mother or child in the course of the birth, so that the child was born disabled (s 1(2)).

A person is 'answerable' to the child if he was liable in tort to the parent for the occurrence, regardless of any limitation point and regardless whether or not the parent suffered any actionable injury from the wrongful act (s 1(3)).

If the 'occurrence' preceded conception the child cannot sue if either parent knew 'at that time' (which presumably means when having intercourse) of the risk created by the 'occurrence' that any child he or she begat might be handicapped (s 1(4)). In other words, if a person knows that he or she is at risk of creating a handicapped child and nevertheless goes on to do so, the child cannot sue the person responsible for creating the risk. (But where the father is the defendant and he alone knew of the risk, the child can sue him. In other words, a man who knows he is at risk of producing a handicapped child, and does not tell the mother, can be sued by the child when it is born disabled (s 1(4)).)

It is specifically provided (it was the law anyway, but it was put in, as the Law Commission Report makes clear, to assuage the fears of the medical profession) that a medical adviser is not liable if he took reasonable care of the parent consistent with the received wisdom of the profession at the time; but that does not mean that he is to be held liable for the reason merely that he did not follow that wisdom (in other words, negligence has to be proved as against the physician in the usual way) (s 1(5)).

Liability to the child may be reduced or extinguished where the defendant could take advantage as against the parent of a term in a contract he made with the parent (s 4(6)) – this should now be read with s 2 of the Unfair Contract Terms Act 1977 which precludes a person, whether by contract or notice, from excluding or restricting his liability for death or personal injury resulting from negligence. Liability may also be reduced to the extent the court thinks just and equitable where it is shown that the parent shared the responsibility for the child being born disabled (this must refer to contributory negligence or some sort of fault on the part of the parent) (s 6(7)).

(There is in fact an exception to the rule that a woman cannot be liable for pre-natal injuries suffered by her child: she has a duty when driving a motor vehicle to take the same care for the child she knows or ought to know she is carrying as she must take for other road users (s 2). This enables the child to recover damages from the mother's motor insurers.)

CAUSATION

The 'occurrence' must be shown to have resulted in the child being born disabled. It is often difficult in the medical negligence action to show that the claimant's condition was caused by the treatment he received, even within the relatively wide scope the law affords to causation (which permits any significant cause, even one among many, to be taken, for the purpose of proving loss, as having caused the damage). But the difficulty is increased in the context of pre-natal injury, where:

> ... often there are difficulties in separating the relative contributions of genetic and environmental effects, and interactions between them ... There must be many pregnant women carrying a fetus with a genetic defect who are exposed to a potential teratogenic [ie capable of deforming a fetus] agent, and many misinterpretations in deciding the cause of damage to the child (*per* Dr Edwards, (1973) 246 Nature 54).

THE DAMAGE

The child sues in respect of the disabilities caused by the original tortious act, the 'occurrence'. This has nothing to do with the unjusticiable action for wrongful life (see Chapter 24).

The Act 'replaces any law in force before its passing, whereby a person could be liable to a child in respect of disabilities with which it might be born' (s 4(5)) (see, for one view on this provision, the last section of Chapter 24).

LIMITATION

It is clear from s 4(3) that the limitation period will be the same as if the injuries had been suffered at birth. It will not begin while the child is still a minor (see Chapter 26). An action could therefore be brought as of right by a claimant aged 20 years in respect of an incident that injured his mother many years before he was born (though the evidence would be hard to collate).

EXAMPLES

Liability was admitted and compensation of over £330,000 awarded to a girl born handicapped due to the negligent transfusion to her mother seven years before her birth of blood which rendered the mother Rhesus incompatible with her husband (*Roberts* v *Johnstone* (1986) Times, 26 July – the Court of Appeal's judgment on damages is reported at [1988] QB 878).

Most cases of injury to the fetus revolve around accusations of negligence during or shortly before labour, and usually no reference is made to the Act, as it is taken for granted. One recent case, however, where the provisions of the Act were set out in the judgment is *Peters* v *University Hospital of Wales NHS Trust* (7 July 2002, unreported), QBD, Purchas J. A consultant acted negligently in carrying out a bladder tap in March

1996 on a woman some four months pregnant, with the result that her child was born missing the whole of the left leg below the knee. The main issue in the case was causation, which was satisfied by proof that probably the damage was caused through vascular injury occurring during the bladder tap.

EXTENSIONS AND RESTRICTIONS

The provisions of the Act are apt to cover negligence in and around *in vitro* fertilisation and artificial insemination.

By s 6(3) of the Consumer Protection Act 1987, that Act applies to the provisions of the Congenital Disabilities (Civil Disability) Act 1976, thus affording its protection to the unborn child (see Chapter 28).

OTHER CASES

Unborn babies cannot be made wards of court (*Re F (in utero)* [1988] Fam 122, CA).

A fetus is not a 'person' distinct from its mother for the purposes of the offence of threatening to kill another person under s 16 of the Offences Against the Person Act 1861 (*R v Tait* [1990] 1 QB 290, CA). See also *A-G's Reference (No 3 of 1994)* [1997] 3 All ER 936, HL.

In *Rance v Mid-Downs Health Authority* MLC 0637, [1991] 1 QB 587, Brooke J held that the words 'a child capable of being born alive' in s 1 of the Infant Life (Preservation) Act 1929 meant capable of existing as a live child, breathing and living by reason of its breathing through its own lungs alone, without deriving any of its living or power of living by or through any connection with its mother, and that, once a fetus had reached such a state of development in the womb that it was capable, if born, of possessing those attributes, it was capable of being born alive within the meaning of the Act. The point of this determination was that the parents of a child born with spina bifida were suing the health authority for not discovering the deformity and terminating the pregnancy. The judge held that, even if it had been discovered, it would have been too late for a lawful abortion as the child was then (he was some 27 weeks in gestation) capable of being born alive.

Chapter 26

Limitation

INTRODUCTION

Limitation is entirely a creature of statute. It has existed since 1623. Its purpose is to prevent stale claims. The present judicial thinking, as per the reforms of Lord Woolf, supports the striking out of actions which are not *brought* or are not *pursued* with expedition. Some members of the Court of Appeal are keener than others to debar old claims and are adept at finding reasons for reversing decisions at first instance in favour of the patient.

THE PERIOD OF LIMITATION

Actions in contract and in court are basically subject to a six-year period of limitation starting from the date when the cause of action arose. However, actions for damages for negligence or breach of duty where the damages claimed consist of or include damages in respect of personal injuries to the claimant or any other person are subject to a three-year period, by virtue of s 11 of the Limitation Act 1980 (replacing the similar provision in the Law Reform (Limitation of Actions) Act 1954).

Further, there are complex provisions for postponing the commencement of the limitation period both in respect of personal injury claims (by virtue of s 14 of the 1980 Act) and other claims in contract and tort (by virtue of the provisions of the Latent Damage Act 1986, which inserted relevant provisions into the 1980 Act as s 11A).

WHAT AMOUNTS TO A PERSONAL INJURY ACTION?

A medical negligence action is not necessarily an action for personal injuries. It may be that the only claim is for financial loss, as where a patient is negligently told not to work any longer. 'Personal injury' includes psychological as well as physical injury.

'Personal injuries' are defined by the interpretation section of the 1980 Act, s 38, as including 'any disease and any impairment of a person's physical or mental condition'. Sometimes it may not be clear if an undisputed consequence is to be regarded as an injury or not; for example, there is judicial authority to support the proposition that an unwanted pregnancy is an 'injury', whereas, if the pregnancy was welcome, it is not an injury (see *Walkin* v *South Manchester Health Authority* (below)).

In *Ackbar* v *C F Green & Co* [1975] QB 582, it was held that a claim against an insurance broker for failing to obtain cover for the claimant was not a claim for damages for personal injuries, although the claim in fact arose out of the claimant's having suffered personal injuries.

In *Norman* v *Aziz* [2000] PIQR P72, the Court of Appeal held that an action against the owner of a motor vehicle for permitting someone to drive it uninsured, the driver then injuring the claimant, was an action in respect of personal injuries and so subject to a three-year limitation period.

But where an injured party claimed under the Third Parties (Rights against Insurers) Act 1930 against the insurers of his employers, who had been wound up, this was held by the Court of Appeal in the context of pre-action disclosure not to be a claim in respect of personal injuries (*Burns* v *Shuttlehurst Ltd* [1999] 1 WLR 1449).

A claim against a solicitor for not pursuing a medical negligence action would not be a claim in respect of personal injuries. In *Broadley* v *Guy Clapham & Co* [1994] 4 All ER 439, CA, it appears to have been accepted without argument that a six-year period applied.

In *Pattison* v *Hobbs* (1985) Times, 11 November, the Court of Appeal held that where, following an allegedly negligently performed vasectomy, damages were claimed only for the cost of raising a healthy child, the action was not one which included a claim for personal injuries. However, in *Walkin* v *South Manchester Health Authority* MLC 0731, [1995] 1 WLR 1543, the Court of Appeal held that a claim for an unwanted pregnancy following a failed sterilisation and for the consequent costs involved in raising the unplanned child was a claim for 'damages in respect of personal injuries', and it was not possible for the claimant to abandon a claim for personal injury, ie the claim for compensation for the unwanted pregnancy, and in that way to assert a six-year period of limitation as for a claim simply for economic loss. In the circumstances of this particular case the decision can be readily understood, because the claimant had already issued, but not served, a writ in the usual form before the expiry of the three-year period. It was only when she realised that a second writ would be outside that period (but within the six-year period) that the claim was reduced to one for economic loss only. However, it is to be noted that Roch LJ said that he had some difficulty in perceiving a normal conception, pregnancy and the birth of a healthy child as 'any disease or any impairment of a person's physical or mental condition' in cases where the only reasons for the pregnancy and subsequent birth being unwanted were financial. He also reserved the question of the proper limitation period in cases of failed male sterilisation because in those circumstances there would be no personal injury to the claimant. Neill LJ also reserved the question whether any personal injury at all would be suffered where a woman who desired to have a child became pregnant as a result of a failed vasectomy. This decision was followed in *Godfrey* v *Gloucestershire Royal Infirmary NHS Trust* [2003] MLC 1010.

In *Bowler* v *Walker* [1996] PIQR P22, the Court of Appeal affirmed the striking out of a claim for *wilful misconduct* against a psychiatrist where it was alleged by a patient that she had caused him psychiatric injury by entering into a sexual relationship with him. The court said that the claim must be brought as a simple claim for *breach of duty*, and as such fell within the normal personal injury limitation provisions.

In the dyslexia case of *Phelps* v *Hillingdon London Borough Council* MLC 0228, [1999] 1 WLR 500 CA; on appeal [2000] 3 WLR 776, HL, the House of Lords reversed the surprising decision of the Court of Appeal, and held that the prolongation of a congenital defect (here dyslexia) could amount to a personal injury.[1]

Assault

It has been held by the House of Lords, in the context of a claim for sexual abuse, that a claim for assault was not a claim in respect of personal injury and therefore the six-year period applied. In that event there is no legislative provision enabling the commencement of the period of limitation to be postponed for lack of knowledge of relevant facts. In this way the court made it impossible for claimants to sue for sexual abuse more than six years after attaining their majority (*Stubbings* v *Webb* [1993] AC 498, HL). An appeal to the European Court of Human Rights was unsuccessful ((1996) 23 EHHR 213). This is an added reason not to sue doctors for assault, but to base allegations of lack of consent on simple negligence.[2]

In *KR* v *Bryn Alyn Community (Holdings) Ltd* [2003] Lloyds Rep Med 175, claims by 14 adults for sexual and/or physical and/or emotional abuse suffered between 1973 and 1991 in children's homes in North Wales, the Court of Appeal said that claims for personal injuries in respect of deliberate conduct, whether considered in the context of vicarious liability or not, did not fall within section 11, and therefore, in the absence of some provable allegation of systemic negligence by the defendant, its employees' deliberate abuse did not fall within section 11 and was therefore governed by a non-extendable six-year period of limitation (rather than an extendable three-year period under ss 11 and 33).[3] This decision was followed in *C* v *Middlesborough Council* [2004] EWCA 1746.

WHEN DOES THE LIMITATION PERIOD BEGIN?

Theoretically, it begins when the cause of action arises (ie when the negligent conduct has given rise to injury, even if the injury is latent), *but* it

---

1   A claim against employers for failing to advise of the possibility of getting benefits for injury suffered during employment was not a personal injury action (*Gaud* v *Leeds Health Authority* (1999) 49 BMLR 105, CA).

2   In *S* v *W* [1995] 1 FLR 862, the Court of Appeal held that an action by a daughter against her mother for not protecting her from abuse by her father was not an action for assault, and so the normal personal injury limitations applied, including s 33 discretion. See also *Rogers* v *Finemodern* (20 October 1999), QBD, Garland J.

3   For the effect of the operation of the Limitation Act 1963 and the Limitation Act 1973 on the six-year statutory bar under the Limitation Act 1939 in the context of a deferred period due to disability, see *McDonnell* v *Congregation of Christian Brothers Trustees* [2004] PIQR P299, HL. These Acts may appear no longer current but this claim, heard in the Lords at the end of 2003, was in fact for alleged abuse between 1941 and 1951!

can usually be postponed in medical negligence claims as it cannot begin until the claimant has acquired the relevant 'knowledge' (s 11(4)). Most limitation issues in medical negligence actions turn on the questions:

* when did the claimant acquire *actual* knowledge?
* did he acquire *constructive* knowledge at an earlier date?
* if he is out of time, should s 33 *discretion* be exercised to permit the action to proceed notwithstanding?

A note on disability

The limitation period will not begin while the claimant remains under a disability, that is to say he is a child (not yet 18) or a 'patient' (ie if he is of unsound mind, in that by reason of mental disorder within the meaning of s 1(2) of the Mental Health Act 1983 – 'mental illness, arrested or incomplete development of the mind, psychopathic disorder, and any other disorder or disability of mind' – he is incapable of managing his property and affairs (Limitation Act 1980, ss 28(1) and 38(3), (4)). For a detailed discussion of capacity in the differing contexts of limitation, legal persona (ie a 'patient' under rules of court), the Court of Protection, the Mental Health Act, and Articles 6 and 8 of the European Convention on Human Rights, see *Masterman-Lister* v *Brutton and Jewell* [2003] Lloyds Rep Med 244.

A supervening disability will not stop the limitation period running, but it should be taken into account on a s 33 application. See *Kirby* v *Leather* (1965) 2 QB 367 and *Rogers* v *Finemodern Ltd* (20 October 1999), QBD, Garland J.

The Court of Appeal

Before dealing with the three main issues in detail (actual knowledge, constructive knowledge and discretion) it should be borne in mind that different members of the Court of Appeal view the prospect of an old claim proceeding with different emotions, ranging from horror to equanimity. So some tribunals cast around for any peg on which to reverse a decision favourable to the claimant, while other tribunals take a more impartial view. Decisions are also influenced by current policy. The current impetus for speedy trials does not favour the presentation of old claims. The current preoccupation with judicial case management influences courts to declare cases out of time so that they themselves get the power (under s 33) to decide whether it is appropriate or not to let them proceed notwithstanding.

A plethora of cases

As Brooke LJ said in *Spargo* v *North Essex District Health Authority* MLC 0651, [1997] 8 Med LR 125, CA, this branch of the law is grossly overloaded with reported cases. As case after case comes to court every judge has his input, telling us, for example, what the word 'know' means, what a reasonable patient would or would not do, and so forth. As long ago as 1985, May LJ said that 'know' was an ordinary English word ('reasonable belief' or 'suspicion' is 'not enough') – *Davis* v *Ministry of Defence*

(1985) Times, 7 August – but that has not stopped our judges from extensive semantic disputation. One of the more remarkable, and certainly more enduring, pieces of sophistry was perpetrated in that same judgment when the Court of Appeal rejected the natural meaning of 'attributable' (ie 'is to be attributed to') and interpreted the word in a novel way, namely to mean '(reasonably) capable of being attributed to'. That interpretation has substantially prejudiced the patient's position as it has enabled courts to find that he has had knowledge where the attribution is only a possibility.

The multitude of reported cases means that the 'devil can find scripture to suit his purpose'. A recent attempt to summarise the relevant law was made by Brooke LJ in the *Spargo* case (see below). But earlier material should not simply be ignored. Perhaps the only useful guideline is that cases at first instance are unlikely to be worth studying as there is so much material on appeal.

KNOWLEDGE

This (by virtue of s 14) involves knowledge:

- that the injury was significant (an injury is significant if the claimant would reasonably have considered it sufficiently serious to justify suing a defendant who did not dispute liability and had the means to pay – s 14(2));
- that the injury is attributable in whole or in part to the act or omission which is alleged to constitute negligence or breach of duty;
- of the identity of the defendant.

The last factor is unlikely to arise in a medical claim, though it is conceivable that it might prove difficult, for example, to identify the GP who treated.[4] If the wrong GP has been sued, the mistake could probably be corrected pursuant to CPR 19.2, 19.5 or 17.4. In *Gregson v Channel Four Television Corpn* (2000) Times, 11 August, CA, the court said, echoing the previous law, that CPR 19.5 applied where the application was to substitute a new party for a party who was named in the claim form in mistake for the new party, and CPR 17.4(3) applied where the intended party was named in the claim form but there was a genuine mistake as to the name of the party and no-one was misled. The court said there was no significant conflict between the two rules. In this case CPR 17.4 applied: it was not a question of substituting a new party, and the judge's discretion in favour of the claimant had been correctly exercised.[5]

Identity may be obscure in employment cases. In *Cressey v E Timm and Son Ltd* [2005] EWCA Civ 763, the commencement of the limitation period was deferred until the claimant could reasonably have known of the identity of his employer at the time of the accident (following *Simpson v Norwest Holst Southern Ltd* (1980) 1 WLR 968).

---

4   It is usually a good idea to sue the practice as a whole on ordinary partnership principles. Where the practice is a primary care trust, as opposed to a primary care group, the trust should be recognised as having legal personality, like any other NHS Trust.

5   See also footnote below, *Henderson v Temple Pier Co* [1998] 1 WLR 1540, CA.

Under s 32(1)(b) of the Act deliberate concealment of relevant facts by a defendant may operate to delay the commencement of the limitation period; see *Williams* v *Fanshaw Porter Williams* [2004] EWCA Civ 157. By s 32(2) a *deliberate* commission of a breach of duty in circumstances in which it is unlikely to be discovered for some time equates with deliberate concealment (see *Cave* v *Robinson Jarvis and Rolf* [2003] 1 AC 384, HL).

Actual knowledge

The claimant has to *know* that he has suffered a *significant* injury that is *attributable* to the alleged negligent act or omission. It is expressly provided that knowledge of *fault*, ie that the relevant act or omission was negligent, is irrelevant (s 14(1)).[6] This does not, however, mean that the limitation date cannot be the date when knowledge of negligence is acquired, because it may be that on that date knowledge of attributability was also for the first time acquired.

'*Know*': – The high point for defence counsel is probably the unfortunate observation of Lord Donaldson in the non-medical case of *Halford* v *Brookes* [1991] 1 WLR 428 at 443, CA, when he said that 'reasonable belief' was usually enough to constitute the required degree of knowledge. Other judicial observations are more acceptable. In *Nash* v *Eli Lilly & Co* [1993] 1 WLR 782, MLC 0021, the Court of Appeal said:

> Knowledge is a condition of mind which imports a degree of certainty and ... the degree of certainty which is appropriate for these purposes is that which, for the particular claimant, may reasonably be regarded as sufficient to justify embarking upon the preliminaries to the making of a claim for compensation such as the taking of legal or other advice.
>
> Whether or not a state of mind for these purposes is properly to be treated by the court as knowledge seems to us to depend, in the first place, upon the nature of the information which the claimant has received, the extent to which he pays attention to the information as affecting him, and his capacity to understand it. There is a second stage at which the information, when received and understood, is evaluated. It may be rejected as unbelievable. It may be regarded as unreliable or uncertain. The court must assess the intelligence of the claimant; consider and assess his assertions as to how he regarded such information as he had; and determine whether he had knowledge of the facts by reason of his understanding of the information.

On the one hand, it is not easy to see why embarking on the preliminaries to the making of the claim for compensation, ie going to see a solicitor, implies knowledge on the part of the claimant. He may go to see a solicitor – in fact he often does – for the very reason that he does not know where he stands or where the truth lies. He may be asking the solicitor to

---

6   This means, among other things, that where one expert reports that there is no cause of action and later another says the opposite, that does not mean that the limitation period begins only with the second report (*Jones* v *Liverpool Health Authority* [1996] PIQR P251, CA).

seek clarification of his lack of understanding of what happened.[7] On the other hand, the court did envisage the possibility that a particular claimant might have been taking the view that, although she had received information on which knowledge could be based, she needed expert confirmation before her belief could attain that degree of firmness to amount to knowledge.

It will be a matter for decision upon the facts of the individual case whether expert confirmation was required for knowledge to be had. *Spargo* v *North Essex District Health Authority* MLC 0651, [1997] 8 Med LR 125 is an example of a case where the Court of Appeal held, not unreasonably, that the judge's finding that expert confirmation had been needed could not be supported (see below). So, too, *Skitt* v *Khan and Wakefield Health Authority* [1997] 8 Med LR 105 (see below). On the other hand, in *Ali* v *Courtaulds Textiles Ltd* [1999] Lloyd's Rep Med 301, the Court of Appeal, reversing the trial judge, held that the claimant, who had taken all reasonable steps to obtain expert knowledge, could not have know that his deafness was attributable to noise rather than age until he got his expert report (Simon Brown questioned this decision in the *Sniezek* case, below).

In *Rowbottom* v *Royal Masonic Hospital* MLC 0553, [2002] Lloyds Rep Med 173 the Court of Appeal held, by a majority, that a claimant who was alleging that he had suffered injury from a failure to administer antibiotics could only have had the relevant knowledge when he received his second expert report. That report told him that lack of antibiotics was responsible for his injury; up till then he had thought it was failure to install a drain. Two recent cases at first instance on this issue of no knowledge until expert report received are *Mirza* v *Birmingham Health Authority* [2001] MLC 0412 and *Burton* v *St Albans and Hemel Hempstead NHS Trust* [2002] MLC 0856.

In *Sniezek* v *Bundy (Letchworth) Ltd* [2000] PIQR P213, [2000] MLC 0225 (Simon Brown, Judge LJJ, Bell J), another case that focused on the meaning of the word 'know', the court equated with knowledge a firm, consistent and convinced belief on the part of the claimant, despite repeated contrary medical advice, that his respiratory problems were caused by his work conditions. On the one hand, the court put much emphasis on the third of Brooke LJ's principles in *Spargo* ([1997] PIQR P235),[8] to the effect that a claimant with a firm belief who goes to a solicitor to seek advice about making a claim for compensation has knowledge (unless – principle four – she is in fact barking up the wrong tree; or her knowledge remains vague, so that she cannot be fairly expected to know what should be investigated; or she believes but is not sure and needs to check with an expert). On the other hand, all three judges deprecated the mountain of past authority analysing and re-analysing the ordinary word 'know'. Simon Brown LJ suggested a simple distinction between a

---

7   At another point in the judgment the court said a claimant would have knowledge where he had sought advice *and taken proceedings* [emphasis added]. This case should not be taken as authority for the proposition that merely going to a solicitor for advice about a possible claim constitutes knowledge (and see below the commentary on the case of *Sniezek*).

8   See below for the principles.

claimant who was a mere believer and one who was a firm believer. This could indeed prove a useful way to end the interminable semantic arguments and analyses about what 'know' means. Stop the endless defining and re-defining and just come to a conclusion on the sense of the matter. Is this a claimant who was convinced of the existence and source of a significant injury, despite (if this be the case) negative medical advice, or was he not convinced but merely highly suspicious?

Bell J similarly distinguished between a firm belief which a claimant retained whatever expert advice he received and a claimant who believed that he may have or even probably had a significant injury attributable to his working conditions but was not sure and felt it necessary to have expert advice on those questions. Judge LJ clearly supported a simple test. He said that the question was one of fact in each case. He doubted whether any considerable legal refinement was necessary or appropriate. He thought that five or ten minutes of argument should enable the judge to make up his mind rather than a long trawl through the authorities, treating a question of fact as a question of law.

A suggestion

I suggest the following. Firm belief can amount to knowledge in appropriate circumstances. It can even amount to knowledge despite contrary negative expert advice in appropriate circumstances. But it needs to be firm enough to amount more or less to an enduring conviction, and is certainly not to be inferred merely from going to a solicitor (note that Judge LJ explicitly said that nothing in the authorities or in the Act supported a conclusion that that time automatically started to run against a claimant who had taken legal advice). The circumstances in which firm belief will amount to knowledge depend on the particular facts of the case and do not call for further defining. The decision in each case can be left to the good sense of the court.

Dyslexia: There have been limitation judgments in the new line of dyslexia cases. In *Robinson* v *St Helens Metropolitan Borough Council* [2002] MLC 0835, [2003] PIQR P129, the Court of Appeal, dismissing the claimant's appeal, agreed that the claimant had obtained actual knowledge (under s 14(1)(b)) when he had received a psychologist's report in 1992 diagnosing severe dyslexia and also knew that he had been badly treated at school. Similarly, in *Rowe* v *Kingston upon Hull City Council* [2003] EWCA Civ 1281, the court allowed the defendants' appeal, finding it sufficient for the purposes of knowledge that by the time he was 18 the claimant knew that he was dyslexic and that the education authorities had failed to help him. That was a significant injury whether or not the claimant knew that it was a suable one (no-one knew that before the House of Lords decision in *Phelps* v *Hillingdon London Borough Council* MLC 0228, [2000] 3 WLR 776, but that simply meant that the claimant did not know he had a legal claim, not that he did not know he had suffered a significant injury).

For constructive knowledge in a case of this sort, see below the *Adams* case, in the section headed 'Constructive knowledge'.

First instance

We may mention one case at first instance at this stage because it is unusual. In *Appleby* v *Walsall Health Authority* [1999] Lloyd's Rep Med 154, MLC 0020, Popplewell J found that a claimant born in 1971 with cerebral palsy affecting only motor control did not acquire the relevant knowledge until 1996, there being no reason for him to question his mother about his birth earlier. Even if his mother had the relevant knowledge years earlier that knowledge could not be imputed to him. The judge also held that, if there had been knowledge, he would nevertheless have exercised his discretion under s 33 to allow the action to proceed (for 'discretion', see below).

If appealed?

One would hope that, where a court of first instance, having heard all the evidence, concluded that the claimant had not had the relevant knowledge until a named date, the Court of Appeal would be reluctant to interfere with that finding. That was certainly the view taken by the Court of Appeal in *Adams* v *Salford and Trafford Health Authority* [2000] MLC 0257, where Kay J had found that the claimant, who had been injured in a road traffic accident, had not known of the possibility that his injuries might have been caused or aggravated by medical negligence until he received his medical records.[9]

'Significant' injury

A patient may not know for a considerable time that she has suffered a significant injury. When did she first know she had suffered any injury? Was she was too ill or disordered to appreciate it? Or perhaps the injury was expected, by her and/or her doctors, to be merely temporary; or perhaps it was latent. For an example of a claimant reasonably believing for a considerable time after an accident (some 18 months) that her back and leg pain were not significant, see *Harding* v *People's Dispensary for Sick Animals* [1994] PIQR P270, CA.

Sometimes there may be argument about what constitutes an injury. In *Dobbie* v *Medway Health Authority* [1994] 1 WLR 1234, MLC 0038, where the claimant underwent removal of a breast upon a mistaken diagnosis of cancer, the Court of Appeal took the view that loss of the breast constituted an injury as it had not in fact been diseased.

A patient is unlikely to succeed in an argument that, although she knew of a minor (but still significant injury), time did not run in respect of a greater injury of which she did not know (*Roberts* v *Winbow* MLC 0074, [1999] Lloyd's Rep Med 31, CA).

---

9   Perhaps the most complex case on 'knowledge' to come before the Court of Appeal in recent years has been *Davis* v *Jacob* (1999) 51 BMLR 42, [1999] MLC 071, where the court, varying the decision of Turner J in a number of respects, considered with minute care the various limitation issues, including discretion. The claimant was alleging negligence in and around prescriptions of dopamine agonists (including by way of clinical trial) for pituitary gland problems, leading to hypomania, changed personality and the urge to commit criminal offences.

Where a patient knows that he is suffering adverse effects from a drug prescribed by his doctor, he cannot argue that that is not a significant injury because the benefit he is getting from it balances out the equation (*Briggs* v *Pitt-Payne and Lias* MLC 0073, [1999] Lloyd's Rep Med 1, CA).

In *Collins* v *Tesco* (24 July 2003, unreported), CA, a claim for injury to the claimant's shoulder at work, the court said that an over-elaborate approach to the question of knowledge was inappropriate. The word 'significant' had to be approached in a common-sense way. While the effect of the injury on a particular claimant might be a factor, the test was an objective test.

If the claim is not for an original injury but for an exacerbation of that injury, the question then is when did the claimant first have knowledge that the exacerbation was significant (*McManus* v *Mannings Marine Ltd* [2001] EWCA Civ 1668).

Attributability

What is it that the claimant has to *know*? He has to know that the significant injury is reasonably *attributable* to the act or omission alleged to constitute negligence. So, in addition to the requirement that he should *know* that he has suffered a *significant injury*, he must also be able to identify a particular act or omission, on which he will later rely as being negligent, as a reasonably possible cause of his injury. This question of attributability has often been the central issue in the reported cases. With what degree of precision must he be able to identify the relevant act or omission? In the case of an *omission* to treat, it is clear that he needs to know not merely that treatment did not take place, but that there was or may well have been a missed opportunity for him to benefit from treatment. *Smith* v *West Lancashire Health Authority* [1995] PIQR P514, CA, was a case where the allegation was one of omission rather than commission (ie that the doctors had failed to do something they should have done rather than done something they should not have done). The patient was treated conservatively at casualty in 1981 for a simple fracture at the base of a ring finger. After two months he was told they would have to operate. He ended up with a disability and lost his job in 1989. Having consulted a solicitor, he obtained a positive medical report in 1991. The court applied the principle of specificity: the question was when did the patient know, or when should he have found out, that he had suffered a significant injury from the act or omission alleged to constitute negligence? Clearly the omission consisted in not operating immediately. The Court of Appeal, reversing the trial judge, said that the patient did not know that was the relevant omission until he got the expert report, nor was there any reason for him to have found it out earlier. He knew he had not had an operation at the outset, but 'he did not know that his problem was in any way associated with the absence of an operation at that time'. The important point is: although this patient ended up with a disability, there was no reason for him to suspect it was attributable to anything done or not done by the doctors (remember that knowledge of fault is irrelevant). This reasoning was endorsed in *Forbes* v *Wandsworth Health Authority* MLC 0671, [1996] 7 Med LR 177, CA (the failure of the Court of Appeal to understand this principle in the case of *Saxby* v *Morgan* MLC 0725, [1997] 8 Med LR 293, led them to a decision that was clearly wrong).[10] Also relevant is *Hayward* v *Sharrard* MLC 0061, [1998] JPIL 326 (patient unaware that an X-ray had been misinterpreted as showing no fracture), and *James* v *East Dorset Health Authority* [1999] MLC 0129, where Sedley LJ said:

> I do not believe that in enacting section 14 Parliament intended to reward those alert to assume that every misfortune is someone else's fault and to place at a disadvantage those who do not assume the worst when there is nothing to alert them to it.

In *Oakes* v *Hopcroft* [2000] Lloyd's Rep Med 394, CA, the claimant, having suffered an accident at work, settled her claim on the basis of a report from the defendant doctor. Years later, after continuing disability and then a further report from a different specialist, she sued the first expert for negligent diagnosis. The court, reversing the judgment below, said that she had not known of the essence of her complaint, nor could have been expected to discover it, until she received the second report.[11]

Knowledge of 'negligence' not necessary

It should always be clearly borne in mind that it is expressly provided by the Act that it is not relevant that the claimant did not know that the relevant act or omission constituted a breach of duty; in other words he does not need to know that the defendant has been negligent (for a recent non-medical case on precisely this issue see *Fennon* v *Anthony Hodari & Co* (21 November 2000, unreported), CA).

Precision

Different courts have offered different glosses on the necessary degree of *precision* with which the vital act or omission has to be identified by the claimant before knowledge can arise. Is it enough to know that the operation or treatment has resulted in an injury, or must the patient know more precisely how it happened?

In *Nash* v *Eli Lilly & Co* [1993] 1 WLR 782, MLC 0021, the Court of Appeal spoke of the need to know 'the essence' of the relevant act or omission. In *Broadley* v *Guy Clapham & Co* [1994] 4 All ER 439, MLC 0043, CA, they spoke of the need for 'specific knowledge' but not so 'detailed' as to permit a detailed pleading, and of knowledge falling short of a complete knowledge of the 'mechanics' of the injury. Then in *Hallam-Eames* v *Merrett Syndicates* MLC 0703, [1996] 7 Med LR 122, they spoke of the act that was 'causally relevant' and said that the claimant 'must have known the facts which can fairly be described as constituting the negligence of which he complains'.

Many cases at first instance on specificity (ie attributability) can be found in the reports. They give a good idea of the view taken by different judges as to the degree of knowledge required to satisfy the test.

---

10 For a full treatment of this unfortunate decision, see the fourth edition of this book.

11 In *Smith* v *National Health Service Litigation Authority* [2001] Lloyd's Rep Med 90, [2001] MLC 0286, Andrew Smith J held that a claimant born in 1973 with a congenitally displaced hip had not known that her disability might be reasonably attributable to an omission in her medical treatment (failure to examine her properly as a baby) until 1994 (however the claim failed on the facts).

Examples are *Davis* v *City and Hackney Health Authority* [1991] 2 Med LR 366; *Driscoll-Varley* v *Parkside Health Authority* [1991] 2 Med LR 346; *Khan* v *Ainslie* MLC 0028, [1993] 4 Med LR 319; and *Baig* v *City and Hackney Health Authority* MLC 0041, [1994] 5 Med LR 221.

Attributability in the Court of Appeal

Broadley v *Guy Clapham & Co* MLC 0043, [1993] 4 Med LR 328, CA and *Dobbie* v *Medway Health Authority* MLC 0038, [1994] 5 Med LR 160 did not pose such problems for the patient as some people thought at the time. In *Broadley*, the patient knew she had come out of the operation on her knee with an unlooked-for result, namely a foot-drop. It was not unreasonable to require her to investigate the injury. *Contra* if she could reasonably have thought that the problem was unconnected with anything the doctors had done. Balcombe LJ's treatment of the attributability question is important, particularly because in latter years it seems to have been lost sight of. He distinguished four categories of knowledge, namely 'broad', 'specific', 'qualitative' and 'detailed', of which the latter two were not necessary to constitute 'knowledge' for the purposes of limitation. He indicated that 'broad' knowledge was not enough in itself, ie knowledge that the operation had been carried out in such a way that something went wrong and resulted in foot-drop. The claimant needed also to have 'specific' knowledge, namely that the operation had been carried out in such a way as to damage a nerve and so cause the injury of foot-drop. 'Qualitative' knowledge was not necessary, ie knowledge that the operation had been carried out 'unreasonably', nor, of course, was 'detailed' knowledge, ie sufficiently detailed to enable the claimants' advisers to draft the claim.

It is a pity the valid distinction the Lord Justice drew between broad and specific knowledge has not been followed in later cases, because those judges in the Court of Appeal who want to make the test as stringent as possible tell us from time to time, in so many words, that a 'broad' knowledge of the facts is sufficient. This may well derive from what Slade LJ said in the early case of *Wilkinson* v *Ancliff* [1986] 1WLR 1352, when he spoke of the 'broad knowledge' of an employee that he had been exposed to dangerous working conditions and of his complaint 'in broad terms' to that effect.

In *Broadley*, Legatt LJ said it was not necessary that the claimant should have knowledge of the *mechanics* of damage; it was enough that soon after the operation she knew something was wrong with her foot which was not an inevitable consequence of it, and therefore she should reasonably have made inquiry.

In *Dobbie*, the patient knew that the breast they had removed had turned out to be non-cancerous. Although the court seems to have taken the view that she had the requisite knowledge at that time, which is doubtful (she would need to know that they could have found this out pre-operatively by further tests), one can hardly quarrel with the requirement that she investigate the matter. It would not be right to attribute actual knowledge to the patient on learning that her breast had not been diseased, because she would not know what act or omission the injury was attributable to until she learnt that, as pleaded in her claim, the pre-operative investigations had been inadequate. It would not be enough to say that she knew her injury was due to the act of removing the breast, because the act/omission alleged to be negligent was not 'removing the breast' but related, more specifically, more accurately and more relevantly, to a failure to conduct appropriate pre-operative investigations.

In *O'Driscoll* v *Dudley Health Authority* MLC 0324, [1998] Lloyd's Rep Med 210, CA, Simon Brown LJ said that the test was whether the claimant knew there was a 'real possibility' that her injury had been cause by the acts complained of.

It is interesting that the Court of Appeal decision most favourable to claimants on limitation issues during this period was the non-medical case of *Hallam-Eames* v *Merrett Syndicates* MLC 0703, [1996] 7 Med LR 122, which was a decision upon one of the economic claims in the Lloyd's Names saga. The limitation provisions of s 14A of the Limitation Act 1980, inserted by the Latent Damage Act 1986, are to all intents and purposes identical with the personal injury provisions of s 14. In short form, the allegation was that the defendants had negligently written contracts for the claimants which involved them in substantial liabilities without having the material on which to assess the potential liabilities. The judges, perhaps more in sympathy with the well-off about to lose their money than they sometimes are with injured patients, appeared to lean over backwards to assert a generous test of 'knowledge', holding that it was not enough for the claimants to have known that the contracts had been written, because they also needed to know that they had been written at a time when the potential liabilities of the parties were impossible to assess. The judgments contain useful glosses on the earlier cases of *Broadley* and *Dobbie*.

Spargo v North Essex District Health Authority

In *Spargo* v *North Essex District Health Authority* [1997] MLC 0651, the Court of Appeal reversed the trial judge's finding that the plaintiff did not have actual knowledge more than three years before the commencement of proceedings. The brief facts were that at the age of four in 1975 the plaintiff was confined to a psychiatric hospital on a mistaken diagnosis of permanent brain damage. Her difficulty on limitation was that, when cross-examined, she said that she knew that she had suffered in hospital for a long time and that she firmly believed that that was because of the mistaken diagnosis. In her mind all her suffering was attributable to the mistaken diagnosis of organic brain damage, and that was her clear view when she first saw her solicitor in October 1986. The trial judge held that this was one of those cases, foreseen by the Court of Appeal in *Nash* v *Eli Lilly* [1993] 1 WLR 782, MLC 0021, where the patient's belief about the attributability of her problem cannot amount to knowledge until an expert report confirms her view. The Court of Appeal disagreed: this plaintiff on her own evidence was convinced that the diagnosis of brain damage had caused her injury (through being confined as a result for a substantial period of time to a mental hospital). She had that conviction as early as 1986 at which time she also had a report on an intelligence test she had taken which indicated that the original diagnosis had been mistaken. The trial judge had actually found that 'she was clear in her mind that the connection was there between the disturbances and what she had suffered'. In those circumstances the decision of the Court of

Appeal which held that she had actual knowledge no later than 1986 is readily understandable.

In *Rowbottom* v *Royal Masonic Hospital* MLC 0553, [2002] Lloyds Rep Med 173, the Court of Appeal held, by a majority, that a claimant who was alleging that he had suffered injury from a failure to administer antibiotics could only have had the relevant knowledge when he received his second expert report. That report told him that lack of antibiotics was responsible for his injury; up till then he had thought it was failure to install a drain. He had been 'barking up the wrong tree'.

Constructive knowledge

Constructive knowledge is particularly important because defence counsel, and judges, often find that they have to accept that the patient did not have actual knowledge until she received her expert report. They then look to see whether the action can be shown to be out of time on the basis that investigation should have been commenced earlier. Section 14(3) provides:

> For the purposes of this section a person's knowledge includes knowledge which he might reasonably have been expected to acquire—
> (a)   from facts observable or ascertainable by him; or
> (b)   from facts ascertainable by him with the help of medical or other appropriate expert advice which it is reasonable for him to seek;
> But a person shall not be fixed under this sub-section with knowledge of a fact ascertainable only with the help of expert advice so long as he has taken all reasonable steps to obtain (and, where appropriate, to act on) that advice.[12]

True to the traditions of English statutory interpretation, the obvious meaning and intent of this subsection have often been obscured by semantic analysis. What it means is that a claimant must make reasonable inquiries at such time as it is reasonable to expect him to do so. If he does not, he is fixed with such knowledge as those inquiries would have given him.

The first point is that, clearly, the court is required to take into account the particular situation of the particular patient before deciding whether he was at fault for not making inquiry earlier. The Court of Appeal in *Nash* v *Eli Lilly* (above) made it clear that the personal characteristics and the situation of the individual claimant should be taken into account. That is obviously right. It was followed in, among other cases, *Coban* v *Allen* MLC 0681, [1997] 8 Med LR 316. It would make little sense for the court to consider what some hypothetical patient should have done. The question is what this particular patient should have done. No doubt the court would use its general understanding of what reasonable people do in coming to its conclusion, but that does not mean that it should ignore the particular characteristics of the individual claimant. The worst

---

12   In *Henderson* v *Temple Pier Co* [1998] 1 WLR 1540, the Court of Appeal held that the claimant was fixed with the knowledge that her solicitors should have acquired earlier about the identity of the defendants. This, incidentally, was the case the absence of knowledge of which by counsel led the Court of Appeal to utter harsh admonitions in *Copeland* v *Smith* [2000] 1 WLR 1371, about the need for counsel to be aware of the relevant authorities!

decision from the Court of Appeal, on this issue as well as on discretion, is *Forbes* (above).[13] One aspect of the (in this writer's view) unacceptable judgments of Stuart-Smith and Evans LJJ was their refusal to follow *Nash* v *Eli Lilly* (above) on this point. It is understandable that they declined to do so, because, otherwise, they would have had to agree with the dissenting judgment of the other member of the court, Roch LJ, and conclude that the fact that the trial judge had seen and heard the patient meant that they could not interfere with his assessment of the question whether that patient should have done more by way of earlier inquiry. The majority were so keen to stop the case that they had to declare the test to be 'objective' (whatever that particular semantic label means), and in that way they were able to declare themselves entitled to decide the question upon their assessment of what the hypothetical reasonable patient would have done. They then announced that that chimera would have investigated earlier and therefore this particular claimant was fixed with the knowledge that the hypothetical patient would have acquired. The majority went on, in my view, to cobble together a raft of unconvincing reasons why the exercise of discretion by the judge was flawed and to substitute their own conclusion, unfavourable to the patient. It is horridly ironic that when the Court of Appeal did stress the need to take the claimant's actual position into account, it rebounded to her disadvantage (see the case of *Gravgaard* below).

Skitt v Khan and Wakefield Health Authority

In *Skitt* v *Khan and Wakefield Health Authority* [1997] 8 Med LR 105, the Court of Appeal went even further, reversing the trial judge on *actual* knowledge, on *constructive* knowledge and on *discretion*. The deceased had been treated by the defendant doctor from 1982 for a persistent lesion on his leg. This was discovered in 1986 to be cancerous. The deceased went without delay to a solicitor, who wrote to the health authority indicating he was holding them liable for negligent failure to make the diagnosis of cancer earlier. The cancer progressed, and the deceased suffered amputation of the leg in November 1987. When legal aid was refused in March 1988 on financial grounds, the deceased made a deliberate decision not to proceed. He died in July 1992. His widow sought to reopen the matter and began proceedings in January 1994.

It has to be said that the finding of the trial judge that the deceased had never had *actual* knowledge more than three years before his death had to be open to challenge. The deceased knew in 1986 that he had developed cancer, knew that it had derived from the original lesion, and knew that the diagnosis had been some years delayed. The rationale of the trial judge's decision was that the deceased needed expert confirmation of his belief that he had suffered an injury attributable to acts or omissions on the part of the defendants before that belief could amount to 'knowledge'. In these circumstances, the finding of the Court of Appeal that he had the necessary knowledge by no later than the time he went to solicitors is understandable.

---

13   For a lengthy criticism of this decision see the fourth edition of this book.

The trial judge had also held that the deceased could not be fixed with *constructive* knowledge because at such time as he might otherwise have been expected to obtain an expert report he was too ill to do so. The Court of Appeal disagreed with the judge here, too, stating that, though it was understandable that the patient did not obtain a report, it was not reasonable of him to have failed to do so. Even though this was not a case where the patient gave evidence before the judge, it is surely unsatisfactory that the appeal court need to do more than, in effect, say 'the judge found that the patient behaved reasonably, but we disagree'.

The Court of Appeal went on to disagree with the judge on *discretion*, too[14] (the judge had said he would have exercised discretion in favour of the claimant if he had found the action to be out of time). They purported to identify a number of matters to which the judge did not 'appear' to have given proper weight so that they could then declare the exercise of his discretion to have been 'flawed' (that is an easy enough exercise; lip-service only is paid to the principle that the appeal court does not interfere with the exercise of discretion merely because they would have decided the issue differently; it is quite clear from the cases that, if the Court of Appeal considers that it would have decided the issue differently, they have no difficulty in finding reasons to do so). They then declared that it would be inequitable to allow the action to proceed, principally because of the delay from 1988, when the deceased had decided not to proceed with his action and the reactivation of the claim some four or five years later, and the death or ill health of defence witnesses.[15]

Note that the burden of establishing a date for constructive knowledge is on the defendant (*Lennon* v *Alvis Industries plc* (27 July 2000, unreported), CA).

In *Gravgaard* v *Aldridge and Brownlee* [2004] EWCA Civ 1529, a claim against solicitors for alleged negligent advice about a mortgage, the Court of Appeal said that, in considering whether knowledge was to be imputed to someone under the Act, the court had to have regard to the position of the actual claimant and not some wholly hypothetical claimant. However, that apparently helpful proposition actually militated against the claimant in this case because it meant that therefore the court could not ignore the claimant's belief that she had a claim even if that belief was unfounded in law.

In *Mellors* v *Perry* [2003] MLC 0900 the Court of Appeal upheld the decision of the trial judge who found that there was no reason to have expected the claimant to have sought an explanation when she came of age why her kidney treatments had been such a failure, because a reasonable person who suffered from a serious problem of apparently

---

14 See below for a full treatment of *discretion*.
15 Another example of the Court of Appeal going to great lengths to reverse the trial judge on discretion is *Whitfield* v *North Durham Health Authority* [1995] 6 Med LR 32. Having found reasons to invalidate the approach of the trial judge to the question of discretion, the court substituted their own contrary view without condescending to any substantive extent to detail.

See also *Fenech* v *East London and City Health Authority* MLC 0130, [2000] Lloyd's Rep Med 35, CA (woman's embarrassment at mentioning to GP her continual perineal problems following her child's birth in 1960 not sufficient reason not to investigate until 1994).

constitutional origin from a very early age could not reasonably be expected to start making inquiries of anyone about whether someone might be to blame when there was no reason to think that there was anything to blame anyone for.

A recent dyslexia claim which surprisingly was accepted as an appeal by the House of Lords offers significant insights into the meaning of constructive knowledge (*Adams* v *Bracknell Forest Borough Council* MLC 1156, [2004] UKHL 29). The claimant was born in March 1972. By a claim issued in June 2002, aged 30, he alleged failure by the education authority to assess his problems between 1981 and 1988 (aged 9 to 16). There were no useful medical notes extant, nor, it appears, much in the way of useful evidence any teacher could give so long after the event. The claimant said he first knew he probably was dyslexic when he was speaking to a friend at a dancing class in November 1999 who happened to be an educational psychologist. That was why he sped off to a solicitor. An expert confirmed severe dyslexia and severe psychological symptoms including panic attacks and social phobia, consequent upon undiagnosed and untreated learning difficulties. Mr Adams, an intelligent man, had not sought any advice about his literacy problems because he wanted to hide them, in other words he did not want to talk about them. He spoke to his doctor about the psychological problems but not about his inability to read and write [was his GP really not aware of this?]. Yet, said Lord Hoffman, no doubt choosing his words carefully as always, if not sympathetically, he 'spilled out the entire story to Ms Harding, a lady nearly 20 years his senior whom he says he hardly knew and had no reason to believe had any expertise in the matter'. The trial judge had found that Mr Adams had known since childhood that he had psychological problems and that they were 'linked in some way to his problems with reading and writing'. But he did not know that the education authority could have helped him. It was this finding that led both courts below to find that he did not have actual earlier knowledge (accepted by the defendants) but which also led them to conclude that there was no reason why he should have got it (before speaking to his lady friend) – which was the issue on which the defendants were to appeal successfully to the House of Lords.

The issue was: is the question as to what the claimant should reasonably be expected to have done in the line of making enquiries or seeking expert help to be answered on a subjective or an objective basis; that is, do you factor in all the personal characteristics of the particular claimant or do you ask what would your average sufferer reasonably have done? Over the years the courts have given totally diverging views on this subjective/objective divide; so clarity from the House of Lords on the issue would be welcome. But although their Lordships favoured the objective test overall, there is no formula possible, no list of relevant and non-relevant factors that can be drawn up. Each case is still going to have to be decided on its own facts. In the case neither side was arguing for a wholly subjective or a wholly objective approach.

Lord Hoffman said the particular character or intelligence of the particular claimant was not relevant. And he said that there was no medical evidence in the case to support the judge's conclusion that extreme reticence was natural to these cases. Lord Hoffman would have expected such a person to reveal the source of his difficulties to his medical adviser; but he added 'in the absence of some special inhibiting factor' which would appear to let in a personal characteristic, albeit one of a special and unusual cogency. Lord Hoffman said that Mr Adams knew his miseries were rooted in his inability to read and write. He had sought help about those miseries. It was 'almost irrational' not to disclose what he felt to be the root cause. The normal expectation is that a person suffering from a significant injury will be curious about its origins. This expectation applies equally to dyslexics.

Lord Scott agreed that personal characteristics such as shyness and embarrassment which would not normally be expected to inhibit others with a like disability should be left out of the equation. 'It is the norms of behaviour of a person in the situation of the claimant that should be the test.' But, one asks, what factors can properly be taken as part of the claimant's 'situation' and what cannot? Lord Scott reckoned that your normal dyslexic who knew that illiteracy was at the back of his serious psychological problems would, when consulting his doctor about those problems, tell the doctor about the illiteracy, though he added that expert evidence to contrary effect about dyslexic sufferers could conceivably lead to another conclusion. The test should be 'mainly objective'. That would create a fair balance between the parties, and would discourage stale claims that should and could have been brought earlier. But if the court thought it nevertheless equitable, it could always exercise its s 33 discretion in favour of the claimant.

Baroness Hale, ever pragmatic, pointed out that it had rarely, if ever, been necessary to resolve the difference between the two tests to decide the case and she wondered if there was in practice much difference between the two approaches. But she agreed that strictly personal characteristics such as shyness or embarrassment were not relevant. So one may hear argument anon to the effect that such and such a characteristic, while admittedly personal, is not strictly personal.

In truth, even on a subjective basis, it is hard to see in the *Adams* case how it was concluded by the courts below that this intelligent claimant could not reasonably have been expected to mention to his doctor, whom he visited on a number of occasions over the years, that the cause of his psychological problems, as he saw it, was his inability to read. The House of Lords allowed the appeal and struck out the claim as out of time.

A note on *Spargo*

The principles which Brooke LJ summarised were as follows:

(1) The knowledge required to satisfy s 14(1)(b) is a broad knowledge of the essence of the causally relevant act or omission to which the injury is attributable.

(2) Attributable in this context means 'capable of being attributed to', in the sense of being a real possibility.

(3) A plaintiff has the requisite knowledge when she knows enough to make it reasonable for her to begin to investigate whether or not she has a case against the defendant. Another way of putting this is to say that she will have such knowledge if she so firmly believes that her condition is capable of being attributed to an act or omission which she can identify (in broad terms) that she goes to a solicitor to seek advice about making a claim for compensation.

(4)   On the other hand, she will not have the requisite knowledge if she thinks she knows the acts or omissions she should investigate but in fact is 'barking up the wrong tree': or if her knowledge of what the defendant did or did not do is so vague or general that she cannot fairly be expected to know what she should investigate, or if her state of mind is such that she thinks her condition is capable of being attributed to the act or omission alleged to constitute negligence, but she is not sure about this, and would need to check with an expert before she could be properly be said to know that it was.

DISCRETION

Section 33 of the Limitation Act 1980 provides:

33.—(1)   If it appears to the court that it would be equitable to allow an action to proceed having regard to the degree to which—
(a)   the provisions of section 11 or 11A or 12 of this Act prejudice the plaintiff or any person whom he represents; and
(b)   any decision of the court under this subsection would prejudice the defendant or any person who he represents;
the court may direct that those provisions shall not apply to the action, or shall not apply to any specified cause of action to which the action relates.
(2)   ...
(3)   in acting under this section the court shall have regard to all the circumstances of the case and in particular to—
(a)   the length of, and the reasons for, the delay on the part of the plaintiff;
(b)   the extent to which, having regard to the delay, the evidence adduced or likely to be adduced by the plaintiff or the defendant is or is likely to be less cogent than if the action had been brought within the time allowed by section 11;
(c)   the conduct of the defendant after the cause of action arose, including the extent (if any) to which he responded to requests reasonably made by the plaintiff for information or inspection for the purpose of ascertaining facts which were or might be relevant to the plaintiff's cause of action against the defendant;
(d)   the duration of any disability[16] of the plaintiff arising after the date of the accrual of the cause of action;
(e)   the extent to which the plaintiff acted promptly and reasonably once he knew whether or not the act or omission of the defendant, to which the injury was attributable, might be capable at that time of giving rise to an action for damages;
(f)   the steps, if any, taken by the plaintiff to obtain medical, legal or other expert advice and the nature of any such advice he may have received.

These are not the only factors to which the court must pay attention. The court must consider the whole of the circumstances.[17] Relevant factors

---

16   An impairment of the claimant's health short of 'disability' may be given due weight by the court: *Davis* v *Jacobs and Camden and Islington Health Authority* MLC 0071, [1999] Lloyd's Rep Med 72 at 86, CA.
17   In *Das* v *Ganju* [1999] PIQR P260, CA, the court rejected the defendant's argument that the claimant should be left to her claim against her solicitors.

include the apparent merits of the claim,[18] whether the issues depend on recollection[19] or extant medical records, whether the claimant has a claim against his solicitors,[20] whether the lapse of time has prejudiced the defendant financially,[21] whether the defendant had reasonably early notice of a possible claim,[22] and, overall, where the balance of prejudice lies and whether a fair trial is still possible. The fact that a defendant is insured is not relevant (*Kelly* v *Bastible* [1997] 8 Med LR 15, CA). The discretion must be exercised reasonably: refusing to allow a case to proceed where it is one day out of time is not reasonable (*Hartley* v *Birmingham City District Council* [1992] 1 WLR 968, CA).

As the court's decision is a matter of discretion, it is very hard to predict in any case what the result is likely to be. Some judges, on some days, in some cases, conclude that it is not equitable to permit the action to proceed even where the claimant is not long out of time. In other cases, other judges take quite a different view. Consider, by way of example (not, of course, by way of precedent, because every case is decided upon its own facts), the following two fairly recent cases at first instance, both involving a claim for physically but not mentally handicapped cerebral palsy victims who issued their writ several years after reaching the age of 21.

In *Pearse* v *Barnet Health Authority* [1998] PIQR P39, Griffiths-Williams QC, sitting as a deputy High Court judge, exercised his discretion in favour a claimant who was born in 1970 and issued his writ in 1994. And in *Bates* v *Leicester Health Authority* MLC 0015, [1998] Lloyd's Rep Med 93 Dyson J, having found for the claimant (born 1968, writ issued 1995) on the issue of knowledge, said that he would have exercised his discretion in his favour, had that been relevant. In each case, the judge placed great weight on the fact that the claim would fall to be decided on the extant medical records, and on the fact that the delay since the claimant had attained the age of 21 would not have involved any additional prejudice.

See also *Roberts* v *Winbow* MLC 0074, [1999] Lloyd's Rep Med 31, where the Court of Appeal, in exercising discretion in favour of the claimant, laid great weight on the fact that the case would be decided largely on expert rather than factual evidence (*contra* the unconvincing argument first advanced by Stuart-Smith LJ in *Forbes* v *Wandsworth Health Authority* (above) that the passage of time made it difficult for experts to speak as to the standard of care years before and, for some reason, more difficult for the defence expert than for the claimants' expert).

We may refer also to *Briody* v *St Helens and Knowsley Area Health Authority* MLC 0099, [1999] Lloyd's Rep Med 185, where the Court of Appeal refused to interfere with the exercise of discretion in the

---

18 But a cast iron case is not a passport to proceed: an untruthful claimant should not be given discretion (*Long* v *Tolchard & Sons Ltd* (2000) Times, 5 January, CA).
19 The court can infer impairment of recollection from the lapse of time – *Price* v *United Engineering Steels Ltd* [1998] PIQR P407, CA – specific evidence of impairment is not required.
20 *Thomson* v *Brown Construction (Ebbw Vale) Ltd* [1981] 1 WLR 744, HL; *Ramsden* v *Lee* [1992] 2 All ER 204, CA.
21 See *McCarthy* v *Recticel Ltd* [2000] PIQR Q74.
22 See *Long* v *Tolchard & Sons Ltd* [2001] PIQR P18, CA.

claimant's favour by Kennedy J for proceedings started nearly 20 years after the perinatal death of her baby.

In *Corbin* v *Penfold Metalising Ltd* [2000] Lloyd's Rep Med 247, the Court of Appeal said that, given proper conduct by a claimant, his solicitor's delay should not be held against him on the issue of discretion. (See also *Steeds* v *Peverel Management Services* (30 March, 2001, unreported), CA.) Nor his expert's delay (*per* Sedley LJ in *James* v *East Dorset Health Authority* MLC 0129, (1999) Times, 7 December, CA, see ML 12/99 pp 2–4).

Other cases on discretion

In *Farthing* v *North East Essex Health Authority* [1998] Lloyd's Rep Med 37, MLC 0053, Simon Brown LJ and Hale J said, in respect of an allegation of negligence around a hysterectomy in 1981, that the case did not turn on the recollection of witnesses as to precisely what was done, but upon the contemporaneous records. And in *Smith* v *Leicestershire Health Authority* [1998] Lloyd's Rep Med 77, the Court of Appeal (Roch, Mantell LJJ, Sir Patrick Russell) reversed a decision of May J whereby he held that a spina bifida patient, born in 1943, who claimed in respect of medical negligence going back some 40 years, had constructive knowledge in 1983 and that it would not be equitable to exercise discretion in her favour. The appeal court held that there was no proper ground for a finding of constructive knowledge and, further, that the judge's exercise of discretion was flawed as he had given too much weight to the mere passage of time and insufficient weight to the fact that a defendant's evidential disadvantage was not great where a case will turn on the extant medical records, and so it pales into insignificance beside the prejudice to the claimant if not permitted to proceed. In such a situation the experts could still make proper analyses.

In *Hammond* v *West Lancashire Health Authority* MLC 0558, [1998] Lloyd's Rep Med 146, Simon Brown LJ, with Ward LJ, confirmed the trial judge's exercise of discretion in favour of the patient. And see the complex case of *Davis* v *Jacobs and Camden and Islington Health Authority* MLC 0071, [1999] Lloyd's Rep Med 72, where the Court of Appeal reversed the judge's refusal to exercise discretion in favour of the patient.[23]

Contra, in *Berry* v *Calderdale Health Authority* [1998] Lloyd's Rep Med 179, CA, Stuart-Smith LJ, with Waller LJ, held that the trial judge's exercise of discretion had been flawed because he had not spelt out his conclusions on the various factors listed in the statute, and then, exercising their own discretion, they reversed his conclusion.

And in *Mold* v *Hayton and Newson* (17 April 2000, unreported), [2000] MLC 0207, CA, the court reversed the exercise of the judge's discretion whereby he permitted an action for failure to examine timeously for vaginal cancer to proceed 18 years out of time, on the ground that it was not appropriate to grant such a huge extension without giving clear reasons

---

23 See also *Hayes* v *Torlo* MLC 0702, where the court reversed the judge on knowledge and on discretion in a dental negligence action begun in 1996 in respect of teeth extraction in 1984 and earlier.

for doing so, and that in the instant case there were no proper grounds for such extension.

Note, incidentally, how ready the appeal judges appear to be to interfere with judicial discretion in the context of limitation while at the same time they are most unwilling to do so where the relevant issue is a procedural issue under the new rules.

In *Buckler* v *J F Finnegan Ltd* [2004] EWCA Civ 920, the Court of Appeal understandably reversed the judge who disapplied the limitation period where a workman who had decided originally not to sue for so slight an injury as pleural thickening to one lung changed his mind years later when he mistakenly thought his condition had deteriorated. *McGhie* v *British Telecommunications plc* [2005] EWCA Civ 48, is a good example of a recent case where the Court of Appeal simply disagreed with the judge's view that the claim could proceed. In other words, as so often, they took over the role of the trial judge.

The rule in *Walkley* v *Precision Forgings*

The discretion is an unfettered one, and the Court of Appeal should be loath to interfere with its exercise by the judge (see *Conry* v *Simpson* [1983] 3 All ER 369; *Firman* v *Ellis* [1978] QB 886; *Bradley* v *Hanseatic Shipping* [1986] 2 Lloyd's Rep 34). However, the judge has to stay within the ambit of the section. Thus, in *Walkley* v *Precision Forgings Ltd* [1979] 1 WLR 606, the House of Lords held that where the plaintiff discontinued an action he had started within the limitation period, the court had no power to permit him to proceed, under s 33, with another action after the limitation period had expired. This was because the prejudice to the plaintiff had not been occasioned by the operation of the limitation provisions of the Act, but by his own conduct (through his solicitors). This somewhat contrived reasoning was extended by the Court of Appeal, albeit reluctantly, to a case where the plaintiff had forgotten to serve his writ within the one year allowed (*Chappell* v *Cooper* [1980] 2 All ER 463). On this particular point, *Firman* v *Ellis* (above) was overruled, although that case is still good authority on the proper approach of the court generally to the exercise of its discretion, which is not limited to 'exceptional' cases.

Walkley v *Precision Forgings* (above) was followed in *Deerness* v *John R Keeble & Son* [1983] 2 Lloyd's Rep 260, HL, where the judge's exercise of discretion in permitting an action to proceed was reversed on the ground that a writ had been issued, but not served within the limitation period, and that therefore there was no jurisdiction to allow a second writ to proceed (because the plaintiff had been prejudiced not by the provisions of s 11 giving him three years to issue a writ, but by the failure of his solicitors to serve the writ within the 12-month period for service). So a claimant who issues a first writ in time, but fails to serve it in time is in a weaker position than one who does not even get around to issuing one in the first place! In such a case, all the claimant can do is ask for the writ to be renewed, but this will almost certainly not be granted (see Chapter 10), and then sue his solicitors.

The rule in *Walkley* v *Precision Forgings* does not apply where the first action was improperly constituted (the defendants had been wrongly titled), notwithstanding that the defect could be corrected. In such a case, the second action is not an abuse of the process of the court (*White* v *Glass* (1989) Times, 18 February, CA). The rule was recently confirmed in *Forward* v *Hendricks* [1997] 2 All ER 395, CA. But the ambit of the rule is nevertheless strictly limited (see *Shapland* v *Palmer* [1999] PIQR P249, CA, and *McEvoy* v *AA Welding and Fabrication* [1998] PIQR P266, CA, for exceptions).

Young v *Western Power Distribution (Soth West) plc* [2004] PIQR P32, CA is a sad case. A workman issued a writ in 1997 for negligent exposure to asbestos causing mesothelioma. The defendants provided evidence to him that 'proved' the disease was adenocarcinoma and therefore unrelated to asbestos. So he discontinued his claim. After his death the postmortem showed he had mesothelioma after all. The widow's claim was held to be caught by the *Walkley* rule; so it was dismissed as the deceased no longer had a cause of action at his death. It is a sad reflection on the law that the fact that the defendants had misled the deceased (and his wife) with their expert report was not sufficient to avoid the *Walkley* rule as it had not been deliberate deception.

Under CPR 19.8(3) proceedings may be commenced against an estate of a deceased person even where no personal representative has yet been appointed, but to continue with the claim a claimant has to apply for an order appointing a PR. In the RTA (road traffic accident) claim of *Piggott* v *Aulton* [2003] EWCA Civ 24 proceedings against an estate were discontinued when it was pointed out by the deceased's insurers that the claimant must make an application for an order for a PR to be appointed. A second action commenced out of time was held not to be caught by the *Walkley* rule as it was not brought against the same party as the first action, seeing that there had been no legal defendant to the first action.

Preliminary trial

Although a preliminary trial on limitation is frequently desirable, it should not be ordered where the limitation issues are intricately bound up in the substantive issues (*Fletcher* v *Sheffield Health Authority* [1994] 5 Med LR 156, MLC 0035; see also *Roberts* v *Winbow* MLC 0074, [1999] Lloyd's Rep Med 31 at 39, CA and *Worsley* v *Tambrands* [2000] MLC 0186, CA).

FATAL ACCIDENT CLAIMS

The limitation period provided by s 12 of the 1980 Act for actions under the Fatal Accidents Act 1976 (amended by s 3 of the Administration of Justice Act 1982) is three years from the date of death, or the date of 'knowledge' of the dependant for whose benefit the action is brought, whichever is the later. If at the date of death the deceased's right of action was already time-barred by s 11, then the dependants' action is also barred, no account being taken of the possibility that the deceased might have got leave to proceed under s 33; but the dependants can on their own account ask for their action to be permitted to proceed under s 33 (by virtue of s 12(1) and (3)). Similarly, if they had a right of action at the deceased's death, his right not having been time-barred by then, but they thereafter permit the limitation period to expire without commencing proceedings, they can ask the court for leave to proceed under s 33.

Dependants are to be considered separately, so that one may be barred where another is within the limitation period because his knowledge arose later, or because he is under a disability (s 13). The court's power to exclude a dependant from participating in the action is limited by s 13(3), which provides that no direction to exclude shall be given if it is shown that if the action were brought exclusively for the benefit of that dependant, it would not be defeated by a defence of limitation.

A fatal accident claim may often include a claim for, eg, terminal suffering or care given to the deceased while he was still alive. That is not a fatal accident head of claim, but is a claim pursuant to the Law Reform (Miscellaneous Provisions) Act 1934, and the limitation period in respect of that claim is not necessarily the same. The relevant provision is s 11(5) which provides that the three-year period runs from the date of death or the date of the personal representative's 'knowledge'. In many cases, the distinction will not be important, but it could be. For example, the personal representative may have acquired the relevant 'knowledge' years before, which will prevent him claiming on behalf of the state or as a dependent (subject to any application for s 33 discretion), whereas the claim by any dependent children will not be affected.

AMENDING A CLAIM

Amending the statement of claim

It often happens in medical negligence actions that the patient needs to add a new party after proceedings have been begun. Perhaps the culprit appears to be a different GP from the current defendant, or perhaps a GP or health authority needs to be added to the frame. The legislative provisions are not particularly easy to understand, but can usefully be summarised by saying that the judge has no general power to add a defendant (or a new cause of action) out of time, except by exercising discretion under s 33 (see s 35(3)). Section 35(4) and (5) lay down guidelines for the enaction of rules of court to permit new claims to be added, but provide that the rules can be more restrictive than the guidelines. Therefore, it is to the rules of court that one has to look upon any such application.

CPR 17.4 (amendments to statements of case after the end of a relevant limitation period) enables amendments to be made where the effect will be to add or substitute a new claim, provided the new claim arises out of the same facts or substantially the same facts as a claim in respect of which the party applying for permission has already claimed a remedy in the proceedings. Genuine mistakes over identity may be corrected under this rule provided the mistake was genuine and not one which would cause reasonable doubt as to the identity of the party in question.[24] Rule 19(5) provides that for the addition or substitution of a party, the relevant limitation period must have been current at the start of the

---

24 See *International Distillers* v *JF Hillebrand (UK) Ltd* (2000) Times, 25 January. See also the commentary above (under 'Knowledge') on *Gregson* v *Channel Four Television Corpn* (2000) Times, 11 August, CA.

proceedings and the amendment must be necessary, which means that the court must be satisfied that the substitution arises out of a mistake, or the change must be made to enable the claim to be properly carried on. There is, of course, power to amend where the court directs, under s 33, that the time limits under ss 11 or 12 shall be disapplied (and it is specifically provided that the issue whether those sections apply is to be determined at trial). These powers depend from s 35 of the Limitation Act 1980.

In *Sayer* v *Kingston and Esher Health Authority* (1989) Independent, 27 March, CA, the Court of Appeal endorsed the judge's decision to permit an amendment of the claim on the eve of the trial whereby the previous case alleging mishandling of the Cesarian section was replaced by allegations of mismanagement earlier in the labour and after delivery. The court said that as the new claims arose out of substantially the same facts as those already pleaded, the judge had discretion to allow the amendment under s 35(5) of the Limitation Act 1980.[25]

In *Welsh Development Agency* v *Redpath Dorman Long Ltd* [1994] 1 WLR 1409, the Court of Appeal held that leave could not be given to add a new claim after the expiry of the limitation period unless it fell within one of the stated exceptions in the Act and the then current rules of court, and that the relevant date for when a new claim should be taken to be made was not the date when the application for leave to amend was issued, but when the amendment was actually made. Reference may also be made to *Howe* v *David Brown Tractors (Retail) Ltd* [1991] 4 All ER 30, CA.

In *Sion* v *Hampstead Health Authority* MLC 0027, [1994] 5 Med LR 170, CA, the defendants' counsel took an obviously bad point on adding a claim after the expiry of the limitation period. It was agreed that the rules permitted a new claim to be added where it arose out of substantially the same facts as a cause of action in respect of which relief had already been claimed in the action, but he said that as the statement of claim in fact disclosed no cause of action, the rule did not apply. The court gave the obvious response, namely that if the pleading could be amended to disclose a cause of action substantially on the facts as pleaded, the precondition to adding a new cause of action was satisfied.

The patient seeking to add a party should try to show that the relevant knowledge was not acquired more than three years before such date as the amendment is likely to be made if it is granted; failing which, she may be able to show a genuine mistake (on this, see *Evans Construction Co Ltd* v *Charrington & Co Ltd and Bass Holdings Ltd* [1983] QB 810, CA, approved in *Signet Group plc* v *Hammerson UK Properties plc* [1998] 03 LS Gaz R 25, CA); failing that possibility, discretion must be sought under s 33. See also *SmithKline Beecham plc* v *Horne-Roberts* [2001] MLC 0667, where an application within the MMR litigation to substitute Smithkline as defendants in place of Merck was permitted because there had been a 'mistake' within the meaning of the Limitation Act 1980, s 35 and the ten-year time limit applicable to the claim was a 'period of limitation' within

---

25   It is useful to note that the Court of Appeal have said that there is no need to amend the pleading every time the medical condition changes, provided that notice in the form of appropriate medical evidence is given to the defendants (*Oksuzoglu* v *Kay* [1998] Lloyd's Rep Med 129).

CPR 19.5(3). See also *Parsons* v *George* [2004] EWCA Civ 1912, where the mistake related to the identity of the claimants' landlord.

In *Senior* v *Pearsons and Ward* (26 January 2001, unreported), CA, the court said that the question whether or not the new claim arose out of the same facts as the existing claim was a matter of impression. The Act and the CPR both focused on the particular facts in each case as being relevant. See also *Savings and Investment Bank* v *Fincken* (2001) Times, 2 March. In the RTA claim of *Goode* v *Martin* [2002] PIQR P333, the Court of Appeal allowed an amendment of the claim out of time whereby the claimant was permitted to plead the different facts alleged in the defence. Although this new claim was, on a strict interpretation of the rule (CPR 17.4), impermissible as not arising out of the same facts as the original claim the court said that, the Human Rights Act having come into operation since the Master's original order disallowing the application, to prevent the claimant from now putting her case on the basis of the facts as pleaded in the defence would constitute an impediment on her access to the court.

Striking a claim out during the currency of the period of limitation

There used to be a rule of practice that a claim would not be struck out during the limitation period, as the claimant could simply start another action. There was an exception where an abuse of court could be discerned.[26] However, all that law seems now to be history. In *Securum Finance Ltd* v *Ashton* [2001] Ch 291, CA, the court said that there was no longer a principle that a second action begun within the limitation period after the first action had been struck out for inordinate and inexcusable delay should not be struck out, save in exceptional circumstances. The pursuit of the new action had to weighed against the overriding objective of dealing with cases justly and, in particular, the court's need to allot its limited resources to other cases (r 1.1(2)(e) is in point here).

---

26 Relevant cases were: *Birkett* v *James* [1978] AC 297, HL; *Tolley* v *Morris* [1979] 2 All ER 561, HL; *Janov* v *Morris* [1981] 1 WLR 1389, CA; *Hogg* v *Hamilton and Northumberland Health Authority* [1993] 4 Med LR 369, CA; *Headford* v *Bristol and District Health Authority* MLC 0033, [1994] 5 Med LR 406.

Chapter 27

Human rights

INTRODUCTION

Following the entry into force in October 2000 of the Human Rights Act 1998, the expected onrush of litigation has materialised. A huge tranche of legal aid money has been taken away from the victims of injury and placed at the disposal of those – lawyers and clients – who can find some human right basis for a claim. This is easy enough as the field is wide open, given the wide – one can say, from the standpoint of an English lawyer, impossibly imprecise – terms in which the articles of the Convention are couched, and the difficulty one has in seeing what the European Court or Commission has actually meant in any of its judgments.[1]

The area where human rights litigation best flourishes is the liberty of the subject. So arrest and detention (including the detention of mental patients (see *R* v *Camden & Islington HA, ex p K* (2001) Times, 15 March, CA)), and any area where the state uses force against a subject (which includes asylum and immigration issues) will be a fruitful field. But the matter goes further than that. Human rights may well be the essential, or the principal, if not the only, basis for some claims, such as immigration and asylum, but, as forecast by early gloomy prognostications, they have sprung up everywhere like weeds, and, although it cannot entirely be said that meantime the coulter rusts that should deracinate such savagery, the courts are not always quick to heed Lord Woolf's words of caution (see the next paragraph). No lawyer dealing with any issue now is worth his salt if he cannot tag on to his claim a human rights plea. Almost every issue one can think of will have some sort of connection with one or more of the hugely comprehensive, fundamental and Protean human rights recognised by the Convention, whether family, life, freedom, access to courts, fair trial or whatever. Those who have carefully read this tome

---

1   When the Convention was first drafted in 1949, Lord Jowett L-C called it a 'half-baked scheme to be administered by some unknown court the language of which is so vague and woolly that it may mean almost anything'. Far more recently Lord McCluskey, when the Act was implemented in Scotland, said: 'We face a field day for crackpots, a pain in the neck for judges and a goldmine for lawyers.' We can certainly agree with the last few words, particularly in view of the aforesaid reallocation of legal aid funds.

this far will have seen how a human rights plea is tagged on to bolster up so very many of the medical claims noted here in whatever field (or chapter!) the claims crop up.[2]

European Union Charter

It is as well to have this document in mind as well, as it may one day be pleadable in our courts.

The Charter was proclaimed at the European Council in Nice on 7 December 2000 by the presidents of the Council, the European Parliament and the Commission. However, it was not then incorporated into the Treaties establishing the European Union.

The Charter has been incorporated as the second part of the draft European Constitution, which is in the process of ratification by the 25 Member States of the European Union. Consequently the Charter is not yet a binding legal document.

Each of the Charter's 50 articles, which set out individuals' rights or freedoms, is taken from a 'precursor' text. This can be another charter, a convention, a treaty or jurisprudence.

Certain rights appear new, such as those relating to bioethics or the protection of personal data, in so far as they seek to respond to the challenges of new technologies in the areas of communication or biotechnology. In fact, a specific Council of Europe convention on bioethics already exists. Likewise, the protection of personal data is the subject of another specific Council of Europe convention, as well as of Community directives. What the Charter does is to express these rights in a new way and raise them to the status of fundamental rights.

If one asks: why have the Charter if these rights already exist?, the response is that the main reason is to make these rights visible for citizens. Whilst the rights deriving from the European Convention on Human Rights were already visible, those deriving from the judgments of the Court of Justice of the European Communities and the European Court of Human Rights were much less so. For example, the right to good administration found in the Charter synthesises a series of decisions of the Court of Justice of the European Communities in this field.

As well as making certain rights more explicit, the Charter is totally innovative in including fundamental economic and social rights, alongside the more traditional civil and political rights and citizens' rights resulting from Community treaties. This is something which has never been done before by any international or European documentation in this field.

The Charter sets out in a single text, for the first time in the European

---

2 It is unlawful for a public authority to act in a way that is incompatible with a right guaranteed under the Convention (s 6 of the Act). The definition of 'public authority' is comprehensive: for our purposes, it will include any health authority or trust, but presumably not a private hospital, as that does not exercise a public function (but one commentator has suggested that health disputes between private parties may well be held to involve a public dimension, as the Health Secretary is ultimately responsible for the provision of all medical treatment – Samuels *Medico-Legal Journal* (2000) p 55). Any victim of an unlawful act may sue – (s 7) (the limitation period is one year from the act complained of).

Union's history, the whole range of civil, political, economic and social rights of European citizens and all persons resident in the EU.

These rights are divided into six sections: Dignity, Freedoms, Equality, Solidarity, Citizens' rights, and Justice. As indicated above, they are based, in particular, on the fundamental rights and freedoms recognised by the European Convention on Human Rights, the constitutional traditions of the EU Member States, the Council of Europe's Social Charter, the Community Charter of Fundamental Social Rights of Workers and other international conventions to which the European Union or its Member States are parties.

It was intended that the European Constitution would give the Charter the status of law within the Community, but certain referenda seem to have put paid to that idea, for the time being at any rate.

If one asks why doesn't the European Union simply sign up to the European Convention?, the response is as follows. The Union itself is unable to sign up to the European Convention on Human Rights because it is not a sovereign state. To enable it to do so, the Convention itself would have to be amended, as would the EU Treaties. The accession of the European Union to the Human Rights Convention is foreseen in Article 1-9 of the draft European Constitution. When (if) the European Constitution enters into force and the Union accesses to the European Convention on Human Rights, the European Court of Human Rights, which is not an EU but a Council of Europe institution, will be in charge of examining how the European Union respects fundamental rights. Thus the Court of Justice of the European Communities will be subject to the control of the European Court of human rights, just like the supreme courts of all the Member States.

The two things – acceding to the Convention and adopting the Union Charter – are not mutually exclusive or contradictory. For the Union, having its own catalogue of rights puts it in the same situation as individual States. Each State has, in its constitution or elsewhere, its own list of fundamental rights and, at the same time, each State has signed up to the Convention. The European Union will have done the same thing.

In some respects the Charter goes further than the ECHR in conferring human rights. It goes further because it contains rights that are not explicitly included in the text of the Convention, which dates from 1950, in particular data protection, bioethics and social rights. But the Charter also goes further to the extent that the Court of Justice of the Communities has itself gone further than the Convention with regard to certain rights: for example, the right to effective judicial recourse. Under the wording of the Convention, effective recourse is not necessarily judicial recourse: States can provide that this recourse be sought before an administrative body and not in court, whilst the Charter requires that this recourse must always be sought before a judge. In addition, under the terms of the Convention, effective recourse needs to be provided only for the defence of fundamental rights. The Charter, on the contrary, provides that judicial recourse must be possible in order to defend all those rights protected by Union law, even where these are not fundamental rights.

Another example is the right of marriage. The text of the Convention speaks of the right of a man and woman to marry. The Charter uses more modern language, in line with national legislation which recognises other ways of creating a family than marriage. Other examples exist where the Charter goes further, even when this involves rights that are based on the Convention, in particular the right not to be tried or punished twice for the same offence.

This right applies not only within the jurisdiction of a particular Member State, as provided for by the European Convention, but also within the jurisdiction of several Union Member States together.

Scope of this chapter

It is clearly impossible, and inappropriate, in this book to attempt any sort of general overview of the human rights context. Better to highlight any reasonably possible areas where a medical claim could be assisted by resort to the Act. At the same time, one notes the warning Lord Woolf gave to the profession in the first reported case where human rights were invoked in a procedural context. In *Daniels* v *Walker* [2000] 1 WLR 1382, CA, the right to a fair trial was invoked to support an appeal against the refusal of the lower court to allow a party to challenge a jointly instructed care expert's report by getting their own expert report. Lord Woolf said that he had had to give short shrift to the argument, notwithstanding his high regard for the counsel responsible for raising the argument, and he said that when the Act became law, counsel would have to show self-restraint if it was not to be discredited (for further details see below under 'The right to a fair trial' and note the observations of the Court of Appeal in *R* v *North West Lancashire Health Authority, ex p A, D and G* below under 'Article 8').[3]

REVIEW

In the following brief review, only those parts of relevant Articles are reproduced such as appear themselves to be clearly relevant. It should, however, be remembered that only the limits of the lawyer's imagination (and lust for litigation) can set boundaries to the possibilities of a human rights plea (though the unwillingness of the judiciary to entertain a human rights debate around every corner may well set a boundary to the success and even the availability of such a plea). As the body of English case law grows, it becomes easier (and, truth to tell, more relevant) to research and find the relevant human rights law within those judgments, rather than trying to ferret it out, and to understand what is actually being said, from the European Court reports. For that reason the accent of this chapter in this edition is on what our judges have made of the Convention and the Human Rights Act.

---

3   Note also *Barclays Bank plc* v *Ellis* (2000) Times, 24 October, CA, where the court said that mere reference to the Convention did not help the court; counsel wishing to rely on the Act had a duty to have available decisions of the ECHR which he relied on or which might help the court.

Article 2: The right to life

1. Everyone's right to life shall be protected by law

How does this provision affect the medical withdrawal of life support or resuscitative treatment?

It has been held by the Commission that the Article does not require that passive euthanasia, by which a person is allowed to die by not being given treatment, be a crime. In *Widmer* v *Switzerland* No 20527/92 (1993, unreported), it was sufficient that Swiss law proved liability for negligent medical treatment causing death.

But can the NHS be compelled to continue to provide life-support for a patient in a vegetative state or a patient that is terminally ill? These questions have heretofore been answered by our courts under the 'best interests' principle (see Chapter 23). In *National Health Service Trust A* v *M* and *National Health Service Trust B* v *H* [2001] 2 WLR 942, [2000] MLC 0272, Butler-Sloss P held that, if artificial nutrition and hydration were withdrawn from two patients who had been for years in permanent vegetative state, there would not be a breach of the Article. She said that the Article did not impose an absolute obligation to treat if such treatment would be futile. The Article only imposed a positive obligation to give life-sustaining treatment in circumstances where, according to responsible medical opinion, such treatment was in the best interests of the patient. The President gave a similar opinion in *NHS Trust* v *H* on 30 March 2001.

In *A National Health Service Trust* v *D* [2000] Lloyd's Rep Med 411, Cazalet J held that a declaration, contrary to the wishes of the parents, permitting doctors to non-resuscitate in the event of the cardiac or respiratory arrest of a 19-month-old boy with irreversible brain damage was not in breach of the Article, as the treatment advised was in the child's best interests, and it also protected his rights under Art 3 not to be subjected to inhuman and degrading treatment, which included the right to die with dignity.

It is surely not enough simply to parrot the high-flown phrases the European Court has used about this Article: 'one of the most fundamental provisions in the Convention', which 'together with Article 3 enshrines one of the basic values of the democratic societies making up the Council of Europe' (*McCann* v *UK* [1996] 21 EHRR 97). The value of life is not absolute; in appropriate cases a balance has to be struck, as the anxious case of the conjoined twins shows ((2000) 57 BMLR 1, Fam D; affd [2000] 4 All ER 961, CA). Further, the general principle of 'proportionality' underpins Strasbourg law, ie that a proper balance should be struck between competing interests.

In *R (on the application of Burke)* v *GMC* [2004] Lloyds Rep Med 451 the claimant suffered from the progressively degenerative disease of cerebellar ataxia. He was of full capacity, but there would come a time when he could only survive by artificial nutrition. His cognitive facilities would remain intact, however. He did not want artificial nutrition to be withdrawn until he died of natural causes. He based his arguments on a number of Articles in the Convention. Munby J held that Article 2 would not be infringed by the withdrawal of nutrition once the patient had lapsed into a coma, but before that time the withdrawal of nutrition would infringe Articles 3 and 8 and hence would be a breach of Article 2 (see further below). Munby J said that Article 2 did not entitle anyone to force life-prolonging treatment on a competent patient who refused to accept it, nor did it entitle anyone to continue with life-prolonging treatment where to do so would expose the patient to 'inhuman or degrading treatment' contrary to Article 3. However, the Court of Appeal ([2005] EWCA Civ 1003), expressing the judgment of the court with more than a degree of asperity throughout, said that litigation need never have been commenced, as the patient could have sought clarity from the General Medical Council about its guidelines for the withdrawal of life-prolonging treatment (instead of apparently letting himself be lured into suing by persons with special agendas), and that the judge had gone far beyond his proper remit in attempting in an extensive judgment to lay down all sorts of general propositions not required by the facts of the particular case (which among other things had the effect of opening the case on appeal to a variety of interveners). The court found it unnecessary to pay much attention to the Convention, certainly not as regards Articles 3 and 8. It said that Article 2 would plainly be violated if a doctor were to bring about the death of a competent patient by withdrawing life-prolonging treatment contrary to the patient's wishes. Where a competent patient indicated his or her wish to be kept alive by the provision of artificial nutrition, any doctor who deliberately brought that patient's life to an end by discontinuing the supply of artificial nutrition would be not merely in breach of duty but would be guilty of murder. Where life depended on the continued provision of artificial nutrition there could be no question of its supply not being clinically indicated *unless a decision had been taken that the life in question should come to an end* (emphasis added). That was not a decision that could lawfully be taken in the case of a competent patient who expressed the wish to remain alive. The court also warned against the selective citing of passages from Munby J's judgment.

In the unhappy case of *Glass* v *United Kingdom* [2004] Lloyds Rep Med 76, where violent disputes had broken out between the family of a seriously ill child and the hospital doctors about the extent of resuscitative procedures to be employed, the ECHR held that a claim under Article 2 was manifestly ill-founded and should be declared inadmissible (claims under Articles 6, 13 and 14 met a similar fate, but the claim under Article 8 was not struck out and later succeeded – see below).

How does the Article affect the demand for expensive, perhaps unaffordable, treatment by a patient who will otherwise die? Or for affordable treatment which the NHS does not provide?

The latter issue was raised – but in the event, did not require an answer – in a case where the parents of a severely disabled child claimed that their daughter had not been allowed free medical treatment by the state (*X* v *Ireland* No 6893/74, 7 DR 78 (1976)).

The Commission has stated that the Article 'enjoins the state not only to refrain from taking life intentionally but, further, to take appropriate steps to safeguard life' (*X* v *UK* No 7154/75, 14 DR 31 (1978)). This might be interpreted to mean that a state is required to take positive steps to make adequate provision for medical care.

It has been suggested by one commentator that this Article will enable the patient to obtain any treatment at all that might be beneficial, regardless of cost. In other words, the suggestion is that the court will not be entitled to have regard to the issue of the allocation by the NHS of limited resources. This is surely fanciful. It would make it impossible to run the NHS. Patients would be litigating in competition with each other to obtain expensive treatment; other patients would not get the otherwise affordable treatment they needed because funds would have been exhausted. If it was held to be the state's responsibility to fund the NHS in that manner, taxes would rise astronomically, and so forth. In *Osman* v *UK* (1998) 29 EHRR 245, [1999] 1 FLR 193, the court said that the obligation under the Convention to take appropriate steps to safeguard life must be interpreted in a way that does not impose an impossible or disproportionate burden on the authorities.

The issue whether a patient was entitled to demand treatment for chronic renal failure where the health body pleaded it could not afford it was debated in the South African Constitutional Court in the case of *Soobramoney* v *Minister of Health, KwaZulu-Natal* (1997) 50 BMLR 224. The court concluded there had been no breach of the right to life afforded by the 1996 Constitution: but it has to be pointed out that the relevant provision specifically required the court, outside of emergencies, to consider the availability of resources.

Where the refusal of treatment is on clinical grounds rather than financial, the Article is unlikely to help the patient or his family, as they would have to prove that it was a reasonable option to give the treatment. If that were so, the patient could simply be transferred to a hospital that shared that view.

It has also been suggested, when enthusiasm has been harnessed to the farther reaches of imagination, that the *Bolam* test could become irrelevant, and even the issue of negligence generally, because the state would have a duty to make adequate provision for medical care, regardless of cost and reasonableness, where the patient's life could be at risk.

One possible line of attack, which seems more reasonable, could be a complaint that the Government failed to give adequate warnings about dangers to health, eg from radiation (see *LCB* v *UK* (1998) 27 EHRR 212), or contaminated food, or a medical product or medical treatment, such as a vaccination programme (see below under Article 8 'Other possibilities').

How does the Article affect the unborn child?

This issue has not yet been clarified. In *Paton* v *UK* No 8416/78, 19 DR 244 (1980), the Commission said that the Article does not recognise the *absolute* right to life of an unborn child (in that case, the abortion of a ten-week fetus to preserve the physical and mental health of the mother was not a breach of the Article). A similar case was *H* v *Norway* No 17004/90 (1992).[4] But does the unborn child have *any* rights under the Article?

---

4   In *Christian Lawyers Association of South Africa* v *Minister of Health* (1998) 50 BMLR 241, McCreath J held in the Transvaal High Court that in the provision in the South African Constitution guaranteeing the right to life to 'everyone', the word 'everyone' did not cover a fetus and therefore legislation permitting abortion in certain circumstances was not in conflict with the constitutional guarantee.

There is, as yet, no clear answer to this question. Note that the action must be brought by a 'victim' within the meaning of Article 25: the potential father qualifies as a victim.

Other issues could concern the taking of hazardous drugs by the mother and issues relating to fetal and embryonic research.

In *An NHS Trust* v *D* MLC 1077, [2004] Lloyds Rep Med 107, Coleridge J held that the carrying out of a termination in accordance with the requirements of the Abortion Act 1967, in circumstances where an incapacitated patient's best interests required it, was a legitimate and proportionate interference with rights (to family life) under Article 8(1) as serving the protection of health under Article 8(2).

In *Simms* v *A (a child)* [2004] Lloyds Rep Med 236, a case concerning the treatment of variant CJD, Dame Elizabeth Butler-Sloss P said a reduced enjoyment of life even at quite a low level was to be respected and protected (under Articles 2 and 8).

In *A NHS Trust* v *S* [2003] MLC 1098, the President held that it was in the best interests of a mentally incapacitated patient suffering from renal dysplasia that haemodialysis via permcath/peritoneal dialysis was used to its fullest extent in order to provide him with the best possible life-sustaining treatment and that, when alternative methods of dialysis were no longer viable, a kidney transplantation should not be rejected on the grounds of the patient's inability to understand the purpose and consequences of the operation or concerns about his management. (For other cases on 'best interests' see Chapter 23.)

Inquests

For the surprising way in which this deceptively simple Article extends to the investigation of deaths and the management of inquests and other procedures, see Chapter 7.

Article 3: Freedom from inhuman treatment

> No-one shall be subjected ... to inhuman ... treatment ...

Although this provision is clearly aimed at quite different contexts than the purely medical (it speaks of torture, degrading treatment and punishment), it certainly applies to the refusal or insufficiency of medical treatment to any detainee.[5] One among many examples must suffice: failure to X-ray a detainee with a fractured rib until six days after he had requested it was a breach of the article (*Hurtado* v *Switzerland* A 280-A (1994)). Forcible medical treatment of mental detainees will not be a breach of the Article if reasonably required to preserve physical and mental health (*Herczegfalvy* v *Austria* A 244 para 82 (1992), *B* v *UK* No 6870/75, 32 DR 5 (1981) – psychiatric treatment of a Broadmoor patient). What is a little surprising is that the Commission have stated in the

---

5   Conditions of detention in Broadmoor (though not specifically the medical attention) have been the subject of criticism from the Commission more than once (*B* v *UK* No 6870/75, 32 DR 5 (1981), *A* v *UK* No 6840/74, (1980) 3 EHRR 131).

more general context that it 'does not exclude that a lack of proper medical care in a case where someone is suffering from a serious illness could in certain circumstances amount to treatment contrary to Article 3' (*Tanko* v *Finland* No 23634/94 (1994)).

Experimental treatment without full consent could come within the terms of the Article; but in such a case, there would presumably be a claim in negligence anyway (though the claim under the Act might obviate possible defences, such as the contention that consent would have been given if properly sought, or that the treatment was in fact beneficial).

In *NHS Trust* v *M* (see above), Butler-Sloss P said that for the prohibition against torture to apply, the victim had to be conscious.

And see above the case of *A National Health Service Trust* v *D* and below, under Article 8, the case of *R* v *North West Lancashire Health Authority, ex p A, D and G*.

Watts v *Primary Care Trust* [2003] EWHC 2228 (Admin), was a claim by a patient to obtain reimbursement for the cost of a replacement hip operation carried out in France. She had been unwilling to wait a few months for the operation under the NHS. Insofar as her claim was based on her Convention rights she relied on Articles 3 and 8. Munby J held that there was no positive obligation to provide treatment, as decided by the *North West Lancashire* case (see below under Article 8). Article 3 did not apply as it was not designed to apply to challenges in relation to policy decisions on the allocation of resources. Also, it was not engaged unless the ill-treatment in question attained a minimum level of severity and involved actual bodily injury or intense physical or mental suffering.

In *Secretary of State for Home Department* v *Wainwright* [2004] 2 AC 406, the House of Lords held that there was no breach of Article 3 where visitors to a prison were strip-searched since the searches did not amount to humiliating and degrading treatment.

Article 6: The right to a fair trial

> In the determination of his civil rights ... everyone is entitled to a fair and public hearing within a reasonable time by an independent and impartial tribunal ...
>
> The right to a fair trial holds so prominent a place in a democratic society that there can be no justification for interpreting Article 6(1) restrictively (*Moreira de Azevedo* v *Portugal* (1990) 13 EHRR 721).

If the expectation among personal injury lawyers had, not unreasonably, been that the procedural constraints on the proper preparation of cases could be challenged under this Article, it appeared to be rudely dispelled by the trenchant observations of Lord Woolf in *Daniels* v *Walker* [2000] 1 WLR 1382, CA. The claimant had been severely injured in a road traffic accident. A joint care report was obtained by consent. The defendants wanted to challenge it by getting their own expert report, as they considered it recommended far more care than was needed. A careful argument was compiled to the effect that to deny them their request would be a breach of the Article. Lord Woolf said:

I will deal with the Human Rights Act point first. It was raised in a supplementary skeleton argument on behalf of the defendant. It relies on Article 6 of the Convention. It refers to *Mantovanelli v France* (1996) 24 EHRR 370, and suggests that, having regard to the provisions of Article 6, the order of the judge in this case conflicted with Article 6 because it amounted either to barring the whole claim of the defendant or barring an essential or fundamental part of that claim ... Article 6 has no possible relevance to this appeal. Quite apart from the fact that the Act is not in force, if the court is not going to be taken down blind alleys it is essential that counsel, and those who instruct counsel, take a responsible attitude as to when it is right to raise a Human Rights Act point. The point was raised in this case and was supported by a skeleton argument which referred to different authorities under the Convention. It covered four pages. It resulted in a supplementary skeleton argument ...

Article 6 could not possibly have anything to add to the issue on this appeal. The provisions of the Civil Procedure Rules, to which I have referred, make it clear that the obligation on the court is to deal with cases *justly*. If, having agreed to a joint expert's report a party subsequently wishes to call evidence, and it would be unjust having regard to the overriding objective of the Civil Procedure Rules not to allow that party to call that evidence, they must be allowed to call it.

In civil jurisdictions the position is different. Expert issues are frequently determined on the basis of a court expert and the parties have to put up with it in the majority of situations. They have an opportunity to question the expert but that was going to be allowed by the judge here in any event. No one suggests that the way matters are conducted in civil jurisdictions could contravene Article 6 in the normal manner, nor could the proper use of the Civil Procedure Rules ...

It would be unfortunate if case management decisions in this jurisdiction involved the need to refer to the learning of the European Court of Human Rights in order for them to be resolved. In my judgment, cases such as this do not require any consideration of human rights issues, certainly not issues under Article 6. It would be highly undesirable if the consideration of case management issues was made more complex by the injection into them of Article 6 style arguments. I hope that judges will be robust in resisting any attempt to introduce those arguments. Certainly, on this occasion, this court gave Mr. Temple short shrift. Notwithstanding my high regard for Mr. Temple, I consider that that was the only way in which that argument could be treated. When the Act of 1998 becomes law, counsel will need to show self-restraint if it is not to be discredited.

In effect, Lord Woolf was saying that considerations of a fair trial in respect of procedural issues have nothing to do with the right to a fair trial under Article 6 and everything to do with the overriding objective under CPR, Pt 1. Justice in this context would be justice under the rules, not under the Convention. Clearly, he was worried that the restraints currently placed on the preparation of cases in the interests of cutting costs and delays could be the subject of innumerable challenges under the Act as the Convention does not explicitly recognise that what is the just solution in a procedural context must be heavily affected by considerations of expense and delay (something that CPR 1 makes abundantly clear). English justice in procedural matters is not the same as European justice. Any challenge to procedural orders, it seemed, would be assessed according to the new age requirements for minimal expense and precipitate trial, not according to any standards which the European Commission or Court may have adopted.[6] However, to be fair, it has not turned out like that. Nothing has deterred the lawyers from attaching an Article 6 plea to any and every interlocutory order of the court or any costs or procedure decision about which they wish to complain. And it is right to say that in many cases such a plea has been taken seriously. Throughout this book we have noted where such a plea has been made – Chapters 5 and 8–13 are particularly relevant.

The right to a fair trial includes the right of access to a court (*Golder* v *UK A 18* (1975), *Osman* v *UK* [1999] 1 FLR 193, 5 BHRC 293). In *Z* v *UK*, in a report adopted on 10 September 1999, the European Commission found unanimously that the decision of the House of Lords in *X (a minor)* v *Bedfordshire County Council* [1995] 2 AC 633) had been in breach of Art 6. This is not, however, an absolute right; restrictions on the right of access may be reasonable in some circumstances (*Ashigdane* v *UK* A 93 para 57 (1985)). Chapter 11 helps us to see to what extent orders under the CPR for summary judgment or strike out are currently being made despite any plea of a breach of this right. In *S* v *Gloucestershire County Council* [2000] 3 All ER 346, CA, the court said that a summary hearing could be a fair hearing within the meaning of the Article. Nevertheless, our courts have already changed their approach to applications for a claim to be struck out as disclosing no cause of action – see *Barrett* v *Enfield London Borough Council* [1999] 3 WLR 79, HL, and the observations of Lord Browne-Wilkinson on the Convention and the European Court's decision in *Osman* (above).[7]

In some circumstances, a state may be required to provide legal aid, particularly where a person cannot plead his case effectively himself, or the where the law makes legal representation compulsory (*Airey* v *Ireland* A 32 (1979)). See Chapter 7 on the relevance of this issue to inquests.

The right to a fair trial includes the right to an oral hearing in person. In civil cases, the right of a party to be present at a hearing, not merely to have a lawyer attend, has not been widely recognised.[8] It is clear that the

---

6   In *R* v *MacLeod* (2000) Times, 20 December, the Court of Appeal said that Art 6 did not add to or alter the normal requirement of English law that trials should be conducted fairly before an independent and impartial tribunal.

7   See Chapter 11 further on this. The European Court's decision in *Osman* was highly significant for English substantive law, not merely procedural law. In the first place, it invalidated the blanket immunity previously afforded by our courts to the police *vis-à-vis* any duty owed to members of the public to investigate cases properly and take appropriate action (an immunity exemplified by *Hill* v *Chief Constable of West Yorkshire* [1989] AC 53, HL, and by the Court of Appeal decision which was being appealed from – *Osman* v *Ferguson* [1993] 4 All ER 344). Second, it showed the extent to which the European Court was willing to use Art 6 not merely to correct procedural abuses, but actually to create duties within the field of substantive law. The right to a fair trial would be infringed not only by procedural bars, but also by the denial by the domestic law of a valid action! (Lord Browne-Wilkinson, among others, has said that this approach by the European Court goes outside their jurisdiction.) Readers are referred to a illuminating article by Robert Weir at [2000] JPIL 208.

8   In *Brabazon-Denning* v *UK Central Council for Nursing Midwifery and Health Visiting* (31 October 2000, unreported), CA, the actions of the defendants in holding a hearing into alleged misconduct by the appellant nurse (while managing a private nursing home) in her absence, despite medical evidence that she was unfit to attend, was held to be in breach of Art 6. Not only did they hold the hearing in her absence, they also struck her off the Register of Nurses!

reluctance now shown by the House of Lords to see a case struck out, where it would have been unlikely some time ago to be so charitable, is largely due to the influence of the 'fair trial' provision in the Convention (see eg *Waters* v *Metropolitan Police Comr* [2000] 1 WLR 1607, HL).[9]

The right to a fair trial includes the right to equality of arms. This has been expressed by saying that a party must have a reasonable opportunity of presenting his case to the court under conditions which do not place him at substantial disadvantage *vis-à-vis* his opponent. In *Dombo Beheer* v *Netherlands* A 274 para 33 (1993), a breach was found where one party was not allowed to call a factual witness relevant to the factual evidence called by the other side. It has been held in other cases that equality of arms requires that the parties be allowed to cross-examine witnesses and be allowed access to facilities on equal terms.

There have been several decisions condemning the failure to allow a party to comment on a report prepared for the court.[10] In *McMichael* v *UK* (1995) 20 EHRR 205, the European Court unanimously held that the refusal at a children's hearing under Scots law (where the mother was seeking to avoid her child going into care), and on appeal at the Sheriff's Court, to disclose to her 'vital' documents, including social reports, was a breach of her right to a fair trial. Compensation of £5,000 was awarded. Meanwhile, her child had been adopted without her consent. The court said that a litigant should have an opportunity to have knowledge of and to comment on observations filed and evinced by another party.

In *McGinley* v *UK* (1998) 42 BMLR 123, where ex-servicemen complained, in relation to the Christmas Island nuclear tests, that the Ministry of Defence had not disclosed available medical records, the court held that there had been no violation of Art 6. It was not established that the UK had in its possession documents relevant to the questions at issue in the pension appeals of the applicants and, in any case, it was open to them to apply for disclosure of the relevant documents under r 6 of the Pension Appeals Tribunals (Scotland) Rules 1981. Since this procedure was provided and the applicants had failed to use it, they were not denied a fair hearing or effective access to the Pensions Appeal Tribunal.

In the case of *Mantovanelli* v *France* (1996) 24 EHRR 370, the parents of a 20-year-old woman who died in hospital after contracting jaundice applied for a declaration that the hospital was responsible for her death; they complained that she had been given excessive doses of halothane during anesthesia. In the course of the proceedings, the parents applied for the appointment of an expert. The appointment was refused. The application was renewed, and an expert was appointed by the court. The applicants complained there had been a breach of Art 6 as the expert prepared his report for the court without the parties having an opportunity to make representations to him. In particular, the expert had interviewed hospital doctors without the parties being present, and without the applicants having an opportunity to examine those witnesses or some of the documents available to the expert. The European Court found that:

---

9   See Chapter 11 further on this .
10   *Van Orshoven* v *Belgium* (1997) 26 EHRR 55; *JJ* v *Netherlands* (1998) 28 EHRR 168; *Reinhardt and Slimane-Kaïd* v *France* (1998) 28 EHRR 59.

... while Mr and Mrs Mantovanelli could have made submissions to the Administrative Court on the content and findings of the report after receiving it, the Court is not convinced that this afforded them a real opportunity to comment effectively on it. The question that the expert was instructed to answer was identical with the one that the court had to determine ... it pertained to a technical field that was not within the Judge's knowledge. Thus, although the Administrative Court was not bound by the expert's findings, his report was likely to have a preponderant effect on the assessment of the facts by that court. Under such circumstances, and in the light also of the Administrative Court's refusal of their application for a fresh expert report, Mr and Mrs Mantovanelli could only have expressed their views effectively before the expert report was lodged ... they were prevented from participating in the interviews ... As to the documents taken into consideration by the expert, the applicants only became aware of them once the report had been completed and transmitted. Mr and Mrs Mantovanelli were thus not able to comment effectively on the main piece of evidence. The proceedings were therefore not fair as required by Article 6(1) of the Convention.[11]

In *H* v *France* (1989) 12 EHRR 74, the European Court considered whether a court's refusal to allow a party to call an expert could constitute a breach of Art 6. On the facts of that case, it was found that no breach had occurred, as it was reasonable for the administrative court to reject the application for a medical expert's report when the applicant had failed to make out a *prima facie* case on the existence of a causal link between the treatment he received and the alleged damage. The court said:

> ... the *Conseil d'Etat's* decision not to order an expert's report might at first sight seem open to criticism in a case concerning medical treatment with a controversial drug ... However, having regard to all the circumstances ... the fact that it did not order an expert's report did not infringe the applicant's right to a fair trial.

A fair hearing also requires a reasoned judgment, albeit only a brief statement of reasons would probably suffice (*Hiro Balani* v *Spain* (1994) 19 EHRR 565; cf *Stefan* v *GMC* [1999] 1 WLR 1293, PC; see also *Hyams* v *Plender* [2000] 1 WLR 32, CA, where the court said that the judge should properly have identified in what way a Practice Direction had not been complied with, rather than leaving it to the claimant to conjecture why his application for permission to appeal had been refused).

Although a claim would seem to be possible along the lines that, for example, there was a breach of the right to fair trial on the equality of arms principle because the patient was only allowed one expert, whereas the defendants had, in addition, the treating doctors to offer their views, it seems clear that Lord Woolf would not approve. It seems that any matter arising out of case management will be decided according to the CPR view of justice. A claim in respect of restrictions

---

11　In *R* v *Marylebone Magistrates Court, ex p Clingham, sub nom C* v *Kensington and Chelsea London Borough Council* (11 January 2001, unreported), CA, the court held that it was not a requirement of the right to fair trial that any admitted hearsay evidence should be subject to cross-examination.

imposed on the specialties for expert reports allowed to a party seems unlikely to succeed.

The exclusion of lawyers from experts' meetings might be a breach of the right to a fair trial; as explained in Chapter 9, it may or may not become the norm that lawyers should be present.

It remains to be seen whether any challenge under the Act will be permitted in respect of alleged dependence or partiality of the court or tribunal. There are several decisions from the European Court in respect of the impartiality of tribunals and the need for a hearing in open court.[12] But as our appeal courts are in any event scrupulous in their application of the bias principle (see eg the *Locabail* case [2000] QB 451, CA; *Roylance* v *General Medical Council* (1999) 47 BMLR 63, PC; *Taylor* v *Lawrence* (25 January 2001, unreported), CA, it is probable that reference to European decisions would not add anything to the strength of a claimant's case. *Quaere*: would a judge who was also a member of an NHS Trust board involve a breach of this right? Would a judge who had gone on record as saying that cerebral palsy awards were bleeding the NHS dry be an acceptable tribunal for assessing quantum? We all know the judges who favour defendants. Medical negligence claims arouse strong and often polarised views. Will we be bolder to challenge the impartiality of a judge in the future?

The GMC, in response to the Act, altered its practice not long ago in relation to disclosure of documents to a complainant. They now follow a more open procedure (see *R* v *GMC, ex p Toth* MLC 0270, [2000] Lloyd's Rep Med 368 at 375).

In *Matthews* v *Ministry of Defence* MLC 0905, [2003] PIQR P392, HL, where an ex-serviceman alleged that the bar to a personal injury action imposed by s 10 of the Crown Proceedings Act 1947 (see Chapter 4) was a breach of Art 6, the House of Lords said that before the Article could be invoked there had to be a civil right that had been infringed, and that a distinction must be drawn between a limitation on a person's right of action which was the product of procedural law and one which was the product of substantive law. The s 10 bar was a substantive law limitation and therefore was not in breach of the Article.

We have previously noted in Chapter 22 the case of *English* v *Emery Reimbold* [2002] EWCA Civ 605, CA, where the court held that the European jurisprudence required that a judge give reasons for his decision but they did not need to be spelt out *in extenso*. We have also noted in Chapter 26 the case of *Goode* v *Martin* [2002] PIQR P333, where the Court of Appeal, influenced by Art 6, took a more relaxed view of an application to amend a statement of case after the expiry of the relevant period of limitation.

---

12 See *Gautrin* v *France* (1998) 28 EHRR 196; *Diennet* v *France* (1995) 21 EHRR 554.

Article 8: The right to respect for private and family life, home and correspondence and Article 12: The right to marry and have a family

1. Everyone has the right to respect for his private and family life, his home and his correspondence.

2. There shall be no interference by a public authority with the exercise of this right except such as is in accordance with the law and is necessary in a democratic society *in the interests of ... public safety, ... for the protection of health or morals, or for the protection of the rights and freedom of others.*[13]

The area where this Article is likely to be relevant is the confidentiality of medical records. What follows should be read with the treatment on confidentiality under domestic law found in Chapter 15.

In *MS* v *Sweden* (1997) 3 BHRC 248, para 41, the European Court acknowledged that the protection of personal data, particularly medical data, is of fundamental importance to a person's enjoyment of his or her right to respect for private and family life. Any state measures which compel disclosure of such information without the consent of the patient call for the 'most careful scrutiny'. Whether interference can be justified will depend upon the reason for disclosure and the safeguards surrounding its use. Although parties are only required to disclose evidence which is relevant, a defendant may not be entitled to inspect all of a claimant's medical/personal records, as this may be unjustified and disproportionate. The Court indicated that the right to privacy is not automatically waived by the mere fact of commencing proceedings, and observed that the disclosure required in that case was limited to the extent that the evidence was material (see also *Z* v *Finland* (1997) 25 EHRR 371). This seems to be in conflict with the normal rule under our law (see eg *Dunn* v *British Coal Corpn* [1993] PIQR P275, CA). Similarly, although this Article might seem to permit a claimant to refuse to undergo a medical examination requested by the defendant, that is not likely to be the way in which our courts will interpret it, given cases such as *Lacey* v *Harrison* [1993] PIQR P10 (see Chapter 12 under 'Medical reports on condition and prognosis').

The collection of medical data and the maintenance of medical records fall within the sphere of 'private life' (*Chare née Jullien* v *France* No 14461/88, 71 DR 141, 155 (1991)). Unjustified collection, and, one would suppose, dissemination of medical information on an individual, will be a breach of the Article (but note again that the exceptions justifying what would otherwise be a breach are widely based).[14]

---

13   The exceptions also include reference to national security, the economic well-being of the country and the prevention of disorder and crime. These are unlikely to be relevant to the medical negligence field. Any 'interference must ... correspond to a pressing social need, and be proportionate to the legitimate aim pursued' – see *Silver* v *UK* (1983) 5 EHRR 347; *Handyside* v *UK* (1976) 1 EHRR 737; *Sporrong* v *Sweden* (1982) 5 EHRR 35).

14   In *Woolgar* v *Chief Constable of Sussex Police* (1999) 50 BMLR 296, CA, an injunction was unsuccessfully sought by the matron of a nursing home to restrain the Chief Constable of Sussex Police from disclosing, to the United Kingdom Central Council for Nursing, Midwifery and Health Visiting (UKCC), the contents of an interview between her and the police which had taken place at Worthing Police Station. The court said that when someone was arrested and interviewed by the police, the content of the interview was confidential, otherwise than in the course of a criminal trial. Article 8 of

The meaning of private life and family life have been so widely interpreted by the European Commission and Court that the expectation of a flood of cases in the Family Division is probably justified. It will not be surprising if imaginative lawyers (the term is not really an oxymoron) also discern medical claims which can invoke this Article. For example, the concept of private life includes sexual relations, so that a woman may have a right to an abortion where conception was unwanted (see *Bruggeman and Scheuten* v *FRG* No 6959/75, 10 DR 100 (1977)).

In *Guerra* v *Italy* (1998) 26 EHRR 357, the Court found a violation of Art 8 in that the relevant authorities had failed to provide members of the public with appropriate information about the health hazards from a nearby chemical factory.

In *Hardman* v *Amin* [2000] Lloyd's Rep Med 498, Henriques J, accepting a claim by parents for the cost of upkeep of an unplanned handicapped child, indicated that to refuse recovery would be in breach of Art 8, as it would have disrupted and prevented the family leading as 'normal' a life as possible (the judge referred to *Marckz* v *Belgium* (1979) 2 EHRR 330).[15]

In *R* v *North and East Devon Health Authority, ex p Coughlan* [2000] 2 WLR 622, [1999] MLC 0105, the Court of Appeal set aside a decision by the health authority to close a home for disabled residents, on the ground that, having told the residents at an earlier date that it would be a permanent home for them, there was no sufficient 'over-reaching public interest' which would justify the health authority breaking that 'home for life promise'. The court was also satisfied that to move the elderly applicant from her home, which had been shown to be likely to be 'emotionally devastating and seriously anti-therapeutic' would, in circumstances where the financial benefit to be gained by such a move would be small, be in breach of Art 8(1).

In *R* v *North West Lancashire Health Authority, ex p A, D and G* [2000] 1 WLR 977, [1999] MLC 0111, the Court of Appeal invalidated the policy of the health authority in relation to the treatment it was or was not prepared to provide to transsexuals, to the effect that such surgery would be refused unless there were exceptional circumstances over and above the clinical need. But the court was not prepared to

---

the European Convention of Human Rights indicated that, to protect private and family life, where information had been obtained in confidence, there should be no disclosure. However, there were exceptional circumstances, recognised by Art 8, where disclosure was justified as being necessary in a democratic society in the interests of national security, public safety or economic well-being of the country, for the prevention of crime and disorder, for the protection of health and morals, or for the protection of rights and freedoms of others. Where a regulatory body such as the UKCC, operating in the field of public health, sought access to confidential material in the possession of the police, being material which the police were reasonably persuaded was of some relevance to the subject matter of the inquiry being conducted by the regulatory body, the police were entitled to disclose the material on the basis that, save in so far as it may be used by the regulatory body for the purposes of its own inquiry, the confidentiality which already attached to the material would be maintained. Even if there was no request from the regulatory body, if the police came into possession of confidential material, which in their reasonable view, in the interests of public health or safety, should be considered by a professional or regulatory body, then the police were free to pass that information to the relevant regulatory body for its consideration.

15 On unplanned pregnancy, see Chapter 24.

find that the refusal of treatment had been in breach of Art 8, because that imposed no positive obligations on the authority to provide treatment and there had been no interference with the applicants' private lives or their sexuality. Nor had it subjected them to inhuman or degrading treatment contrary to Art 3. It is not surprising that the court complained that an unfocused recourse to the jurisprudence deriving from the Convention was positively unhelpful to the court, cluttering up its consideration of adequate and more precise domestic principles and authorities governing the issues in play.

In *Glass* v *United Kingdom* (9 March 2004), MLC 1092, ECHR (see above for summary of the facts) the parents succeeded in obtaining from the European Court a declaration that a hospital's decision that it could take no active steps to prolong their disabled child's life was in breach of Article 8 in the absence of authorisation by a court. They also obtained €10,000 by way of non-pecuniary loss.

In *Briody* v *St Helens and Knowsley Area Health Authority* [2001] MLC 0165, where the claimant, who had through negligent treatment lost her womb, put forward a head of damages for the cost of surrogacy, Hale LJ said:

> While everyone has the right to try to have their own children by natural means, no-one has the right to be provided with a child. Mr Irwin prayed in aid Article 12 of the European Convention on Human Rights:
>
> > *'Men and women of marriageable age have the right to marry and to found a family, according to the national laws governing the exercise of this right.'*
>
> So far, the European jurisprudence has linked these two rights: the right to found a family is a family founded by marriage; the right to marry is limited to traditional marriage between persons of opposite biological sex: see *Rees* v *United Kingdom* (1986) 9 EHRR 56. More importantly, these are freedoms which should not be arbitrarily restricted, for example by preventing prisoners from marrying; this may well preclude placing arbitrary or disproportionate restrictions upon access to the reproductive services which are generally available. But that is quite different from having a right to be supplied with a child (or a spouse): see the recent decision of this Court in *R* v *Secretary of State for the Home Department, ex p Mellor, The Times,* 1 May 2001.

One wonders wryly whether the right to marry enshrined by the Convention will soon be extended, as it has been in some countries already, to homosexual marriage.

The Pinochet case

In *R* v *Secretary of State for Home Department, ex p Kingdom of Belgium* [2000] MLC 0271, the Court of Appeal ordered disclosure, limited to four named states who had unsuccessfully sought General Pinochet's extradition, of the medical reports which had led the Home Secretary to refuse extradition. The court, while confirming the basic right to confidentiality, said that in the circumstances, the integrity of the international criminal justice system needed to be demonstrated, and that the governing interest was the public interest in operating a procedure which would be perceived and accepted by the great majority to be fair, an imperative which outweighed any private interest. The disclosure fell within the exceptions of Art 8 of the Convention as being both 'in accordance with the law' and 'necessary in a democratic society ... for the prevention of disorder or crime'.

Confidentiality and the press

In *Ashworth Hospital Authority* v *MGN Ltd* [2001] 1 All ER 991, [2000] MLC 0285, the Court of Appeal held that there was no breach of the Convention when they upheld an order requiring a journalist to disclose the source of his information gained from medical records held at Ashworth on one of the Moors murderers. The court said only in exceptional circumstances, where vital public or individual interests were at stake, could an order requiring journalists to disclose their sources be justified (as *per Goodwin* v *UK* (1996) 22 EHRR 123), but this was an exceptional case because the disclosure of confidential medical records to the press was misconduct which was not merely of concern to the individual establishment in which it occurred; it was an attack on an area of confidentiality which should be safeguarded in any democratic society and the protection of patient information was of vital concern to the NHS.

Private ceremonies

When Michael Douglas sought to protect the privacy of his wedding from the paparazzi of *Hello!* magazine, the Court of Appeal, in a seminal judgment on the right to privacy, said that English law recognised the right to privacy afforded by the Convention, but that it was also clear that the European Court recognised different degrees of privacy, and the relevant degree of privacy affected the interaction between the right to privacy under Art 8 and the right to freedom of expression under Art 12. Although the couple were likely to succeed at trial, they had already compromised their privacy by selling the rights to the wedding photos to another magazine.[16] In those circumstances, the court was not prepared to grant the proposed injunction, but would leave the claimants to their remedy in damages (*Douglas* v *Hello! Ltd* [2000] All ER (D) 2435, [2001] 2 WLR 292). This action was the preface to the multi-stranded litigation in which damages were sought for breach of confidential information, ie the unlawful use and publication of the wedding pictures (see *Douglas* v *Hello!* [2005] EWCA Civ 595).

In *Archer* v *Williams* [2003] EMLR 38, Jackson J, Lady Archer obtained an injunction restraining the defendant from disclosing confidential details of her employment with the claimant. The judge said that the defendant's right to freedom of expression under Art 10 did not supersede the claimant's right to family life under Art 8. There was no overriding public interest in the disclosure of sensitive personal information relating to the claimant. In *D* v *L* [2003] EWCA Civ 1169, the balancing exercise that had to be carried out as between Arts 8 and 10 resulted in no injunction being granted, principally because the information which was

---

16 So very different from the genuine desire for privacy shown by the other superstar couple marrying the following year in the wilder reaches of Scotland.

sought to be protected was already in the public domain and, in any event, the defendant had not published or threatened to publish it.

In *Greenfield* v *Irwin* [2001] MLC 0341, CA, a claim for loss of mother's earnings while looking after an unplanned healthy child, the court gave short shrift to an application by the claimant to plead that the judge's rejection of this head of loss was in breach of Art 8 (for unplanned pregnancy see Chapter 24).

In *Secretary of State for Home Department* v *Wainwright* [2004] 2 AC 406, HL (see above) the House of Lords said there was no general cause of action in English common law for invasion of privacy. The *Michael Douglas* case was for breach of confidence. All English law need do would be to provide a remedy where there had been a breach of Art 8(1) which could not be justified under 8(2).

Other possibilities

There may be scope for a claim where the Government fails to give adequate public warning of health risks. In *Guerra* v *Italy* [1998] 4 BHRC 63, a failure to warn residents of a village of the risks of an explosion at a chemical works nearby was held to be a breach of Art 8, as was a failure to warn the inhabitants of Christmas Island of the dangers of a nuclear test (*LCB* v *UK* (1998) 27 EHRR 212). Perhaps one may extend this sort of obligation to the proper dissemination of any health information the withholding of which could adversely affect the enjoyment of family or private life. Where the adverse effects threaten life itself, Art 2 could be invoked.

In *Dobson* v *North Tyneside Health Authority* [1997] 1 WLR 596, CA, the Court of Appeal held that there was no right of property in the brain of a deceased and that there was no duty to preserve the brain after post mortem and after the rest of the body had been buried, and the claim was therefore struck out. However, this issue is likely to be more carefully ventilated following the revelations about hospitals removing and then preserving or destroying organs, particularly of children, without proper consent; and a court may possibly find that in such circumstances there has been a breach of Art 8 (though 'family *life*' might seem an unhappily inapposite basis for a claim in such a context).

Article 10: Freedom of expression

> Everyone has the right to freedom of expression. This right shall include freedom to hold opinions and to receive and impart information and ideas without interference by public authority and regardless of frontiers.
>
> [These freedoms may be restricted in the interests of national security, public safety etc.]

In *R* v *Secretary of State for Health, ex p Wagstaff* [2000] MLC 0232, the Court of Appeal found that the decision by the Secretary of State to hold the Shipman inquiry in private was a breach of this Article in that it constituted unjustified governmental interference with the reception of information that others wished or might be willing to impart.

Eady J made reference to this Article in the case of *Moran* v *Heathcote*, MLC 0344. A claimant's orthopedic expert gave a negative opinion which resulted in the discharge of the legal aid certificate. The patient continued on his own and lost at trial. He then told the expert he was going to publish an account of his dealings with the expert on the internet. The expert, fearing he would be defamed, sought an injunction against publication. Eady J declined to grant one, being satisfied that the limited ambit of the patient's commentary, as explained to him by the patient, would not attack the expert's integrity. The judge said that the importance of free speech in general terms was highlighted by Art 12 and also, in the particular context of interlocutory relief, by s 12 of the Act itself.

Damages

Although we are all naturally excited about human rights possibilities, we should bear in mind that the European Court's awards of damages are generally a lot lower than we are accustomed to. General damages are often not awarded at all, on the ground that the finding of the court in favour of the applicant is sufficient compensation. When they are awarded, they rarely exceed £10,000. Also, the Court is not keen to make awards for future speculative loss. This question of damages is well covered in the Law Commission Report No 266 *Damages under the Human Rights Act* (Cmnd 4853 October 2000).

Chapter 28

Strict liability

INTRODUCTION

This chapter considers various contexts in which liability may attach in respect of a claim for a medical accident without the need to prove fault. These include the Consumer Protection Act 1987, the Vaccine Damage Payments Act 1979, and any proposed system of no-fault compensation.

THE CONSUMER PROTECTION ACT 1987

This Act came into force on 1 March 1988. Strict liability for damage caused is imposed on the producers and certain suppliers of any product falling within the Act and supplied after that date. The definition of 'product' is apt to cover medical products, equipment and drugs. It may also cover blood and blood-based materials.

Section 2 of the Act provides that where any damage is caused wholly or partly by a defect in a product (the relevant party) shall be liable for the damage.

Section 2(1) reads:

Subject to the following provisions of this Part, where damage is caused wholly or partly by a defect in a product, every person to whom subsection (2) applies shall be liable for the damage.

Section 3(1) of the Act defines the meaning of 'defect' and reads:

Subject to the following provisions of this section, there is a defect in a product for the purposes of this Part if the safety of the product is not such as persons generally are entitled to expect; and for those purposes 'safety', in relation to a product, shall include safety with respect to products comprised in that product and safety in the context of risks after damage to property, as well as in the context of risks of death or personal injury.

Section 3(2) reads:

In determining for the purposes of sub-section (1) above what persons generally are entitled to expect in relation to a product all the circumstances shall be taken into account, including—
   '(a) the manner in which, and purposes for which, the product has been marketed, its get-up, the use of any mark in relation to the product and

any instructions for, or warnings with respect to, doing or refraining from doing anything with or in relation to the product;

'(b)   what might reasonably be expected to be done with or in relation to the product; and

'(c)   the time when the product was supplied by its producer to another;

and nothing in this section shall require a defect to be inferred from the fact alone that the safety of a product which is supplied after that time is greater than the safety of the product in question.

This legislation, following the EC Product Liability Directive (85/374/EEC), was expected (wrongly, as it turned out), *inter alia*, to put an end to the insuperable difficulties experienced by, for example, thalidomide victims in establishing negligence. One expected to have to prove that the drug had a defect and that the patient suffered an injury from ingesting the drug (ie that his condition was not due to progress of his underlying illness). But one did not expect the so-called strict liability to be, as explained below, watered down to the point where it adds very little to ordinary principles of liability for negligence under the common law.

The supplier will be liable if he cannot name the producer. If he can identify the producer he will not be liable even if the producer cannot satisfy a judgment.

Defect

A product is deemed to have a defect if its safety is not such as persons generally are entitled to expect. This suggests a form of *res ipsa loquitur*, in that the proof of the pudding may be said to be in the eating – you are entitled, one would hope, not to expect to be injured by a prescribed drug. However, the Department of Trade in 1985 sounded a warning note about the variability of the safety factor:

> The safety which a person is entitled to expect raises particularly complex issues in respect of medicinal products and adverse reactions to them. Establishing the existence of a defect in a medicine administered to a patient is complicated by the fact that not only is the human body a highly complex organism but at the time of treatment is already subject to an adverse pathological condition. In order to avoid an adverse reaction a medicine will have to be able to cope successfully with already faulty organs, disease and almost infinite variations in individual susceptibility to the effect of medicines from person to person. The more active the medicine, and the greater its beneficial potential, the more extensive its effects are likely to be, and therefore the greater the chances of an adverse effect. A medicine used to treat a life-threatening condition is likely to be much more powerful than a medicine used in the treatment of a less serious condition, and the safety that one is reasonably entitled to expect of such a medicine may therefore be correspondingly lower.

Drugs are never without risk. All one can hope is that proper and full clinical trials are carried out by independent parties (ie not dependent on the manufacturer) before the drug is marketed.

The 'development risks' defence

Unfortunately a lot of the bite of this Act is taken away by the fact that the Government (who no doubt find the pharmaceutical companies to be powerful – and wealthy – lobbyists) opted to enact the so-called 'development risks' defence, so that it is a defence to show that:

> ... the state of scientific and technical knowledge at the relevant time was not such that a producer of products of the same description as the product in question might be expected to have discovered the defect if it had existed in his products while they were under his control (s 4(1)(e)).

It appears that this provision has the effect of preserving the position at common law. If the producer is excused if he could not be expected to have discovered the defect, what point of strict liability is left? If he could have discovered it but did not, then, assuming it would have been reasonable for him to take steps to remedy it (which, with a potentially lethal drug, would surely be the case), he would be negligent under the common law. All one can really say has been achieved for the patient by this complex legislation is that the burden of proof has shifted to the defendants to show that they were not 'negligent', ie they could not have been expected to know that the product was unsafe. That is not a negligible advantage to the claimant, but it is a far cry from strict liability without proof of fault.

In fact, the defence that is given as an option in the EC Directive is not as wide as the formulation of the Act: the defendant is excused according to the Directive (Art 7(e)) if he proves 'that the state of scientific and technical knowledge at the time when he put the product into circulation was not such as to enable the existence of the defect to be discovered' – in other words, there is no limitation, as to persons who could have discovered the defect, to producers of products of the same description.

Limitation

An injured person has a three-year limitation period within which to issue his writ, on much the same principles as those that apply to a 'normal' action for personal injuries (see Chapter 26), subject, however, to an overall limitation period of ten years from the date of the relevant supplying.

The Act can usefully be invoked in the context of an otherwise routine medical negligence action where an instrument breaks during a procedure. It is usually impossible to show that the instrument was handled incompetently, or that the hospital failed to inspect or maintain, so recourse may be had to the manufacturer or importer and the burden of disproof is on them.

Cases

There are few reported cases on medical Consumer Protection Act (CPA) claims.

In *Richardson* v *LRC Products* [2000] Lloyd's Rep Med 280 (see Chapter 24, the section headed *Marian Richardson* v *LRC Products Ltd*), an unsuccessful claim was brought against a condom manufacturer when during use the product fractured across the teat line. It was alleged the fracture of the condom had been caused by a weakening of the latex by ozone occurring before the condom left the factory and also that the fact of the fracture itself evidenced the existence of a defect for the purposes of the Act in any event. In the result, Kennedy J found that nothing the manufacturer had done had contributed to the damage. He had this to say about the Act:

> Section 3 speaks of the safety of the product being such as persons generally are entitled to expect. The question of what persons are entitled to expect includes, as one might suppose, all the circumstances including the manner in which and the purposes for which the product is being marketed, its get up, the use of any mark in relation to the product, and any instructions or warnings with respect to doing or refraining from doing anything with or in relation to the product. Naturally enough the user's expectation is that a condom will not fail. There are no claims made by the defendants, one will never fail and no-one has ever supposed that any method of contraception intended to defeat nature will be 100% effective. This must particularly be so in the case of a condom where the product is required to a degree at least to be, in the jargon, 'user friendly'.
>
> So to the question: does a fracture prove a defect? I would answer, no, not by itself. Dr Rosenberg has shown that there are inexplicable failures, for all the condoms that he used in his trials would have been manufactured to United States standards and the defendants' are manufactured, or were manufactured, to a standard in excess of the relevant British standard. That standard has since been heightened and the defendants' tests have been changed, but that is another question. So for those reasons I have reached the conclusion that the claimant has not established a breach of the section by either of the routes which she has sought to follow.
>
> It is argued by the defendants that section 4 of the Act would have come to their aid if my conclusion had been against them. I do not think that this is so unless the case had shown that there was a defect of whose possible existence the leading edge of available scientific knowledge was ignorant. The test provided by the statute is not what the defendants knew but what they could have known if they had consulted those who might be expected to know the state of research and all available literature sources. This provision is, to my mind, not apt to protect a defendant in the case of a defect of a known character merely because there is no test which is able to reveal its existence in every case.

In *Worsley* v *Tambrands Ltd (No 2)* [2000] MLC 0280, an unsuccessful claim under the Act was dismissed without evidence being required from the defence. The claim had been presented (both for negligence at common law and under the Act) for damages for toxic shock syndrome (TSS) allegedly caused by the use of Tampax Regular tampons as a result of failure properly to warn of the risks associated with their use. Ebsworth J said:

> The test therefore is objective and the Act imposes a form of strict liability. The claimant must show that the tampon was defective within the meaning of s 2 and that the damage was caused wholly or in part by the defect. This case turns on the nature and extent of the warning and information accompanying the relevant tampons. Were they adequate to warn the claimant of the potential risk associated with tampon use, having regard to the nature of the risk and the potentially life-threatening consequences of TSS?

and:

> ... The reality of this case is that the claimant had lost the relevant leaflet and, for some inexplicable reason, misremembered its contents as to the onset of the illness. That does not render the box or the leaflet defective, and the claim must fail. The defendant had done what a menstruating woman was, in all the circumstances, entitled to expect: (1) they had a clearly legible warning on the outside of the box directing the user to the leaflet; (2) the leaflet was legible, literate,

and unambiguous and contained all the material necessary to convey both the warning signs and the action required if any of them were present; and (3) they cannot cater for lost leaflets or for those who choose not to replace them, as the claimant could have done after the Tuesday when she discovered the loss.

In those circumstances, whilst it is a sad fact that the claimant suffered a frightening and near fatal illness, there must be judgment for the defendant on its submission of no case to answer.

Abouzaid v *Mothercare (UK) Ltd* (2001) Times, 20 February, CA, was a successful CPA claim, upheld by the Court of Appeal, where the young claimant was awarded nearly £40,000 damages for injuries to his eye sustained in 1990 when attempting to fasten a fleece-lined sleeping bag known as a Cosytoes to his young brother's pushchair by means of elasticated straps. The strap slipped from his grasp and the buckle hit him in the eye. Expert evidence was to the effect that the hazard had not been recognised by anyone in the business in 1990, but ten years later such a product could be said to have a safety defect. The judge said that if it had one now, it had one then. The Court of Appeal agreed. The public's expectation had not changed since 1990. The judge said that the product was unsafe due to failure to provide proper instructions, particularly in the case of younger children, and the manufacturer should have appreciated the risk. The Court of Appeal was not satisfied that there was liability at common law, but endorsed the finding of liability under the Act, although saying the case was borderline. The defence under s 4(1)(e) (that the state of scientific and technical knowledge at the time was not such that the defect could be discovered), relying as it did on the absence of any record of similar accident, was not valid, as such evidence did not fall within the meaning of scientific and technical knowledge.

The AvMA database of settlements reveals three cases where the Act was used to good effect. In *G* v *Fry Surgical International Ltd and Nottingham Health Authority* (1992), damages were obtained against the importers of arthroscopy scissors which fractured during a lateral meniscectomy in 1988, a fragment being lost in the patient's knee. Although at first the importers blamed the surgeon, thus requiring the health authority to be joined, they offered no evidence when the patient's expert showed that the instrument had been defective. In *Clarke* v *Stockport Health Authority and William Cook (Europe) Ltd* (1994), unreported, an Omega C balloon catheter fractured during a renal angioplasty. A claim was brought for common law negligence against the operator, and one under the Act against the second defendant as manufacturer or supplier of the instrument. The latter denied any involvement. The patient settled for £16,000, though it is not clear from the report if it was the health authority that paid up (presumably then also paying the manufacturer's costs). In *Poole* v *Boots Co plc* (1997), unreported, the manufacturers of baclofen pumps (baclofen treats spasticity of limbs) settled this claim under the Act, and a number of similar claims, when it was found that the aspirate from the pump had become contaminated by *pseudomonas pickettii*.

Most actions under the Act for defects in medical products are likely to be group actions (for reasons of expense and because the product, particularly if it is a medicinal product, is likely to have harmed a number of patients). However, as we have seen, there are circumstances where a single claimant might reasonably bring an action, eg an action for injury in hospital caused by a defective instrument. The condom case above is another example (if one may call a condom a medical product). Whether in respect of single or multiple claimants:

> ... the new theory of liability under the CPA available to claimants in respect of damage caused by products supplied after 1 March 1988 has been very sparingly used. A recent survey conducted on behalf of the European Commission established that this cause of action had been pleaded in a mere handful of cases around the European Union and for nothing very serious.[1]

Group actions

The history of group actions in this country in relation to medical products has for the most part been dismal, whether alleging common law negligence or (where the Act was in force at the relevant time) a breach of the statutory provisions. Some claims have resulted in modest settlements. Many have been discontinued. One claim that lost in court, the pertussis vaccine claim, is considered in more detail in the next section. Some claims, like the MMR vaccine claim[2] struggle on. The human growth hormone litigation has, to date, achieved a fair degree of success,[3] the hemophilia litigation more so (see below). Legal aid is hard to obtain, and maintain, for such actions. This is not surprising as the legal aid authority is still traumatised by the £30m bill for the totally unsuccessful benzodiazepine litigation.[4] So it will often be a contest between the skill of the solicitors in uncovering the potential for a group action and creating appropriate evidence to support an application for legal aid to begin a lucrative suit, and the apparent desire of the legal aid authority and the Government to spend next to nothing on medical claims of any sort. Until recently, assistance could be obtained from a study of medical group actions in interpreting the provisions of the Consumer Protection Act. Group actions themselves are not within the ambit of this book. The interested reader would do well to consult *Multi-party Actions*, a practitioners' guide to pursuing group claims by Martyn Day, Paul Balen and Geraldine McCool (published in association with APIL).

In the Hepatitis C litigation (*A v The National Blood Authority* [2001] Lloyds Rep Med 187, MLC 0348) the short facts were that at various dates after the Act had come into force the claimants had become infected with the Hepatitis C virus as a result of being given transfusions of infected blood. The defendants had known that some bags of blood were bound to be infected (they had known since the 1970s that there was a problem with infected blood), but they had no way of discovering which were the infected bags until a date later than the date of the transfusions (by the early 1990s new screening tests had all but eliminated the problem). The judgment, some 300 pages of it, by Burton J is the first fully reasoned English decision within the consumer protection context in a group action for a medical product and without doubt the whole judgment repays careful study

---

1   *Per* Mark Mildred in *Clinical Negligence* (3rd edn, 2000) p 644.
2   See [1999] MLC 0117, [2000] MLC 0253 and [2000] MLC 0281.
3   See 54 BMLR 95, 100, 104, 111, 174, and the recent announcements of further settlements in the pipeline.
4   Wyeth's had to resort to litigation to recover against their insurers for the huge costs of defending the group action (*John Wyeth & Brother Ltd* v *Signa Insurance Co of Europe* (9 February 2001, unreported), CA).

(indeed by all European lawyers practising in the field), but for present purposes we can highlight the following factors:

(1) It was agreed by lawyers and judge that as the Act of 1987 derived from the 1985 Product Liability Directive (see above) it was upon the terms of the latter that their attention should be focused;

(2) Article 6 enacted that a product was defective where it did not provide the safety which a person was entitled to expect taking all circumstances into account. The judge held that the question of the avoidability of the defect (whether in terms of practicability or cost or whatever) was irrelevant under Art 6, as was any proof that the product was on the whole beneficial to the public. The Directive was intended to eliminate proof of fault or negligence;

(3) It was for the court to decide what the legitimate expectations of the public were. The court concluded that the public had not accepted that a proportion of the products would be defective (ie they had not accepted the non-standard nature of the defective product). The defendants' contention that all that the public had a right to expect (ie their legitimate expectation) was that the defendants had carried out all reasonable precautions was rejected;

(4) Further, there could be no valid defence under Art 7(e) which provided that a producer would not be liable if he proved that 'the state of scientific and technical knowledge at the time when he put the product into circulation as not such as to enable the existence of the defect to be discovered'. The risk *was* known. The fact that the particular defective products could not reasonably be identified among all the products was of no assistance to the defendants. Where a producer knew that he was continuing to produce products some of which were bound to be defective he did so at his own risk.

XYZ v *Schering Health Care, Organon Laboratories and John Wyeth and Brother* [2002] MLC 0796, was a trial of seven lead claims in respect of cardiovascular injuries allegedly caused by 'third generation' combined oral contraceptives. The claimants contended the products were defective within the meaning of the Act of 1987, but they failed to convince Mackay J that the third generation drugs carried any substantively higher risk than the second generation ones.

In *Bogle* v *McDonald's Restaurants Ltd* [2002] EWHC 490 (QB) it appears, *mirabile dictu*, that enough customers had been scalded by the defendant's coffee to form a group action. However, Field J found that the coffee was served at a temperature which was reasonable for its purposes, the cups were not unsafe, and there was no breach of the 1987 Act.

Meanwhile the MMR/MR vaccine litigation grinds along under the governance of Keith J, with various claimants falling by the wayside from time to time. For the discontinuances and the continuances (of both consumer and negligence claims) see *Sayers* v *SmithKline Beecham plc* [2005] EWHC 539 (QB). Claimants seek to establish a link between the vaccine and various disorders.[5] It will be surprising (to me) if they

---

5   The claimants who have had legal aid funding recently restored are those who are not alleging disorders in the autistic spectrum or inflammatory bowel disorder. Disorders acceptable (for the time being) to the legal aid authority include deafness, epilepsy and arthritis.

succeed. I wrote that last sentence before the October 2005 Cochrane Review which surely will put an end to this hopeful and hopeless litigation.

DHSS circular

The DHSS produced a Health Notice, HN(88)3 HN(FP)(88)5, which deals with the implications of this legislation for the NHS. First, hospitals are advised that a health authority may be liable as the supplier of a defective product to a patient, unless either the producer or the authority's supplier can be identified. So records should clearly show from whom and when a product was obtained, and to whom and when it was supplied, including any serial or batch number, the date of its issue to wards, clinics, etc, and it should be noted that all due warnings and instructions about use were passed on. Second, it is stated that the health authority may be liable as a keeper for damage from defective products that it uses, if its supplier or the producer show that the equipment has not been maintained, calibrated or used in accordance with the instructions. This is an added reason for keeping full records of such maintenance. Third, the NHS may also be liable as a producer, eg of medicines, appliances, dressings, blood products, products from hospital pharmacies. So as well as taking great care in the manufacture, the advice is to keep records which demonstrate conformity with proper standards.

The basic rule is to maintain clear, accurate and comprehensive records relating to the procurement, use, modification and supply of products, to be kept at least until the end of the ten-year period of limitation.

VACCINE DAMAGE PAYMENTS ACT 1979

No common law claim for vaccine-induced injuries has yet succeeded in England or Wales. The 1979 Act provided for a lump sum payment of £10,000 (increased thereafter, with top-up awards for all previous recipients) to be paid, regardless of fault, to any person who suffered severe disablement (which originally meant 80% disablement but has been reduced to 60% by the Regulatory Reform (Vaccine Damage Payments Act 1979) Order 2002) as a result of one of the specified vaccinations administered after July 1948. The claim must be brought before the age of 21 (the previous limitation was six years), or, by the Order of 2002, within six years of the date of the vaccination; if the claimant has died, the claim must be made by the date he would have reached 21. The claimant must have been vaccinated when under 18 years of age, except in the case of rubella or poliomyelitis. The Act was passed as a result of anxiety arising in the early 1970s over the possibility that the whooping cough vaccine, which, along with other vaccines, was being strongly urged on the populace by the Government, could cause brain damage. The Act is, however, of minor significance in the context of medical negligence and the no-fault compensation debate. The area in which it is operative is highly specialised and the compensation provided for a severely disabled person, though substantially increased in 2000 from £40,000 to £100,000, is still very modest compared to the awards of several million pounds and more to those claimants who can prove medical negligence. The payments are designed as compensation to those who may have been injured through following the Government's advice to be vaccinated.[6]

Vaccination of pre-school children is not compulsory, but parents are encouraged, sometimes pressured, to accept it. Currently, there is a vaccination at two, three and four months for diphtheria, tetanus, pertussis (whooping cough), Hib (Hemophilus influenza type b), polio and meningitis C; at 12–18 months for measles, mumps and rubella (MMR); and at four to five years for diphtheria, tetanus, polio, measles, mumps and rubella. As we saw in the preceding section, group litigation over the MMR/MR vaccination rumbles on.

Causation has to be proved on the balance of probabilities to the satisfaction of the tribunal. It does not appear that the tribunal was originally particularly slow to find a nexus between the vaccination and the injury if the case appeared an appropriate one for compensation. However, the situation suffered a sea-change in the light of the decision in *Loveday* v *Renton* [1990] 1 Med LR 117, a common law action where the claimant sought, as a preliminary point, to establish that the whooping cough vaccine could cause brain damage. Stuart-Smith LJ found, after a long and complex trial, that it had not been established that the whooping cough vaccine was capable of causing permanent brain damage in young children. He said that all four of the suggested mechanisms for the nexus between the vaccine and the damage were improbable. He also added, *obiter*, that even if that nexus had been established, the claimant would surely find it impossible to show that the GP had been negligent in vaccinating.

That same judge had already held, in *Department of Health and Social Security* v *Kinnear* (1984) 134 NLJ 886, N-J&B 308, that no action could be maintained against the Department for adopting in good faith a policy of whooping cough immunisation pursuant to the provisions of s 26 of the National Health Service Act 1946 (the legislation then in force).[7]

---

6   The Court of Appeal reversed a finding that a GP had been negligent to advise parents not to accept vaccination in *Thomson* v *James* [1998] Lloyd's Rep Med 187.

7   It is worth noting at this point that in fact Stuart-Smith LJ did not strike out the claims insofar as they alleged the giving by the DHSS of negligent and misleading advice to local health authorities regarding the circumstances in which such inoculation should be performed and the factors to be applied in determining whether a given individual should or should not be inoculated. The *Kinnear* decision was followed in part in the Scottish Court of Session in *Ross* v *Secretary of State for Scotland* [1990] 1 Med LR 235, where a pursuer's direct case against the Scottish Home and Health Department alleging that she suffered brain damage as a result of being vaccinated against smallpox was dismissed because it was based on considerations of ministerial policy and matters of discretion and was, therefore, irrelevant in the absence of averments of bad faith. The *Kinnear* decision was distinguished in part in that the judge, Lord Milligan, said that that part of the *Kinnear* claim that was permitted to proceed appeared to be of an 'operational' nature and so not of assistance in his case. A similar decision on the main issue had been reached by Lord Grieve in the Scottish case of *Bonthrone* v *Secretary of State for Scotland* 1987 SLT 34, where the pursuer's claim for injury allegedly sustained as a result of vaccination against whooping cough, diphtheria and tetanus without there having been given adequate warning of the risk of encephalopathy or other side effects had been struck out as attacking the ambit of exercise of a discretion rather than action taken to implement a discretionary decision. It is unlikely that that sort of reasoning would be followed today given the reluctance to strike out cases without some ventilation of the issues (see Chapter 5).

The child Loveday had also pursued compensation through the Vaccine Damage Tribunal in a long series of hearings: the tribunal and the appeal tribunal did not accept the nexus between injury and vaccination; the High Court ordered a rehearing before a different tribunal on the ground that the tribunals had not given proper thought to the matter. The new tribunal also refused an award. The High Court quashed that decision for certain procedural and evidential irregularities, but both it, and on appeal the Court of Appeal, refused to direct that the tribunal find the nexus established (*R* v *Vaccine Damage Tribunal, ex p Loveday* [1985] 2 Lancet 1137).

In *Bonthrone* v *Millan* [1985] 2 Lancet 1137, Scottish Court of Session, an action for negligence by a child against doctor and health visitor for administering the second dose of the pertussis vaccine despite an adverse reaction from the first, Lord Jauncey, dismissing the claim, said that, despite an earlier finding by a tribunal that injury had been caused to the pursuer by the second dose, there was no proved causal link between the injury and the vaccine (cf *Bonthrone* v *Secretary of State for Scotland* (footnote 7 above)).

Compare *Best* v *Wellcome Foundation Ltd* [1994] 5 Med LR 81, where the Supreme Court of Ireland endorsed the judge's findings that there was at the relevant time a possibility, known to the defendants, that the pertussis component in the vaccine could in rare cases cause encephalopathy, that the tests carried out by the defendants in regard to the batch from which the injection in question came were inadequate, and that they were therefore negligent in releasing the batch; but the Supreme Court also held that the judge's reason for rejecting the claim, namely that the evidence suggested that the claimant's first convulsion was not sufficiently proximate to the injection, was untenable. Therefore, the claimant succeeded and a new trial on damages was ordered. It is understood that the action was later settled for a sum in the area of £2.75m.

Thompson v *Bradford* [2004] MLC 1182, was an unusual case involving the polio vaccination. The child developed a vaccine strain of poliomyelitis. Wilkie J held that the GP had been negligent in not telling the parents that they could, if they wished, postpone the vaccination until the child's perianal abscess had healed; that (despite the fact that the GP's advice would have been that there were no contra-indications to having the vaccination at that time) the parents would have opted to postpone it; and that the child would then probably not have contracted the disease as it was probably the weakened state of the muscle tissue due to the abscess that let in the polio infection. But, see preface for Court of Appeal reversal.

NO-FAULT COMPENSATION

From time to time over the years one hears calls for the introduction, in varying forms, of a no-fault system of compensation for those who are injured by medical accidents.[8] Usually, the caller stands, himself or his

---

8   In October 1988, the Florida legislature introduced a scheme of no-fault compensation for 'birth-related neurological injury', the stated objective being that the obstetricians 'whom Florida so desperately needs' should return to the deserted delivery rooms.

group, to gain from such a scheme; he may be a doctor, or he may be an NHS official or supporter. Sometimes he may be an independent voice who genuinely believes that such a scheme would be for the good of society generally (one such voice, and a highly influential one, has been that of Lord Justice Otton).

A no-fault scheme would considerably relieve doctors emotionally, and the NHS financially, and would advantage the claimant from the strictly legal point of view that he would not have to prove that he received negligent care; but he would still have the difficult task of proving causation (for the enormous importance of causation in contested medical negligence action, see Chapter 17).

One riposte to the clamour for a no-fault scheme that is often stressed is that the principle of accountability is being overlooked, and that there would be less incentive to maintain, let alone raise, standards if the question of fault was no longer to be investigated. One has also to be aware that the claimant will often be more interested in publicising the failure of care and getting an admission of liability from the hospital than in obtaining financial compensation. One so often hears the claimant say that his main purpose in bringing an action is to try to ensure that the same thing does not happen to any other patient. Although a great deal is currently being done to improve risk management in medicine, a lot of the incentive for this good work is provided by patients' complaints supported by litigation.

And there are other considerations which need careful thought and investigation before one concludes that no-fault compensation would be a solution to the problems posed by the slow, anxious, uncertain and, as some would have it, unfair English litigious process.

It does seem to be assumed by those who call for a no-fault system that it would provide a simple and satisfactory solution to the perceived inadequacies and inequalities of the present fault-based tort system; any patient whose operation was not a total success, any child born handicapped, would receive substantial compensation (though it is not made clear where the money would come from). Reference is often made to the two no-fault systems of New Zealand and Sweden, as if what suits a sparsely populated, predominantly rural community where the pioneering spirit is still alive or a highly developed socialist state with a wide range of welfare benefits from cradle to grave would necessarily be appropriate here. This is wishful thinking, born, no doubt, of a genuine compassion for the innocent victims of misfortune and an understandable revulsion at the often titanic struggle that is involved in obtaining compensation under the present system. The first emotion makes us consider the rationale for compensating our fellow citizens for misfortunes that befall them, the second the procedure for so doing. It seems to be often overlooked that the first point is prior to the second, and needs to be clarified first.

The philosophy of compensation

It may be that the fault-based system is a hangover from the Victorian ideals of self-help and has no place in a modern welfare state, but it is not philosophically, even if it is politically, indefensible. A citizen has a right to expect that his fellows will conduct themselves with reasonable care in their dealings with him, and if they do not, and so cause him injury, then, given a breach of the duty of reasonable care, they will have to make good all his loss, insofar as that can be made good by money. But if he suffers one of the multifarious misfortunes that the vicissitudes of life are ever dealing us he has no right to demand that his fellows compensate him for that. He can always arrange his own insurance against such events.

That philosophy has perhaps a superficial attraction, if only for clarity and concision, but it takes no account of the theme of group endeavour which is the well-spring of the welfare state. One has to ask in what circumstances, as well as to what extent, should a citizen be compensated by his fellows for a misfortune, regardless of fault. Where he is injured giving his labour to the common weal there is clearly a case for compensation (hence industrial injury compensation). So, too, where he is injured acting on government recommendations or orders (hence the Vaccine Damage Payments Act 1979 and disability pensions for the armed forces). If he is willing to work but the state cannot find him work, or he would be working but for illness, his fellow citizens owe him a bare living. Examples can be multiplied.

The Pearson Commission suggested that no-fault compensation for motor accidents should be introduced (for the drunken or reckless driver, too?). This could be done without too much difficulty as the definition of injury through a motor accident is unlikely to give rise to much argument. But to what extent is it appropriate that medical misfortunes should be singled out as an area for compensation beyond the benefits that the welfare state already provides to ill or disabled citizens? Is it simply a practical suggestion because under the present tort-based system it is a particularly laborious and lengthy business to prove negligence against the medical profession, as well as unpleasant for all parties and hardly conducive to promoting good doctor-patient relations, as well as a financial drain on the NHS? Surely there is nothing particularly deserving of no-fault compensation in the medical misfortune, as opposed, say, to the misfortune of being struck by a falling branch or a tile dislodged unforeseeably by a high wind, or indeed the simple but all too common misfortune of an illness.

A decision to permit no-fault recovery for medical misfortunes only has no philosophical justification and can only be defended on the basis that practical considerations demand it and society is ready to accept it. To be sure, one can wax indignant that the parents of a handicapped child may recover several million pounds if they can prove, against all the odds, that some medical slip or other was made at or around the time of birth, whereas, if they cannot prove that, they will, after years of hassle and heartache, get nothing. But what if the handicap was congenital and not due to medical handling? Why should those parents not be similarly compensated? Why should the woman who has a heart attack under anesthesia receive a compensation and not the woman who has a heart attack walking down the road? There is no neat answer to these questions, so one need to think about this prior issue of the justification for a no-fault scheme in the medical context before proposing one.

The parameters of a no-fault scheme

It is not possible to decide what are the parameters for awarding compensation without at the same time being clear about what compensation you propose to award. We will assume agreement here that we are not trying to cover all injuries through accident, as has been the case in New Zealand, but only medical and drug-induced ones, as in Sweden.

It seems to be agreed that where the patient's condition is due to the progress of his disease, ie where medical intervention or omission did not contribute to it, there is no case for compensation, for that would be tantamount to compensating a person for becoming ill. That is the case in Sweden, where compensation is paid for injury or illness resulting from any procedure related to health care, and in New Zealand, where 'accident' includes medical and surgical misadventure, although it was hoped originally to include compensation for illness simpliciter. So the amount of compensation is inextricably linked with the incidence of compensation. In fact the New Zealand government has relaxed previously strict criteria for access to its 'no fault' accident compensation scheme for claims arising from medical misadventure. Patients who sustained injury from medical mishaps could previously access the Accident Compensation Corporation's scheme only if they met certain criteria. To access the scheme the adverse consequence either had to be rare – 'occurring in one per cent or less of cases where that treatment is given' – or required a finding of fault on the part of a practitioner or organisation. Thus a victim of a car crash could get compensation from the scheme without first having to prove fault, but the same did not necessarily apply to patients who sustained an injury as a result of medical treatment. The government said removal of the two thresholds would 'end the inconsistencies between how an injury was incurred and make it a true "no fault" scheme'.

But, even so, it is not necessarily every medical misfortune that falls to be compensated. What if the 'accident' was a recognised risk of the operation? The Swedish system does not cover misfortunes which were within the area of foreseeable risk of a medically justified act, though this is as much an 'accident' as an unforeseeable complication. It must be extremely difficult to show that an injury or adverse condition was not the natural progression of a disease or injury and also was not a foreseeable risk or side effect of treatment, but was in fact both the result of the treatment and a result that was not within the area of foreseeable risk. It could be said that most medical 'accidents' came within the area of foreseeable risk, for there are always a number of risks attendant upon any medical intervention. In the case of drugs, it may well be easier to show that the condition complained of was not a foreseeable consequence of taking the drug, as their capacity to injure is far-reaching and usually unknown, but it is likely to be difficult to prove that the drug caused the injury.

So we have got as far now as asking the advocates of a no-fault medical scheme to justify its introduction and define its intended scope. Now we ask them what sort of compensation they have in mind.

The amount of compensation

What will be paid to the victim of a medical accident? It is not presumably suggested that a high earner who comes out of a properly conducted operation unable to resume work because something went accidentally wrong should be paid what he would get in the tort scheme, say £50,000 times a multiplier of 20 equals £1m, plus, say, a million and more for private health care for the rest of his life, etc. Clearly, the money is not available for this level of compensation. So it needs to be clearly understood that compensation under a no-fault scheme, however useful it may be to patients who cannot prove fault, would be very different from what it is under the tort-based system. It will probably involve a range of periodic payments, which top up or extend existing available welfare benefits (as in Sweden). Those who see the parents of handicapped children being awarded without proof of fault the sort of compensation that they would get if they proved fault are simply deluding themselves. And, if that be so, one can see that a patient who is able to prove fault is not going to be satisfied with the no-fault level of compensation. Therefore, the tort system should remain as an alternative, which only serves to emphasise my point that the no-fault scheme will do no more than extend the range of available welfare or similar benefits as and where need arises. (The treatment of this issue by the Pearson Commission could be seen as somewhat disingenuous, as they seem to think that welfare benefits provide a more or less satisfactory scheme and level of compensation, a view which few who enjoy them would be likely to endorse.)

But how extensive any increased benefits should be is unclear. For example, a handicapped child is likely already to receive some degree of care and support in the field of therapy and education, as well as help at home for aids and equipment.[9] It is most unlikely that a 'no-fault' tribunal will be awarding thousands of pounds to the mother for nursing care or paying for the latest in electronic communication aids or trips to foreign remedial institutes, all of which are, if not standard, at any rate common items in tort-based awards. Advocates of these no-fault schemes need to be very clear about the sort of compensation that they envisage being paid before they ask us to pay it.

It may be instructive to consider what has happened to the Criminal Injuries Compensation Scheme. After years of awards being made on the same basis as any tort-based award in the civil courts, the Government decided it was spending too much on the scheme, and so introduced a tariff scheme, which, as you would expect, pays a claimant a great deal less. Is this what the reformers have in mind? If so, one needs to stress the difference between a claim by the victim of violence who has no other claim (because his assailant is unknown or has no money or insurance to satisfy a judgment) and a medical claim, which, unless these claims are taken wholly out of the forensic arena,[10] can be pursued in the courts.

Proposed legislation

The Labour Party originally produced a draft of a Compensation for Medical Injury Bill, creating a Compensation for Medical Injury Scheme,

---

9 This statement may be rather optimistic in the present climate of cutbacks.

10 This drastic step is proposed from time to time, accompanied by statistics cobbled together for the purpose and designed to show that the NHS is about to collapse due to litigation (to which the appropriate response is: let it avoid negligent mistakes and it will not be sued, not successfully at any rate).

to be supervised by a Medical Injury Compensation Board: this would have provided unspecified compensation for medical injury that had caused death, more than ten days in-patient treatment or more than 28 days off work, but it excluded injury caused by a number of specified factors including reasonable diagnostic error, unavoidable complications of a proper procedure and the use of a drug in accordance with the manufacturer's instructions; so its ambit was substantially limited.

A second effort, called the NHS (Compensation) Bill, was refused a second reading by 193 votes to 81 in February 1991. It had been proposed by Mrs Rosie Barnes, MP. The drafting was inept but the ideas were interesting. The Board would assess compensation for NHS patients who suffered injuries due to 'mishap' during NHS care. 'Mishap', however, was nowhere defined save to say that it included but was not restricted to any act or omission which gave rise to an action at common law or for breach of statutory duty, and excluded any foreseeable or reasonable result of the medical care or the patient's pre-existing condition. It is not easy to know what was meant by a 'reasonable result', but presumably one should run the two epithets together and read 'reasonably foreseeable result'. The mishap would have to be such as to result in death, in-patient treatment for at least ten days, inability to engage in normal activities for at least 28 days, or significant pain, disability, harm, distress, or loss of amenity, or a reduction in life expectancy.

The present position

Support for a no-fault scheme ebbs and flows. In 1997 I wrote:

> Currently no-fault is on the back burner. In fact, I would say that the gas is off and unlikely to be turned on again. The jurisprudential difficulties, as explained earlier in this chapter, allied to the apparent false economies of such a scheme, seem to have done for it permanently.

In 2001 I wrote:

> Given the present Government's attitude to public expense, and given that there are always influential voices baying, *inter alia*, about the 'greed' of patients, defensive medicine, the financial plight of the NHS and the astronomical awards now being made, it would not be altogether surprising if legislation were introduced to nullify in the medical field the traditional and fundamental principle of our law giving a citizen the right to recover compensation from a tortfeasor for negligently caused injury.

Now, in 2006, I do not see the latter happening. I do see no-fault as being dead in the water. This is because the Government is pinning its hopes on the *Redress* system. No-fault would be hugely expensive, but if patients can be forced, by financial pressures if not legal ones, into accepting a *Redress* adjudication of their claims, it will cost the public purse much less than litigation, because it will be much less generous (and, I dare say, will result in fewer successful claims). See, further, the discussion of the scheme in Chapter 2.

Epilogue

Epilogue

Chapter 29

Epilogue

'Where do we go from here? What does the future hold for patients' claims, for the children who would have been born normal and healthy if they had not received incompetent medical attention, for the men and women whose lives have been ruined or substantially impaired through negligent medical care? The worst scenario is that the Government will pull the plug on such claims, desperate to save both the legal aid fund and the NHS coffers from any further depletion; that it will annul the funda-mental principle of our whole legal structure, the right to sue a tortfeasor for compensation for negligently caused injury, and put in its place with an ungenerous tariff a system of set awards for medical accidents (this last no doubt defined in some way or another so as to give rise to further litigation). This sort of move might well provoke a human rights chal-lenge. Short of that dramatic and wholly unacceptable 'solution', one can envisage the possibility that legal aid will be withdrawn from medical claims, even if perhaps retained for the investigative stages (thereafter to be progressed on a conditional fee basis, if at all). The investigative stages may be paid for at even worse rates than at present.'

I wrote the above paragraph for the last edition in 2001. I do not now see any real possibility of the Government annulling the right to sue. But I do see it placing every possible obstacle in the way of a claimant. It is pinning its hopes on something like the 'system of set awards' I suggested above. It is pinning its hopes on the system of *Redress*, proposed not long ago by the Chief Medical Officer. That system is discussed at some length in Chapter 2. The legal aid authority is likely (acting on governmental orders) to refuse to fund litigation, trumping up some reason or other in each case for its decision. Whether its reason will be that the patient must accept the *Redress* scheme remains to be seen. Probably not. But there are a host of reasons they use to deny funding already or to debili-tate a claim through underfunding (eg the case is too old, it is not worth enough, it is costing too much, use the great new internal complaints pro-cedure please, the claimant has at least sixpence ha'penny in the savings bank, the evidence does not look very strong to us, we are not in the giving vein – and so forth, if not exactly *ad infinitum*, then at least *ad nauseam*).

We are likely to see new ploys devised by the legal aid authority to reduce expense, to pay lawyers even less, to reduce financial eligibility for legal aid yet further, and so on. We may well also see, once the *Redress* scheme is up and running, amendments made to it which would be designed to cut down on awards – the common governmental ploy of luring people in and then altering the terms on which they were initially attracted.

It is fair to say that the process of a medical claim has been made speedier, and possibly less costly, by the new Civil Procedure Rules and the management of claims by some (but by no means all) of the judicial officers who have charge of them, notably the experienced Queen's Bench Masters. Defendants, by which is meant the NHSLA (for the medical defence societies remain as reasonable as they have ever been), are making progress towards living up to their boast that they assess cases early and do not hold back on admitting liability where it should be admitted. But they need to understand that their not infrequent ploy of offering a sum by way of settlement in a big case before the claimant's lawyers have obtained any reports on quantum and thereby been able to do at least some part of the necessary calculations is a pointless exercise. This is particularly the case where a child is involved, as any settlement needs to be explained in detail to the court in order to get approval. The pre-action protocol has proved helpful, if only because it gets the parties to state their respective case at an early stage. It should promote early admissions and in those cases should obviate the need to start proceedings (waivers should be offered on limitation). The provision for Part 36 offers by a claimant has received general approval; it helps to concentrate the mind of the opponent and gets settlement seriously considered at an earlier stage.

My views on mediation need not be repeated here. They can be found in Chapter 2. There is currently a new direction in the north of England whereby parties in a clinical negligence action have to meet for a round table conference at an appropriate time. This is highly desirable. No mediator is necessary. The experienced lawyers for each side will sit down to negotiate and very likely come up with a settlement. This is what I have always argued for. It may well be that such a direction will be extended across the country in due course. Although not strictly within the purview of this book, I would add that the powers the court now has to impose periodical payments has changed the whole scenario for what we have heretofore called structured settlements. It has put the claimant in a much stronger position, in that no discount need now be given to the NHSLA for agreeing to fund a structure. We are likely to see more settlements which are based and calculated on the annual needs of a claimant.

Whatever the future holds, we still need to ensure that the rule-makers allow justice to whisper as persuasively in their ear as Mammon, so that clear and provable medical negligence resulting in substantive injury attracts reasonable compensation by way of claims properly investigated and presented. At the same time, those who act for claimants, both lawyers and experts, need to ensure that they do not bolster weak claims with specious argument, battering their experts about the ears until they manage to discern a case, just as those who defend patients' claims must do so fairly and honourably. And let neither faction stoop to the hackneyed oratory of the demagogue (one may say, tautologically, the politician), the one side condemning all doctors as uncaring and unwilling to be accountable, the other condemning all lawyers, and patients who bring claims, as money-grubbers.

Meanwhile we can hope that the various moves that have been and continue to be made to put the medical profession's house in order (eg risk management strategies, appropriate monitoring of Trust performance and of individual doctors by the NHS and by the GMC, and quick reaction to problem areas) will mean that fewer patients will have legitimate complaints.

Appendix I

Statutes, Regulations and Rules

Contents

[See Appendix II for protocol for instruction of experts.]

1. DAMAGES*

Law Reform (Personal Injuries) Act 1948 (11 & 12 Geo 6 c 41)

2. *Measure of damages* ...

(4) In an action for damages for personal injuries (including any such action arising out of a contract), there shall be disregarded, in determining the reasonableness of any expenses, the possibility of avoiding those expenses or part of them by taking advantage of facilities available under the National Health Service Act 1977, or the National Health Service (Scotland) Act 1978, or of any corresponding facilities in Northern Ireland.

[NB: there is a growing lobby for the repeal of this section. If ever enacted, this would have the effect of substantially reducing compensation in many cases.]

Administration of Justice Act 1982 (1982 c 53)

Abolition of certain claims for damages etc

Abolition of right to damages for loss of expectation of life

1.–(1) In an action under the law of England and Wales or the law of Northern Ireland for damages for personal injuries –

  (a) no damages shall be recoverable in respect of any loss of expectation of life caused to the injured person by the injuries; but

  (b) if the injured person's expectation of life has been reduced by the injuries, the court, in assessing damages in respect of pain and suffering caused by the injuries, shall take account of any suffering caused or likely to be caused to him by awareness that his expectation of life has been so reduced.

(2) The reference in subsection (1)(a) above to damages in respect of loss of expectation of life does not include damages in respect of loss of income.

Abolition of actions for loss of services etc

2. No person shall be liable in tort under the law of England and Wales or the law of Northern Ireland –

  (a) a husband on the ground only of his having deprived him of the services or society of his wife;

  (b) to a parent (or person standing in the place of a parent) on the ground only of his having deprived him of the services of a child; or

  (c) on the ground only –

  (i) of having deprived another of the services of his menial servant;

  (ii) of having deprived another of the services of his female servant by raping or seducing her; or

  (iii) of enticement of a servant or harbouring a servant.

Fatal Accidents Act 1976

3.–The following sections shall be substituted for sections 1 to 4 of the Fatal Accidents Act 1976 –

'. . .

Bereavement

1A.–(1) An action under this Act may consist of or include a claim for damages for bereavement.

---

*   The sections reproduced are printed as amended, where appropriate

(2) A claim for damages for bereavement shall only be for the benefit –
    (a) of the wife or husband of the deceased; and
    (b) where the deceased was a minor who was never married –
        (i) of his parents, if he was legitimate; and
        (ii) of his mother, if he was illegitimate.

(3) Subject to subsection (5) below, the sum to be awarded as damages under this section shall be £3,500. [£7,500 for deaths from April 1991]

(4) Where there is a claim for damages under this section for the benefit of both the parents of the deceased the sum awarded shall be divided equally between them (subject to any deduction falling to be made in respect of costs not recovered from the defendant).

(5) The Lord Chancellor may by order made by statutory instrument, subject to annulment in pursuance of a resolution of either House of Parliament, amend this section by varying the sum for the time being specified in subsection (3) above.
   . . .'

Claims not surviving death

Exclusion of Law Reform (Miscellaneous Provisions) Act 1934

4.–(1) The following subsection shall be inserted after section 1(1) of the Law Reform (Miscellaneous Provisions) Act 1934 (actions to survive death) –

'(1A) The right of a person to claim under section 1A of the Fatal Accidents Act 1976 (bereavement) shall not survive for the benefit of his estate on his death.'.

(2) The following paragraph shall be substituted for subsection (2)(a) –

'(a) shall not include –
    (i) any exemplary damages;
    (ii) any damages for loss of income in respect of any period after that person's death;'.

Maintenance at public expense to be taken into account in assessment of damages

5. In an action under the law of England and Wales or the law of Northern Ireland for damages for personal injuries (including any such action arising out of a contract) any saving to the injured person which is attributable to his maintenance wholly or partly at public expense in a hospital, nursing home or other institution shall be set off against any income lost by him as a result of his injuries.

2. LIMITATION

Limitation Act 1980 (1980 c 58)

[*The sections reproduced below are printed as amended, where appropriate.*]

An Act to consolidate the Limitations Acts 1939 to 1980. [13th November 1980]

PART I

ORDINARY TIME LIMITS FOR DIFFERENT CLASSES OF ACTION

Time limits under Part I subject to extension or exclusion under Part II

Time limits under Part I subject to extension or exclusion under Part II

1.–(1) This Part of this Act gives the ordinary time limits for bringing actions of the various classes mentioned in the following provisions of this Part.

(2) The ordinary time limits given in this Part of this Act are subject to extension or exclusion in accordance with the provisions of Part II of this Act.

Actions founded on tort

Time limit for actions founded on tort

2. An action founded on tort shall not be brought after the expiration of six years from the date on which the cause of action accrued.

Actions founded on simple contract

Time limit for actions founded on simple contract

5. An action founded on simple contract shall not be brought after the expiration of six years from the date on which the cause of action accrued.

Actions in respect of wrongs causing personal injuries or death

Special time limit for actions in respect of personal injuries

11.–(1) This section applies to any action for damages for negligence, nuisance or breach of duty (whether the duty exists by virtue of a contract or of provision made by or under a statute or independently of any contract or any such provision) where the damages claimed by the plaintiff for the negligence, nuisance or breach of duty consist of or include damages in respect of personal injuries to the plaintiff or any other person.

(1A) This section does not apply to any action brought for damages under section 3 of the Protection from Harrassment Act 1997.

(2) None of the time limits given in the preceding provisions of this Act shall apply to an action to which this section applies.

(3) An action to which this section applies shall not be brought after the expiration of the period applicable in accordance with subsection (4) or (5) below.

(4) Except where subsection (5) below applies, the period applicable is three years from –

    (a) the date on which the cause of action accrued; or

    (b) the date of knowledge (if later) of the person injured.

(5) If the person injured dies before the expiration of the period mentioned in subsection (4) above, the period applicable as respects the cause of action surviving for the benefit of his estate by virtue of section 1 of the Law Reform (Miscellaneous Provisions) Act 1934 shall be three years from –

    (a) the date of death; or

    (b) the date of the personal representative's knowledge;
whichever is the later.

(6) For the purposes of this section 'personal representative' includes any person who is or has been a personal representative of the deceased, including an

executor who has not proved the will (whether or not he has renounced probate) but not anyone appointed only as a special personal representative in relation to settled land; and regard shall be had to any knowledge acquired by any such person while a personal representative or previously.

(7) If there is more than one personal representative, and their dates of knowledge are different, subsection (5)(b) above shall be read as referring to the earliest of those dates.

Actions in respect of defective products

11A.–(1) This section shall apply to an action for damages by virtue of any provision of Part I of the Consumer Protection Act 1987.

(2) None of the time limits given in the preceding provisions of this Act shall apply to an action to which this section applies.

(3) An action in which this section applies shall not be brought after the expiration of the period of ten years from the relevant time, within the meaning of section 4 of the said Act of 1987; and this subsection shall operate to extinguish a right of action and shall do so whether or not that right of action had accrued, or time under the following provisions of this Act had begun to run, at the end of the said period of ten years.

(4) Subject to subsection (5) below, an action to which this section applies in which the damages claimed by the plaintiff consist of or include damages in respect of personal injuries to the plaintiff or any other person for loss of or damage to any property, shall not be brought after the expiration of the period of three years from whichever is the later of –

    (a) the date on which the cause of action accrued; and

    (b) the date of knowledge of the injured person or, in the case of loss of or damage to property, the date of knowledge of the plaintiff or (if earlier) of any person in whom this cause of action was previously vested.

(5) If in a case where the damages claimed by the plaintiff consist of or include damages in respect of personal injuries to the plaintiff or any other person the injured person died before the expiration of the period mentioned in subsection (4) above, that subsection shall have effect as respects the cause of action surviving for the benefit of his estate by virtue of section 1 of the Law Reform (Miscellaneous Provisions) Act 1934 as if for the reference to that period there were substituted a reference to the period of three years from whichever is the later of –

    (a) the date of death; and

    (b) the date of the personal representative's knowledge.

(6) For the purposes of this section 'personal representative' includes any person who is or has been a personal representative of the deceased, including an executor who has not proved the will (whether or not he has renounced probate) but not anyone appointed only as a special personal representative in relation to settled land; and regard shall be had to any knowledge acquired by any such person while a personal representative or previously.

(7) If there is more than one personal representative and their dates of knowledge are different, subsection (5)(b) above shall be read as referring to the earliest of those dates.

(8) Expressions used in this section or section 14 of this Act and in Part I of the Consumer Protection Act 1987 have the same meanings in this section or that section as in that Part; and section 1(1) of that Act (Part I to be construed as enacted for the purpose of complying with the product liability Directive) shall apply for the purpose of construing this section and the following provisions of this Act so far as they relate to any action by virtue of any provision of that Part as it applies for the purpose of construing that part.

Special time limit for actions under Fatal Accidents legislation

12.–(1) An action under the Fatal Accidents Act 1976 shall not be brought if the death occurred when the person injured could no longer maintain an action and recover damages in respect of the injury (whether because of a time limit in this Act or in any other Act, or for any other reason).

Where any such action by the injured person would have been barred by the time limit in section 11 or 11A of this Act, no account shall be taken of the possibility of that time limit being overridden under section 33 of this Act.

(2) None of the time limits given in the preceding provisions of this Act shall apply to an action under the Fatal Accidents Act 1976, but no such action shall be brought after the expiration of three years from –

    (a) the date of death; or

    (b) the date of knowledge of the person for whose benefit the action is brought;

whichever is the later.

(3) An action under the Fatal Accidents Act 1976 shall be one to which sections 28, 33 and 35 of this Act apply, and the application to any such action of the time limit under subsection (2) above shall be subject to section 39; but otherwise Parts II and III of this Act shall not apply to any such action.

Operation of time limit under section 12 in relation to different dependants

13.–(1) Where there is more than one person for whose benefit an action under the Fatal Accidents Act 1976 is brought, section 12(2)(b) of this Act shall be applied separately to each of them.

(2) Subject to subsection (3) below, if by virtue of subsection (1) above the action would be outside the time limit given by section 12(2) as regards one or more, but not all, of the persons for whose benefit it is brought, the court shall direct that any person as regards whom the action would be outside that limit shall be excluded from those for whom the action is brought.

(3) The court shall not give such a direction if it is shown that if the action were brought exclusively for the benefit of the person in question it would not be defeated by a defence of limitation (whether in consequence of section 28 of this Act or an agreement between the parties not to raise the defence, or otherwise).

Definition of date of knowledge for purposes of sections 11 and 12

14.–(1) Subject to subsection (1A) below, in sections 11 and 12 of this Act references to a person's date of knowledge are references to the date on which he first had knowledge of the following facts –

    (a) that the injury in question was significant; and

    (b) that the injury was attributable in whole or in part to the act or omission which is alleged to constitute negligence, nuisance or breach of duty; and

    (c) the identity of the defendant; and

    (d) if it is alleged that the act or omission was that of a person other than the defendant, the identity of that person and the additional facts supporting the bringing of an action against the defendant;

and knowledge that any acts or omissions did or did not, as a matter of law, involve negligence, nuisance or breach of duty is irrelevant.

(1A) In section 11A of this Act and in section 12 of this Act so far as that section applies to an action by virtue of section 6(1)(a) of the Consumer Protection Act 1987 (death caused by defective product) references to a person's date of knowledge are references to the date on which he first had knowledge of the following facts –

(a) such facts about the damage caused by the defect as would lead a reasonable person who had suffered such damage to consider it sufficiently serious to justify his instituting proceedings for damages against a defendant who did not dispute liability and was able to satisfy a judgment; and

(b) that the damage was wholly or partly attributable to the facts and circumstances alleged to constitute the defect; and

(c) the identity of the defendant;

but, in determining the date on which a person first had such knowledge there shall be disregarded both the extent (if any) of that person's knowledge on any date of whether particular facts or circumstances would or would not, as a matter of law, constitute a defect and, in a case relating to loss of or damage to property, any knowledge which that person had on a date on which he had no right of action by virtue of Part I of that Act in respect of the loss or damage.

(2) For the purposes of this section an injury is significant if the person whose date of knowledge is in question would reasonably have considered it sufficiently serious to justify his instituting proceedings for damages against a defendant who did not dispute liability and was able to satisfy a judgment.

(3) For the purposes of this section a person's knowledge includes knowledge which he might reasonably have been expected to acquire –

(a) from facts observable or ascertainable by him; or

(b) from facts ascertainable by him with the help of medical or other appropriate expert advice which it is reasonable for him to seek;

but a person shall not be fixed under this subsection with knowledge of a fact ascertainable only with the help of expert advice so long as he has taken all reasonable steps to obtain (and, where appropriate, to act on) that advice.

Actions in respect of latent damage not involving personal injuries

Special time limit for negligence actions where facts relevant to cause of action are not known at date of accrual

14A.–(1) This section applies to any action for damages for negligence, other than one to which section 11 of this Act applies, where the starting date for reckoning the period of limitation under subsection (4)(b) below falls after the date on which the cause of action accrued.

(2) Section 2 of this Act shall not apply to an action to which this section applies.

(3) An action to which this section applies shall not be brought after the expiration of the period applicable in accordance with subsection (4) below.

(4) That period is either –

(a) six years from the date on which the cause of action accrued; or

(b) three years from the starting date as defined by subsection (5) below, if that period expires later than the period mentioned in paragraph (a) above

(5) For the purposes of this section, the starting date for reckoning the period of limitation under subsection (4)(b) above is the earliest date on which the plaintiff or any person in whom the cause of action was vested before him first had both the knowledge required for bringing an action for damages in respect of the relevant damage and a right to bring such an action.

(6) In subsection (5) above 'the knowledge required for bringing an action for damages in respect of the relevant damage' means knowledge both –

(a) of the material facts about the damage in respect of which damages are claimed; and

(b) of the other facts relevant to the current action mentioned in subsection (8) below.

(7) For the purposes of subsection 6(a) above, the material facts about the

damage are such facts about the damage as would lead a reasonable person who had suffered such damage to consider it sufficiently serious to justify his instituting proceedings for damages against a defendant who did not dispute liability and was able to satisfy a judgment.

(8) The other facts referred to in subsection (6)(b) above are –

(a) that the damage was attributable in whole or in part to the act or omission which is alleged to constitute negligence; and

(b) the identity of the defendant; and

(c) if it is alleged that the act or omission was that of a person other than the defendant, the identity of that person and the additional facts supporting the bringing of an action against the defendant.

(9) Knowledge that any acts or omissions did or did not, as a matter of law, involve negligence is irrelevant for the purposes of subsection (5) above.

(10) For the purposes of this section a person's knowledge includes knowledge which he might reasonably have been expected to acquire –

(a) from facts observable or ascertainable by him; or

(b) from facts ascertainable by him with the help of appropriate expert advice which it is reasonable for him to seek;

but a person shall not be taken by virtue of this subsection to have knowledge of a fact ascertainable only with the help of expert advice so long as he has taken all reasonable steps to obtain (and, where appropriate, to act on) that advice.

Overriding time limit for negligence actions not involving personal injuries

14B.–(1) An action for damages for negligence, other than one to which section 11 of this Act applies, shall not be brought after the expiration of fifteen years from the date (or, if more than one, from the last of the dates) on which there occurred any act or omission –

(a) which is alleged to constitute negligence; and

(b) to which the damage in respect of which damages are claimed is alleged to be attributable (in whole or in part).

(2) This section bars the right of action in a case to which subsection (1) above applies notwithstanding that –

(a) the cause of action has not yet accrued; or

(b) where section 14A of this Act applies to the action, the date which is for the purposes of that section the starting date for reckoning the period mentioned in subsection (4)(b) of that section has not yet occurred;

before the end of the period of limitation prescribed by this section.

PART II

EXTENSION OR EXCLUSION OF ORDINARY TIME LIMITS

Disability

Extension of limitation period in case of disability

28.–(1) Subject to the following provisions of this section, if on the date when any right of action accrued for which a period of limitation is prescribed by this Act, the person to whom it accrued was under a disability, the action may be brought at any time before the expiration of six years from the date when he ceased to be under a disability or died (whichever first occurred) notwithstanding that the period of limitation has expired.

(2) This section shall not affect any case where the right of action first accrued to some person (not under a disability) through whom the person under a disability claims.

(3) When a right of action which has accrued to a person under a disability

accrues, on the death of that person while still under a disability, to another person under a disability, no further extension of time shall be allowed by reason of the disability of the second person.

(4) No action to recover land or money charged on land shall be brought by virtue of this section by any person after the expiration of thirty years from the date on which the right of action accrued to that person or some person through whom he claims.

(4A) If the action is one to which section 4A of this Act applies, subsection(1) above shall have effect –

> (a) in the case of an action for libel or slander, as if for the words from 'at any time' to 'occurred' there were substituted the words 'by him at any time before the expiration of one year from the date on which he ceased to be under a disability'; and
>
> (b) in the case of an action for slander of title, slander of goods or other malicious falsehood, as if for the words 'six years' there were substituted the words 'one year'.

(5) If the action is one to which section 10 of this Act applies, subsection (1) above shall have effect as if for the words 'six years' there were substituted the words 'two years'.

(6) If the action is one to which section 11 or 12(2) of this Act applies, subsection (1) above shall have effect as if for the words 'six years' there were substituted the words 'three years'.

(7) If the action is one to which section 11A of this Act applies or one by virtue of section 6(1)(a) of the Consumer Protection Act 1987 (death caused by defective product), subsection (1) above –

> (a) shall not apply to the time limit prescribed by subsection (3) of the said section 11A or to that time limit as applied by virtue of section 12(1) of this Act; and
>
> (b) in relation to any other time limit prescribed by this Act shall have effect as if for the words 'six years' there were substituted the words 'three years'.

Extension for cases where the limitation period is the period under section 14A(4)(b)

28A.–(1) Subject to subsection (2) below, if in the case of any action for which a period of limitation is prescribed by section 14A of this Act –

> (a) the period applicable in accordance with subsection (4) of that section is the period mentioned in paragraph (b) of that subsection;
>
> (b) on the date which is for the purposes of that section the starting date for reckoning that period the person by reference to whose knowledge that date fell to be determined under subsection (5) of that section was under a disability; and
>
> (c) section 28 of this Act does not apply to the action;

the action may be brought at any time before the expiration of three years from the date when he ceased to be under a disability or died (whichever first occurred) notwithstanding that the period mentioned above has expired.

(2) An action may not be brought by virtue of subsection (1) above after the end of the period of limitation prescribed by section 14B of this Act.

Fraud, concealment and mistake

Postponement of limitation period in case of fraud, concealment or mistake

32.–(1) Subject to subsections (3) and (4A) below, where in the case of any action for which a period of limitation is prescribed by this Act, either –

> (a) the action is based upon the fraud of the defendant; or

(b) any fact relevant to the plaintiff's right of action has been deliberately concealed from him by the defendant; or

(c) the action is for relief from the consequences of a mistake;

the period of limitation shall not begin to run until the plaintiff has discovered the fraud, concealment or mistake (as the case may be) or could with reasonable diligence have discovered it.

References in this subsection to the defendant include references to the defendant's agent and to any person through whom the defendant claims and his agent.

(2) For the purposes of subsection (1) above, deliberate commission of a breach of duty in circumstances in which it is unlikely to be discovered for some time amounts to deliberate concealment of the facts involved in that breach of duty.

(3) Nothing in this section shall enable any action –

(a) to recover, or recover the value of, any property; or

(b) to enforce any charge against, or set aside any transaction affecting, any property;

to be brought against the purchaser of the property or any person claiming through him in any case where the property has been purchased for valuable consideration by an innocent third party since the fraud or concealment or (as the case may be) the transaction in which the mistake was made took place.

(4) A purchaser is an innocent third party for the purposes of this section –

(a) in the case of fraud or concealment of any fact relevant to the plaintiff's right of action, if he was not a party to the fraud or (as the case may be) to the concealment of that fact and did not at the time of the purchase know or have reason to believe that the fraud or concealment had taken place; and

(b) in the case of mistake, if he did not at the time of the purchase know or have reason to believe that the mistake had been made.

(4A) Subsection (1) above shall not apply in relation to the time limit prescribed by section 11A(3) of this Act or in relation to that time limit as applied by virtue of section 12(1) of this Act.

(5) Sections 14A and 14B of this Act shall not apply to any action to which subsection (1)(b) above applies (and accordingly to the period of limitation referred to in that subsection, in any case to which either of those sections would otherwise apply, is the period applicable under section 2 of this Act).

Discretionary exclusion of time limit for actions in respect of personal injuries or death

Discretionary exclusion of time limit for actions in respect of personal injuries or death

33.–(1) If it appears to the court that it would be equitable to allow an action to proceed having regard to the degree to which –

(a) the provisions of section 11 or 11A or 12 of this Act prejudice the plaintiff or any person whom he represents; and

(b) any decision of the court under this subsection would prejudice the defendant or any person whom he represents;

the court may direct that those provisions shall not apply to the action, or shall not apply to any specified cause of action to which the action relates.

(1A) The court shall not under this section disapply –

(a) subsection (3) of section 11A; or

(b) where the damages claimed by the plaintiff are confined to damages for loss of or damage to any property, any other provision in its application to an action by virtue of Part I of the Consumer Protection Act 1987.

(2) The court shall not under this section disapply section 12(1) except where the reason why the person injured could no longer maintain an action was because of the time limit in section 11 or subsection (4) of section 11A.

If, for example, the person injured could at his death no longer maintain an action under the Fatal Accidents Act 1976 because of the time limit in Article 29 in Schedule 1 to the Carriage by Air Act 1961, the court has no power to direct that section 12(1) shall not apply.

(3) In acting under this section the court shall have regard to all the circumstances of the case and in particular to –

    (a) the length of, and the reasons for, the delay on the part of the plaintiff;

    (b) the extent to which, having regard to the delay, the evidence adduced or likely to be adduced by the plaintiff or the defendant is or is likely to be less cogent than if the action had been brought within the time allowed by section 11, by section 11A or (as the case may be) by section 12;

    (c) the conduct of the defendant after the cause of action arose, including the extent (if any) to which he responded to requests reasonably made by the plaintiff for information or inspection for the purpose of ascertaining facts which were or might be relevant to the plaintiff's cause of action against the defendant;

    (d) the duration of any disability of the plaintiff arising after the date of the accrual of the cause of action;

    (e) the extent to which the plaintiff acted promptly and reasonably once he knew whether or not the act or omission of the defendant, to which the injury was attributable, might be capable at that time of giving rise to an action for damages;

    (f) the steps, if any, taken by the plaintiff to obtain medical, legal or other expert advice and the nature of any such advice he may have received.

(4) In a case where the person injured died when, because of section 11 or subsection (4) of section 11A, he could no longer maintain an action and recover damages in respect of the injury, the court shall have regard in particular to the length of, and the reasons for, the delay on the part of the deceased.

(5) In a case under subsection (4) above, or any other case where the time limit, or one of the time limits, depends on the date of knowledge of a person other than the plaintiff, subsection (3) above shall have effect with appropriate modifications, and shall have effect in particular as if references to the plaintiff included references to any person whose date of knowledge is or was relevant in determining a time limit.

(6) A direction by the court disapplying the provisions of section 12(1) shall operate to disapply the provisions to the same effect in section 1(1) of the Fatal Accidents Act 1976.

(7) In this section 'the court' means the court in which the action has been brought.

(8) References in this section to section 11 or 11A include references to that section as extended by any of the preceding provisions of this Part of this Act or by any provision of Part III of this Act.

PART III

MISCELLANEOUS AND GENERAL

New claims in pending actions: rules of court

35.–(1) For the purposes of this Act, any new claim made in the course of any action shall be deemed to be a separate action and to have been commenced –

    (a) in the case of a new claim made in or by way of third party proceedings, on the date on which those proceedings were commenced; and

    (b) in the case of any other new claim, on the same date as the original action.

(2) In this section a new claim means any claim by way of set-off or counterclaim, and any claim involving either –

(a) the addition or substitution of a new cause of action; or

(b) the addition or substitution of a new party;

and 'third party proceedings' means any proceedings brought in the course of any action by any party to the action against a person not previously a party to the action, other than proceedings brought by joining any such person as defendant to any claim already made in the original action by the party bringing the proceedings.

(3) Except as provided by section 33 of this Act or by rules of court, neither the High Court nor any county court shall allow a new claim within subsection (1)(b) above, other than an original set-off or counterclaim, to be made in the course of any action after the expiry of any time limit under this Act which would affect a new action to enforce that claim.

For the purposes of this subsection, a claim is an original set-off or an original counterclaim if it is a claim by way of set-off or (as the case may be) by way of counterclaim by a party who has not previously made any claim in the action.

(4) Rules of court may provide for allowing a new claim to which subsection (3) above applies to be made as there mentioned, but only if the conditions specified in subsection (5) below are satisfied, and subject to any further restrictions the rules may impose.

(5) The conditions referred to in subsection (4) above are the following –

(a) in the case of a claim involving a new cause of action, if the new cause of action arises out of the same facts or substantially the same facts as are already in issue on any claim previously made in the original action; and

(b) in the case of a claim involving a new party, if the addition or substitution of the new party is necessary for the determination of the original action.

(6) The addition or substitution of a new party shall not be regarded for the purposes of subsection (5)(b) above as necessary for the determination of the original action unless either –

(a) the new party is substituted for a party whose name was given in any claim made in the original action in mistake for the new party's name; or

(b) any claim already made in the original action cannot be maintained by or against any existing party unless the new party is joined or substituted as plaintiff or defendant in that action.

(7) Subject to subsection (4) above, rules of court may provide for allowing a party to any action to claim relief in a new capacity in respect of a new cause of action notwithstanding that he had no title to make that claim at the date of the commencement of the action.

This subsection shall not be taken as prejudicing the power of rules of court to provide for allowing a party to claim relief in a new capacity without adding or substituting a new cause of action.

(8) Subsections (3) to (7) above shall apply in relation to a new claim made in the course of third party proceedings as if those proceedings were the original action, and subject to such other modifications as may be prescribed by rules of court in any case or class of case.

(9) [*Repealed*]

Interpretation

38.–(1) In this Act, unless the context otherwise requires –

'action' includes any proceedings in a court of law, including an ecclesiastical court;

'land' includes corporeal hereditaments, tithes and rentcharges and any legal or equitable estate or interest therein, but except as provided above in this definition does not include any incorporeal hereditament;

'personal estate' and 'personal property' do not include chattels real;

'personal injuries' includes any disease and any impairment of a person's physical or mental condition, and 'injury' and cognate expressions shall be construed accordingly;

'rent' includes a rentcharge and a rentservice;

'rentcharge' means any annuity or periodical sum of money charged upon or payable out of land, except a rentservice or interest on a mortgage on land;

'settled land', 'statutory owner' and 'tenant for life' have the same meanings respectively as in the Settled Land Act 1925;

'trust' and 'trustee' have the same meanings respectively as in the Trustee Act 1925; and

(2) For the purposes of this Act a person shall be treated as under a disability while he is an infant, or of unsound mind.

(3) For the purposes of subsection (2) above a person is of unsound mind if he is a person who, by reason of mental disorder *within the meaning of the Mental Health Act 1983, is incapable of managing and administering his property and affairs* [is incapable of managing and administering his property and affairs; and in this section 'mental disorder' has the same meaning as in the Mental Health Act 1983].

(4) Without prejudice to the generality of subsection (3) above, a person shall be conclusively presumed for the purposes of subsection (2) above to be of unsound mind –

> (a)   while he is liable to be detained or subject to guardianship under the Mental Health Act 1983 (otherwise than by virtue of section 35 or 89); and
>
> (b)   while he is receiving treatment [for mental disorder] as an in-patient in any hospital within the meaning of the Mental Health Act 1983 *or mental nursing home within the meaning of the Nursing Homes Act 1975* [or independent hospital or care home within the meaning of the Care Standards Act 2000] without being liable to be detained under the said Act of 1983 (otherwise than by virtue of section 35 or 89), being treatment which follows without any interval a period during which he was liable to be detained or subject to guardianship under the Mental Health Act 1959, or the said Act of 1983 (otherwise than by virtue of section 35 or 89) or by virtue of any enactment repealed or excluded by the Mental Health Act 1959.

(5) Subject to subsection (6) below, a person shall be treated as claiming through another person if he became entitled by, through, under, or by the act of that other person to the right claimed, and any person whose estate or interest might have been barred by a person entitled to an entailed interest in possession shall be treated as claiming through the person so entitled.

(6) A person becoming entitled to any estate or interest by virtue of a special power of appointment shall not be treated as claiming through the appointor.

(7) References in this Act to a right of action to recover land shall include references to a right to enter into possession of the land or, in the case of rentcharges and tithes, to distrain for arrears of rent or tithe, and references to the bringing of such an action shall include references to the making of such an entry or distress.

(8) References in this Act to the possession of land shall, in the case of tithes and rentcharges, be construed as references to the receipt of the tithe or rent, and references to the date of dispossession or discontinuance of possession of land shall, in the case of rentcharges, be construed as references to the date of the last receipt of rent.

(9) References in Part II of this Act to a right of action shall include references to –

> (a)   a cause of action;

(b) a right to receive money secured by a mortgage or charge on any property;

(c) a right to recover proceeds of the sale of land; and

(d) a right to receive a share or interest in the personal estate of a deceased person.

(10) References in Part II to the date of the accrual of a right of action shall be construed –

(a) in the case of an action upon a judgment, as references to the date on which the judgment became enforceable; and

(b) in the case of an action to recover arrears of rent or interest, or damages in respect of arrears of rent or interest, as references to the date on which the rent or interest became due.

[Note: Words in italic repealed and words in square brackets substituted by the Care Standards Act 2000, from a date to be appointed.]

3. CONGENITAL DISABILITIES (CIVIL LIABILITY) ACT 1976

(1976 c 28)

An Act to make provision as to civil liability in the case of children born disabled in consequence of some person's fault; and to extend the Nuclear Installations Act 1965, so that children so born in consequence of a breach of duty under that Act may claim compensation.

[22nd July 1976]

Civil liability to child born disabled

1.–(1) If a child is born disabled as a result of such an occurrence before its birth as is mentioned in subsection (2) below, and a person (other than the child's own mother) is under this section answerable to the child in respect of the occurrence, the child's disabilities are to be regarded as damage resulting from the wrongful act of that person and actionable accordingly at the suit of the child.

(2) An occurrence to which this section applies is one which –

    (a) affected either parent of the child in his or her ability to have a normal, healthy child; or

    (b) affected the mother during her pregnancy, or affected her or the child in the course of its birth, so that the child is born with disabilities which would not otherwise have been present.

(3) Subject to the following subsections, a person (here referred to as 'the defendant') is answerable to the child if he was liable in tort to the parent or would, if sued in time, have been so; and it is no answer that there could not have been such liability because the parent suffered no actionable injury, if there was a breach of legal duty which, accompanied by injury would have given rise to the liability.

(4) In the case of an occurrence preceding the time of conception, the defendant is not answerable to the child if at that time either or both of the parents knew the risk of their child being born disabled (that is to say, the particular risk created by the occurrence); but should it be the child's father who is the defendant, this subsection does not apply if he knew of the risk and the mother did not.

(5) The defendant is not answerable to the child, for anything he did or omitted to do when responsible in a professional capacity for treating or advising the parent, if he took reasonable care having due regard to then received professional opinion applicable to the particular class of case; but this does not mean that he is answerable only because he departed from received opinion.

(6) Liability to the child under this section may be treated as having been excluded or limited by contract made with the parent affected, to the same extent and subject to the same restrictions as liability in the parent's own case; and a contract term which could have been set up by the defendant in an action by the parent, so as to exclude or limit his liability to him or her, operates in the defendant's favour to the same, but no greater, extent in an action under this section by the child.

(7) If in the child's action under this section it is shown that the parent affected shared the responsibility for the child being born disabled, the damages are to be reduced to such extent as the court thinks just and equitable having regard to the extent of the parent's responsibility.

Extension of section 1 to cover infertility treatments

1A.–(1) In any case where –

    (a) a child carried by a woman as the result of the placing in her of an embryo or of sperm and eggs or her artificial insemination is born disabled,

   (b) the disability results from an act or omission in the course of the selection, or the keeping or use outside the body, of the embryo carried by her or of the gametes used to bring about the creation of the embryo, and

   (c) a person is under this section answerable to the child in respect of the act or omission,

the child's disabilities are to be regarded as damage resulting from the wrongful act of that person and actionable accordingly at the suit of the child.

(2) Subject to subsection (3) below and the applied provisions of section 1 of this Act, a person (here referred to as 'the defendant') is answerable to the child if he was liable in tort to one or both of the parents (here referred to as 'the parent or parents concerned') or would, if sued in due time, have been so; and it is no answer that there could not have been such liability because the parent or parents concerned suffered no actionable injury, if there was a breach of legal duty which, accompanied by injury, would have given rise to the liability.

(3) The defendant is not under this section answerable to the child if at the time the embryo, or the sperm and eggs, are placed in the woman or at the time of her insemination (as the case may be) either or both of the parents knew the risk of their child being born disabled (that is to say, the particular risk created by the act or omission).

(4) Subsections (5) to (7) of section 1 of this Act apply for the purposes of this section as they apply for the purposes of that but as if references to the parent or the parents affected were references to the parent or parents concerned.

[Note: Section 1A was inserted by s 44(1) of the Human Fertilisation and Embryology Act 1990.]

Liability of woman driving when pregnant

2. A woman driving a motor vehicle when she knows (or ought reasonably to know) herself to be pregnant is to be regarded as being under the same duty to take care for the safety of her unborn child as the law imposes on her with respect to the safety of other people; and if in consequence of her breach of that duty her child is born with disabilities which would not otherwise have been present, those disabilities are to be regarded as damage resulting from her wrongful act and actionable accordingly at the suit of the child.

Disabled birth due to radiation

3.–(1) Section 1 of this Act does not affect the operation of the Nuclear Installations Act 1965 as to liability for, and compensation in respect of, injury or damage caused by occurrences involving nuclear matter or the emission of ionising radiations.

(2) For the avoidance of doubt anything which –

   (a) affects a man in his ability to have a normal, healthy child; or

   (b) affects a woman in that ability, or so affects her when she is pregnant that her child is born with disabilities which would not otherwise have been present,

is an injury for the purposes of that Act.

(3) If a child is born disabled as the result of an injury to either of its parents caused in breach of a duty imposed by any of sections 7 to 11 of that Act (nuclear site licensees and others to secure that nuclear incidents do not cause injury to persons, etc), the child's disabilities are to be regarded under the subsequent provisions of that Act (compensation and other matters) as injuries caused on the same occasion, and by the same breach of duty, as was the injury to the parent.

(4) As respects compensation to the child, section 13(6) of that Act (contributory fault of person injured by radiation) is to be applied as if the reference there to fault were to the fault of the parent.

(5) Compensation is not payable in the child's case if the injury to the parent

preceded the time of the child's conception and at that time either or both of the parents knew the risk of their child being born disabled (that is to say, the particular risk created by the injury).

Interpretation and other supplementary provisions

4.–(1) References in this Act to a child being born disabled or with disabilities are to its being born with any deformity, disease or abnormality, including predisposition (whether or not susceptible of immediate prognosis) to physical or mental defect in the future.

(2) In this Act –
- (a) 'born' means alive (the moment of a child's birth being when it first has a life separate from its mother), and 'birth' has a corresponding meaning; and
- (b) 'motor vehicle' means a mechanically propelled vehicle intended or adapted for use on roads;

[and references to embryos shall be construed in accordance with section 1 of the Human Fertilisation and Embryology Act 1990.]

(3) Liability to a child under section 1 [or 1A] or 2 of this Act is to be regarded–
- (a) as respects all its incidents and any matters arising or to arise out of it; and
- (b) subject to any contrary context or intention, for the purpose of construing references in enactments and documents to personal or bodily injuries and cognate matters,

as liability for personal injuries sustained by the child immediately after its birth.

(4) No damages shall be recoverable under [any] of those sections in respect of any loss of expectation of life, nor shall any such loss be taken into account in the compensation payable in respect of a child under the Nuclear Installations Act 1965 as extended by section 3, unless (in either case) the child lives for at least 48 hours.

(4A) In any case where a child carried by a woman as the result of the placing in her of an embryo or of sperm and eggs or her artificial insemination is born disabled, any reference in section 1 of this Act to a parent includes a reference to a person who would be a parent but for sections 27 to 29 of the Human Fertilisation and Embryology Act 1990.

(5) This Act applies in respect of births after (but not before) its passing, and in respect of any such birth it replaces any law in force before its passing, whereby a person could be liable to a child in respect of disabilities with which it might be born; but in section 1(3) of this Act the expression 'liable in tort' does not include any reference to liability by virtue of this Act, or to liability by virtue of any such law.

(6) References to the Nuclear Installations Act 1965 are to that Act as amended; and for the purposes of section 28 of that Act (power by Order in Council to extend the Act to territories outside the United Kingdom) section 3 of this Act is to be treated as if it were a provision of that Act.

[Note: Sub-s. (4A) was inserted by s 35 of the Human Fertilisation and Embryology Act 1990, and the words in square brackets in sub-ss (2), (3) and (4) were substituted by s 44 of that Act.]

Crown application

5. This Act binds the Crown.

Citation and extent

6.–(1) This Act may be cited as the Congenital Disabilities (Civil Liability) Act 1976.

(2) This Act extends to Northern Ireland but not to Scotland.

4. THE NATIONAL HEALTH SERVICE

(There is a mass of complex and much amended legislation on the NHS. This is not an encyclopedia, so I have selected just a few passages which I think could be of use and interest in and about the medical negligence action.)

(a) National Health Service Act 1977 (1977 c 49)

An Act to consolidate certain provisions relating to the health service for England and Wales; and to repeal certain enactments relating to the health service which have ceased to have any effect. [29th July 1977]

PART I

SERVICES AND ADMINISTRATION

Functions of the Secretary of State

Secretary of State's duty as to health service

1.–(1) It is the Secretary of State's duty to continue the promotion in England and Wales of a comprehensive health service designed to secure improvement –
>   (a) in the physical and mental health of the people of those countries, and
>   (b) in the prevention, diagnosis and treatment of illness,
and for the purpose to provide or secure the effective provision of services in accordance with this Act.

(2) The services so provided shall be free of charge except in so far as the making and recovery of charges is expressly provided for by or under any enactment, whenever passed.

Secretary of State's general power as to services

2. Without prejudice to the Secretary of State's powers apart from this section, he has power –
>   (a) to provide such services as he considers appropriate for the purpose of discharging any duty imposed on him by this Act; and
>   (b) to do any other thing whatsoever which is calculated to facilitate, or is conducive or incidental to, the discharge of such a duty.
This section is subject to section 3(3) below.

Services generally

3.–(1) It is the Secretary of State's duty to provide throughout England and Wales, to such extent as he considers necessary to meet all reasonable requirements –

(a)   hospital accommodation;

(b)   other accommodation for the purpose of any service provided under this Act;

(c)   medical, dental, nursing and ambulance services;

(d)   such other facilities for the care of expectant and nursing mothers and young children as he considers are appropriate as part of the health service;

(e)   such facilities for the prevention of illness, the care of persons suffering from illness and the after-care of persons who have suffered from illness as he considers appropriate as part of the health service;

(f)   such other services as are required for the diagnosis and treatment of illness.

(2) Where any hospital provided by the Secretary of State in accordance with this Act was a voluntary hospital transferred by virtue of the National Health Service Act 1946, and –

(a)   the character and association of that hospital before its transfer were such as to link it with a particular religious denomination, then

(b)   regard shall be had in the general administration of the hospital to the preservation of that character and those associations.

(3) Nothing in section 2 above or in this section affects the provisions of Part II of this Act (which relates to arrangements with practitioners for the provision of medical, dental, ophthalmic and pharmaceutical services).

High security psychiatric services

4.–(1) The duty imposed on the Secretary of State by section 1 above to provide services for the purposes of the health service includes a duty to provide hospital accommodation and services for persons who are liable to be detained under the Mental Health Act 1983 and in his opinion require treatment under conditions of high security on account of their dangerous, violent or criminal propensities.

(2) The hospital accommodation and services mentioned in subsection (1) above are in this Act referred to as 'high security psychiatric services'.

(3) High security psychiatric services shall be provided only at hospital premises at which services are provided only for the persons mentioned in subsection (1) above; and for this purpose 'hospital premises' means—

(a)   a hospital; or

(b)   any part of a hospital which is treated as a separate unit.

Other services

5.–(1) It is the Secretary of State's duty –

(a)   to provide for the medical inspection at appropriate intervals of pupils in attendance at schools maintained by local education authorities and for the medical treatment of such pupils;

(b)   to arrange, to such extent as he considers necessary to meet all reasonable requirements in England and Wales, for the giving of advice on contraception, the medical examination of persons seeking advice on contraception, the treatment of such persons and the supply of contraceptive substances and appliances.

(1A) It is also the Secretary of State's duty to provide, to such extent as he considers necessary to meet all reasonable requirements –

(a)   for the dental inspection of pupils in attendance at schools maintained by local education authorities;

    (b) for the dental treatment of such pupils; and

    (c) for the education of such pupils in dental health.

(1B) Schedule 1 to this Act shall have effect.

(2) The Secretary of State may –

    (a) provide invalid carriages for persons appearing to him to be suffering from severe physical defect or disability and, at the request of such a person, may provide for him a vehicle other than an invalid carriage (and the additional provisions set out in Schedule 2 to this Act have effect in relation to this paragraph);

    (b) arrange to provide accommodation and treatment outside Great Britain for persons suffering from respiratory tuberculosis;

    (c) provide a microbiological service, which may include the provisions of laboratories, for the control of the spread of infectious diseases and to carry on such other activities as in his opinion can conveniently be carried on in conjunction with that service;

    (d) conduct, or assist by grants or otherwise (without prejudice to the general powers and duties conferred on him under the Ministry of Health Act 1919) any person to conduct research into any matters relating to the causation, prevention, diagnosis or treatment of illness, and into any such other matters connected with any service provided under this Act as he considers appropriate.

(2A) Charges may be made for services or materials supplied by virtue of paragraph (c) of subsection (2) above; and the powers conferred by that paragraph may be exercised both for the purposes of the health service and for other purposes.

(2B) The Secretary of State's function may be performed outside England and Wales, insofar as they relate –

    (a) to holidays for patients

    (b) to the transfer of patients to and from Scotland, Northern Ireland, the Isle of Man or the Channel Islands; or

    (c) to the return of patients who have received treatment in England and Wales to countries or territories outside the British Islands.

(3) *[Repealed]*

(4) The Public Health Laboratory Service Board continues in being for the purpose of exercising such functions with respect to the powers conferred by paragraph (c) of subsection (2) above as the Secretary of State may determine.

(5) The Board shall continue to be constituted in accordance with Part I of Schedule 3 to this Act, and the additional provisions set out in Part II of that Schedule have effect in relation to the Board.

[Note: this section is printed as amended by the Public Health Laboratory Service Act 1979, the Health and Social Security Act 1984 and the Social Security Act 1988.]

(b) National Health Service and Community Care Act 1990 (1990 c 19)

Removal of Crown immunities

60.–(1) Subject to the following provisions of this section, on and after the day appointed for the coming into force of this subsection, no health service body shall be regarded as the servant or agent of the Crown or as enjoying any status, immunity, or privilege of the Crown; and so far as concerns land in which the Secretary of State has an interest, at any time when –

    (a) by virtue of directions under any provision of the National Health Service Act 1977, the Mental Health (Scotland) Act 1984 or the Health and Medicines Act 1988 or by virtue of orders under section 2 or section 10 of the National Health Service (Scotland) Act 1978, powers of disposal or management with respect to the land are conferred on a health service body, or

(b) the land is otherwise held, used or occupied by a health service body,
the interest of the Secretary of State shall be treated for the purposes of any
enactment or rule of law relating to Crown land or interests as if it were an interest held otherwise than by the Secretary of State (or any other emanation of the
Crown).

(2) In Schedule 8 to this Act –

    (a) Part I has the effect to continue certain exemptions for health service
        bodies and property held, used or occupied by such bodies;

    (b) the amendments in Part II have effect, being amendments consequen-
        tial on subsection (1) above; and

    (c) the transitional provisions in Part III have effect in connection with the
        operation of subsection (1) above.

(3) Where, as a result of the provision of subsection (1) above, by virtue of his
employment during any period after the day appointed for the coming into force
of that subsection –

    (a) an employee has contractual rights against a health service body to
        benefits in the event of his redundancy, and

    (b) he also has statutory rights against the health service body under Part
        XI of the Employment Rights Act 1996 (redundancy payments).

any benefits provided to him by virtue of the contractual rights referred to in
paragraph (a) above shall be taken as satisfying his entitlement to benefits under
that Part of that Act.

(4) Nothing in subsection (1) above affects the extent of the expression 'the
services of the Crown' where it appears in –

    (a) Schedule 1 to the Registered Designs Act 1949 (provisions as to the use
        of registered designs for the services of the Crown etc.); and

    (b) sections 55 to 59 of the Patents Act 1977 (use of patented inventions for
        the services of the Crown);

and, accordingly, services provided in pursuance of any power or duty of the
Secretary of State under Part I of the National Health Service Act 1977 or Part I
or Part III of the National Health Service (Scotland) Act 1978 shall continue to be
regarded as included in that expression, whether the services are in fact provided
by a health service body, a National Health Service trust or any other person.

(5) The Secretary of State may by order made by statutory instrument provide
that, in relation to any enactment contained in a local Act and specified in the
order, the operation of subsection (1) above shall be excluded or modified to the
extent specified in the order.

(6) No order shall be made under subsection (5) above unless a draft of it has
been laid before, and approved by a resolution of, each House of Parliament.

(7) In this section 'health service body' means –

    (a) a Health Authority established under section 8 of the National Health
        Service Act 1977;

    (aa) a Special Health Authority established under section 11 of that Act;

    (b) a Health Board or Special Health Board constituted under section 2 of
        the National Health Service (Scotland) Act 1978;

    (c) a State Hospital Management Committee constituted under section
        91 of the Mental Health (Scotland) Act 1984;

    (e) the Common Services Agency for the Scottish Health Service;

    (f) the Dental Practice Board;

    (g) the Scottish Dental Practice Board; and

    (h) the Public Health Laboratory Service Board.

5. DISCOVERY

Supreme Court Act 1981

Powers of High Court exercisable before commencement of action

33.–(1) On the application of any person in accordance with rules of court, the High Court shall, in such circumstances as may be specified in the rules, have power to make an order providing for any one or more of the following matters, that is to say –

    (a)   the inspection, photographing, preservation, custody and detention of property which appears to the court to be property which may become the subject matter of subsequent proceedings in the High Court, or as to which any question may arise in any such proceedings; and

    (b)   the taking of samples of any such property as is mentioned in paragraph (a), and the carrying out of any experiment on or with any such property.

(2) On the application, in accordance with rules of court, of a person who appears to the High Court to be likely to be a party to subsequent proceedings in that court, the High Court shall, in such circumstances as may be specified in the rules, have power to order a person who appears to the court to be likely to be a party to the proceedings and to be likely to have or to have had in his possession, custody or power any documents which are relevant to an issue arising or likely to arise out of that claim –

    (a)   to disclose whether those documents are in his possession, custody or power; and

    (b)   to produce such of those documents as are in his possession, custody or power to the applicant or, on such conditions as may be specified in the order –

       (i)   to the applicant's legal advisers; or

      (ii)   to the applicant's legal advisers and any medical or other professional adviser of the applicant; or

     (iii)   if the applicant has no legal adviser, to any medical or other professional adviser of the applicant.

Power of High Court to order disclosure of documents, inspection of property etc in proceedings for personal injuries or death

34.–(1) [*Repealed*]

(2) On the application, in accordance with rules of court, of a party to any proceedings, the High Court shall, in such circumstances as may be specified in the rules, have power to order a person who is not a party to the proceedings and who appears to the court to be likely to have in his possession, custody or power any documents which are relevant to an issue arising out of the said claim –

    (a)   to disclose whether those documents are in his possession, custody or power; and

    (b)   to produce such of those documents as are in his possession, custody or power to the applicant or, on such conditions as may be specified in the order –

       (i)   to the applicant's legal advisers; or

      (ii)   to the applicant's legal advisers and any medical or other professional adviser of the applicant; or

     (iii)   if the applicant has no legal adviser, to any medical or other professional adviser of the applicant.

(3) On the application, in accordance with rules of court, of a party to any proceedings, the High Court shall, in such circumstances as may be specified in the rules, have power to make an order providing for any one or more of the following matters, that is to say –

(a)   the inspection, photographing, preservation, custody and detention of property which is not the property of, or in the possession of, any party to the proceedings but which is the subject-matter of the proceedings or as to which any question arises in the proceedings;

(b)   the taking of samples of any such property as is mentioned in paragraph (a) and the carrying out of any experiment on or with any such property.

(4) The preceding provisions of this section are without prejudice to the exercise by the High Court of any power to make orders which is exercisable apart from those provisions.

Provisions supplementary to ss 33 and 34

35.–(1) The High Court shall not make an order under section 33 or 34 if it considers that compliance with the order, if made, would be likely to be injurious to the public interest.

(2) Rules of court may make provision as to the circumstances in which an order under section 33 or 34 can be made; and any rules making such provision may include such incidental, supplementary and consequential provisions as the rule-making authority may consider necessary or expedient.

(3) Without prejudice to the generality of subsection (2), rules of court shall be made for the purpose of ensuring that the costs of and incidental to proceedings for an order under section 33(2) or 34 incurred by the person against whom the order is sought shall be awarded to that person unless the court otherwise directs.

(4) Sections 33(2) and 34 and this section bind the Crown; and section 33(1) binds the Crown so far as it relates to property as to which it appears to the court that it may become the subject-matter of subsequent proceedings involving a claim in respect of personal injuries to a person or in respect of a person's death.

In this subsection references to the Crown do not include references to Her Majesty in Her private capacity or to Her Majesty in right of Her Duchy of Lancaster or to the Duke of Cornwall.

(5) In sections 32A, 33 and 34 and this section –

'property' includes any land, chattel or other corporeal property of any description;

'personal injuries' includes any disease and any impairment of a person's physical or mental condition.

6. EVIDENCE

(a) Civil Evidence Act 1995 (1995 c 38)

An Act to provide for the admissibility of hearsay evidence, the proof of certain documentary evidence and the admissibility and proof of official actuarial tables in civil proceedings; and for connected purposes [8th November 1995]

Admissibility of hearsay evidence

Admissibility of hearsay evidence

1.–(1) In civil proceedings evidence shall not be excluded on the ground that it is hearsay.
    (2) In this Act –
        (a) 'hearsay' means a statement made otherwise than by a person while giving oral evidence in the proceedings which is tendered as evidence of the matters stated; and
        (b) references to hearsay include hearsay of whatever degree.
    (3) Nothing in this Act affects the admissibility of evidence admissible apart from this section.
    (4) The provision of sections 2 to 6 (safeguards and supplementary provisions relating to hearsay evidence) do not apply in relation to hearsay evidence admis-

sible apart from this section, notwithstanding that it may also be admissible by virtue of this section.

Safeguards in relation to hearsay evidence

Notice of proposal to adduce hearsay evidence

2.–(1) A party proposing to adduce hearsay evidence in civil proceedings shall, subject to the following provisions of this section, give to the other party or parties to the proceedings –
> (a) such notice (if any) of that fact, and
> (b) on request, such particulars of or relating to the evidence,
as is reasonable and practicable in the circumstances for the purpose of enabling him or them to deal with any matters arising from its being hearsay.

(2) Provision may be made by rules of court –
> (a) specifying classes of proceedings or evidence in relation to which subsection(1) does not apply, and
> (b) as to the manner in which (including the time within which) the duties imposed by that subsection are to be complied with in the cases where it does apply.

(3) Subsection (1) may also be excluded by agreement of the parties; and compliance with the duty to give notice may in any case be waived by the person to whom notice is required to be given.

(4) A failure to comply with subsection (1), or with rules under subsection (2)(b), does not affect the admissibility of the evidence but may be taken into account by the court –
> (a) in considering the exercise of its powers with respect to the course of proceedings and costs, and
> (b) as a matter adversely affecting the weight to be given to the evidence in accordance with section 4.

Power to call witness for cross-examination on hearsay statement

3. Rules of court may provide that where a party to civil proceedings adduces hearsay evidence of a statement made by a person and does not call that person as a witness, any other party to the proceedings may, with the leave of the court, call that person as a witness and cross-examine him on the statement as if he had been called by the first-mentioned party and as if the hearsay statement were his evidence in chief.

Considerations relevant to weighing of hearsay evidence

4.–(1) In estimating the weight (if any) to be given to hearsay evidence in civil proceedings the court shall have regard to any circumstances from which any inference can reasonably be drawn as to the reliability or otherwise of the evidence.

(2) Regard may be had, in particular, to the following –
> (a) whether it would have been reasonable and practicable for the party by whom the evidence was adduced to have produced the maker of the original statement as a witness;
> (b) whether the original statement was made contemporaneously with the occurrence or existence of the matters stated;
> (c) whether the evidence involves multiple hearsay;
> (d) whether any person involved has any motive to conceal or misrepresent matters;
> (e) whether the original statement was an edited account, or was made in collaboration with another or for a particular purpose;
> (f) whether the circumstances in which the evidence is adduced as hearsay are such as to suggest an attempt to prevent proper evaluation of its weight.

Supplementary provisions as to hearsay evidence

Competence and credibility

5.–(1) Hearsay evidence shall not be admitted in civil proceedings if or to the extent that it is shown to consist of, or to be proved by means of, a statement made by a person who at the time he made the statement was not competent as a witness.

For this purpose 'not competent as a witness' means suffering from such mental or physical infirmity, or lack of understanding, as would render a person incompetent as a witness in civil proceedings; but a child shall be treated as competent as a witness if he satisfies the requirements of section 96(2)(a) and (b) of the Children Act 1989 (conditions for reception of unsworn evidence of child).

(2) Where in civil proceedings hearsay evidence is adduced and the maker of the original statement, or of any statement relied upon to prove another statement, is not called as a witness –

    (a) evidence which if he had been so called would be admissible for the purpose of attacking or supporting his credibility as a witness is admissible for that purpose in the proceedings; and

    (b) evidence tending to prove that, whether before or after he made the statement, he made any other statement inconsistent with it is admissible for the purpose of showing that he had contradicted himself.

Provided that evidence may not be given of any matter of which, if he had been called as a witness and had denied that matter in cross-examination, evidence could not have been adduced by the cross-examining party.

Previous statements of witnesses

6.–(1) Subject as follows, the provisions of this Act as to hearsay evidence in civil proceedings apply equally (but with any necessary modifications) in relation to a previous statement made by a person called as a witness in the proceedings.

(2) A party who has called or intends to call a person as a witness in civil proceedings may not in those proceedings adduce evidence of a previous statement made by that person, except –

    (a) with the leave of the court, or

    (b) for the purpose of rebutting a suggestion that his evidence has been fabricated.

This shall not be construed as preventing a witness statement (that is, a written statement of oral evidence which a party to the proceedings intends to lead) from being adopted by a witness in giving evidence or treated as his evidence.

(3) Where in the case of civil proceedings section 3, 4 or 5 of the Criminal Procedure Act 1865 applies, which make provision as to –

    (a) how far a witness may be discredited by the party producing him,

    (b) the proof of contradictory statements made by a witness, and

    (c) cross-examination as to previous statements in writing,

this Act does not authorise the adducing of evidence of a previous inconsistent or contradictory statement otherwise than in accordance with those sections.

This is without prejudice to any provision made by rules of court under section 3 above (power to call witness for cross-examination on hearsay statement).

(4) Nothing in this Act affects any of the rules of law as to the circumstances in which, where a person called as a witness in civil proceedings is cross-examined on a document used by him to refresh his memory, that document may be made evidence in the proceedings.

(5) Nothing in this section shall be construed as preventing a statement of any description referred to above from being admissible by virtue of section 1 as evidence of the matters stated.

Evidence formerly admissible at common law

7.–(1) The common law rule effectively preserved by section 9(1) and (2)(a) of the Civil Evidence Act 1968 (admissibility of admissions adverse to a party) is superseded by the provisions of this Act.

(2) The common law rules effectively preserved by section 9(1) and (2)(b) to (d) of the Civil Evidence Act 1968, that is, any rule of law whereby in civil proceedings –

    (a) published works dealing with matters of a public nature (for example, histories, scientific works, dictionaries and maps) are admissible as evidence of facts of a public nature stated in them,

    (b) public documents (for example, public registers, and returns made under public authority with respect to matters of public interest) are admissible as evidence of facts stated in them, or

    (c) records (for example, the records of certain courts, treaties, Crown grants, pardons and commissions) are admissible as evidence of facts stated in them,

shall continue to have effect.

(3) The common law rules effectively preserved by section 9(3) and (4) of the Civil Evidence Act 1968, that is, any rule of law whereby in civil proceedings –

    (a) evidence of a person's reputation is admissible for the purpose of proving his good or bad character, or

    (b) evidence of reputation or family tradition is admissible –

        (i) for the purpose of proving or disproving pedigree or the existence of a marriage, or

        (ii) for the purpose of proving or disproving the existence of any public or general right or of identifying any person or thing,

shall continue to have effect in so far as they authorise the court to treat such evidence as proving or disproving that matter.

Where any such rule applies, reputation or family tradition shall be treated for the purposes of this Act as a fact and not as a statement or multiplicity of statements about the matter in question.

(4) The words in which a rule of law mentioned in this section is described are intended only to identify the rule and shall not be construed as altering it in any way.

Proof of statements contained in documents

8.–(1) Where a statement contained in a document is admissible as evidence in civil proceedings, it may be proved –

    (a) by the production of that document, or

    (b) whether or not that document is still in existence, by the production of a copy of that document or of the material part of it,

authenticated in such manner as the court may approve.

(2) It is immaterial for this purpose how many removes there are between a copy and the original.

Proof of records of business or public authority

9.–(1) A document which is shown to form part of the records of a business or public authority may be received in evidence in civil proceedings without further proof.

(2) A document shall be taken to form part of the records of a business or public authority if there is produced to the court a certificate to that effect signed by an officer of the business or authority to which the records belong.

For this purpose –

    (a) a document purporting to be a certificate signed by an officer of a business or public authority shall be deemed to have been duly given by such an officer and signed by him; and

(b) a certificate shall be treated as signed by a person if it purports to bear a facsimile of his signature.

(3) The absence of an entry in the records of a business or public authority may be proved in civil proceedings by affidavit of an officer of the business or authority to which the records belong.

(4) In this section –

'records' means records in whatever form;

'business' includes any activity regularly carried on over a period of time, whether for profit or not, by any body (whether corporate or not) or by an individual;

'officer' includes any person occupying a responsible position in relation to the relevant activities of the business or public authority or in relation to its records; and

'public authority' includes any public or statutory undertaking, any government department and any person holding office under Her Majesty.

(5) The court may, having regard to the circumstances of the case, direct that all or any of the above provisions of this section do not apply in relation to a particular document or record, or description of documents or records.

Admissibility and proof of Ogden Tables

[**10.**–(1) The actuarial tables (together with explanatory notes) for use in personal injury and fatal accident cases issued from time to time by the Government Actuary's Department are admissible in evidence for the purpose of assessing, in an action for personal injury, the sum to be awarded as general damages for future pecuniary loss.

(2) They may be proved by the production of a copy published by Her Majesty's Stationery Office.

(3) For the purposes of this section –

(a) 'personal injury' includes any disease and any impairment of a person's physical or mental condition; and

(b) 'action for personal injury' includes an action brought by virtue of the Law Reform (Miscellaneous Provisions) Act 1934 or the Fatal Accidents Act 1976.]

[Note: Section 10 is not yet in force.]

General

Meaning of 'civil proceedings'

11. In this Act 'civil proceedings' means civil proceedings, before any tribunal, in relation to which the strict rules of evidence apply, whether as a matter of law or by agreement of the parties.

References to 'the court' and 'rules of court' shall be construed accordingly.

Provisions as to rules of court

12.–(1) Any power to make rules of court regulating the practice or procedure of the court in relation to civil proceedings includes power to make such provision as may be necessary or expedient for carrying into effect the provisions of this Act.

(2) Any rules of court made for the purposes of this Act as it applies in relation to proceedings in the High court apply, except in so far as their operation is excluded by agreement, to arbitration proceedings to which this Act applies, subject to such modifications as may be appropriate.

Any question arising as to what modifications are appropriate shall be determined, in default of agreement, by the arbitrator or umpire, as the case may be.

Interpretation

13. In this Act –

'civil proceedings' has the meaning given by section 11 and 'court' and 'rules of court' shall be construed in accordance with that section;

'document' means anything in which information of any description is recorded, and 'copy', in relation to a document, means anything onto which information recorded in the document has been copied, by whatever means and whether directly or indirectly;

'hearsay' shall be construed in accordance with section 1(2);

'oral evidence' includes evidence which, by reason of a defect of speech or hearing, a person called as a witness gives in writing or by signs;

'the original statement', in relation to hearsay evidence, means the under-lying statement (if any) by –

   (a) in the case of evidence of fact, a person having personal knowledge of that fact, or

   (b) in the case of evidence of opinion, the person whose opinion it is; and

'statement' means any representation of fact or opinion, however made.

Savings

14.–(1) Nothing in this Act affects the exclusion of evidence on grounds other than that it is hearsay.

This applies whether the evidence falls to be excluded in pursuance of any enactment or rule of law, for failure to comply with rules of court or an order of the court, or otherwise.

(2) Nothing in this Act affects the proof of documents by means other than those specified in section 8 or 9.

(3) Nothing in this act affects the operation of the following enactments –

   (a) section 2 of the Documentary Evidence Act 1868 (mode of proving certain official documents);

   (b) section 2 of the Documentary Evidence Act 1882 (documents printed under the superintendence of Stationery Office);

   (c) section 1 of the Evidence (Colonial Statutes) Act 1907 (proof of statutes of certain legislatures);

   (d) section 1 of the Evidence (Foreign Dominion and Colonial Documents) Act 1933 (proof and effect of registers and official certificates of certain countries);

   (e) section 5 of the Oaths and Evidence (Overseas Authorities and Countries) Act 1963 (provision in respect of public registers of other countries).

Consequential amendments and repeals

15.–(1) The enactments specified in Schedule 1 are amended in accordance with that Schedule, the amendments being consequential on the provisions of this Act.

(2) The enactments specified in Schedule 2 are repealed to the extent specified.

Short title, commencement and extent

16.–(1) This Act may be cited as the Civil Evidence Act 1995.

(2) The provisions of this Act come into force on such day as the Lord Chancellor may appoint by order made by statutory instrument, and different days may be appointed for different provisions and for different purposes.

(3) Subject to subsection (3A), the provisions of this Act shall not apply in relation to proceedings begun before commencement.

(3A) Transitional provisions for the application of the provisions of the Act to proceedings begun before commencement may be made by rules of court or practice directions.

(4) This Act extends to England and Wales.

(5) *Section 10 (admissibility and proof of Ogden Tables) also extends to Northern Ireland.*

As it extends to Northern Ireland, the following shall be substituted for subsection (3)(b) –

'*(b) 'action for personal injury' includes an action brought by virtue of the Law Reform (Miscellaneous Provisions) (Northern Ireland) Act 1937 or the Fatal Accidents (Northern Ireland) Order 1977.*

(6) The provisions of Schedules 1 and 2 (consequential amendments and repeals) have the same extent as the enactments respectively amended or repealed.

[Note: Sub-s (5) repealed with savings by the Civil Evidence (Northern Ireland) Order 1997, SI 1997/2983, art 13(2), Sch 2.]

(b) Civil Evidence Act 1972 (1972 c 30)

[*The sections reproduced below are printed as amended, where appropriate.*]

An Act to make, for civil proceedings in England and Wales, provision as to the admissibility in evidence of statements of opinion and the reception of expert evidence; and to facilitate proof in such proceedings of any law other than that of England and Wales.   [12th June 1972]

Application of Part I of Civil Evidence Act 1968 to statements of opinion

1. [*Repealed*]

Rules of court with respect to expert reports and oral expert evidence

2.–(1) [*Repealed*]

(2) [*Repealed*]

(3) Notwithstanding any enactment or rule of law by virtue of which documents prepared for the purpose of pending or contemplated civil proceedings or in connection with the obtaining or giving of legal advice are in certain circumstances privileged from disclosure, provision may be made by rules of court –

   (a)   for enabling the court in any civil proceedings to direct, with respect to medical matters or matters of any other class which may be specified in the direction, that the parties or some of them shall each by such date as may be so specified (or such later date as may be permitted or agreed in accordance with the rules) disclose to the other or others in the form of one or more expert reports the expert evidence on matters of that class which he proposed to adduce as part of his case at the trial; and

   (b)   for prohibiting a party who fails to comply with a direction given in any such proceedings under rules of court made by virtue of paragraph (a) above from adducing in evidence, except with the leave of the court, any statement (whether of fact or opinion) contained in any expert report whatsoever in so far as that statement deals with matters of any class specified in the direction.

(4) Provision may be made by rules of court as to the conditions subject to which oral expert evidence may be given in civil proceedings.

(5) Without prejudice to the generality of subsection (4) above, rules of court made in pursuance of that subsection may make provision for prohibiting a party who fails to comply with a direction given as mentioned in subsection (3)(b) above from adducing, except with the leave of the court, any oral expert evidence whatsoever with respect to matters of any class specified in the direction.

(6) Any rules of court made in pursuance of this section may make different provision for different classes of cases, for expert reports dealing with matters of different classes, and for other different circumstances.

(7) References in this section to an expert report are references to a written report by a person dealing wholly or mainly with matters on which he is (or would if living be) qualified to give expert evidence.

(8) Nothing in the foregoing provisions of this section shall prejudice the generality of section 75 of the County Courts Act 1984, section 144 of the Magistrates' Courts Act 1980 or any other enactment conferring power to make rules of court; and nothing in section 75(2) of the County Courts Act 1984 or any other enactment restricting the matters with respect to which rules of court may be made shall prejudice the making of rules of court in pursuance of this section or the operation of any rules of court so made.

Admissibility of expert opinion and certain expressions of non-expert opinion

3.–(1) Subject to any rules of court made in pursuance of this Act, where a person is called as a witness in any civil proceedings, his opinion on any relevant matter on which he is qualified to give expert evidence shall be admissible in evidence.

(2) It is hereby declared that where a person is called as a witness in any civil proceedings, a statement of opinion by him on any relevant matter on which he is not qualified to give expert evidence, if made as a way of conveying relevant facts personally perceived by him, is admissible as evidence of what he perceived.

(3) In this section 'relevant matter' includes an issue in the proceedings in question.

Interpretation, application to arbitrations etc, and savings

5.–(1) In this Act 'civil proceedings' means civil proceedings, before any tribunal, in relation to which the strict rules of evidence apply, whether as a matter of law or by agreement, of the parties; and references to 'the court' shall be construed accordingly.

(2) The rules of court made for the purposes of the application of sections 2 and 4 of this Act to proceedings in the High Court apply, except in so far as their application is excluded by agreement, to proceedings before tribunals other than the ordinary courts of law, subject to such modifications as may be appropriate.

Any question arising as to what modifications are appropriate shall be determined, in default of agreement, by the tribunal.

(3) Nothing in this Act shall prejudice –

(a) any power of a court, in any civil proceedings, to exclude evidence (whether by preventing questions from being put or otherwise) at its discretion; or

(b) the operation of any agreement (whenever made) between the parties to any civil proceedings as to the evidence which is to be admissible (whether generally or for any particular purpose) in those proceedings.

Short title, extent and commencement

6.–(1) This Act may be cited as the Civil Evidence Act 1972.

(2) This Act shall not extend to Scotland or Northern Ireland.

(3) This Act, except sections 4(2) to (5) shall come into force on 1 January 1973, and sections 4(2) to (5) shall come into force on such day as the Lord Chancellor may by order made by statutory instrument appoint; and different days may be so appointed for different purposes or for the same purposes in relation to different courts or proceedings or otherwise in relation to different circumstances.

7. CIVIL PROCEDURE RULES

. . .

Part 1

Overriding Objective

. . .

1.1 The overriding objective

(1) These Rules are a new procedural code with the overriding objective of enabling the court to deal with cases justly.

(2) Dealing with a case justly includes, so far as is practicable –

    (a) ensuring that the parties are on an equal footing;

    (b) saving expense;

    (c) dealing with the case in ways which are proportionate –

        (i)   to the amount of money involved;

        (ii) to the importance of the case;

        (iii) to the complexity of the issues; and

        (iv) to the financial position of each party;

    (d) ensuring that it is dealt with expeditiously and fairly; and

    (e) allotting to it an appropriate share of the court's resources, while taking into account the need to allot resources to other cases.

1.2 Application by the court of the overriding objective

The court must seek to give effect to the overriding objective when it –

    (a) exercises any power given to it by the Rules; or

    (b) interprets any rule.

1.3 Duty of the parties

The parties are required to help the court to further the overriding objective.

1.4 Court's duty to manage cases

(1) The court must further the overriding objective by actively managing cases.

(2) Active case management includes –

    (a) encouraging the parties to co-operate with each other in the conduct of the proceedings;

    (b) identifying the issues at an early stage;

    (c) deciding promptly which issues need full investigation and trial and accordingly disposing summarily of the others;

    (d) deciding the order in which issues are to be resolved;

    (e) encouraging the parties to use an alternative dispute resolution[GL] procedure if the court considers that appropriate and facilitating the use of such procedure;

    (f) helping the parties to settle the whole or part of the case;

    (g) fixing timetables or otherwise controlling the progress of the case;

    (h) considering whether the likely benefits of taking a particular step justify the cost of taking it;

    (i) dealing with as many aspects of the case as it can on the same occasion;

    (j) dealing with the case without the parties needing to attend at court;

    (k) making use of technology; and

    (l) giving directions to ensure that the trial of a case proceeds quickly and efficiently.

Part 3

The Court's Case Management Powers

. . .

3.4 Power to strike out a statement of case

(1) In this rule and rule 3.5, reference to a statement of case includes reference to part of a statement of case.

(2) The court may strike out[(GL)] a statement of case if it appears to the court –

   (a) that the statement of case discloses no reasonable grounds for bringing or defending the claim;

   (b) that the statement of case is an abuse of the court's process or is otherwise likely to obstruct the just disposal of the proceedings; or

   (c) that there has been a failure to comply with a rule, practice direction or court order.

(3) When the court strikes out a statement of case it may make any consequential order it considers appropriate.

(4) Where –

   (a) the court has struck out a claimant's statement of case;

   (b) the claimant has been ordered to pay costs to the defendant; and

   (c) before the claimant pays those costs, he starts another claim against the same defendant, arising out of facts which are the same or substantially the same as those relating to the claim in which the statement of case was struck out,

the court may, on the application of the defendant, stay[(GL)] that other claim until the costs of the first claim have been paid.

(5) Paragraph (2) does not limit any other power of the court to strike out[(GL)] a statement of case.

3.8 Sanctions have effect unless defaulting party obtains relief

(1) Where a party has failed to comply with a rule, practice direction or court order, any sanction for failure to comply imposed by the rule, practice direction or court order has effect unless the party in default applies for and obtains relief from the sanction.

(Rule 3.9 sets out the circumstances which the court may consider on an application to grant relief from a sanction.)

(2) Where the sanction is the payment of costs, the party in default may only obtain relief by appealing against the order for costs.

(3) Where a rule, practice direction or court order –

   (a) requires a party to do something within a specified time, and

   (b) specifies the consequence of failure to comply,

the time for doing the act in question may not be extended by agreement between the parties.

3.9 Relief from sanctions

(1) On an application for relief from any sanction imposed for a failure to comply with any rule, practice direction or court order the court will consider all the circumstances including –

   (a) the interests of the administration of justice;

   (b) whether the application for relief has been made promptly;

   (c) whether the failure to comply was intentional;

   (d) whether there is a good explanation for the failure;

   (e) the extent to which the party in default has complied with other rules, practice directions, court orders and any relevant pre-action protocol[(GL)];

(f) whether the failure to comply was caused by the party or his legal representative;

(g) whether the trial date or the likely trial date can still be met if relief is granted;

(h) the effect which the failure to comply had on each party; and

(i) the effect which the granting of relief would have on each party.

(2) An application for relief must be supported by evidence.

3.10 General power of the court to rectify matters where there has been an error of procedure

Where there has been an error of procedure such as a failure to comply with a rule or practice direction –

(a) the error does not invalidate any step taken in the proceedings unless the court so orders; and

(b) the court may make an order to remedy the error.

. . .

Part 7

How to Start Proceedings – The Claim Form

. . .

7.2 How to start proceedings

(1) Proceedings are started when the court issues a claim form at the request of the claimant.

(2) A claim form is issued on the date entered on the form by the court.

(A person who seeks a remedy from the court before proceedings are started or in relation to proceedings which are taking place, or will take place, in another jurisdiction must make an application under Part 23.)

(Part 16 sets out what the claim form must include.)

[(The costs practice direction sets out the information about a funding arrangement to be provided with the claim form where the claimant intends to seek to recover an additional liability).

("Funding arrangements" and "additional liability" are defined in rule 43.2).]

. . .

7.4 Particulars of claim

(1) Particulars of claim must –

(a) be contained in or served with the claim form; or

(b) subject to paragraph (2) be served on the defendant by the claimant within 14 days after service of the claim form.

(2) Particulars of claim must be served on the defendant no later than the latest time for serving a claim form.

(Rule 7.5 sets out the latest time for serving a claim form.)

(3) Where the claimant serves particulars of claim separately from the claim form in accordance with paragraph (1)(b), he must, within 7 days of service on the defendant, file a copy of the particulars together with a certificate of service.

(Part 16 sets out what the particulars of claim must include.)

(Part 22 requires particulars of claim to be verified by a statement of truth.)

(Rule 6.10 makes provision for a certificate of service.)

7.5 Service of a claim form

(1) After a claim form has been issued, it must be served on the defendant.

(2) The general rule is that a claim form must be served within 4 months after the date of issue.

(3) The period for service is 6 months where the claim form is to be served out of the jurisdiction.

7.6 Extension of time for serving a claim form

(1) The claimant may apply for an order extending the period within which the claim form may be served.

(2) The general rule is that an application to extend the time for service must be made –

    (a) within the period for serving the claim form specified by rule 7.5; or

    (b) where an order has been made under this rule, within the period for service specified by that order.

(3) If the claimant applies for an order to extend the time for service of the claim form after the end of the period specified by rule 7.5 or by an order made under this rule, the court may make such an order only if –

    (a) the court has been unable to serve the claim form; or

    (b) the claimant has taken all reasonable steps to serve the claim form but has been unable to do so; and

    (c) in either case, the claimant has acted promptly in making the application.

(4) An application for an order extending the time for service –

    (a) must be supplied by evidence; and

    (b) may be made without notice.

. . .

Part 15

Defence and Reply

. . .

15.2 Filing a defence

A defendant who wishes to defend all or part of a claim must file a defence. (Part 14 contains further provisions which apply where the defendant admits a claim.)

15.3 Consequence of not filing a defence

If a defendant fails to file a defence, the claimant may obtain default judgment if Part 12 allows it.

15.4 The period for filing a defence

(1) The general rule is that the period for filing a defence is –

    (a) 14 days after service of the particulars of claim; or

    (b) if the defendant files an acknowledgment of service under Part 10, 28 days after service of the particulars of claim.

(Rule 7.4 provides for the particulars of claim to be contained in or served with the claim form or served within 14 days of service of the claim form.)

(2) The general rule is subject to the following rules –

    (a) rule 6.23 (which specifies how the period for filing a defence is calculated where the claim form is served out of the jurisdiction);

    (b) rule 11 (which provides that, where the defendant makes an application disputing the court's jurisdiction, he need not file a defence before the hearing);

    (c)   rule 24.4(2) (which provides that, if the claimant applies for summary judgment before the defendant has filed a defence, the defendant need not file a defence before the summary judgment hearing); and

    (d)   rule 6.16(4) (which requires the court to specify the period for responding to the particulars of claim when it makes an order under that rule).

15.5 Agreement extending the period for filing a defence

(1) The defendant and the claimant may agree that the period for filing a defence specified in rule 15.4 shall be extended by up to 28 days.

(2) Where the defendant and the claimant agree to extend the period for filing a defence, the defendant must notify the court in writing.

. . .

Part 16

Statements of Case

. . .

16.2 Contents of the claim form

(1) The claim form must –

    (a)   contain a concise statement of the nature of the claim;

    (b)   specify the remedy which the claimant seeks;

    (c)   where the claimant is making a claim for money, contain a statement of value in accordance with rule 16.3; and

    (d)   contain such other matters as may be set out in a practice direction.

(1A) In civil proceedings against the Crown, as defined in rule 66.1(2), the claim form must also contain –

    (a)   the names of the government departments and officers of the Crown concerned; and

    (b)   brief details of the circumstances in which it is alleged that the liability of the Crown arose.

(2) If the particulars of claim specified in rule 16.4 are not contained in or are not served with the claim form, the claimant must state on the claim form that the particulars of claim will follow.

(3) If the claimant is claiming in a representative capacity, the claim form must state what that capacity is.

(4) If the defendant is sued in a representative capacity, the claim form must state what that capacity is.

(5) The court may grant any remedy to which the claimant is entitled even if that remedy is not specified in the claim form.

(Part 22 requires a claim form to be verified by a statement of truth.)

[(The costs practice direction sets out the information about a funding arrangement to be provided with the statement of case where the defendant intends to seek to recover an additional liability.)

("Funding arrangement" and "additional liability" are defined in rule 43.2.)]

16.3 Statement of value to be included in the claim form

(1) This rule applies where the claimant is making a claim for money.

(2) The claimant must, in the claim form, state –

    (a)   the amount of money which he is claiming;

    (b)   that he expects to recover –

        (i)   not more than £5,000;

        (ii) more than £5,000 but not more than £15,000; or

        (iii) more than £15,000; or

    (c)   that he cannot say how much he expects to recover.

(3) In a claim for personal injuries, the claimant must also state in the claim form whether the amount which he expects to recover as general damages for pain, suffering and loss of amenity is –

    (a) not more than £1,000; or

    (b) more than £1,000.

(4) In a claim which includes a claim by a tenant of residential premises against his landlord where the tenant is seeking an order requiring the landlord to carry out repairs or other work to the premises, the claimant must also state in the claim form –

    (a) whether the estimated costs of those repairs or other work is –

        (i) not more than £1,000; or

        (ii) more than £1,000; and

    (b) whether the financial value of any other claim for damages is –

        (i) not more than £1,000; or

        (ii) more than £1,000.

(5) If the claim form is to be issued in the High Court it must, where this rule applies –

    (a) state that the claimant expects to recover more than £15,000;

    (b) state that some other enactment provides that the claim may be commenced only in the High Court and specify that enactment;

    (c) if the claim is a claim for personal injuries state that the claimant expects to recover £50,000 or more; or

    (d) state that the claim is to be in one of the specialist High Court lists and state which list.

(6) When calculating how much he expects to recover, the claimant must disregard any possibility –

    (a) that he may recover –

        (i) interest;

        (ii) costs;

    (b) that the court may make a finding of contributory negligence against him;

    (c) that the defendant may make a counterclaim or that the defence may include a set-off; or

    (d) that the defendant may be liable to pay an amount of money which the court awards to the claimant to the Secretary of State for Social Security under section 6 of the Social Security (Recovery of Benefits) Act 1997 (1).

(7) The statement of value in the claim form does not limit the power of the court to give judgment for the amount which it finds the claimant is entitled to.

16.4 Contents of the particulars of claim

(1) Particulars of claim must include –

    (a) a concise statement of the facts on which the claimant relies;

    (b) if the claimant is seeking interest, a statement to that effect and the details set out in paragraph (2);

    (c) if the claimant is seeking aggravated damages[GL] or exemplary damages[GL], a statement to that effect and his grounds for claiming them;

    (d) if the claimant is seeking provisional damages, a statement to that effect and his grounds for claiming them; and

    (e) such other matters as may be set out in a practice direction.

(2) If the claimant is seeking interest he must –

    (a) state whether he is doing so –

        (i) under the terms of a contract;

        (ii) under an enactment and if so which; or

        (iii) on some other basis and if so what that basis is; and

   (b) if the claim is for a specified amount of money, state –
      (i)   the percentage rate at which interest is claimed;
      (ii) the date from which it is claimed;
      (iii) the date to which it is calculated, which must not be later than the
            date on which the claim form is issued;
      (iv) the total amount of interest claimed to the date of calculation; and
      (v)   the daily rate at which interest accrues after that date.
(Part 22 requires particulars of claim to be verified by a statement of truth.)

16.5 Contents of defence

 (1) In his defence, the defendant must state –
      (a) which of the allegations in the particulars of claim he denies;
      (b) which allegations he is unable to admit or deny, but which he requires
           the claimant to prove; and
      (c) which allegations he admits.
 (2) Where the defendant denies an allegation –
      (a) he must state his reasons for doing so; and
      (b) if he intends to put forward a different version of events from that
           given by the claimant, he must state his own version.
 (3) A defendant who –
      (a) fails to deal with an allegation; but
      (b) has set out in his defence the nature of his case in relation to the issue
           to which that allegation is relevant,
shall be taken to require that allegation to be proved.
 (4) Where the claim includes a money claim, a defendant shall be taken to
require that any allegation relating to the amount of money claimed be proved
unless he expressly admits the allegation.
 (5) Subject to paragraphs (3) and (4), a defendant who fails to deal with an allegation shall be taken to admit that allegation.
 (6) If the defendant disputes the claimant's statement of value under rule 16.3
he must –
      (a) state why he disputes it; and
      (b) if he is able, give his own statement of the value of the claim.
 (7) If the defendant is defending in a representative capacity, he must state
what that capacity is.
 (8) If the defendant has not filed an acknowledgment of service under Part 10,
he must give an address for service.
(Part 22 requires a defence to be verified by a statement of truth.)
(Rule 6.5 provides that an address for service must be within the jurisdiction.)

. . .

Part 17

Amendments to Statements of Case

. . .

17.1 Amendments to statements of case

 (1) A party may amend his statement of case at any time before it has been
served on any other party.
 (2) If his statement of case has been served, a party may amend it only –
      (a) with the written consent of all the other parties; or
      (b) with the permission of the court.

(3) If a statement of case has been served, an application to amend it by removing, adding or substituting a party must be made in accordance with rule 19.4.

. . .

(Part 22 requires amendments to a statement of case to be verified by a statement of truth unless the court orders otherwise.)

17.2 Power of court to disallow amendments made without permission

(1) If a party has amended his statement of case where permission of the court was not required, the court may disallow the amendment.

(2) A party may apply to the court for an order under paragraph (1) within 14 days of service of a copy of the amended statement of case on him.

17.3 Amendments to statements of case with the permission of the court

(1) Where the court gives permission for a party to amend his statement of case, it may give directions as to –
    (a) amendments to be made to any other statement of case; and
    (b) service of any amended statement of case.

(2) The power of the court to give permission under this rule is subject to –
    (a) rule 19.1 (change of parties – general);
    (b) rule 19.4 (special provisions about adding or substituting parties after the end of a relevant limitation period[(GL)]); and
    (c) rule 17.4 (amendments of statement of case after the end of a relevant limitation period).

17.4 Amendments to statements of case after the end of a relevant limitation period

(1) This rule applies where –
    (a) a party applies to amend his statement of case in one of the ways mentioned in this rule; and
    (b) a period of limitation has expired under –
        (i) the Limitation Act 1980;
        (ii) the Foreign Limitation Periods Act 1984; or
        (iii) any other enactment which allows such an amendment, or under which such an amendment is allowed.

(2) The court may allow an amendment whose effect will be to add or substitute a new claim, but only if the new claim arises out of the same facts or substantially the same facts as a claim in respect of which the party applying for permission has already claimed a remedy in the proceedings.

(3) The court may allow an amendment to correct a mistake as to the name of a party, but only where the mistake was genuine and not one which would cause reasonable doubt as to the identity of the party in question.

(4) The court may allow an amendment to alter the capacity in which a party claims if the new capacity is one which that party had when the proceedings started or has since acquired.

(Rule 19.5 specifies the circumstances in which the court may allow a new party to be added or substituted after the end of a relevant limitation period[(GL)].)

. . .

Part 18

Further Information

. . .

18.1 Obtaining further information

(1) The court may at any time order a party to –
    (a) clarify any matter which is in dispute in the proceedings; or
    (b) give additional information in relation to any such matter,
whether or not the matter is contained or referred to in a statement of case.

(2) Paragraph (1) is subject to any rule of law to the contrary.

(3) Where the court makes an order under paragraph (1), the party against whom it is made must –
    (a) file his response; and
    (b) serve it on the other parties,
within the time specified by the court.

(Part 22 requires a response to be verified by a statement of truth.)

(Part 53 (defamation) restricts requirements for providing further information about sources of information in defamation claims.)

Part 19

Parties and Group Litigation

. . .

19.4 Procedure for adding and substituting parties

[(1) The court's permission is required to remove, add or substitute a party, unless the claim form has not been served.

(2) An application for permission under paragraph (1) may be made by –
    (a) an existing party; or
    (b) a person who wishes to become a party.

(3) An application for an order under rule 19.2(4) (substitution of a new party where existing party's interest or liability has passed) –
    (a) may be made without notice; and
    (b) must be supported by evidence.

(4) Nobody may be added or substituted as a claimant unless –
    (a) he has given his consent in writing; and
    (b) that consent has been filed with the court.

(4A) The Commissioners for HM Revenue and Customs may be added as a party to proceedings only if they consent in writing.

(5) An order for the removal, addition or substitution of a party must be served on –
    (a) all parties to the proceedings; and
    (b) any other person affected by the order.

(6) When the court makes an order for the removal, addition or substitution of a party, it may give consequential directions about –
    (a) filing and serving the claim form on any new defendant;
    (b) serving relevant documents on the new party; and
    (c) the management of the proceedings.]

19.4A Human Rights

Section 4 of the Human Rights Act 1998

(1) The court may not make a declaration of incompatibility in accordance with section 4 of the Human Rights Act 1998 unless 21 days' notice, or such other period of notice as the court directs, has been given to the Crown.

(2) Where notice has been given to the Crown a Minister, or other person permitted by that Act, shall be joined as a party on giving notice to the court.

(Only courts specified in section 4 of the Human Rights Act 1998 can make a declaration of incompatibility.)

Section 9 of the Human Rights Act 1998

(3) Where a claim is made under that Act for damages in respect of a judicial act –

    (a) that claim must be set out in the statement of case or the appeal notice; and

    (b) notice must be given to the Crown.

(4) Where paragraph (3) applies and the appropriate person has not applied to be joined as a party within 21 days, or such other period as the court directs, after the notice is served, the court may join the appropriate person as a party.

(A practice direction makes provision for these notices.)

19.5 Special provisions about adding or substituting parties after the end of a relevant limitation period

(1) This rule applies to a change of parties after the end of a period of limitation under –

    (a) the Limitation Act 1980;

    (b) the Foreign Limitation Periods Act 1984; or

    (c) any other enactment which allows such a change, or under which such a change is allowed.

(2) The court may add or substitute a party only if –

    (a) the relevant limitation period[(GL)] was current when the proceedings were started; and

    (b) the addition or substitution is necessary.

(3) The addition or substitution of a party is necessary only if the court is satisfied that –

    (a) the new party is to be substituted for a party who was named in the claim form in mistake for the new party;

    (b) the claim cannot properly be carried on by or against the original party unless the new party is added or substituted as claimant or defendant; or

    (c) the original party has died or had a bankruptcy order made against him and his interest or liability has passed to the new party.

(4) In addition, in a claim for personal injuries the court may add or substitute a party where it directs that –

    (a)

        (i) section 11 (special time limit for claims for personal injuries); or

        (ii) section 12 (special time limit for claims under fatal accidents legislation),

        of the Limitation Act 1980 shall not apply to the claim by or against the new party; or

    (b) the issue of whether those sections apply shall be determined at trial.

(Rule 17.4 deals with other changes after the end of a relevant limitation period[(GL)].)

. . .

Part 21

Children and Patients

. . .

21.1 Scope of this Part

(1) This Part –
  (a) contains special provisions which apply in proceedings involving children and patients; and
  (b) sets out how a person becomes a litigation friend.
(2) In this Part –
  (a) "child" means a person under 18; and
  (b) "patient" means a person who by reason of mental disorder within the meaning of the Mental Health Act 1983 is incapable of managing and administering his own affairs.
(Rule 6.6 contains provisions about the service of documents on children and patients.)
(Rule 48.5 deals with costs where money is payable by or to a child or patient.)

21.2 Requirement for litigation friend in proceedings by or against children and patients

(1) A patient must have a litigation friend to conduct proceedings on his behalf.
(2) A child must have a litigation friend to conduct proceedings on his behalf unless the court makes an order under paragraph (3).
(3) The court may make an order permitting the child to conduct proceedings without a litigation friend.
(4) An application for an order under paragraph (3) –
  (a) may be made by the child;
  (b) if the child already has a litigation friend, must be made on notice to the litigation friend; and
  (c) if the child has no litigation friend, may be made without notice.
(5) Where –
  (a) the court has made an order under paragraph (3); and
  (b) it subsequently appears to the court that it is desirable for a litigation friend to conduct the proceedings on behalf of the child, the court may appoint a person to be the child's litigation friend.

21.3 Stage of proceedings at which a litigation friend becomes necessary

(1) This rule does not apply where the court has made an order under rule 21.2(3).
(2) A person may not, without the permission of the court –
  (a) make an application against a child or patient before proceedings have started; or
  (b) take any step in proceedings except –
    (i)   issuing and serving a claim form; or
    (ii) applying for the appointment of a litigation friend under rule 21.6,
until the child or patient has a litigation friend.
(3) If a party becomes a patient during proceedings, no party may take any step in the proceedings without the permission of the court until the patient has a litigation friend.
(4) Any step taken before a child or patient has a litigation friend shall be of no effect unless the court otherwise orders.

21.4 Who may be a litigation friend without a court order

(1) This rule does not apply if the court has appointed a person to be a litigation friend.

(2) A person authorised under Part VII of the Mental Health Act 1983 to conduct legal proceedings in the name of a patient or on his behalf is entitled to be the litigation friend of the patient in any proceedings to which his authority extends.

(3) If nobody has been appointed by the court or, in the case of a patient, authorised under Part VII, a person may act as a litigation friend if he –

    (a) can fairly and competently conduct proceedings on behalf of the child or patient;

    (b) has no interest adverse to that of the child or patient; and

    (c) where the child or patient is a claimant, undertakes to pay any costs which the child or patient may be ordered to pay in relation to the proceedings, subject to any right he may have to be repaid from the assets of the child or patient.

21.5 How a person becomes a litigation friend without a court order

(1) If the court has not appointed a litigation friend, a person who wishes to act as a litigation friend must follow the procedure set out in this rule.

(2) A person authorised under Part VII of the Mental Health Act 1983 must file an official copy[(GL)] of the order or other document which constitutes his authorisation to act.

(3) Any other person must file a certificate of suitability stating that he satisfies the conditions specified in rule 21.4(3).

(4) A person who is to act as a litigation friend for a claimant must file –

    (a) the authorisation; or

    (b) the certificate of suitability,

at the time when the claim is made.

(5) A person who is to act as a litigation friend for a defendant must file –

    (a) the authorisation; or

    (b) the certificate of suitability,

at the time when he first takes a step in the proceedings on behalf of the defendant.

(6) The litigation friend must –

    (a) serve the certificate of suitability on every person on whom, in accordance with rule 6.6 (service on parent, guardian etc), the claim form should be served; and

    (b) file a certificate of service when he files the certificate of suitability.

(Rule 6.10 sets out the details to be contained in a certificate of service.)

. . .

21.10 Compromise etc by or on behalf of child or patient

(1) Where a claim is made –

    (a) by or on behalf of a child or patient; or

    (b) against a child or patient,

no settlement, compromise or payment and no acceptance of money paid into court shall be valid, so far as it relates to the claim by, on behalf of or against the child or patient, without the approval of the court.

(2) Where –

    (a) before proceedings in which a claim is made by or on behalf of, or against a child or patient (whether alone or with any other person) are begun, an agreement is reached for the settlement of the claim; and

    (b) the sole purpose of proceedings on that claim is to obtain the approval of the court to a settlement or compromise of the claim,

the claim must –
  (i) be made using the procedure set out in Part 8 (alternative proce-
       dure for claims); and
  (ii) include a request to the court for approval of the settlement or
       compromise.
(Rule 48.5 contains provisions about costs where money is payable to a child or
patient.)

21.11 Control of money recovered by or on behalf of child or patient

  (1) Where in any proceedings –
  (a) money is recovered by or on behalf of or for the benefit of a child or
       patient; or
  (b) money paid into court is accepted by or on behalf of a child or patient,
       the money shall be dealt with in accordance with directions given by
       the court under this rule and not otherwise.
  (2) Directions given under this rule may provide that the money shall be wholly
or partly paid into court and invested or otherwise dealt with.

. . .

Part 24

Summary Judgment

. . .

24.2 Grounds for summary judgment

The court may give summary judgment against a claimant or defendant on the
whole of a claim or on a particular issue if –
  (a) it considers that –
       (i) that claimant has no real prospect of succeeding on the claim or
            issue; or
       (ii) that defendant has no real prospect of successfully defending the
            claim or issue; and
  (b) there is no other compelling reason why the case or issue should be dis-
       posed of at a trial.
(Rule 3.4 makes provision for the court to strike out[(GL)] a statement of case or part
of a statement of case if it appears that it discloses no reasonable grounds for
bringing or defending a claim.)

. . .

Part 29

The Multi-Track

. . .

29.2 Case management

  (1) When it allocates a case to the multi-track, the court will –
  (a) give directions for the management of the case and set a timetable for
       the steps to be taken between the giving of directions and the trial; or
  (b) fix –
       (i) a case management conference; or
       (ii) a pre-trial review,
or both, and give such other directions relating to the management of the case as
it sees fit.

(2) The court will fix the trial date or the period in which the trial is to take place as soon as practicable.

(3) When the court fixes the trial date or the trial period under paragraph (2), it will –

    (a) give notice to the parties of the date or period; and

    (b) specify the date by which the parties must file a listing questionnaire.

29.3 Case management conference and pre-trial review

(1) The court may fix –

    (a) a case management conference; or

    (b) a pre-trial review,

at any time after the claim has been allocated.

(2) If a party has a legal representative, a representative –

    (a) familiar with the case; and

    (b) with sufficient authority to deal with any issues that are likely to arise,

        must attend case management conferences and pre-trial reviews.

(Rule 3.1(2)(c) provides that the court may require a party to attend the court.)

29.4 Steps taken by the parties

If –

    (a) the parties agree proposals for the management of the proceedings (including a proposed trial date or period in which the trial is to take place); and

    (b) the court considers that the proposals are suitable,

it may approve them without a hearing and give directions in the terms proposed.

29.5 Variation of case management timetable

(1) A party must apply to the court if he wishes to vary the date which the court has fixed for –

    (a) a case management conference;

    (b) a pre-trial review;

    (c) the return of a listing questionnaire under rule 29.6;

    (d) the trial; or

    (e) the trial period.

(2) Any date set by the court or these Rules for doing any act may not be varied by the parties if the variation would make it necessary to vary any of the dates mentioned in paragraph (1).

(Rule 2.11 allows the parties to vary a date by written agreement except where the rules provide otherwise or the court orders otherwise.)

29.6 Pre-trial check list (listing questionnaire)

(1) The court will send the parties a pre-trial check list (listing questionnaire) for completion and return by the date specified in directions given under rule 29.2(3) unless it considers that the claim can be listed for trial without the need for a listing questionnaire.

(2) Each party must file the completed pre-trial check list by the date specified by the court.

(3) If no party files the completed pre-trial checklist by the date specified, the court will order that unless a completed pre-trial checklist is filed within 7 days from service of that order, the claim, defence and any counterclaim will be struck out without further order of the court.

(4) If –

    (a) a party files a completed pre-trial checklist but another party does not;

    (b) a party has failed to give all the information requested by the pre-trial checklist; or

(c) the court considers that a hearing is necessary to enable it to decide what directions to give in order to complete preparation of the case for trial,

the court may give such directions as it thinks appropriate.

29.7 Pre-trial review

If, on receipt of the parties' pre-trial check lists, the court decides –
    (a) to hold a pre-trial review; or
    (b) to cancel a pre-trial review which has already been fixed,
it will serve notice of its decision at least 7 days before the date fixed for the hearing or, as the case may be, the cancelled hearing.

29.8 Setting a trial timetable and fixing or confirming the trial date or week

As soon as practicable after –
    (a) each party has filed a completed pre-trial check list;
    (b) the court has held a listing hearing under rule 29.6(3); or
    (c) the court has held a pre-trial review under rule 29.7,
the court will –
        (i) set a timetable for the trial unless a timetable has already been fixed, or the court considers that it would be inappropriate to do so;
        (ii) fix the date for the trial or the week within which the trial is to begin (or, if it has already done so, confirm that date); and
        (iii) notify the parties of the trial timetable (where one is fixed under this rule) and the date or trial period.

29.9 Conduct of trial

Unless the trial judge otherwise directs, the trial will be conducted in accordance with any order previously made.

. . .

Part 31

Disclosure and Inspection of Documents

31.14 Documents referred to in statements of case etc

(1) A party may inspect a document mentioned in –
    (a) a statement of case;
    (b) a witness statement;
    (c) a witness summary; or
    (d) an affidavit [GL].
    (e) [Revoked].
(2) Subject to rule 35.10(4), a party may apply for an order for inspection of any document mentioned in an expert's report which has not already been disclosed in the proceedings.
(Rule 35.10(4) makes provision in relation to instructions referred to in an expert's report.)

31.15 Inspection and copying of documents

Where a party has a right to inspect a document –
    (a) that party must give the party who disclosed the document written notice of his wish to inspect it;
    (b) the party who disclosed the document must permit inspection not more than 7 days after the date on which he received the notice; and

(c) that party may request a copy of the document and, if he also undertakes to pay reasonable copying costs, the party who disclosed the document must supply him with a copy not more than 7 days after the date
on which he received the request.

(Rules 31.3 and 31.14 deal with the right of a party to inspect a document.)

...

31.16 Disclosure before proceedings start

(1) This rule applies where an application is made to the court under any Act
for disclosure before proceedings have started.

(2) The application must be supported by evidence.

(3) The court may make an order under this rule only where –

  (a) the respondent is likely to be a party to subsequent proceedings;

  (b) the applicant is also likely to be a party to those proceedings;

  (c) if proceedings had started, the respondent's duty by way of standard
disclosure, set out in rule 31.6, would extend to the documents or
classes of documents of which the applicant seeks disclosure; and

  (d) disclosure before proceedings have started is desirable in order to –

    (i)   dispose fairly of the anticipated proceedings;

    (ii) assist the dispute to be resolved without proceedings; or

    (iii) save costs.

(4) An order under this rule must –

  (a) specify the documents or the classes of documents which the respondent must disclose; and

  (b) require him, when making disclosure, to specify any of those documents –

    (i) which are no longer in his control; or

    (ii) in respect of which he claims a right or duty to withhold inspection.

(5) Such an order may –

  (a) require the respondent to indicate what has happened to any documents which are no longer in his control; and

  (b) specify the time and place for disclosure and inspection.

31.17 Orders for disclosure against a person not a party

(1) This rule applies where an application is made to the court under any Act
for disclosure by a person who is not a party to the proceedings.

(2) The application must be supported by evidence.

(3) The court may make an order under this rule only where –

  (a) the documents of which disclosure is sought are likely to support the
case of the applicant or adversely affect the case of one of the other parties to the proceedings; and

  (b) disclosure is necessary in order to dispose fairly of the claim or to save
costs.

(4) An order under this rule must –

  (a) specify the documents or the classes of documents which the respondent must disclose; and

  (b) require the respondent, when making disclosure, to specify any of those
documents –

    (i)   which are no longer in his control; or

    (ii) in respect of which he claims a right or duty to withhold inspection.

(5) Such an order may –

  (a) require the respondent to indicate what has happened to any documents which are no longer in his control; and

  (b) specify the time and place for disclosure and inspection.

...

Part 32

Evidence

. . .

32.1 Power of court to control evidence

(1) The court may control the evidence by giving directions as to –
   (a) the issues on which it requires evidence;
   (b) the nature of the evidence which it requires to decide those issues; and
   (c) the way in which the evidence is to be placed before the court.

(2) The court may use its power under this rule to exclude evidence that would otherwise be admissible.

(3) The court may limit cross-examination[(GL)].

32.2 Evidence of witnesses – general rule

(1) The general rule is that any fact which needs to be proved by the evidence of witnesses is to be proved –
   (a) at trial, by their oral evidence given in public; and
   (b) at any other hearing, by their evidence in writing.

(2) This is subject –
   (a) to any provision to the contrary contained in these Rules or elsewhere; or
   (b) to any order of the court.

32.3 Evidence by video link or other means

The court may allow a witness to give evidence through a video link or by other means.

32.4 Requirement to serve witness statements for use at trial

(1) A witness statement is a written statement signed by a person which contains the evidence which that person would be allowed to give orally.

(2) The court will order a party to serve on the other parties any witness statement of the oral evidence which the party serving the statement intends to rely on in relation to any issues of fact to be decided at the trial.

(3) The court may give directions as to –
   (a) the order in which witness statements are to be served; and
   (b) whether or not the witness statements are to be filed.

32.5 Use at trial of witness statements which have been served

(1) If –
   (a) a party has served a witness statement; and
   (b) he wishes to rely at trial on the evidence of the witness who made the statement, he must call the witness to give oral evidence unless the court orders otherwise or he puts the statement in as hearsay evidence.

(Part 33 contains provisions about hearsay evidence.)

(2) Where a witness is called to give oral evidence under paragraph (1), his witness statement shall stand as his evidence in chief[(GL)] unless the court orders otherwise.

(3) A witness giving oral evidence at trial may with the permission of the court –
   (a) amplify his witness statement; and
   (b) give evidence in relation to new matters which have arisen since the witness statement was served on the other parties.

(4) The court will give permission under paragraph (3) only if it considers that there is good reason not to confine the evidence of the witness to the contents of his witness statement.

(5) If a party who has served a witness statement does not –
    (a) call the witness to give evidence at trial; or
    (b) put the witness statement in as hearsay evidence,
any other party may put the witness statement in as hearsay evidence.

32.6 Evidence in proceedings other than at trial

(1) Subject to paragraph (2), the general rule is that evidence at hearings other than the trial is to be by witness statement unless the court, a practice direction or any other enactment requires otherwise.

(2) At hearings other than the trial, a party may . . . rely on the matters set out in –
    (a) his statement of case; or
    (b) his application notice,
if the statement of case or application notice is verified by a statement of truth.

32.7 Order for cross-examination

(1) Where, at a hearing other than the trial, evidence is given in writing, any party may apply to the court for permission to cross-examine the person giving the evidence.

(2) If the court gives permission under paragraph (1) but the person in question does not attend as required by the order, his evidence may not be used unless the court gives permission.

32.8 Form of witness statement

A witness statement must comply with the requirements set out in the relevant practice direction.
(Part 22 requires a witness statement to be verified by a statement of truth.)

32.9 Witness summaries

(1) A party who –
    (a) is required to serve a witness statement for use at trial; but
    (b) is unable to obtain one,
may apply, without notice, for permission to serve a witness summary instead.

(2) A witness summary is a summary of –
    (a) the evidence, if known, which would otherwise be included in a witness statement; or
    (b) if the evidence is not known, the matters about which the party serving the witness summary proposes to question the witness.

(3) Unless the court orders otherwise, a witness summary must include the name and address of the intended witness.

(4) Unless the court orders otherwise, a witness summary must be served within the period in which a witness statement would have had to be served.

(5) Where a party serves a witness summary, so far as practicable rules 32.4 (requirement to serve witness statements for use at trial), 32.5(3) (amplifying witness statements), and 32.8 (form of witness statement) shall apply to the summary.

32.10 Consequence of failure to serve witness statement or summary

If a witness statement or a witness summary for use at trial is not served in respect of an intended witness within the time specified by the court, then the witness may not be called to give oral evidence unless the court gives permission.

32.11 Cross-examination on a witness statement

Where a witness is called to give evidence at trial, he may be cross-examined on his witness statement whether or not the statement or any part of it was referred to during the witness's evidence in chief[GL].

. . .

32.18 Notice to admit facts

(1) A party may serve notice on another party requiring him to admit the facts, or the part of the case of the serving party, specified in the notice.

(2) A notice to admit facts must be served no later than 21 days before the trial.

(3) Where the other party makes any admission in response to the notice, the admission may be used against him only –

    (a) in the proceedings in which the notice to admit is served; and

    (b) by the party who served the notice.

(4) The court may allow a party to amend or withdraw any admission made by him on such terms as it thinks just.

32.19 Notice to admit or produce documents

(1) A party shall be deemed to admit the authenticity of a document disclosed to him under Part 31 (disclosure and inspection of documents) unless he serves notice that he wishes the document to be proved at trial.

(2) A notice to prove a document must be served –

    (a) by the latest date for serving witness statements; or

    (b) within 7 days of disclosure of the document, whichever is later.

Part 33

Miscellaneous Rules about Evidence

. . .

33.1 Introductory

In this Part –

    (a) "hearsay" means a statement, made otherwise than by a person while giving oral evidence in proceedings, which is tendered as evidence of the matters stated; and

    (b) references to hearsay include hearsay of whatever degree.

33.2 Notice of intention to rely on hearsay evidence

(1) Where a party intends to rely on hearsay evidence at trial and either –

    (a) that evidence is to be given by a witness giving oral evidence; or

    (b) that evidence is contained in a witness statement of a person who is not being called to give oral evidence;

that party complies with section 2(1)(a) of the Civil Evidence Act 1995 by serving a witness statement on the other parties in accordance with the court's order.

(2) Where paragraph (1)(b) applies, the party intending to rely on the hearsay evidence must, when he serves the witness statement –

    (a) inform the other parties that the witness is not being called to give oral evidence; and

    (b) give the reason why the witness will not be called.

(3) In all other cases where a party intends to rely on hearsay evidence at trial, that party complies with section 2(1)(a) of the Civil Evidence Act 1995 by serving a notice on the other parties which –

    (a) identifies the hearsay evidence;

 (b) states that the party serving the notice proposes to rely on the hearsay evidence at trial; and

 (c) gives the reason why the witness will not be called.

(4) The party proposing to rely on the hearsay evidence must –

 (a) serve the notice no later than the latest date for serving witness statements; and

 (b) if the hearsay evidence is to be in a document, supply a copy to any party who requests him to do so.

33.3 Circumstances in which notice of intention to rely on hearsay evidence is not required

Section 2(1) of the Civil Evidence Act 1995 (duty to give notice of intention to rely on hearsay evidence) does not apply –

 (a) to evidence at hearings other than trials;

 [(aa) to an affidavit or witness statement which is to be used at trial but which does not contain hearsay evidence;]

 (b) to a statement which a party to a probate action wishes to put in evidence and which is alleged to have been made by the person whose estate is the subject of the proceedings; or

 (c) where the requirement is excluded by a practice direction.

33.4 Power to call witness for cross-examination on hearsay evidence

(1) Where a party –

 (a) proposes to rely on hearsay evidence; and

 (b) does not propose to call the person who made the original statement to give oral evidence,

the court may, on the application of any other party, permit that party to call the maker of the statement to be cross-examined on the contents of the statement.

(2) An application for permission to cross-examine under this rule must be made not more than 14 days after the day on which a notice of intention to rely on the hearsay evidence was served on the applicant.

33.5 Credibility

(1) Where a party –

 (a) proposes to rely on hearsay evidence; but

 (b) does not propose to call the person who made the original statement to give oral evidence; and

 (c) another party wishes to call evidence to attack the credibility of the person who made the statement,

the party who so wishes must give notice of his intention to the party who proposes to give the hearsay statement in evidence.

(2) A party must give notice under paragraph (1) not more than 14 days after the day on which a hearsay notice relating to the hearsay evidence was served on him.

. . .

Part 35

Experts and Assessors

35.1 Duty to restrict expert evidence

Expert evidence shall be restricted to that which is reasonably required to resolve the proceedings.

35.2 Interpretation

A reference to an "expert" in this Part is a reference to an expert who has been instructed to give or prepare evidence for the purpose of court proceedings.

35.3 Experts – overriding duty to the court

(1) It is the duty of an expert to help the court on the matters within his expertise.

(2) This duty overrides any obligation to the person from whom he has received instructions or by whom he is paid.

35.4 Court's power to restrict expert evidence

(1) No party may call an expert or put in evidence an expert's report without the court's permission.

(2) When a party applies for permission under this rule he must identify –
  (a)   the field in which he wishes to rely on expert evidence; and
  (b)   where practicable the expert in that field on whose evidence he wishes to rely.

(3) If permission is granted under this rule it shall be in relation only to the expert named or the field identified under paragraph (2).

(4) The court may limit the amount of the expert's fees and expenses that the party who wishes to rely on the expert may recover from any other party.

35.5 General requirement for expert evidence to be given in a written report

(1) Expert evidence is to be given in a written report unless the court directs otherwise.

(2) If a claim is on the fast track, the court will not direct an expert to attend a hearing unless it is necessary to do so in the interests of justice.

35.6 Written questions to experts

(1) A party may put to –
  (a)   an expert instructed by another party; or
  (b)   a single joint expert appointed under rule 35.7,
written questions about his report.

(2) Written questions under paragraph (1) –
  (a)   may be put once only;
  (b)   must be put within 28 days of service of the expert's report; and
  (c)   must be for the purpose only of clarification of the report,
  unless in any case,
      (i)   the court gives permission; or
      (ii) the other party agrees.

(3) An expert's answers to questions put in accordance with paragraph (1) shall be treated as part of the expert's report.

(4) Where –
  (a)   a party has put a written question to an expert instructed by another party in accordance with this rule; and
  (b)   the expert does not answer that question,

the court may make one or both of the following orders in relation to the party who instructed the expert –

(i)   that the party may not rely on the evidence of that expert; or

(ii)   that the party may not recover the fees and expenses of that expert from any other party.

35.7 Court's power to direct that evidence is to be given by a single joint expert

(1) Where two or more parties wish to submit expert evidence on a particular issue, the court may direct that the evidence on that issue is to be given by one expert only.

(2) The parties wishing to submit the expert evidence are called "the instructing parties".

(3) Where the instructing parties cannot agree who should be the expert, the court may –

(a)   select the expert from a list prepared or identified by the instructing parties; or

(b)   direct that the expert be selected in such other manner as the court may direct.

35.8 Instructions to a single joint expert

(1) Where the court gives a direction under rule 35.7 for a single joint expert to be used, each instructing party may give instructions to the expert.

(2) When an instructing party gives instructions to the expert he must, at the same time, send a copy of the instructions to the other instructing parties.

(3) The court may give directions about –

(a)   the payment of the expert's fees and expenses; and

(b)   any inspection, examination or experiments which the expert wishes to carry out.

(4) The court may, before an expert is instructed –

(a)   limit the amount that can be paid by way of fees and expenses to the expert; and

(b)   direct that the instructing parties pay that amount into court.

(5) Unless the court otherwise directs, the instructing parties are jointly and severally liable^(GL) for the payment of the expert's fees and expenses.

35.9 Power of court to direct a party to provide information

Where a party has access to information which is not reasonably available to the other party, the court may direct the party who has access to the information to –

(a)   prepare and file a document recording the information; and

(b)   serve a copy of that document on the other party.

35.10 Contents of report

(1) An expert's report must comply with the requirements set out in the relevant practice direction.

(2) At the end of an expert's report there must be a statement that –

(a)   the expert understands his duty to the court; and

(b)   he has complied with that duty.

(3) The expert's report must state the substance of all material instructions, whether written or oral, on the basis of which the report was written.

(4) The instructions referred to in paragraph (3) shall not be privileged^(GL) against disclosure but the court will not, in relation to those instructions –

(a)   order disclosure of any specific document; or

(b)   permit any questioning in court, other than by the party who instructed the expert, unless it is satisfied that there are reasonable grounds to consider the statement of instructions given under paragraph (3) to be inaccurate or incomplete.

35.11 Use by one party of expert's report disclosed by another

Where a party has disclosed an expert's report, any party may use that expert's report as evidence at the trial.

35.12 Discussions between experts

(1) The court may, at any stage, direct a discussion between experts for the purpose of requiring the experts to –
    (a)   identify and discuss the issues in the proceedings; and
    (b)   where possible, reach an agreed opinion on those issues.
(2) The court may specify the issues which the experts must discuss.
(3) The court may direct that following a discussion between the experts they must prepare a statement for the court showing –
    (a)   those issues on which they agree; and
    (b)   those issues on which they disagree and a summary of their reasons for disagreeing.
(4) The content of the discussion between the experts shall not be referred to at the trial unless the parties agree.
(5) Where experts reach agreement on an issue during their discussions, the agreement shall not bind the parties unless the parties expressly agree to be bound by the agreement.

35.13 Consequence of failure to disclose expert's report

A party who fails to disclose an expert's report may not use the report at the trial or call the expert to give evidence orally unless the court gives permission.

35.14 Expert's right to ask court for directions

(1) An expert may file a written request for directions to assist him in carrying out his function as an expert.
(2) An expert must, unless the court orders otherwise, provide a copy of any proposed request for directions under paragraph (1) –
    (a)   to the party instructing him, at least 7 days before he files the request; and
    (b)   to all other parties, at least 4 days before he files it.
(3) The court, when it gives directions, may also direct that a party be served with a copy of the directions.

. . .

Practice direction – experts and assessors

This Practice Direction supplements CPR Part 35

Contents of this Practice Direction

EXPERT EVIDENCE – GENERAL REQUIREMENTS
FORM AND CONTENT OF EXPERT'S REPORTS
INFORMATION
INSTRUCTIONS
QUESTIONS TO EXPERTS
SINGLE EXPERT
ORDERS
[ASSESSORS]

Part 35 is intended to limit the use of oral expert evidence to that which is reasonably required. In addition, where possible, matters requiring expert evidence should be dealt with by a single expert. Permission of the court is always required either to call an expert or to put an expert's report in evidence. There is annexed to this Practice Direction a protocol for the instruction of experts to give evidence in civil claims. Experts and those instructing them are expected to have regard to the guidance contained in the protocol. *(NB: the protocol will be found in this book at Appendix II)*

Expert evidence – general requirements

1.1 It is the duty of an expert to help the court on matters within his own expertise: rule 35.3(1). This duty is paramount and overrides any obligation to the person from whom the expert has received instructions or by whom he is paid: rule 35.3(2).

1.2 Expert evidence should be the independent product of the expert uninfluenced by the pressures of litigation.

1.3 An expert should assist the court by providing objective, unbiased opinion on matters within his expertise, and should not assume the role of an advocate.

1.4 An expert should consider all material facts, including those which might detract from his opinion.

1.5 An expert should make it clear:
   (a) when a question or issue falls outside his expertise; and
   (b) when he is not able to reach a definite opinion, for example because he has insufficient information.

1.6 If, after producing a report, an expert changes his view on any material matter, such change of view should be communicated to all the parties without delay, and when appropriate to the court.

Form and content of expert's reports

2.1 An expert's report should be addressed to the court and not to the party from whom the expert has received his instructions.

2.2 An expert's report must:
   (1) give details of the expert's qualifications;
   (2) give details of any literature or other material which the expert has relied on in making the report;
   (3) contain a statement setting out the substance of all facts and instructions given to the expert which are material to the opinions expressed in the report or upon which those opinions are based;
   (4) make clear which of the facts stated in the report are within the expert's own knowledge;

(5)   say who carried out any examination, measurement, test or experiment which the expert has used for the report, give the qualifications of that person, and say whether or not the test or experiment has been carried out under the expert's supervision;

(6)   where there is a range of opinion on the matters dealt with in the report –
    (a)   summarise the range of opinion, and
    (b)   give reasons for his own opinion;

(7)   contain a summary of the conclusions reached;

(8)   if the expert is not able to give his opinion without qualification, state the qualification; and

(9)   contain a statement that the expert understands his duty to the court, and has complied and will continue to comply with that duty.

2.3   An expert's report must be verified by a statement of truth as well as containing the statements required in paragraph 2.2(8) and (9) above.

2.4   The form of the statement of truth is as follows:
    "I confirm that insofar as the facts stated in my report are within my own knowledge I have made clear which they are and I believe them to be true, and that the opinions I have expressed represent my true and complete professional opinion."

2.5   Attention is drawn to rule 32.14 which sets out the consequences of verifying a document containing a false statement without an honest belief in its truth.
    (For information about statements of truth see Part 22 and the practice direction which supplements it.)

Information

3   Under Rule 35.9 the court may direct a party with access to information which is not reasonably available to another party to serve on that other party a document which records the information. The document served must include sufficient details of all the facts, tests, experiments and assumptions which underlie any part of the information to enable the party on whom it is served to make, or to obtain, a proper interpretation of the information and an assessment of its significance.

Instructions

4   The instructions referred to in paragraph 2.2(3) will not be protected by privilege (see rule 35.10(4)). But cross-examination of the expert on the contents of his instructions will not be allowed unless the court permits it (or unless the party who gave the instructions consents to it). Before it gives permission the court must be satisfied that there are reasonable grounds to consider that the statement in the report of the substance of the instructions is inaccurate or incomplete. If the court is so satisfied, it will allow the cross-examination where it appears to be in the interests of justice to do so.

Questions to experts

5.1   Questions asked for the purpose of clarifying the expert's report (see rule 35.6) should be put, in writing, to the expert not later than 28 days after receipt of the expert's report (see paragraphs 1.2 to 1.5 above as to verification).

5.2   Where a party sends a written question or questions direct to an expert, a copy of the questions should, at the same time, be sent to the other party or parties.

5.3 The party or parties instructing the expert must pay any fees charged by that expert for answering questions put under rule 35.6. This does not affect any decision of the court as to the party who is ultimately to bear the expert's costs.

Single expert

6 Where the court has directed that the evidence on a particular issue is to be given by one expert only (rule 35.7) but there are a number of disciplines relevant to that issue, a leading expert in the dominant discipline should be identified as the single expert. He should prepare the general part of the report and be responsible for annexing or incorporating the contents of any reports from experts in other disciplines.

Orders

6A Where an order requires an act to be done by an expert, or otherwise affects an expert, the party instructing that expert must serve a copy of the order on the expert instructed by him. In the case of a jointly instructed expert, the claimant must serve the order.

Part 36

Offers to Settle and Payments into Court

. . .

36.1 Scope of this Part

(1) This Part contains rules about –
- (a) offers to settle and payments into court; and
- (b) the consequences where an offer to settle or payment into court is made in accordance with this Part.

(2) Nothing in this Part prevents a party making an offer to settle in whatever way he chooses, but if that offer is not made in accordance with this Part, it will only have the consequences specified in this Part if the court so orders.
(Part 36 applies to Part 20 claims by virtue of rule 20.3.)

36.2 Part 36 offers and Part 36 payments – general provisions

(1) An offer made in accordance with the requirements of this Part is called –
- (a) if made by way of a payment into court, "a Part 36 payment";
- (b) otherwise "a Part 36 offer".
(Rule 36.3 sets out when an offer has to be made by way of a payment into court.)
(2) The party who makes an offer is the "offeror".
(3) The party to whom an offer is made is the "offeree".
(4) A Part 36 offer or a Part 36 payment –
- (a) may be made at any time after proceedings have started; and
- (b) may be made in appeal proceedings.
(5) A Part 36 offer or a Part 36 payment shall not have the consequences set out in this Part while the claim is being dealt with on the small claims track unless the court orders otherwise.
(Part 26 deals with allocation to the small claims track.)
(Rule 27.2 provides that Part 36 does not apply to small claims.)

36.2A Personal injury claims for future pecuniary loss

(1) This rule applies to a claim for damages for personal injury which is or includes a claim for future pecuniary loss.

(2) An offer to settle such a claim will not have the consequences set out in this Part unless it is made by way of a Part 36 offer under this rule, and where such an offer is or includes an offer to pay the whole or part of any damages in the form of a lump sum, it will not have the consequences set out in this Part unless a Part 36 payment of the amount of the lump sum offer is also made.

(3) Where both a Part 36 offer and a Part 36 payment are made under this rule –
- (a) the offer must include details of the payment, and
- (b) rules 36.11(1) and (2) and 36.13(1) and (2) apply as if there were only a Part 36 offer.

(4) A Part 36 offer to which this rule applies may contain an offer to pay, or an offer to accept –
- (a) the whole or part of the damages for future pecuniary loss in the form of –
  - (i) either a lump sum or periodical payments, or
  - (ii) both a lump sum and periodical payments,
- (b) the whole or part of any other damages in the form of a lump sum.

(5) A Part 36 offer to which this rule applies –
- (a) must state the amount of any offer to pay the whole or part of any damages in the form of a lump sum;
- (b) may state what part of the offer relates to damages for future pecuniary loss to be accepted in the form of a lump sum;
- (c) may state, where part of the offer relates to other damages to be accepted in the form of a lump sum, what amounts are attributable to those other damages;
- (d) must state what part of the offer relates to damages for future pecuniary loss to be paid or accepted in the form of periodical payments and must specify –
  - (i) the amount and duration of the periodical payments,
  - (ii) the amount of any payments for substantial capital purchases and when they are to be made, and
  - (iii) that each amount is to vary by reference to the retail prices index (or to some other named index, or that it is not to vary by reference to any index); and
- (e) must state either that any damages which take the form of periodical payments will be funded in a way which ensures that the continuity of payment is reasonably secure in accordance with section 2(4) of the Damages Act 1996 or how such damages are to be paid and how the continuity of their payment is to be secured.

(6) Where a Part 36 payment includes a lump sum for damages for future pecuniary loss, the Part 36 payment notice may state the amount of that lump sum.

(7) Where the defendant makes a Part 36 offer to which this rule applies and which offers to pay damages in the form of both a lump sum and periodical payments, the claimant may only give notice of acceptance of the offer as a whole.

36.3 A defendant's offer to settle a money claim requires a Part 36 payment

(1) Subject to rules 36.5(5) and 36.23, an offer by a defendant to settle a money claim will not have the consequences set out in this Part unless it is made by way of a Part 36 payment.

(2) A Part 36 payment may only be made after proceedings have started.
(Rule 36.5(5) permits a Part 36 offer to be made by reference to an interim payment.)
(Rule 36.10 makes provision for an offer to settle a money claim before the commencement of proceedings.)
(Rule 36.23 makes provision for where benefit is recoverable under the Social Security (Recovery of Benefit) Act 1997.)

36.4 Defendant's offer to settle the whole of a claim which includes both a money claim and a non-money claim

(1) This rule applies where a defendant to a claim which includes both a money claim and a non-money claim wishes –
    (a) to make an offer to settle the whole claim which will have the consequences set out in this Part; and
    [(b) to make a money offer in respect of the money claim and a non-money offer in respect of the non-money claim].

(2) The defendant must –
    (a) make a Part 36 payment in relation to the money claim; and
    (b) make a Part 36 offer in relation to the non-money claim.

(3) The Part 36 payment notice must –
    (a) identify the document which sets out the terms of the Part 36 offer; and
    (b) state that if the claimant gives notice of acceptance of the Part 36 payment he will be treated as also accepting the Part 36 offer.

(Rule 36.6 makes provision for a Part 36 payment notice.)

(4) If the claimant gives notice of acceptance of the Part 36 payment, he shall also be taken as giving notice of acceptance of the Part 36 offer in relation to the non-money claim.

36.5 Form and content of a Part 36 offer

(1) A Part 36 offer must be in writing.

(2) A Part 36 offer may relate to the whole claim or to part of it or to any issue that arises in it.

(3) A Part 36 offer must –
    (a) state whether it relates to the whole of the claim or to part of it or to an issue that arises in it and if so to which part or issue;
    (b) state whether it takes into account any counterclaim; and
    (c) if it is expressed not to be inclusive of interest, give the details relating to interest set out in rule 36.22(2).

(4) A defendant may make a Part 36 offer limited to accepting liability up to a specified proportion.

(5) A Part 36 offer may be made by reference to an interim payment.
(Part 25 contains provisions relating to interim payments.)

(6) A Part 36 offer made not less than 21 days before the start of the trial must –
    (a) be expressed to remain open for acceptance for 21 days from the date it is made; and
    (b) provide that after 21 days the offeree may only accept it if –
        (i) the parties agree the liability for costs; or
        (ii) the court gives permission.

(7) A Part 36 offer made less than 21 days before the start of the trial must state that the offeree may only accept it if –
    (a) the parties agree the liability for costs; or
    (b) the court gives permission.

(Rule 36.8 makes provision for when a Part 36 offer is treated as being made.)

(8) If a Part 36 offer is withdrawn it will not have the consequences set out in this Part.

36.6 Notice of a Part 36 payment

(1) A Part 36 payment may relate to the whole claim or part of it or to an issue that arises in it.

(2) A defendant who makes a Part 36 payment must file with the court a notice ("Part 36 payment notice") which –
    (a) states the amount of the payment;

(b) states whether the payment relates to the whole claim or to part of it or to any issue that arises in it and if so to which part or issue;

(c) states whether it takes into account any counterclaim;

(d) if an interim payment has been made, states that the defendant has taken into account the interim payment; and

(e) if it is expressed not to be inclusive of interest, gives the details relating to interest set out in rule 36.22(2).

(Rule 25.6 makes provision for an interim payment.)

(Rule 36.4 provides for further information to be included where a defendant wishes to settle the whole of a claim which includes a money claim and a non-money claim.)

(Rule 36.23 makes provision for extra information to be included in the payment notice in a case where benefit is recoverable under the Social Security (Recovery of Benefit) Act 1997.)

(3) The offeror must –

(a) serve the Part 36 payment on the offeree; and

(b) file a certificate of notice of the service

(4) [*omitted*]

(5) A Part 36 payment may be withdrawn or reduced only with the permission of the court.

36.7 Offer to settle a claim for provisional damages

(1) A defendant may make a Part 36 payment in respect of a claim which includes a claim for provisional damages.

(2) Where he does so, the Part 36 payment notice must specify whether or not the defendant is offering to agree to the making of an award of provisional damages.

(3) Where the defendant is offering to agree to the making of an award of provisional damages the payment notice must also state –

(a) that the sum paid into court is in satisfaction of the claim for damages on the assumption that the injured person will not develop the disease or suffer the type of deterioration specified in the notice;

(b) that the offer is subject to the condition that the claimant must make any claim for further damages within a limited period; and

(c) what that period is.

(4) Where a Part 36 payment is –

(a) made in accordance with paragraph (3); and

(b) accepted within the relevant period in rule 36.11, the Part 36 payment will have the consequences set out in rule 36.13, unless the court orders otherwise.

(5) If the claimant accepts the Part 36 payment he must, within 7 days of doing so, apply to the court for an order for an award of provisional damages under rule 41.2.

(Rule 41.2 provides for an order for an award of provisional damages.)

(6) The money in court may not be paid out until the court has disposed of the application made in accordance with paragraph (5).

36.8 Time when a Part 36 offer or a Part 36 payment is made and accepted

(1) A Part 36 offer is made when received by the offeree.

(2) A Part 36 payment is made when written notice of the payment into court is served on the offeree.

(3) An improvement to a Part 36 offer will be effective when its details are received by the offeree.

(4) An increase in a Part 36 payment will be effective when notice of the increase is served on the offeree.

(5) A Part 36 offer or Part 36 payment is accepted when notice of its acceptance is received by the offeror.

36.9 Clarification of a Part 36 offer or a Part 36 payment notice

(1) The offeree may, within 7 days of a Part 36 offer or payment being made, request the offeror to clarify the offer or payment notice.

(2) If the offeror does not give the clarification requested under paragraph (1) within 7 days of receiving the request, the offeree may, unless the trial has started, apply for an order that he does so.

(3) If the court makes an order under paragraph (2), it must specify the date when the Part 36 offer or Part 36 payment is to be treated as having been made.

36.10 Court to take into account offer to settle made before commencement of proceedings

(1) If a person makes an offer to settle before proceedings are begun which complies with the provisions of this rule, the court will take that offer into account when making any order as to costs.

(2) The offer must –

    (a) be expressed to be open for at least 21 days after the date it was made;

    (b) if made by a person who would be a defendant were proceedings commenced, include an offer to pay the costs of the offeree incurred up to the date 21 days after the date it was made; and

    (c) otherwise comply with this Part.

(3) Subject to paragraph (3A), if the offeror is a defendant to a money claim –

    (a) he must make a Part 36 payment within 14 days of service of the claim form; and

    (b) the amount of the payment must be not less than the sum offered before proceedings began.

(3A) In a claim to which rule 36.2A applies, if the offeror is a defendant who wishes to offer to pay the whole or part of any damages in the form of a lump sum –

    (a) he must make a Part 36 payment within 14 days of service of the claim form; and

    (b) the amount of the payment must be not less than the lump sum offered before proceedings began.

(4) An offeree may not, after proceedings have begun, accept –

    (a) an offer made under paragraph (2); or

    (b) a Part 36 payment made under paragraph (3) or (3A),

without the permission of the court.

(5) An offer under this rule is made when it is received by the offeree.

36.11 Time for acceptance of a defendant's Part 36 offer or Part 36 payment

(1) A claimant may accept a Part 36 offer or a Part 36 payment made not less than 21 days before the start of the trial without needing the court's permission if he gives the defendant written notice of acceptance not later than 21 days after the offer or payment was made.

(Rule 36.13 sets out the costs consequences of accepting a defendant's offer or payment without needing the permission of the court.)

(2) If –

    (a) a defendant's Part 36 offer or Part 36 payment is made less than 21 days before the start of the trial; or

    (b) the claimant does not accept it within the period specified in paragraph (1) –

        (i) if the parties agree the liability for costs, the claimant may accept the offer or payment without needing the permission of the court;

(ii) if the parties do not agree the liability for costs the claimant may only accept the offer or payment with the permission of the court.

(3) Where the permission of the court is needed under paragraph (2) the court will, if it gives permission, make an order as to costs.

36.12 Time for acceptance of a claimant's Part 36 offer

(1) A defendant may accept a Part 36 offer made not less than 21 days before the start of the trial without needing the court's permission if he gives the claimant written notice of acceptance not later than 21 days after the offer was made.

(Rule 36.14 sets out the costs consequences of accepting a claimant's offer without needing the permission of the court.)

(2) If –
(a) a claimant's Part 36 offer is made less than 21 days before the start of the trial; or
(b) the defendant does not accept it within the period specified in paragraph (1) –
(i)   if the parties agree the liability for costs, the defendant may accept the offer without needing the permission of the court;
(ii) if the parties do not agree the liability for costs the defendant may only accept the offer with the permission of the court.

(3) Where the permission of the court is needed under paragraph (2) the court will, if it gives permission, make an order as to costs.

36.13 Costs consequences of acceptance of a defendant's Part 36 offer or Part 36 payment

(1) Where a Part 36 offer or a Part 36 payment is accepted without needing the permission of the court the claimant will be entitled to his costs of the proceedings up to the date of serving notice of acceptance.

(2) Where –
(a) a Part 36 offer or a Part 36 payment relates to part only of the claim; and
(b) at the time of serving notice of acceptance the claimant abandons the balance of the claim,
the claimant will be entitled to his costs of the proceedings up to the date of serving notice of acceptance, unless the court orders otherwise.

(3) The claimant's costs include any costs attributable to the defendant's counterclaim if the Part 36 offer or the Part 36 payment notice states that it takes into account the counterclaim.

(4) Costs under this rule will be payable on the standard basis if not agreed.

36.14 Costs consequences of acceptance of a claimant's Part 36 offer

Where a claimant's Part 36 offer is accepted without needing the permission of the court the claimant will be entitled to his costs of the proceedings up to the date upon which the defendant serves notice of acceptance.

36.15 The effect of acceptance of a Part 36 offer or a Part 36 payment

(1) If a Part 36 offer or Part 36 payment relates to the whole claim and is accepted, the claim will be stayed[(GL)].

(2) In the case of acceptance of a Part 36 offer which relates to the whole claim –
(a) the stay[(GL)] will be upon the terms of the offer; and
(b) either party may apply to enforce those terms without the need for a new claim.

(3) If a Part 36 offer or a Part 36 payment which relates to part only of the claim is accepted –

(a) the claim will be stayed$^{(GL)}$ as to that part; and

(b) unless the parties have agreed costs, the liability for costs shall be decided by the court.

(4) If the approval of the court is required before a settlement can be binding, any stay$^{(GL)}$ which would otherwise arise on the acceptance of a Part 36 offer or a Part 36 payment will take effect only when that approval has been given.

(5) Any stay$^{(GL)}$ arising under this rule will not affect the power of the court –

(a) to enforce the terms of a Part 36 offer;

(b) to deal with any question of costs (including interest on costs) relating to the proceedings;

(c) to order payment out of court of any sum paid into court.

(6) Where –

(a) a Part 36 offer has been accepted; and

(b) a party alleges that –

(i) the other party has not honoured the terms of the offer; and

(ii) he is therefore entitled to a remedy for breach of contract,

the party may claim the remedy by applying to the court without the need to start a new claim unless the court orders otherwise.

36.16 Payment out of a sum in court on the acceptance of a Part 36 payment

Where a Part 36 payment is accepted the claimant obtains payment out of the sum in court by making a request for payment in the practice form.

36.17 Acceptance of a Part 36 offer or a Part 36 payment made by one or more, but not all, defendants

(1) This rule applies where the claimant wishes to accept a Part 36 offer or a Part 36 payment made by one or more, but not all, of a number of defendants.

(2) If the defendants are sued jointly or in the alternative, the claimant may accept the offer or payment without needing the permission of the court in accordance with rule 36.11(1) if –

(a) he discontinues his claim against those defendants who have not made the offer or payment; and

(b) those defendants give written consent to the acceptance of the offer or payment.

(3) If the claimant alleges that the defendants have a several liability$^{(GL)}$ to him the claimant may –

(a) accept the offer or payment in accordance with rule 36.11(1); and

(b) continue with his claims against the other defendants [if he is entitled to do so].

(4) In all other cases the claimant must apply to the court for –

(a) an order permitting a payment out to him of any sum in court; and

(b) such order as to costs as the court considers appropriate.

36.18 Other cases where a court order is required to enable acceptance of a Part 36 offer or a Part 36 payment

(1) Where a Part 36 offer or a Part 36 payment is made in proceedings to which rule 21.10 applies –

(a) the offer or payment may be accepted only with the permission of the court; and

(b) no payment out of any sum in court shall be made without a court order.

(Rule 21.10 deals with compromise etc by or on behalf of a child or patient.)

(2) Where the court gives a claimant permission to accept a Part 36 offer or payment after the trial has started –

   (a) any money in court may be paid out only with a court order; and

   (b) the court must, in the order, deal with the whole costs of the proceedings.

(3) Where a claimant accepts a Part 36 payment after a defence of tender before claim(GL) has been put forward by the defendant, the money in court may be paid out only after an order of the court.

(Rule 37.3 requires a defendant who wishes to rely on a defence of tender before claim(GL) to make a payment into court.)

36.19 Restriction on disclosure of a Part 36 offer or a Part 36 payment

   (1) A Part 36 offer will be treated as "without prejudice(GL) except as to costs".

   (2) The fact that a Part 36 payment has been made shall not be communicated to the trial judge until all questions of liability and the amount of money to be awarded have been decided.

   (3) Paragraph (2) does not apply –

     (a) where the defence of tender before claim(GL) has been raised;

     (b) where the proceedings have been stayed(GL) under rule 36.15 following acceptance of a Part 36 offer or Part 36 payment; or

     (c) where –

       (i) the issue of liability has been determined before any assessment of the money claimed; and

      (ii) the fact that there has or has not been a Part 36 payment may be relevant to the question of the costs of the issue of liability.

36.20 Costs consequences where claimant fails to do better than a Part 36 offer or a Part 36 payment

   (1) This rule applies where at trial a claimant –

     (a) fails to better a Part 36 payment; or

     (b) fails to obtain a judgment which is more advantageous than a defendant's Part 36 offer.

     (c) in a claim to which rule 36.2A applies, fails to obtain a judgment which is more advantageous than the Part 36 offer made under that rule.

   (2) Unless it considers it unjust to do so, the court will order the claimant to pay any costs incurred by the defendant after the latest date on which the payment or offer could have been accepted without needing the permission of the court.

(Rule 36.11 sets out the time for acceptance of a defendant's Part 36 offer or Part 36 payment.)

36.21 Costs and other consequences where claimant does better than he proposed in his Part 36 offer

   (1) This rule applies where at trial –

     (a) a defendant is held liable for more; or

     (b) the judgment against a defendant is more advantageous to the claimant,

than the proposals contained in a claimant's Part 36 offer including a Part 36 offer made under rule 36.2A.

   (2) The court may order interest on the whole or part of any sum of money (excluding interest) awarded to the claimant at a rate not exceeding 10% above base rate(GL) for some or all of the period starting with the latest date on which the defendant could have accepted the offer without needing the permission of the court.

   (3) The court may also order that the claimant is entitled to –

     (a) his costs on the indemnity basis from the latest date when the defendant could have accepted the offer without needing the permission of the court; and

     (b) interest on those costs at a rate not exceeding 10% above base rate(GL).

(4) Where this rule applies, the court will make the orders referred to in paragraphs (2) and (3) unless it considers it unjust to do so.
(Rule 36.12 sets out the latest date when the defendant could have accepted the offer.)

(5) In considering whether it would be unjust to make the orders referred to in paragraphs (2) and (3) above, the court will take into account all the circumstances of the case including –

    (a) the terms of any Part 36 offer;

    (b) the stage in the proceedings when any Part 36 offer or Part 36 payment was made;

    (c) the information available to the parties at the time when the Part 36 offer or Part 36 payment was made; and

    (d) the conduct of the parties with regard to the giving or refusing to give information for the purposes of enabling the offer or payment into court to be made or evaluated.

(6) Where the court awards interest under this rule and also awards interest on the same sum and for the same period under any other power, the total rate of interest may not exceed 10% above base rate$^{(GL)}$.

36.22 Interest

(1) Unless –

    (a) a claimant's Part 36 offer which offers to accept a sum of money; or

    (b) a Part 36 payment notice,

indicates to the contrary, any such offer or payment will be treated as inclusive of all interest until the last date on which it could be accepted without needing the permission of the court.

(2) Where a claimant's Part 36 offer or Part 36 payment notice is expressed not to be inclusive of interest, the offer or notice must state –

    (a) whether interest is offered; and

    (b) if so, the amount offered, the rate or rates offered and the period or periods for which it is offered.

36.23 Deduction of benefits

(1) This rule applies where a payment to a claimant following acceptance of a Part 36 offer or Part 36 payment into court would be a compensation payment as defined in section 1 of the Social Security (Recovery of Benefits) Act 1997.

(2) A defendant to a money claim may make an offer to settle the claim which will have the consequences set out in this Part, without making a Part 36 payment if –

    (a) at the time he makes the offer he has applied for, but not received, a certificate of recoverable benefit; and

    (b) he makes a Part 36 payment not more than 7 days after he receives the certificate.

(Section 1 of the 1997 Act defines "recoverable benefit".)

(3) A Part 36 payment notice must state –

    (a) the amount of gross compensation;

    (b) the name and amount of any benefit by which that gross amount is reduced in accordance with section 8 and Schedule 2 to the 1997 Act; and

    (c) that the sum paid in is the net amount after deduction of the amount of benefit.

(4) For the purposes of rule 36.20, a claimant fails to better a Part 36 payment if he fails to obtain judgment for more than the gross sum specified in the Part 36 payment notice.

(5) Where –

    (a) a Part 36 payment has been made; and

(b) application is made for the money remaining in court to be paid out, the court may treat the money in court as being reduced by a sum equivalent to any further recoverable benefits paid to the claimant since the date of payment into court and may direct payment out accordingly.

...

Part 41

Provisional Damages

...

41.1 Application and definitions

(1) This Part applies to proceedings to which SCA s 32A or CCA s 51 applies.

(2) In this Part –

    (a) "SCA s 32A" means section 32A of the Supreme Court Act 1981;

    (b) "CCA s 51" means section 51 of the County Courts Act 1984; and

    (c) "award of provisional damages" means an award of damages for personal injuries under which –

        (i) damages are assessed on the assumption referred to in SCA s 32A or CCA s 51 that the injured person will not develop the disease or suffer the deterioration; and

        (ii) the injured person is entitled to apply for further damages at a future date if he develops the disease or suffers the deterioration.

41.2 Order for an award of provisional damages

(1) The court may make an order for an award of provisional damages if –

    (a) the particulars of claim include a claim for provisional damages; and

    (b) the court is satisfied that SCA s 32A or CCA s 51 applies.

(Rule 16.4(1)(d) sets out what must be included in the particulars of claim where the claimant is claiming provisional damages.)

(2) An order for an award of provisional damages –

    (a) must specify the disease or type of deterioration in respect of which an application may be made at a future date;

    (b) must specify the period within which such an application may be made; and

    (c) may be made in respect of more than one disease or type of deterioration and may, in respect of each disease or type of deterioration, specify a different period within which a subsequent application may be made.

(3) The claimant may make more than one application to extend the period specified under paragraph (2)(b) or (2)(c).

41.3 Application for further damages

(1) The claimant may not make an application for further damages after the end of the period specified under rule 41.2(2), or such period as extended by the court.

(2) Only one application for further damages may be made in respect of each disease or type of deterioration specified in the award of provisional damages.

(3) The claimant must give at least 28 days written notice to the defendant of his intention to apply for further damages.

(4) If the claimant knows –

    (a) that the defendant is insured in respect of the claim; and

    (b) the identity of the defendant's insurers,

he must also give at least 28 days written notice to the insurers.

(5) Within 21 days after the end of the 28 day notice period referred to in paragraphs (3) and (4), the claimant must apply for directions.

Periodical payments under The Damages Act 1996

41.4 Scope and interpretation

(1) This Section of this Part contains rules about the exercise of the court's powers under section 2(1) of the 1996 Act to order that all or part of an award of damages in respect of personal injury is to take the form of periodical payments.
(2) In this Section –
    (a) "the 1996 Act" means the Damages Act 1996;
    (b) "damages" means damages for future pecuniary loss; and
    (c) "periodical payments" means periodical payments under section 2(1) of the 1996 Act.

41.5 Statement of case

(1) In a claim for damages for personal injury, each party in its statement of case may state whether it considers periodical payments or a lump sum is the more appropriate form for all or part of an award of damages and where such statement is given must provide relevant particulars of the circumstances which are relied on.
(2) Where a statement under paragraph (1) is not given, the court may order a party to make such a statement.
(3) Where the court considers that a statement of case contains insufficient particulars under paragraph (1), the court may order a party to provide such further particulars as it considers appropriate.

41.6 Court's indication to parties

The court shall consider and indicate to the parties as soon as practicable whether periodical payments or a lump sum is likely to be the more appropriate form for all or part of an award of damages.

41.7 Factors to be taken into account

When considering –
    (a) its indication as to whether periodical payments or a lump sum is likely to be the more appropriate form for all or part of an award of damages under rule 41.6; or
    (b) whether to make an order under section 2(1)(a) of the 1996 Act,
the court shall have regard to all the circumstances of the case and in particular the form of award which best meets the claimant's needs, having regard to the factors set out in the practice direction.

41.8 The award

(1) Where the court awards damages in the form of periodical payments, the order must specify –
    (a) the annual amount awarded, how each payment is to be made during the year and at what intervals;
    (b) the amount awarded for future –
        (i) loss of earnings and other income; and
        (ii) care and medical costs and other recurring or capital costs;
    (c) that the claimant's annual future pecuniary losses, as assessed by the court, are to be paid for the duration of the claimant's life, or such other period as the court orders; and

    (d) that the amount of the payments shall vary annually by reference to the retail prices index, unless the court orders otherwise under section 2(9) of the 1996 Act.

(2) Where the court orders that any part of the award shall continue after the claimant's death, for the benefit of the claimant's dependants, the order must also specify the relevant amount and duration of the payments and how each payment is to be made during the year and at what intervals.

(3) Where an amount awarded under paragraph (1)(b) is to increase or decrease on a certain date, the order must also specify –

    (a) the date on which the increase or decrease will take effect; and

    (b) the amount of the increase or decrease at current value.

(4) Where damages for substantial capital purchases are awarded under paragraph (1)(b)(ii), the order must also specify –

    (a) the amount of the payments at current value;

    (b) when the payments are to be made; and

    (c) that the amount of the payments shall be adjusted by reference to the retail prices index, unless the court orders otherwise under section 2(9) of the 1996 Act.

41.9 Continuity of payment

(1) An order for periodical payments shall specify that the payments must be funded in accordance with section 2(4) of the 1996 Act, unless the court orders an alternative method of funding.

(2) Before ordering an alternative method of funding, the court must be satisfied that –

    (a) the continuity of payment under the order is reasonably secure; and

    (b) the criteria set out in the practice direction are met.

(3) An order under paragraph (2) must specify the alternative method of funding.

...

8. PRACTICE DIRECTIONS AND PROTOCOLS

Practice Direction – Protocols

Contents of this Practice Direction

GENERAL
COMPLIANCE WITH PROTOCOLS
PRE-ACTION BEHAVIOUR IN OTHER CASES
INFORMATION ABOUT FUNDING ARRANGEMENTS
COMMENCEMENT

General

1.1   This Practice Direction applies to the pre-action protocols which have been approved by the Head of Civil Justice.

1.2   The pre-action protocols which have been approved are set out in para 5.1. Other pre-action protocols may subsequently be added.

1.3   Pre-action protocols outline the steps parties should take to seek information from and to provide information to each other about a prospective legal claim.

1.4   The objectives of pre-action protocols are –

(1)   to encourage the exchange of early and full information about the prospective legal claim,

(2)   to enable parties to avoid litigation by agreeing a settlement of the claim before the commencement of proceedings,

(3)   to support the efficient management of proceedings where litigation cannot be avoided.

Compliance with protocols

2.1   The Civil Procedure Rules enable the court to take into account compliance or non-compliance with an applicable protocol when giving directions for the management of proceedings (see CPR rules 3.1(4) and (5) and 3.9(e)) and when making orders for costs (see CPR rule 44.3(a)).

2.2   The court will expect all parties to have complied in substance with the terms of an approved protocol.

2.3   If, in the opinion of the court, non-compliance has led to the commencement of proceedings which might otherwise not have needed to be commenced, or has led to costs being incurred in the proceedings that might otherwise not have been incurred, the orders the court may make include –

(1)   an order that the party at fault pay the costs of the proceedings, or part of those costs, of the other party or parties;

(2)   an order that the party at fault pay those costs on an indemnity basis;

(3)   if the party at fault is a claimant in whose favour an order for the payment of damages or some specified sum is subsequently made, an order depriving that party of interest on such sum and in respect of such period as may be specified, and/or awarding interest at a lower rate than that at which interest would otherwise have been awarded;

(4)   if the party at fault is a defendant and an order for the payment of damages or some specified sum is subsequently made in favour of the claimant, an order awarding interest on such sum and in respect of such period as may be specified at a higher rate, not exceeding 10% above base rate (cf. CPR rule 36.21(2)), than the rate at which interest would otherwise have been awarded.

2.4   The court will exercise its powers under paragraphs 2.1 and 2.3 with the object of placing the innocent party in no worse a position than he would have been in if the protocol had been complied with.

3.1   A claimant may be found to have failed to comply with a protocol by, for example –
  (a)   not having provided sufficient information to the defendant, or
  (b)   not having followed the procedure required by the protocol to be followed (e.g. not having followed the medical expert instruction procedure set out in the Personal Injury Protocol).

3.2   A defendant may be found to have failed to comply with a protocol by, for example –
  (a)   not making a preliminary response to the letter of claim within the time fixed for that purpose by the relevant protocol (21 days under the Personal Injury Protocol, 14 days under the Clinical Negligence Protocol),
  (b)   not making a full response within the time fixed for that purpose by the relevant protocol (3 months of the letter of claim under the Clinical Negligence Protocol, 3 months from the date of acknowledgement of the letter of claim under the Personal Injury Protocol),
  (c)   not disclosing documents required to be disclosed by the relevant protocol.

3.3   The court is likely to treat this practice direction as indicating the normal, reasonable way of dealing with disputes. If proceedings are issued and parties have not complied with this practice direction or a specific protocol, it will be for the court to decide whether sanctions should be applied.

3.4   The court is not likely to be concerned with minor infringements of the practice direction or protocols. The court is likely to look at the effect of non-compliance on the other party when deciding whether to impose sanctions.

3.5   This practice direction does not alter the statutory time limits for starting court proceedings. A claimant is required to start proceedings within those time limits and to adhere to subsequent time limits required by the rules or ordered by the court. If proceedings are for any reason started before the parties have followed the procedures in this practice direction, the parties are encouraged to agree to apply to the court for a stay of the proceedings while they follow the practice direction.

Pre-action behaviour in other cases

4.1   In cases not covered by any approved protocol, the court will expect the parties, in accordance with the overriding objective and the matters referred to in CPR 1.1(2)(a), (b) and (c), to act reasonably in exchanging information and documents relevant to the claim and generally in trying to avoid the necessity for the start of proceedings.

4.2   Parties to a potential dispute should follow a reasonable procedure, suitable to their particular circumstances, which is intended to avoid litigation. The procedure should not be regarded as a prelude to inevitable litigation. It should normally include –
  (a)   the claimant writing to give details of the claim;
  (b)   the defendant acknowledging the claim letter promptly;
  (c)   the defendant giving within a reasonable time a detailed written response; and
  (d)   the parties conducting genuine and reasonable negotiations with a view to settling the claim economically and without court proceedings.

4.3   The claimant's letter should –
  (a)   give sufficient concise details to enable the recipient to understand and investigate the claim without extensive further information;

(b) enclose copies of the essential documents which the claimant relies on;

(c) ask for a prompt acknowledgement of the letter, followed by a full written response within a reasonable stated period;
(For many claims, a normal reasonable period for a full response may be one month.)

(d) state whether court proceedings will be issued if the full response is not received within the stated period;

(e) identify and ask for copies of any essential documents, not in his possession, which the claimant wishes to see;

(f) state (if this is so) that the claimant wishes to enter into mediation or another alternative method of dispute resolution; and

(g) draw attention to the court's powers to impose sanctions for failure to comply with this practice direction and, if the recipient is likely to be unrepresented, enclose a copy of this practice direction.

4.4 The defendant should acknowledge the claimant's letter in writing within 21 days of receiving it. The acknowledgement should state when the defendant will give a full written response. If the time for this is longer than the period stated by the claimant, the defendant should give reasons why a longer period is needed.

4.5 The defendant's full written response should as appropriate –
(a) accept the claim in whole or in part and make proposals for settlement; or
(b) state that the claim is not accepted.
If the claim is accepted in part only, the response should make clear which part is accepted and which part is not accepted.

4.6 If the defendant does not accept the claim or part of it, the response should –
(a) give detailed reasons why the claim is not accepted, identifying which of the claimant's contentions are accepted and which are in dispute;
(b) enclose copies of the essential documents which the defendant relies on;
(c) enclose copies of documents asked for by the claimant, or explain why they are not enclosed;
(d) identify and ask for copies of any further essential documents, not in his possession, which the defendant wishes to see; and
(The claimant should provide these within a reasonably short time or explain in writing why he is not doing so.)
(e) state whether the defendant is prepared to enter into mediation or another alternative method of dispute resolution.

4.7 If the claim remains in dispute, the parties should promptly engage in appropriate negotiations with a view to settling the dispute and avoiding litigation. The courts increasingly take the view that litigation should be a last resort, and that claims should not be issued prematurely when a settlement is still likely. Therefore, the parties should consider whether some form of alternative dispute resolution procedure would be more suitable than litigation, and if so, endeavour to agree which form to adopt. The Legal Services Commission has published a booklet on 'Alternatives to Court', CLS Direct information leaflet 23 (www.clsdirect.org.uk/legal-help/leaflet23.jsp), which lists a number of organisations that provide alternative dispute resolution services.
The parties may be required by the Court to provide evidence that alternative means of dispute resolution were considered

4.8 Documents disclosed by either party in accordance with this practice direction may not be used for any purpose other than resolving the dispute, unless the other party agrees.

4.9   The resolution of some claims, but by no means all, may need help from an expert. If an expert is needed, the parties should wherever possible and to save expense engage an agreed expert.

4.10   Parties should be aware that, if the matter proceeds to litigation, the court may not allow the use of an expert's report, and that the cost of it is not always recoverable.

Information about funding arrangements

4A.1   Where a person enters into a funding arrangement within the meaning of rule 43.2(1)(k) he should inform other potential parties to the claim that he has done so.

4A.2   Paragraph 4A.1 applies to all proceedings whether proceedings to which a pre-action protocol applies or otherwise.

(Rule 44.3B(1)(c) provides that a party may not recover any additional liability for any period in the proceedings during which he failed to provide information about a funding arrangement in accordance with a rule, practice direction or court order.)

Commencement

5.1   The following table sets out the protocols currently in force, the date they came into force and their date of publication:

Protocol	Coming into force	Publication
Personal Injury	26 April 1999	January 1999
Clinical Negligence	26 April 1999	January 1999
Professional Negligence	16 July 2001	May 2001

5.2   The court will take compliance or non-compliance with a relevant protocol into account where the claim was started after the coming into force of that protocol but will not do so where the claim was started before that date.

5.3   Parties in a claim started after a relevant protocol came into force, who have, by work done before that date, achieved the objectives sought to be achieved by certain requirements of that protocol, need not take any further steps to comply with those requirements. They will not be considered to have not complied with the protocol for the purposes of paragraphs 2 and 3.

5.4   Parties in a claim started after a relevant protocol came into force, who have not been able to comply with any particular requirements of that protocol because the period of time between the publication date and the date of coming into force was too short, will not be considered to have not complied with the protocol for the purposes of paragraphs 2 and 3.

Pre-action Protocol for the Resolution of Clinical Disputes

Clinical Disputes Forum

December 1998

EXECUTIVE SUMMARY

1.   The Clinical Disputes Forum is a multi-disciplinary body which was formed in 1997, as a result of Lord Woolf's 'Access to Justice' inquiry. One of the aims of the Forum is to find less adversarial and more cost-effective ways of resolving disputes about healthcare and medical treatment. The names and addresses of the Chairman and Secretary of the Forum can be found at Annex E.

2.   This protocol is the Forum's first major initiative. It has been drawn up carefully, including extensive consultations with most of the key stakeholders in the medico-legal system.

3.   The protocol –
   •   encourages a climate of openness when something has 'gone wrong' with a patient's treatment or the patient is dissatisfied with that treatment and/or the outcome. This reflects the new and developing requirements for clinical governance within healthcare;
   •   provides general guidance on how this more open culture might be achieved when disputes arise;
   •   recommends a timed sequence of steps for patients and healthcare providers, and their advisers, to follow when a dispute arises. This should facilitate and speed up exchanging relevant information and increase the prospects that disputes can be resolved without resort to legal action.

4.   This protocol has been prepared by a working party of the Clinical Disputes Forum. It has the support of the Lord Chancellor's Department, the Department of Health and NHS Executive, the Law Society, the Legal Aid Board and many other key organisations.

1   WHY THIS PROTOCOL?

Mistrust in Healthcare Disputes

1.1   The number of complaints and claims against hospitals, GPs, dentists and private healthcare providers is growing as patients become more prepared to question the treatment they are given, to seek explanations of what happened, and to seek appropriate redress. Patients may require further treatment, an apology, assurances about future action, or compensation. These trends are unlikely to change. The Patients' Charter encourages patients to have high expectations, and a revised NHS Complaints Procedure was implemented in 1996. The civil justice reforms and new Rules of Court should make litigation quicker, more user friendly and less expensive.

1.2   It is clearly in the interests of patients, healthcare professionals and providers that patients' concerns, complaints and claims arising from their treatment are resolved as quickly, efficiently and professionally as possible. A climate of mistrust and lack of openness can seriously damage the patient/clinician relationship, unnecessarily prolong disputes (especially litigation), and reduce the resources available for treating patients. It may also cause additional work for, and lower the morale of, healthcare professionals.

1.3   At present there is often mistrust by both sides. This can mean that patients fail to raise their concerns with the healthcare provider as early as possible. Sometimes patients may pursue a complaint or claim which has little merit, due to a lack of sufficient information and understanding. It can also mean that patients become reluctant, once advice has been taken on a potential claim, to disclose sufficient information to enable the provider to investigate that claim efficiently and, where appropriate, resolve it.

1.4   On the side of the healthcare provider this mistrust can be shown in a reluctance to be honest with patients, a failure to provide prompt clear explanations, especially of adverse outcomes (whether or not there may have been negligence) and a tendency to 'close ranks' once a claim is made.

What needs to change?

1.5   If that mistrust is to be removed, and a more co-operative culture is to develop –
- healthcare professionals and providers need to adopt a constructive approach to complaints and claims. They should accept that concerned patients are entitled to an explanation and an apology, if warranted, and to appropriate redress in the event of negligence. An overly defensive approach is not in the long-term interest of their main goal: patient care;
- patients should recognise that unintended and/or unfortunate consequences of medical treatment can only be rectified if they are brought to the attention of the healthcare provider as soon as possible.

1.6   A protocol which sets out 'ground rules' for the handling of disputes at their early stages should, if it is to be subscribed to, and followed –
- encourage greater openness between the parties;
- encourage parties to find the most appropriate way of resolving the particular dispute;
- reduce delay and costs;
- reduce the need for litigation.

Why this protocol now?

1.7   Lord Woolf in his Access to Justice Report in July 1996, concluded that major causes of costs and delay in medical negligence litigation occur at the pre-action stage. He recommended that patients and their advisers, and healthcare providers, should work more closely together to try to resolve disputes co-operatively, rather than proceed to litigation. He specifically recommended a pre-action protocol for medical negligence cases.

1.8   A fuller summary of Lord Woolf's recommendations is at Annex D.

Where the protocol fits in

1.9   Protocols serve the needs of litigation and pre-litigation practice, especially –
- predictability in the time needed for steps pre-proceedings;
- standardisation of relevant information, including records and documents to be disclosed.

1.10 Building upon Lord Woolf's recommendations, the Lord Chancellor's Department is now promoting the adoption of protocols in specific areas, including medical negligence.

1.11 It is recognised that contexts differ significantly. For example: patients tend to have an ongoing relationship with a GP, more so than with a hospital; clinical staff in the National Health Service are often employees, while those in the private sector may be contractors; providing records quickly may be relatively easy for GPs and dentists, but can be a complicated procedure in a large multi-department hospital. The protocol which follows is intended to be sufficiently broadly based, and flexible, to apply to all aspects of the health service: primary and secondary; public and private sectors.

Enforcement of the protocol and sanctions

1.12   The civil justice reforms will be implemented in April 1999. One new set of Court Rules and procedures is replacing the existing rules for both the High Court and county courts. This and the personal injury protocol are being published with the Rules, practice directions and key court forms. The courts will be able to treat the standards set in protocols as the normal reasonable approach to pre-action conduct.

1.13   If proceedings are issued it will be for the court to decide whether non-compliance with a protocol should merit sanctions. Guidance on the court's likely approach will be given from time to time in practice directions.

1.14   If the court has to consider the question of compliance after proceedings have begun it will not be concerned with minor infringements, eg failure by a short period to provide relevant information. One minor breach will not entitle the 'innocent' party to abandon following the protocol. The court will look at the effect of non-compliance on the other party when deciding whether to impose sanctions.

2   THE AIMS OF THE PROTOCOL

2.1   The *general* aims of the protocol are –
  • to maintain/restore the patient/healthcare provider relationship;
  • to resolve as many disputes as possible without litigation.

2.2   The *specific* objectives are –

Openness
  • to encourage early communication of the perceived problem between patients and healthcare providers;
  • to encourage patients to voice any concerns or dissatisfaction with their treatment as soon as practicable;
  • to encourage healthcare providers to develop systems of early reporting and investigation for serious adverse treatment outcomes and to provide full and prompt explanations to dissatisfied patients;
  • to ensure that sufficient information is disclosed by both parties to enable each to understand the other's perspective and case, and to encourage early resolution;

Timeliness
  • to provide an early opportunity for healthcare providers to identify cases where an investigation is required and to carry out that investigation promptly;
  • to encourage primary and private healthcare providers to involve their defence organisations or insurers at an early stage;
  • to ensure that all relevant medical records are provided to patients or their appointed representatives on request, to a realistic timetable by any healthcare provider;
  • to ensure that relevant records which are not in healthcare providers' possession are made available to them by patients and their advisers at an appropriate stage;
  • where a resolution is not achievable to lay the ground to enable litigation to proceed on a reasonable timetable, at a reasonable and proportionate cost and to limit the matters in contention;
  • to discourage the prolonged pursuit of unmeritorious claims and the prolonged defence of meritorious claims.

Awareness of options
  • to ensure that patients and healthcare providers are made aware of the available options to pursue and resolve disputes and what each might involve.

2.3　This protocol does not attempt to be prescriptive about a number of related clinical governance issues which will have a bearing on healthcare providers' ability to meet the standards within the protocol. Good clinical governance requires the following to be considered –

(a)　**Clinical risk management:** the protocol does not provide any detailed guidance to healthcare providers on clinical risk management or the adoption of risk management systems and procedures. This must be a matter for the NHS Executive, the National Health Service Litigation Authority, individual trusts and providers, including GPs, dentists and the private sector. However, effective, co-ordinated, focused clinical risk management strategies and procedures can help in managing risk and in the early identification and investigation of adverse outcomes.

(b)　**Adverse outcome reporting:** the protocol does not provide any detailed guidance on which adverse outcomes should trigger an investigation. However, healthcare providers should have in place procedures for such investigations, including recording of statements of key witnesses. These procedures should also cover when and how to inform patients that an adverse outcome has occurred.

(c)　**The professional's duty to report:** the protocol does not recommend changes to the codes of conduct of professionals in healthcare, or attempt to impose a specific duty on those professionals to report known adverse outcomes or untoward incidents. Lord Woolf in his final report suggested that the professional bodies might consider this. The General Medical Council is preparing guidance to doctors about their duty to report adverse incidents and to co-operate with inquiries.

3　　THE PROTOCOL

3.1　This protocol is not a comprehensive code governing all the steps in clinical disputes. Rather it attempts to set out **a code of good practice** which parties should follow when litigation might be a possibility.

3.2　The **commitments** section of the protocol summarises the guiding principles which healthcare providers and patients and their advisers are invited to endorse when dealing with patient dissatisfaction with treatment and its outcome, and with potential complaints and claims.

3.3　The **steps** section sets out in a more prescriptive form, a recommended sequence of actions to be followed if litigation is a prospect.

Good practice commitments

3.4　**Healthcare providers** should –

(i)　ensure that **key staff**, including claims and litigation managers, are appropriately trained and have some knowledge of healthcare law, and of complaints procedures and civil litigation practice and procedure;

(ii)　develop an approach to **clinical governance** that ensures that clinical practice is delivered to commonly accepted standards and that this is routinely monitored through a system of clinical audit and clinical risk management (particularly adverse outcome investigation);

(iii)　set up **adverse outcome reporting systems** in all specialties to record and investigate unexpected serious adverse outcomes as soon as possible. Such systems can enable evidence to be gathered quickly, which makes it easier to provide an accurate explanation of what happened and to defend or settle any subsequent claims;

(iv)　use the results of **adverse incidents and complaints positively** as a guide to how to improve services to patients in the future;

(v) ensure **that patients receive clear and comprehensible infor-mation** in an accessible form about how to raise their concerns or complaints;

(vi) establish **efficient and effective systems of recording and stor-ing patient records**, notes, diagnostic reports and X-rays, and to retain these in accordance with Department of Health guidance (cur-rently for a minimum of eight years in the case of adults, and all obstetric and paediatric notes for children until they reach the age of 25);

(vii) **advise patients** of a serious adverse outcome and provide on request to the patient or the patient's representative an oral or writ-ten explanation of what happened, information on further steps open to the patient, including where appropriate an offer of future treat-ment to rectify the problem, an apology, changes in procedure which will benefit patients and/or compensation.

3.5 **Patients and their advisers** should –

(i) **report any concerns and dissatisfaction** to the healthcare provider as soon as is reasonable to enable that provider to offer clin-ical advice where possible, to advise the patient if anything has gone wrong and take appropriate action;

(ii) consider the **full range of options** available following an adverse outcome with which a patient is dissatisfied, including a request for an explanation, a meeting, a complaint, and other appropriate dis-pute resolution methods (including mediation) and negotiation, not only litigation;

(iii) **inform the healthcare provider when the patient is satisfied** that the matter has been concluded: legal advisers should notify the provider when they are no longer acting for the patient, particularly if proceedings have not started.

Protocol steps

3.6 The steps of this protocol which follow have been kept deliberately simple. An illustration of the likely sequence of events in a number of healthcare situations is at Annex A.

Obtaining the health records

3.7 Any request for records by the **patient** or their adviser should –

- **provide sufficient information** to alert the healthcare provider where an adverse outcome has been serious or had serious conse-quences;
- be as **specific as possible** about the records which are required.

3.8 Requests for copies of the patient's clinical records should be made using the Law Society and Department of Health approved **standard forms** (enclosed at Annex B), adapted as necessary.

3.9 The copy records should be provided **within 40 days** of the request and for a cost not exceeding the charges permissible under the Access to Health Records Act 1990 (currently a maximum of £10 plus photocopying and postage).

3.10 In the rare circumstances that the healthcare provider is in difficulty in complying with the request within 40 days, the **problem should be explained** quickly and details given of what is being done to resolve it.

3.11 It will not be practicable for healthcare providers to investigate in detail each case when records are requested. But healthcare providers should **adopt a policy on which cases will be investigated** (see paragraph 3.5 on clinical governance and adverse outcome reporting).

3.12 If the healthcare provider fails to provide the health records within 40 days, the patient or their adviser can then apply to the court for an **order**

for pre-action disclosure. The new Civil Procedure Rules should make pre-action applications to the court easier. The court will also have the power to impose costs sanctions for unreasonable delay in providing records.

3.13   If either the patient or the healthcare provider considers **additional health records are required from a third party**, in the first instance these should be requested by or through the patient. Third party health-care providers are expected to co-operate. The Civil Procedure Rules will enable patients and healthcare providers to apply to the court for pre-action disclosure by third parties.

Letter of claim

3.14   Annex C1 to this protocol provides **a template for the recommended contents of a letter of claim**: the level of detail will need to be varied to suit the particular circumstances.

3.15   If, following the receipt and analysis of the records, and the receipt of any further advice (including from experts if necessary – see Section 4), the patient/adviser decides that there are grounds for a claim, they should then send, as soon as practicable, to the healthcare provider/potential defendant, a **letter of claim.**

3.16   This letter should contain a **clear summary of the facts** on which the claim is based, including the alleged adverse outcome, and the **main allegations of negligence**. It should also describe the **patient's injuries**, and present condition and prognosis. The **financial loss** incurred by the plaintiff should be outlined with an indication of the heads of damage to be claimed and the scale of the loss, unless this is impracticable.

3.17   In more complex cases a **chronology** of the relevant events should be provided, particularly if the patient has been treated by a number of different healthcare providers.

3.18   The letter of claim **should refer to any relevant documents**, including health records, and if possible enclose copies of any of those which will not already be in the potential defendant's possession, eg any relevant general practitioner records if the plaintiff's claim is against a hospital.

3.19   **Sufficient information** must be given to enable the healthcare provider defendant to **commence investigations** and to put an initial valuation on the claim.

3.20   Letters of claim are **not** intended to have the same formal status as a **pleading**, nor should any sanctions necessarily apply if the letter of claim and any subsequent statement of claim in the proceedings differ.

3.21   **Proceedings should not be issued until after three months from the letter of claim**, unless there is a limitation problem and/or the patient's position needs to be protected by early issue.

3.22   The patient or their adviser may want to make an **offer to settle** the claim at this early stage by putting forward an amount of compensation which would be satisfactory (possibly including any costs incurred to date). If an offer to settle is made, generally this should be supported by a medical report which deals with the injuries, condition and prognosis, and by a schedule of loss and supporting documentation. The level of detail necessary will depend on the value of the claim. Medical reports may not be necessary where there is no significant continuing injury, and a detailed schedule may not be necessary in a low value case. The Civil Procedure Rules are expected to set out the legal and procedural requirements for making offers to settle.

The response

3.23   Attached at Annex C2 is a template for the suggested contents of the **letter of response.**

3.24   The healthcare provider should **acknowledge** the letter of claim **within 14 days of receipt** and should identify who will be dealing with the matter.

3.25   The healthcare provider should, **within three months** of the letter of claim, provide a **reasoned answer** –
- if the **claim is admitted** the healthcare provider should say so in clear terms;
- if only **part of the claim is admitted** the healthcare provider should make clear which issues of breach of duty and/or causation are admitted and which are denied and why;
- if it is intended that any **admissions will be binding**;
- if the claim is denied, this should include specific comments on the allegations of negligence, and if a synopsis or chronology of relevant events has been provided and is disputed, the healthcare provider's version of those events;
- where additional documents are relied upon, eg an internal protocol, copies should be provided.

3.26   If the patient has made an offer to settle, the healthcare provider should **respond to that offer** in the response letter, preferably with reasons. The provider may make its own offer to settle at this stage, either as a counter-offer to the patient's, or of its own accord, but should accompany any offer by any supporting medical evidence, and/or by any other evidence in relation to the value of the claim which is in the healthcare provider's possession.

3.27   If the parties reach agreement on liability, but time is needed to resolve the value of the claim, they should aim to agree a reasonable period.

4   EXPERTS

4.1   In clinical negligence disputes expert opinions may be needed –
- on breach of duty and causation;
- on the patient's condition and prognosis;
- to assist in valuing aspects of the claim.

4.2   The civil justice reforms and the new Civil Procedure Rules will encourage economy in the use of experts and a less adversarial expert culture. It is recognised that in clinical negligence disputes, the parties and their advisers will require flexibility in their approach to expert evidence. Decisions on whether experts might be instructed jointly, and on whether reports might be disclosed sequentially or by exchange, should rest with the parties and their advisers. Sharing expert evidence may be appropriate on issues relating to the value of the claim. However, this protocol does not attempt to be prescriptive on issues in relation to expert evidence.

4.3   Obtaining expert evidence will often be an expensive step and may take time, especially in specialised areas of medicine where there are limited numbers of suitable experts. Patients and healthcare providers, and their advisers, will therefore need to consider carefully how best to obtain any necessary expert help quickly and cost-effectively. Assistance with locating a suitable expert is available from a number of sources.

5   ALTERNATIVE APPROACHES TO SETTLING DISPUTES

5.1   It would not be practicable for this protocol to address in any detail how a patient or their adviser, or healthcare provider, might decide which method to adopt to resolve the particular problem. But, the courts increasingly expect parties to try to settle their differences by agreement before issuing proceedings.

5.2   Most disputes are resolved by discussion and negotiation. Parties should bear in mind that carefully planned face-to-face meetings may be particularly helpful in exploring further treatment for the patient, in reaching understandings about what happened, and on both parties' positions, in narrowing the issues in dispute and, if the timing is right, in helping to settle the whole matter.

5.3   Summarised below are some other alternatives for resolving disputes –

- The revised NHS Complaints Procedure, which was implemented in April 1996, is designed to provide patients with an explanation of what happened and an apology if appropriate. It is not designed to provide compensation for cases of negligence. However, patients might choose to use the procedure if their only, or main, goal is to obtain an explanation, or to obtain more information to help them decide what other action might be appropriate.

- Mediation may be appropriate in some cases: this is a form of facilitated negotiation assisted by an independent neutral party. It is expected that the new Civil Procedure Rules will give the court the power to stay proceedings for one month for settlement discussions or mediation.

- Other methods of resolving disputes include arbitration, determination by an expert, and early neutral evaluation by a medical or legal expert. The Legal Services Commission has published a booklet on 'Alternatives to Court', LSC August 2001, CLS information leaflet number 23, which lists a number of organisations that provide alternative dispute resolution services.

ANNEX A

ILLUSTRATIVE FLOWCHART

Patient (P)   *Healthcare Provider* (HCP)

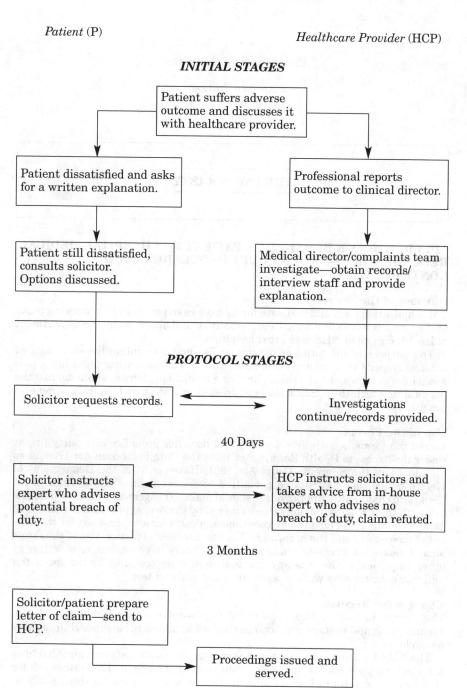

INITIAL STAGES

Patient suffers adverse outcome and discusses it with healthcare provider.

Patient dissatisfied and asks for a written explanation.

Professional reports outcome to clinical director.

Patient still dissatisfied, consults solicitor. Options discussed.

Medical director/complaints team investigate—obtain records/ interview staff and provide explanation.

PROTOCOL STAGES

Solicitor requests records.

Investigations continue/records provided.

40 Days

Solicitor instructs expert who advises potential breach of duty.

HCP instructs solicitors and takes advice from in-house expert who advises no breach of duty, claim refuted.

3 Months

Solicitor/patient prepare letter of claim—send to HCP.

Proceedings issued and served.

ANNEX B
A PROTOCOL FOR OBTAINING HOSPITAL MEDICAL RECORDS

Civil Litigation Committee

Revised Edition
June 1998

THE LAW SOCIETY

APPLICATION ON BEHALF OF A PATIENT FOR HOSPITAL MEDICAL RECORDS FOR USE WHEN COURT PROCEEDINGS ARE CONTEMPLATED

Purpose of the Forms
This application form and response forms have been prepared by a working party of the Law Society's Civil Litigation Committee and approved by the Department of Health for use in NHS and Trust hospitals.

The purpose of the forms is to standardise and streamline the disclosure of medical records to a patient's solicitors, who are investigating pursuing a personal injury claim against a third party, or a medical negligence claim against the hospital to which the application is addressed and/or other hospitals or general practitioners.

Use of the Forms
Use of the forms is entirely voluntary and does not prejudice any party's right under the Access to Health Records Act 1990, the Data Protection Act 1984, or ss 33 and 34 of the Supreme Court Act 1981. However, it is the Department of Health policy that patients be permitted to see what has been written about them, and that healthcare providers should make arrangements to allow patients to see all their records, not only those covered by the Access to Health Records Act 1990. The aim of the forms is to save time and costs for all concerned for the benefit of the patient and the hospital and in the interests of justice. Use of the forms should make it unnecessary in most cases for there to be exchanges of letters or other enquiries. If there is any unusual matter not covered by the form, the patient's solicitor may write a separate letter at the outset.

Charges for Records
The Access to Health Records Act 1990 prescribes a maximum fee of £10. Photocopying and postage costs can be charged in addition. No other charges may be made.

The NHS Executive guidance makes it clear to healthcare providers that 'it is a perfectly proper use' of the 1990 Act to request records in that framework for the purpose of potential or actual litigation, whether against a third party or against the hospital or trust.

The 1990 Act does not permit differential rates of charges to be levied if the application is made by the patient, or by a solicitor on his or her behalf, or whether the response to the application is made by the healthcare provider directly (the medical records manager or a claims manager) or by a solicitor.

The NHS Executive guidance recommend that the same practice should be followed with regard to charges when the records are provided under a voluntary agreement as under the 1990 Act, except that in those circumstances the £10 access fee will not be appropriate.

The NHS Executive also advises:
That the cost of photocopying may include 'the cost of staff time in making copies' and the costs of running the copier (but not costs of locating and sifting records).

That the common practice of setting a standard rate for an application or charging an administration fee is not acceptable because there will be cases when this fails to comply with the 1990 Act.

Records: What might be included
X-rays and test results form part of the patient's records. Additional charges for copying X-rays are permissible. If there are large numbers of X-rays, the records officer should check with the patient/solicitor before arranging copying.

Reports on an 'adverse incident' and reports on the patient made for risk management and audit purposes may form part of the records and be discloseable: the exception will be any specific record or report made solely or mainly in connection with an actual or potential claim.

Records: Quality Standards
When copying records healthcare providers should ensure:

1   All documents are legible, and complete, if necessary by photocopying at less than 100% size.
2   Documents larger than A4 in the original, eg ITU charts, should be reproduced in A3, or reduced to A4 where this retains readability.
3   Documents are only copied on one side of paper, unless the original is two sided.
4   Documents should not be unnecessarily shuffled or bound and holes should not be made in the copied papers.

Enquiries/Further Information
Any enquiries about the forms should be made initially to the solicitors making the request. Comments on the use and content of the forms should be made to the Secretary, Civil Litigation Committee, The Law Society, 113 Chancery Lane, London WC2A 1PL, telephone 020 7320 5739, or to the NHS Management Executive, Quarry House, Quarry Hill, Leeds LS2 7UE.

The Law Society
May 1998

APPLICATION ON BEHALF OF A PATIENT FOR HOSPITAL MEDICAL RECORDS FOR USE WHEN COURT PROCEEDINGS ARE CONTEMPLATED

This should be completed as fully as possible

Insert Hospital Name and Address	**TO: Medical Records Officer** **Hospital**

1   Full name of patient (including
     (a)   Previous surnames)

     (b)   Address now

     (c)   Address at start of treatment

     (d)   Date of birth (and death, if applicable)

     (e)   Hospital ref. no if available

     (f)   N.I. number, if available

2   This application is made because the patient is
     considering

     (a)   a claim against your hospital as detailed in
            para 7 overleaf
                                        YES/NO

     (b)   Pursuing an action against someone else
                                        YES/NO

3   Department(s) where treatment was received

4   Name(s) of consultant(s) at your hospital in charge
     of the treatment

5   Whether treatment at your hospital was private or
     NHS, wholly or in part

6   A description of the treatment received, with
     approximate dates

7   If the answer to Q2(A) is "Yes" details of
     (a)   the likely nature of the claim,
     (b)   grounds for the claim,
     (c)   approximate dates of the events involved

8   If the answer to Q2(B) is "Yes" insert

     (i)   the names of the proposed defendants

     (ii)   whether legal proceedings yet begun   YES/NO

     (iii) if appropriate, details of the claim and action
            number

9   We confirm we will pay reasonable copying charges

10   We request prior details of

     (i)   photocopying and administration charges for
            medical records
                                              YES/NO

     (ii)   number of and cost of copying x-ray and scan
            films
                                              YES/NO

11   Any other relevant information, particular
     requirements, or any particular documents <u>not</u>
     required (eg copies of computerised records)

Signature of Solicitor

Name

Address

Ref.

Telephone Number

Fax number

Please print name beneath each signature.
Signature by child over 12 but under
18 years also requires signature by parent.

Signature of patient

Signature of parent or next friend if appropriate

Signature of personal representative where patient
has died

FIRST RESPONSE TO APPLICATION FOR HOSPITAL RECORDS

NAME OF PATIENT Our ref Your ref		
1	Date of receipt of patients application	
2	We intend that copy medical records will be dispatched within 6 weeks of that date	YES/NO
3	We require pre-payment of photocopying charges	YES/NO
4	If estimate of photocopying charges requested or pre-payment required the amount will be	£ / notified to you
5	The cost of x-ray and scan films will be	£ / notified to you
6	If there is any problem, we shall write to you within those 6 weeks	YES/NO
7	Any other information Please address further correspondence to Signed Direct telephone number Direct fax number Dated	

SECOND RESPONSE ENCLOSING PATIENT'S HOSPITAL MEDICAL RECORDS

Address	Our Ref. Your Ref.

NAME OF PATIENT:

1   We confirm that the enclosed copy medical
     records are all those within the control of the
     hospital, relevant to the application which
     you have made to the best of our knowledge
     and belief, subject to paras 2–5 below

                                                            YES/NO

2   Details of any other documents which have
     not yet been located

3   Date by when it is expected that these will
     be supplied

4   Details of any records which we are not
     producing

5   The reasons for not doing so

6   An invoice for copying and administration
     charges is attached   YES/NO

     Signed

     Date

ANNEX C
TEMPLATES FOR LETTERS OF CLAIM AND RESPONSE

Annex C1   Letter of Claim

Essential Contents

1   Client's name, address, date of birth, etc.
2   Dates of allegedly negligent treatment
3   Events giving rise to the claim:
       an outline of what happened, including details of other relevant treatments to the client by other healthcare providers
4   Allegation of negligence and causal link with injuries:
       an outline of the allegations or a more detailed list in a complex case; an outline of the causal link between allegations and the injuries complained of
5   The client's injuries, condition and future prognosis
6   Request for clinical records (if not previously provided);
       use the Law Society form if appropriate or adapt; specify the records required; if other records are held by other providers, and may be relevant, say so;
       state what investigations have been carried out to date, eg information from client and witnesses, any complaint and the outcome, if any clinical records have been seen or experts advice obtained
7   The likely value of the claim
       an outline of the main heads of damage, or in straightforward cases the details of loss

Optional Information
What investigations have been carried out
An offer to settle without supporting evidence
Suggestions for obtaining expert evidence
Suggestions for meetings, negotiations, discussion or mediation

Possible Enclosures
Chronology
Clinical records request form and client's authorisation
Expert report(s)
Schedules of loss and supporting evidence

Annex C2   Letter of Response

Essential Contents

1   Provide requested records and invoice for copying:
       explain if records are incomplete or extensive records are held and ask for further instructions
       request additional records from third parties
2   Comments on events and/or chronology:
       if events are disputed or the healthcare provider has further information or documents on which they wish to rely, these should be provided, eg internal protocol
       details of any further information needed from the patient or a third party should be provided.
3   If breach of duty and causation are accepted:
       suggestions might be made for resolving the claim and/or requests for further information
       a response should be made to any offer to settle

4   If breach of duty and/or causation are denied:
         a bare denial will not be sufficient. If the healthcare provider has other
         explanations for what happened, these should be given at least in outline
         suggestions might be made for the next steps, eg further investigations,
         obtaining expert evidence, meetings/negotiations or mediation, or an invi-
         tation to issue proceedings

Optional Matters
an offer to settle if the patient has not made one, or a counter offer to the patient's
with supporting evidence

Possible Enclosures
Clinical records
Annotated chronology
Expert reports

ANNEX D

LORD WOOLF'S RECOMMENDATIONS

1   Lord Woolf in his Access to Justice Report in July 1996, following a detailed review of the problems of medical negligence claims, identified that one of the major sources of costs and delay is at the pre-litigation stage because:—

(a)   Inadequate incident reporting and record keeping in hospitals, and mobility of staff, make it difficult to establish facts, often several years after the event.

(b)   Claimants must incur the cost of an expert in order to establish whether they have a viable claim.

(c)   There is often a long delay before a claim is made.

(d)   Defendants do not have sufficient resources to carry out a full investigation of every incident, and do not consider it worthwhile to start an investigation as soon as they receive a request for records, because many cases do not proceed beyond that stage.

(e)   Patients often give the Defendant little or no notice of a firm intention to pursue a claim. Consequently, many incidents are not investigated by the defendants until after proceedings have started.

(f)   Doctors and other clinical staff are traditionally reluctant to admit negligence or apologise to, or negotiate with, claimants for fear of damage to their professional reputations or career prospects.

2   Lord Woolf acknowledged that under the present arrangements healthcare providers, faced with possible medical negligence claims, have a number of practical problems to contend with:—

(a)   Difficulties of finding patients' records and tracing former staff, which can be exacerbated by late notification and be the health care provider's own failure to identify adverse incidents.

(b)   The healthcare provider may have only treated the patient for a limited time or for a specific complaint: the patient's previous history may be relevant but the records may be in the possession of one of several other healthcare providers.

(c)   The large number of potential claims do not proceed beyond the stage of a request for medical records, or an explanation, and that is difficult for healthcare providers to investigate fully every case whenever a patient asks to see the records.

Appendix II

Guidelines

Contents

CIVIL JUSTICE COUNCIL

1 PROTOCOL FOR THE INSTRUCTION OF EXPERTS TO GIVE EVIDENCE IN CIVIL CLAIMS

1. Introduction

Expert witnesses perform a vital role in civil litigation. It is essential that both those who instruct experts and experts themselves are given clear guidance as to what they are expected to do in civil proceedings. The purpose of this Protocol is to provide such guidance. It has been drafted by the Civil Justice Council and reflects the rules and practice directions current [in June 2005], replacing the Code of Guidance on Expert Evidence. The authors of the Protocol wish to acknowledge the valuable assistance they obtained by drawing on earlier documents produced by the Academy of Experts and the Expert Witness Institute, as well as suggestions made by the Clinical Dispute Forum. The Protocol has been approved by the Master of the Rolls.

2. Aims of Protocol

2.1 This Protocol offers guidance to experts and to those instructing them in the interpretation of and compliance with Part 35 of the Civil Procedure Rules (CPR 35) and its associated Practice Direction (PD 35) and to further the objectives of the Civil Procedure Rules in general. It is intended to assist in the interpretation of those provisions in the interests of good practice but it does not replace them. It sets out standards for the use of experts and the conduct of experts and those who instruct them. The existence of this Protocol does not remove the need for experts and those who instruct them to be familiar with CPR 35 and PD 35.

2.2 Experts and those who instruct them should also bear in mind para 1.4 of the Practice Direction on Protocols which contains the following objectives, namely to:

(a) encourage the exchange of early and full information about the expert issues involved in a prospective legal claim;

(b) enable the parties to avoid or reduce the scope of litigation by agreeing the whole or part of an expert issue before commencement of proceedings; and

(c) support the efficient management of proceedings where litigation cannot be avoided.

3. Application

3.1 This Protocol applies to any steps taken for the purpose of civil proceedings by experts or those who instruct them on or after 5th September 2005.

3.2 It applies to all experts who are, or who may be, governed by CPR Part 35 and to those who instruct them. Experts are governed by Part 35 if they are or have been instructed to give or prepare evidence for the purpose of civil proceedings in a court in England and Wales (CPR 35.2).

3.3 Experts, and those instructing them, should be aware that some cases may be 'specialist proceedings' (CPR 49) where there are modifications to the Civil Procedure Rules. Proceedings may also be governed by other Protocols. Further, some courts have published their own Guides which supplement the Civil Procedure Rules for proceedings in those courts. They contain provisions affecting expert evidence. Expert witnesses and those instructing them should be familiar with them when they are relevant.

3.4 Courts may take into account any failure to comply with this Protocol when making orders in relation to costs, interest, time limits, the stay of proceedings and whether to order a party to pay a sum of money into court.

Limitation

3.5 If, as a result of complying with any part of this Protocol, claims would or might be time barred under any provision in the Limitation Act 1980, or any other legislation that imposes a time limit for bringing an action, claimants may commence proceedings without complying with this Protocol. In such circumstances, claimants who commence proceedings without complying with all, or any part, of this Protocol must apply, giving notice to all other parties, to the court for directions as to the timetable and form of procedure to be adopted, at the same time as they request the court to issue proceedings. The court may consider whether to order a stay of the whole or part of the proceedings pending compliance with this Protocol and may make orders in relation to costs.

4. Duties of experts

4.1 Experts always owe a duty to exercise reasonable skill and care to those instructing them, and to comply with any relevant professional code of ethics. However when they are instructed to give or prepare evidence for the purpose of civil proceedings in England and Wales they have an overriding duty to help the court on matters within their expertise (CPR 35.3). This duty overrides any obligation to the person instructing or paying them. Experts must not serve the exclusive interest of those who retain them.

4.2 Experts should be aware of the overriding objective that courts deal with cases justly. This includes dealing with cases proportionately, expeditiously and fairly (CPR 1.1). Experts are under an obligation to assist the court so as to enable them to deal with cases in accordance with the overriding objective. However the overriding objective does not impose on experts any duty to act as mediators between the parties or require them to trespass on the role of the court in deciding facts.

4.3   Experts should provide opinions which are independent, regardless of the pressures of litigation. In this context, a useful test of 'independence' is that the expert would express the same opinion if given the same instructions by an opposing party. Experts should not take it upon themselves to promote the point of view of the party instructing them or engage in the role of advocates.

4.4   Experts should confine their opinions to matters which are material to the disputes between the parties and provide opinions only in relation to matters which lie within their expertise. Experts should indicate without delay where particular questions or issues fall outside their expertise.

4.5   Experts should take into account all material facts before them at the time that they give their opinion. Their reports should set out those facts and any literature or any other material on which they have relied in forming their opinions. They should indicate if an opinion is provisional, or qualified, or where they consider that further information is required or if, for any other reason, they are not satisfied that an opinion can be expressed finally and without qualification.

4.6   Experts should inform those instructing them without delay of any change in their opinions on any material matter and the reason for it.

4.7   Experts should be aware that any failure by them to comply with the Civil Procedure Rules or court orders or any excessive delay for which they are responsible may result in the parties who instructed them being penalised in costs and even, in extreme cases, being debarred from placing the experts' evidence before the court. In *Phillips* v *Symes* Peter Smith J held that courts may also make orders for costs (under section 51 of the Supreme Court Act 1981) directly against expert witnesses who by their evidence cause significant expense to be incurred, and do so in flagrant and reckless disregard of their duties to the Court.

5. Conduct of experts instructed only to advise

5.1 Part 35 only applies where experts are instructed to give opinions which are relied on for the purposes of court proceedings. Advice which the parties do not intend to adduce in litigation is likely to be confidential; the Protocol does not apply in these circumstances.

5.2   The same applies where, after the commencement of proceedings, experts are instructed only to advise (eg to comment upon a single joint expert's report) and not to give or prepare evidence for use in the proceedings.

5.3   However this Protocol does apply if experts who were formerly instructed only to advise are later instructed to give or prepare evidence for the purpose of civil proceedings.

6. The need for experts

6.1   Those intending to instruct experts to give or prepare evidence for the purpose of civil proceedings should consider whether expert evidence is appropriate, taking account of the principles set out in CPR Parts 1 and 35, and in particular whether:

(a)   it is relevant to a matter which is in dispute between the parties.
(b)   it is reasonably required to resolve the proceedings (CPR 35.1);
(c)   the expert has expertise relevant to the issue on which an opinion is sought;
(d)   the expert has the experience, expertise and training appropriate to the value, complexity and importance of the case; and whether
(e)   these objects can be achieved by the appointment of a single joint expert (see section 17 below).

6.2 Although the court's permission is not generally required to instruct an expert, the court's permission is required before experts can be called to give evidence or their evidence can be put in (CPR 35.4)

7. *The appointment of experts*

7.1 Before experts are formally instructed or the court's permission to appoint named experts is sought, the following should be established:
  (a) that they have the appropriate expertise and experience;
  (b) that they are familiar with the general duties of an expert;
  (c) that they can produce a report, deal with questions and have discussions with other experts within a reasonable time and at a cost proportionate to the matters in issue;
  (d) a description of the work required;
  (e) whether they are available to attend the trial, if attendance is required; and
  (f) there is no potential conflict of interest.

7.2 Terms of appointment should be agreed at the outset and should normally include:
  (a) the capacity in which the expert is to be appointed (eg party appointed expert, single joint expert or expert advisor);
  (b) the services required of the expert (eg provision of expert's report, answering questions in writing, attendance at meetings and attendance at court);
  (c) time for delivery of the report;
  (d) the basis of the expert's charges (either daily or hourly rates and an estimate of the time likely to be required, or a total fee for the services);
  (e) travelling expenses and disbursements;
  (f) cancellation charges;
  (g) any fees for attending court;
  (h) time for making the payment;
  (i) whether fees are to be paid by a third party; and
  (j) if a party is publicly funded, whether or not the expert's charges will be subject to assessment by a costs officer.

7.3 As to the appointment of single joint experts, see section 17 below.

7.4 When necessary, arrangements should be made for dealing with questions to experts and discussions between experts, including any directions given by the court, and provision should be made for the cost of this work.

7.5 Experts should be informed regularly about deadlines for all matters concerning them. Those instructing experts should promptly send them copies of all court orders and directions which may affect the preparation of their reports or any other matters concerning their obligations.

Conditional and contingency fees

7.6 Payments contingent upon the nature of the expert evidence given in legal proceedings, or upon the outcome of a case, must not be offered or accepted. To do so would contravene experts' overriding duty to the court and compromise their duty of independence.

7.7 Agreement to delay payment of experts' fees until after the conclusion of cases is permissible as long as the amount of the fee does not depend on the outcome of the case.

8. Instructions

8.1   Those instructing experts should ensure that they give clear instructions, including the following:

    (a)   basic information, such as names, addresses, telephone numbers, dates of birth and dates of incidents;

    (b)   the nature and extent of the expertise which is called for;

    (c)   the purpose of requesting the advice or report, a description of the matter(s) to be investigated, the principal known issues and the identity of all parties;

    (d)   the statement(s) of case (if any), those documents which form part of standard disclosure and witness statements which are relevant to the advice or report;

    (e)   where proceedings have not been started, whether proceedings are being contemplated and, if so, whether the expert is asked only for advice;

    (f)   an outline programme, consistent with good case management and the expert's availability, for the completion and delivery of each stage of the expert's work; and

    (g)   where proceedings have been started, the dates of any hearings (including any Case Management Conferences and/or Pre-Trial Reviews), the name of the court, the claim number and the track to which the claim has been allocated.

8.2   Experts who do not receive clear instructions should request clarification and may indicate that they are not prepared to act unless and until such clear instructions are received.

8.3   As to the instruction of single joint experts, see section 17 below.

9. Experts' acceptance of instructions

9.1   Experts should confirm without delay whether or not they accept instructions. They should also inform those instructing them (whether on initial instruction or at any later stage) without delay if:

    (a)   instructions are not acceptable because, for example, they require work that falls outside their expertise, impose unrealistic deadlines, or are insufficiently clear;

    (b)   they consider that instructions are or have become insufficient to complete the work;

    (c)   they become aware that they may not be able to fulfil any of the terms of appointment;

    (d)   the instructions and/or work have, for any reason, placed them in conflict with their duties as an expert; or

    (e)   they are not satisfied that they can comply with any orders that have been made.

9.2   Experts must neither express an opinion outside the scope of their field of expertise, nor accept any instructions to do so.

10. Withdrawal

10.1   Where experts' instructions remain incompatible with their duties, whether through incompleteness, a conflict between their duty to the court and their instructions, or for any other substantial and significant reason, they may consider withdrawing from the case. However, experts should not withdraw without first discussing the position fully with those who instruct them and considering carefully whether it would be more appropriate to make a written request for directions from the court. If experts do withdraw, they must give formal written notice to those instructing them.

11. Experts' right to ask court for directions

11.1   Experts may request directions from the court to assist them in carrying out their functions as experts. Experts should normally discuss such matters with those who instruct them before making any such request. Unless the court otherwise orders, any proposed request for directions should be copied to the party instructing the expert at least seven days before filing any request to the court, and to all other parties at least four days before filing it. (CPR 35.14).

11.2   Requests to the court for directions should be made by letter, containing.
    (a)   the title of the claim;
    (b)   the claim number of the case;
    (c)   the name of the expert;
    (d)   full details of why directions are sought; and
    (e)   copies of any relevant documentation.

12. Power of the court to direct a party to provide information

12.1   If experts consider that those instructing them have not provided information which they require, they may, after discussion with those instructing them and giving notice, write to the court to seek directions (CPR 35.14).

12.2   Experts and those who instruct them should also be aware of CPR 35.9. This provides that where one party has access to information which is not readily available to the other party, the court may direct the party who has access to the information to prepare, file and copy to the other party a document recording the information. If experts require such information which has not been disclosed, they should discuss the position with those instructing them without delay, so that a request for the information can be made, and, if not forthcoming, an application can be made to the court. Unless a document appears to be essential, experts should assess the cost and time involved in the production of a document and whether its provision would be proportionate in the context of the case.

13. Contents of experts' reports

13.1   The content and extent of experts' reports should be governed by the scope of their instructions and general obligations, the contents of CPR 35 and PD 35 and their overriding duty to the court.

13.2   In preparing reports, experts should maintain professional objectivity and impartiality at all times.

13.3   PD 35, para 2 provides that experts' reports should be addressed to the court and gives detailed directions about the form and content of such reports. All experts and those who instruct them should ensure that they are familiar with these requirements.

13.4   Model forms of experts' reports are available from bodies such as the Academy of Experts or the Expert Witness Institute.

13.5   Experts' reports must contain statements that they understand their duty to the court and have complied and will continue to comply with that duty (PD 35, para 2.2(9)). They must also be verified by a statement of truth. The form of the statement of truth is as follows:
> 'I confirm that insofar as the facts stated in my report are within my own knowledge I have made clear which they are and I believe them to be true, and that the opinions I have expressed represent my true and complete professional opinion.'

This wording is mandatory and must not be modified.

Qualifications

13.6   The details of experts' qualifications to be given in reports should be commensurate with the nature and complexity of the case. It may be sufficient merely to state academic and professional qualifications. However, where highly specialised expertise is called for, experts should include the detail of particular training and/or experience that qualifies them to provide that highly specialised evidence.

Tests

13.7   Where tests of a scientific or technical nature have been carried out, experts should state:
(a)   the methodology used; and
(b)   by whom the tests were undertaken and under whose supervision, summarising their respective qualifications and experience.

Reliance on the work of others

13.8   Where experts rely in their reports on literature or other material and cite the opinions of others without having verified them, they must give details of those opinions relied on. It is likely to assist the court if the qualifications of the originator(s) are also stated.

Facts

13.9   When addressing questions of fact and opinion, experts should keep the two separate and discrete.

13.10   Experts must state those facts (whether assumed or otherwise) upon which their opinions are based. They must distinguish clearly between those facts which experts know to be true and those facts which they assume.

13.11   Where there are material facts in dispute experts should express separate opinions on each hypothesis put forward. They should not express a view in favour of one or other disputed version of the facts unless, as a result of particular expertise and experience, they consider one set of facts as being improbable or less probable, in which case they may express that view, and should give reasons for holding it.

Range of opinion

13.12   If the mandatory summary of the range of opinion is based on published sources, experts should explain those sources and, where appropriate, state the qualifications of the originator(s) of the opinions from which they differ, particularly if such opinions represent a well-established school of thought.

13.13   Where there is no available source for the range of opinion, experts may need to express opinions on what they believe to be the range which other experts would arrive at if asked. In those circumstances, experts should make it clear that the range that they summarise is based on their own judgement and explain the basis of that judgement.

Conclusions

13.14   A summary of conclusions is mandatory. The summary should be at the end of the report after all the reasoning. There may be cases, however, where the benefit to the court is heightened by placing a short summary at the beginning of the report whilst giving the full conclusions at the end. For example, it can assist with the comprehension of the analysis and with the absorption of the detailed facts if the court is told at the outset of the direction in which the report's logic will flow in cases involving highly complex matters which fall outside the general knowledge of the court.

Basis of report: material instructions

13.15   The mandatory statement of the substance of all material instructions should not be incomplete or otherwise tend to mislead. The imperative is transparency. The term 'instructions' includes all material which solicitors place in front of experts in order to gain advice. The omission from the statement of 'off-the-record' oral instructions is not permitted. Courts may allow cross-examination about the instructions if there are reasonable grounds to consider that the statement may be inaccurate or incomplete.

14. After receipt of experts' reports

14.1   Following the receipt of experts' reports, those instructing them should advise the experts as soon as reasonably practicable whether, and if so when, the report will be disclosed to other parties; and, if so disclosed, the date of actual disclosure.

14.2   If experts' reports are to be relied upon, and if experts are to give oral evidence, those instructing them should give the experts the opportunity to consider and comment upon other reports within their area of expertise and which deal with relevant issues at the earliest opportunity.

14.3   Those instructing experts should keep experts informed of the progress of cases, including amendments to statements of case relevant to experts' opinion.

14.4   If those instructing experts become aware of material changes in circumstances or that relevant information within their control was not previously provided to experts, they should without delay instruct experts to review and, if necessary, update the contents of their reports.

15. Amendment of reports

15.1   It may become necessary for experts to amend their reports:
    (a)   as a result of an exchange of questions and answers;
    (b)   following agreements reached at meetings between experts; or
    (c)   where further evidence or documentation is disclosed.

15.2   Experts should not be asked to, and should not, amend, expand or alter any parts of reports in a manner which distorts their true opinion, but may be invited to amend or expand reports to ensure accuracy, internal consistency, completeness and relevance to the issues and clarity. Although experts should generally follow the recommendations of solicitors with regard to the form of reports, they should form their own independent views as to the opinions and contents expressed in their reports and exclude any suggestions which do not accord with their views.

15.3   Where experts change their opinion following a meeting of experts, a simple signed and dated addendum or memorandum to that effect is generally sufficient. In some cases, however, the benefit to the court of having an amended report may justify the cost of making the amendment.

15.4   Where experts significantly alter their opinion, as a result of new evidence or because evidence on which they relied has become unreliable, or for any other reason, they should amend their reports to reflect that fact. Amended reports should include reasons for amendments. In such circumstances those instructing experts should inform other parties as soon as possible of any change of opinion.

15.5   When experts intend to amend their reports, they should inform those instructing them without delay and give reasons. They should provide the amended version (or an addendum or memorandum) clearly marked as such as quickly as possible.

16. Written questions to experts

16.1   The procedure for putting written questions to experts (CPR 35.6) is intended to facilitate the clarification of opinions and issues after experts' reports have been served. Experts have a duty to provide answers to questions properly put. Where they fail to do so, the court may impose sanctions against the party instructing the expert, and, if there is continued non-compliance, debar a party from relying on the report. Experts should copy their answers to those instructing them.

16.2   Experts' answers to questions automatically become part of their reports. They are covered by the statement of truth and form part of the expert evidence.

16.3   Where experts believe that questions put are not properly directed to the clarification of the report, or are disproportionate, or have been asked out of time, they should discuss the questions with those instructing them and, if appropriate, those asking the questions. Attempts should be made to resolve such problems without the need for an application to the court for directions.

Written requests for directions in relation to questions

16.4   If those instructing experts do not apply to the court in respect of questions, but experts still believe that questions are improper or out of time, experts may file written requests with the court for directions to assist in carrying out their functions as experts (CPR 35.14). See Section 11 above.

17. Single joint experts

17.1   CPR 35 and PD 35 deal extensively with the instruction and use of joint experts by the parties and the powers of the court to order their use (see CPR 35.7 and 35.8, PD 35, para 5).

17.2   The Civil Procedure Rules encourage the use of joint experts. Wherever possible a joint report should be obtained. Consideration should therefore be given by all parties to the appointment of single joint experts in all cases where a court might direct such an appointment. Single joint experts are the norm in cases allocated to the small claims track and the fast track.

17.3   Where, in the early stages of a dispute, examinations, investigations, tests, site inspections, experiments, preparation of photographs, plans or other similar preliminary expert tasks are necessary, consideration should be given to the instruction of a single joint expert, especially where such matters are not, at that stage, expected to be contentious as between the parties. The objective of such an appointment should be to agree or to narrow issues.

...

17.5   Experts who have previously advised a party (whether in the same case or otherwise) should only be proposed as single joint experts if other parties are given all relevant information about the previous involvement.

17.6   The appointment of a single joint expert does not prevent parties from instructing their own experts to advise (but the costs of such expert advisers may not be recoverable in the case).

Joint instructions

17.7   The parties should try to agree joint instructions to single joint experts, but, in default of agreement, each party may give instructions. In particular, all parties should try to agree what documents should be included with instructions and what assumptions single joint experts should make.

17.8   Where the parties fail to agree joint instructions, they should try to agree where the areas of disagreement lie and their instructions should make this clear. If separate instructions are given, they should be copied at the same time to the other instructing parties.

17.9   Where experts are instructed by two or more parties, the terms of appointment should, unless the court has directed otherwise, or the parties have agreed otherwise, include:

(a)   a statement that all the instructing parties are jointly and severally liable to pay the experts' fees and, accordingly, that experts' invoices should be sent simultaneously to all instructing parties or their solicitors (as appropriate); and

(b)   a statement as to whether any order has been made limiting the amount of experts' fees and expenses (CPR 35.8(4)(a)).

17.10   Where instructions have not been received by the expert from one or more of the instructing parties the expert should give notice (normally at least 7 days) of a deadline to all instructing parties for the receipt by the expert of such instructions. Unless the instructions are received within the deadline the expert may begin work. In the event that instructions are received after the deadline but before the signing off of the report the expert should consider whether it is practicable to comply with those instructions without adversely affecting the timetable set for delivery of the report and in such a manner as to comply with the proportionality principle. An expert who decides to issue a report without taking into account instructions received after the deadline should inform the parties who may apply to the court for directions. In either event the report must show clearly that the expert did not receive instructions within the deadline, or, as the case may be, at all.

Conduct of the single joint expert

17.11   Single joint experts should keep all instructing parties informed of any material steps that they may be taking by, for example, copying all correspondence to those instructing them.

17.12   Single joint experts are Part 35 experts and so have an overriding duty to the court. They are the parties' appointed experts and therefore owe an equal duty to all parties. They should maintain independence, impartiality and transparency at all times.

17.13   Single joint experts should not attend any meeting or conference which is not a joint one, unless all the parties have agreed in writing or the court has directed that such a meeting may be held and who is to pay the experts' fees for the meeting.

17.14   Single joint experts may request directions from the court – see Section 11 above.

17.15   Single joint experts should serve their reports simultaneously on all instructing parties. They should provide a single report even though they may have received instructions which contain areas of conflicting fact or allegation. If conflicting instructions lead to different opinions (for example, because the instructions require experts to make different assumptions of fact), reports may need to contain more than one set of opinions on any issue. It is for the court to determine the facts.

Cross-examination

17.16　Single joint experts do not normally give oral evidence at trial but if they do, all parties may cross-examine them. In general written questions (CPR 35.6) should be put to single joint experts before requests are made for them to attend court for the purpose of cross-examination.

18. Discussions between experts

18.1　The court has powers to direct discussions between experts for the purposes set out in the Rules (CPR 35.12). Parties may also agree that discussions take place between their experts.

18.2　Where single joint experts have been instructed but parties have, with the permission of the court, instructed their own additional Part 35 experts, there may, if the court so orders or the parties agree, be discussions between the single joint experts and the additional Part 35 experts. Such discussions should be confined to those matters within the remit of the additional Part 35 experts or as ordered by the court.

18.3　The purpose of discussions between experts should be, wherever possible, to:
  (a)　identify and discuss the expert issues in the proceedings;
  (b)　reach agreed opinions on those issues, and, if that is not possible, to narrow the issues in the case;
  (c)　identify those issues on which they agree and disagree and summarise their reasons for disagreement on any issue; and
  (d)　identify what action, if any, may be taken to resolve any of the outstanding issues between the parties.

Arrangements for discussions between experts

18.4　Arrangements for discussions between experts should be proportionate to the value of cases. In small claims and fast-track cases there should not normally be meetings between experts. Where discussion is justified in such cases, telephone discussion or an exchange of letters should, in the interests of proportionality, usually suffice. In multi-track cases, discussion may be face to face, but the practicalities or the proportionality principle may require discussions to be by telephone or video conference.

18.5　The parties, their lawyers and experts should co-operate to produce the agenda for any discussion between experts, although primary responsibility for preparation of the agenda should normally lie with the parties' solicitors.

18.6　The agenda should indicate what matters have been agreed and summarise concisely those which are in issue. It is often helpful for it to include questions to be answered by the experts. If agreement cannot be reached promptly or a party is unrepresented, the court may give directions for the drawing up of the agenda. The agenda should be circulated to experts and those instructing them to allow sufficient time for the experts to prepare for the discussion.

18.7　Those instructing experts must not instruct experts to avoid reaching agreement (or to defer doing so) on any matter within the experts' competence. Experts are not permitted to accept such instructions.

18.8　The parties' lawyers may only be present at discussions between experts if all the parties agree or the court so orders. If lawyers do attend, they should not normally intervene except to answer questions put to them by the experts or to advise about the law.

18.9　The content of discussions between experts should not be referred to at trial unless the parties agree (CPR 35.12(4)). It is good practice for any such agreement to be in writing.

18.10   At the conclusion of any discussion between experts, a statement should be prepared setting out:

(a)   a list of issues that have been agreed, including, in each instance, the basis of agreement;

(b)   a list of issues that have not been agreed, including, in each instance, the basis of disagreement;

(c)   a list of any further issues that have arisen that were not included in the original agenda for discussion;

(d)   a record of further action, if any, to be taken or recommended, including as appropriate the holding of further discussions between experts.

18.11   The statement should be agreed and signed by all the parties to the discussion as soon as may be practicable.

18.12   Agreements between experts during discussions do not bind the parties unless the parties expressly agree to be bound by the agreement (CPR 35.12(5)). However, in view of the overriding objective, parties should give careful consideration before refusing to be bound by such an agreement and be able to explain their refusal should it become relevant to the issue of costs.

19. Attendance of experts at court

19.1   Experts instructed in cases have an obligation to attend court if called upon to do so and accordingly should ensure that those instructing them are always aware of their dates to be avoided and take all reasonable steps to be available.

19.2   Those instructing experts should:

(a)   ascertain the availability of experts before trial dates are fixed;

(b)   keep experts updated with timetables (including the dates and times experts are to attend) and the location of the court;

(c)   give consideration, where appropriate, to experts giving evidence via a video-link.

(d)   inform experts immediately if trial dates are vacated.

19.3   Experts should normally attend court without the need for the service of witness summonses, but on occasion they may be served to require attendance (CPR 34). The use of witness summonses does not affect the contractual or other obligations of the parties to pay experts' fees.

2 GUIDELINES ON EXPERTS' DISCUSSIONS IN THE CONTEXT OF CLINICAL DISPUTES

Note that the Protocol from the Civil Justice Council (see above) has a section on discussions, so it may be that this document has lost much of its cogency

1. Purpose of the Guidelines

To provide guidance for lawyers and experts to arrange discussions between the experts in clinical negligence cases within the ambit of Part 35.

2. Application of the Guidelines

The court may direct a discussion between the experts in accordance with Part 35.12 of the Civil Procedure Rules (CPR), alternatively there may be a discussion by consent between the parties; in each case the guidelines apply.

3. Time for Expert Discussion

(1)   The court has power to direct that a discussion be held at any stage of the proceedings. This will usually be after exchange of experts' reports.

(2)   Discussions may take place by agreement at any time including before proceedings are commenced provided that the issues have been sufficiently identified to justify discussions.

4. Purpose of Expert Discussions

The purpose of expert discussion is to identify:

(1)   the extent of the agreement between the experts;

(2)   the points of disagreement and the reasons for disagreement;

(3)   action, if any, which may be taken to resolve the outstanding points of disagreement;

(4)   any further material questions not raised in the agenda and the extent to which those issues may be agreed.

5. Arrangements for Expert Discussions

(1)   The Agenda
There must be a detailed agenda. Unless the parties agree otherwise the agenda should be prepared by the claimant's lawyers (with expert assistance) and supplemented by the defendants' lawyers, if so advised, and mutually agreed. The agenda should consist as far as possible of closed questions, that is questions which can be answered 'yes' or 'no'. The questions should be clearly stated and relate directly to the legal and factual issues in the case.

(2)   The nature of the discussion
The discussion should take place face to face or by video link. Exceptionally, and having regard to proportionality, the discussion may take place by telephone. Save in exceptional circumstances these guidelines (and in particular paragraph 6 below) should apply whatever the form of the discussion.
It is usually advisable to have separate agenda and discussions between experts in different disciplines.

(3)   The experts should be provided with the following documents before the discussion:
   (a)   the medical records;
   (b)   if proceedings have been issued, the statements of case, the claimant's chronology, the defendants' comments on the chronology, the witness statements and the expert's reports as exchanged;
   (c)   if proceedings have not been issued then the parties should agree a chronology and provide this to the experts with witness statements and such experts' opinion as has been exchanged.

(4)   Unless the lawyers for all parties agree or the court orders otherwise lawyers for all parties will attend the discussions of experts. If lawyers do attend such discussions they should not normally intervene save to answer questions put to them by the experts or advise them on the law.

(5)   Timing
   (a)   A draft agenda should be served on the defendants' lawyers for comments 28 days before the agreed date for the expert discussion. The defendants should, within 14 days of receipt, agree the agenda or propose amendments; and
   (b)   7 days thereafter the claimant's lawyers shall agree the agenda. If in exceptional circumstances agreement cannot be reached, the parties should apply to the court.

6. Conclusion of the Discussion

(A) At the conclusion of a face to face discussion a statement must be prepared setting out:

(1) A list of the agreed answers to the question in the agenda.

(2) A list of the questions which have not been agreed.

(3) Where possible a summary of the reasons for non-agreement.

(4) An account of any agreed action which needs to be taken to resolve the outstanding questions in (2) above.

(5) A list of any further material questions identified by the experts, not in the agenda, and the extent to which they are agreed or alternatively, the action (if any) which needs to be taken to resolve these further outstanding questions.

Individual copies of this statement must be signed by all the experts before leaving any face to face meeting.

(B) Before the conclusion of a discussion at a distance, identical statements setting out all the information required in paragraph (A) above must be prepared and signed by each expert. Unaltered signed copies must be exchanged immediately.

7. The experts' duty is to the court and those instructing experts must not give and no expert should accept instructions not to agree any item on the agenda.

3 GUIDELINES ON INSTRUCTING SINGLE JOINT EXPERTS

Note that the Protocol from the Civil Justice Council (see above) has a section on single joint experts, so it may be that this document has lost much of its cogency

Consultation draft – September 2001

I. The purpose of the guidelines

The remit of the group was to produce guidelines for the instruction and conduct of single joint experts in situations where the parties had agreed, or the court had ordered, that a single joint expert should be instructed. The Forum has formed no view as to whether the instruction of single joint experts is in principle or in any particular circumstances desirable and this was not within the remit of the group.

In these guidelines 'expert' means 'single joint expert'.

II. General principles governing the use of the single joint experts

Experts (and those instructing them) should act at all times in accordance with the Civil Procedure Rules 1999 and the Code of Guidance on Expert Evidence. Their conduct should be governed by the following principles.

1. **Fairness** and **equality of access**. The expert must be equally accessible to all the parties. The fact that one party has sent the instructions to the expert does not give that party the right to any favourable treatment by the expert. The expert should be scrupulous to treat all instructing parties equally.

2. **Transparency** – all instructions and responses to and from the expert should be equally visible to all the parties in the action. To achieve this

(a) No instruction should be given or accepted which is not seen by all other parties;

(b) The expert should communicate nothing to any party that is invisible to any other party;

(c) All such communications shall be in writing. It is the responsibility of the author or originator of every document to send copies of it to all instructing parties at the same time;

(d) So that there should be no doubt about whether this has been done every letter should be marked with the names of the persons to whom it is being copied;

(e) Where these guidelines provide that a particular party will normally have the responsibility for initiating an action, and that party fails to do so within a reasonable time, another instructing party should initiate the action.

3. **Agreement**. Every contact each party has with the expert must be within the terms agreed between the parties.

III. Running an action with single joint experts involved; a narrative guide

(1) Identifying speciality, ambit of instruction, and choice of expert

(i) Parties should agree

    (a) on the expert speciality on which it is desired to achieve a joint instruction;

    (b) on the ambit of the instruction to such expert, following which

    (c) they should endeavour to agree on the choice of an individual expert to perform that role.

(ii) No expert previously instructed in the same matter by either party should be instructed unless the other party is made privy to all the instructions to and advice given by that expert.

(iii) The party who agrees to arrange the involvement of the expert is responsible for making sure that the expert accepts the conditions of involvement, including the fee limit and the action timetable as provided for below.

(2) Arrangements for and limits set for fees

(i) Parties should agree on what fees are to be paid to the expert, both on a limit to the initial report fee and an hourly rate for further work.

(ii) Experts should observe the fee limit.

(iii) Fee notes must clearly state both the total fee charged in the matter and the share of the fee to the party being billed.

(iv) All the parties being billed for the fee must be sent a separate fee note.

(v) The instructing parties are jointly and severally liable for the whole of the expert's fee. Should an instructing party default for three months, the other party or parties must pay the fee.

(3) Establishing the management plan for the action

(i) In every matter it will be necessary to produce a written memorandum of what has been agreed between the parties as to how the instruction of the expert is to be managed and to circulate it to the expert and others involved in the action.

(ii) In complex matters the parties will need to agree on a detailed management plan clearly stating who is to perform which task by which date in order to comply with any directions in the action.

(iii) It will normally be the responsibility of the claimant's solicitor to produce the first draft of the memorandum or action plan and to submit it to the solicitors for the defendant(s) for agreement or amendment.

(iv)   It will normally be the responsibility of the claimant's solicitor to keep the plan up to date, should changes be necessary.

(v)   The plan should specify whose responsibility it is to circulate the plan to which experts, counsel and other persons involved in the action, after agreeing any amendments with the other party.

(vi)   The plan should have annexed a contact list detailing the name, address, telephone numbers and email addresses of all persons involved in the case.

(vii)   Where proceedings have been issued, the list should include the name and contact details of the Master or District Judge to whom the matter is assigned and to whom the expert can apply for directions or guidance, pursuant to Civil Procedure Rules Part 35.14.

(viii)   The management plan should stipulate whether and on what terms experts may discuss the case with other expert(s) (whether joint or not) instructed in the action, and if they are to be free to do this then the full contact list should be provided to them.

(4) Arrangements for drafting instructions

(i)   It is recommended that the parties make every effort to agree on the terms of a joint letter of instruction to the expert.

(ii)   The defendant's solicitor will normally produce the first draft of the instruction to the expert. If there is more than one defendant in the case the first defendant will normally, in default of agreement to the contrary, have this duty. This will be submitted to the claimant for completion, amendment and approval. The claimant's solicitor will submit the amended draft to the defendant for approval and then when it is approved send the instructions to the expert with the appropriate documentation, which must be identified to or copied to the other parties.

(iii)   In the exceptional case that they cannot agree on the terms of a joint letter of instruction, they may each send their own letter of instruction, in accordance with Part 35 Rule 8 of the Civil Procedure Rules 1999 and paragraph 29 of the Code of Guidance to experts. In that event each party must copy his letter to the other instructing parties.

(iv)   When a joint letter of instruction is to be used, this must not be sent to the expert until all instructing parties have formally agreed the draft and a copy of the final instructing letter should also be sent to the other instructing parties. If instructions are on an agreed basis, the other instructing parties must then write to the expert confirming that they agree with the instructions.

(v)   Any further instructions to the expert must also be agreed between the parties.

(vi)   If the parties cannot agree on the ambit of any instruction, whether initial or supplemental, then the parties must return to the court for a ruling on whether the party who wants this further advice may instruct the expert, on terms to be agreed between the parties, to provide it. If proceedings have not begun, and the parties cannot agree, the party in question must instruct another expert.

(vii)   All documentation or other material discloseable in the action, which is relevant to the expert's instruction, must be provided to the expert, unless all instructing parties agree that some is unnecessary.

(viii)   All instructions to the expert must be in writing (which includes email) and so must all the expert's responses. The only exception is that the parties may agree on a conference call involving the expert and all instructing parties.

(ix) Parties should agree on whether they want to receive copies of all communications to the expert at the time when they are made, or want to be periodically updated.

(5) Arranging the expert's access to the claimant and other persons

(i) The parties should agree initially on whether the expert needs access to the claimant or any other person, where appropriate after consulting the nominated expert, and under what terms.

(ii) They should then leave it to the expert to arrange such access, at reasonable notice and with regard to the convenience of the claimant, unless other parties object.

(6) Delivery of reports

(i) It is the responsibility of the expert to deliver his or her report within the time agreed and to send it at the same time to each of the instructing solicitors, together with a copy of any accompanying letter.

(ii) The same conditions and practices as set out above apply to supplemental reports.

(7) Questions to the experts

(i) Questions can only be put to the experts if they are within the ambit of CPR Part 35.6, or agreed between the parties, or sanctioned by the court.

(8) Conferences and meetings

(i) The parties may choose to have a joint conference, with jointly instructed experts.

(ii) Alternatively, any instructing party may arrange a conference with the expert but must in that event offer the other instructing parties an opportunity to attend and take part in the part of the conference which the expert is to attend.

(iii) The party organising the conference must where practicable fix such a meeting for the convenience of all instructing parties after a period of notice which is reasonable in the circumstances. Where this is not practicable then the meeting may take place. However, if the other instructing parties do not wish to send a representative or are unable to do so they shall be entitled to be provided with the convening solicitor's note (which should be that made for his own file) of the part of the meeting which included discussion with the expert. This note should be supplied as soon as reasonably possible after the meeting and in any event within two working days.

(iv) The expert must not be asked to be present at any part of the meeting to which the other instructing parties are not invited.

(9) Trial

(i) Any discussions with experts, which take place outside court or otherwise in the context of a trial should be treated as conferences and the guidelines set out in (8) above should be followed.

4 THE PRE-ACTION PROTOCOL – WHERE NEXT?

Introduction

The clinical negligence pre-action protocol was created by the Forum and, more than 2 years ago was adopted by the government and annexed to the CPR.

Earlier this year the Forum decided to try to find out how satisfactorily the protocol was working. We did this by way of a structured questionnaire, sent to a wide range of consultees. We received about 100 responses. We know that the Lord Chancellor's Department and the Law Society are conducting more general research into changes in pre-action conduct post CPR which should be published early next year.

...

The Main Findings

These are very positive. The main objectives of the protocol appear to be met:

- Better communication
- Better exchange of information
- Earlier investigation by defendants
- Improved opportunities for settlement

Very few changes to the protocol were suggested by respondents.

Recommendations to the Forum re the Protocol

The CDF Protocol Working Party has considered the response and is minded to recommend to the Forum:

- The results of the survey should be disseminated – by posting on the CDF website and in articles in the medical and legal press
- A few changes to the text of the protocol to reflect comments on:
  - Health records – if the claimant has relevant 'third party' health records, copies should be provided to the defendant within 40 days of a request – Protocol para 3.13
  - Health records – defendants should include in routine disclosure complaints documents relevant to the (potential) claim – Protocol para 3.7
  - Letter of claim – to clarify that the letter should indicate the nature of alleged breaches of duty and their causative effect – Protocol para 3.16
  - Response time for defendants – to add that claimants should not unreasonably refuse extensions of time beyond 3 months if the defendant provides good reasons for needing more time – Protocol para 3.25
  - When defendants admit liability – they too should be specific about which breaches of duty and causation are admitted and why – Protocol para 3.25
  - Conditional fee agreements – the protocol should make it clear that the existence of a CFA, but not the success fee or insurance premium, should be disclosed in the letter of claim or within 7 days of the party entering into the CFA.

Recommendations to LCD

- Compliance with the protocol – that judges need to be more robust and proactive in applying sanctions for non-compliance
- Part 36 offers – CPR Part 36 should be amended to clarify that the time for responding to an offer to settle made with the letter of claim is 21 days from when the response is due, not 21 days from the receipt of the offer.

Conclusion

Associates are invited to:
- add their views to the questionnaire response
- comment constructively on how the protocol might be amended
- suggest any other changes to pre-action steps/rules which the LCD or others might consider.

Suzanne Burn
August 2001

5 EXPERT'S DECLARATION

The expert's declaration can take different forms. The Expert Witness Institute has suggested the following:

1. I understand that my overriding duty is to the court, both in preparing reports and in giving oral evidence. I have complied and will continue to comply with that duty.

2. I have set out in my report what I understand from those instructing me to be the questions in respect of which my opinion as an expert are required.

3. I have done my best, in preparing this report, to be accurate and complete. I have mentioned all matters which I regard as relevant to the opinions I have expressed. All of the matters on which I have expressed an opinion lie within my field of expertise.

4. I have drawn to the attention of the court all matters, of which I am aware, which might adversely affect my opinion.

5. Wherever I have no personal knowledge, I have indicated the source of factual information.

6. I have not included anything in this report which has been suggested to me by anyone, including the lawyers instructing me, without forming my own independent view of the matter.

7. Where, in my view, there is a range of reasonable opinion, I have indicated the extent of that range in the report.

8. At the time of signing the report I consider it to be complete and accurate. I will notify those instructing me if, for any reason, I subsequently consider that the report requires any correction or qualification.

9. I understand that this report will be the evidence that I will give under oath, subject to any correction or qualification I may make before swearing to its veracity.

10. I have attached to this report a statement setting out the substance of all facts and instructions given to me which are material to the opinions expressed in this report or upon which these opinions are based. I confirm that insofar as the facts stated in my report are within my own knowledge I have made clear which they are and I believe them to be true, and the opinion I have expressed represents my true and complete professional opinion.

The Protocol from the Civil Justice Council has simply this:

'I confirm that insofar as the facts stated in my report are within my own knowledge I have made clear which they are and I believe them to be true, and that the opinions I have expressed represent my true and complete professional opinion.'

Appendix III

Directions

SUGGESTED MODEL DIRECTIONS FOR CLINICAL NEGLIGENCE
CASES BEFORE MASTER UNGLEY AND MASTER YOXALL[1]

Version 3 (11/3/05)

Introductory Note

These directions are based on orders that have been made and obeyed; they need
not be slavishly followed, but used as guidelines only. The following specimen
paragraphs can be used to prepare a draft order before a case management hearing. If this is not served with the application, it should be sent to all other parties
in sufficient time for them to consider it before the hearing. [It is especially helpful if the draft order is double-spaced with wide margins to allow for corrections
at the time the order is made.]

[The passages in italics are to assist parties, but should not normally be
included in the draft order.]

Note: [*Periodical payments. Parties should, at the first CMC, be prepared to give
their <u>provisional</u> view as to whether the case is one in which a periodical payments
order might be appropriate.*]

ORDER

Allocation

Allocate to Multi-Track. [*In most cases allocation will have been dealt with on
Allocation Questionnaires.*]

Preservation of Evidence

The Defendant do retain and preserve safely the original clinical notes relating to
this action pending the trial. The Defendant do give facilities for inspection by the
Claimant, the Claimant's legal advisers and experts of the said original notes
upon 7 days written notice to do so.

Maintenance of Records and Reports

Legible copies of the medical records of the Claimant/Deceased/Claimant's
Mother are to be placed in a separate paginated bundle at the earliest opportunity

---

1   These model directions, reproduced by kind permission of Master Ungley, will of course
    be varied as and when the needs of the case demands some variation. They are not
    written in stone.

by the Claimant's Solicitors and kept up to date. All references to medical notes in any report are to be made by reference to the pages in that bundle.

All reports coming into existence for the purpose of the case disclosed by any party are to be placed in a separate paginated bundle at the earliest opportunity by the Claimant's Solicitors and kept up to date. Upon reports being added to such bundle the Claimants are to serve a revised index to such bundle upon all other parties. All references to such reports in subsequent reports shall include a reference to the relevant pages in that bundle.

Split Trial

[*An order 'that there be a split trial' is inappropriate. The following is suggested.*]

'A preliminary issue shall be tried between the Claimant and the Defendant as to whether or not the Defendant is liable to the Claimant by reason of the matters alleged in the Particulars of Claim and, if so, whether or not any of the injuries pleaded were caused thereby; if any such injuries were so caused, the extent of the same.'

Amendments

Permission to Claimant/Defendant to amend the Particulars of Claim/Defence in accordance with the draft initialled, the Defendant to serve an amended Defence by / /05. If an amended Defence is served, permission to Claimant to serve a reply within ...... days thereafter. Costs of and occasioned by the amendments to be borne by (the party seeking permission to amend) [*where no draft is available, but the form of the amendments is not contentious*] (party wishing to amend) to serve draft amended Statement of Case by / /05. If no objection to the draft amendments, response to be served by / /05, if objection is taken to the draft, permission to restore.

Disclosure

Standard disclosure by list/category to be effected by / /05/(within ..... days after a reply is served or due).

Any initial request for inspection or copy documents is to be made within 7/14 days of service of the lists.

Witness Statements

Each party shall exchange all factual evidence on issues of liability, causation and quantum in the form of signed and dated witness statements to be disclosed by simultaneous exchange on or before / /05 and shall serve Civil Evidence Act notices by the same date. Evidence of all concerned with the treatment and care of the Claimant at the time of the matters alleged against the Defendant shall be disclosed in accordance with this paragraph.

Expert Evidence
A. Joint Single Experts

Permission to the parties to rely upon the evidence of joint single experts in the fields of [*state the disciplines*], identity of the experts to be agreed by / /05. Instructions to be provided to the expert by / /05, report to be prepared by / /05. If the parties are unable to agree on the identity of the expert to be instructed, parties to apply to restore before the Master. [*At such hearing the parties are to provide details of the CVs, availability and the estimated fee of the expert they propose and reasoned objections to any other proposed.*]

B. Separate Experts

Each party shall exchange all expert evidence on liability and causation in the form of expert reports to take place by simultaneous exchange on or before / /05 and such evidence to be limited to a report from one expert in each of the following disciplines: [*state the disciplines*] permission being given to call the makers of the same to give oral evidence as to matters remaining in issue.

Permission to the Claimant and all Defendants, Defendants acting jointly, (*unless otherwise ordered*) to rely on expert evidence on quantum, condition and prognosis in the form of expert reports limited to one expert from each of the following fields. [*State the disciplines*] permission being given to call the makers of the same to give oral evidence as to matters remaining in issue.

Reports to be served as follows, Claimant's by / /05. Defendants' by / /05. [*Usually about 3 months after the Claimant's.*]

Any unpublished literature upon which any expert witness proposes to rely shall be served at the same time as service of his statement together with a list of published literature. Any supplementary literature upon which any expert witness proposes to rely shall be notified to all other parties at least one month before trial. No expert witness shall rely upon any publications that have not been disclosed in accordance with this direction without leave of the trial judge on such terms as to costs as he deems fit.

Experts' Discussions

Unless otherwise agreed by all parties' solicitors, after consulting with the experts, the experts of like discipline for the parties shall discuss the case on a without prejudice basis by / /05.

(a)   The purpose of the discussions is to identify:
   (i)   The extent of the agreement between the experts;
   (ii)   The points of disagreement and short reasons for disagreement;
   (iii) Action, if any, which may be taken to resolve the outstanding points of disagreement;
   (iv) Any further material points not raised in the Agenda and the extent to which these issues are agreed;

(b)   **Unless otherwise agreed** by all parties' solicitors, after consulting with the experts, a draft Agenda in the form of questions capable, as far as possible, of being answered 'yes' or 'no' shall be prepared jointly by the Claimant's solicitors and experts and sent to the Defendant's solicitors for comment at least 35 days before the agreed date for the experts' discussions; [*The Agenda should assist the experts by directing them to the issues identified between the parties in the pleadings and should not be in the form of leading questions.*]

(c)   The Defendants shall within 14 days of receipt agree the Agenda, or propose amendments;

(d)   Seven days thereafter all solicitors shall use their best endeavours to agree the Agenda; in default both versions shall be considered at the discussions. Agendas, when used, shall be provided to the experts not less than 7 days before the date fixed for discussions.

[*Where it has been impossible to agree a single Agenda, it is of assistance to the experts if the second Agenda is consecutively numbered to the first, ie if the first Agenda has 16 questions in it, the second Agenda is numbered from 17 onwards.*]

Experts give their own opinions to assist the court and should attend discussions on the basis that they have full authority to sign the joint statement. The experts should not require the authorisation of solicitor or counsel before signing a joint statement. [*Note to the parties: this does not affect Rule 35.12 which provides that where experts reach agreement on an issue during their discussions, the agreement shall not bind the parties unless the parties expressly agree to be bound by the agreement.*]

If an expert radically alters his or her opinion, the joint statement should include a note or addendum by that expert explaining the change of opinion

Unless otherwise ordered by the Court, or unless agreed by all parties, including the experts, the parties' solicitors shall not attend such discussions. If solicitors do attend, the experts may if they so request, hold a part of their discussions in the absence of the solicitors. Where solicitors do attend, they should not normally intervene, save to answer questions put to them by the experts or to advise them upon the law. A statement shall be prepared by the experts dealing with (a) (i)–(iv) above. Individual copies of such statements shall be signed by the experts at the conclusion of the discussion, or as soon thereafter as practicable and in any event within 7 days. Copies of the statements are to be provided to the parties' solicitors thereafter.

Experts instructed by the parties in accordance with this Order shall be provided with a copy of this Order within 7 days after it is sealed, or at the time of instruction, whichever is the later.

Schedules

Claimant to serve by / /05 a final Schedule of loss and damage costed to the date of trial.

Defendant to serve by / /05 a Counter Schedule. [*Note: parties are encouraged to exchange Schedules in a form which enables the Counter Schedule to be based on the Claimant's Schedule ie by delivering a disk with the hard copy, or by sending it as an e-mail attachment.*]

Trial Directions

The Claimant's Solicitors shall apply on or before ...... [*usually no later than 6 weeks after the CMC at which the disciplines of the experts are fixed*] to the Clerk of the Lists in London/[the Listing Officer in the venue] for a listing appointment for a trial period for hearing within the trial window. Pre-trial check lists to be filed as directed by the Clerk of the Lists. [*Note: the Clerk of the Lists, in order to maintain the necessary degree of flexibility for listing, will give a 'trial period' rather than a fixed date, but, in order to accommodate parties need for certainty as to dates for experts to attend, will, if an approach is made closer to the beginning of the trial period, confirm the date for the trial to begin as the first day of the trial period.*]

Mode of Trial: Judge Alone. London
Listing category: [*usually 'B'*]
Estimated time:
Trial Window: / / 05 to / /05
Certified fit for trial by High Court Judge, if available.

Alternative Dispute Resolution

The parties shall by / /05 [*a date usually about 3 months before the trial window opens*] consider whether the case is capable of resolution by ADR. If any party considers that the case is unsuitable for resolution by ADR, that party shall be prepared to justify that decision at the conclusion of the trial, should the trial judge consider that such means of resolution were appropriate, when he is considering the appropriate costs order to make. Such means of ADR as shall be adopted shall be concluded not less than 35 days prior to the trial.

The party considering the case unsuitable for ADR shall, not less than 28 days before the commencement of the trial, file with the Court a Witness Statement, without prejudice save as to costs, giving the reasons upon which they rely for saying that the case was unsuitable. The Witness Statement shall not be disclosed to the trial Judge until the conclusion of the case.

[*'ADR' includes 'round table' conferences, at which the parties attempt to define and narrow the issues in the case, including those to which expert evidence is directed, early neutral evaluation, mediation and arbitration. The object is to try* to reduce the number of cases settled 'at the door of the Court', which are wasteful both of costs and judicial time.]

Trial Bundles

Parties to agree the contents of the Trial bundle and exchange skeleton arguments not less than 7 days before the hearing. Claimant to lodge the skeleton arguments and the Trial bundle under PD 39.3 [*Note: the object is to ensure that <u>all</u> the relevant material is provided at one time to the Clerk of the Lists to pass to the trial Judge. The PD sets out both the contents of the bundle and the time when it must be lodged.*]

Restoration of Hearing

Further CMC Room E 101/109 on / /05 at .... Time estimate . . . mins. [*Note: if all directions have been complied with and there are no further directions to be made, the further CMC can be vacated by consent, preferably giving the Master as much notice as possible.*]

Permission to restore the application for further directions [*Note: an application to restore will be made as follows, <u>provided that the time estimate is 20 mins or less.</u> The parties will apply directly to Master Ungley / Master Yoxall by joint letter stating that the application will take no longer than 20 mins and giving 3 dates on which both parties are available. The application will be listed by the Master at 10.00 a.m. on the first available of those dates. Applications estimated to take more than 20 mins should be applied for as private room appointments in the usual way.*]

[*Both Masters are willing, in appropriate cases, to hear applications by telephone link, provided sufficient notice is given <u>directly to the Master concerned</u> and the relevant papers are provided in advance. E-mails are an acceptable means of communication, provided that they are copied to all parties.*]

Costs in case/(or other costs order sought)

Claimant to draw and file this Order by / /05 and serve the Defendant(s)

E-mail addresses (to be used only for case management purposes):

master.ungley@courtservice.gsi.gov.uk

master.yoxall@courtservice.gsi.gov.uk

[*Note: the Court File in cases proceeding before the Masters will not be placed before the Master. Parties wishing for it to be produced should notify the Registry in Room E07 FIVE CLEAR DAYS in advance of the appointment. In all other cases parties should bring with them copies of any filed documents upon which they intend to rely.*]

Appendix IV

Common Hieroglyphs and Abbreviations

Here is a list of common abbreviations and hieroglyphs, reproduced by kind permission of Ann Winyard.

Common hieroglyphs

+ + +	much/many
#	fracture
Δ	diagnosis
diff. Δ or $\Delta\Delta$	differential diagnosis
℞	treatment
J° (no jaundice)	nil/nothing/no
†	up, increasing
N,→	constant, normal or lateral shift (eg of apex of heart)
↓	down, decreasing
⊥	central (of the trachea)
$\frac{1}{7}$	one day
$\frac{2}{52}$	two weeks
$\frac{3}{12}$	three months
T32.C°C	temperature 38.6
T–14	term (ie date baby due) less two weeks
T+7	term plus one week
$\frac{35+4}{40}$	35 weeks and 4 days
$\frac{37+3}{40}$	37 weeks and 3 days

Common abbreviations

AAL	Anterior axillary line
ATCH	Adrenocorticotrophic hormone
AE	Air entry
AFB	Acid fast bacillus (TB)

AFP	Alpha-fetoprotein (maternal serum and occasionally amniotic fluid levels tested in pregnancy to screen for neural tube defect in fetus).
AJ	Ankle jerk (reflex: see also BJ, KJ, SJ, TJ)
Anti-D	This gamma globulin must be given by injection to Rhesus negative mother who delivers/aborts Rhesus positive child/fetus to prevent mother developing antibodies which could damage a subsequent Rhesus positive baby.
Apgar	Apgar score: means of recording baby's condition at birth by observing and 'scoring' (0, 1 or 2) 5 parameters
A/V	Anteverted
BJ	Biceps jerk (reflex: see AJ)
BNF (plus date)	British National Formulary (prescriber's 'bible' supplied free to all NHS doctors). New edition each year. You can buy one (about £10 from medical bookshops).
BO	Bowels open
BP (plus date)	British pharmacopoeia
BP	Blood pressure
BS	(a) Breath sounds
	(b) Bowel sounds
	(c) Blood sugar
c̄	With (Latin: cum)
C_2H_5OH	Alcohol
Ca	(a) Carcinoma/cancer
	(b) Calcium
Caps	Capsules
CAT scan	Computed axial tomograph
CNS	Central nervous system
CO	Complaining of
CO_2	Carbon dioxide
COETT	Cuffed oral endotracheal tube (see COT and ETT)
COT	Cuffed oral tube (endotracheal tube used for ventilating a patient who cannot breath unaided)
CPD	Cephalo-pelvic disproportion (baby too big to fit through pelvis)
CSF	Cerebo-spinal fluid
CTG	Cardiotocograph (trace duing labour of baby's heart and mum's contractions)
CVA	Cerebo-vascular accident (stroke)
CVS	Cardio-vascular system
Cx	Cervix
CXR	Chest X-ray
DNA	(a) Did not attend
	(b) Deoxyribonucleic acid
D & V	Diarrhoea and vomiting
DOA	Dead on arrival
DVT	Deep vein thrombosis
Dx	Diagnosis
EGG	Electro-cardiogram/graph (electri heart recording)
ECT	Electro-convulsive therapy
EDC	Expected date of confinement
EDD	Expected date of delivery
EEG	Electroencephalogram/graph (brain scan)
ERCP	Endoscopic retrograde choledochopancreatico/graphy/scopy

ERPC	Evacuation of retained products of conception
ESR	Erythrocyte sedimentation rate (blood)
EtOH	Another code for alcohol
ETT	Endotracheal tube (see COT above)
FB	Finger's breadth
FBC	Full blood count
FBS	Fetal blood sampling (carried out during labour to check baby's condition)
FH	Family history
FHH	Fetal heart heard
FHHR	Fetal heart heard regular
FHR	Fetal heart rate
FLK	(Used by pediatricians) Funny looking kid
FMF	Fetal movements felt
FSE	Fetal scalp electrode
FSH	(a) Family and social history
	(b) Follicle-stimulating hormone (produced in pregnancy)
GA	General anesthetic
GFR	Glomerular filtration rate
GIT	Gastro-intestinal tract
GTT	Glucose tolerance test (for diabetes)
GUT	Genito-urinary tract
Hb	Hemoglobin (blood)
HPC	History of presenting complaint
HS	Heart sounds
HVS	High vaginal swab
Hx	History
ICS	Intercostal space (usually as xICS, where x = a number from 1 to 11)
IJ	Internal jugular vein
IM	Intramuscular
IVI	Intravenous infusion (drip)
JVP	Jugular vein pressure
K	Potassium
KJ	Knee jerk (reflex: see AJ)
kPa	Kilopascal, approximately 7.5 mmHg
L	Litre
LA	Local anesthetic
LFTs	Liver function tests
LIH	Left inguinal hernia
LMP	Last menstrual period
LN	Lymph node
LOA	Left occiput anterior (position of baby's head at delivery; see also LOP, ROA, ROP)
LOC	Loss of consciousness
LOL	Left occipitolateral
LOP	Left occiput posterior (see LOA above)
LSCS	Lower segment cesarean section (the 'normal' type of cesarean)
LSKK	Liver, spleen and kidneys
mcg	Microgram
MCL	Mic clavicular line
μg	Microgram

mg	Milligram
mist	Mixture
ml	Mililitre
mmHG	Milimitres of mercury (pressure)
mMOL	Milimol
N & V	Nausea and vomiting
Na	Sodium
NaHCO$_3$	Sodium bicarbonate (alkaline substance: *inter alia* given to counteract metabolic acidosis following oxygen deprivation)
NAD	Nothing abnormal diagnosed/detected
NBM	Nil by mouth
ng	Nanogram
NG	Carcinoma/cancer (neoplastic growth)
NMCS	No malignant cells seen
NOF	Neck of femur
N/S	Normal size
O$_2$	Oxygen
OA	Occipito-posterior
P	Pulse
π	Period
Pco$_2$	Partial pressure of carbon dioxide (normally in blood)
PERLA	Pupils are equal and react to light and accommodation
PE	(a) Pulmonary embolism
	(b) Pre-eclampsia
PET	Pre-eclamptic toxemia
pg	Picogram
pH	Negative log of hydrogen icon activity: 'acidity and alkalinity' scale. Low is acidic. High is alkaline. pH7 is about neutral.
PH	Past/previous history
PID	(a) Pelvic inflammatory disease
	(b) Prolapsed intevertebral disc
PMH	Past/previous medical history
PN(R)	Percussion note (resonant)
PO$_2$	Partial pressure of oxygen (normally in blood)
POH	Past/previous obstetric history
po	Per os (by mouth)
pr	Per rectum (by the rectum)
prn	As required – of, eg, pain killers
pv	Per vaginam (by the vagina)
RBC	Red blood cell (erythrocyte)
Rh	Rhesus (blood type, can cause problems in pregnancy if mother is Rhesus *negative* and father Rhesus *positive*)
RIH	Right inguinal hernia
ROA	Right occiput anterior (see LOA above)
ROL	Right occipito-lateral
ROM	Range of movement
ROP	Right occiput posterior (see LOA above)
RS	Respiratory system
RTI	Respiratory tract infection
s̄	Without (Latin: sine)
S/B	seen by
S/D	Systolic/diastolic (heart and circulation)
SH	Social history

SJ	Supinator jerk (reflex: see AJ)
SOA	Swelling of ankles
SOB (OE)	Short of breath (on exertion)
SOS	(a) si opus sit (if necessary)
	(b) see other sheet
SROM	Spontaneous rupture of membranes (labour)
SVC	Superior vena cava
SVD	Spontaneous vaginal delivery
SVT	Supraventricular tachycardia
TCI/52	To come in, in 2 weeks' time
TGH	To go home
THR	Total hip replacement
TIA	Transient ischemic attack
TJ	Triceps jerk (reflex: see AJ)
TVF	Tactile vocal fremitus
U & E	Urea and electrolytes (biochemical tests)
URTI	Upper respiratory tract infection
UTI	Urinary tract infection
VE	Vaginal examination
VF	Ventricular fibrillation
VT	Ventricular tachycardia
V/V	Vulva and vagina
WBC	White blood corpuscle/white blood cell count
XR	X-ray

Appendix V

Hippocratic Oath

This oath, taken at the time of graduation by medical students at some universities, dates back to the 4th century BC. It was handed down as part of the *Hippocratic Collection*, a philosophy developed by the Greeks from the writings of Hippocrates and others, from which the whole of their science grew. One version of the oath states:

I will look upon him who shall have taught me this Art even as one of my parents. I will share my substance with him, and I will supply his necessities, if he be in need. I will regard his offspring even as my own brethren, and I will teach them this Art, if they would learn it, without fee or covenant. I will impart this Art by precept, by lecture and by every mode of teaching, not only to my own sons, but to the sons of him who taught me, and to disciples bound by covenant and oath, according to the Law of Medicine.

The regimen I adopt shall be for the benefit of my patients according to my ability and judgment, and not for their hurt or for any wrong. I will give no deadly drug to any, though it be asked of me, nor will I counsel such, and especially I will not aid a woman to procure abortion. Whatsoever house I enter, there will I go for the benefit of the sick, refraining from all wrongdoing or corruption, and especially from any act of seduction of male or female, of bond or free. Whatsoever things I see or hear concerning the life of men, in my attendance on the sick, or even apart therefrom, which ought not to be noised abroad, I will keep silence thereon, counting such things to be as sacred secrets.

Appendix VI

Access to Justice *(Final Report)* *by Lord Woolf*

CHAPTER 15 MEDICAL NEGLIGENCE

Reasons for looking at medical negligence

1. Why have I singled out medical negligence for the most intensive examination during Stage 2 of my Inquiry? (I am using the term 'medical negligence' in this report to refer to any litigation involving allegations of negligence in the delivery of health care, whether by doctors, nurses or other health professionals.) It may appear a surprising choice, because medical negligence cases have no special procedures or rules of court. They are a sub-species of professional negligence actions, and they also belong to what is numerically the largest category of cases proceeding to trial, personal injury. Neither of these is singled out for special attention.

2. The answer is that early in the Inquiry it became increasingly obvious that it was in the area of medical negligence that the civil justice system was failing most conspicuously to meet the needs of litigants in a number of respects.

    (a) The disproportion between costs and damages in medical negligence is particularly excessive, especially in lower value cases.

    (b) The delay in resolving claims is more often unacceptable.

    (c) Unmeritorious cases are often pursued, and clear-cut claims defended, for too long.

    (d) The success rate is lower than in other personal injury litigation.

    (e) The suspicion between the parties is more intense and the lack of co-operation frequently greater than in many other areas of litigation.

3. The cost of medical negligence litigation is now so high that smaller claims can rarely be litigated because of the disproportionate cost. It is difficult for patients to pursue a claim of any value unless they are eligible for legal aid. In the Supreme Court Taxing Office survey (see Annex 3 to this report), 92 per cent of successful parties in medical negligence cases were legally aided. An analysis by the Law Society of a survey by Action for Victims of Medical Accidents (AVMA) of 376 cases conducted by solicitors' firms on its specialist panel indicates that 90 per cent of cases which reached the stage of litigation were legally aided. If these figures are representative of medical negligence litigation generally, then in the vast majority of cases both sides are funded from the public purse. Here the cause for concern is the amount of money spent by NHS trusts and other defendants on legal costs: money which would be much better devoted to compensating victims or, better still, to improving standards of care so that future mistakes are avoided.

4. The new system of case management by the courts which I proposed in my interim report could do much to reduce cost and delay in medical negligence, and to encourage a more co-operative approach, enabling cases to settle on appropriate terms at an earlier stage. In particular:

(a) Clearer statements of claim and fully pleaded defences should speed up the progress of cases by helping to establish a factual matrix and define the real issues at an earlier stage.

(b) Claimant's offers will encourage earlier settlements on realistic terms.

(c) Extended summary judgment may help to weed out weak claims or defences at an earlier stage.

(d) Improved training and greater specialisation should help judges to identify weak cases, narrow and determine issues and limit the scope of evidence.

(e) More use of split trials will limit unnecessary work on quantum of damages in cases where liability is in issue (although this should not inhibit early work on quantum in cases where a valuation of the claim is possible).

(f) Greater emphasis on early definition of issues between experts should encourage a more co-operative approach and reduce cost and delay.

5. The difficulty of proving both causation and negligence, which arises more acutely in medical negligence than in other personal injury cases, accounts for much of the excessive cost. The root of the problem, however, lies less in the complexity of the law or procedure than in the climate of mutual suspicion and defensiveness which is still all too prevalent in this area of litigation. Patients feel let down when treatment goes wrong, sometimes because of unrealistic expectations as to what could be achieved. Doctors feel they are under attack from aggrieved patients and react defensively. The patients' disappointment is then heightened by what they perceive to be a refusal to acknowledge fault and an attempt to cover up.

6. Case management alone cannot provide the answer to this. A key requirement for achieving the necessary change is designing procedures for handling these cases, both at the pre-litigation stage and by the courts, so that a more co-operate and conciliatory approach to dispute resolution is achieved.

7. A Medical Negligence Working Group was convened for my Inquiry by Sarah Leigh. This has already laid the foundation for the more co-operative approach which is so urgently needed in this area of litigation. It has brought together a considerable number of those involved on all sides of medical negligence litigation to discuss for the first time the problems which exist. I am particularly pleased to report that the group has established a new 'umbrella' organisation which will be open to all those with an interest in medical negligence litigation. One of this organisation's principal tasks will be to discuss and advance the further reforms which are needed after the Inquiry has finished.

The broader context

8. My Inquiry has coincided with a period of significant change in the handling of claims within the NHS. The National Health Service Litigation Authority (NHSLA) came into existence in November 1995. It now administers a voluntary scheme which, in effect, almost acts as a mutual insurer of those NHS trusts which opt for membership. This is known as the Clinical Negligence Scheme for Trusts (CNST). Its membership already comprises about 384 NHS trusts, 89.5 per cent of the trusts in England. The CNST's coverage is limited to claims involving incidents which occurred after 1 April 1995. Because of the timescale involved in resolving this class of claims it will be some time before the full effect of the scheme will become apparent. However, its creation is undoubtedly a positive move which should result in a more satisfactory approach being adopted by defendants.

9. A separate scheme, effective from 1 April 1996 and also administered by the NHSLA, covers all claims against NHS bodies relating to incidents which occurred before 1 April 1995. This is the Existing Liabilities Scheme, under which an NHS body can apply to the NHSLA for reimbursement of any payment out under a claim, provided it has complied with the conditions imposed by the scheme.

10. As an indication of the scale of the task faced by the NHSLA, it is estimated that there are currently about 20,000 claims outstanding against the NHS. About 2,500 of these have a value in excess of £100,000. About 5,000 claims are settled or adjudicated each year, but the number of settlements is matched by the number of new claims entering the system.

11. I am glad to say that the recently appointed Chairman of the NHSLA, Sir Bruce Martin QC, has responded positively to the general thrust of my proposed reforms, and has made it clear that the NHSLA will support any steps taken to improve the legal process.

12. Different arrangements apply to claims against general practitioners and doctors of consultant status working in private hospitals. These are still dealt with by the defence organisations of which the medical practitioners involved are members, and which formerly dealt with all claims against hospital doctors. (One of these organisations, the Medical Protection Society, is about to take on a role within the management of the CNST.) The defence organisations have also made it clear that they support my objectives. Junior doctors and nursing and other staff working in private hospitals are indemnified by their employers who in turn have insurance arrangements.

13. I have no doubt that these changes, combined and with reforms of court procedure, will lay the foundation for a much improved system of handling medical negligence claims which will be to the advantage of both patients and doctors.

14. Two further significant changes were introduced in the NHS on 1 April 1996, as part of the Government's response to the Wilson report on complaints handling in the NHS. The first is a new, more open complaints procedure, covering all NHS staff, which includes an independent review stage. The new machinery has been widely welcomed in principle, but the detailed way in which it is intended to operate has attracted some criticism, in particular because cases where the patient has indicated an intention to claim compensation are excluded.

15. The second change is an extension of the Health Service Ombudsman's statutory jurisdiction to include clinical complaints against all NHS staff, normally provided that the complainant has exhausted the internal complaints system. The particular advantages of the Ombudsman scheme are that it is free of charge to claimants and that it provides an inquisitorial approach, with a single, neutral investigation, but the Ombudsman's extended jurisdiction will not cover claims for financial compensation.

16. A system for resolving disputes about medical treatment must be designed to meet the needs of doctors and other health professionals as well as patients. It should not be designed to suit the interests or convenience of lawyers, except in so far as this is necessary to ensure that the work is done properly.

17. Many people involved in medical negligence litigation have justifiably pointed out to me the importance of establishing at the outset what an injured patient wants. Proceedings often start because the claimant cannot get the information he is seeking, or an explanation or apology, from the doctor or hospital. Historically, solicitors have had no alternative but to advise legal action, which is unlikely to be appropriate in all cases unless the client's main or only objective is to obtain financial compensation.

18. Patients' needs and wishes may not be the same in all cases, and are not always compatible with those of health professionals. An obvious point is that both sides want to win, and for some individuals this may override considerations of speed, economy, or even fairness. Some patients want financial compensation, but they may also want to prevent a repetition of the mistreatment or misdiagnosis which occurred, or to get an apology or explanation for what went wrong. Sometimes, especially in cases where the physical injury was less serious, these non-monetary factors are the most important. Whatever form of redress they are seeking, most patients probably want:

    (a) impartial information and advice, including an independent medical assessment;

    (b) fair compensation for losses suffered;

    (c) a limited financial commitment;

    (d) a speedy resolution of the dispute;

    (e) a fair and independent adjudication; and

    (f) (sometimes) a day in court.

19. Doctors and other healthcare professionals agree with patients in wanting a speedy resolution of any disputes, but this is not always compatible with their understandable wish for a fair assessment of their conduct, with a right of comment and hearing. Doctors in particular also want:

    (a) a discreet, private adjudication, which some would prefer to be by a medical rather than a legal tribunal;

    (b) an expert of their own or their solicitor's choice; and

    (c) an economical system, which does not encourage NHS trusts to settle cases over their heads, regardless of liability.

20. There is no easy way of satisfying everyone, but I hope to provide a set of practical and sensible recommendations which will have an impact on costs and delay while ensuring that all parties are treated fairly.

A change of culture

21. The extent of patients' mistrust of doctors and other hospital staff is illustrated by the submission I have received from Action for Victims of Medical Accidents (AVMA). They argue that the real reason for defendants' reluctance to investigate complaints where there is a possibility of legal action is a concern that such an investigation might indeed disclose negligence:

[The defendants] do not in fact want a relatively simple and cheap way of investigating a complaint which might expose that there has been negligence.

22. If that mistrust is to be removed, the medical profession and the NHS administration must demonstrate their commitment to patients' well-being by adopting a constructive approach to claims handling. It must be clearly accepted that injured patients are entitled to redress, and that professional solidarity or individual self-esteem are not sufficient reasons for resisting or obstructing valid claims.

23. Patients and their representatives, for their part, must recognise that some degree of risk is inherent in all medical treatment, and that even the best practitioners do sometimes make mistakes. They should not pursue unrealistic claims, and should make every effort to resolve disputes without recourse to litigation.

24. It is fundamental to my approach to civil litigation in general that legal proceedings should be treated as a last resort, to be used only when other means of resolving a dispute are inappropriate or have failed. When someone has a potential negligence claim against a doctor or hospital, the first essential step is to find out what the patient wants to achieve. If his other main need is for substantial financial compensation to cover future loss of earnings or the cost of continuing care, then litigation may be (but is not always) the best way to proceed. If the patient is chiefly concerned to get an explanation or apology for what went wrong, or to ensure that procedures are changed so that future accidents can be avoided, then litigation is less likely to be the best course. Recourse to the NHS complaints procedures and, if necessary, the Health Service Ombudsman, may offer a more appropriate means of redress.

25. The existing litigation system may allow an untenable case to come to court, several years after the event, in which there has at no stage been any personal contact between the healthcare professionals involved and the injured patient or his family. That simply should not happen, and doctors, trusts and lawyers all have a part to play in preventing it. In some cases, an explanation from the doctor of what went wrong, coupled with a personal apology, would resolve the matter without any further action. Many claims managers, who act as the hospital's first point of contact with aggrieved patients, concentrate on trying to achieve this in suitable cases.

26. One innovative suggestion which has been put to me is that there should be a new, non-pecuniary remedy available from the courts. A patient would, in effect, be able to apply to the court for a formal statement from the hospital explaining the incident of alleged negligence.

27. This idea has some attraction, but I do not recommend it because I think it would send out the wrong signals about the role of the courts and might even encourage unnecessary litigation. It is, as I have already stated, a fundamental part of my approach to access to justice that litigation should be treated as a last resort, and it is far better for patients and hospitals to resolve their disputes through other channels wherever possible.

28. The best way of dealing with the problem of delay before claims are started would be a policy of more open communication on the part of hospital staff. Effective communication of course needs to start before things go wrong. All patients who are about to undergo treatment should understand that the outcome of medical treatment can be uncertain, and should be told about the range of possible outcomes in their particular case. Wherever practicable, the advice should be confirmed in writing. Doctors and hospitals should encourage patients to report any unsatisfactory outcome as soon as possible, and to seek an explanation direct from the individual doctor or hospital before going to a solicitor.

29. Every patient who has suffered an adverse outcome is entitled to an explanation, and, where appropriate, an apology. In appropriate cases, there is no reason why an offer of compensation should not be made before any legal claim is notified, provided the patient is encouraged to seek independent advice on the offer. I understand that some hospitals offer to pay for such advice, to ensure that patients are not deterred from seeking it through fear of the cost.

30. I can understand why this approach is unwelcome to many doctors, in particular. There is a natural reluctance to admit that one has been at fault, and sometimes a fear that any form of apology will amount to an admission of legal liability. Such an admission could have implications for the doctor's professional reputation and career prospects. A face to face meeting with an injured patient may be a very daunting prospect for the doctor concerned. From the trust's point of view, an immediate offer of compensation may not appear to be an effective or produce use of resources.

31. There are, nevertheless, good reasons for adopting such an approach. Most importantly, unless the patient himself opts to go elsewhere, the hospital and the individual doctor have a continuing obligation to care for a patient who has been injured by negligent treatment. In some cases, at least, that obligation includes the provision of financial compensation to pay for rehabilitation. Secondly, from the hospital's point of view it will be easier to trace the relevant records and carry out an investigation if a potential claim is identified as early as possible. Finally, an open approach is also in the interest of the doctor because an explanation or apology will resolve some cases without the need for litigation.

32. In my discussions and correspondence with doctors, I have been encouraged by the extent to which this more open and enlightened approach to patients is now increasingly recognised and accepted as a matter of good practice. This is, however, far from universally the case, although the system of clinical audit encourages doctors to report adverse outcomes. Doctors need support in any subsequent investigation or litigation and disciplinary proceedings against the minority of incompetent doctors should be clearly separate from this procedure.

33. I have no doubt that the more systematic and professional approach to claims management which the NHSLA is encouraging will help to achieve the necessary change of culture. This is, however, not the only way of tackling the problem. The fear of litigation among so many doctors is often based on ignorance of the legal system. I have heard, for example, of doctors who were unclear about the difference between civil and criminal proceedings, and afraid they might be sent to prison if they were 'found guilty' of medical negligence. To ensure that they are properly informed, I believe that all doctors should be given, as part of their basic medical training, an introduction to the legal context of their work, including an indication of what is involved in a claim for negligence.

34. One specific suggestion which has been made to me in the course of the Inquiry is that there should be an obligation on doctors, as part of their ethical code, to inform their patients if they discover an act or omission in their care and treatment which may have caused injury, and that doctors who fail to comply with such a duty should be subject to disciplinary action. It is suggested that nurses, midwives and other healthcare professionals should have corresponding obligations. There is a comparable requirement in the Law Society's code of professional conduct for solicitors to notify their clients when they become aware of a possible negligent act or omission.

35. It is, in fact, arguable that such an obligation already exists under the common law. In 1987 Sir John Donaldson, then Master of the Rolls, said:

> I personally think that in professional negligence cases, and in particular in medical negligence cases, there is a duty of candour resting on the professional man ... It is but one aspect of the general duty of care, arising out of the patient/medical practitioner or hospital authority relationship ... (*Naylor* v *Preston Area Health Authority* [1987] 2 All ER 353 at 360)

There has, however, been no binding decision of the courts as to the existence of such a duty.

36. I recognise that there may be considerable difficulties in defining such an obligation so that it could be meaningfully embodied in a rule of conduct. What is appropriate for lawyers cannot be assumed to be right for doctors, because of the very different ways in which the work of the two professions is organised. Moreover, the doctor/patient relationship is a uniquely personal and sensitive one. Nevertheless, I suggest that the General Medical Council and other regulatory bodies could usefully consider how to clarify and promulgate the responsibilities of healthcare professionals in these circumstances.

Pre-litigation procedure

37. Some of the major sources of cost and delay in medical negligence cases arise at the pre-litigation stage.

(a) Inadequate incident reporting and record keeping in hospitals, and mobility of staff, make it difficult to establish facts, often several years after the event.

(b) Claimants must incur the cost of an expert investigation in order to establish whether they have a viable claim.

(c) There is often a long delay before a claim is made.

(d) Defendants do not have sufficient resources to carry out a full investigation of every incident, and do not consider it worthwhile to start an investigation as soon as they receive a request for records, because many cases do not proceed beyond that stage.

(e) Patients often give the defendant little or no notice of a firm intention to sue. Consequently, many incidents are not investigated by the defendant until after proceedings have started.

(f) Doctors and hospital staff in general are traditionally reluctant to admit negligence or apologise to or negotiate with claimants, for fear of damage to their professional reputation or career prospects.

38. An effective pre-action procedure for medical negligence cases therefore needs to:

    (a) encourage early communication between claimants and defendants, and ensure that any appropriate apology or explanation is always offered to the claimant;

    (b) set a challenging but realistic target for disclosure of medical records by defendants;

    (c) ensure that the claimant knows what options are available (including ADR) and what each will involve;

    (d) require the parties to consider whether joint instructions to an expert would be possible, at least on some of the issues in the case; and

    (e) provide an early opportunity for defendants to identify cases where a full investigation is required.

39. Under the present arrangements a hospital faced with the possibility of a medical negligence claim has a number of very real practical problems to contend with. The difficulties of finding patients' records and tracing former staff are endemic problems which, in many cases, are unfortunately exacerbated by late notification of the claim to the defendant, and by the hospital's own failure to record adverse incidents. When a medical procedure goes wrong, it is natural that the first reaction of both doctor and patient is to take restorative measures. The patient may not even consider the possibility of a claim until a protracted course of treatment has been completed. Late notification of a claim creates difficulty for the claimant in establishing liability, while the defendant is faced with all the problems of carrying out an investigation possibly several years after the event, when records may have been lost and staff who have moved away are difficult to trace. This is a situation which can only accentuate the lack of trust between the two sides.

40. In the NHS the establishment of the NHSLA is likely to have a significant impact on the standards of record keeping and incident reporting in hospitals. Imported technology and information systems could, in any event, have a significant impact on record storage and retrieval. I am very encouraged by what I have learnt about the current practice of the more progressive NHS trusts, which have already appointed professional claims managers to adopt a more proactive approach to risk management. I look forward to a more general movement in this direction once the administrative changes come fully into effect. I am pleased to say that my Inquiry has already contributed to this development, by providing a forum for discussion and spreading the message about best practice among doctors and health service administrators.

41. Patients seeking access to their medical records for possible use in litigation had, in the past, been faced with a slow and expensive procedure. This situation has improved following the Access to Health Records Act 1990, which makes it more difficult for a hospital or trust to justify withholding records which a patient is entitled to see under the Act. The NHS Code of Practice on Openness, which has been in force since June 1995, is non-statutory and does not add to the rights of access created by the 1990 Act, but it should contribute to a climate of greater openness in the NHS. Those who are unable to gain access to the information they request from the responsible NHS body may complain to the Health Service Ombudsman.

42. There was a further step forward in August 1995 when the Law Society, with the support of the Department of Health, launched a protocol designed to make the process quicker and cheaper through the use of standard forms of application and response. This is a very encouraging development, although I understand that the protocol is not yet universally followed either by claimants' solicitors or by hospital trusts. It is, in any event, limited in scope. I hope that in due course it will be possible to build on this approach by introducing an extended protocol covering pre-litigation activity more generally.

43. There are occasionally disputes between parties on the breadth of discovery to be provided in a potential clinical negligence claim. Under the existing rules of court a potential claimant can apply to the court before proceedings have commenced for discovery (disclosure) of documents by the potential defendant, but cannot apply for disclosure by a third party until after the issue of proceedings. This may cause difficulty in medical negligence cases, where the patient's previous medical history is often relevant to the claim and access is needed to records held by the patient's general practitioner or by another hospital. Time and money may be wasted if an expert writes his initial report on the basis of an incomplete history, and then changes his view once the rest of the records become available. I therefore recommend that legislation should be amended to enable potential claimants to apply to the court for pre-action disclosure of documents by someone who is not a party to the proposed litigation.

44. The problem of tracing former staff should, in time, become less serious as procedures in general are speeded up. In the meantime, however, more positive ways of tackling this need to be considered. At present I understand that NHS trusts normally keep employment records for around 6 years, and superannuation records are kept permanently. There may be some scope for extending this or making more use of the existing information.

45. I have already mentioned that one of the difficulties faced by NHS trusts is that of deciding whether a potential claim is worth investigating, and at what stage. The point has been made to me (by, among others, the Law Society) that it is anomalous that potentially serious negligence claims are not automatically investigated until proceedings are issued, whereas the new NHS complaints procedure requires an investigation of all complaints.

46. I agree that any attempt to distinguish 'complaints' from 'claims' must in some respects be artificial. To the extent that a valid distinction can be drawn, it would appear more logical to concentrate resources on the investigation of the more serious complaints, which are likely to include those involving allegations of negligence. I do accept, however, that it would be unreasonable to expect hospitals to instigate a full investigation every time a patient asks for disclosure of medical records, given the number of potential claims which do not proceed beyond that stage. A more proactive system of incident reporting in hospitals should facilitate a more informed and rational approach to the identification of cases in need of investigation. I am glad to hear that this is already beginning to happen, particularly in hospitals where professional claims managers have been appointed. It would also help if claimants gave an indication with their request for records that they are considering making a claim and not simply asking for information.

47. So far I have concentrated on the part to be played by health providers in constructive pre-litigation activity. Claimants (or potential claimants) and their legal advisers must also make a significant contribution. First, if a genuine change in ethos is to be achieved, it is important that solicitors acting for patients to do not adopt an unduly adversarial attitude, and that they find out at an early stage what their clients want. It should always be remembered that clients do have their own views, and it is particularly important to establish whether they are mainly seeking financial compensation. Solicitors should not automatically advise litigation, but should explore and provide information about any available alternatives such as mediation or the Ombudsman service. The primary objective of their initial approach to the prospective defendant should be to obtain the relevant information about the patient's treatment (unless the patient has already done this) and then to resolve any dispute by discussion or negotiation. The possibility of mediation or some other form of alternative dispute resolution should be considered at all stages of the case.

48. Once the patient has made a firm decision to litigate, that decision should be notified to the defendant in a letter before action. Wherever possible, the defendant should be given at least three months' notice that a statement of claim is to be served. The letter before action should give the fullest available information about the basis of the intended claim, in the light of the expert evidence obtained by the patient, and, whenever possible, include an offer to settle. At that stage, defendants who have not already done so should initiate a full investigation of the claim, unless they agree to settle on the claimant's terms. If liability is disputed, defendants must provide a reasoned answer. As part of my proposed system of case management by the courts, any unreasonable delay by either side should be taken into account by the court in setting timetables and making directions for the conduct of the case, and in the award of costs.

49. I understand that the new 'umbrella' organisation has undertaken, as one of its initial tasks, to carry forward the development of a pre-litigation protocol for medical negligence cases. I believe that the adoption of such a protocol will reduce the volume of medical negligence litigation by diverting some cases to alternative methods of dispute resolution and promoting settlement in others. For cases where litigation is unavoidable, the benefits of the protocol should become apparent in an early definition of the issues between the parties and a speedier resolution than is normally possible under the existing, less co-operative approach.

Alternative dispute resolution

50. There is in existence an expanding range of alternative dispute resolution mechanisms for medical negligence claims which may be better suited than litigation to the needs of both patients and doctors. This applies especially to smaller claims, and to those where financial compensation is not the patient's main or only requirement. It is, however, important to ensure that informal procedures do not put claimants at a disadvantage because of the inevitable imbalance of knowledge and power between patients and hospitals.

51. The first possibility, at least for hospitals with professional claims managers, is in-house resolution. This need not have any cost to the patient, has the advantage of speed and informality, and is most likely to be effective when the claims manager has full authority to agree financial compensation up to a limit set by senior managers. It also has the flexibility to provide non-monetary redress when that is what the patient wants. In-house resolution does, however, carry the risk – whether real or perceived – of providing a solution which under-compensates the patient or fails to take his or her interests fully into account. I believe that the benefits outweigh the risks provided that claims managers are properly trained and act responsibly. They should recognise their obligation to put the patient's interests first, and should be able to identify cases which are too complex, or where the potential quantum is too high, for informal resolution. Above all, they should always advise patients as to the need for independent advice, and consider advancing the cost of this. Provided these conditions are met, I believe that in-house resolution may be the best means of settling relatively small and simple claims.

52. Mediation offers a further possibility for out of court resolution. In April 1995 the Department of Health set up pilot mediation schemes for medical negligence cases in two regions: Anglia and Oxford, and Northern and Yorkshire. Participation in the schemes is voluntary, and they are concentrating on cases where legal proceedings have already started. There will be an independent evaluation which is due to report in the autumn of 1997. The Department of Health has also considered the possibility of an arbitration scheme for medical negligence cases, but concluded after consultation that claimants would be unlikely to accept the binding nature of an arbitration award.

53. Work carried out by the ADR sub-group of the Medical Negligence Working Group suggests that it may be possible to mediate cases successfully before proceedings are started, provided the claim can be valued. Exchange of experts' reports and witness statements may in some cases be unnecessary; the basic requirements are for both sides to have a condition and prognosis report which they are happy to use, a reliable estimate of value, copies of the medial records and their own expert reports.

54. I regard this as a very promising development, and one which could result in a significant number of medical negligence claims being resolved without litigation. I understand that work on pre-litigation mediation is continuing, and I hope that in due course it will be possible for guidelines to be produced and incorporated in a pre-action protocol. As I have said elsewhere in this report, this approach will be more effective if legal aid is made available for pre-litigation resolution and ADR.

55. I have considered the suggestion that some form of ADR should be a compulsory precursor to litigation, at least in smaller medical negligence cases. Such a requirement would not, in any event, be realistic at present, given the limited availability of ADR, and as a matter of principle I think it is preferable to encourage rather than to compel its use, as I proposed in the interim report. If the development of in-house resolution and mediation continues, these are likely to prove attractive options for smaller cases on economic grounds. Their use can be encouraged by protocols, and failure to follow the protocol should be taken into account by the court in any subsequent proceedings.

Do medical negligence cases need special treatment by the courts?

56. Medical negligence cases in the High Court are at present treated as part of the general business of the Queen's Bench Division. I proposed in my interim report (chapter 12, paragraph 25) that the work of that Division should be divided between a general list (to be known as the General, Personal Injury and Damages List) and a number of special lists. Medical negligence work is significantly different from, and in many cases more complex than, ordinary personal injury cases, and effective case management (including trial management) requires a degree of familiarity with standard medical practices and procedures which is unlikely to be acquired by judges who only occasionally deal with medical negligence cases. I have therefore concluded that the special lists in the Queen's Bench Division should include a separate medical negligence list. I believe that this arrangement will foster the appropriate degree of special experience and expertise among the judiciary which is needed for the efficient and effective disposal of these cases.

57. Outside London, I propose that medical negligence cases, at both High Court and county court level, should be handled at specially designated court centres where both the judiciary and staff will have the opportunity to build up experience and expertise in this work. I have received clear indications that litigants and their legal representatives would be prepared to travel a considerable distance to have access to specialist procedural and trial judges. The problems of distance will be overcome in time by the use of video conferencing and other technology, and there is already scope for using telephone conferencing facilities for straightforward procedural matters.

58. Depending on the volume of cases there should be regional lists, or perhaps a national list, to facilitate the flexible allocation of cases for trial and reduce delay. The precise solution to be adopted will depend on the volume of cases going through the courts, which will need to be ascertained as part of the process of implementing my proposals for case management generally.

59. The question of specialisation leads naturally to that of training. Medical negligence is a highly technical area where judges (unless they happen to belong to the minority who have medical as well as legal qualifications) will inevitably know a great deal less about the subject matter of the litigation than other participants, notably the defendant, the expert witnesses, and the lawyers who are becoming increasingly specialist in this area of litigation. If case management is to work effectively, it will be essential for the procedural judge to have some understanding of the substantive issues in the case. I believe that trial judges would also benefit from specialist training, although I have no doubt that it is possible for a trial judge to acquire enough background information on a particular case to make a reasoned decision on the issues. Indeed, it is one of the functions of the parties' representatives, and in particular of the expert witnesses, to ensure that he does so. However, it takes longer to conduct a case if the judge has to be 'educated' in this way. It is also difficult for the judge to have the authority needed to manage a case well if he is less experienced than the lawyers who are appearing before him.

60. There are ways in which it can be made easier for both the procedural judge and the trial judge to assimilate the essential knowledge for a particular case. For example, the parties' advisers can produce summaries of technical documents, core bundles of essential papers, or a glossary or synopsis of the relevant medical issues. Some judges, I know, would gladly accept this level of help, but do not see the need for any wider training in medical issues.

61. Again, while I can understand that position, I do not think it goes far enough. Under the new system of civil litigation which I have outlined in my interim report, both procedural judges and trial judges will play a much more active part than they do at present in the management of cases. They will be expected, for example, to narrow and define issues as the case progresses, and will have extended powers to exclude evidence. They will not be able to carry out this new role effectively if their grasp of the technical background to the case is solely dependent on briefing from the parties and their advisers; they will need to have sufficient confidence to form an independent judgment and overrule the parties when necessary.

62. For these reasons I believe that some form of training in medical issues is essential for judges who seek to become specialists in this area, to reinforce the expertise they will acquire through regular handling of these cases. I therefore recommend that the Judicial Studies Board should investigate, with the help of appropriate medical experts, the scope and content of training in medical issues for procedural and trial judges; and organise the necessary training. I have no doubt that the appropriate expert help can be provided by the various medical royal colleges and by AVMA, all of whom have told me in the course of the Inquiry of their willingness to assist, for example by giving advice or providing specialist lecturers.

Expert evidence

63. Medical negligence differs from other personal injury litigation in the parties' greater reliance on expert medical evidence for issues of causation and liability as well as quantum. Causation is more difficult to establish than in other personal injury cases. This is because the effects of the allegedly negligent treatment must be distinguished from those of the patient's underlying condition which gave rise to the need for treatment. Liability is often very difficult to establish. It must be determined by the principle stated in *Bolam v Friern Hospital Committee* [1957] 1 WLR 582:

> [A doctor] is not guilty of negligence if he has acted in accordance with a practice accepted as proper by a responsible body of medical men skilled in that particular art ... Putting it the other way round, a man is not negligent, if he acts in accordance with such a practice, merely because there is a body of opinion who would take a contrary view.

64. This is not significantly different from the test used in any professional negligence litigation, but it causes greater difficulty for the courts than would a claim for negligence against, say, a lawyer or an accountant, because of the technical issues involved. The assessment of damages, although essentially a similar exercise in all personal injury cases, is often complicated in medical negligence, because the court must compare the claimant's actual condition and prognosis with the hypothetical condition and prognosis if the patient had received competent medical treatment. The court must only compensate for the injuries caused by negligent treatment, not for any underlying condition.

65. For the resolution of all three issues – causation, liability and quantum of damages – the parties and the courts are dependent on medical and other expert evidence. This is not only expensive, especially if experts from several specialities are used by each side, but may also be a source of delay because of the time taken by the experts to produce their reports. Generally speaking, expert witnesses in the medical field have less time to spare for legal work than experts in other fields.

66. All practitioners in this field know the peculiar difficulty of finding the information necessary to determine whether a potential claimant has a case. This is not simply a matter of establishing the facts, although that in itself is often difficult enough, but of finding an expert medical opinion to support the claim.

67. Traditionally, there has been an understandable reluctance on the part of doctors and other healthcare professionals to criticise their colleagues. Their reluctance was accentuated by the fact that the defence in the majority of medical negligence cases was conducted by the medical protection bodies, of which doctors themselves were members. This resulted in a shortage of medical experts who were willing to work on behalf of claimants, which in turn led to heavy demands on those who were prepared to do the work, and to a tendency for them to spend more time preparing medico-legal reports than providing treatment. The end result was that their standing in the profession was lowered, and other doctors were even more reluctant to be associated with claimants.

68. It would be difficult to exaggerate the effect on potential claimants of the problems they encounter in obtaining information, coupled with the knowledge that defendants have easy access to medical information and opinion. I am glad to say there have been some improvements since my own experience in practice, but many claimants still feel strongly that the system is weighted against them, and in particular that professional solidarity among doctors is a barrier to justice for ordinary people. Whether or not this feeling is always justified, I have no doubt that it is encouraged by the lack of openness between parties which still prevails in this area of litigation.

69. My general approach to expert evidence in the context of a case-managed system was set out in chapter 23 of the interim report. I recommended that the scope of expert evidence in a particular case should be under the control of the court; that a single expert (whether jointly instructed by the parties or appointed by the court) should be used wherever possible; and that, where this was not appropriate, the issues between opposing experts should be narrowed and outstanding areas of disagreement defined as early as possible.

70. In chapter 13 of this report I have given an account of the Inquiry's work on experts since the interim report, and explained how my general approach is to be put into effect through the new code of procedural rules. I revert to the subject in the present chapter in order to consider how the approach will work in the specific context of medical negligence litigation.

71. The vast majority of people consulted by the Medical Negligence Working Group, including many with whom I have discussed the matter personally, see no scope for the joint appointment of liability experts in medical negligence, except perhaps in the smallest and most straightforward cases. The most commonly cited reason for this is the special nature of the Bolam test (see paragraph 63 above), which requires the court to be appraised of the whole range of acceptable medical practice in a given speciality.

72. I accept that in some medical negligence cases the issues of causation and liability will be too complex to be decided on the basis of evidence from one medial expert in the relevant speciality or specialities. I do not, however, agree that it is an inevitable consequence of the Bolam test that each side must instruct its own experts on all issues in every case. In a straightforward case it may be perfectly possible, and appropriate, for a consultant to advise the court not only of his own practice in relation to the alleged negligence, but of the range of practices regarded as acceptable by his colleagues. Conversely, in an exceptionally complex case, or one where the treatment given was at the 'cutting edge' of medical science, it is by no means self-evidence that two opposing experts will be able to represent the whole spectrum of professional opinion.

73. It is part of my approach to expert evidence in general, as set out in chapter 13 of this report, that parties must consider whether a particular case or issue could be dealt with by a jointly instructed expert. In medical negligence cases, I suggest this will apply in particular to:

    (a) quantum issues, such as future care costs;

    (b) medical issues which are uncontroversial (such as the precise nature of a tumour, for example);

    (c) condition and prognosis in straightforward claims; and

    (d) liability in claims under £10,000.

74. As I see it, one of the fundamental problems in medical negligence litigation is polarisation of experts: the situation is all too common where neither side knows until a very late stage in the case on what evidence the other is to rely. Joint instruction of an expert by both parties is clearly one way of overcoming the problem; but, as I have already discussed, that will not be appropriate in all cases. In cases where opposing experts are involved, it must be a prime objective to identify areas of agreement and disagreement between the experts as early as possible, and, if the case proceeds to trial, to ensure that the outstanding issues are clearly identified for the court.

75. The principle of mutual and simultaneous disclosure of expert evidence is well established in medical negligence litigation, and is strongly supported by a number of those who have contributed to this part of the Inquiry. Nevertheless, I believe it is worth reconsidering. Sequential rather than simultaneous disclosure of expert evidence could, at least in theory, reduce delay and cut down the amount of work needed on medical negligence claims. Defendants tend to support this, on the basis that the claimant's report would be disclosed first and might persuade some defendants to settle without going to the expense of obtaining their own reports. The opposing argument which has been put to me is that simultaneous disclosure is a more effective way of establishing the true facts of the case. On this view, sequential disclosure encourages the defendant's expert to focus on (and possibly attack) the points made by the claimant's expert, instead of carrying out a full and independent investigation. This, it is said, is in neither party's real interest, because a factually inaccurate view of the incident is unsafe and likely to be exposed at trial, sometimes at enormous expense.

76. For ordinary personal injury litigation, pre-action protocols are being developed on the basis that the claimant will instruct an expert who is approved by the defendant, and that the defendant will accept the claimant's report without instructing a separate expert. In principle, I see no reason why a similar approach could not be adopted in medical negligence, at least for the smaller and more straightforward cases. For the time being, I have to recognise that this would not be acceptable to claimants, but I strongly urge that it should be seriously considered by those concerned as part of the more co-operative approach which I am aiming to establish.

77. It emerged from the working group's consultation exercise that meetings between opposing experts were rarely used in medical negligence cases, but that there was a strong view that they might be a helpful way forward. I have dealt with the arguments for and against experts' meetings in chapter 13 of this report, where I concluded that in the majority of cases the benefits should outweigh any disadvantages in terms of cost and inconvenience. I mentioned the particular problem in medical negligence that private meetings between experts would not be acceptable to patients. To meet this, I proposed that experts' meetings should normally be held in private, but that when the court directs a meeting the parties may apply to the court for any special arrangements.

Quantification of medical negligence claims

78. One particular feature of medical negligence litigation (and, indeed, of personal injury claims in general) which has come to my attention in the course of the Inquiry is the enormous amount of time and money which is spent on quantification of the more substantial claims. There are a number of ways to tackling this, all of which will require a greater emphasis on co-operation and joint planning of quantum resolution. Particularly, in larger cases, this is a matter that should be dealt with, either by the parties themselves or with the help of the procedural judge, as part of the case management process.

79. First, to avoid waste of resources, it is important to ensure that detailed quantification work is done at the most appropriate stage of the case. Defendants want claimants to value cases at an early stage, because it encourages early settlement or at least enables the defendant to estimate his liability. But in complex cases where prognosis and needs are unclear, this is too expensive and leads to repetition. Early quantification can also be wasteful of resources when there is a real dispute on liability; in such cases, consideration should be given to deferring quantum evidence until the issue of liability has been dealt with.

80. Working out the detailed costs of a care regime for a severely injured patient requires contributions from experts in a number of different fields, including, for example, architects, employment consultants, nurses, physiotherapists, and accountants. Wider use of single experts in each speciality will go some way to reducing the cost of the exercise, but without a more radical approach this is likely to produce only limited savings. Standard tables should be drawn up and, wherever possible, used to reduce the need for separate calculation in individual cases.

Case management in the multi-track

81. Chapter 5 of this report explains how my proposals for case management on the multi-track will be embodied in the new rules. My overall approach is that uniform rules should apply, so far as possible, to all types of cases, with special provisions kept to a minimum. The general rules will be sufficiently flexible to accommodate appropriate variations of practice and procedure for particular categories of cases, such as medical negligence, or for individual cases. For example, the standard time allowed for filing of a defence will be 28 days, which is unlikely to be sufficient in any but the most straightforward medical negligence cases. The rule will permit parties to agree an extension up to three months, and to apply to the court for any further extensions.

82. As experience is gained of the new system, I would expect the rules to be supplemented by judicial practice directions, and published practice guides, which will indicate how the rules are to be applied to different classes of cases. Ideally, the production of the various guides should be supervised by the Civil Justice Council whose establishment I recommended in the interim report. In the particular instance of medical negligence, the work could be started at an early date by the new 'umbrella' organisation, building on the detailed work on case management and procedure which has already been done by the working group.

How to deal with smaller cases

83. I have already pointed out that the problem of disproportionate cost is particularly acute in smaller medical negligence cases. This creates a drain on the legal aid fund, as well as on the resources of the NHS. It also denies access to justice for potential claimants who are not eligible for legal aid, and for whom litigation would be uneconomic.

84. In the interim report I proposed a new 'fast track' procedure, which would enable most straightforward cases up to about £10,000 to be litigated simply, quickly and at a proportionate cost. A more detailed procedure is set out in chapter 35 of this report.

85. I accept that the standard fast track will not be suitable for the vast majority of the smaller medical negligence cases. Preliminary investigations can be just as lengthy and expensive whatever the value of the claim, and expert evidence on liability may be just as strongly contested. These are the main factors which would make it impossible to impose the normal fast track timetable and costs limit in small medical negligence cases.

86. I have considered in chapter 2 of this report the arguments put forward by APIL and others that proportionality of costs to compensation would be a denial of access to justice because parties must be allowed to argue their cases fully, regardless of cost. This view has been expressed particularly forcibly by some contributors to the Inquiry in respect of medical negligence. I agree that the special features of medical negligence claims, which I have already identified, make them more expensive to litigate than ordinary personal injury cases of equivalent value, and that this must be reflected in the level of recoverable costs. Even on the standard fast track, as I have explained in chapter 4, I accept that there will need to be different levels of costs for the straightforward and the more complex cases. In other words, strict proportionality, in the sense of a fixed percentage to apply to all cases of the same value, is not a realistic proposition.

87. This does not mean, however, that we should abandon all attempt to achieve a more proportionate use of resources in medical negligence, or in any other areas of litigation. On the contrary, I believe that the disproportionate use of resources in this area is unsustainable. Excessive costs and delay deny access to justice and divert scarce human and financial resources in the NHS away from its primary objective of providing health care.

88. In February 1996 Nottingham Law School organised a one-day conference for the Inquiry on the scope for a fast track for medical negligence cases. It was set up as a hypothetical case study, moderated by Lord Justice Otton and assembled in sections for claimant lawyers, defendant lawyers, managers, doctors and neutrals. There was an interactive voting system which enabled conferred delegates to give their views on a range of questions at various stages of the proceedings. One of the most significant findings, in my view, was that the majority of people thought the present cost of litigating small medical negligence claims was too high.

89. With the help of the working group, and of other contributors to the Inquiry, I have explored various options for dealing with smaller medical negligence claims in a more proportionate way. The three main options to emerge from this work, which were examined at Nottingham Law School's conference by reference to two hypothetical case studies, are:

(a) a 'modified fast track', with
    (i)   a simplified procedure focusing on joint instruction of a single jointly chosen expert;
    (ii) only one lawyer for each side attending the trial;
    (iii) an overall costs cap of £3,500 applying to all cases on the fast track;

(b) a 'best practice' approach which:
    (i)   is based on existing procedure but assumes a more efficient approach by litigators and the courts;
    (ii) does not attempt an arbitrary pre-set costs limit, but suggests a budget related to defined stages of litigation which would amount to a total of around £4,000 on each side; and

(c) the 'streamlined track' which I have proposed in chapter 5 of this report for cases at the lower end of the multi-track, and which would include:
    (i)   a tailor-made procedure and pre-set budget for each case;
    (ii) a target maximum timescale of 18 months;
    (iii) a requirement for joint instruction of a single expert after the case management conference, to act as adviser to the court and neutral evaluator of the evidence put forward by the parties' experts.

90. Any of these options would achieve the objective of enabling smaller medical negligence cases to be litigated on a modest budget known in advance. I believe it would be inappropriate at this stage to prescribe a single, mandatory system, and that the Court Service should facilitate pilot studies enabling each of the possible approaches to be tested at selected courts.

91. I have already mentioned that alternatives to litigation may provide the best solution for smaller medical negligence cases. There is a view, held, among others, by the Law Society, that it is better to channel smaller medical negligence claims out of the court system than to make it easier for them to be litigated. The Society has accordingly proposed that claims up to £10,000 should be dealt with under a modified version of the new NHS complaints procedure, as a compulsory precursor to litigation. I have some sympathy with the idea of a combined procedure for complaints and claims, particularly for cases where the monetary value is below £5,000. It would not, however, be realistic to recommend it at present, given that the new NHS procedures are expressly designed to deal with complaints separately from claims for compensation. In any event, I have reservations about making such a system compulsory, especially since the length of the proposed procedure (up to 18 months) would cause serious delay in cases which could not be resolved without subsequent litigation. I hope, however, that the scope for including smaller medical negligence claims will be reconsidered in the context of any future changes to the NHS complaints system.

The future

92. If my recommendations for reform in this area of litigation are successfully implemented, the overall result should be that more patients who have suffered negligent medical treatment obtain the redress they are seeking (whether financial or otherwise) within a shorter timescale and at a significantly reduced cost. That does not necessarily imply a large growth in the volume of litigation, provided that informal negotiation and alternative dispute resolution mechanisms are used in the ways I have suggested. The system should be fairer and more open than it is at present, and I believe that the benefits of this will be felt by doctors, other healthcare professionals and health service administrators as well as by patients.

93. Some contributors to the Inquiry have suggested that more radical change is needed, such as a modification of the test of negligence which is currently applied by the courts or replacement of tort-based litigation with a system of no-fault compensation for some or all medial negligence claims. These matters are not within the remit of my Inquiry; consideration of them is a matter for others if they think it is appropriate.

Recommendations

My recommendations are as follows.
  (1) The training of health professionals should include an introduction to the legal context of medical work, including an indication of what is involved in a claim for negligence.
  (2) The General Medical Council and other regulatory bodies should consider whether a rule of professional conduct is needed to clarify the responsibility of healthcare professionals to their patients when they discover an act or omission in which they may have been negligent in their care and treatment.
  (3) The NHS should consider tackling the problem of tracing former hospital staff, by improving hospital record systems or making more use of existing information.
  (4) A pre-litigation protocol for medical negligence cases should be developed. As part of the protocol, claimants should be required to notify defendants of a firm intention to sue in a letter before action. The letter should include the fullest available information about the basis of the intended claim, and should wherever possible give at least three months' notice that a statement of case is to be served. If liability is disputed, defendants should be required to provide a reasoned answer.

(5)   The use of alternative dispute resolution mechanisms should be encouraged in medical negligence, especially for smaller claims. Solicitors acting for patients should not automatically advise litigation but should inform their clients of all the available options, including the Health Service Ombudsman, and consider the possibility of alternative dispute resolution at all stages of the case.

(6)   The specialist lists in the Queen's Bench Division of the High Court should include a separate medical negligence list.

(7)   Outside London, medical negligence cases at both High Court and county court level should be handled at specially designated court centres.

(8)   There should be regional lists, or a single national list, to facilitate the flexible allocation of cases for trial and reduce delay.

(9)   The Judicial Studies Board should investigate, with appropriate medical experts, the scope and content of training in medical issues for procedural and trail judges, and organise the necessary training.

(10) Standard tables should be used wherever possible to reduce the cost of quantifying complex medical negligence (and other personal injury) claims.

(11) There should be a practice guide to indicate how the new rules on case management and procedure will apply in detail to medical negligence litigation. The guide should be developed by the new 'umbrella' organisation for medical negligence or under the aegis of the Civil Justice Council.

(12) The Court Service should facilitate a pilot study of the various options for dealing with medical negligence claims below £10,000, to establish which is the most effective procedure for enabling these cases to be litigated on a modest budget.

Appendix VII

Reference Guide to Consent for Examination or Treatment

CONTENTS

INTRODUCTION

1.　It is a general legal and ethical principle that valid consent must be obtained before starting treatment or physical investigation, or providing personal care, for a patient. This principle reflects the right of patients to determine what happens to their own bodies, and is a fundamental part of good practice. A health professional who does not respect this principle may be liable both to legal action by the patient and action by their professional body. Employing bodies may also be liable for the actions of their staff.

2.　While there is no English statute setting out the general principles of consent, case law ("common law") has established that touching a patient without valid consent may constitute the civil or criminal offence of battery. Further, if health professionals fail to obtain proper consent and the patient subsequently suffers harm as a result of treatment, this may be a factor in a claim of negligence against the health professional involved. Poor handling of the consent process may also result in complaints from patients through the NHS complaints procedure or to professional bodies.

3.　This booklet provides guidance on English law concerning consent to physical interventions on patients – from major surgery and the administration or prescription of drugs to assistance with dressing – and is relevant to all health care professionals (including students) who carry out interventions of this nature. Guidance is provided on the legal requirements for obtaining valid consent and on the situations where the law recognises exceptions to the common law requirement to obtain consent. References to the cases on which this guidance is based are given in Appendix C. It should be noted that this guidance is specific to consent for physical interventions on living patients, and the following areas are therefore not included:

- participation in observational studies;
- the use of personal information;
- the use of organs or tissue after death (see below, paragraph 6).

4.　Case law on consent has evolved significantly over the last decade. Further legal developments may occur after this guidance has been issued, and health professionals must remember their duty to keep themselves informed of legal developments which may have a bearing on their practice. Legal advice should always be sought if there is any doubt about the legal validity of a proposed intervention. While much of the case law refers specifically to doctors, the same principles will apply to other health professionals involved in examining or treating patients.

5.   The *Human Rights Act 1998* came into force in October 2000, giving further effect in the UK to the rights enshrined in the European Convention on Human Rights. In future, courts will be expected to take into account the case law of the European Court of Human Rights in Strasbourg, as well as English case law. Although it is too early to predict how the *Human Rights Act* will affect English medical law, the guidance in this booklet is compatible with the existing case law of the European Court of Human Rights. The main articles which are likely to be relevant in medical case law are Article 2 (protection of right to life), Article 3 (prohibition of torture, inhuman or degrading treatment or punishment), Article 5 (right to liberty and security), Article 8 (right to respect for private and family life), Article 9 (freedom of thought, conscience and religion), Article 12 (right to marry and found a family) and Article 14 (prohibition of discrimination in enjoyment of Convention rights).

6.   The removal of organs or tissue from patients who have been declared dead, whether for diagnostic, therapeutic or research purposes, is governed by particular legislation, the *Human Tissue Act 1961*, whose terms currently focus on "lack of objection" rather than consent. The Government has indicated that it intends to amend the law in this area, to give increased emphasis to the wishes of the relatives of the deceased person.[1] Questions concerning the use of organs or tissue after death are beyond the scope of this Guidance.

7.   The standards expected of health professionals by their regulatory bodies may at times be higher than the minimum required by the law. Although this Guidance focuses primarily on the legal position, it will also indicate where regulatory bodies have set out more stringent requirements. It should be noted that the legal requirements in negligence cases (see chapter 1, paragraph 5) have historically been based on the standards set by the professions for their members, and hence where standards required by professional bodies are rising, it is likely that the legal standards will rise accordingly.

1   SEEKING CONSENT

Valid consent

1.   For consent to be valid, it must be given voluntarily by an appropriately informed person (the patient or where relevant someone with parental responsibility for a patient under the age of 18[2]) who has the capacity to consent to the intervention in question. Acquiescence where the person does not know what the intervention entails is not "consent".

Does the patient have capacity?

2.   For a person to have capacity, he or she must be able to comprehend and retain information material to the decision, especially as to the consequences of having or not having the intervention in question, and must be able to use and weigh this information in the decision-making process.

2.1   Thus, patients may have capacity to consent to some interventions but not to others. Adults are presumed to have capacity, but where any doubt exists the health professional should assess the capacity of the patient to take the decision in question. This assessment and the conclusions drawn from it should be recorded in the patient's notes. The British Medical Association has published advice on the assessment of capacity.[3]

---

1   Department of Health, *The removal, retention and use of human organs and tissue from post-mortem examination: advice from the Chief Medical Officer*, 2001
2   See chapter 3
3   BMA and The Law Society, *Assessment of mental capacity: guidance for doctors and lawyers*, 1995

2.2   A patient's capacity to understand may be temporarily affected by factors such as confusion, panic, shock, fatigue, pain or medication. However the existence of such factors should not be assumed automatically to render the patient incapable of consenting. Temporary incapacity is discussed further in chapter 2.

2.3   Capacity should not be confused with a health professional's assessment of the reasonableness of the patient's decision. The patient is entitled to make a decision which is based on their own religious belief or value system, even if it is perceived by others to be irrational, as long as the patient understands what is entailed in their decision. An irrational decision has been defined as one which is so outrageous in its defiance of logic or of accepted moral standards that no sensible person who had applied his or her mind to the question could have arrived at it.

2.4   However, if the decision which appears irrational is based on a misperception of reality, as opposed to an unusual value system – for example a patient who, despite the obvious evidence, denies that his foot is gangrenous, or a patient with anorexia nervosa who is unable to comprehend her failing physical condition – then the patient may not be able to comprehend and make use of the relevant information and hence may lack capacity to make the decision in question.

2.5   In practice patients also need to be able to communicate their decision. Care should be taken not to underestimate the ability of a patient to communicate, whatever their condition. Health professionals should take all steps which are reasonable in the circumstances to facilitate communication with the patient, using interpreters or communication aids as appropriate. The Department has issued guidance on reasonable steps which should be taken to communicate with patients with sensory disabilities.[4]

2.6   Care should also be taken not to underestimate the capacity of a patient with a learning disability to understand. Many people with learning disabilities have the capacity to consent if time is spent explaining to the individual the issues in simple language, using visual aids and signing if necessary.

2.7   Where appropriate, those who know the patient well, including their family, carers and staff from professional or voluntary support services, may be able to advise on the best ways to communicate with the person.

Is the consent given voluntarily?

3.   To be valid, consent must be given voluntarily and freely, without pressure or undue influence being exerted on the patient either to accept or refuse treatment. Such pressure can come from partners or family members as well as health or care professionals. Professionals should be alert to this possibility and where appropriate should arrange to see the patient on their own to establish that the decision is truly that of the patient.

3.1   When patients are seen and treated in environments where involuntary detention may be an issue, such as prisons and mental hospitals, there is a potential for treatment offers to be perceived coercively, whether or not this is the case. Coercion invalidates consent and care must be taken to ensure that the patient makes a decision freely. Coercion should be distinguished from providing the patient with appropriate reassurance concerning their treatment, or pointing out the potential benefits of treatment for the patient's health. However, threats such as withdrawal of any privileges or loss of remission of sentence for refusing consent, or using such matters to induce consent, are not acceptable.

---

4   Department of Health circulars HSC 1999/093 and HSC 1999/156 (www.doh.gov.uk/publications/coinh.html)

Has the patient received sufficient information?

4. To give valid consent the patient needs to understand in broad terms the nature and purpose of the procedure. Any misrepresentation of these elements will invalidate consent. Where relevant, information about anaesthesia should be given as well as information about the procedure itself.

4.1 Clear information is particularly important when students or trainees carry out procedures to further their own education. Where the procedure will further the patient's care – for example taking a blood sample for testing – then, assuming the student is appropriately trained in the procedure, the fact that it is carried out by a student does not alter the nature and purpose of the procedure. It is therefore not a legal requirement to tell the patient that the clinician is a student, although it would always be good practice to do so. In contrast, where a student proposes to conduct a physical examination which is not part of the patient's care, then it is essential to explain that the purpose of the examination is to further the student's training and to seek consent for that to take place.

5. Although informing patients of the nature and purpose of procedures enables valid consent to be given as far as any claim of battery is concerned, this is *not* sufficient to fulfil the legal duty of care to the patient. Failure to provide other relevant information may render the professional liable to an action for negligence if a patient subsequently suffers harm as a result of the treatment received.

5.1 The requirements of the legal duty to inform patients have been significantly developed in case law during the last decade. In 1985, the House of Lords decided in the *Sidaway*[5] case that the legal standard to be used when deciding whether adequate information had been given to a patient should be the same as that used when judging whether a doctor had been negligent in their treatment or care of a patient: a doctor would not be considered negligent if their practice conformed to that of a responsible body of medical opinion held by practitioners skilled in the field in question (known as the "Bolam test").[6] Whether the duty of care had been satisfied was therefore primarily a matter of medical opinion. However, *Sidaway* also stated that it was open to the courts to decide that information about a particular risk was so obviously necessary that it would be negligent not to provide it, even if a "responsible body" of medical opinion would not have done so.

5.2 Since *Sidaway*, judgements in a number of negligence cases (relating both to the provision of information and to the standard of treatment given) have shown that courts are willing to be critical of a "responsible body" of medical opinion. It is now clear that the courts will be the final arbiter of what constitutes responsible practice, although the standards set by the health professions for their members will still be influential.

5.3 In considering what information to provide, the health professional should try to ensure that the patient is able to make a balanced judgement on whether to give or withhold consent. Case law on this issue is evolving. It is therefore advisable to inform the patient of any "material" or "significant" risks in the proposed treatment, any alternatives to it, and the risks incurred by doing nothing. A recent Court of Appeal judgement stated that it will normally be the responsibility of the doctor to inform a patient of "a significant risk which would affect the judgement of a reasonable patient".[7]

5.4 The General Medical Council has gone further, stating in guidance that doctors should do their best to find out about patients' *individual* needs and priorities when providing information about treatment options. The

---

5   *Sidaway v Board of Governors of the Bethlem Royal Hospital* [1985] AC 871
6   *Bolam v Friern Hospital Management Committee* [1957] 2 All ER 118
7   *Pearce v United Bristol Healthcare NHS Trust* (1999) 48 BMLR 118

guidance also emphasises that if the patient asks specific questions about the procedure and associated risks these should be answered truthfully.[8]

5.5　In the very rare event that the health professional believes that to follow the guidance in paragraphs 5.3 and 5.4 in full would have a deleterious effect on the patient's health, the GMC guidance states that this view, and the reasons for it, should be recorded in the patient's notes. When such concerns arise it is advisable to discuss the issue within the team caring for the patient. In an individual case the courts may accept such a justification but would examine it with great care. The mere fact that the patient might become upset by hearing the information, or might refuse treatment, is *not* sufficient to act as a justification.

5.6　Some patients may wish to know very little about the treatment which is being proposed. If information is offered and declined, it is good practice to record this fact in the notes. However, it is possible that patients' wishes may change over time, and it is important to provide opportunities for them to express this. The GMC guidance encourages doctors to explain to patients the importance of knowing the options open to them, and states that basic information should always be provided.

Additional procedures

6.　During an operation it may become evident that the patient could benefit from an additional procedure that was not within the scope of the original consent. If it would be unreasonable to delay the procedure until the patient regains consciousness (for example because there is a threat to the patient's life) it may be justified to perform the procedure on the grounds that it is in the patient's best interests. However, the procedure should not be performed merely because it is convenient. A hysterectomy should never be performed during an operation without explicit consent, unless it is necessary to do so to save life.

6.1　As noted in paragraph 19 below, if a patient has refused certain additional procedures before the anaesthetic (for example, specifying that a mastectomy should not be carried out after a frozen section biopsy result) this must be respected if the refusal is applicable to the circumstances. The GMC guidance states that it is good practice to seek the views of the patient on possible additional procedures when seeking consent to the original intervention.

Subsequent use of removed tissue

7.　The legal status of tissue (including clinical samples such as blood samples) which has been removed from a patient during the course of a procedure is at present unclear. Tissue left over after routine pathological examination may have a range of potentially beneficial uses, for example in basic and applied research, in drug testing and in teaching. Further, excess human tissue from medical procedures, such as bone from hip replacements, may have therapeutic uses for others.

7.1　In the past, there seems to have been an assumption that such tissue has been "abandoned" by patients and that it may be freely used for any ethically acceptable purpose without the patient's consent being sought. This assumption is increasingly being challenged, on the basis that patients should be given the opportunity to give or refuse their consent for such use. The Chief Medical Officer has recommended that there should be a review of the existing law on the taking, storing and use of tissue, both before and after death, and the Government has accepted this recommendation.[9] Both

---

8　GMC, *Seeking patients' consent: the ethical considerations*, November 1998
9　Department of Health, *The removal, retention and use of human organs and tissue from post-mortem examination: advice from the Chief Medical Officer*, 2001

the Royal College of Pathologists and the Medical Research Council are also currently undertaking work with the aim of ensuring that appropriate consent for tissue use is sought and is communicated to laboratory staff.

Consent to video recordings and clinical photography

8. Video recordings of treatment may be used both as a medical record or treatment aid in themselves, and as a tool for teaching, audit or research. The purpose and possible future use of the video must be clearly explained to the person, before their consent is sought for the recording to be made. If the video is to be used for teaching, audit or research, patients must be aware that they can refuse without their care being compromised and that when required or appropriate the video can be anonymised. As a matter of good practice, the same principles should be applied to clinical photography.

Who should seek consent?

9. The clinician providing the treatment or investigation is responsible for ensuring that the patient has given valid consent before treatment begins, although the consultant responsible for the patient's care will remain ultimately responsible for the quality of medical care provided. The GMC guidance states that the task of seeking consent may be delegated to another health professional, as long as that professional is suitably trained and qualified. In particular, they must have sufficient knowledge of the proposed investigation or treatment, and understand the risks involved, in order to be able to provide any information the patient may require. Inappropriate delegation (for example where the clinician seeking consent has inadequate knowledge of the procedure) may mean that the "consent" obtained is not valid. Clinicians are responsible for knowing the limits of their own competence and should seek the advice of appropriate colleagues when necessary.

When should consent be sought?

10. The seeking and giving of consent is usually a process, rather than a one-off event. For major interventions, it is good practice where possible to seek the patient's consent to the proposed procedure well in advance, when there is time to respond to the patient's questions and provide adequate information (see above paragraphs 4-5). Clinicians should then check, before the procedure starts, that the patient still consents. If a patient is not asked to signify their consent until just before the procedure is due to start, at a time when they may be feeling particularly vulnerable, there may be real doubt as to its validity. In no circumstances should patients be given routine pre-operative medication before being asked for their consent to proceed with the treatment.

Form of consent

11. The validity of consent does not depend on the form in which it is given. Written consent merely serves as evidence of consent: if the elements of voluntariness, appropriate information and capacity have not been satisfied, a signature on a form will not make the consent valid.

11.1 Although completion of a consent form is in most cases not a legal requirement (exceptions include certain requirements of the *Mental Health Act 1983* and of the *Human Fertilisation and Embryology Act 1990*) the use of such forms is good practice where an intervention such as surgery is to be undertaken. Where there is any doubt about the patient's capacity, it is important, *before* the patient is asked to sign the form, to establish both that they have the capacity to consent to the intervention and that they have received enough information to enable valid consent to be given. Details of the assessment of capacity, and the conclusion reached, should be recorded in the case notes.

11.2 If the patient has capacity, but is illiterate, the patient may be able to make their mark on the form to indicate consent. It would be good practice for the mark to be witnessed by a person other than the clinician seeking consent, and for the fact that the patient has chosen to make their mark in this way to be recorded in the case notes. Similarly, if the patient has capacity, and wishes to give consent, but is physically unable to mark the form, this fact should be recorded in the notes. If consent has been validly given, the lack of a completed form is no bar to treatment.

12. Consent may be expressed verbally or non-verbally: an example of non-verbal consent would be where a patient, after receiving appropriate information, holds out an arm for their blood pressure to be taken. It is good practice to obtain written consent for any significant procedure such as a surgical operation or when the patient participates in a research project or a video recording (even if only minor procedures are involved).

Requirements concerning gametes

13. It is a legal requirement under the *Human Fertilisation and Embryology Act 1990* that consent to the storage and use of gametes must be given in writing after the person has received such relevant information as is proper and had an opportunity to receive counselling. Where these requirements are not satisfied, it is unlawful to store or use the person's gametes. Clinicians should ensure that written consent to storage exists before retrieving gametes.

13.1 Outside specialist infertility practice, these requirements may be relevant to health care professionals whose patients are about to undergo treatment which may render them sterile (such as chemotherapy or radiotherapy) where a patient may wish to have gametes, or ovarian or testicular tissue, stored prior to the procedure. Health professionals may also receive requests to remove gametes from a person unable to give consent. Further guidance is available from the Human Fertilisation and Embryology Authority.[10]

Additional legal requirements

14. Before a live transplant of an organ (as defined in the *Human Organ Transplants Act 1989*) can take place from one living person to another to whom the individual is not genetically related (as defined in the same Act) approval must first be sought from the Unrelated Live Transplant Regulatory Authority, from whom further information may be obtained.[11] Where the individuals are genetically related, this fact may need to be demonstrated and specialist advice should be sought.

14.1 The potential benefits of a live transplant for a sick relative may be such that a family member may feel under considerable emotional pressure to donate. As noted in paragraph 3 above, it is important to establish that the decision of the potential donor is truly their own. The position of child bone marrow donors is covered in more detail below (see chapter 3, paragraph 16).

---

10   Paxton House, 30 Artillery Lane, London E1 7LS. Tel: 020 7377 5077
11   ULTRA Secretariat, Rm 421, Wellington House, London SE1 8UG. Tel: 020 7972 4812; fax: 020 7972 4852

Research and innovative treatment

15. The same legal principles apply when seeking consent from patients for research purposes as when seeking consent for investigations or treatment. However, in acknowledgement of the fact that research may not have direct benefits for the patients involved, the GMC states that "particular care" should be taken to ensure that possible research subjects have the fullest possible information about the proposed study and sufficient time to absorb it. Patients should never feel pressurised to take part, and advice must be given that they can withdraw from the research project at any time, without their care being affected. If patients are being offered the opportunity to participate in a clinical trial, they should have clear information on the nature of the trial.

15.1 If the treatment being offered is of an experimental nature, but not actually part of a research trial, this fact must be clearly explained to patients before their consent is sought, along with information about standard alternatives. It is good practice to give patients information about the evidence to date of the effectiveness of the new treatment, both at national/international level and in the practitioner's own experience, including information about known possible side-effects.

Duration of consent

16. When a patient gives valid consent to an intervention, in general that consent remains valid for an indefinite duration unless it is withdrawn by the patient. However, if new information becomes available regarding the proposed intervention (for example new evidence of risks or new treatment options) between the time when consent was sought and when the intervention is undertaken, the GMC guidance states that a doctor or member of the healthcare team should inform the patient and reconfirm their consent. In the light of paragraphs 4-5 above, the clinician should consider whether the new information should be drawn to the attention of the patient and the process of seeking consent repeated on the basis of this information. Similarly, if the patient's condition has changed significantly in the intervening time, it may be necessary to seek consent again, on the basis that the likely benefits and/or risks of the intervention may also have changed.

16.1 If consent has been obtained a significant time before undertaking the intervention, it is good practice to confirm that the person who has given consent (assuming he or she retains capacity) still wishes the intervention to proceed even if no new information needs to be provided or further questions answered. The position of patients who lack capacity is covered in chapter 2.

When consent is refused

17. If an adult with capacity makes a voluntary and appropriately informed decision to refuse treatment this decision must be respected, except in circumstances defined by the *Mental Health Act 1983* (see chapter 5). This is the case even where this may result in the death of the patient and/or the death of an unborn child, whatever the stage of the pregnancy. Refusal of treatment by those under the age of 18 is covered in chapter 3.

Withdrawal of consent

18. A patient with capacity is entitled to withdraw consent at any time, including during the performance of a procedure. Where a patient does object during treatment, it is good practice for the practitioner, if at all possible, to stop the procedure, establish the patient's concerns, and explain the consequences of not completing the procedure. At times an apparent objection may reflect a cry of pain rather than withdrawal of consent, and appropriate

reassurance may enable the practitioner to continue with the patient's consent. If stopping the procedure at that point would genuinely put the life of the patient at risk, the practitioner may be entitled to continue until this risk no longer applies.

18.1 Assessing capacity during a procedure may be difficult and, as noted above, factors such as pain, panic and shock may diminish capacity to consent. The practitioner should try to establish whether at that time the patient has capacity to withdraw a previously given consent. If capacity is lacking, it may sometimes be justified to continue in the patient's best interests (see chapter 2), although this should not be used as an excuse to ignore distress.

Advance refusals of treatment

19. Patients may have a "living will" or "advance directive" specifying how they would like to be treated in the case of future incapacity. While professionals cannot be required by such directives to provide particular treatments (which might be inappropriate), case law is now clear that an advance refusal of treatment which is valid and applicable to subsequent circumstances in which the patient lacks capacity is **legally binding**. An advance refusal is valid if made voluntarily by an appropriately informed person with capacity. Failure to respect such an advance refusal can result in legal action against the practitioner.

19.1 If there is doubt about the validity of an advance refusal a ruling should be sought from the court. It is not legally necessary for the refusal to be made in writing or formally witnessed, although such measures add evidentiary weight to the validity of the refusal. A health professional **may not** override a valid and applicable advance refusal on the grounds of the professional's personal conscientious objection to such a refusal.

19.2 Although the issue has not yet come before a court, it has been suggested that as a matter of public policy individuals should not be able to refuse in advance measures which are essential to keep a patient comfortable.[12] This is sometimes referred to as "basic" or "essential" care, and includes keeping the patient warm and clean and free from distressing symptoms such as breathlessness, vomiting, and severe pain. However, some patients may prefer to tolerate some discomfort if this means they remain more alert and able to respond to family and friends.

19.3 However, although basic/essential care would include the offer of oral nutrition and hydration, it would **not** cover force feeding an individual or the use of artificial nutrition and hydration. The courts have recognised that a competent individual has the right to choose to go on a "hunger strike", although this may be qualified if the person has a mental disorder. Towards the end of such a period an individual is likely to lose capacity (become incompetent) and the courts have stated that if the individual has, whilst competent, expressed the desire to refuse food until death supervenes, the person cannot be force fed or fed artificially when incompetent. If the patient is refusing food as a result of mental disorder and is detained under the *Mental Health Act 1983*, different considerations may apply and more specialist guidance should be consulted.[13]

---

12 British Medical Association, *Advance statements about medical treatment* (1995) BMA Publishing Group: London

13 eg Mental Health Act Commission, *Guidance Note 3 – Guidance on the treatment of anorexia nervosa under the Mental Health Act 1983* (issued August 1997 and updated March 1999)

Self harm

20.   Cases of self harm present a particular difficulty for health professionals. Where the patient is able to communicate, an assessment of their mental capacity should be made as a matter of urgency. If the patient is judged not to be competent, they may be treated on the basis of temporary incapacity (see paragraph 5 in chapter 2). Similarly, patients who have attempted suicide and are unconscious should be given emergency treatment if any doubt exists as to either their intentions or their capacity when they took the decision to attempt suicide.

20.1 However, as noted in paragraphs 17 and 19 above, competent patients **do** have the right to refuse life-sustaining treatment (other than treatment for mental disorder under the *Mental Health Act 1983*), both at the time it is offered and in the future. If a competent patient has harmed themselves and refuses treatment, a psychiatric assessment should be obtained. If the use of the *Mental Health Act 1983* is not appropriate, then their refusal must be respected. Similarly, if practitioners have good reason to believe that a patient genuinely intended to end their life and was competent when they took that decision, and are satisfied that the *Mental Health Act* is not applicable, then treatment should not be forced upon the patient although clearly attempts should be made to encourage him or her to accept help.

2   ADULTS WITHOUT CAPACITY

General principles

1.   Under English law, no one is able to give consent to the examination or treatment of an adult unable to give consent for him or herself (an "incapable" adult). Therefore, parents, relatives or members of the healthcare team can **not** consent on behalf of such an adult. However, in certain circumstances, it will be lawful to carry out such examinations or treatment.

2.   In general the refusal of an intervention made by a patient before their loss of capacity cannot be over-ridden if the refusal is valid and applicable to the situation (see advance refusals in chapter 1, paragraph 19). There are certain statutory exceptions to this principle, treatment for mental disorder under the *Mental Health Act 1983* being the main example, which are set out briefly in chapter 5.

3.   A key principle concerning treatment of the incapable adult is that of the person's best interests. "Best interests" are not confined to best *medical* interests:[14] case law has established that other factors which may need to be taken into account include the patient's values and preferences when competent, their psychological health, well-being, quality of life, relationships with family or other carers, spiritual and religious welfare and their own financial interests. It is good practice for the healthcare team to involve those close to the patient in order to find out about the patient's values and preferences before loss of capacity, unless the patient has previously made clear that particular individuals should not be involved.

4.   Where there is doubt about an individual's capacity or best interests, the High Court can give a ruling on these matters and on the lawfulness or unlawfulness of a proposed procedure. The duty officer of the Official Solicitor can advise on the appropriate procedure if necessary.[15] The court

---

14 *Re MB* (1997) 38 BMLR 175
15 The Official Solicitor can be contacted through the Urgent Court Business Officer out of office hours on 020 7947 6000. This should usually be done through the legal department of the NHS body involved.

has given guidance on making applications to the court, which is reproduced at Appendix A. It is good practice to seek the views of the court prior to undertaking certain interventions, listed in paragraph 8 below, which arouse particular concern.

Temporary incapacity

5.   An adult who usually has capacity may become temporarily incapable, for example whilst under a general anaesthetic or sedation, or after a road accident. Unless a valid advance refusal of treatment is applicable to the circumstances (see chapter 1, paragraph 19), the law permits interventions to be made which are necessary and no more than is reasonably required in the patient's best interests pending the recovery of capacity. This will include, but is not limited to, routine procedures such as washing and assistance with feeding. If a medical intervention is thought to be in the patient's best interests but can be delayed until the patient recovers capacity and can consent to (or refuse) the intervention, it must be delayed until that time.

Permanent or long-standing incapacity

6.   Where the adult's incapacity is permanent or likely to be long-standing, it will be lawful to carry out any procedure which is in the "best interests" of the adult. The House of Lords has suggested that action taken "to preserve the life, health or well-being" of a patient will be in their best interests, and subsequent court judgements have emphasised that a patient's best interests go beyond their best medical interests, to include much wider welfare considerations (see paragraph 3 above). The principle of caring for patients in their best interests also covers such routine procedures as dressing, washing, putting to bed and assisting with the consumption of food and drink. Where treatment is given to an incapable adult on this basis, the standard consent form should not be signed by either relatives or healthcare professionals. It is good practice to note either in the records or in a "patient unable to consent" form why the treatment was believed to be in the patient's best interests.

6.1   Where the patient has never been competent, it is clearly impossible to determine their best interests by reference to earlier, competent, beliefs and values. In such cases, family and friends close to the patient will often be in the best position to advise health professionals on the patient's needs and preferences.

Fluctuating capacity

7.   It is possible for capacity to fluctuate. In such cases, it is good practice to establish whilst the person has capacity their views about any clinical intervention that may be necessary during a period of incapacity and to record these views. The person may wish to make an advance refusal of certain types of treatment (see chapter 1, paragraph 19). If the person does not make any relevant advance refusal, the person's treatment when incapacitated should accord with the principles for treating the temporarily incapacitated (paragraph 5 above).

Referral to court

8.   The courts have identified certain circumstances when referral should be made to them for a ruling on lawfulness before a procedure is undertaken. These are:

   •   sterilisation for contraceptive purposes;
   •   donation of regenerative tissue such as bone marrow;

- withdrawal of nutrition and hydration from a patient in a persistent vegetative state;
- where there is doubt as to the patient's capacity or best interests.

8.1 It is unlikely that an adult without the capacity to consent would ever be considered as a donor of a solid organ, and even less likely that such a procedure would be in that adult's best interests. In the event that such an intervention was ever considered, referral should also be made to the court.

8.2 The courts have stated that neither sterilisation which is incidental to the management of detrimental effects of menstruation nor abortion need automatically be referred to court, if there is no doubt that this is the most appropriate therapeutic response. However, these procedures can give rise to special concern about the best interests and rights of a person who lacks capacity. The need for such procedures occasionally arises in relation to women with a severe learning disability. It is good practice to involve a consultant in the psychiatry of learning disability, the multidisciplinary team, and the patient's family as part of the decision-making process, and to document their involvement. Less invasive or reversible options should always be considered before permanent sterilisation. Where there is disagreement as to the patient's best interests, a reference to court may be appropriate.

8.3 It should be noted that the courts may extend the list of procedures concerning which court reference is good practice in the future.

8.4 Although some procedures may not require court approval, their appropriateness may give rise to concern. For example, some patients with learning disability may exhibit challenging behaviour, such as biting or self-injury. If such behaviour is severe, interventions such as applying a temporary soft splint to the teeth or using arm splints to prevent self-injury are exceptionally considered, within a wider therapeutic context. As with hysterectomies undertaken for menstrual management purposes, great care must be taken in determining the best interests of such patients as distinct from dealing with the needs of carers and others concerned with the individual's treatment.

Research

9. The lawfulness of medical research on adults or children who lack capacity has never been considered by an English court and therefore no definitive statement of the law can be made. General principles may provide some guidance. Ethically, any research project which is carried out on human beings should be approved by an independent research ethics committee. In the NHS this will be the Local Research Ethics Committee, and additionally where appropriate the Multi-Centre Research Ethics Committee. However, ethics committee approval does not absolve the clinicians carrying out the research from ethical or legal responsibility for their own actions.

9.1 Treatment for many conditions is imperfect, but new treatments are constantly being developed. In some cases, a competent patient will be offered the opportunity to enter into a clinical trial of two alternative therapies, on the basis that on the evidence available at the time the new therapy is at least as likely to benefit the patient as the standard therapy. Where children lack capacity to consent for themselves, parents may give consent for their child to be entered into a trial where the evidence is that the trial therapy may be at least as beneficial to the patient as the standard therapy. It is undesirable to carry out such research on adults without capacity if that research can equally well be carried out on those with capacity. However, where the standard treatment is non-existent or of very limited effectiveness, it may be in the best interests of an incapacitated adult to be entered into such a trial, unless there are reasons to believe that, when competent, the patient would not have wished to do so.

9.2   The position concerning research which does not have the potential immediately to benefit the person's health is a legally uncharted area. This type of research should never be undertaken on incapable patients if it is possible instead to carry out the research on persons capable of giving consent.

9.3   Although research has not been specifically considered, the courts have considered whether it would be legal to carry out a medical intervention with no therapeutic purpose on children lacking capacity. It was held that a person with parental responsibility can consent to an intervention which, although not in the best interests of that child, is not against the interests of such a child (the case in question concerned a blood test for non-therapeutic reasons). From this the idea has developed that research which is not of direct benefit to such children may be lawful (with consent from a person with parental responsibility) if it is **not against** the interests of the child and imposes no greater than minimal burden. The burden on the child must be assessed individually for each child: children's attitudes to blood tests and injections, for example, vary considerably.

9.4   Professional bodies such as the Medical Research Council and the Royal College of Physicians have suggested that it can, similarly, be ethical to perform research which involves minimal intervention on incapable adults, if certain stringent conditions are met. The research must be approved by the relevant Research Ethics Committee, it must relate to the condition from which the incapable adult is suffering, and it must be demonstrated that the research is not against their interests.[16]

9.5   The alternative view is that such research would only be lawful if it was in the best interests of the adult, taking into account all the factors listed in paragraph 3 above. Only the courts can rule on this issue, and until there is such a ruling this type of research should be considered with caution.

3   CHILDREN AND YOUNG PEOPLE

1.   The legal position concerning consent and refusal of treatment by those under the age of 18 is different from the position for adults, in particular where treatment is being refused. In the following paragraphs the terms 'child' and 'young person' are used interchangeably.

Young people aged 16–17

2.   By virtue of section 8 of the *Family Law Reform Act 1969*, people aged 16 or 17 are entitled to consent to their own medical treatment, and any ancillary procedures involved in that treatment, such as an anaesthetic. As for adults, consent will be valid only if it is given voluntarily by an appropriately informed patient capable of consenting to the particular intervention. However, unlike adults, the refusal of a competent person aged 16-17 may in certain circumstances be over-ridden by either a person with parental responsibility or a court (see below paragraphs 8-8.5).

2.1   Section 8 of the *Family Law Reform Act* applies only to the young person's own treatment. It does not apply to an intervention which is not potentially of direct health benefit to the young person, such as blood donation or non-therapeutic research on the causes of a disorder. However, a young person may be able to consent to such an intervention under the standard of Gillick competence, considered below.

---

16   Medical Research Council, *The ethical conduct of research on the mentally incapacitated*, 1991 and The Royal College of Physicians of London, *Guidelines on the practice of ethics committees in medical research involving human subjects*, 3rd Edn, 1996

3. In order to establish whether a young person aged 16 or 17 has the requisite capacity to consent to the proposed intervention, the same criteria as for adults should be used (see paragraph 2 of chapter 1).

4. If the requirements for valid consent are met, it is not legally necessary to obtain consent from a person with parental responsibility for the young person in addition to that of the young person. It is, however, good practice to involve the young person's family in the decision-making process, unless the young person specifically wishes to exclude them.

Children under 16 – the concept of *"Gillick* competence"

5. Following the case of *Gillick*,[17] the courts have held that children who have sufficient understanding and intelligence to enable them to understand fully what is involved in a proposed intervention will also have the capacity to consent to that intervention. This is sometimes described as being *"Gillick* competent" and may apply to consent for treatment, research or tissue donation. As the understanding required for different interventions will vary considerably, a child under 16 may therefore have the capacity to consent to some interventions but not others. As with adults, assumptions that a child with a learning disability may not be able to understand the issues should never be made automatically (see chapter 1, paragraph 2.6).

5.1 The concept of *Gillick* competence is said to reflect the child's increasing development to maturity. In some cases, for example because of a mental disorder, a child's mental state may fluctuate significantly so that on some occasions the child appears *Gillick* competent in respect of a particular decision and on other occasions does not. In cases such as these, careful consideration should be given to whether the child is truly *Gillick* competent at any time to take this decision.

6. If the child is *Gillick* competent and is able to give voluntary consent after receiving appropriate information, that consent will be valid and additional consent by a person with parental responsibility will not be required. However where the decision will have on-going implications, such as long-term use of contraception, it is good practice to encourage the child to inform his or her parents unless it would clearly not be in the child's best interests to do so.

The requirement of voluntariness

7. Although a child or young person may have the capacity to give consent, valid consent must be given voluntarily. This requirement must be considered carefully. Children and young people may be subject to undue influence by their parents, other carers, or a potential sexual partner, and it is important to establish that the decision is that of the individual him or herself.

Child or young person with capacity refusing treatment

8. Where a young person of 16 or 17 who could consent to treatment in accordance with section 8 of the *Family Law Reform Act*, or a child under 16 but *Gillick* competent, refuses treatment, such a refusal can be over-ruled either by a person with parental responsibility for the child or by the court. If more than one person has parental responsibility for the young person, consent by any one such person is sufficient, irrespective of the refusal of any other individual.

---

17 *Gillick v West Norfolk and Wisbeach AHA* [1996] AC 112

8.1   This power to over-rule must be exercised on the basis that the welfare of the child/young person is paramount. As with the concept of best interests, "welfare" does not just mean physical health. The psychological effect of having the decision over-ruled must also be considered. While no definitive guidance has been given as to when it is appropriate to over-rule a competent young person's refusal, it has been suggested that it should be restricted to occasions where the child is at risk of suffering "grave and irreversible mental or physical harm".

8.2   The outcome of such decisions may have a serious impact on the individual concerned. Examples might include a young person with capacity refusing an abortion or further chemotherapy for cancer in the knowledge of a poor prognosis. When a person with parental responsibility wishes to over-rule such decisions, consideration should be given to applying to the court for a ruling prior to undertaking the intervention. Such applications can be made at short notice if necessary.

8.3   For parents to be in a position to over-rule a competent child's refusal, they must inevitably be provided with sufficient information about their child's condition, which the child may not be willing for them to receive. While this will constitute a breach of confidence on the part of the clinician treating the child, this may be justifiable where it is in the child's best interests. Such a justification may only apply where the child is at serious risk as a result of their refusal of treatment.

8.4   Refusal by a competent child and all persons with parental responsibility for the child can be over-ruled by the court if the welfare of the child so requires.

8.5   A life-threatening emergency may arise when consultation with either a person with parental responsibility or the court is impossible, or the persons with parental responsibility refuse consent despite such emergency treatment appearing to be in the best interests of the child. In such cases the courts have stated that doubt should be resolved in favour of the preservation of life and it will be acceptable to undertake treatment to preserve life or prevent serious damage to health.

Child or young person without capacity

9.   Where a child lacks capacity to consent, consent can be given on their behalf by any one person with parental responsibility or by the court. As is the case where patients are giving consent for themselves, those giving consent on behalf of child patients must have the capacity to consent to the intervention in question, be acting voluntarily, and be appropriately informed. The power to consent must be exercised according to the "welfare principle": that the child's "welfare" or "best interests" must be paramount. Even where a child lacks capacity to consent on their own behalf, it is good practice to involve the child as much as possible in the decision-making process.

9.1   Where necessary the courts can, as with competent children, over-rule a refusal by a person with parental responsibility. It is recommended that certain important decisions, such as sterilisation for contraceptive purposes, should be referred to the courts for guidance, even if those with parental responsibility consent to the operation going ahead.

10.   The *Children Act 1989* sets out persons who may have parental responsibility. These include:
   •   the child's parents if married to each other at the time of conception or birth;
   •   the child's mother, but not father if they were not so married unless the father has acquired parental responsibility via a court order or a parental responsibility agreement or the couple subsequently marry;

- the child's legally appointed guardian;[18]
- a person in whose favour the court has made a residence order concerning the child;
- a Local Authority designated in a care order in respect of the child;
- a Local Authority or other authorised person who holds an emergency protection order in respect of the child.

Section 2(9) of the *Children Act 1989* states that a person who has parental responsibility for a child "may arrange for some or all of it to be met by one or more persons acting on his behalf". Such a person might choose to do this, for example, if a childminder or the staff of a boarding school have regular care of their child. As only a person exercising parental responsibility can give valid consent, in the event of any doubt specific enquiry should be made. Foster parents do not automatically have parental responsibility.

11. Consent given by one person with parental responsibility is valid, even if another person with parental responsibility withholds consent. However, the courts have stated that a "small group of important decisions" should not be taken by one person with parental responsibility against the wishes of another, citing in particular non-therapeutic male circumcision.[19] Where persons with parental responsibility disagree as to whether non-therapeutic procedures are in the child's best interests, it is advisable to refer the decision to the courts. It is possible that major experimental treatment, where opinion is divided as to the benefits it may bring the child, might also fall into this category of important decisions, although such a case has not yet been considered in the English courts.

12. In order to consent on behalf of a child, the person with parental responsibility must themselves have capacity. Where the mother of a child is herself under 16, she will only be able to give valid consent for her child's treatment if she herself is *Gillick* competent (see paragraphs 5-6 above). Whether or not she has capacity may vary, depending on the seriousness of the decision to be taken.

13. Where a child is a ward of court, no important step may be taken in the life of the ward without the prior consent of the court. This is likely to include more significant medical interventions but not treatment for minor injuries or common diseases of childhood.

14. In an emergency, it is justifiable to treat a child who lacks capacity without the consent of a person with parental responsibility, if it is impossible to obtain consent in time and if the treatment is vital to the survival or health of the child. The Department of Health will be issuing guidance to health professionals in 2001 which will include coverage of situations where parents refuse consent to examination, and abuse or neglect is suspected.

Research

15. The legal position concerning research on patients unable to consent is discussed in chapter 2 paragraphs 9-9.5. Where children lack capacity to consent for themselves, parents may give consent for their child to be entered into a trial where the evidence is that the trial therapy may be at least as beneficial to the patient as the standard therapy. It may also be compatible with the welfare principle for a person with parental responsibility to give consent to a research intervention which is not strictly in the best interests

---

18 Under section 5 of the *Children Act 1989*, courts may appoint a guardian for a child who has no parent with parental responsibility. Parents with a parental responsibility may also appoint a guardian in the event of their own death.

19 Female circumcision is always prohibited, under the *Prohibition of Female Circumcision Act 1985*

of the child, but is not against the interests of the child. Such an intervention must involve only minimal burden to the child.

Using children lacking capacity as bone marrow donors

16.   Donation of bone marrow can be painful and carries some significant risks. It is not a minimal intervention. Children lacking capacity have on some occasions provided bone marrow to assist in the treatment of a sibling. To have such a transplant may clearly be in the best interests of the sibling. However, in relation to medical interventions it is not acceptable for the needs of one sibling to be balanced against the needs of another. The legal test is whether donating bone marrow is in the best interests of the healthy child.

16.1 It may be extremely difficult for a person with parental responsibility who has one dying child to take a dispassionate view of the best interests of that child's healthy sibling. Factors to be taken into account in a best interests assessment are described in chapter 2, paragraph 3. Health professionals may also find it difficult to assess the needs of the children independently. However, without such dispassionate assessment the treatment may not be lawful.

16.2 The Council of Europe's Convention on Human Rights and Biomedicine requires that authorisation for organ or tissue removal from a person not able to consent (whether adult or child) must be approved by a 'competent body'. States have discretion in how they implement this requirement. Although the UK has not yet signed the Convention, best practice requires some form of independent scrutiny of the healthy child's best interests. Examples might include use of an assessor who is independent of the team responsible for the sick child, or consideration of the case by a hospital clinical ethics committee or other multidisciplinary board convened for the purpose. If there is any doubt about the healthy child's best interests, a ruling from the court should be sought before undertaking the intervention.

4   WITHDRAWING AND WITHHOLDING LIFE-PROLONGING TREATMENT

General principles

1.   The same legal principles apply to withdrawing and withholding life-prolonging treatment as apply to any other medical intervention. However, the gravity and sensitivity of these decisions are such that the assessment of capacity and of best interests are particularly important. Sometimes decisions will need to be made immediately – for example whether it is appropriate to attempt resuscitation after severe trauma.[20] When more time is available and the patient is an adult or child without capacity, all those concerned with the care of the patient – relatives, partners, friends, carers and the multidisciplinary team – can potentially make a contribution to the assessment. The discussions and the basis for decisions should be recorded in the notes.

2.   Legally, the use of artificial nutrition and hydration (ANH) constitutes medical treatment. Thus the legal principles which apply to the use of ANH are the same as those which apply to all other medical treatments such as medication or ventilation. The courts have confirmed that the current case law in this area is compatible with the *Human Rights Act 1998*.

3.   There is an important distinction between withdrawing or withholding treatment which is of no clinical benefit to the patient or is not in the

---

20   See circular HSC 2000/28 for further guidance on resuscitation decisions

patient's best interests, and taking a deliberate action to end the patient's life. A deliberate action which is intended to cause death is unlawful. Equally, there is no lawful justification for continuing treatment which is not in an incompetent patient's best interests.

Adults and children with capacity

4. Except in circumstances governed by the *Mental Health Act 1983*, if an adult with the capacity to make the decision refuses treatment, or requests that it be withdrawn, practitioners **must** comply with the patient's decision.
5. However, if a child with capacity makes such a request or refusal, this may be over-ridden, as noted in chapter 3, by either a person with parental responsibility or by the courts, if this is believed to be necessary for the welfare of the child. Moreover, the courts consider that to take a decision which may result in the individual's death requires a very high level of understanding, so that many young people who would have the capacity to take other decisions about their medical care would lack the capacity to make such a grave decision.
5.1 Refusal of treatment by a child with capacity must always be taken very seriously, even though legally it is possible to over-ride their objections. It is not a legal requirement to continue a child's life-prolonging treatment in all circumstances. For example, where the child is suffering an illness where the likelihood of survival even with treatment is poor, and treatment will pose a significant burden to the child, it may not be in the best interests of the child to continue treatment.

Adults and children lacking capacity

6. If a child lacks capacity it is still good practice to involve the child as far as is possible and appropriate in the decision. The decision to withdraw or withhold life-prolonging treatment must be founded on the welfare of the child. If there is disagreement between those with parental responsibility for the child and the clinical team concerning the appropriate course of action, a ruling should be sought from the court.
7. If an adult lacks capacity, and has not made an advance refusal of treatment which is valid and applicable to the circumstances, the decision must be based on the best interests of the adult, again involving the patient as far as this is possible.
7.1 The British Medical Association has suggested that extra safeguards should be followed before a decision to withhold or withdraw ANH is made: that a senior clinician not otherwise involved in the patient's care should formally review the case; that details of cases where ANH has been withdrawn should later be made available for clinical audit; and, where the patient is in PVS or a state closely resembling PVS, that legal advice should be sought. Further, the courts have stated that it is good practice for court approval to be sought before ANH is withdrawn from patients in PVS.

Brain stem death

8. "Best interests" is a concept which only applies to the living. The courts in England have recognised what were originally referred to as the "brain death criteria" as part of the law for the purposes of diagnosing death. The criteria are more accurately described as "brain stem death criteria". Updated guidance on the diagnosis of brain stem death is available.[21]

---

21 HSC 1998/35: *A code of practice for the diagnosis of brain stem death*

8.1   When the diagnosis of brain stem death has been confirmed, all clinical interventions can be withdrawn. If, subject to the requirements of the *Human Tissue Act 1961*, the deceased person will become an organ donor, medical interventions to facilitate donation, such as maintaining electrolyte balance, may be continued.

8.2   If a patient is expected to die shortly but brain stem death has not been established, the Department of Health has issued guidance based on legal advice that artificial ventilation with the sole aim of preserving organ function is unlawful.[22] Its purpose is not to benefit the patient and may run the risk of causing serious harm. It is therefore not in the best interests of the patient.

5   OTHER EXCEPTIONS TO THE PRINCIPLES

1.   Certain statutes set out specific exceptions to the principles noted in the previous chapters. These are briefly noted below. Those concerned with the operation of such statutes should consult more detailed guidance.

2.   Part IV of the *Mental Health Act 1983* sets out circumstances in which patients detained under the Act may be treated without consent for their mental disorder. It has no application to treatment for physical disorders unrelated to the mental disorder, which remains subject to the common law principles described in previous chapters. Chapters 15 and 16 of the *Mental Health Act Code of Practice* offer guidance on consent and medical treatment in this context.[23]

2.1   Neither the existence of mental disorder nor the fact of detention under the 1983 Act should give rise to an assumption of incapacity. The patient's capacity must be assessed in every case in relation to the particular decision being made. The capacity of a person with mental disorder may fluctuate.

2.2   Significant reforms to the 1983 Act have been described in the White Paper, *Reforming the Mental Health Act*, published in December 2000.[24] However, these reforms should not affect the principle that treatment for physical disorders, unrelated to the mental disorder for which the patient is receiving compulsory treatment, does not come within the scope of mental health legislation.

3.   The *Public Health (Control of Disease) Act 1984* provides that, on an order made by a magistrate, persons suffering from certain notifiable infectious diseases can be medically examined, removed to, and detained in a hospital without their consent. Although the Act has a power for regulations to be made concerning the treatment of such persons without their consent, such regulations have not been made and thus the treatment of such persons must be based on the common law principles previously described.

4.   Section 47 of the *National Assistance Act 1948* provides for the removal to suitable premises of persons in need of care and attention without their consent. Such persons must either be suffering from grave chronic disease or be aged, infirm or physically incapacitated and living in insanitary conditions. In either case, they must be unable to devote to themselves (and are not receiving from others) proper care and attention. The Act does not give a power to treat such persons without their consent and therefore their treatment is dependent on common law principles.

---

22   HSG(94)41: *Identification of potential donors of organs for transplantation*
23   Department of Health and Welsh Office, *Code of Practice: Mental Health Act 1983* (1999) The Stationery Office: London
24   Department of Health and Home Office, *Reforming the Mental Health Act*, Cm 5016-I (2000) The Stationery Office; London

APPENDIX A: PRINCIPLES TO BE FOLLOWED REGARDING APPLICATIONS TO THE COURT WHEN THE PATIENT'S CAPACITY TO CONSENT IS IN DOUBT

Extract from the Court of Appeal's decision in St. George's Healthcare NHS Trust v S:[25]

"The case highlighted some major problems which could arise for hospital authorities when a pregnant woman presented at hospital, the possible need for Caesarean surgery was diagnosed, and there was serious doubt about the patient's capacity to accept or decline treatment. To avoid any recurrence of the unsatisfactory events recorded in this judgement, and after consultations with the President of the Family Division and the Official Solicitor, and in the light of the written submissions from Mr Havers and Mr Gordon, we shall attempt to repeat and expand the advice given in *Re MB* [1997] 2 FCR 541, 38 BMLR 175. This advice also applies to any cases involving capacity when surgical or invasive treatment may be needed by a patient, whether female or male. References to 'she' and 'her' should be read accordingly. It also extends, where relevant, to medical practitioners and health professionals generally as well as to hospital authorities.

The guidelines depend on basic legal principles, which we summarise:

i)   They have no application where the patient is competent to accept or refuse treatment. In principle a patient may remain competent notwithstanding detention under the Mental Health Act.

ii) If the patient is competent and refuses consent to the treatment, an application to the High Court for a declaration would be pointless. In this situation the advice given to the patient should be recorded. For their own protection hospital authorities should seek unequivocal assurances from the patient (to be recorded in writing) that the refusal represents an informed decision: that is that she understands the nature of and reasons for the proposed treatment, and the risks and likely prognosis involved in the decision to refuse or accept it. If the patient is unwilling to sign a written indication of this refusal, this too should be noted in writing. Such a written indication is merely a record for evidential purposes. It should not be confused with or regarded as a disclaimer.

iii) If the patient is incapable of giving or refusing consent, either in the long term or temporarily (eg. due to unconsciousness), the patient must be cared for according to the authority's judgement of the patient's best interests. Where the patient has given an advance directive, before becoming incapable, treatment and care should normally be subject to the advance directive. However, if there is reason to doubt the reliability of the advance directive (eg. it may sensibly be thought not to apply to the circumstances which have arisen), then an application for a declaration may be made.

Concern over capacity

iv) The authority should identify as soon as possible whether there is concern about a patient's competence to consent to or refuse treatment.

v)   If the capacity of the patient is seriously in doubt it should be assessed as a matter of priority. In many such cases the patient's general practitioner or other responsible doctor may be sufficiently qualified to make the necessary assessment, but in serious or complex cases involving difficult issues about the future health and well-being or even the life of the patient, the issue of capacity should be examined by an independent psychiatrist, ideally one

---

25   *St George's Healthcare NHS Trust v S* [1998] 3 All ER 673.

approved under s12(2) of the Mental Health Act. If following this assessment there remains a serious doubt about the patient's competence, and the seriousness or complexity of the issues in the particular case may require the involvement of the court, the psychiatrist should further consider whether the patient is incapable by reason of mental disorder of managing her property or affairs. If so the patient may be unable to instruct a solicitor and will require a guardian *ad litem* in any court proceedings.

The authority should seek legal advice as quickly as possible. If a declaration is to be sought, the patient's solicitors should be informed immediately and if practicable they should have a proper opportunity to take instructions and apply for legal aid where necessary. Potential witnesses for the authority should be made aware of the criteria laid down in *Re MB* and this case, together with any guidance issued by the Department of Health, and the British Medical Association.

vi)   If the patient is unable to instruct solicitors, or is believed to be incapable of doing so, the authority or its legal advisers must notify the Official Solicitor and invite him to act as guardian *ad litem*. If the Official Solicitor agrees he will no doubt wish, if possible, to arrange for the patient to be interviewed to ascertain her wishes and to explore the reasons for any refusal of treatment. The Official Solicitor can be contacted through the Urgent Court Business Officer out of office hours on 020 7947 6000.

The hearing

vii)   The hearing before the judge should be *inter partes*. As the order made in her absence will not be binding on the patient unless she is represented either by a guardian *ad litem* (if incapable of giving instructions) or (if capable) by counsel or solicitor, a declaration granted *ex parte* is of no assistance to the authority. Although the Official Solicitor will not act for a patient if she is capable of instructing a solicitor, the court may in any event call on the Official Solicitor (who has considerable expertise in these matters) to assist as an *amicus curiae*.

viii)   It is axiomatic that the judge must be provided with accurate and all the relevant information. This should include the reasons for the proposed treatment, the risks involved in the proposed treatment, and in not proceeding with it, whether any alternative treatment exists, and the reason, if ascertainable, why the patient is refusing the proposed treatment. The judge will need sufficient information to reach an informed conclusion about the patient's capacity, and, where it arises, the issue of best interest.

ix)   The precise terms of any order should be recorded and approved by the judge before its terms are transmitted to the authority. The patient should be accurately informed of the precise terms.

x)   Applicants for emergency orders from the High Court made without first issuing and serving the relevant applications and evidence in support have a duty to comply with the procedural requirements (and pay the court fees) as soon as possible after the urgency hearing.

Conclusion

There may be occasions when, assuming a serious question arises about the competence of the patient, the situation facing the authority may be so urgent and the consequences so desperate that it is impracticable to attempt to comply with these guidelines. The guidelines should be approached for what they are, that is guidelines. Where delay may itself cause serious damage to the patient's health or put her life at risk then formulaic compliance with these guidelines would be inappropriate."

APPENDIX B: FURTHER READING

Alderson, P & Montgomery J, *Health care choices: making decisions with children* (1996) IPPR: London.

Association of Anaesthetists of Great Britain and Ireland, *Information and consent for anaesthesia* (1999) Association of Anaesthetists of Great Britain and Ireland: London. (www.aagbi.org)

British Medical Association, *Advance statements about medical treatment* (1995) BMA Publishing Group: London. (www.bma.org.uk)

British Medical Association, *Consent, rights and choices in health care for children and young people* (2001) BMJ Books: London. (www.bmjpg.com/consent)

British Medical Association, Royal College of Nursing and Resuscitation Council (UK), *Decisions relating to cardiopulmonary resuscitation* (2001) BMA: London. (web.bma.org.uk/cpr)

British Medical Association, *The impact of the Human Rights Act 1998 on medical decision-making* (2000) BMA: London. (www.bma.org.uk)

British Medical Association, *Withdrawing and withholding life prolonging treatment: guidance for decision making*, 2nd edition (2000) BMJ Books: London. (www.bmjpg.com/withwith/ww.htm)

Department of Health and Welsh Office, *Code of Practice: Mental Health Act 1983* (1999) The Stationery Office: London. (www.doh.gov.uk/mhact1983.htm)

Department of Health, current edition of *Immunisation against infectious diseases*, The Stationery Office: London (contains chapter on consent for immunisation).

Department of Health, HSC 1998/35: *A code of practice for the diagnosis of brain stem death*, and attached booklet *A code of practice for the diagnosis of brain stem death including guidelines for the identification and management of potential organ and tissue donors*. (www.doh.gov.uk/publications/coinh.html, circular only)

Department of Health, *Working together to safeguard children: a guide to inter-agency working to safeguard and promote the welfare of children* (1999) The Stationery Office: London.

Department of Health, *The removal, retention and use of human organs and tissue from post-mortem examination: advice from the Chief Medical Officer* (2001) The Stationery Office: London. (www.doh.gov.uk/orgretentionadvice)

General Dental Council, *Maintaining standards: guidance to dentists on professional and personal conduct* (May 2000) GDC: London.

General Medical Council, *Seeking patients' consent: the ethical considerations* (1998) GMC: London. (www.gmc-uk.org)

GMC guidance, *Making and using visual and audio recordings of patients* (1997) GMC: London. (www.gmc-uk.org)

Keywood, K et al, *Best practice? Health care decision making by, with and for adults with learning disabilities* (1999) National Development Team: Manchester.

Royal College of Pathologists, *Guidelines for the retention of tissues and organs at post-mortem examination* (2000) Royal College of Pathologists: London. (www.rcpath.org)

Royal College of Physicians of London, *Guidelines on the practice of ethics committees in medical research involving human subjects*, 3rd edition (1996) Royal College of Physicians: London.

Royal College of Surgeons of England, *Good surgical practice* (2000) Royal College of Surgeons of England: London. (www.rcseng.ac.uk/publications/list.asp?menu=publications)

Senate of Surgery of Great Britain and Ireland, *The surgeon's duty of care* (1997) Senate of Surgery of Great Britain and Ireland: London.

United Kingdom Central Council for Nursing, Midwifery and Health Visiting, *Code of professional conduct* (1992) UKCC: London. (www.ukcc.org.uk/cms/content/Publications/)

United Kingdom Central Council for Nursing, Midwifery and Health Visiting, *Guidelines for professional practice* (1996) UKCC: London. (www.ukcc.org.uk/cms/content/Publications/)

United Kingdom Central Council for Nursing, Midwifery and Health Visiting, *Guidelines for mental health and learning disabilities nursing* (1998) UKCC: London. (www.ukcc.org.uk/cms/content/Publications/)

United Kingdom Central Council for Nursing, Midwifery and Health Visiting, *Midwives Rules and Code of Practice* (1998) UKCC: London. (www.ukcc.org.uk/cms/content/Publications/)

In addition to the codes of practice of the regulatory bodies cited above, the professional bodies of each of the allied health professions publish codes of conduct which include requirements on seeking consent. These codes of conduct are normally congruent with the 'statements regarding infamous conduct' which regulate all the professions covered by the Council for Professions Supplementary to Medicine.

APPENDIX C: LEGAL REFERENCES

References to the main cases and professional guidance from which the principles set out in this guidance are derived are given below, by paragraph number.

Chapter 1

1. *Re F (mental patient: sterilisation)* [1990] 2 AC 1
2. *Re MB (an adult: medical treatment)* (1997) 38 BMLR 175; *Re T (adult: refusal of treatment)* [1993] Fam 95
3. *Re T (adult: refusal of treatment)* [1993] Fam 95
4. *Chatterton v Gerson* [1981] 1 All ER 257; *Appleton v Garrett* (1995) 34 BMLR 23
5. *Sidaway v Board of Governors of the Bethlem Royal Hospital* [1985] AC 871; *Smith v Tunbridge Wells HA* (1994) 5 Med LR 334; *Bolitho v City & Hackney HA* [1997] 4 All ER 771; *Pearce v United Bristol Healthcare NHS Trust* (1999) 48 BMLR 118
6. This issue has never been directly addressed in English case law, but academic commentators suggest that English courts would be likely to follow the Canadian cases of *Marshall v Curry* [1994] 3 DLR 260 and *Murray v McMurchy* [1949] 2 DLR 442; *Re T (adult: refusal of treatment)* [1993] Fam 95 (regarding advance refusals)
7. No English cases as yet
8. GMC guidance, *Making and using visual and audio recordings of patients*, September 1997
9. *Re F (mental patient: sterilisation)* [1990] 2 AC 1; General Medical Council, *Seeking patients' consent: the ethical considerations*, November 1998; UKCC, *Code of professional conduct*, June 1992

10. *Re MB (an adult: medical treatment)* (1997) 38 BMLR 175 highlights temporary factors such as fear which may affect a patient's capacity to consent and advocates identifying 'potential problems' (in that case a patient's fear of needles) as far in advance as possible

11. *Chatterton v Gerson* [1981] 1 All ER 257

12. No direct English cases, but a well-established principle, based on the Massachusetts case of *O'Brien v Cunard SS Co* (1891) 28 NE 266 (Mass Sup Jud Ct)

13. Schedule 3 of the *Human Fertilisation and Embryology Act 1990*

14. Section 2 of the *Human Organ Transplants Act 1989*

15. *Chatterton v Gerson* [1981] 1 All ER 257; General Medical Council, *Seeking patients' consent: the ethical considerations*, November 1998, paragraphs 35-36

16. General Medical Council, *Seeking patients' consent: the ethical considerations*, November 1998, paragraph 32

17. *Re C (adult: refusal of medical treatment)* [1994] 1 All ER 819; *Re MB (an adult: medical treatment)* (1997) 38 BMLR 175; *St George's Healthcare NHS Trust v S* [1998] 3 All ER 673

18. No direct English case law, but Canadian Supreme Court judgement *Ciarlariello v Schacter* (1993) 100 DLR (4th) 609

19. *Re T (adult: refusal of treatment)* [1993] Fam 95; *Re C (adult: refusal of medical treatment)* [1994] 1 All ER 819; *Re MB (an adult: medical treatment)* (1997) 38 BMLR 175; *St George's Healthcare NHS Trust v S* [1998] 3 All ER 673; *Secretary of State for the Home Department v Robb* [1995] 1 All ER 677 (on refusal of food)

20. *Re T (adult: refusal of treatment)* [1993] Fam 95; *B v Croydon District HA* [1995] Fam 133

Chapter 2

1. *Re F (mental patient: sterilisation)* [1990] 2 AC 1

2. *Re T (adult: refusal of treatment)* [1993] Fam 95

3. *Re MB (an adult: medical treatment)* (1997) 38 BMLR 175 (best interests not restricted to best medical interests); Kennedy and Grubb, eds, *Principles of Medical Law* (1998), pp 247-252, draws together numerous cases in which 'best interests' have been discussed by the courts in the clinical context

4. *St George's Healthcare NHS Trust v S* [1998] 3 All ER 673

5. *Re F (mental patient: sterilisation)* [1990] 2 AC 1

6. *Re F (mental patient: sterilisation)* [1990] 2 AC 1

7. *Re F (mental patient: sterilisation)* [1990] 2 AC 1

8. *Re F (mental patient: sterilisation)* [1990] 2 AC 1 (sterilisation for contraceptive purposes); *Re Y (mental patient: bone marrow donation)* [1997] Fam 110 (donation of regenerative tissue); *Airedale NHS Trust v Bland* [1993] AC 789 (withdrawal of artificial nutrition and hydration); *St George's Healthcare NHS Trust v S* [1998] 3 All ER 673 (where doubt as to patient's capacity); *Re SG (a patient)* (1990) 6 BMLR 95 (abortion); *F v F* (1991) 7 BMLR 135 (hysterectomy for serious menorrhagia declared lawful); *Re S (adult patient: sterilisation)* [2000] 3 WLR 1288 (hysterectomy for menorrhagia declared unlawful)

9. No directly relevant English cases as yet, but *S v S, W v Official Solicitor* [1972] AC 24 ruled that a blood test to establish paternity was "not against the interests" of a child

Chapter 3

1. The *Children Act 1989*; *Gillick v West Norfolk and Wisbech AHA* [1986] AC 112; *Re R (a minor) (wardship: consent to treatment)* [1992] Fam 11; *Re W (a minor) (medical treatment)* [1992] 4 All ER 627

2.   Section 8 of the *Family Law Reform Act 1969*
3.   Section 8 of the *Family Law Reform Act 1969*
4.   Section 8 of the *Family Law Reform Act 1969*
5.   *Gillick v West Norfolk and Wisbech AHA* [1986] AC 112; *Re R (a minor) (wardship: consent to treatment)* [1992] Fam 11
6.   *Gillick v West Norfolk and Wisbech AHA* [1986] AC 112
7.   *Re T (adult: refusal of treatment)* [1993] Fam 95; *Re S (a minor) (consent to medical treatment)* [1994] 2 FLR 1065
8.   *Re W (a minor) (medical treatment)* [1992] 4 All ER 627; *Re C (a minor) (evidence: confidential information)* (1991) 7 BMLR 138; *Gillick v West Norfolk and Wisbech AHA* [1986] AC 112 (resolving doubts in favour of saving life)
9.   Sections 1 and 3 of the *Children Act 1989*; *Re B (a minor) (wardship: sterilisation)* [1988] AC 199; *Re E (a minor) (medical treatment)* (1991) 7 BMLR 117
10.   Sections 2, 4, 5, 12, 33 and 44 of the *Children Act 1989*
11.   Section 2(7) of the *Children Act 1989*; *Re J (child's religious upbringing and circumcision)* (1999) 52 BMLR 82
12.   *Gillick v West Norfolk and Wisbech AHA* [1986] AC 112
13.   *Re D (a minor) (wardship: sterilisation)* [1976] Fam 185
14.   *Gillick v West Norfolk and Wisbech AHA* [1986] AC 112
15.   No directly relevant English cases as yet, but *S v S, W v Official Solicitor* [1972] AC 24 ruled that a blood test to establish paternity was "not against the interests" of a child
16.   No English cases yet involving children, but *Re Y (mental patient: bone marrow donation)* [1997] Fam 110 sets out the "best interests" approach for incompetent adults; Council of Europe, *Convention on Human Rights and Biomedicine*, Article 20(2)(iv)

Chapter 4

1.   *Airedale NHS Trust v Bland* [1993] AC 789
2.   *Airedale NHS Trust v Bland* [1993] AC 789; *NHS Trust A v Mrs M: NHS Trust B v Mrs H* [2001] 1 All ER 801
3.   *Airedale NHS Trust v Bland* [1993] AC 789
4.   *Re C (adult: refusal of medical treatment)* [1994] 1 All ER 819; *Re MB (an adult: medical treatment)* (1997) 38 BMLR 175; *St George's Healthcare NHS Trust v S* [1998] 3 All ER 673
5.   *Re W (a minor) (medical treatment)* [1992] 4 All ER 627
6.   *R v Portsmouth Hospitals NHS Trust, ex parte Glass* (1999) 50 BMLR 269
7.   *Airedale NHS Trust v Bland* [1993] AC 789
8.   *Re A (a minor)* [1992] 3 Med LR 303

This guidance has been prepared with the assistance of the Good Practice in Consent Advisory Group, whose membership is listed below.

Chair: Dr. Sheila Adam, Health Services Director, Department of Health

Members

(including details of organisations nominating individuals)

Mr. Clive Appleby (Epping Forest PCT, representing the NHS Confederation)

Ms. Sarah Bazin (Birmingham Heartlands and Solihull NHS Trust nominated by DH to represent the allied health professions)

Professor Joe Collier (St. George's Hospital Medical School, representing the Council of Heads of Medical Schools)

Dr. Jane Cowan (Medical Protection Society)

Professor Andrew Grubb (Cardiff Law School)

Mr. Barry Jackson (Royal College of Surgeons of England)

Dr. Iona Heath (Royal College of General Practitioners)

Professor Peter Hill (Postgraduate Dean (Northern) Northern and Yorkshire Region)

Mr. James Johnson (Joint Consultants Committee)

Professor John Lilleyman (President of the Royal College of Pathologists, representing the Academy of Medical Royal Colleges)

Mr. Brian McGinnis (Mencap)

Ms. Polly Moreton (Action for Sick Children)

Ms. Dora Opoku (United Kingdom Central Council for Nursing, Midwifery and Health Visiting)

Ms. Jane O'Brien (General Medical Council)

Dr. Gina Radford (Regional Director of Public Health, Eastern Regional Office)

Mrs. Shahwar Sadeque (member of the Royal College of Physicians' committee on medical ethics; particular interest in ethnic minority health issues)

Dame Margaret Seward (Chief Dental Officer)

Dr. Ewen Sim (Junior Doctors Committee, BMA)

Professor Terry Stacey (Central Office of Research Ethics Committees)

Ms. Moira Wheeler (Head of Midwifery and Nursing Services, Epsom and St. Helier NHS Trust, representing the Royal College of Midwives)

Ms. Rosie Wilkinson (Royal College of Nursing)

Dr. Michael Wilks (BMA)

Ms. Micky Willmott (Age Concern England)

Co-opted member: Mr. Steve Walker of the NHS Litigation Authority

Secretariat

Dr. Elaine Gadd

Ms. Katharine Wright

© Crown Copyright
Produced by Department of Health
23617 1p 50k Mar 01 (COL)

Further copies of this document are available free from:
Department of Health, PO Box 777,
London SE1 6XH.
Or you could call the NHS Response Line
on: 0541 555 455

It is also on our website on: www.doh.gov.uk/consent

Index

All references are to page numbers